Software
Engineering
for Real-Time
Systems

We work with leading authors to develop the
strongest educational materials in computer
science, bringing cutting-edge thinking and best
learning practice to a global market.

Under a range of well-known imprints, including
Addison-Wesley, we craft high-quality print and
electronic publications which help readers to understand
and apply their content, whether studying or at work.

To find out more about the complete range of our
publishing, please visit us on the World Wide Web at:
www.pearsoneduc.com

Software

Engineering

for Real-Time

Systems

JIM COOLING

 ADDISON-WESLEY

An imprint of Pearson Education

Harlow, England • London • New York • Boston • San Francisco • Toronto
Sydney • Tokyo • Singapore • Hong Kong • Seoul • Taipei • New Delhi
Cape Town • Madrid • Mexico City • Amsterdam • Munich • Paris • Milan

Pearson Education Limited
Edinburgh Gate
Harlow
Essex CM20 2JE
England

and Associated Companies throughout the world

Visit us on the World Wide Web at:
www.pearsoneduc.com

First published 2003

ISBN: 978-0201-596205

British Library Cataloguing-in-Publication Data
A catalogue record for this book is available from the British Library

Library of Congress Cataloging-in-Publication Data
Cooling, J. E.
    Software engineering for real-time systems / Jim Cooling.
        p. cm.
    Includes bibliographical references and index.
    ISBN 0-201-59620-2 (pbk.)
    1. Software engineering. 2. Real-time data processing. I. Title.
QA76.758 .C695 2002
005.1—dc21   2002025422

Transferred to Digital Print on Demand 2012

Typeset in 9/12.5pt Stone Serif by 35
Printed and bound by CPI Group (UK) Ltd, Croydon, CR0 4YY

For Jo (Joanne)

To thank her for bringing so much to our lives

Beidh fáilte romhat ag aon tam

And for my grandson
Finnian James Cooling

Contents

Preface

....

What is this book about?

This book sets out to provide a firm foundation in the knowledge and skills needed to develop and produce real-time (and in particular, embedded) systems.

Let us be clear right up front what it does *not* aim to do. It does not teach you how to be a designer. It does not show you, in fine detail, how to design real-time software. It is not a programming text. What it does, however, is actually more fundamental (and in reality, more important): it deals with the *engineering* of real-time systems.

Who should read this book?

Those working – or intending to work – in the field of software development for real-time systems. It has been written with four audiences in mind:

- Students.
- Engineers, scientists and mathematicians moving into software systems.
- Professional and experienced software engineers entering the embedded field.
- Programmers having little or no formal education in the underlying principles of software-based real-time systems.

Why should you read this book?

First let's assume that your major interest is in the real-time area. Why should you part with your hard-earned money (though for students it may be somebody else's money) for this textbook? Well, it's essential to realize that many skills are needed to produce quality real-time software. Being able to program is but one step. The whole process involves a range of activities, involving (among others) problem analysis, software and program design, testing, debugging, documentation, reviews and configuration management. This book covers the essential features of such topics.

How relevant is the material?

This is the successor to my earlier book *Software Design for Real-time Systems*, published in 1991. Relevant comments made by reviewers include:

'Congratulations on producing an excellent book on Software Design for Real-time Systems', Stuart Bennett, University of Sheffield.

'We have for a long time been searching for a good and suitable book for our courses on embedded systems. We are very pleased to have found your book after trying out a number of others ... it very well suits our course Design of Software for Embedded Real-Time Control Systems. We are also using it in a similar external industrial course', Martin Torngren, Royal Institute of Technology, Stockholm.

'I am full of admiration and hope that your book has the needed effect on software engineering', Cliff Dilloway, in Software World Series.

'In conclusion I applaud the author for what I found to be an excellent book', Richard Tinker, BT Research Labs, in Software Testing and Verification.

'As the book spans the whole range of embedded development (apart from coding) I highly recommend this book to all embedded engineers', Chris Hills, Association of C and C++ Users.

I have used the material from the 1991 book to form the basis for this new one. The original material has been extensively updated to reflect the significant changes in the software industry of the past decade. Moreover, it has been extended to include a greater range of topics, such as critical systems and performance engineering. Hence I am sure that readers will find it relevant, topical and, most important, useful.

At what level is this book pitched?

Taken as a whole, few assumptions are made about the background of the reader. Ideally he (shorthand for he/she) will have a broad grasp of microprocessor systems, a basic understanding of programming and an appreciation of elementary digital logic. These aren't essential but they help in understanding the reasoning used at many points in the text. Some experience of assembly language and high-level language programming would also be helpful here.

How is this book organized?

The material is organized to cater for both new and experienced readers. It provides full coverage for those new to software engineering and real-time systems. At the same time it allows experienced software engineers to move rapidly onto the more practical-oriented aspects of the subject. This it does by grouping the material into three sections:

Part I: Foundations – Chapters 1–5.

Part II: Designing and developing real-time software – Chapters 6–10.

Part III: Implementation and performance issues – Chapters 11–15.

In general there is a logical progression from start to finish (hardly startling but useful). Chapters, where possible, have been written to stand alone. Thus some repetition and duplication will be found (see also later remarks concerning diagramming aspects). Occasionally forward referencing will be met, but this is used mainly as a pointer to future topics.

What are the objectives and contents of Part I?

The aim of Part I is to give a good grounding in the basics of the subject. The material, which forms the foundations for later chapters, is essential reading for those new to real-time software.

It begins by describing what real-time systems are, their structures and applications, and the impact of these on software design in general. This should be especially useful to readers having a software background only.

Following this is a chapter which shows clearly that to achieve reliable, safe and correct operation, a professional approach to software design is imperative. It explains how and why software errors occur, what qualities are desirable (e.g. feasibility, suitability, robustness, etc.), discusses error avoidance and defensive programming and finishes by looking at design styles.

The problems of deducing and defining system specifications and performance requirements are covered next, including the topics of rapid and animation prototyping. This leads into the basic concepts of software and program design, including modularization, structured programming and mainstream design methods (specifically functional, object-oriented (OO) and data flow techniques).

Rounding off Part I is an introduction to real-time operating systems. The purpose of this is to explain in general terms what these do, why we use them and how they work. It covers the basics of the subject, including scheduling, mutual exclusion, inter-task communication and memory management.

What are the objectives and contents of Part II?

The purpose of Part II is to introduce key practical issues met in the analysis, design and development of real-time software. It is especially relevant to those actively involved in such work.

Chapters 6–9 deal with three distinct aspects of the overall process: operating systems, diagramming and code-related issues. Chapter 10 brings things together, illustrating various methods and methodologies via design examples.

Opening Part II is a chapter dealing with practical aspects of real-time operating systems (RTOSs). It is written primarily from the point of view of building applications on top of commercial RTOSs, taking into account structures, features, performance, overheads, development environments and portability. Following this are two chapters (7 and 8) concerned with a core aspect of modern software development: diagramming. Chapter 7 is a groundwork chapter. It explains why diagrams and diagramming are important, what we achieve by using diagrams and the types used in the software development process. Chapter 8 extends this material showing diagrams which are in common use, are integral to mainstream design methods and are supported by computer-based tools. For sound practical reasons the topic is set in the context of structured, data flow and object-oriented design techniques.

Next to be covered (Chapter 9) are essentially code-related topics, including code development, code organization and packaging and the integration of program units. Issues handled include fundamental program design and construction techniques, the use of component technology in software development, the programming needs of embedded systems, and how mainstream programming languages (Ada 95, C, C++ and Java) meet these requirements. It concludes by showing how the Unified Modelling Language (UML) can be used to document code-related work.

The concluding chapter of Part II (Chapter 10) shows the application of these aspects to practical software development. It looks at the overall specification-to-coding process using both structured/data flow methods (mainly Yourdon) and object-oriented techniques (supported by UML notation).

What are the objectives and contents of Part III?

Part III has two objectives. One aim is to cover important implementation subjects, including analysing and testing source code in both host and target systems and documenting development work. This work applies to all real-time software developments. The second aim is to explain why criticality and performance are key design-drivers in many applications and to give a sound grounding in these topics.

Opening this final section is Chapter 11, 'Analysing and testing source code'. It explains the underlying concepts of source code testing, describes static and dynamic analysis, introduces code complexity metrics and coverage analysis, and deals with OO-specific issues. Following this, Chapter 12, is a description of the last stage of software development, that of producing debugged code in the target system. Topics include software debugging on host and target systems, debugging in host/target combinations, the use of performance analysis tools, emulators and progammers, and integrated development environments.

The next two chapters are essentially stand-alone ones (although their content has a major impact on practical design, development and implementation methods). Chapter 13 explains what critical and fault-tolerant systems are and why their design strategies differ from run-of-the-mill software systems. It is a very wide-ranging chapter, dealing with many diverse aspects important to the development of critical systems. These include the categorization of critical systems, formal specification methods, numerical operations, the development of robust software, dealing with real-world interfacing, operating systems, handling processor and memory malfunctions, and using hardware-based techniques to limit the effects of software failures.

Chapter 14 sets out to show why it is important to design for performance, especially where systems have demanding timing requirements. It shows where such requirements come from, how software performance relates to system performance, and how performance targets get translated into deliverables. It also shows the value of modelling and simulation for analysis, prediction and evaluation of software performance. Lastly it illustrates the techniques of top-down, middle-out and bottom-up performance analysis.

Chapter 15, which deals with documentation, rounds off this section. It describes the relevance and importance of system test and documentation, from functional specification through module description and test operations to maintenance documents. The importance and implementation of configuration management and version control techniques are also covered.

How should the book be read?

If you are new to real-time microprocessor-based systems, start with Chapter 1.

If you are new to software engineering, the following sequence is recommended: all of Part I, all of Part II, Chapters 11, 12 and 15.

For experienced software engineers new to real-time systems: check the contents of Part I, then go on to Part II, followed by Chapters 11, 12 and 15.

Chapters 13 and 14 are very much self-contained.

Why is diagramming covered so extensively?

Now read this

Diagramming is the one area where there may appear to be a fair degree of repetition of material (so I think it's important to discuss this just in case you think it's a ploy to produce a larger book and make more money). One of the reasons for coming up with the structure of this book is that it worked well in its predecessor.

However, at that time the major battle was to convince software designers that diagramming really is an integral part of the design process. Ten years on (and 33 years after my first use of flow charts) things have changed. We find (from our commercial software engineering training courses) that where diagramming is concerned there are fundamentally three groups of people:

1. Those who don't see the need for diagrams and who use expressions like 'the code is my design' (frequently made by those producing write-only C++ programs).
2. Those who, because of the influence of UML, see that diagramming is 'good', but appear to have little understanding of its effective use.
3. Those who truly understand the value of diagramming, practise it and attempt to integrate it within their design processes.

We have also had a sea-change in attitude, with UML becoming the *de facto* standard for OO-based designs.

Part I deals with fundamentals, not diagramming *per se*. As you can see, 'pictures' are used to demonstrate and illustrate points throughout this section. It just seemed common-sense to use standard UML and Yourdon notation rather than *ad hoc* methods wherever appropriate. The material here, especially in Chapters 3–5, is aimed at demonstrating, by example, how useful diagramming is. Moreover, it is hoped that readers new to software will have gradually absorbed information, making it easier to assimilate the material in later stages.

The intent of Chapter 7, 'Diagramming – an introduction', is to show exactly why we should be using diagrams. As the material is mostly conceptual, it could have come early in the book. However, there are a number of reasons for putting it here. First, if the lessons (many implicit) of Part I have been taken on board, then there is little need to sell the 'message' of the chapter. Second, by covering the material at this point, the reader can readily see how it relates to software processes introduced earlier. Third, it acts as a natural lead-in to practical diagramming methods, the subject of Chapter 8. You will find diagrams from earlier chapters repeated here but set in a different context. Here in Chapter 8 the intent is to describe the syntax and semantics of Yourdon and UML notation. Repeating material also allows chapters to be self-contained and complete, so eliminating the need for constant backward references. More experienced readers who choose to skip Part I will appreciate this feature.

The intent of Chapters 9 and 10 is to show how diagrams can be used when developing real systems. Chapter 9 uses them to model code-specific aspects such as component dependencies, class packaging and software deployment. The final chapter of Part II, 'Software analysis and design – methods and methodologies', uses diagrams as part of two specific development processes. Two processes, based on structured/data flow and OO methods, are modelled using the notation (diagrams) defined in Chapter 8.

Acknowledgements

Critics and assessors

First and foremost, I must thank all those friends and colleagues who, by their advice, comments and criticism helped this book into its final state. In particular I would like to mention Adrian Stephens, Barbara Korousic-Seljak, and Stuart Bennett. Special thanks also go to my son Niall for giving over so much time to reviewing the material (well beyond the call of filial duty). The advice of two anonymous referees has helped very much in arriving at the final version. Overall the result has been a much-improved book.

Advice, assistance and contributions

Thanks are also due to a number of people who provided practical assistance in developing material for the book: Matthew Brady of McCabe & Associates UK Ltd, who produced the McCabe control flow graphs of Chapter 11; Ian Gilchrist of IPL Software Products Group, who provided much material on static and dynamic testing; Chris Hills and Michael Beach of Hitex Ltd, for their technical assistance concerning development tools (and also thanks to Chris for his review of Chapter 12); and Alex Robinson, who did such a good job in producing many of the diagrams used in this book. My appreciation must also go to Steven Harris of Wind River Systems for his generous assistance and advice in preparing material for the real-time operating systems chapters. Unfortunately, the most useful material he provided hasn't appeared in the book, as we changed the scope of the text. Next time, perhaps?

I am grateful to my friend Brian Kirk, not only for providing interesting material for Chapter 14, but also for being an inspiration to preach the gospel of good software engineering – and then to practise what I preach. His company, Robinson Associates, is a shining example of quality in our real-time software industry.

Sustenance and relaxation

Owing to business commitments this book has been a long haul (I've seen off two commissioning editors and one editor-in-chief since it started). So those things that contributed to sanity, sustenance and relaxation during this period deserve a special mention: the Bull's Head, Markfield (in conjunction with Arthur Guinness and Sons Ltd), Mistral Windsurfing and Portland Harbour, Flaine and snowboarding and Coed Y Brenin and mountain biking.

Jim Cooling
Markfield, December 2001
(Drained, exhausted, dying for a pint, never going to write another book – until the next time.)

Publisher's acknowledgements

We are grateful to the following for permission to reproduce copyright material:

MDBA Missile Systems for Figure 1.7; BAE Systems (Combat and Radar Systems) Ltd for Figure 1.8; Thales Defence Ltd. for Figure 1.9; MEI for Figure 1.10; Professor D.J. Allerton for Figure 3.50; Taylor & Francis Ltd. (http://www.tandf.co.uk/journals) for Figure 7.19 from 'Pictures of programs and other processes, or how to do things with lines' by T.R.G. Green, *Behaviour and Information Technology*, Vol. 1, No. 1, 1982, pp. 3–36; *Ada User Journal* for Figure 9.50; McCabe & Associates UK Ltd. for Figures 11.11 and 11.12; IPL Information Processing Ltd. for Figures 11.17–11.28; Green Hills Software, Inc. for Figures 12.67, 12.68 and 12.69. MULTI® is a registered trademark of Green Hills Software, Inc.; Hitex (UK) Ltd. for Figures 15.10 and 15.11; Robinson Associates Ltd. for Figure 15.12.

While every effort has been made to trace the owners of copyright material, in a few cases this has proved impossible and we would be grateful to hear from anyone with information which would enable us to do so.

part 1

Foundations

chapter 1

Real-Time Systems – Setting the Scene

Forty years ago software development was widely seen as consisting only of programming. And this was regarded more as an art than a science (and certainly not as an engineering discipline). Perhaps that's why this period is associated with so many gloomy tales of project failure [BRO75]. Well, the industry matured. Along the way we had new languages, real design methods and, in 1968, the distinction between computer science and software engineering.

The microprocessor arrived circa 1970 and set a revolution in motion. But experienced software developers played little part in this. For, until the late 1970s, most developers of microcomputer software were electronic, electrical or control engineers. And they proceeded to make exactly the same mistakes as their predecessors. Now why didn't they learn from the experience of earlier workers? There were three main reasons for this. In the first place, there was little contact between electronic engineers (and the like) and computer scientists. In the second place, many proposed software design methods weren't suitable for real-time applications. Thirdly, traditional computer scientists were quite dismissive of the difficulties met by microprocessor systems designers. Because programs were small the tasks were trivial (or so it was concluded).

Over the years the industry has changed considerably. The driving force for this has been the need to:

● Reduce costs.
● Improve quality, reliability and safety.
● Reduce design, development and commissioning timescales.

3

- Design complex systems.
- Build complex systems.

Without this pressure for change the tools, techniques and concepts discussed in this book would probably still be academic playthings.

Early design methods can be likened to hand-crafting, while the latest ones are more like automated manufacture. But, as in any industry, it's no good automating the wrong tools; we have to use the right tools in the right place at the right time. This chapter lays the groundwork for later work by giving a general picture of real-time systems. It:

- Highlights the differences between general-purpose computer applications (e.g. information technology, management information systems, etc.) and real-time systems.
- Looks at the types of real-time systems met in practice.
- Describes the environmental and performance requirements of embedded real-time systems.
- Describes typical structures of modern microprocessors and microcomputers.
- Shows, in general, how software design and development techniques are influenced by these factors.

The detailed features of modern software methods are covered in later chapters.

1.1 Categorizing computer systems

How are computer systems categorized? There are many answers to this, sometimes conflicting, sometimes overlapping. But if we use speed of response as the main criterion, then three general groups emerge:

- Batch: I don't mind when the computer results arrive, within reason (the time taken may be hours or even days in such systems).
- Interactive on-line: I *would like* the results within a fairly short time, typically a few seconds.
- Real-time: I *need* the results within definite timescales, otherwise the system just won't work properly.

Let's consider these in turn.

An example of a modern batch system is shown in Figure 1.1. Methods like this are used where computing resources are scarce and/or expensive as it is a very efficient technique. Here the user usually pre-processes all programs and information, perhaps storing data on a local computer. At some convenient time, say at the start of an evening shift, this job is passed over the data link to a remote site (often a number of jobs are transmitted as a single job-lot). When all jobs are finished the results are transmitted back to the originating site.

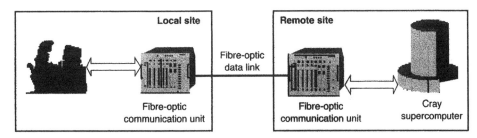

Figure 1.1   Modern batch system.

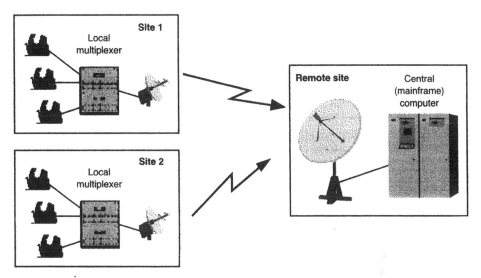

Figure 1.2   Typical interactive on-line computer system.

Interactive on-line computer systems are widely used in banking, holiday booking and mail-order systems. Here, for private systems, access to the system is made using (typically) PC-based remote terminals, Figure 1.2. Local processing of data isn't normally done in this instance. Instead, all transactions are handled by the central computer in a time-sliced fashion. Routing and access control is the responsibility of the front-end processors and local multiplexers. Many readers will, of course, have experience of such systems through their use of the Internet and the Web (perhaps the importance of timeliness in interactive systems is summed up by the definition of www. as standing for 'world wide wait'). A further point to take note of is that response times depend on the amount of activity. All systems slow down as load builds up, sometimes seizing up at peak times. For time-critical applications this type of response is unacceptable, as, for example, in auto cruise-control systems, Figure 1.3. Here the driver dials in the desired cruising speed. The cruise control computer notes this and compares it with the actual vehicle speed. If there is a

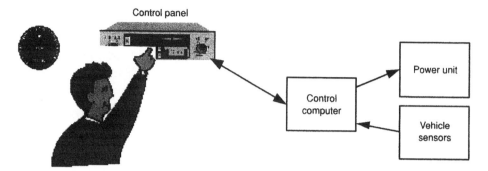

Control panel

Power unit

Control computer

Vehicle sensors

Figure 1.3 Real-time computer system.

difference, correcting signals are sent to the power unit. The vehicle will either speed up or slow down, depending on the desired response. Provided control is executed quickly the vehicle will be powered in a smooth and responsive manner. But if there is a significant delay in the computer, a kangaroo-like performance occurs. Clearly, in this case, the computer is worse than useless: it degrades the car's performance.

In this text 'real-time' is taken to imply time-bounded response constraints. Should computer responses exceed specific time bounds then performance degradation and/or malfunction results. So, *within this definition*, batch and interactive on-line systems are not considered to operate in real time.

 ## 1.2 Real-time computer systems

1.2.1 Time and criticality issues

From what's been said so far, one factor distinguishes real-time systems from batch and on-line applications: timeliness. Unfortunately, this is a rather limited definition; a more precise one is needed. Many ways of categorizing real-time systems have been proposed and are in use. One particular pragmatic scheme, based on time and criticality, is shown in Figure 1.4. An arbitrary boundary between slow and fast is one second (chosen because problems shift from individual computing issues to overall system aspects at around this point). The related attributes are given in Figure 1.5

Time ⇒ Criticality ⇓	Slow	Fast
Soft	Machine condition monitoring	Man–machine interfacing
Hard	Missile point defence system	Airbag control system

Figure 1.4 Real-time system categorization.

Attribute ⇒ Category ⇓	Execution time	Deadlines	Software size	Software complexity
Hard-Fast	****	****	*	*
Hard-Slow	*	****	* → ***	* → ****
Soft-Fast	****	**	* → ***	* → ***
Soft-Slow	**	**	* → ****	* → ****

   *   *Low weighting*
 ****   *High weighting*

Figure 1.5 ┊ Attributes of real-time systems.

Hard, fast embedded systems tend, in computing terms, to be small (or may be a small, localized part of a larger system). Computation times are short (typically in the tens of milliseconds or faster), and deadlines are critical. Software complexity is usually low, especially in safety-critical work. A good example is the airbag deployment system in motor vehicles. Late deployment defeats the whole purpose of airbag protection.

Hard, slow systems do not fall into any particular size category (though many, as with process controllers, are small). An illustrative example of such an application is an anti-aircraft missile-based point-defence system for fast patrol boats. Here the total reaction time is in the order of 10 seconds. However, the consequences of failing to respond in this time frame are self-evident.

Larger systems usually include comprehensive, and sometimes complex, man–machine interfaces (MMIs). Such interfaces may form an integral part of the total system operation, as, for instance, in integrated weapon fire–control systems. Fast operator responses may be required, but deadlines are not critical as in the previous cases. Significant tolerance can be permitted (in fact, this is generally true when humans form part of system operation). MMI software tends to be large and complex.

The final category, soft–slow, is typified by condition monitoring, trend analysis and statistics analysis in, for example, factory automation. Frequently such software is large and complex. Applications like these may be classified as *information processing* (IP) systems.

1.2.2   Real-time system structures

It is clear that the fundamental difference between real-time and other (i.e. batch and interactive) systems is one of timeliness. However, this in itself tells us little about the structure of such computer systems. So, before looking at modern real-time systems, it's worth digressing to consider the set-up of IT-type mainframe installations. While most modern mainframe systems are large and complex (and may be used for a whole variety of jobs) they have many features in common. In the first case, the essential architectures are broadly similar; the real differences lie in the applications themselves and the application software. Second, the physical environments are usually benign ones, often including air conditioning. Peripheral devices include terminals, PCs, printers, plotters, disks, tapes, communication links; and little else. Common to many mainframe installations is the use of terabytes of disk and tape storage. The installation itself is staffed and maintained by professional DP personnel. It requires maintenance in the broadest sense, including that for upgrading and modifying programs. In such a setting it's not surprising that *the computer* is the focus of attention and concern.

By contrast, real-time systems come in many types and sizes. The largest, in geographical terms, are telemetry control systems, Figure 1.6. Such systems are widely used in the space, gas, oil, water and electricity industries. They provide centralized control and monitoring of remote sites from a single control room.

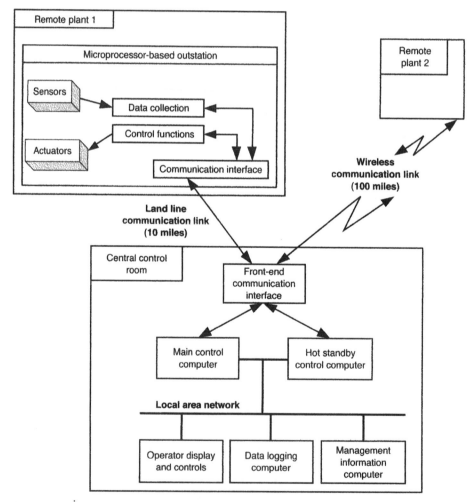

Figure 1.6 Telemetry control system.

Figure 1.7 Sea Skua missile system (reproduced with permission from MBDA Missile Systems).

Smaller in size, but probably more complex in nature, are missile control systems, Figure 1.7. Many larger embedded applications involve a considerable degree of complex man–machine interaction. Typical of these are the command and control systems of modern naval vessels (Figure 1.8). And of course one of the major application areas of real-time systems is that of avionics, Figure 1.9. These, in particular, involve numerous hard, fast and safety-critical systems.

On the industrial scene there are many installations which use computer-based stand-alone controllers (often for quite dedicated functions). Applications include vending machines (Figure 1.10), printer controllers, anti-lock braking, burglar alarms; the list is endless. These examples differ in many detailed ways from DP installations, such factors being discussed below. There are, though, two fundamental points. First, as stated above, the computer is seen to be merely one component of a larger system. Second, the user does not normally have the requirements – or facilities – to modify programs on a day-to-day basis. In practice, most users won't have the knowledge or skill to re-program the machine.

Embedded systems use a variety of hardware architectures ('platforms'), Figure 1.11.

Many are based on special-to-purpose ('bespoke') designs, especially where there are significant constraints such as:

● Environmental aspects (temperature, shock, vibration, humidity, etc.).

● Size and weight (aerospace, auto, telecomms, etc.).

● Cost (auto, consumer goods, etc.).

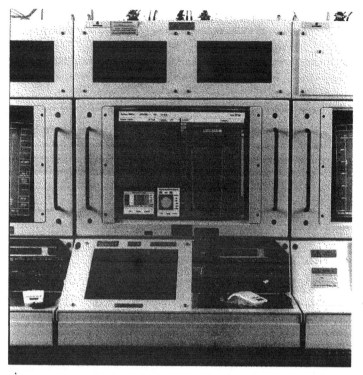

Figure 1.8 Submarine command and control system console (reproduced with permission from BAE Systems).

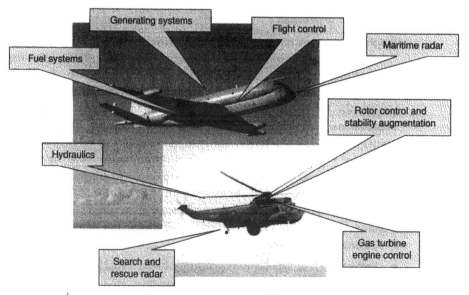

Figure 1.9 Typical avionic platforms (reproduced with permission from Thales Ltd).

Figure 1.10 Microprocessor-based vending machine units (reproduced with permission from Mars Electronics International).

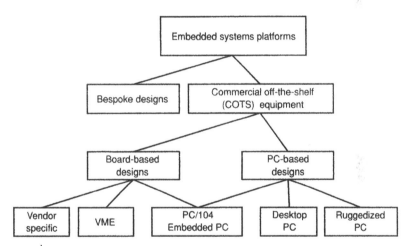

Figure 1.11 Embedded systems platforms.

The advantage of bespoke systems is that products are optimized for the applications. Unfortunately, design and development is a costly and time-consuming process. A much cheaper and faster approach is to use ready-made items, a commercial off-the-shelf (COTS) buying policy. Broadly speaking there are two alternative approaches:

● Base the hardware design on the use of sets of circuit boards, or
● Implement the design using some form of PC.

In reality these aren't mutually exclusive.

COTS board-based designs

Many vendors offer single-board computer systems, based on particular processors and having a wide range of peripheral boards. In some cases these may be compatible with standard PC buses such as PCI (peripheral component interconnect). For embedded applications, it is problematic whether boards from different suppliers can be mixed and matched with confidence. However, where boards are designed to comply with well-defined standards, this can be done (generally) without worry. One great advantage with this is that it doesn't tie a company to one specific supplier. Two standards are particularly important in the embedded world: VME [VME87] and PC/104 [PC01].

VME was originally introduced by a number of vendors in 1981, and was later standardized as IEEE standard 1014-1987. It is especially important to developers of military and similar systems, as robust, wide-temperature-range boards are available. A second significant standard for embedded applications is PC/104, a cheaper alternative to VME. It is essentially a PC but with a different physical construction, being based on stackable circuit boards (it gets its name from its PC roots and the number of pins used to connect the boards together (104)). At present it is estimated that more than 150 vendors manufacture PC/104 compatible products.

COTS PC-based designs

Clearly PC/104 designs are PC-based. However, an alternative to the board solution is to use ready-made personal computers. These may be tailored to particular applications by using specialized plug-in boards (e.g. stepper motor drives, data acquisition units, etc.). If the machine is to be located in say an office environment, then a standard desktop computer may be satisfactory. However, these are not designed to cope with conditions met on the factory floor, such as dust, moisture, etc. In such situations ruggedized, industrial standard PCs can be used. Where reliability, durability and serviceability are concerned, these are immensely superior to the desktop machines.

1.2.3 Characteristics of embedded systems

Embedded computers are defined to be those where the computer is used as a component within a system: not as a computing engine in its own right. This definition is the one which, at heart, separates embedded from non-embedded designs (note that, from now on, 'embedded' implicitly means 'real-time embedded').

Embedded systems are characterized (Figure 1.12) by:

- The environments they work in.
- The performance expected of them.
- The interfaces to the outside world.

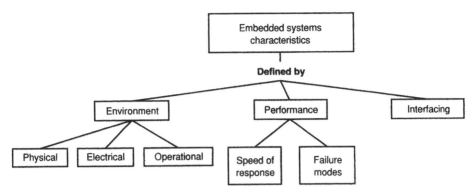

Figure 1.12 Embedded systems characteristics.

Environmental aspects

Environmental factors may, at first glance, seem to have little bearing on software. Primarily they affect:

● Hardware design and construction.

● Operator interaction with the system.

But these, to a large extent, determine how the complete system works – and that defines the overall software requirements. Consider the physical effects of:

● Temperature.

● Shock and vibration.

● Humidity.

● Size limits.

● Weight limits.

The temperature ranges commonly met in embedded applications are shown in Figure 1.13. Many components used in commercial computers are designed to operate in the band 0–30 degrees centigrade. Electronic components aren't usually a problem. Items like terminals, display units, floppy and hard disks are the weaknesses. As a result, the embedded designer must either do without them or else provide them with a protected environment – which can be a costly solution. When the requirements to withstand shock, vibration and water penetration are added, the options narrow. For instance, the ideal way to re-program a system might be to update the system using a flash card. But if we can't use this technology because of environmental factors, then what?

Size and weight are two factors uppermost in the minds of many embedded systems designers. For vehicle systems, such as automobiles, aircraft, armoured fighting vehicles and submarines, they may be *the* crucial factors. Not much to do

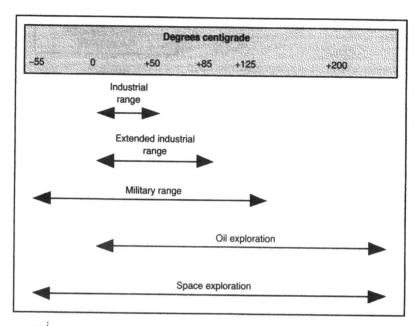

Figure 1.13 Typical temperature specifications for real-time applications.

with software, you may think. But suppose a design requirement can only be met by using a single-chip micro (see later). Further, suppose that this device has only 256 bytes of random access memory (RAM). How does that affect our choice of programming language?

The electrical environments of industrial and military systems are not easy to work in. Yet most systems are expected to cope with extensive power supply variations in a predictable manner. To handle problems like this we may have to resort to defensive programming techniques (Chapter 2). Program malfunction can result from electrical interference; again, defensive programming is needed to handle this. A further complicating factor in some systems is that the available power may be limited. This won't cause difficulties in small systems. But if your software needs 512 megabytes of dynamic RAM to run in, the power system designers are going to face problems.

Let's now turn to the operational environmental aspects of embedded systems. Normally we expect that when the power is turned on the system starts up safely and correctly. It should do this every time, *and* without any operator intervention. Conversely, when the power is turned off, the system should also behave safely. What we design for are 'fit and forget' functions.

In many instances embedded systems have long operational lives, perhaps from 10 to 30 years. Often it is required to upgrade the equipment a number of times in its lifetime. So, the software itself will also need upgrading. This aspect of software, its maintenance, may well affect how we design it in the first place.

Performance

Two particular factors are important here:

- How fast does a system respond?
- When it fails, what happens?

The speed of response

All required responses are time-critical (although these may vary from microseconds to days). Therefore the designer should predict the delivered performance of the embedded system. Unfortunately, with the best will in the world, it may not be possible to give 100% guarantees. The situation is complicated because there are two distinct sides to this issue, both relating to the way tasks are processed by the computer.

Case one concerns demands to run jobs at regular, pre-defined intervals. A typical application is that of closed-loop digital controllers having fixed, preset sampling rates. This we'll define to be a 'synchronous' or 'periodic' task event (synchronous with some real-time clock – Figure 1.14). Case two occurs when the computer must respond to (generally) external events which occur at random ('asynchronous' or 'aperiodic'). And the event must be serviced within a specific maximum time period. Where the computer handles only periodic events, response times can be determined reasonably well. This is also true where only one aperiodic event drives the system (a rare event), Figure 1.15. When the system has to cope with a number of asynchronous events, estimates are difficult to arrive at. But by setting task priorities, good estimates of worst case performance can be deduced (Figure 1.16). As shown here task 1 has higher priority than task 2.

Where we get into trouble is in situations which involve a mixture of periodic and aperiodic events, which are usual in real-time designs. Much thought and skill are needed to deal with the response requirements of periodic and aperiodic tasks (especially when using just one processor).

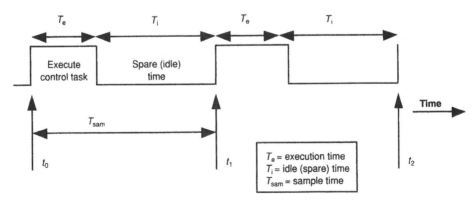

Figure 1.14 Computer loading – single synchronous (periodic) task.

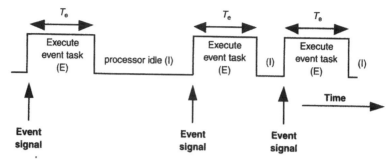

Figure 1.15 : Computer loading – single asynchronous (aperiodic) task.

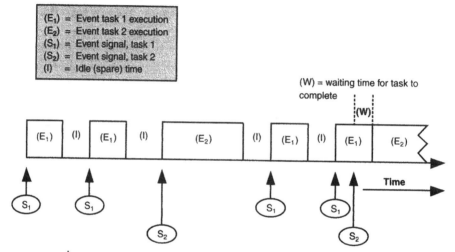

Figure 1.16 : Computer loading – multiple asynchronous (aperiodic) tasks.

Failures and their effects

All systems go wrong at some time in their lives. It may be a transient condition or a hard failure; the cause may be hardware or software or a combination of both. It really doesn't matter; accept that it will happen. What we have to concern ourselves with are:

- The consequences of such faults and failures.
- Why the problem(s) arose in the first place.

Because a system can tolerate faults without sustaining damage doesn't mean that such performance is acceptable. Nuisance tripping out of a large piece of plant, for instance, is not going to win many friends. *All* real-time software must therefore be designed in a professional manner to handle all foreseen problems, that is, 'exception' handling (an exception is defined here to be an error or fault which produces program malfunction, see Chapter 2; it may originate within the program itself or be due to external factors). If, on the other hand, software packages are bought in, their quality must be assessed. Regularly claims are made concerning the benefits of using Windows™ operating systems in real-time applications. Yet users of such systems often experience unpredictable behaviour, including total system hang-up. Could this really be trusted for plant control and similar applications?

In other situations we may not be able to cope with unrectified system faults. Three options are open to us. In the first, where no recovery action is possible, the system is put into a fail-safe condition. In the second, the system keeps on working, but with reduced service. This may be achieved, say, by reducing response times or by servicing only the 'good' elements of the system. Such systems are said to offer 'graceful' degradation in their response characteristics. Finally, for fault tolerant operation, full and safe performance is maintained in the presence of faults.

Interfacing

The range of devices which interface to embedded computers is extensive. It includes sensors, actuators, motors, switches, display panels, serial communication links, parallel communication methods, analogue-to-digital converters, digital-to-analogue converters, voltage-to-frequency converters, pulse-width modulated controllers, and so on. Signals may be analogue (d.c. or a.c.) or digital; voltage, current or frequency encoding methods may be used. In anything but the smallest systems hardware size is dominated by the interfacing electronics. This has a profound effect on system design strategies concerning processor replication and exception handling.

When the processor itself is the major item in a system, fitting a back-up to cope with failures is feasible and sensible. Using this same approach in an input–output (I/O) dominated system makes much less sense (and introduces much complexity).

Conventional exception-handling schemes are usually concerned with detecting internal (program) problems. These include stack overflow, array bound violations and arithmetic overflow. However, for most real-time systems a new range of problems has to be considered. These relate to factors such as sensor failure, illegal operator actions, program malfunction induced by external interference, etc. Detecting such faults is one thing; deciding what to do subsequently can be an even more difficult problem. Exception-handling strategies need careful design to prevent faults causing system or environmental damage (or worse – injury or death).

1.3 The computing elements of real-time systems

1.3.1 Overview

In real-time systems, computing elements are destined for use in either general-purpose or specialized applications, Figure 1.17. To use these effectively, the software designer should have a good understanding of their features. After all, what might be an excellent design solution for one application might be ghastly (or even unusable) in others.

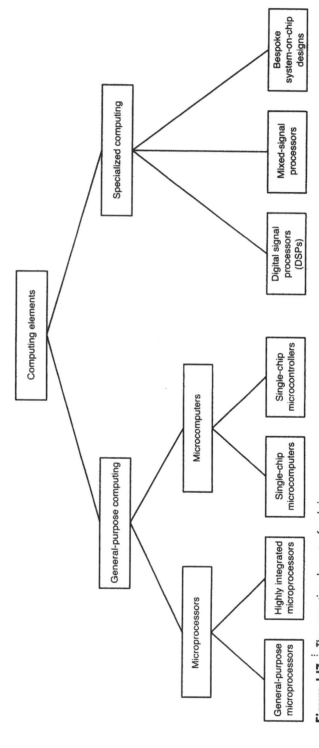

Figure 1.17 The computing elements of real-time systems.

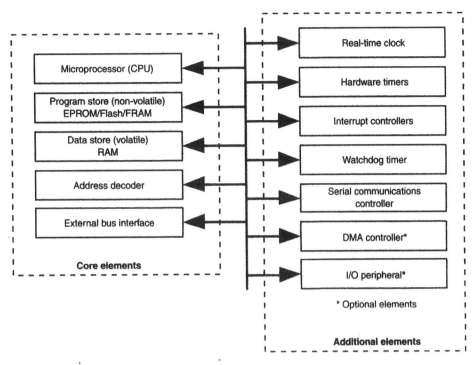

Figure 1.18 Elements of a microcomputer system.

1.3.2 General-purpose microprocessors

General-purpose microprocessors are the single largest group, including, for example, the Intel X86, Infineon C166, Motorola PowerPC and Hitachi H series devices. But, by itself, the processor is only one element within the microprocessor system. To turn it into a computing machine certain essential elements need to be added (Figure 1.18). The program code itself is stored in memory which, for embedded systems, must be retained on power-down. That is, the memory must be 'non-volatile'. Older designs typically used ultraviolet erasable (electrically) programmable ROM (EPROM). The drawback with this device is that (normally) it must be removed from the computer for erasure and re-programming. However, where in-circuit re-programming is required, code is located in electrically erasable/programmable non-volatile storage, the alternatives being:

● Electrically erasable programmable ROM (EEPROM).

● Flash memory (a particular type of EEPROM technology).

● Ferroelectric random access memory (FRAM).

Flash memory has, to a large extent, replaced EPROM in new designs.

When large production quantities are concerned, two approaches may be used:

- Mask-programmable devices.
- One-time programmable ROM (OTPROM).

In the first case the program is set in the memory by the chip manufacturer; as such it is unalterable. The second method is essentially an EPROM device without a light window. Nowadays this market sector usually uses single-chip microcomputers rather that general-purpose ones.

All data which is subject to regular change is located in read–write 'random access' memory (a confusing term, as memory locations, for most devices, can be accessed randomly). This includes program variables, stack data, process descriptors and dynamic data items.

The final element is the address decoder unit. Its function is to identify the element being accessed by the processor.

Taken together, these items form the heart of the microcomputer. However, to make it usable in real-time applications, extra elements need to be added. The key items are:

- Real-time clock.
- Hardware timers.
- Interrupt controller.
- Watchdog timer.
- Serial communication controller.

Items which should also be considered at the design stage include:

- Direct memory access (DMA) controllers.
- I/O peripheral controllers (only where large volume data transfer is required).

These may be essential in some systems but not in others.

Interrupt controllers

As pointed out earlier, real-time systems must support both periodic and aperiodic tasks. In most designs 'guaranteed' response times are obtained by using interrupts.

Real-time clock

The function of the real-time clock is to provide a highly accurate record of elapsed time. It is normally used in conjunction with an interrupt function. Real-time clocks shouldn't be confused with calendar clocks (although they may be used for calendar functions). When an operating system is incorporated within the software the clock acts as the basic timing element (the 'tick').

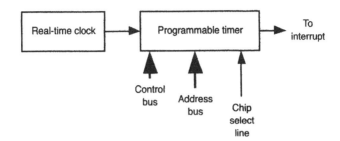

Figure 1.19 : Timing in hardware.

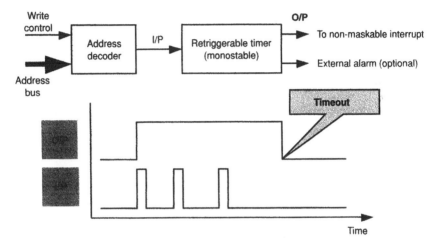

Figure 1.20 : Watchdog timer.

Hardware timers

Accurate timing, especially that involving long time periods, cannot normally be done in software. Without the timing support of the tick in an operating system, hardware timers have to be used. Even when an operating system is used, these timers provide great flexibility. Generally these are software programmable (Figure 1.19), both in terms of timing and modes of operation (e.g. square-wave generation, 'one-shot' pulse outputs and retriggerable operation).

Watchdog timer

The purpose of the watchdog timer is to act as the last line of defence against program malfunction. It normally consists of a retriggerable monostable or one-shot timer, activated by program command (Figure 1.20). Each time the timer is addressed it is retriggered, the output staying in the 'normal' state. If for any reason it isn't retriggered then time-out occurs, and the output goes into alarm conditions. The usual course of action is to then generate a non-maskable interrupt (NMI), so setting a recovery program into action. In some instances external warnings are also produced. In others, especially digital control systems, warnings are produced and the controller then isolated from the controller process.

Address decoding of the watchdog timer is, for critical systems, performed over all bits of the address. In these circumstances the address is a unique one; hence retriggering by accident is virtually eliminated.

Serial communications controllers

Serial communications facilities are integral parts of many modern embedded systems. However, even where this isn't needed, it is well worth while to design in an RS232 compatible communication channel [EIA69]. This can be used as a major aid in the development and debugging of the application software (Chapter 12).

DMA controllers

The DMA controller (Figure 1.21) is used where data has to be moved about quickly and/or in large amounts (data rates can exceed 100 MBytes/s). DMA techniques are

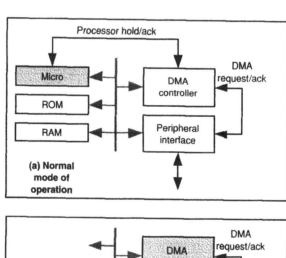

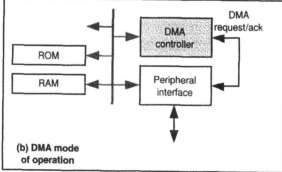

Figure 1.21 DMA operation.

widely used in conjunction with bulk memory storage devices such as hard disks and compact disks. For many real-time systems they are used where high-speed serial communication links have to be supported. In normal circumstances (the 'normal' mode of operation, Figure 1.21a), the controller acts just like any other slave device, being controlled by the processor. However, when a DMA request is generated by a peripheral device, control is taken over by the DMA controller (Figure 1.21b). In this case the micro is electrically disconnected from the rest of the system. Precise details of data transfer operations are usually programmed into the controller by the micro.

I/O peripheral

I/O peripherals are used either as controllers or as interfacing devices. When used as a controller, their function is to offload routine I/O processing, control and high-speed transfer work from the processor itself, Figure 1.22. One of the most common uses of such devices is to handle high-speed large-volume data transfers to and from hard disk. They are especially useful in dealing with replicated memory storage units, as with replicated arrays of independent disk (RAID) technology. Other applications include intelligent bus, network and communications interfacing.

The I/O controller's basic operation is similar to that of a DMA controller, but with two major differences. First, it can work co-operatively with the processor, using system resources when the processor is busy. Second, I/O processors are much more powerful than DMA devices. For example, the Intel 80303 IOP includes (amongst other items) a high-speed parallel bus bridge, a specialized serial bus interface, internal DMA controllers and a performance monitoring unit.

In other applications I/O devices are used to provide compact, simple and low-cost interfaces between the processor and peripheral equipment, Figure 1.23. I/O pins are user-programmable to set up the desired connections to such equipment. These interface chips function as slave devices to the processing unit.

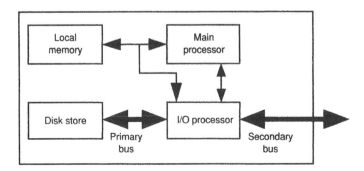

Figure I.22 : Intelligent I/O processing.

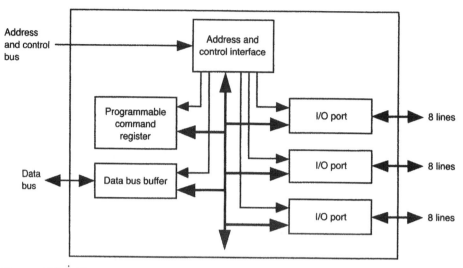

Figure 1.23 | I/O interface peripheral.

1.3.3 Highly integrated microprocessors

Highly integrated processors are those which contain many of the standard elements of a microcomputer system on a single chip. Typical of these are the Intel 386 and the Motorola MPC8240 integrated PowerPC microprocessor (Figure 1.24).

A comparison of Figure 1.18 and Figure 1.24 shows just what can be achieved on one chip (the MPC8240, for example, reduces the chip count from five to one). Naturally, such processors are more expensive than the basic general-purpose device. However, the integration of many devices onto one chip usually reduces overall system cost. Moreover, it makes a major impact on board-packing densities. It also reduces manufacturing and test costs. In short, these are highly suited for use in embedded systems design.

1.3.4 Single-chip microcomputers

With modern technology complete microcomputers can be implemented on a single chip, eliminating the need for external components. Using the single-chip solution reduces the:

- Package count.
- Size.
- Overall costs.

One widely used device of this type is the 8052 microcomputer, a Philips Semiconductor variant being shown in Figure 1.25.

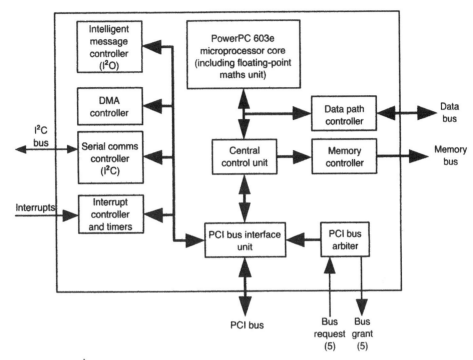

Figure 1.24 Highly integrated processor – Motorola MPC8240.

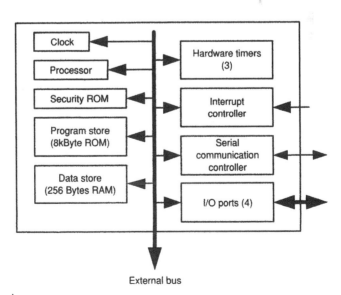

Figure 1.25 Single-chip microcomputer – Philips Semiconductor 8052.

By now all the on-chip devices will be familiar. Note that the interfacing to the outside world may be carried out through the I/O port subsystem. This is a highly flexible structure which, in smaller systems, minimizes component count. But with only 8 kBytes of ROM and 256 bytes of RAM, it is clearly intended for use in small systems (the memory size can, of course, be extended by using external devices).

1.3.5 Single-chip microcontrollers

Microcontrollers are derivatives of microcomputers, but aimed specifically at the embedded control market (though the boundary between the two is becoming some-what blurred). Like the single-chip microcomputer, they are designed to provide all computing functions in a single package. The interfacing hardware, internal register structure and the instruction set are usually optimized for use with fast real-time systems. An example of such a device is the Fujitsu MB91F361, Figure 1.26.

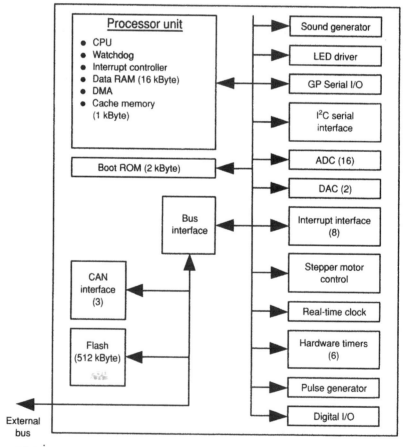

Figure 1.26 Single-chip microcontroller – Fujitsu MB91F361.

This particular micro is tailored for use with CAN (controller area network) embedded applications (e.g. industrial and auto systems).

From the hardware point of view the most obvious additions relate to I/O interfacing. This includes:

- CAN network interfacing.

- Simpler serial communication interfacing.

- Stepper motor control.

- High-current LED drivers.

- 16-channel analogue-to-digital converter (10 bit resolution).

- Two-channel digital-to-analogue converter (10 bit resolution).

- Eight interrupts.

- Real-time clock.

- Pulse modulated output drives.

- Sound driver.

- Timers.

- On-chip power-down reset circuitry.

- Digital input and output channels.

It also contains 16 kBytes of RAM and 512 kBytes of OTPROM or Flash.

1.3.6 Digital signal processors

There are numerous applications which need to process analogue signals very quickly. These include instrumentation, speech processing, telecommunications, radar, sonar and control systems. In the past such processing was done using analogue techniques. But because of the disadvantages of analogue processors (filters), designers have, where possible, moved to digital techniques. Important characteristics of such systems are:

- Extremely high throughputs.

- Optimization for numerical operations.

- Employment of a small number of repetitive numerical calculations and often

- Low-cost.

These needs have been met by the digital signal processor (DSP), optimized for digital filtering calculations. Such calculations are typified by sets of multiply and add (accumulate) instructions, the so-called 'sum of products' computation.

To achieve high processing speeds, the basic computing engine is organized around a high-speed multiplier/accumulator combination (Figure 1.27). In these designs the Von Neumann structure is replaced by the Harvard architecture, having separate

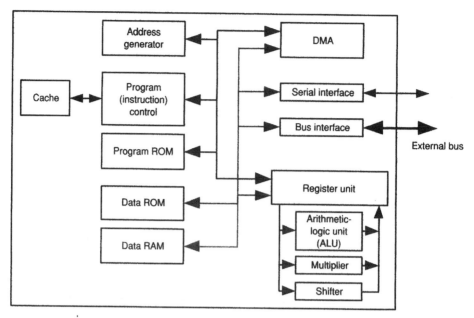

Figure 1.27 | Digital signal processor structure.

paths for instruction and data. The system form shown in Figure 1.27 is fairly typical of digital signal processors. Obviously, specific details vary from processor to processor, see [DSP01] for further information.

Programming DSPs is a demanding task, especially working at assembly language level. The instruction sets are optimized to perform fast and efficient arithmetic. Among those instructions are those which invoke complex multipurpose operations. Added to this is the need to produce compact and efficient code if the whole program is to fit into the on-chip ROM. And finally, there is the need to handle extensive fixed-point computations without running into overflow problems. It has been said that, in fixed-point DSP programming, '90% of the effort goes into worrying about where the decimal point is' [DET86].

1.3.7 Mixed-signal processors

Mixed-signal processors, as their name suggests, are designed to interface simultaneously to analogue and digital components. The Texas MSP430, for example (Figure 1.28), is aimed at battery-powered applications (such as multimeters, intelligent sensing, etc.) where low power consumption is paramount.

Quoted figures (typical) for power requirements are:

- Active: 250 µA at 2.2 volts.
- Standby: 0.8 µA at 2.2 volts.

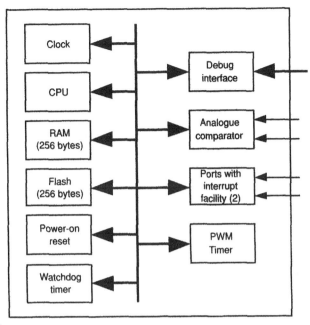

Figure 1.28 Mixed-signal processor structure – Texas MSP430.

Work like this *could* be done by a standard microcontroller, but this is a relatively costly solution. Hence mixed-signal processors are optimized for use in low-cost, high-volume products. This particular device sells at $0.99 – provided you buy 10,000 at a time!

1.3.8 Bespoke system-on-chip designs

System-on-chip (SOC) components are essentially single-chip *application-specific* designs. Applications include digital cameras, wireless communication, engine management, specialized peripherals and complex signal processing.

Figure 1.29 is a representative structure of an SOC unit, though by definition there are many variations of such structures. At first glance it seems very much like other single-chip devices, incorporating a variety of familiar subsystems. However, there are two very distinct differences between these products: design/fabrication methods and subsystem type.

With SOC technology, all design and fabrication is carried out by (or under the control of) the chip designer. Electronic engineers have for many years produced application-specific devices using, for example, field programmable gate arrays (FPGAs) and application-specific integrated circuits (ASICs). Such products are good examples of custom designs, being produced for very specific purposes (e.g. discrete

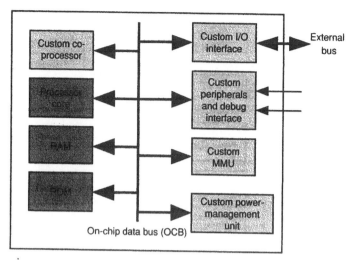

Figure 1.29 Example system-on-a-chip design.

Fourier analysis, DFT). Design itself is normally done using computer-aided design (CAD) methods, often based on very high-level description languages (VHDL). An SOC design is fundamentally the same, but much more complex. In particular, SOC devices incorporate microprocessor(s) and memory devices, etc. to form full on-chip microcomputers.

In Figure 1.29, the subsystems fall into two groups: 'custom' and other. Anything designed by the chip designer is labelled custom; the others represent bought-in items (e.g. microprocessor, RAM, ROM). Of course, because this is chip-fabrication, we cannot 'plug-in' such items onto the chip. What happens typically is that *VHDL descriptions* [VHD01] of the components are used within the overall design process. Naturally these must be obtained from the designers of such products. Such components are usually called 'virtual components', 'virtual cores' (VCs) or 'intellectual property' (IP) cores. Note also that the latest generation of FPGA devices incorporates processor cores in the crips.

1.4 Software for real-time applications – some general comments

In later chapters the total design process for real-time systems is described. We'll be looking for answers to questions such as:

- What truly needs to be done?
- How should we specify these needs?
- How do we ensure that we're doing the *right job* (satisfy the system requirements)?

- How can we make sure that we're doing the *job right* (perform the design correctly)?
- How can we test the resulting designs for correctness, performance and errors?
- How do we get programs to work correctly in the target system itself?

Before doing this, let's consider some general problems met in real-time systems work and also dispel a few software myths. And a useful word of advice: don't believe everything you read – question any unsupported assertions (even in this book).

The quotations used below have been made (in print) by experienced software practitioners.

'For real-time systems . . . programs tend to be large, often in the order of tens of thousands or even of hundreds of thousands of lines of code'. This generalization is wrong, especially for embedded systems. Here programs are frequently small, having object code sizes in the range 2–40 kBytes (however, two factors in particular tend to bloat embedded code: support for highly interactive graphical user interfaces and support for Internet communication protocols). An oft-made mistake frequently made is to apply the rules of large systems to small ones.

'At the specification stage . . . *all* the functional requirements, performance requirements and design constraints must be specified'. In the world of real-time system design this is an illusion. Ideas like these have come about mostly from the DP world. There, systems such as stock control, accounting, management reporting methods and the like *can* be specified in their entirety before software design commences. In contrast, specifications for real-time systems tend to follow an evolutionary development. We may start with an apparently clear set of requirements. At a much later stage (usually some time after the software has been delivered) the final, clear, but quite different specifications are agreed.

'Software costs dominate . . .'. This is rarely true for embedded systems. It all depends on the size of the job, the role of software within the total system, and the number of items to be manufactured.

'Software is one of the most complex things known to man . . . Hundreds of man years to develop system XXX'. Well, yes, software is complex. But let's not go overboard about it. Just consider that the development of a new nuclear propulsion for submarines took more than 5000 man-years (at a very conservative estimate). And it involved large teams, skilled in many engineering disciplines, and based at various geographically separate sites. Is this an 'easy' task compared with software development?

'Software, by its nature, is inherently unreliable'. I think the assumption behind this is that software is a product of thought, and isn't bounded by natural physical laws. Therefore there is a much greater chance of making mistakes. This is rather like saying that as circuit theory underpins electronic design, hardware designs are intrinsically less prone to errors. Not so. Delivered hardware is generally free of fault because design, development and manufacture is (or should be) rigorous, formal and systematic. By contrast, software has for far too long been developed in a sloppy manner in cottage industry style. The industry (especially the industrial embedded world) has lacked design formality, has rarely used software design tools, and almost completely ignored the use of documentation and configuration control mechanisms. Look out for the classic hacker comment: 'my code is the design'.

The final point for consideration concerns the knowledge and background needed by embedded systems software designers. In the early days of microprocessor systems there was an intimate bond between hardware and software. It was (and, in many cases, still is) essential to have a very good understanding of the hardware: especially so for the I/O activities. Unfortunately, in recent years a gulf has developed between hardware and software engineers. As a result it is increasingly difficult to find engineers with the ability to bridge this gap effectively. Moreover, larger and larger jobs are being implemented using microprocessors. Allied to this has been an explosion in the use of software-based real-time systems. As a result, more and more software is being developed by people who have little knowledge of hardware or systems. We may not like the situation, but that's the way it is. To cope with this, there has been a change in software design methodologies. Now the design philosophy is to provide a 'software base' for handling hardware and system-specific tasks. This is sometimes called 'foundation' or 'service' software. Programmers can then build their application programs on the foundation software, needing only a minimal understanding of the system hardware. The greatest impact of this has been in the area of real-time operating systems.

Review

You should now:

- Clearly understand the important features of real-time systems.

- Know what sets them apart from batch and interactive application.

- See how real-time systems may be categorized in terms of speed and criticality.

- Have a general understanding of the range of real-time (and especially embedded) applications.

- Realize that environmental and performance factors are key drivers in real-time systems design.

- Know the basic component parts of real-time computer units.

- Appreciate the essential differences between microprocessors, microcomputers and microcontrollers.

- Realize why there is a large market for specialized processors.

References and further reading

[BRO75] *The mythical man-month*, F.P. Brooks, Addison-Wesley, ISBN 0-201-00650-2, 1975.

[DET86] *Digital signal processors*, R. Dettmer, Electronics and Power, pp 124–128, Feb. 1986.

[DSP01] http://www.bdti.com/procsum/index.htm.

[EIA69] *EIA standard 232: Interface between data terminal equipment and data communication equipment employing serial binary data interchange*, Electronic Industries Association, 1969.

[PC01] *PC/104 embedded solutions*, www.pc104.org.

[SOC01] *Surviving the SOC revolution*, H. Chang *et al.* Kluwer Academic Publishers, ISBN 0-7923-8679-5, 2001. www.wkap.nl/book.htm/0-7923-8679-5.

[VHD01] *The designers guide to VHDL*, Peter Ashenden, Morgan Kaufmann, ISBN 1558606742, 2001.

[VME87] *VME – Versa Module Europa, IEEE Std. 1014-1987*, 1987. www.vmebus-systems.com.

chapter 2

The Search for Dependable Software

Many steps have to be taken to combat the problems of poor software. Proper system specification, defined design methods, high-level language support and good development tools all contribute toward a solution. But to appreciate their use (instead of merely knowing what they do), we must understand what they aim to achieve. To answer that we need to know where, why and how software problems arise. Then at least we can define the features of software and software design which can eliminate such problems.

The aims of this chapter are to:

- Show where, why and how software errors arise.
- Explain why, in the real world, development of fault-free systems cannot be achieved.
- Distinguish between correct, reliable and safe software.
- Establish that dependable software should be a primary design aim.
- Highlight the importance and influence of the software operating environment.
- Establish the basics of good software.
- Describe the need for, and use of, defensive programming.
- Show that, in a professional software design environment, codes of practice are a key element.

2.1 What do we want in our software?

In an ideal world, what do we look for in our software? There are many answers to this question, but, more than anything else, one stands out: the production of totally fault-free software. We look for that because, we reason, given such software, our systems should work exactly as planned. But will they? Unfortunately not necessarily so, as will be shown later. When designing software a total system view must be taken. There are too many opportunities to get designs and implementations wrong; it isn't just confined to the code-writing stage.

In this chapter we'll first look at the root problems of such errors. Then we'll define the qualities of software which attempt to eliminate these. One must be realistic about them, however. Given the current state of design tools it is impossible to guarantee the delivery of fault-free systems (on a personal note, I believe that totally fault-free systems are a myth).

Therefore, if fault-free systems are unattainable, what should we aim for? A different, realistic, criterion is needed: that of 'dependable software', having the qualities shown in Figure 2.1. Many people, when asked to define fault-free software, talk about 'correct' software. But what *is* correct software? *The Dictionary of Computing* (1984) [OED84] defines correctness as 'the static property that a program is consistent with its specification'. In other words, if we check the code against the job specification, it does exactly what is asked of it.

On the other hand, reliability is concerned with the intended *function* of the system. The IEEE definition of software reliability is 'the extent to which a program can be expected to perform its intended function with required precision' [IEEE79]. That is, it defines how well a program carries out the required task when asked to do so. Thus it is a measure of the dynamic performance of the software.

Can a correct program be unreliable? Conversely, can an incorrect program be reliable? The answer in each case is, surprisingly, *yes*. Consider the first question. Let's suppose that a program has been checked out statically and shown to be correct. Subsequently, when installed in a system, it behaves in an unexpected way. In this situation it hasn't performed its intended function. So the program is deemed

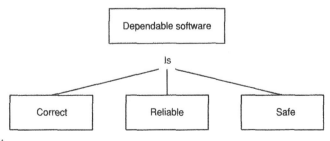

Figure 2.1 Qualities of dependable software.

to be unreliable. This really means that the design specification wasn't right in the first place.

Now let's turn to the second one. Assume that we've written a program to implement a control algorithm in a closed-loop control system. This should produce results with a given, pre-defined, accuracy. If it fails to do this then clearly it is incorrect. Yet, if the errors are small, the control loop will work quite well. In this instance it performs its intended function satisfactorily. Thus the program is deemed to be reliable.

The terms 'safe software' and 'reliable software' are often used loosely to mean the same thing. They are, in fact, very different. In extreme cases, the aims of reliability and safety may conflict. Where software is designed with safety in mind, it is concerned with the *consequences* of failure. Such consequences usually involve injury or death and/or material damage. Reliability is concerned with failures *per se*. A system can be 100% reliable, yet be totally unsafe. And, as a ludicrous example, a system can be 100% safe but 0% reliable if it is never switched on.

All designs aim for high reliability (it goes without saying that we would like our programs to be correct as well). By contrast the emphasis put on safeness depends on each particular task. Any real system will throw up a fault at some point in its life. Therefore, we need to decide at the design stage exactly *how* the system should behave when faults occur. The broad division is between those which carry on working and those that don't (Figure 2.2).

Within the first group are two subgroups. First there are those which provide full service even in the presence of faults ('fail-operational'). These are usually found in highly critical applications where failure would be catastrophic (e.g. a passenger aircraft flight control system). Second are 'fail-soft' systems (also called 'fail-active'), designed to keep on working with faults present, but with reduced performance. For instance, some automobiles use simplified back-up engine management systems to cater for failures of the main unit. Both systems (fail-operational and fail-soft) are defined to be fault-tolerant ones, described in detail in Chapter 13.

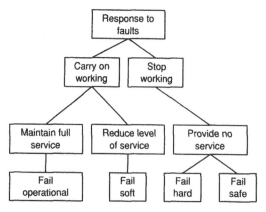

Figure 2.2 | System behaviour under fault conditions.

Those that stop working can be grouped into two types, fail-hard and fail-safe. Hard failures are those which, while they persist, may well cause the whole system to grind to a halt. These problems are often met in personal computers. In such applications they usually don't cause damage (though they are extremely irritating). This failure mode may be acceptable in some applications.

Fail-safe systems make no effort to meet normal operational requirements. Instead they aim to limit the danger or damage caused by the fault. Such techniques are applicable to aircraft weapon stores management systems, nuclear reactor control equipment and the like.

Most real-time software needs some attention paid to its safety aspects. In many applications hard software failures are tolerable because external devices are used to limit their effects. For more stringent functions, or where external back-ups aren't available, fail-soft methods are used. Finally, fail-safe methods are generally used only in safety-critical operations, a small but important area of real-time systems design.

On a last note, although we talk about 'unsafe software', in fact only hardware (or people) can do physical damage.

2.2 Software errors

2.2.1 Overview

In this text a software error is defined to be 'any feature of a program which produces a system malfunction'. This is a very broad definition, really quite unfair to software developers. In many instances of system misbehaviour the code is blameless; but we still talk of 'faulty software'. What it does, though, is emphasize that it isn't sufficient to eliminate errors at the software design stage; other factors need to be taken into account (Figure 2.3). These are looked at in more detail below.

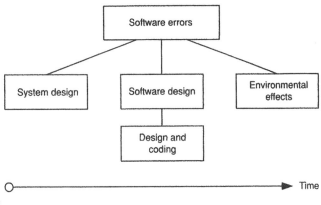

Figure 2.3 Types of software errors.

2.2.2 System design errors

System design takes place right at the front end of a project. Quite often software engineers are excluded from this stage. Many system designers have the attitude of 'well, we'll go out and buy a box to control the plant (once we've worked out how to put it together)'. Mistakes made here usually show only when system trials begin (or worse still, when the system is in service). It doesn't matter whether we're talking about mechanical, electrical or software designs; getting it wrong at this point can have dramatic consequences. For instance, on one type of Royal Navy destroyer the radar mast was located just aft of the funnel. During sea trials the paint burnt off the mast. Only then was it realized that the design was suitable only for steam propulsion, not gas turbines (as fitted).

During the system design phase the designer has to make many assumptions about the system and its operational environment. These form the basis for the specification against which the software is designed. If this is wrong then everything else from then on is also wrong (no matter how many times the program is validated and verified). The following examples illustrate this:

- 'A wing-mounted missile on an F18 aircraft failed to separate from the launcher after ignition because a computer program signalled the missile retaining mechanism to close before the rocket had built up sufficient thrust to clear the missile from the wing. An erroneous assumption had been made about the length of time that this would take. The aircraft went violently out of control' [LEV86].

- 'HMS Sheffield's radar system identified an incoming Argentinian Exocet missile as non-Soviet and thus friendly. No alarm was raised. The ship was sunk with considerable loss of life' [SEN3].

The moral for the software designer is to make the software flexible because you never know when you'll need to change it.

2.2.3 Design and coding errors

In software design, a concept is translated into computer code without any sign of a physical product. In essence it is an intellectual effort by the designer. Thus errors introduced at the point must be due to faulty thinking about the problem or its solution.

Design and coding errors fall into four categories, Figure 2.4. The only way we can catch mistakes of this type is to force the designer to externalize his thinking (a rather up-market way of saying 'get it out of him'). That is the essence of modern software design practices.

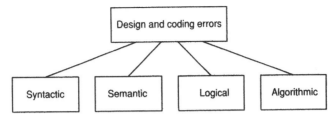

Figure 2.4 : Errors in the design process.

Figure 2.5 : A problem of syntax.

Syntax errors

The *Oxford English Dictionary* defines syntax to be 'the grammatical arrangement of words in speech or writing' (Figure 2.5). In software terms, syntax is the definition and arrangement of program symbols that the computer will accept. Such symbols include program words and delimiters – semicolons, full stops (periods), brackets, etc.

There are two distinct types of syntax error. In the first, the wrong symbol is used. In the second the symbol is used wrongly. As an example of the first suppose that, in an Ada 95 program, we write:

```
ShaftSpeed: Integer:
```

Here the final delimiter, ':', is incorrect. It should be ';'. Mistakes like this are, almost without exception, picked up by the compiler. So although they're frustrating, no damage is done.

However, consider writing:

```
X = Y ...
```

in a C program when what was wanted was:

```
X == Y .....
```

Both are valid constructs; yet they produce quite different results. If it so happens that the statements are accepted by the compiler then the program is guaranteed to malfunction. This may not appear to be all that significant, except that:

> 'a misplaced comma in one NASA program sent a Voyager spacecraft towards Mars instead of Venus' [HAM86].

Problems like these fall into the general category of 'errors of user intent'. They can be extremely difficult to identify because programs which contain them appear to be correct.

The best way to combat syntax errors is to use the right language for the job. This doesn't mean that one, and only one, language should be used. It's more a question of having the right basic features to support good design practices (discussed later). Nowadays, unless there are special reasons, code should be written in a modern high-level language (HLL). The text produced is compact and readable, two very good reasons for using such languages. Furthermore, the less we write, the fewer chances there are of making mistakes. And the less there is to read, the easier it is to grasp its meaning. On top of this, modern HLL compilers usually have powerful error-checking features. Executable code produced in this way should be syntactically quite trustworthy – but never forget that compilers themselves can have residual errors.

Semantic errors

Semantics 'relate to the meaning in language' (*Oxford English Dictionary*). Semantic errors (Figure 2.6) can arise in two ways. First, we may not properly understand what the software is supposed to do. So we end up translating the wrong solution into code. Second, we may understand the problem but translate it wrongly into code. This second point is the one most often talked about under the heading of semantic errors (the *Dictionary of Computing* defines these to be 'programming errors that arise from a misunderstanding of the meaning or effect of some construct in a programming language').

An example of the first type of mistake is that which resulted in an accident involving a chemical reactor [KLE83]. Due to human and software problems a reactor overheated, discharging its contents into the atmosphere. Afterwards, during the accident investigation, the system specifications were examined. In these the

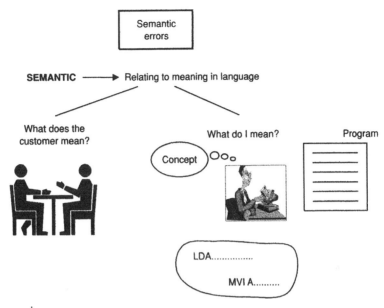

Figure 2.6 : A problem of semantics.

programmers were told that if a fault occurred in the plant, they were to leave all controlled variables as they were and sound the alarm. But it was also found that they didn't properly understand this directive. Did this mean that the valve which controlled the flow of cooling water to the reactor should freeze its position? Or, should the temperature of the reactor itself be held steady? The systems engineers clearly thought they'd specified the second response. Unfortunately the programmers had done it the other way round.

Problems caused by not having a full and proper understanding of programming languages are very common. Mistakes are made mostly by inexperienced programmers. But they also crop up when software teams begin to use new programming languages. An example of such a mistake was made by a fairly experienced assembly language programmer when using an HLL for the first time. The design task was to produce a series of recursive filter algorithms, implemented as procedures. But because he didn't appreciate the difference between static and dynamic variables, these algorithms just refused to work.

Both problems described here are also 'errors of intent'. As pointed out earlier, these are extremely hard to catch before software is tested. To eliminate the first we need to set down an agreed design specification. And to do that we have to extract full and correct information from the system designers. *Then* we have to show them that we understand it.

Having a set specification helps us attack the second issue. From such specifications we can produce the source code. This can then be checked against the

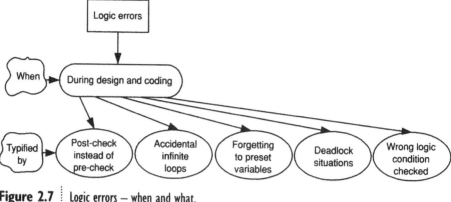

Figure 2.7　Logic errors – when and what.

original requirement to verify that it is correct. In safety-critical systems we may have to use formal mathematical techniques in the verification process. The more complex the language the more likely it is that blunders will be made (and the longer it'll take to find them). Assembly language working certainly produces many more problems of this type compared with HLLs.

Logic errors

These are also errors of user intent, made during program design and coding phases (Figure 2.7). As a result these programs don't behave in a logically correct manner. This can show up in a number of ways. For instance, the program may appear to run correctly but keeps on giving the wrong answers. Doing post-checks instead of pre-checks leads to this. Forgetting to preset variables produces similar results; we may violate assumptions upon which the logic operations are built. In other cases systems hang-up as a result of carrying out logical actions. Infinite loops and deadlocks in multiprocessing/tasking are well-known examples. Mistakes of logic aren't always found in test. And when they do the results can be costly:

'Mariner 18 lost due to missing NOT statement in program' [SEN2].

It's important to realize that logical errors are easily made. And, when programs are coded in assembly language, the errors are quite difficult to detect before the test stage. Fundamentally this is due to the highly detailed nature of low-level coding methods. When using these it is almost impossible to see the *structure* of the logic. Hence it is difficult to spot logical errors just by reading through the source code. By contrast, when using a high-level language, such errors are less likely to be made in the first place; the inbuilt constructs ('while-do', 'repeat-until') force us to do the right thing. Even when mistakes are made they are much easier to find and correct because of improved program readability.

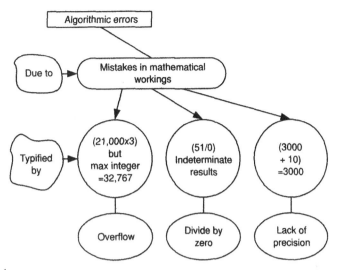

Figure 2.8 Algorithmic errors.

Algorithmic errors

These occur during mathematical operations (Figure 2.8), for a variety of reasons. In some situations basic mathematical rules are broken, as in trying to divide by zero. In other cases the capabilities of the computer system are exceeded. Every machine has limits on the size and range of its number system, affecting:

- The largest number which the machine can hold.

- The smallest number.

- The ratio of the largest to the smallest number which can be manipulated simultaneously.

- The degree of precision (resolution) of numbers.

- The range of values which input–out devices handle.

What are the effects of algorithmic errors? Here are some examples:

- 'A Shuttle laser experiment failed because the computer data was in nautical miles instead of feet' [SEN3].

- 'The Mars Climate Orbiter spacecraft was destroyed (a 'fly-by' became a 'fly-into') because of failure to translate English units into metric units in a segment of the mission software' [NAS99]

- 'The Vancouver Stock Exchange Index rose by 50% when two years of round-off errors were corrected' [SEN4].

- 'The first Ariane 5 launch ended in disaster with the destruction of the launcher itself. It was a result of number overflow of the horizontal velocity value' [ARI96].

Algorithmic errors are a significant factor in control system and signal processing work. When coding is done at assembler level it is a painstaking and time-consuming task. These tasks are much more controllable and testable when working in an HLL. But designers still need to understand fully the number system used by their machines (see Chapter 13).

2.2.4 Environmental factors

This is a broad-ranging topic because it concerns how software behaves within its normal working environment. Far too often designers regard software as something which is complete in itself. They forget that it is just one part of a larger process. And, in most real-time applications, this involves not only hardware but also humans. For such designs it's not good enough to produce software which is correct. We must also ensure that the system in which it is incorporated also works correctly.

These problems often surface for the first time when full system testing is carried out. In other cases they lie dormant for long periods until the right set of circumstances occurs; then they can strike catastrophically. There is *no* way that we can eliminate environmental problems at the design stage; there are just too many different ways in which they can occur (see below). All we can do is to minimize the number of potential trouble-spots by deep and extensive design analysis. It also helps, as a matter of sanity, to accept Murphy's law ('anything that can go wrong, will').

- 'A computer issued a "close weapons bay door" command on a B-1A aircraft at a time when a mechanical inhibit had been put in place in order to perform maintenance on the door. The "close" command was generated when someone in the cockpit punched the close switch on the control panel during a test. Two hours later, when maintenance was completed and the inhibit removed, the door unexpectedly closed. Luckily nobody was injured. The software was later altered to discard any commands not complete within a certain time frame, but this situation had never been considered during testing' [FRO84].

- 'A mechanical malfunction in a fly-by-wire flight control system set up an accelerated environment for which the flight control computer was not programmed. The aircraft went out of control and crashed' [FRO84].

- 'Just before the Apollo 11's moon landing, the software sent out an alarm indicating that it was overloaded with tasks and had to reset itself continually to service critical functions. The program was still functional, so the landing went ahead. Later it was found that an astronaut had mistakenly been instructed to turn on a sensor that sent a continuous stream of interrupts to the processor, causing the overload' [HAM86].

- 'An F16 autopilot flipped the plane upside down whenever it crossed the equator' [SEN2]. The fact that this occurred in a simulator doesn't lessen the gravity of the mistake.

- 'In one case, a 62 year old man died abruptly during treatment. Interference from the therapeutic microwaves had reset his pacemaker, driving his already injured heart to beat at 214 times a minute. It couldn't do it.' [SEN5].

2.2.5 Why do we get poor software?

There isn't a formal definition for 'poor' software. This term is meant to cover all aspects of the problem, including software which is:

- Incorrect.
- Unreliable.
- Unsafe.
- Late.
- Expensive.

The last two items are usually closely bound up with the first three.

What gives rise to poor software? Many answers to this question will by now be obvious. What doesn't always show is that, frequently, more fundamental problems exist. There are three general aspects to this (Figure 2.9).

Company ethos

This is all tied up with how software activities are understood at a senior level within a firm. Basically, the characteristic spirit of a company determines how well jobs are done. A company with negative attitudes has:

- Poor senior management response to problems.
- Lack of formal and rigorous company software design and documentation procedures.
- Inadequate tools.
- Lack of professionalism and discipline in the software team.

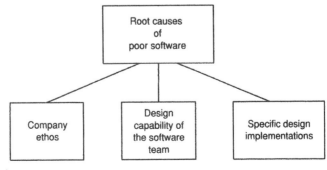

Figure 2.9 Poor software – the reasons.

If senior management doesn't (or doesn't want to) understand the needs of software development then poor software becomes endemic. No effort is made to bring formality and rigour into the design and development process. No specifications are set for documentation. No provision is made for the costs of design documentation. Development tools are obtained only with the greatest of difficulty, often much later than needed. The inevitable consequences are that design teams become demoralized. Good people opt out, either by leaving or just by giving in to the system. It is no accident that one very large company which epitomizes these qualities had – in its 'management by accident phase' – lost money, contracts and prestige in large amounts. It had government contracts terminated. It had one of its major projects investigated and evaluated by a rival software house (this being paid for by a highly disillusioned customer). And its software effort on one defence project was described as being run by 'one man and his dog'.

Design capability

Management decisions have a strong bearing on the levels of competence and expertise achieved by software teams. You don't get good software by accident. It requires experienced, professional and dedicated designers. And you don't hold such people without the right support and encouragement from senior management. Indicators of a suspect design team are:

- Lack of appreciation of software complexity.
- Little formal documentation.
- Little use of software design tools.
- No system prototyping.
- Designing from scratch (no reuse of software).

These directly affect just how well individual jobs are handled.

Specific design implementations

Given the situation outlined above, it isn't surprising that inferior software designs commonly have:

- Hazy system requirements specifications.
- An overrun on time.
- An overrun on budget.
- Faulty delivered software.
- Negligible documentation.

Contributory factors are:

- Simultaneous development of hardware and software.
- Incorrect trade-off of resources.

Let's look at how these all combine to turn a software project into a nightmare.

In the first place it's not unusual to find that nobody can define exactly what the system is supposed to do. Everybody thinks they know what should happen, but frequently these just don't add up. Because little is committed to paper during the design stage such discrepancies fail to surface.

As the design progresses, three factors cause it to become late. It often turns out that the software is much more complex than first envisaged. Second, much more effort is required. Finally, implementing it without decent software design tools makes it a long (and often error-prone) task. And, because no use is made of reusable software, *all* of it has to be designed from scratch.

The overall system may involve new hardware. This presents the software designers with a task over and above that of writing the application software; that is, the need to develop programs to interface to the physical level, the 'system' software. It's not enough just to allow for the time and effort needed to do this. In these circumstances the development phase takes on a new dimension. System programs can't be tested out until the hardware is ready. And application software can't be fully tested until both these are complete. Concurrent development of hardware, system software and application software is a recipe for long, long development timescales.

During this period various trade-offs have to be made which affect the resulting software. For instance, an early decision concerns the choice of a programming language and/or compiler. This has a profound impact on productivity, visibility and, ultimately, dependability. At the same time the hardware–software balance has to be decided on. Later, specific effects of the language have to be checked out, concerning items such as memory usage and program run-time. It takes experience and knowledge to get these right.

All of these combine to make the job late, and as a result it costs more than planned. And, the first set of software is delivered as the final item: there is no prototyping effort as in normal engineering design. So it is not surprising that the software fails to work correctly on delivery. It then takes a massive effort to eliminate all the faults (this last items seems to be a way of life in much commercial software; it has been said that some firms regard customers as extensions to their software teams, acting as fault finders).

The factors outlined above influence the general nature of software design in a company. As an analogy, visualize management as providing hygienic facilities, the software teams being hygiene attendants. If facilities are poor then the attendants are unlikely to produce a safe environment – no matter how hard they work. The end result is that the user's health is under threat.

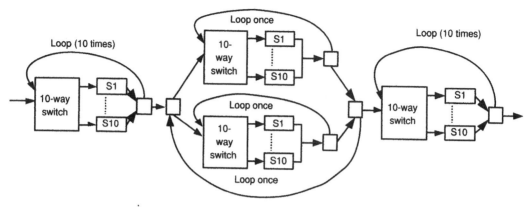

Figure 2.10 | A flow-chart problem.

2.2.6 Testing – how useful?

The testing of software is a contentious issue, particularly for safety-critical applications. Testing *is* an important part of the development process but its limits must be recognized. Design flaws can often be picked up early on by running the program in an emulated environment. Consider, for instance, where source code is written, compiled and linked using a personal computer (PC). It may be possible to exercise it subsequently under the control of the PC operating system. The behaviour of the program can be examined and any faults rectified. But there is a limit to what we can do at this point; some errors will always get through to the final hardware. Unfortunately, these errors tend to be the really difficult ones to sort out. The only solution then is to use specialized test gear such as in-circuit emulators.

There are sound objections to using tests for proving that software works. Consider the flow-chart example (Figure 2.10) set out by Boehm [JEN79].

The questions are:

- How many paths through this section of program?

- How long would it take to check out each and every path at 10 μsec per path?

The answers are (approximately) 4×10^{10} paths and 111 hours (almost five days of fully automated testing).

This shows that statements which say that 'full and complete testing of the program has been carried out' must be treated with scepticism. Fortunately, in practice, things are not quite so gloomy. Usually a smaller number of tests exercise a sufficient, statistically significant number of paths through the program [JEN79]. While this is very encouraging it has a profound implication. That is, testing of this kind cannot *prove* that the software is error-free.

There is a second, more fundamental, point implicit in this technique. What we have tested is the *correctness* of the program. But this, as has already been pointed out, is not sufficient. Correctness testing only shows how well the program meets its specification. It cannot point out where the specifications may be wrong. Further, such testing is static. We really need to verify that it will behave *reliably*. Consequently, many real-time systems developers use simulation as a test method. This gives much greater confidence in the behaviour of the software. But it still leaves questions unanswered because:

- Most testing is done by simulation of the environment.
- It is difficult to provide realistic test exercises and set-ups.
- In many cases the test strategy is based on assumptions about the total system and its environment. There is no guarantee that these are right.
- It is difficult to predict and simulate all failure modes of the system. Hardware failures complicate the matter.
- The behaviour of the software may vary with time or environmental conditions. This requires testing to be dynamic.
- Following on from this, it may become impossible to carry out complete and exhaustive tests for real-time systems.

Don't get paranoid about software problems. Be assured that all engineering project managers would instantly recognize the difficulties listed above. Just be realistic about what can and can't be achieved by the testing of software.

2.3 The basics of good software

2.3.1 General

'Good' software is dependable, is delivered on time and is done within budget. Whether we can achieve this depends on many factors. Some relate to major sections of the development process. Others affect quite specific design activities.

What then, do we need to do to create a quality software product? At the minimum, we should:

- Develop a clear statement of requirements for the software.
- Ensure that the design solution is capable of achieving this.
- Organize the development so that the project is manageable.
- Organize the development so that the timescales can be met.
- Make sure that the design can be changed without major rewrites.
- Design for testability.
- Minimize risks by using tried and trusted methods.
- Ensure that safety is given its correct priority.
- Make sure that the project doesn't completely rely on particular individuals.
- Produce a maintainable design.

Mind you, there is a bit of the 'wish' element here.

Let's now look at items which determine precisely how well we can achieve these aims.

2.3.2 Specification correctness

There is only one way to make sure that the software specification is right. Talk to the users. Explain what you're doing. Put it down on paper in a way that they can understand. Get to know the job yourself. Keep on talking to the users. And never delude yourself that the requirements' documents are set in concrete. In reality they never stop changing.

Specification methods and related topics are covered in detail in Chapter 3.

2.3.3 Feasibility and suitability

Here we seek to answer the general questions 'will it work?' (feasibility) and 'how well?' (suitability). Specifically we need to assess the:

- Time allowed to complete tasks.
- Accuracy and completeness of input information.
- Required accuracy of mathematical operations.
- Operator interaction with the system.
- Special operating conditions, such as data retention on a power loss.
- Power supply parameters.
- Special performance parameters, such as radiation hardness.

It may seem that decisions concerning the last two items should be left to hardware engineers. But these can have a major impact on the software development. For instance, if a battery-powered system is specified then a CMOS processor will probably have to be used. Likewise, if radiation hardness is required it may be that bipolar technology has to be used. Any choices made must take into account their effects on the software aspects of the project. So they need consideration at the feasibility design stage.

We then need to consider the overall hardware and software structure, and determine:

- Is the language correct for the job?
- Are there proper support tools for the chosen language?
- Is there enough code and data store space?
- Will task execution times meet their specifications?
- If, at test time, task execution times are excessive, how can we handle the problem?
- Will the system be able to respond sufficiently fast to asynchronous events?

This part of the development process isn't easy to get right. It is carried out at an early stage when there are many unknowns in the project. Frequently the size of the problem is underestimated. Combine that with the usual optimism of designers and it's not surprising that so many projects have problems.

2.3.4 Modularization

One of the most highly refined structures for the handling of major projects in set timescales is that of the military (Figure 2.11). The military command structure is hierarchical, grouping men together as a set of distinct units (or 'modules'). Without this structure all we'd have would be a disorganized rabble. But with it, the organization becomes manageable and effective. With this simple chain of command, control is easy to maintain. Large jobs can be tackled by the group as a whole. Yet, at the lowest level, the jobs taken on by separate platoons are 'visible'. Individual progress and performance can be monitored and assessed. When troubles arise they can be dealt with quickly and effectively.

Software which is organized in a modular way exhibits the same properties:

- The overall project is manageable and flexible.
- Low-level tasks can be made small enough for one person to work on.
- Software can be designed as a set of parallel (concurrent) actions.

Even within the work of one person, modularization gives the same sort of benefits.

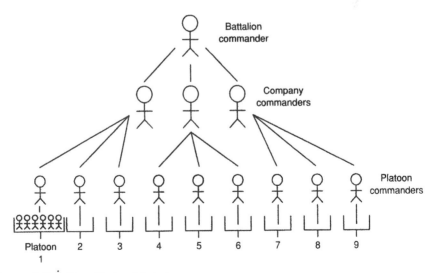

Figure 2.11 : Hierarchical modularized structure.

What is not so obvious is that modularization can make a program very stable. That is, localized changes produce very little of a ripple-through effect in the program as a whole. For exactly the same reasons a modular program is much easier to test and maintain (but this is also closely tied up with program design methods, Chapter 4).

2.3.5 Portability and reusability

Most manufacturers of microprocessor systems produce a range of products (Figure 2.12). Typically these range from simple single-board computers (SBCs) through multiple rack units. In many cases a number of microprocessor types are used. To a lesser extent different operating systems may be in use. If each configuration requires unique software, development is expensive and time-consuming – and threatens to generate a whole new range of software faults. Ideally we would like one set of programs capable of running on all configurations – fully portable software. Portability is a measure of the effort needed to transfer programs between:

● Computers which use different processors.

● Different configurations based on the same processor.

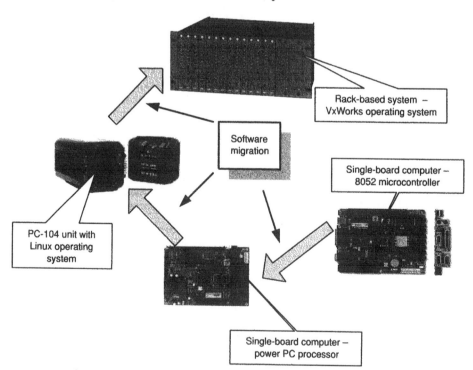

Figure 2.12 Microprocessor system configurations.

- Configurations which use different operating systems.
- Different compilers, given the same language and same hardware.

If programs need a complete rewrite before being transferred they are totally non-portable.

It is true that, in the past, most real-time software was non-portable. Now there is much greater emphasis on portability, especially for professional work. There are still many barriers to achieving this goal, the major ones being:

- Computer hardware.
- Number representation, range and precision.
- Programming language.
- Operating system structures.
- Communication structures and protocols.

For embedded systems, fully portable software can never be attained. The stumbling block is that hardware structures almost always differ from job to job. But, given the right design approach and the right programming language, very high levels of portability *can* be achieved.

Reusability is a measure of how easily we can use existing software, especially that which is tried and trusted. Doing this saves us from (to quote a very hackneyed but true cliché) 're-inventing the wheel'. There's no doubt that high portability produces high reusability (and vice versa).

What exactly do we gain by having a suite of portable and reusable software? The advantages are that:

- Design and coding times are reduced.
- Development effort is reduced.
- Less manpower is needed.
- Less debugging is needed (use of proven software).
- Costs are reduced.
- Correct and reliable designs are more easily achieved.

In recent years one item has emerged as being key to the development of reusable software: the *component*. Unfortunately, trying to precisely define what this is – and get everyone else to agree with you – seems difficult to achieve. Brown and Wallnau [BRO98] found at least four different definitions of a software component. We'll somewhat fudge the issue by using the following definition: 'A component is an independent part of a larger ("parent") system. It is intended to carry out specific functions; these may or may not depend on the nature and/or role of the parent system. It may be implemented as a single software unit or as a logical collection of such units. In all cases it must provide a set of clearly specified interfaces.'

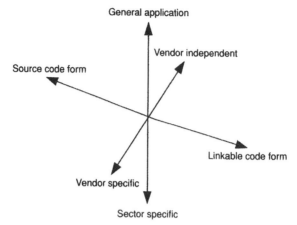

Figure 2.13 | Component categorization.

Components by themselves are not a universal remedy for poor design techniques. They must be organized in terms of clearly defined functions, and be easy
to use. Otherwise they are likely to make it more, not less, difficult to implement
a design. How, though, can components be categorized? Many ways are possible;
the criteria given in Figure 2.13 are those of our choice.

This gives us eight groups:

● General application, source code form, vendor independent. Example: Linux
operating system [RTL01].

● General application, source code form, vendor specific. Example: MultiGraph-2,
graphics support library for the Modula-2 language [MUL95].

● General application, linkable code form, vendor independent. Example: CORBA,
the Common Object Request Broker Architecture [ORF97].

● General application, linkable code form, vendor specific. Example: DCOM, the
Distributed Component Model from Microsoft [MIC99].

● Sector specific, source code form, vendor independent. Example: CAMP, the
Common Ada Missile Packages project [AND88].

● Sector specific, source code form, vendor specific. Example: OSEFA, the Open
Software Framework for Manufacturing [SCH96].

● Sector specific, linkable code form, vendor independent. Example: embedded
TCP/IP stacks.

● Sector specific, linkable code form, vendor specific. Example: real-time operating
system for embedded applications, RTKernel-32 [ONT01].

Closely related to these developments is the growing use of commercial off-the-shelf
(COTS) components as a way of building software systems. These are especially
useful in large or/and complex projects.

Just to clarify things:

- 'Vendor independent' means that any vendor may produce the product in accordance with a defined specification or standard.
- 'Linkable code form' includes binary files which are linked into the application code and 'software in silicon' object code provided in programmable devices.

2.3.6 Error avoidance and defensive programming – robust programs

How can we deal with error situations? Start off by accepting that, in any real project, mistakes *will* be made. Therefore we need to design software to limit the effects of such mistakes – damage limitation. But to do this we must have some idea of the general (and sometimes specific) nature of error sources. Exactly how, when, why and where do these problems arise? Generally they are due to:

- The human factor.
- Computational problems.
- Hardware failure.

(a) The human factor
The problem can originate outside the system due to the behaviour of people (assuming they can interact with the software). For instance, consider using a processor as a controller for a closed-loop control system. Normally the controller is expected to carry out tasks additional to that of controlling the loop. So, under normal conditions, the control task runs at regular and preset times; other tasks are executed in the remaining time. Assume that the operator can set the system sampling rate as desired. If this is set too fast the processor will execute nothing but the loop-control algorithm; all other tasks are ignored. Despite the fact that the software may be faultless, the system fails to work correctly.

(b) Computational problems
One of the well-known mistakes here is not allowing for invalid mathematical operations. These, such as dividing by zero, produce indeterminate results. Other items, such as going outside the correct limits of array bounds, also fall into this category.

(c) Hardware failure
The following example typifies the problems of hardware failure. A control program instructs an analogue-to-digital converter to begin conversation. It then polls the converter, looking for the end of conversion signal. But for some reason the converter fails to generate this signal. The result is that the program just sits there *ad infinitum* (or until the power is switched off); control of the system is completely lost.

The technique used to handle these situations is called 'defensive programming'. Fundamentally, this method accepts that errors will occur, originating inside the computer system and/or external to it. It aims to:

- Prevent faults being introduced into the system in the first place.
- Detect faults if they do occur.
- Control the resulting response of the system.

Software which behaves like this combines the attributes of fault resistance with fault tolerance.

In the case of (a) above we would limit the range of sample times which are accepted as valid. In (b) and (c) we can't control the occurrence of a fault. Instead, once having detected the fault, we must put the system into a safe mode ('*exception handling*'). An ideal design includes a specific test and a corresponding response for each possible error condition. In practice this is very unlikely to be achieved. But, for real-time systems, this isn't our chief concern. If we can identify the cause of the problem, fine. But it's usually much more important to respond to faults quickly, safely, and in a deterministic manner.

All these factors are summed up in a quality called the 'robustness' of the program. This is defined by the *Dictionary of Computing* as 'a measure of the ability of a system to recover from error conditions, whether generated externally or internally, e.g. a robust system would be tolerant to errors in input data or to failures of internal components. Although there may be a relationship between robustness and reliability, the two are distinct measures. A system never required to recover from error conditions may be reliable without being robust. By contrast a highly robust system that recovers and continues to operate – despite numerous error conditions – may still be regarded as unreliable. The reason? Quite simply it fails to provide essential services in a timely fashion on demand.'

2.3.7 Design codes of practice – style, clarity and documentation

First, it is important not only that software specifications and the corresponding design solutions are correct; they must be seen to be so. Second, the resulting program must be understandable and unambiguous. And not just to the original designer. Finally, the ability to assess the effects of program modifications easily and quickly is very desirable.

These items are not so concerned with how well we do a design (design quality is considered to be an implicit requirement). Rather, it relates to the quality and completeness of design methods and documentation.

Design style defines the way in which the development as a whole is tackled. It covers all aspects of the work, from initial feasibility studies to post-design services. Most engineering firms have, for many years, used 'codes of practice' to establish design styles. In large organizations such practices are fairly formal; small companies can afford to work informally. The purpose is to create working conditions and attitudes which:

- Encourage the production of high-quality work.

- Ensure that timescales are met.

- Ensure that budgets are met.

Codes of practice may be written for detailed as well as general design activities. For instance, one company which used C++ as a programming language was concerned about the quality of their existing implementations. As a result company standards were issued limiting the language constructs that its programmers could use. The purpose of this was to:

- Eliminate unsafe programming practices.

- Get rid of 'clever' (i.e. obscure) programming tricks.

- Produce understandable programs (clarity).

- Avoid (or minimize) the use of undefined, unspecified and locale-specific language constructs (affects portability).

This aspect of design is normally termed 'programming style'.

Clarity is not just restricted to program writing; it is essential that the design as a whole should be easy to understand. At all stages we should be able to answer the 'what, why and how' questions. This is why good, clear, comprehensive documentation is such an important item.

2.4 A final comment

It is only in the last few years that the ideas and methods described here have been put into action by the software industry. Much still remains to be done, especially in view of the 'cottage industry' mentality of many developers. It's not as if professionals didn't recognize the problems of software design and development. In fact, many tools and techniques have been proposed with a fervour normally associated with evangelical rallies. Most of the early developments came from the DP field, a trend which has continued with OO technology. Unfortunately, these have little to offer for real-time work. Now the sheer size of the software problem (time, cost, reliability, etc.) is acting as the driving force for the development of:

- New and better tools specifically for the real-time market.

- Powerful integrated development environments.

- Design formality.

- Defined documentation standards.

- High standards of professionalism (as exhibited by software engineers).

All these are combining to raise software quality standards.

Review

Having finished this chapter you should now:

- Realize why, in the real world, we can never guarantee to produce fault-free systems.

- Know what is meant by correct, reliable and safe software.

- Know what is meant by dependable software and why it should be a primary design aim.

- Understand that software errors arise from problems to do with system design, software design and environmental factors.

- See that developing real-time software without taking system factors into account can lead to major problems.

- Appreciate some of the root causes of poor software.

- Recognize what has to be done to produce a quality software product.

- Be aware of the need for and use of codes of practice in a professional development environment.

- Be able to describe the need for, and use of, defensive programming.

References and further reading

[AND88] *The CAMP approach to software reuse*, C. Anderson, Defense Computing, pp 25–29, Sept./Oct. 1988.

[ARI96] *ARIANE 5 flight 501 failure report by the inquiry board*, http://www.mssl.ucl.ac.uk/www_plasma/missions/cluster/ariane5rep.html, July 1996.

[BRO98] *Component-based software engineering*, A.W. Brown and K.C. Wallnau, IEEE Software, Vol. 15, No. 5, pp 37–46, Sept./Oct. 1998.

[FRO84] *System safety in aircraft management*, F.R. Frola and C.O. Miller, Logistics Management Institute, Washington, DC, January 1984.

[HAM86] *Zero-defect software: the elusive goal*, M.H. Hamilton, IEEE Spectrum, pp 48–53, March 1986.

[IEEE79] *Computer Dictionary*, M.H. Weik, IEEE Computer Society Standards, 1979.

[JEN79] *Software Engineering*, R.W. Jensen and C.C. Tonies, Prentice Hall, ISBN 0-13-82214-8, 1979.

[KLE83] *Human problems with computer control, hazard prevention*, T. Kletz, Journal of the System Safety Society, pp 24–26, March/April 1983.

[LEV86] *Software safety: why, what and how*, Nancy Leveson, ACM Computing Surveys, Vol. 18, No. 2, pp 125–163, June 1986.

[LEV95] *Safeware – system safety and computers*, Nancy Leveson, Addison-Wesley, ISBN 0-201-11972-2, 1995.

[MIC99] www.microsoft.com/com/.

[MUL95] *Multigraph 2 graphics support library for the Modula-2 language*, Shareware software, A. Iakovlev and D. Maslov, Moscow, 1995.

[NAS99] Mars climate orbiter failure, NASA release H99-134, http://spaceflight.nasa.gov/spacenews/releases/h-99-134.html.

[OED84] *Dictionary of computing*, Oxford University Press, ISBN 0-19-853905-3, 1984.

[ONT01] *RTKernel-32 real-time scheduler*, On Time Informatik GmbH, www.on-time.com, 2001.

[ORF97] *Instant CORBA*, R. Orfali, D. Harkey and J. Edwards, Wiley, ISBN 0-471-18333-4, 1997.

[RTL01] Real-time Linux organization, http://RealTimeLinux.org.

[SAM97] *Software engineering with reusable components*, J. Sametinger, Springer-Verlag, ISBN 3-540-62695-6, 1997.

[SCH96] *Creating applications from components: A manufacturing framework design*, H.A. Schmid, IEEE Software, Vol. 13, No. 6, pp 67–75, Nov. 1996.

[SEN1] ACM Software Engineering Notes, Vol. 8, No. 3.

[SEN2] ACM Software Engineering Notes, Vol. 5, No. 2.

[SEN3] ACM Software Engineering Notes, Vol. 10, No. 3.

[SEN4] ACM Software Engineering Notes, Vol. 9, No. 1.

[SEN5] ACM Software Engineering Notes, Vol. 5, No. 1.

[WIE94] *Digital woes – why we should not depend on software*, Ruth Wiener, Helix Books, ISBN 0-201-40796-5, 1994.

chapter 3

First Steps – Requirements Analysis and Specification

One of the most difficult tasks in any project is to establish precisely what the system requirements are. This is a problem faced by project managers from time immemorial, who recognize that getting it right at the start of a job is of the utmost importance. Engineers have long realized that a disciplined, organized and formalized approach must be used when evaluating systems requirements (whether that's always been practised is another matter). This hasn't been done through a sense of 'doing the right thing'. No. Experience, frequently painful, has shown that such methods are necessary. In particular, with projects of any real size, they are essential.

What is the situation concerning software projects? Considering the number of major failure stories in circulation, the answer must be 'pretty awful'. In the past this situation has frequently been condoned on the grounds that software is inherently highly complex; one can't expect anything else in such projects. This is nonsense. The real problem was that anything smacking of organization and discipline was considered to impinge upon the programmer's creativity. Eventually, though, the point came when such an approach to professional software couldn't be tolerated any longer. Consequently, requirements analysis and software specification are now regularly practised as a formal aspect of quality software design.

The purpose of this chapter is to:

- Distinguish between mythical and realistic software life-cycle models.
- Show where requirements analysis and software specification (the requirements stage) fits into the life cycle.
- Highlight the importance of the requirements stage.
- Explain why and how mistakes are made during this period.
- Discuss practical analysis and specification methods.
- Introduce the topic of software prototyping.

In reality this isn't about software; it's project engineering.

3.1 The software life-cycle

3.1.1 Introduction

There is a long path between recognizing the need for a product and satisfying this need. Many activities take place along this 'life-cycle' path, involving system, software and hardware designers. In an attempt to formalize the process, models have been developed describing what the process consists of and how it functions. Although these cover all aspects of system development they have generally become known as 'software life-cycle models'. Software engineering textbooks describe these in varying degrees of detail, such descriptions usually being quite plausible. Regrettably many suffer from the 'wish' syndrome – as in 'I wish it was like this' – ignoring the realities of life. Consequently, models usually belong to one of two distinct groups – mythical and real. And, for the inexperienced engineer, it can be difficult to tell them apart on a first meeting.

3.1.2 A mythical model of the software life-cycle

The simplistic 'waterfall' structure shown in Figure 3.1 is an example of a mythical software life-cycle model. Let's see how this model is supposed to function. The process begins when a prospective customer arrives looking for a solution to a clearly defined requirement. Frequently this is a desire to automate an existing manual system, such as accounts handling, stock control, or bookings and reservations. The computing task is seen primarily as a software one, even though hardware forms part of the design solution. Hardware is subordinated to software because the equipment fit is usually based on standard items, configured specifically for each application. Moreover, by using standard hardware, there isn't a need to develop system software; the primary objective is the production of application software only.

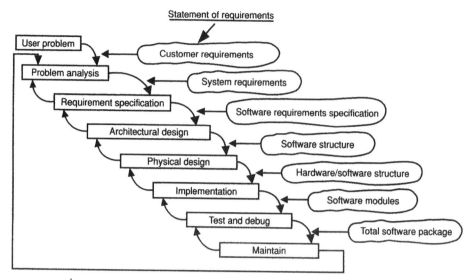

Figure 3.1 The mythical software life-cycle model.

At this point the software house sends its top men – the system's analysts – to investigate the client's existing system. Their objectives are to:

● Analyse the problem presented to them (i.e. the existing system).

● Establish precisely what the new system is supposed to do.

● Document these aspects in a clear and understandable way.

The output from the problem analysis phase is the system's requirements document. Using this the system's analysts, together with senior software designers, define what the software must do to meet these requirements. This includes the:

● Objectives of the software.

● Constraints placed on the software developers.

● Overall software work plan.

Such features are described in the software specification document, issued at the end of the requirements specification phase. Note that usually there is iteration around the analysis and specification loop, to resolve errors, ambiguities, etc. Note also that similar iterations take place at all stages in the model.

Only now does software design commence, in a nearly compartmentalized manner, Figure 3.2. Experienced designers, working with a clear, complete and correct software specification document, begin software architectural design. Their purpose is to identify and model the overall software structure, based on the software specification supplied to them. The resulting software structure document defines

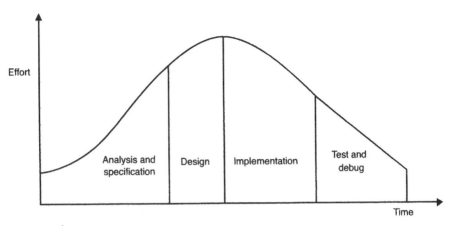

Figure 3.2 Project effort distribution – another myth.

the essential components of the system, how these fit together and how they com-municate. In essence it describes an abstract model of the software, ignoring imple-mentation aspects (i.e. processor hardware, communication links, etc.). During the next stage, that of physical design, the abstract structure is partitioned or 'mapped' onto actual system hardware. In some applications this may be a complex task – but it is considerably simplified by using standard hardware. The outcome of this work is a hardware/software structure-defining document, forming the input to the implementation phase. The function of *this* phase is to take the physical design structures and translate them into source code. Once the code is written it can be tested and debugged. Normally this is first done on a host development system; later it is tested in the target system (in most cases the host and target computers are identical).

One of the assumptions underlying this simplistic approach is that system hard-ware requires configuration, installation and commissioning; but not development. It also assumes that such activities proceed in parallel with the design task; that the hardware is fully functional when application software tests commence on the target system. Such testing is, of course, always needed to show that the finished code performs as specified. Thus the integration of software and hardware is a straight-forward and fairly painless task.

Once the customer is convinced that the system performs as required it is put into operational use; the maintenance phase begins. This involves two major factors. First, not all errors are detected during the testing phase; such residual bugs need to be eradicated from the software. Second, upgrades and enhancements are usually demanded by the customer during the life of the system. Minor changes involve tinkering with the source code (the minor iteration). But significant altera-tions take us back to the analysis stage of the life-cycle model, the major iteration loop.

3.1.3 Bringing realism to the life cycle

So, what's wrong with the model described so far? It seems reasonable, clearly describing the major activities and outputs relating to software production. It also defines what these involve, where they occur and how they relate to each other. Quite true. The problem is not with the definition and use of the individual activities. These are perfectly valid, forming a sound basis for software design methodologies. Fundamentally it is due to many underlying false assumptions within this model, the first relating to the customer's requirements.

Most real-time software designs form part of larger systems (it's also worth pointing out that software costs dominate hardware costs only if a very narrow view of hardware is taken, i.e. the computer installation itself). In such applications it isn't a case of putting processor-based equipment into a company to perform a computing task; the problems are much more complex. Moreover, although there may be a single end user, other bodies often have vested interests in the project. It isn't easy to generalize about real-time developments because projects are so diverse. But let's take the following example which shows how complex the situation can become.

Assume that the Defence Staff have perceived a potential air warfare threat. Decisions are made to develop a new air interceptor fighter aircraft to counter this, its requirements being stated in very general terms. At this stage the need is seen, but the solution isn't. Studies are then carried out by defence procurement agencies, research establishments and the end user. Aircraft and avionic companies are invited to bid. They in turn perform tender studies which involve their system suppliers (e.g. flight control, weapon management, etc.). Only at this level are hard decisions made concerning mechanical, electrical, electronic and software systems, etc.

One can define system requirements at each and every point in this chain. The content of such requirements and the issues involved vary from level to level. So when we talk about requirements analysis, we have to define precisely the issues which concern us. In this text attention is focused on the lowest level discussed above.

The customer (in this case the aircraft manufacturer, say) has a perceived need, and is looking for a way to meet this need. Internal discussions within the company – and possibly external studies by consultants – lead to the production of an informal specification of requirements (Figure 3.3). These are firmed up in terms of concepts, achievable targets, on-line costs, etc. during informal discussions with potential suppliers of equipment. The process is repeated until the customer is sure that the requirements are realizable, both technically and financially – and within desired timescales. Eventually he produces a formal tendering document requesting bids by suppliers. Replies are analysed, the responses usually leading to changes in the tendering document. This is then re-issued in modified form, requesting further bids. Finally, a single supplier is identified as the best contender and nominated for the job. When contracts are awarded, the tendering document is converted into a statement of requirements (SOR) for the task. This then becomes

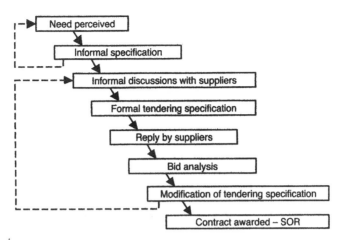

Figure 3.3 ┊ Formulating the user statement of requirements (SOR).

the binding legal document for all further developments. Note that even before the design process proper begins many decisions have already been made. These concern system structure, performance targets, size, weight, timescales, as well as project management functions. So although work hasn't yet started many constraints apply to the job – compounded by one major factor. The specifications *always* change in such complex systems. This is an immutable rule which can't be proved but always holds true. It is inherent in the evolutionary aspects of the design process.

So, we start the life cycle with what appears to be a complete, correct and full statement of requirements of the problem; in reality, it is nothing of the sort. It is, though, the best we can do given the nature of the problem. Consequently much greater effort is needed at the requirements analysis stage to clarify the customer's requirements. The effect of this is to introduce a new major iteration step between the analysis and problem definition (the SOR) stages, Figure 3.4.

The steps through requirements specification and architectural design tend to follow the earlier pattern. In practice there may be a major change in design methodology between these steps. Problems encountered in these stages are usually reasonably easy to solve, unless they are fundamental (for instance, it just won't work). It's at the physical design stage that some really difficult problems surface, involving computer power, speed, memory, size, weight and cost. If the designer had a free hand there wouldn't be a problem; but he hasn't. Constraints set at the tendering phase act as a straitjacket, limiting the designer's choices. If the effects are significant they usually lead to a major iteration, going right back to the user problem. Surprisingly, critical problems at the physical design level can often be eliminated by making simple changes to the SOR.

During the implementation phase minor changes may be made in the physical design structure. For instance, tasks may be partitioned in more efficient ways, better modular structures formed, etc. Generally this part of the work doesn't raise

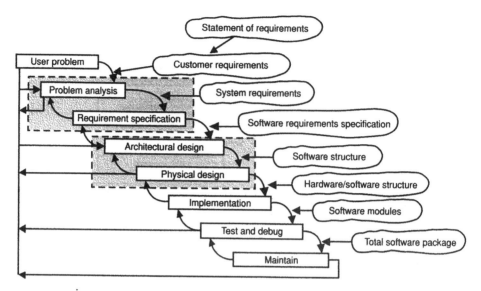

Figure 3.4 | A more realistic software life-cycle model.

real difficulties, provided proper development tools are available. However, the next set of major stumbling blocks occur in the test, integration and debug phase. This is a wide-ranging activity which includes:

- Testing software in a host environment.
- Testing software in a target environment.
- Integrating separately designed software packages.
- Integrating software and hardware.
- Integrating subsystems.
- System trials.
- System commissioning.

This phase, which embraces much more than just software, is often *the* major activity in the development of processor-based systems, as shown in Figure 3.5 [FAR75].

Project	Requirements and design	Implementation	Test, debug and integration
SAGE	39	14	47
NTDS	30	20	50
GEMINI	36	17	47
SATURN V	32	24	44
OS/360	33	17	50
TRW Survey	46	20	34

Figure 3.5 | Distribution of software effort.

There are many reasons for the size of this activity. Testing and debugging software in a target environment is a difficult and time-consuming process. This is compounded by the fact that target systems are usually quite different from the hosts. Integration of systems, whether software, electronic, mechanical, etc. is always fraught with problems. Some system testing *can* take place in a simulated environment. Mostly it has to be done within the real environment, with all its attendant problems. Like, for instance, operating hundreds of miles from base, with limited test facilities, working long hours in arduous conditions, trying to meet near impossible timescales. Grave problems may be found for the first time at this stage, particularly concerning processing power (not enough), available memory size (too small) and response times (too slow). Solving these involves iteration back to the architectural design stage (at the very least). In really dramatic cases it may be impossible to meet the user requirements under any circumstances. So we need to go right back to the SOR to try to resolve the problem.

Maintenance aspects are similar to those described earlier, only the whole process is more difficult to carry out. It may be tedious to hunt for bugs in an accounts recording system. By contrast, trying to pin down a fault in the flight control software of a supersonic fighter can be a Herculean task. Upgrading systems can also present major problems. With DP systems the emphasis is on software upgrading; for real-time applications it includes software, hardware, subsystems and even whole systems.

Lack of precision in the initial SOR, together with continual changes in this document, alter the way a project progresses. Project effort distribution becomes more like that shown in Figure 3.6 than that of Figure 3.2. This is a simplified model; precise details vary from project to project. But they all exhibit one common feature: the overlapping of phases. This implies a much higher degree of interaction between stages than that predicted by the simple waterfall model. It also highlights the need for firm, organized project management and formal quality assurance techniques.

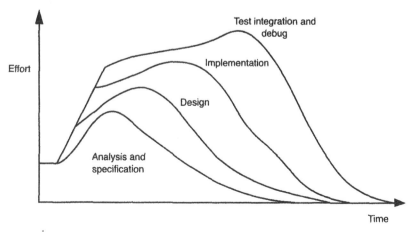

Figure 3.6 ┊ Project effort distribution – reality.

3.1.4　Requirements issues – a practical approach

The differences between ideal and realistic approaches to requirements analysis and specification should now be pretty clear. We can now look at a practical, realistic model of the process. The scenario it applies to is the overall development of the air interceptor fighter aircraft (Figure 3.7). Although this is repeating some material, it presents it in a somewhat different way. Two factors are key to this model:

- A layered process.
- Incremental development.

At the project outset the most important players on the scene are the defence agencies. Also, from the project point of view, these are the end client(s). Work begins with an analysis of the air defence requirements which the system is required to meet. And this is probably the *only* stage in which pure analysis is carried out. Subsequently, analysis and design are carried out as an interlocking pair of operations. But there are a number of distinct sets of A/D operations, each having a 'ceiling' (the input) and a 'floor' (the output).

For the defence staff, the floor of activities is the generation of the statement of requirements (SOR) for the complete system. These act as the ceiling for the main contractor, whose first task is to analyse the requirements. Next, subsystem design is performed, using as input the information provided within the SOR. The floor activity of this work layer is the production of sets of subsystem specifications (one being the navigation and weapons aiming – NAV/WAS – subsystem). Subsequent events are depicted in Figure 3.7. For simplicity, only the software development phase is included at the bottom level.

It is important to understand that you, as a software engineer, are likely to be involved in the bottom layer of work. Know your place in the scheme of things, and recognize that the computer is essentially a component within a complete system. Thus system – not computer – requirements predominate.

Now let us look at how software development itself proceeds in real life. It does not occur in a 'big-bang' fashion. Rather it takes place gradually, as illustrated in Figure 3.8. The inputs to (the ceiling of) the design process are the software requirements specifications. Work proceeds by evaluating the specifications and then developing – in conceptual form – suitable software structuring.

Next is the design process itself, which translates concepts into design solutions. Following on is the implementation phase, the outcome being source code. This is not the finish, however. Generally issues which come to light during the development lead us to review the design. In turn this leads to a greater understanding of the problem; frequently it also results in changes to the design specification itself. At this stage we retread the path, using our new (or better) knowledge to improve the software product.

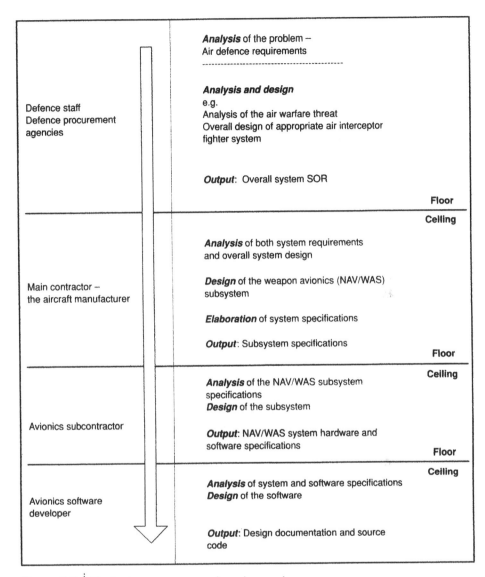

Figure 3.7 ⋮ The development process – a layered approach.

The model of Figure 3.8 describes the concrete aspects of software development for real-time systems. In the past few companies formalized this process; generally their methods evolved in an *ad hoc* way. Now, though, more rigour is gradually being introduced, reinforced by the use of modern tools and techniques. The rest of this chapter concentrates specifically on the front-end stages of analysis and specification; other aspects are discussed later in the text.

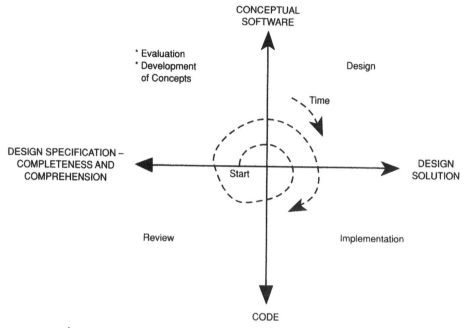

Figure 3.8 Incremental development of software.

3.2 The importance of the requirements stage

Why are the front-end stages so important? Because they have a profound effect on overall software error rates and productivity. And these are closely related to system costs.

Let's first consider software errors. There's no need to ask where they occur. The answer, as pointed out in Chapter 2, is *everywhere*. More importantly, what is the distribution of these occurrences? Figure 3.9, based on statistics obtained by Tom DeMarco [DEM78], gives a good general guide.

It's not surprising that high error levels occur in the requirements phase. It is, after all, a highly complex procedure to specify fully the requirements of a system. More on this later.

A second important point is the cost impact of these errors. Figure 3.10 illustrates this, again using the statistics from DeMarco. Given that Figure 3.9 is correct, this shouldn't be a surprise. Any mistake made at the beginning of a project affects all subsequent phases, a 'ripple-down' effect. So when requirements errors are discovered at the final stage of development, corrections have to be made throughout the complete design. The resulting corrective costs are extremely high. Mistakes made in later stages have much less impact. In theory there should be no ripple-up effect;

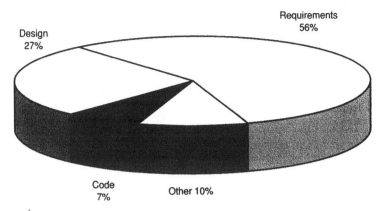

Figure 3.9 | Distribution of software errors.

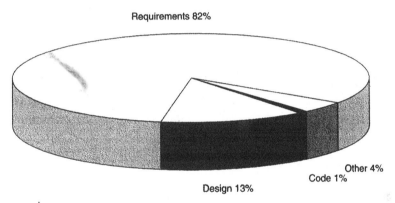

Figure 3.10 | Cost of rectifying software errors.

in practice, though, this *can* happen. For instance, suppose a major error occurs at the physical design level. It may actually be easier to change the software specification and structure rather than redesign the physical level.

The second issue, costs, is very closely bound up with the first one. Mistakes take time to find and correct. Therefore as the error rate increases the amount of deliverable code per unit time decreases – with consequent cost penalties.

It should now be clear that the requirements stage is the most important aspect of the life-cycle process. Unfortunately, many customers and suppliers fail to realize exactly how important it is. Getting this wrong can produce dreadful downstream effects. Most situations are recoverable – at a cost. But there are also well-documented cases where whole projects have been ditched as a result of requirements errors. Paradoxically, this stage has the fewest development and support tools within the total software toolset.

3.3 Making mistakes – sources and causes

3.3.1 A general comment

Why and how do we make mistakes? Figure 3.11 attempts, in a light-hearted way, to highlight some of the issues involved. It may be simplistic but it does get to the heart of the matter, because it shows that three major factors are at work here:

- How we convert what we think into what we say.
- How we express ourselves.
- How we convert what we see (receive) into thought.

How do these apply to the requirements stage of a project? Let's first look at the customer–supplier relationship in more detail, as modelled in Figure 3.12.

This model also applies to the system designer–software designer relationship. So rules derived to enhance customer–supplier interactions can also be applied later in the software development cycle. The first step in procuring any new system is to define exactly what is needed. The customer, using his acquired knowledge and available information, formulates a set of requirements. These are communicated (by whatever means are suitable) to the supplier. He in turn evaluates these requirements, and produces a design solution based on the evaluation. This looks simple enough. But then why is it that the delivered product often fails to match up with what was wanted in the first place? The answer, of course, is that it isn't simple at all. It's important to recognize the source of these mismatch problems because then we can:

- Understand the weaknesses of informal systems (past–current practice).
- Appreciate the use of rigorous analysis/specification tools (current practice).
- Perceive the advantages in using prototyping techniques (current–future practice).

There are four major reasons why mismatches occur (Figure 3.13). First, we don't formulate the requirements properly. Secondly, we don't communicate these requirements correctly. Thirdly, we fail to understand properly these improperly communicated requirements. Finally, because requirements continually change, not all changes may be acted on correctly. How much effect do these errors have, and how significant are they? It depends mainly on two factors: expertise and methods. Experienced people make fewer mistakes and are more likely to find errors in other people's work. Unfortunately this is a process we can't automate; there is no substitute for good people. What we *can* do is produce tools which help in formulating and analysing problems and communicating ideas. Furthermore, it is essential that these tackle the root cause of errors (Figure 3.14), otherwise they're useless.

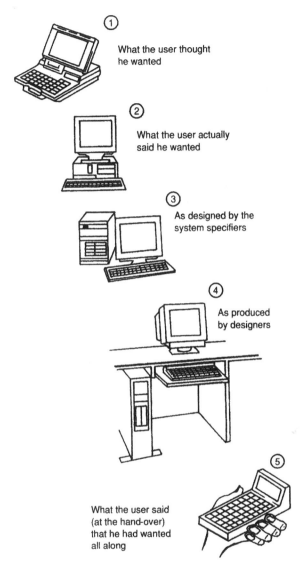

What the user thought
he wanted

What the user actually
said he wanted

As designed by the
system specifiers

As produced
by designers

What the user said
(at the hand-over)
that he had wanted
all along

Figure 3.11 Making mistakes.

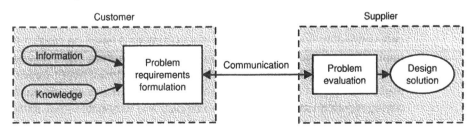

Figure 3.12 Simplistic view of the customer–supplier relationship.

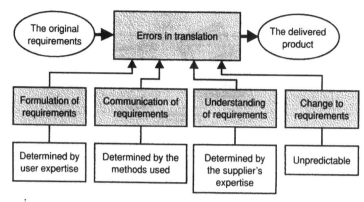

Figure 3.13 : Sources of requirements/deliverables mismatch problems.

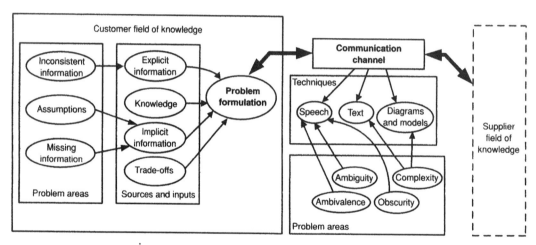

Figure 3.14 : Causes of requirements/deliverables mismatch problems.

3.3.2 Problems in formulating specifications

First let's consider what goes on when the customer attempts to put together an SOR. In an ideal situation full information relating to the requirement is explicitly defined. In reality the requirement document is based on explicit information, implicit information and knowledge. Further, in putting together a specification, many conflicting demands are made by involved parties; hence trade-offs must be made. Each aspect has associated problems. And problems are compounded by specifying requirements which appear to be clear and reasonable – but actually are quite imprecise (and sometimes untestable). For instance, what does 'mimic displays shall be clear and uncluttered' mean? How does one define 'clear' and 'uncluttered'?

Explicit information

This may seem a clear-cut situation. True, but the major problem here is inconsistency of the information supplied. Specification documents are usually weighty items (in both a physical and literary sense). It can be extremely difficult to identify conflicts in such circumstances.

Implicit information

Implicit information is that which, to the specifier, appears to be present in, or deducible from, the SOR – but isn't. In some instances it is a simple case of missing information. In others, information is omitted or overlooked because assumptions are made concerning the supplier's understanding of the requirements. For instance, the operational temperature range of an equipment might be omitted from its specification. But because the application is an avionic one, say, everybody knows what this requirement is. Really?

Knowledge

This is a difficult area to describe precisely; there are many facets to it. Problems arise because the customer has a much greater knowledge of the system than the supplier; and much of it is unstated. For instance, there is always some relationship between the system being specified and other systems. The specifier has a good understanding of this, and aims to ensure that system integration is achieved correctly. Unfortunately the supplier is unlikely to have the same knowledge. Hence, during software design, decisions are made which seem perfectly correct for the system being constructed, yet may adversely affect other systems.

There is usually some overlap between this aspect and that of implicit information. The following example, relating to a very large computer-controlled rotating machine, illustrates this point. On initial trials the protection system kept shutting the machine down during start-up operations. It turned out that nobody had bothered to tell the software designers that the machine took a full minute to run up to speed – the assumption was that everybody knew about this. Unfortunately the software engineers didn't, and invoked an underspeed trip far too early in the run-up process.

Another factor, that of balance of judgement, can have significant cost and performance effects on the final product. Consider, for instance, where a particular requirement is extremely difficult to satisfy. The supplier isn't in a position to judge its importance; it's just another target to be met. So the target *is* achieved – but only with the greatest of difficulty, possibly affecting both software and hardware. Yet the customer may be the only person who knows that the requirement isn't especially important. Thus the specification could well be relaxed, with attendant savings to time and money.

3.3.3   Problems in communicating requirements

Four basic methods can be used to communicate information: speech, text, pictures and physical models. Models tend to play a much greater role in the later stages of system development, and their importance cannot be underestimated. It's well known that car manufacturers build models of new vehicles, but less well known is that a full-scale wooden mock-up was built of the Swiftsure class nuclear-powered hunter–killer submarine. For software systems different, non-physical, models are needed. This topic is discussed further in the section on prototyping.

One view of the communication process is that information is transmitted along a communication channel from sender to receiver. In the ideal world, what is sent is also what is received. But in reality this isn't true; information is corrupted by 'noise' along the way. The major sources of noise are:

- Ambiguity – I don't know what it means.
- Ambivalence – it could mean either this OR that: or both.
- Obscurity – it just isn't clear at all, I'm quite confused.
- Complexity – I hear what you say but I'm now totally confused.

Speech (and here is implied face-to-face contact) is probably the most important and significant communication process. Yet it is the one most prone to noise corruption. It's impossible to eliminate this noise – it is part of human nature. One must accept that there are inherent problems in speech communication; therefore other methods are needed to compensate for them.

Text description is, after speech, the most common method of communicating information. It too suffers from the problems outlined above, but generally these are easier to correct. Unfortunately, as a result of trying to eliminate these deficiencies, textual material becomes extremely complex (have a look at some legal documents). For technical systems we frequently end up with specification documents which are massive, dull and virtually unusable. Some authors of specification documents have an unshakeable belief in their effectiveness – even when experience proves the contrary point.

Pictures (diagrams) are one of the most effective means of communicating information (just think of the amount of money spent on eye-catching television advertisements). Diagrams have two major advantages over other forms of communication. First, they let us express our thoughts easily. Second, they make it much easier (compared with text descriptions) to assimilate information. Engineers have used this as a primary communication tool for centuries; yet for years it was almost entirely neglected by the computer science industry.

The role of diagramming is discussed in much more detail in Chapter 7. Suffice it to say that, as far as specification methods are concerned, diagrams are becoming an important technique. Note that in this context structured text is considered to be a diagram.

Finally, this description has only considered information flow from the customer to the supplier. In practice it is a two-way process – with all the consequent noise corruption effects on return messages.

3.3.4 Problems in understanding requirements

Even if the specifications delivered by the customer are totally correct, unambiguous, etc., mistakes are still going to be made. First, the supplier interprets the specifications from his point of view (or 'domain'). This is usually very different from that of the customer. Second, difficulties arise as he attempts to convey his response to the customer. He has exactly the same problems as those experienced by the customer when formulating the specification. Is it surprising then that the customer may not quite understand what the supplier is doing, how he's doing it and why he's doing it in a particular way? Therefore it is essential that the supplier uses techniques which make his work meaningful: both to him and to the customer.

3.4 Practical approaches to analysis and specification

3.4.1 General aspects

What is the fundamental purpose of the analysis and specification – the requirements – phase? It is to define *what* a proposed system is to do, not *how* it is supposed to do it; 'how' is the function of the design process. However, in practice there isn't always a sharp boundary between requirements and design. And the problem is compounded because some design methods make little distinction between the two. We can see why these overlap by considering the make-up of the requirements work-stage, Figure 3.15.

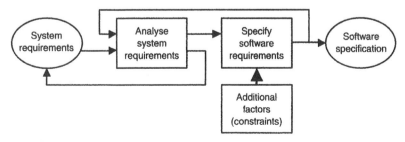

Figure 3.15 The requirements phase – analysis and specification.

The first part of this process is concerned with analysing and recording the system *requirements*. Note this well. Many traditional (i.e. DP) descriptions discuss the analysis of systems, but you can only analyse a system if one already exists.

In the initial run-through, design factors shouldn't affect the outcome of the analysis work. Using the information acquired during the analysis phase the software requirements are now specified. Constraints are usually applied here: programming language, design methods and documentation procedures, for instance. Now this is the point where design aspects *do* enter the process. There isn't much point in specifying a software requirement if the required system can't be:

- Achieved.

- Completed within the required timescale.

- Done within budget.

Implementation difficulties, actual or anticipated, cause us to review and re-analyse system requirements. As a result the software specifications are, if necessary, changed to a more sensible form. In some cases, though, it may be impossible to do this and still meet the original system requirements. Consequently a further review of the SOR must be carried out. Where possible this document should be amended to take implementation factors into account. This is a normal and accepted part of any development process – most problems can be tackled in this way. Occasionally obstacles arise which are impossible to overcome within the given requirement objectives. There are only two courses of action. Either major changes are made to these objectives, or else the whole project must be abandoned.

We've already said that requirements and design may not be easy to separate. But they *are* very distinct parts of the development process. Therefore the software developer should always strive to treat them in this way. The main attributes of the requirements phase are the:

- Basic strategy used.

- Acquisition and presentation of information.

- Information content.

- Choice of method and tool support.

The first question to answer is what the specification document should contain. Sensibly it should provide a good description of the intended system, Figure 3.16. This description includes system:

- Function.

- Performance.

- Interfaces.

- Constraints.

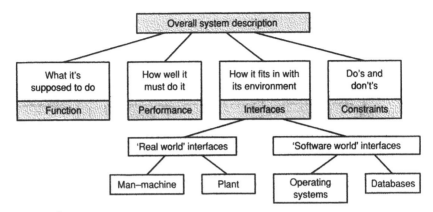

Figure 3.16 Overall system description.

Interfaces include those which connect to the physical environment – the 'real world' – and to other software entities.

The description/document must be structured so that it can be understood both by the customer and the supplier. This means, most definitely, that it should not use obscure notation, complex structures or definitions using computer language terms. This latter approach has been advocated by a number of authors. It may be a very useful technique for the architectural design stage, but it cannot be recommended as a way of stating system requirements. We really need methods which are:

- Formal (that is, there are defined rules which must be obeyed).
- Visible (no implicit information).
- Expressive (easy to state what we mean).
- Understandable (making communication simpler).
- Easy to use (an obvious need, yet frequently ignored).

We also need proper tools to support these methods. In structural terms three specific functions should be present in any requirements tool: elicitation, representation and analysis (Figure 3.17). These cover the actions of gathering information, formally recording this information, and then checking it for consistency, conflicts and completeness. Such information is derived from a variety of sources, including users (humans), equipment data and formal documents such as the SOR. It should be appreciated that only the customer can provide this information. In an ideal world these three actions would be performed once, as a set of sequential operations. In practice the process is an ongoing one, with regular overlapping of actions. There are constant iterations through these steps as new data is acquired, ideas refined, and old information modified or discarded.

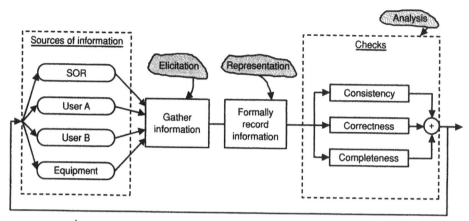

Figure 3.17 Requirements elicitation, representation and analysis.

What's been described so far takes place in all engineering projects. Requirements-handling strategies in engineering are usually quite formalized: but only on a company basis. The techniques are well known and practised, adapted as necessary to suit particular local conditions. Specific prescriptive methods, which can be applied across a variety of applications, are virtually unknown. This hasn't been a problem, though, because of the rigour and discipline inherent in engineering projects. Unfortunately, in the past (only the past?), rigour and program development have been mutually exclusive events. To rectify this situation – at least as far as the requirements phases are concerned – a number of methods have been developed. Some have been designed for very specific uses; others intended for general usage.

3.4.2 Tool support and automation

Defined *methods* are fine. They are the first step in formalizing analysis and specification techniques. Unfortunately there is one problem on which methods themselves make little impact: information complexity. How can we really be sure that, when dealing with complex requirements, information is:

- Consistent (we haven't made mistakes in gathering and recording the data)?
- Correct (there aren't wrong or conflicting requirements laid down within the requirements themselves)?
- Complete (items haven't been omitted)?

It's extremely difficult, time-consuming and tedious to do this manually. Clearly, automated tools are needed. Then the question arises: what can we sensibly automate? Ideas, concepts, meaning: all are beyond automation. We can only work with facts. Now, systems can be described in terms of their internal data, the data flow

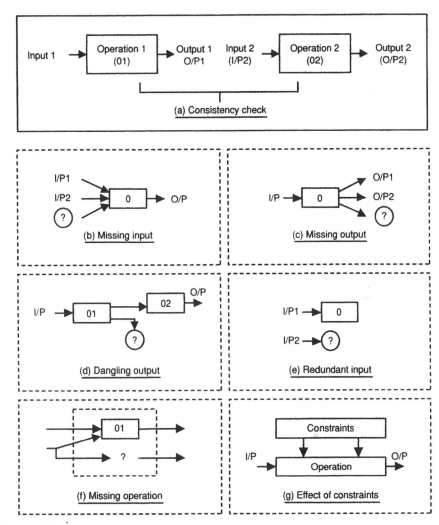

Figure 3.18 | Automated checking rules.

through them, and actions performed on this data. To a large extent we can auto-mate this description, as shown in Figure 3.18.

First we describe individual operations within the system, together with their inputs and outputs. It is then possible to check for consistency between operations, as in Figure 3.18a. Assume, for instance, that the requirements specification defines that the output of operation 01 acts as the input to 02. Thus both output1 and input2 represent the same entity. If during the recording process different entities are assigned to these, the error can be quickly identified, provided all information is held in a common store. Thus any automated tool has at its heart a common database. Many other errors can be picked up in this way. These include:

- Missing inputs; Figure 3.18b (an operation, to produce the desired output, needs three inputs; but only two are provided).

- Missing outputs, Figure 3.18c (an operation must produce three outputs to satisfy system structure and operation; however, only two are specified in the SOR).

- Dangling outputs, Figure 3.18d (specified operations produce outputs which aren't used anywhere).

- Redundant inputs, Figure 3.18e (inputs are specified in the SOR, but no operations are performed on these within the system).

- Missing operations, Figure 3.18f (inputs are provided, outputs are expected, but no operations are specified in the requirements document).

Constraint effects can also be introduced, Figure 3.18g. We can, for instance, define that:

- Operations may be controlled by specific enabling/disabling conditions.

- Selection of operations may be required.

- Repeated activation of operations may be invoked.

3.4.3   Viewpoint analysis

Now what we've said so far is splendid, but its effectiveness depends on how well we can define the set of operations in the first place. One concept which has been highly effective here is that of viewpoint analysis.

The notion of viewpoints is based on common sense; that is, we all see things from our own point of view. Consider a system which consists of a propulsion engine driving a ship's propeller via gearing and shafting, Figure 3.19. Attached to the engine is a digital control unit, its functions being to modulate engine speed. To the marine engineer the controller is insignificant when compared with the mechanical systems. Yet the software engineer responsible for the controller programs may have

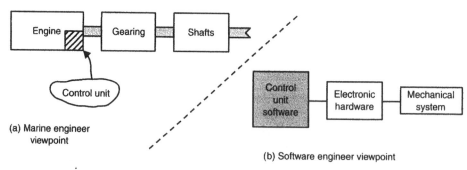

(a) Marine engineer
viewpoint

(b) Software engineer viewpoint

Figure 3.19   Viewpoint concept.

a totally different perception of the situation. He may regard software as *the* single most important item in the whole system, electronic hardware being a poor second. Mechanical systems almost disappear from sight.

The viewpoint analysis concept recognizes that systems cannot be adequately described from a single point of view; many must be taken into account. By setting out a system description as seen from all relevant viewpoints, consistency, correctness and completeness can be monitored. We can then produce a software specification which is totally consistent, correct and complete – but only in terms of the information recorded in the first place. Be warned: total completeness is another myth.

Now let's see how viewpoint analysis works in practice. Assume that we have been asked to supply a digital controller for the system shown in Figure 3.20. How many viewpoints should be taken into account? There isn't a unique answer to this; it really depends on each particular case. One tendency is to think only in terms of inanimate objects; we frequently forget people and their interactions with the system. For this example we will describe the system as seen from the points of view of the operator and other major system items, Figure 3.21.

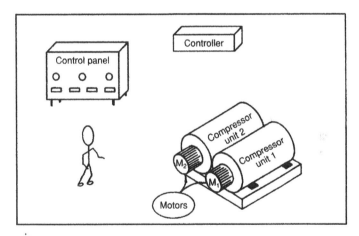

Figure 3.20 Specimen system.

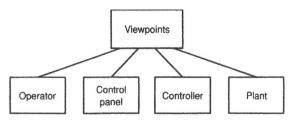

Figure 3.21 Viewpoint diagram for specimen system.

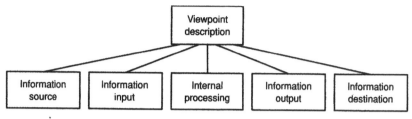

Figure 3.22 | Viewpoint contents.

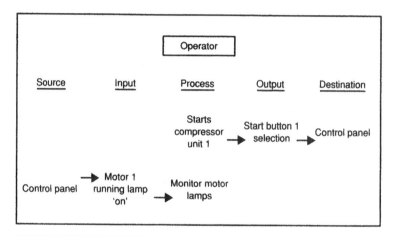

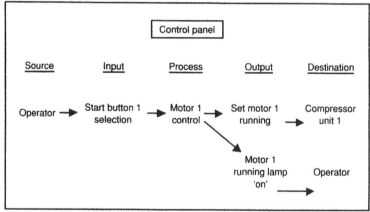

Figure 3.23 | Viewpoint description diagrams.

Each viewpoint is described in terms of its inputs, actions (processing) and outputs, Figure 3.22. The appropriate information is usually recorded in tabular form, precise details depending on the particular analysis method used. In the case of CORE (Controlled Requirements Expression [COR86]), the layout follows the pattern of Figure 3.23.

Here part descriptions are given for the operator and control panel viewpoints. The diagram, which is self-explanatory, highlights the important features of viewpoints and viewpoint description diagrams:

- Each viewpoint describes one or more system processing operations.

- Any particular processing operations takes place in one, and only one, viewpoint.

- Inputs and outputs must balance across the full set of diagrams.

There are two aspects of viewpoint analysis which cannot be automated. First, a set of viewpoints has to be established in the first place. Secondly, *all* relevant information needs to be recorded. It is perfectly possible to have a balance across the set of diagrams and yet have essential data missing.

3.4.4   Viewpoints – analysis versus specification

Viewpoint analysis is an effective way of extracting, evaluating and collating information. The result should be a comprehensive description of the required system behaviour and its attributes. But two important features still need to be defined: what precisely happens within each process, and how do these relate in time (the system dynamic behaviour)? To describe these we need to show three features:

- The data flow through a system.

- Detailed processing of this data.

- When such processing events occur.

One practical technique does this by combining data flow and events in a single description diagram, Figure 3.24. Note that here we aren't really concerned with absolute time, more the sequence of events. Diagrams like these can be formed for each viewpoint, being decomposed as necessary to show more detailed information. By recording this information in the same database as the viewpoint diagrams,

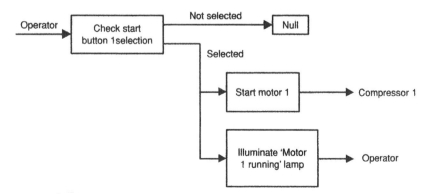

Figure 3.24   Combining data flow and events (control panel viewpoint).

consistency is maintained. Moreover, detailed descriptions can be re-composed to eliminate mistakes which may have occurred during decomposition.

3.4.5 Use case analysis

Fundamentals

Without a doubt, the analysis methodology of Ivar Jacobson [JAC92] has made an immense impact on the software scene. The technique – called a 'use-case driven approach' – has become very widely used in recent years. It is probably *the* dominant requirements analysis and specification method in the software world of business systems. Although it isn't so widely applied in the real-time area, its use is spreading rapidly. So what then are the fundamental ideas of use cases? Before answering that, though, there is one other important question to tackle. Exactly *what* does the method set out to achieve? The answer is a sixfold one. Use case techniques provide us with a way to:

- Analyse client requirements.
- Organize and present requirements in a way that is useful, meaningful and complete.
- Minimize confusion and misunderstanding between clients and suppliers.
- Validate system-level designs.
- Develop specifications for the software system itself.
- Define the outlines of system acceptance tests (for function, performance and usage).

The underlying ideas are really quite simple (but it usually takes talented people to develop such concepts). They are based on the fact that people are users of systems, Figure 3.25. And, in general, system requirements are related to the whats, whens and hows of people–system interactions. *That* is what we set out to define as part of the requirements analysis process.

Of course, the real world contains many people and many systems. First we must establish exactly what is of interest to us, which could be shown as in Figure 3.26. Although this is a step in the right direction, the diagram has one great shortcoming. We have no idea *why* the people use such systems. This leads on to the basics of the use case diagram, Figure 3.27.

It shows (Figure 3.27a):

- The system of concern is a bookshop.
- There are two users (specifically two individuals).
- The individuals are using the system to order a book (or books). Any illustration of the use of a system is defined to be a 'use case'; hence this example is the use case 'order book'.

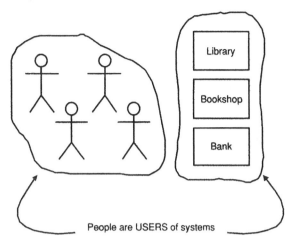

Figure 3.25 Use cases – setting the scene.

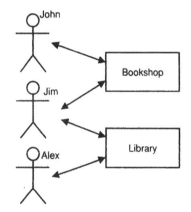

Figure 3.26 Systems and their users.

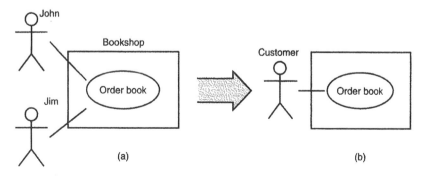

(a)

(b)

Figure 3.27 The basics of the use case diagram.

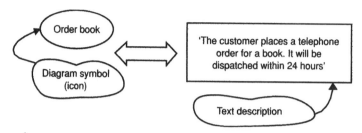

Figure 3.28 The two components of a use case.

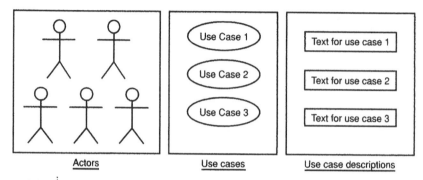

Figure 3.29 The components of the use case model.

From the system's point of view the two users are essentially the same; both are customers. Therefore, rather than focusing on individuals, we try to identify the 'roles' they play in the interaction. In this example both people are 'customers', Figure 3.27b.

At this stage most of the ideas of the use case model have been established. However, it still isn't complete; we have no idea what actually goes on when a customer tries to order a book. Thus the diagram symbol needs to be backed up by a text description, Figure 3.28. Here we have the essential components of a use case: a diagram symbol and a text description of the user–system interaction (there is, in fact, no need to limit yourself to text; anything which imparts information can be used – but more of that later).

From this it is but a small step to establish the components of the use case *model*, Figure 3.29. This consists of actors, use cases and use case descriptions. Each system will have its own model, with actors depicting users (more correctly, roles performed by users). The reasons why these actors are using the system are shown as a set of use cases within the system boundary. Supporting these are the use case descriptions. Two simple examples are given in Figure 3.30. Each system is drawn as a rectangular box, with the relevant use cases shown as ellipses inside them. Outside the system boundary are the actors, connected via lines to the use cases. In (a), both the navigator actor and the pilot actor interact with the navigation/weapon

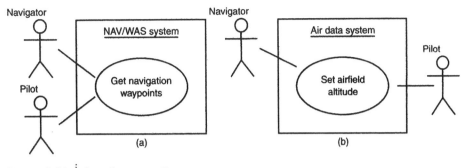

Figure 3.30 Example use case diagrams.

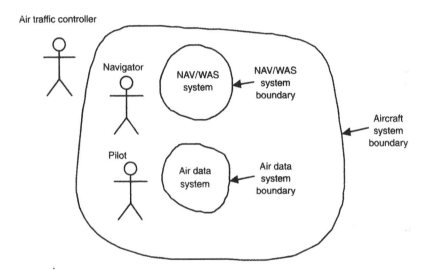

Figure 3.3I System boundaries.

aiming (NAV/WAS) system in the same way; they use it to find out what the navigation waypoints are. Information flow is a two-way process. In (b), the navigator uses the air data system to set airfield altitude: again a two-way process. However, in this case the pilot merely receives output (information) from the system; the role played by the actor is thus a 'passive' one.

Summarizing things to date: the use case diagram shows all users of the system and their reasons for using the system. It should go without saying that all items on the diagram must have useful, relevant and meaningful names. Moreover, we have to be clear exactly where our system boundary lies. In the example given, both systems are within the overall aircraft system (Figure 3.31). Therefore, from the perspective of an air traffic controller, the pilot and navigator form part of the *aircraft* system.

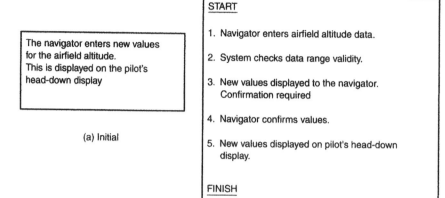

(a) Initial

(b) Expanded

Figure 3.32 Text description — initial and expanded versions.

Two small asides at this point. First, the term 'use case' is often used to denote two items: the symbol on the use case diagram and the description of the related user–system interaction. In practice this isn't a problem; you can usually see which one is being referred to. Second, there are many definitions of the term itself (Alistair Cockburn states 'I have personally encountered over 18 different definitions of use case, given by different, each expert, teachers and consultants' [COC97]). One widely accepted, formalized, description is [BOO98] 'a description of a set of sequences of actions, including variants, that a system performs that yield an observable result of value to an actor'. However, we'll take a more laid-back approach with 'a way that an actor uses a system to achieve some desired result'. This result or 'goal' should determine the wording used on the use case diagram. If you can't express your goals simply then you don't understand what you're trying to do.

Describing and structuring use cases

Now let us look into the use case text descriptions in more detail. It is *strongly* recommended that the first attempt should be short, clear and use ordinary language, Figure 3.32a. A structured, formalized version can be used to expand on this at a later stage, Figure 3.32b. Trying to do this in the beginning is often a hindrance to clear thinking.

Observe that the text is enclosed between a START and a FINISH marker. The starting point is pretty self-evident: when the actor begins to use the system. Thus a use case always has a single starting point. This, however, is not necessarily true for the finish condition, a point of much confusion. Cockburn's definition is clear and practical: 'a use case is finished when the goal is achieved or abandoned'. That's good enough for me. And this nicely leads into the topic of *scenarios*, Figure 3.33.

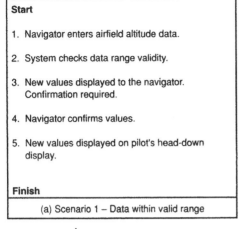

Start		Start
1. Navigator enters airfield altitude data.		1. Navigator enters ____
2. System checks data range validity.		2. System checks data range validity.
		2.1 System rejects data.
		2.2 Requests re-entry of data.
		2.3 Go to action 1.
3. New values displayed to the navigator. Confirmation required.		3. New values _ _ _
4. Navigator confirms values.		4. Navigator confirms_ _ _
		5. New values _ _ _
5. New values displayed on pilot's head-down display.		
Finish		Finish
(a) Scenario 1 – Data within valid range		(b) Scenario 2 – Data not in valid range

Figure 3.33 Scenarios.

Figure 3.33a is a description of what happens assuming that everything is OK. This is one *scenario* (a particular sequence of actions and interactions) for the use case 'set airfield altitude'. The scenario, identified as 'data within valid range', has a single finish point. But what of the situation where the data entered is *not* within the pre-defined range? The interactions which take place in those circumstances are shown in Figure 3.33b. Here, if the data is invalid it is rejected and a request made for new data. This is a second, valid sequence of interactions for the use case, a second scenario.

We can simplify our paperwork by combining scenarios as shown in Figure 3.34a. Moreover, if it helps, we can use diagrams to show the logic of the scenarios, Figure 3.34b. This also brings out that there are two distinct routes through the use case text: therefore two scenarios.

There are three kinds of scenarios, describing:

● Normal (error-free) use of the system.

● Uses where errors occur but which can be dealt with as part of the interaction process (e.g. entering invalid data).

● Uses where errors occur but which cannot be dealt with as part of the normal processing (exceptions).

A major failing of analysts is in spending insufficient time and brain-power on the issues of errors and error-handling. And yet these are, if anything, more important than the normal or 'happy day' scenarios.

As we combine more and more scenarios, text documents soon become complex, difficult to read, and difficult to understand. Hardly a step forward for mankind, as the whole point of use cases is to make things understandable. One way of simplifying documents is to take a leaf out of programming techniques: use the equivalent

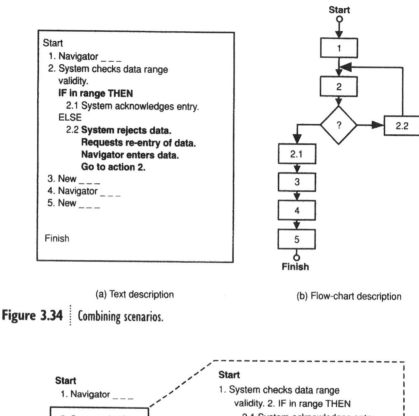

(a) Text description

(b) Flow-chart description

Figure 3.34 Combining scenarios.

Figure 3.35 Simplifying use case descriptions.

of subprograms and subprogram calls (Figure 3.35). Here we aim to write the 'top-level' text as a set of sequential operations; where necessary these can be expanded in a separate text document. In fact, the separate text can be treated as a use case in its own right, Figure 3.36. The use case 'set airfield altitude' – the *base* use case – is considered to include that of 'validate data range'; this is defined to be an *includes* relationship. We can read the diagram to mean that the base use case *will* use the behaviour of the included use; moreover it will do so at explicit points. One last aspect of the includes relationship: the included use case should always form some part of a base use case. It is not meant to be a use case in its own right. Moreover,

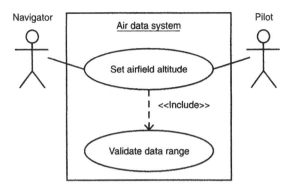

Figure 3.36 Use case diagram for Figure 3.35 – the include relationship.

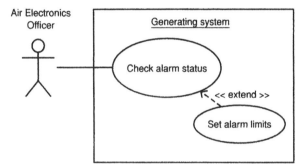

Figure 3.37 The extend relationship.

the included use case is an integral part of the base one; without this the base use case is incomplete. Observe the notation used and the direction of the arrow.

Now there are situations where a base use case is complete, as per the 'check alarm status' of Figure 3.37. Here the Air Electronics Officer starts the base use case 'check alarm status' to check out the generating system alarms. Most of the time this is the only action which is carried out. However, on certain occasions it may be necessary to (re)set alarm limits. In these circumstances extra functions are performed, defined in the use case 'set alarm limits'. Thus the functionality of the base use case is *extended* by the second one. This is denoted by drawing an arrowed line from the extended class to the base class.

The distinction between includes and extends causes much confusion. One way to resolve this is to ask the question 'if I remove the (included/extended) use case, is the base use case complete?' Another view is that:

- Include use cases collect in one place behaviour which is common to a number of base use cases (Figure 3.38a).
- Extend use cases show variations on a theme (Figure 3.38b).

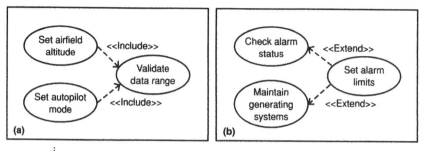

Figure 3.38 Comparing the includes and extends relationships.

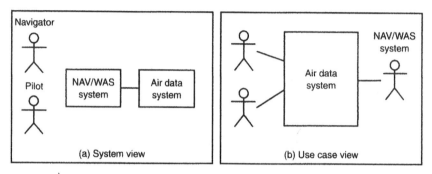

Figure 3.39 External systems as actors.

Unfortunately the distinction between the two isn't always clear-cut. The only advice worth giving is really not to worry too much; do whatever seems right for the problem facing you.

Up to this point we have used actors to represent the roles of people. But frequently systems interact, not only with people, but with other systems, Figure 3.39a. Here the NAV/WAS system uses information provided by the air data system. Thus, from the point of view of the air data system, the NAV/WAS system is merely another actor, Figure 3.39b.

Preparing for design

If our brief was to analyse the system requirements and so produce a general set of requirements we would probably stop at this point. But as specifications for software systems, they lack depth and perhaps rigour. More work is needed. In particular we need to specify in detail the flow of information to and from the software system.

The first and obvious statement is that people cannot directly interact with software; user interfaces (hardware) are required (Figure 3.40). Here we have specified our scope of interest using a system scope diagram, Figure 3.40a, or something similar. Including the interface devices (i.e. keypad, display) is most important.

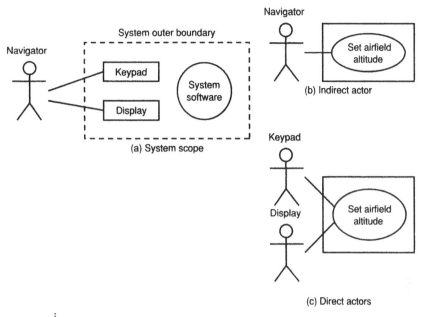

Figure 3.40 System scope, direct and indirect actors.

Now, from the point of view of the software the navigator becomes an *indirect* actor, Figure 3.40b; the devices themselves are the *direct* ones, Figure 3.40c.

What we have done is changed the focus of attention from the system to the software. In effect Figure 3.40c defines the context of the software within the system. It is imperative that all interface signals are defined and listed as part of this process. Relevant parameters should be noted, initially from a system perspective. Later these can be elaborated to include electronic and software features, viz.:

Signal: Lye temperature.
Initial definition:
    Temperature range 0 to 70°C.
Interim update:
    Analogue signal, 0 to 10 volts d.c. 0 volts ≡ 0°C, 10 volts ≡ 100°C.
Later update:
    Input on: ADC board.
    Channel: 4.
    Digitization: 8 bits.
    Format: straight binary.
    Memory address: 5000(h) (absolute)

Existing use case descriptions may, if desired, be updated to take the changes into account. However, a very effective way forward is to show such actor–system interactions in graphical form as in Figure 3.41. Cross-refer this to Figure 3.40a. You will

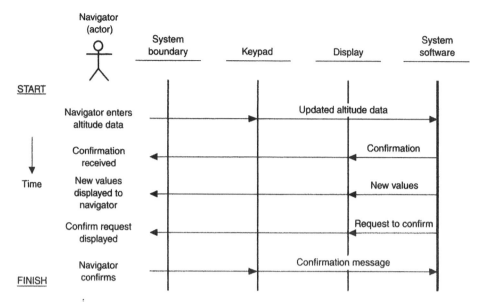

Figure 3.41 A graphical display of actor–system interaction.

see that all items in this diagram are repeated in Figure 3.41. Each one has its own time line or *trace*, where time runs from top to bottom of the diagram. Messages going between the different items are shown as horizontal lines, arrows denoting direction. You will also see that the system boundary has been placed on the diagram.

You will only understand the value of this diagram when you use it in a real design. It is one of *the* major bridging pieces between high-level (system) and software-level design. In effect it guarantees that we at least *start* software design from the right place. Furthermore, you will find it to be of immense value when carrying out design traceability exercises.

Some final points

Just where do you start when faced with having to do high-level analysis/design of a new system (from a use case perspective, that is)? Just how do you go about developing the use case model? Generally, real-time systems have fewer actors (in the people sense) than business or IT systems. Thus identification of users should be a first priority. So define the system boundary so that only users and external systems are shown as actors. Now proceed to identify the way in which these use the system under consideration. Much information will be contained in the system SORs, for example:

● 'The system will produce a graphical display of plant parameters when requested to do so' – a particular operational requirement.

- 'The active suspension system will provide hard, firm and soft rides in response to driver input commands' – a mission requirement.

- 'The line operator must have facilities to override the automatic control system' – a specific reference to a user (people).

With business systems it may be feasible to proceed into software design before fully completing the use case model. A regularly quoted figure in OO literature is to aim for an initial completion figure of 80% – but there appears to be no evidence to back this up. For real-time (and especially embedded) systems doing this is akin to digging a hole into which you will later fall. Always complete your use case model before going forward to hardware and software design (or if you don't, make sure the omissions are justified *and* red-lined).

And finally, use cases are not the holy grail of software; they are just one more weapon in the armoury of analysis and design tools.

3.4.6 Functional, non-functional and development requirements specifications

So far we have concentrated on what is required of a system. Now let us look specifically at the issue of software specification. Our objective during the specification phase is to produce a definitive document that states what the system is required to do. Fundamentally each requirements specification document consists of three parts: functional, non-functional and development requirements, Figure 3.42. This model of the software requirements specification is based on that defined in STARTS [STA87]. Functional requirements specifications relate to system behaviour as shown in Figure 3.43. They describe system operation from three perspectives: what systems do, when they do it, and how they respond to deviations of normal behaviour. Note that they should not define *how* these requirements are to be satisfied.

Observe that data input to the system, output from the system and that contained within the system itself forms part of the specification model.

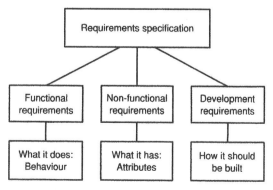

Figure 3.42 ⋮ Software specification features.

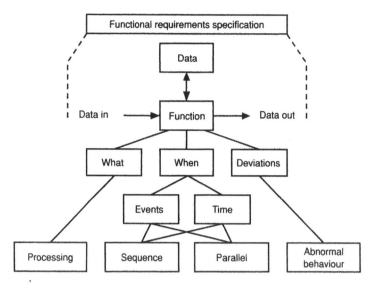

Figure 3.43 Aspects of functional requirements specifications.

The 'when' aspect expresses the dynamic behaviour of systems, both in terms of system events and real time. Events *may* be time dependent; but here the important point is their relationship to each other. For instance, it should not be possible to launch a missile until its hatch cover is removed. Time may be absolute, being defined in terms of the normal calendar time clock. Alternatively it may be a relative value, as in 'the low oil pressure alarm is to be inhibited for 40 seconds after the start switch is pressed'. It's also important that, when specifying dynamic behaviour, we distinguish between parallel actions and sequential ones. This can have a profound effect on resulting design decisions.

All real-time systems must be designed to cope with abnormal conditions to ensure safe operation. Where possible all significant deviations should be defined, together with appropriate exception-handling responses.

The information and diagrams produced previously form the basis for the software requirements specification document. These identify the various functions, the data flows, processing of data, dependencies and deviant behaviour. The major working diagrams are those which combine system data and events; viewpoint descriptions are less useful. These diagrams need to be augmented by text specifications to provide a full description of the function. There isn't a particular prescriptive format for these documents; only guidelines can be given. The following listing (Figure 3.44) is a very simplified high-level description of part of a flight control system.

Non-functional system requirements specifications are shown in Figure 3.45. These define:

- How well a function should be performed (performance).

- How the system connects to its environment (interfaces).

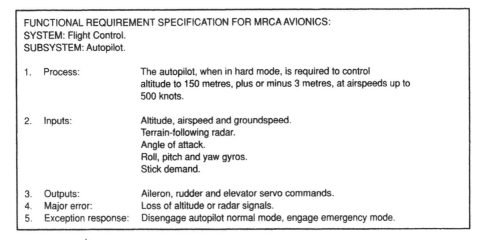

Figure 3.44 : Specimen functional requirements specification.

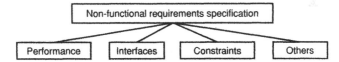

Figure 3.45 : Non-functional requirements specification.

- What limitations are placed on the design (constraints).

- Anything which doesn't fit into these three groupings (others).

It's impossible to define precisely what non-functional specifications should contain. Much depends on the particular system being assessed. However, guidance can be given. As an example, consider the system described by the functional specification of Figure 3.44. Its corresponding non-functional specification is given on the following page (Figure 3.46). This, of course, is a highly simplified version; the real one would occupy many pages of text.

It can be seen here that there is overlap between sections. For instance, use of the VRTX executive is listed both as an interface requirement and as a design constraint. But this is necessary because it applies to both areas of design. Furthermore, it's not always easy to decide which category items fit into. The temperature-range requirement is listed here as an 'other' constraint; but it could equally well be viewed as a design constraint.

Functional specifications are highly visible parts of any development. Therefore, no matter what analysis and specification technique is used, it's normally fairly easy to identify these factors. Non-functional specifications are equally important. Unfortunately, when using informal techniques, they can disappear in the detail. To minimize this problem – and that's all we can ever hope for – methods must

NON-FUNCTIONAL REQUIREMENT SPECIFICATION FOR MRCA AVIONICS:
SYSTEM: flight Control.
SUBSYSTEM: Autopilot.

1. PERFORMANCE:
    Computation: The control algorithm is of the form

    $Ka[(1+ST_1)(1+ST_2)]/[(1+ST_3)(1+ST_4)]$

    Computation time: This must be achieved in 5 milliseconds.
    Computation accuracy: Calculations must be accurate to within 0.01%.
    Control loop update rates: 100 per second.
    Variation on loop sampling time: 1 millisecond from sample to sample.
    Response to loss of altitude signal: 100 microseconds maximum.
    Redundancy: Quad redundant processor system.
    System fault handling: Majority voting on processor outputs.
    Mean Time Between Failures (MTBF) per control channel: 5000 hours.
    Reliability per control channel: 99.98%.
    Mean Time To Repair (MTTR) per control channel: 1 hour.
    Storage capacity: 1 MByte.

2. INTERFACES.
2.1 Interfaces – MMI.
    The pilots will be able to select hard, medium or soft rides via a touch screen facility on the head
    down display.
2.2 Interfaces – Aircraft.
    (a) Analogue input signals: These are derived from the following sources:
        Altitude, airspeed and groundspeed.
        Terrain-following radar.
        Angle of attack.
        Roll, pitch and yaw gyros.
        Stick demand.
    All are digitized using a 12 bit analogue-to-digital converter having a
    conversion time of 10 microseconds.
    (b) Analogue output signals: These are fed to the following items:
        Aileron, rudder and elevator servo controllers.
    A 12 bit digital-to-analogue converter is used on the output of the controller.
    (c) Avionics data bus: All state information is to be fed out onto the aircraft Mil-Std 1553 data bus.
2.3 Interfaces – Software.
    The application software will be designed to interface to the VRTX32 real-time executive.

3. DESIGN CONSTRAINTS.
    Programming language: Ada95.
    Operating system: VRTX32.
    Avionic's data bus communication protocols: Mil-Std 1553b.
    Processor type: Motorola PC604.
    Maximum memory capacity (including expansion capability): 500 Kbytes.
    Spare processor performance capacity on delivery: 50% min.
    Documentation: JSP188.

4. OTHER CONSTRAINTS.
    Maximum size: Half ATR case size.
    Maximum weight: 10 lb.
    Temperature range: –55 to +125 degrees centigrade.
    Servicing policy: Line replaceable unit.
    Test: Built-in test to identify faults to unit level.

Figure 3.46 Specimen non-functional requirements specification.

be used which bring these factors formally into the design process. They then remain visible throughout the rest of the software life cycle.

The third component of software requirements specifications, development requirements, varies considerably from application to application. In the simplest situation the customer and supplier agree on:

- What is to be supplied.
- When it is to be supplied and installed.

At the other extreme requirements cover:

- The extent of supply.
- Delivery and installation.
- Formal acceptance testing.
- Project management structures and techniques.
- Formal progress reporting procedures.
- Configuration control systems.
- Design methods, methodologies and plans.
- Quality assurance.
- Reliability aspects.
- Legal, contractual and certification aspects.

One generalization can be made. As projects get larger the number of system requirements needing formal consideration increases. Even if the customer hasn't demanded such formality the supplier should impose it. Because without strict project management, formal rules, defined reporting procedures, proper recording techniques and configuration control, chaos is always likely to break out.

3.5 Communication aspects – the role of prototyping

3.5.1 Prototyping – an introduction

In engineering a prototype is a pre-production version of a manufactured product such as a component, subassembly, system, etc. The purpose of building a prototype is to prove design and manufacturing aspects as early as possible, before resources are committed to full-scale production. A number of questions are evaluated during prototyping, including:

- Is the product actually feasible? In other words, are problems present which are fundamentally impossible to overcome?
- Are there unforeseen high-risk technical and cost aspects?

- Are the design and build correct? That is, has the correct product been built (validation), and has the product been built correctly (verification)?
- Can it be built in a manufacturing environment (as opposed to the hand-crafting methods of the prototyping phase)?
- Can it be built for the right price?

Once this phase is completed manufacture can commence with a very high level of confidence in the final product (even then success isn't guaranteed).

Normally prototypes are built to full scale. In some cases, though, scaled down versions are cheaper and easier to produce. For instance, a three-eighths scale remotely controlled F15 aircraft research vehicle was used to evaluate digital flight control systems. But no matter which method is used, prototyping is carried out for one basic reason: to answer the questions set out above. Once this is done the proto-type is usually consigned to the scrap-heap; it has served its purpose.

3.5.2 Software prototyping

Prototyping of real software systems is, at this time, still in its infancy (perhaps its omission from the software design cycle says more about the attitudes of software practitioners than pages of words). Fortunately, though, software engineers are now beginning to understand that prototyping can bring real benefits to professional designs. Put in a nutshell, it helps us to produce the right jobs, on time, and within budget. It can be applied in a number of different ways – and at different times – in the software life cycle, Figure 3.47. Please note that the terminology used for prototyping is not consistent across the software community.

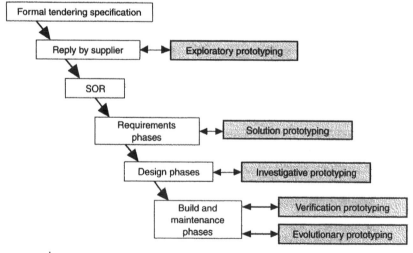

Figure 3.47 Prototyping within the software life cycle.

Exploratory prototyping

This is used as a tool in the development of the SOR to a point where it is acceptable to both parties. A particular version of this is animation prototyping. This involves the use of animated graphics to enhance communication between the customer and the supplier.

Solution prototyping

Here the system software requirements are prototyped, typically using commercial visual software tools. Frequently these prototyping tools produce executable code.

Investigative prototyping

This enables the designer to evaluate alternative software solutions at the design stage. Again, visual software tools may be used for this work.

Verification prototyping

This method is used to evaluate source code produced by using formal specification methods.

Evolutionary prototyping

This describes the use of working prototypes to evaluate the effects of modifications and upgrades.

A number of points need to be made here concerning definitions, usage and prototype facilities.

First, definitions. The definitions given here are not necessarily generally accepted. This is especially true of evolutionary prototyping. For many workers, true evolutionary prototyping spans the whole life cycle.

Secondly, usage of the prototyping methods is not simple and clear-cut. For instance, investigative prototyping can be (and frequently is) implemented using tools designed for solution prototyping.

Thirdly, prototype facilities vary considerably. At one extreme are models designed for use in very specific parts of the software life cycle – and destined to be thrown away after use. At the other end of the scale are general-purpose models from which actual production systems emerge.

This chapter is concerned with the 'front-end' section of the software development cycle, up to the start of the design phases. Two aspects of prototyping are relevant to this area: exploratory and solution methods. The following sections discuss these in more detail.

3.5.3 Requirements prototyping

In this section the combination of exploratory and solution prototyping is, for brevity, defined as 'requirements prototyping'. There is, in fact, another reason for grouping them together. Basically they attempt to solve the same problems.

Central to requirements prototyping is the use of models ('prototypes') to demonstrate the essential features of the proposed system. Equally important is the provision of tools for constructing and manipulating these models. Requirements prototypes serve a number of purposes, the primary ones being to:

- Act as a reference point for supplier–customer communication.
- Allow both parties to increase their understanding of the proposed system.
- Allow both parties to appreciate properly the content and implications of the requirements documents.
- Highlight important qualities such as dynamic behaviour, response times, exception handling, etc.

Figure 3.48 describes the prototyping cycle as applied to either the tendering or the requirements phases, or both.

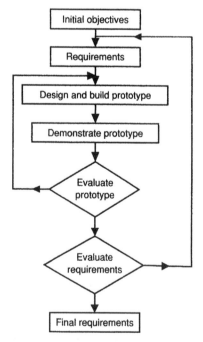

Figure 3.48 The prototyping cycle for requirements extraction.

From some initial objectives a set of requirements is formed, expressed in a preliminary defining document. This, together with verbal and other sources of information, form guidelines for the construction of a prototype. Once the prototype is built it is demonstrated and evaluated, being modified until it satisfies the initial specification. At this point the requirements themselves can be evaluated using the prototype facilities. Problems found here normally result in changes to the requirements until they are acceptable to both parties. The outcome is a definitive requirements specification. In the first instance this forms the SOR; later it acts as the basis for the software specification (in practice, of course, events don't take place quite so neatly).

What are the limitations of prototypes? In other words, how do they differ from the final (production) version of the system? This isn't an easy question to answer. There aren't at the present time, clear, defined and agreed guidelines. Prototypes vary from simple static text type models through to those which are virtually full simulations. As a general rule prototypes should behave like the real system but with reduced functionality. Differences occur because prototypes:

- May be required to illustrate only part of the final system.

- Might require the use of computer resources which aren't available in the target system (e.g. the model itself may require 500 kBytes of RAM space to run in, yet the target system may only have 128 kBytes available).

- Do not aim – or may be unable – to produce real-time responses.

- May not be powerful enough to demonstrate all operational functions.

All prototyping methods should be economical, fast and adaptable, for the reasons given below.

Economical

Requirements prototyping is used right at the front end of the software development cycle. One possible conclusion of the analysis phase is that the proposed system is unattainable. Now, whether the project is abandoned at this stage or pursued in a modified form, the first lot of work is a write-off. Therefore costs must be kept to a minimum. This also implies a short timescale.

Fast

Answers need to be produced quickly, especially prior to and during the tendering phases of the project.

Adaptable

Development of prototypes is a continual – and not a once through – process. Thus it is essential that the model can be modified easily and quickly.

Unless these targets are attained three problems may be encountered:

- Slowness in responding to customer enquiries and requirements. This leads to a lack of confidence by the customer in the supplier's abilities.

- Inflexible models. The consequence is that substantial effort is needed to modify and upgrade prototypes as time goes by.

- Excessive effort in developing prototypes in the first place. Prototyping is *not* an alternative to design.

Methods designed to satisfy the aims outlined above are categorized as 'rapid prototyping' – the process of building and evaluating quickly a set of prototypes.

3.5.4 Practical rapid prototyping of system requirements

Rapid prototyping has its origins in the development of interactive information systems. From this, three major factors were identified: the user interface, the modelling environment and an output support system, Figure 3.49.

Such work showed that effective tools are needed if prototyping is to be an economical proposition. Without these it takes as much effort to develop a prototype as the production system itself. This perception led to the development of computer aided rapid prototyping, also called *fast prototyping*. Central to this are a software design database, design tools specific to the prototyping method, and an overall design management subsystem. The function of the user interface is self-explanatory, but output support system features are tool specific. The output system is primarily concerned with demonstrating prototype operation and attributes. At its simplest level it produces fixed static descriptions in text form. At the other extreme it provides dynamic interaction features, representation of requirements in programming language form and debugging facilities.

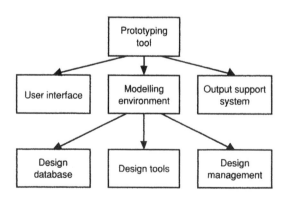

Figure 3.49 Elements of a prototyping tool.

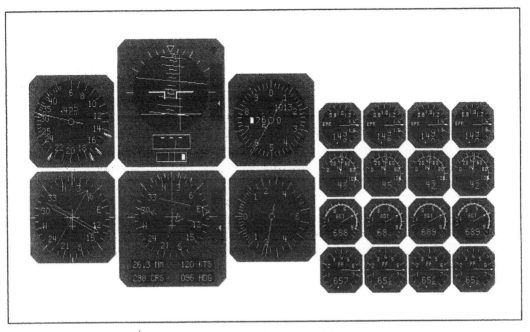

Figure 3.50 Screen prototype – proposed avionics cockpit instrument layout (courtesy of Professor D.J. Allerton, Cranfield University).

Requirements prototyping in real-time systems has two distinct aspects. The first describes user interaction with display systems – interactive information handling (IIH). The second relates to the interaction of a system with its external environment.

Interactive information handling is associated with human–computer interactions (HCI), usually involving screen displays. Here 'screen' prototyping is used to elicit user feedback on the 'feel' of the interface before its design is finalized. An example of this, Figure 3.50, is a mock-up of a proposed avionics cockpit instrument layout

HCI operations rarely involve complex information processing or logic functions, the primary concern being the presentation of information. The purpose of screen prototyping is to ensure that operator responses are efficient, correct and timely. IIH in real-time systems is broadly similar to that in batch and on-line systems. These have features which are common to all applications, and which recur with great regularity. This includes menu formats, report generation and screen painters.

The same cannot be said for system–environment interactions. Tools designed to prototype these functions must support very diverse activities. At the present time this is a rapidly growing area of work. Experience has shown that mimicking system actions (*animation prototyping*) is a powerful and meaningful way of demonstrating system behaviour [COO93]. Moreover, with such tools it is possible to add interactive animation facilities to basic screen prototypes.

3.5.5 Animation prototyping – concepts and application

First, some definitions. Animation prototyping is 'the visualization and demonstration of *intended* system behaviour'. Central to this is that behavioural aspects are *pre-defined*. Simulation, by contrast, is 'a prediction and demonstration of *actual* system behaviour'; behaviour is normally *computed* as the simulator runs.

The application of animation prototyping to real-time systems can be illustrated using the nitrogen plant of Figure 3.51. This represents a chemical plant, designed to take in gas at atmospheric pressure and compress it into liquid form. This liquid is deposited, at high pressure, into a storage vessel. Two compressors are used, connected in parallel. A variety of valves are fitted which, together with the compressors, provide control of plant operation. It is required to equip this system with a processor-based controller having appropriate man–machine interfaces. Let us look at how animation prototyping can be applied here.

First, it is essential to clearly understand the nature of the prototyping run-time and development environment (Figures 3.52 and 3.53). The user interacts with the prototype via the screen model (which can also accept user inputs). Details of the screen display are defined in the model properties database (or file). The behaviour of the screen model is determined by the animation engine, taking into account time and/or user inputs.

Usually the screen model is built using a graphics-based model building tool (most modern tools are PC-based). Such models can be constructed rapidly, easily and

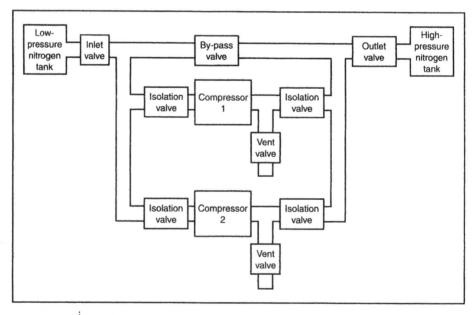

Figure 3.51 Nitrogen plant schematic diagram.

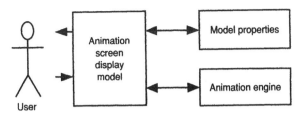

Figure 3.52 Animation prototyping – typical run-time environment.

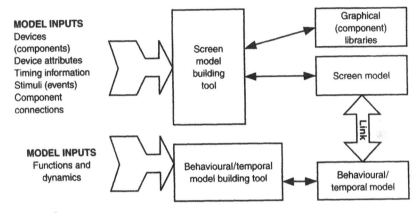

Figure 3.53 Animation prototyping – typical development environment.

cheaply if a comprehensive graphical component library is provided. An example is given in Figure 3.54. This shows:

- Figure 3.54a: a selected icon – a toggle switch – from the pre-defined library of components. It is customized by editing its associated property dialog box.

- Figure 3.54b: the customized icon, together with the completed property dialog box details.

However, in engineering, many symbols, icons, etc. are domain-specific; hence it is essential that the user has facilities to create these as and when required.

Associated with the screen model is the behavioural/temporal model, Figure 3.53. This is usually built as a separate item and then linked up with the screen model. Both functional and dynamic information is provided to the model as it is built. A variety of methods can be used to build this model, Figure 3.55. This is usually based on information supplied by the customer. An example animated screen model is that of the nitrogen plant, Figure 3.56. This serves two purposes. First, it shows the intended functionality and layout of the plant local control panel. Second, because it is animated, it can be used to verify the ease of use, clarity of display and correctness of behaviour of the interface. Without a doubt the technique is a powerful one for resolving HCI requirements in real-time systems.

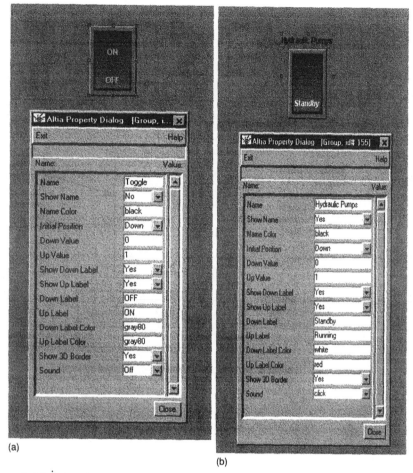

(a)

(b)

Figure 3.54 Example steps in building the screen model (constructed using the Altia Faceplate tool).

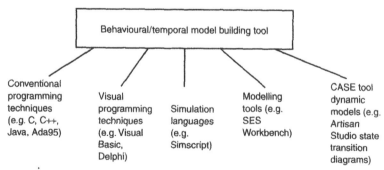

Figure 3.55 Methods for developing the behavioural/temporal model.

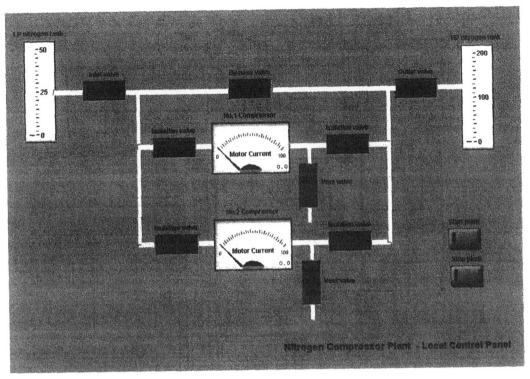

Figure 3.56   Nitrogen plant – animated screen model.

Screen prototyping, as a method of describing interactions between the plant and its environment, is quite limited. Instead, animating plant operation itself is highly effective as a learning and communication tool, Figure 3.57. Given here are particular frames from the animation, showing power-up, normal running and fail-safe conditions. Attached to each frame is the corresponding section from the SOR. In the initial stage of analysis each component is described in 'black box' terms; little internal detail is provided. Even so the model allows the user to step through various sequences and to interact with the display. As development progresses the model can be elaborated and refined. In particular, time constraints, component performance factors and safety features can be included. Thus the prototype is developed in an evolutionary manner, ultimately approaching the performance of a simulator.

Just to recap: rapid prototyping is an effective and realistic requirements analysis method, but to be commercially practical three criteria must be satisfied. First, models must be produced quickly, ranging from a few days to a few weeks. Second, the model should represent the problem in terms of the customer's viewpoint. Third, both the customer and the supplier must be allowed to interact with the model.

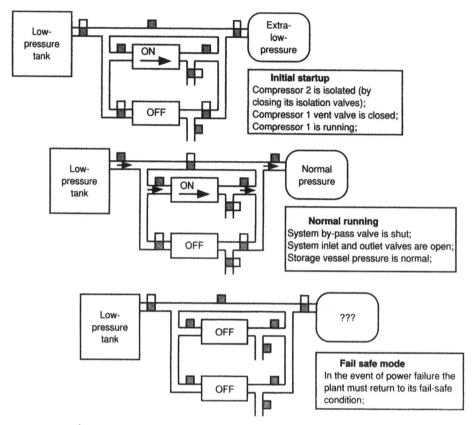

Figure 3.57 Animated operation of the nitrogen plant.

Review

On completing this chapter you should now:

- Be able to explain the realistic development of software in real-time systems.
- Appreciate how important it is to properly and fully establish the true requirements of systems before plunging into design.
- Recognize the problems associated with formulating, communicating and understanding requirements.
- See why tool support is important for developing and maintaining analysis and specification documents.
- Understand the basics of viewpoint and use case analysis and appreciate that these are complementary, not conflicting, techniques.
- Understand the basic role of prototyping in establishing system requirements.
- Appreciate how rapid and animation prototyping can be used effectively as front-end techniques in defining system and software requirements.

Exercises

1. Your company provides a range of computer-based business systems. A client requests the provision of one of the more expensive implementations for his application. However, on evaluating his requirements, you realize that a much simpler, cheaper solution would be satisfactory. When you propose to do this you are told that your business is to make as much money as possible for your employer – give the customer what was asked for in the first place. What are your views on the ethics of this? What would you do?

2. As a project manager, you are requested to evaluate a software development plan. This gives details of a two-year software design and development project. Within this time frame, three months are allocated to integration and testing. What comments would you make concerning this? Justify them with reference to appropriate statistics.

3. You have been appointed manager of an embedded software development group in a company that makes diesel engines for many industries. Currently, relations between the software group and clients – both external and internal – are poor. Much criticism has been made of the 'remoteness' of software developers and their failure to understand the real needs of the business. List the procedures, practices and tools (if appropriate) which you might use to improve this situation. Explain your reasoning.

4. Explain how use case techniques could be applied in developing systems for factory control room operation (this involves remote monitoring and control of production processes, using computer-based display techniques).

5. Present a case to your senior management which explains how and why animation prototyping can be a cost-effective development technique.

References and further reading

[BOO98] *The Unified Modelling Language User Guide*, G. Booch, J. Rumbaugh and I. Jacobson, Addison-Wesley, ISBN 0-201-57168-4, 1998.

[COC97] *Structuring use cases with goals*, A. Cockburn, Journal of Object Oriented Programming, Sept./Oct. pp 45–51, 1997.

[COO93] *Animation prototyping of real-time embedded systems*, J.E. Cooling and T.S. Hughes, Microprocessors and Microsystems, Vol. 17, No. 6, pp 315–324, 1993.

[COR86] *Controlled Requirements Expression*, Systems Designers plc, Hampshire, UK, 1986.

[DEM78] *Structured analysis and system specification*, T. De Marco, Yourdon Press, ISBN 0-138-54380-1, 1978.

[FAR75] *Reliable computer software – what it is and how to get it, project report*, Defense Systems Management School, Fort Belvoir, Virginia, Nov. 1975.

[JAC92] *Object-oriented software engineering: A use-case driven approach*, I. Jacobson *et al.*, Addison-Wesley, ISBN 0-201-54435-0, 1992.

[KOT98] *Requirements engineering – processes and techniques*, G. Kotonya and I. Sommerville, Wiley, ISBN 0-471-97208-8, 1998.

[PUL93] *Graphical animation as a form of prototyping real-time software systems*, R. Pulli *et al.*, Real-Time Systems, 5, pp 173–195, 1993.

[SID96] *Special feature: requirements engineering*, Editors, J. Siddiqi and M.C. Shekaran, IEEE Software, Vol. 12, No. 6, pp 15–64, March 1996.

[SOM95] *Software engineering, 5th edition*, I. Sommerville, Addison-Wesley, ISBN 0-201-42765-6, 1995.

[SOM97] *Requirements engineering – a good practice guide*, I. Sommerville and P. Sawyer, Wiley, ISBN 0-471-97444-7, 1997.

[STA87] *The STARTS guide – a guide to methods and software tools for the construction of large real-time systems*, NCC Publications, Manchester, ISBN 0-85012-619-3, 1987.

chapter 4

Software and Program Design Concepts

The effects produced by poor software – covered in Chapter 2 – can't be dismissed lightly. Equipment damage, personal injury and deaths have resulted from mistakes in software. Even where such disasters are avoided software liabilities can financially cripple a company. Three factors are usually at work here: late delivery of the software, overrun on budget and massive installation/maintenance efforts. Therefore the primary goal of any software team is to eliminate the possibility of such events. To do this it must deliver dependable software, on time, within cost. These 'high-level' objectives can be attained only by using professional design methods. Such methods enable designers to achieve specific 'low-level' targets for quality code production. These features, already discussed in Chapter 2, include:

- Formal and rigorous design methods.
- Properly documented software.
- Understandable designs.
- Robust and stable software.
- Maintainable programs.
- Portable and re-usable software.

These are the goals of the software engineer. How well they are achieved depends considerably on both the tools and techniques used in the design process. Here we limit ourselves to techniques, the purpose of the chapter being to:

- Outline fundamental design strategies and design factors incorporated within these strategies.

- Describe how and why modular design is essential for the production of good software.

- Show the influence of structured programming on software design.

- Describe modern design methodologies, including functionally structured, object-oriented and data flow methods.

Chapters 7 and 8 extend this by showing how such methods are used to produce working design documents. Chapter 10 describes these in the context of specific design methodologies.

4.1 Design fundamentals

4.1.1 The design and development process – an introduction

Design and development is the process of turning ideas (the specification) into reality (the product), Figure 4.1. There are a number of distinct stages in this operation; each one can be analysed and described as a separate item. Here we'll

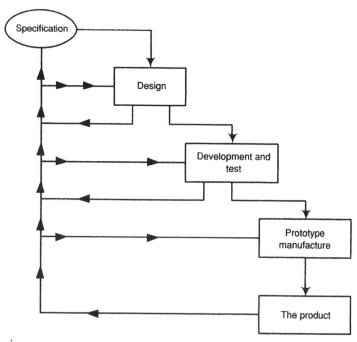

Figure 4.1 The design and development process.

concentrate on that identified as 'design'. But remember, in producing the product, they are highly interactive. The idea that design is a once-through activity, never to be repeated, belongs to the world of science fiction. Consequently any useful design method must be able to handle change easily, simply and efficiently.

The purpose of this section is to describe the design process in general conceptual terms. However, many people find that abstract descriptions of processes aren't especially helpful. So the approach used here takes a particular (fictional) auto-engineering design problem and shows alternative ways of solving it. It then generalizes from these specific ideas and methods to the more abstract design concepts.

Assume that the objective is to design a vehicle power-train system. The fuel source is diesel, the final drive method being two road wheels. From this simplified specification the designer organizes his ideas, in the first case expressing the solution in very general terms. As with most forms of engineering this involves the use of diagrams (Figure 4.2). Here the design specification is translated into a number of feasible alternatives. The expanded descriptions are more detailed and refined, but still operate at the conceptual level. Now the designer can move – in stages – to the general design level (Figure 4.3). At this stage the 'best' solution is identified, and work proceeds into the detailed design phase (Figure 4.4).

This approach should sound reasonable and logical. Good. But you may then well ask 'what's so special about this? Isn't it what we'd expect to happen?' Yes, but because the approach is 'sensible' we tend not to see the profound design concepts inherent in the method. Let's look at it again, stage by stage.

First, there is translation from a specification to a conceptual solution. This is a creative activity which cannot be taught; it must be learned. Here there is no substitute for experience and knowledge. Moreover, even at this very abstract stage, the designer is guided by his knowledge of what is practicable. So, note point one: creativity and knowledge.

The second stage, expanding the basic ideas, is one which involves both design creativity and design technique. Expansion takes place in a controlled, organized and logical manner. Note point two: method and organization.

Observe here that two solutions have been generated (many others are possible). This highlights the fact that there isn't a unique answer to each problem. A good designer will try first to identify realistic alternatives and then assess their qualities. Here, for instance, the assessment factors involve cost, performance, technology level, manufacturing aspects, etc. Point three: identification and evaluation of design options.

It may seem surprising that it is easier to assess information when dealing with an abstract model. But what this does is allow us to ignore detail and concentrate on the big picture (the really important view). Point four: postponement of detailed design decisions for as long as possible.

When the descriptive model is expanded into something fairly specific the following factors can be tackled:

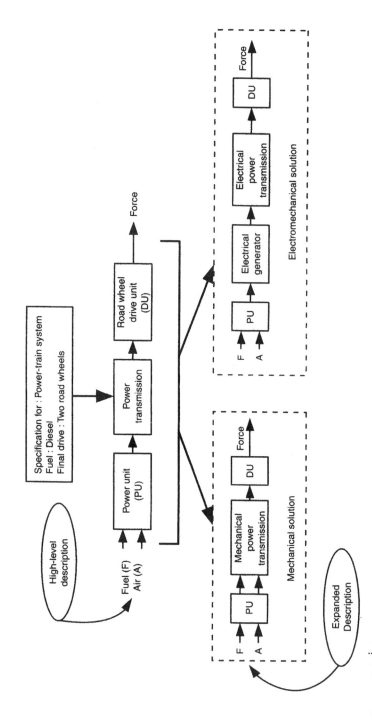

Figure 4.2 Specification translation — high-level description.

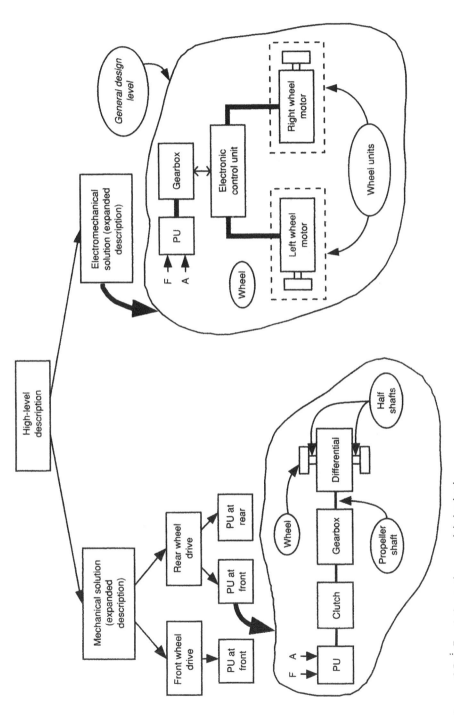

Figure 4.3 Translation to the general design level.

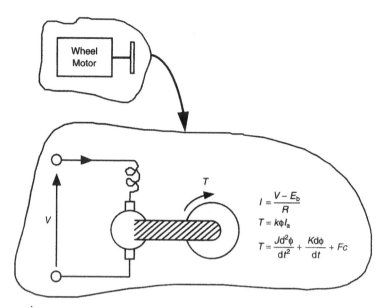

Figure 4.4 : Detailed design level.

- Identification of functions and partitioning by subsystems.
- Identification of interfaces between subsystems.
- Evaluation of subsystem interaction.
- Identification of work-loading and allocation.
- Assessment of manpower requirements.

Point five: general design evaluation.

At this stage the basic feasibility of the project has been assured. Detailed design calculations can be carried out knowing, at least, that the right problem is being tacked. Point six: solve the right problem.

The process described here is one of working from a very general top-level view of the problem to a specific design solution. This approach is usually called 'top-down'. However, no real design proceeds in this way. The designer always guides the work towards feasible solutions (often unconsciously). That is, he uses knowledge relating to the bottom end of the design process, a 'bottom-up' method. Added to this is a further complicating factor. Frequently the designer identifies high-risk areas early on in the design exercise (in the example here for instance, the use of electrical power transmission may raise special technical difficulties). Such problems are likely to be tackled early (and in some detail), a 'middle-out' design approach.

Gathering all these facts, recommendations and ideas together enables us to define the rules of workable design techniques:

- Use method and organization in the design process.
- First define the problem solution in general concepts.
- Identify and evaluate all sensible design options.
- Postpone detailed design decisions for as long as possible.
- Identify system functions.
- Partition the overall system into manageable subsystems.
- Identify interfaces between subsystems.
- Evaluate subsystem interaction.
- Solve the right problem.
- Base the design method on a top-down approach augmented by bottom-up and middle-out actions.
- Always review and, where necessary, re-do designs (iterate).
- Be prepared to throw away awkward, complex or redundant design parts (no matter how attached to them you become).

By using these rules we've introduced order and logic into system design, that is, structure. Now, you'll see the words 'structured design' in every textbook on software engineering. Some computer scientists actually believe that this general methodology was invented by the software community. In fact all good engineering design is structured; the Egyptians practised it thousands of years ago when they built the Pyramids.

4.1.2 Fundamental design strategies

A number of design methods are currently used by the software community. Therefore, to explain the concepts and principles involved, let us look at the problem outlined below.

The overall task in question is the design of a vehicle anti-skid braking system. Its purpose is to eliminate vehicle skidding by preventing lock-up of the wheels. The software-based control system measures the speed of each wheel, calculates acceleration/deceleration values, and, using this data, detects the onset of wheel lock-up. Should lock-up occur then command signals back-off the braking effect. Speed sensors and brake actuators (hydraulic servo units) are fitted as appropriate.

Figure 4.5 shows two possible system design solutions to this problem.

The reasons for showing these are to reinforce several important points:

- Software engineers do not design embedded *systems*.
- The purpose of the software is to make the system work correctly (in other words, to carry out very specific functions).

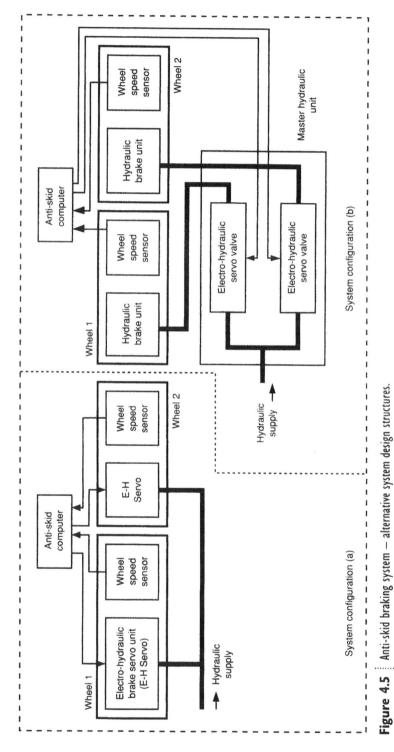

Figure 4.5 Anti-skid braking system – alternative system design structures.

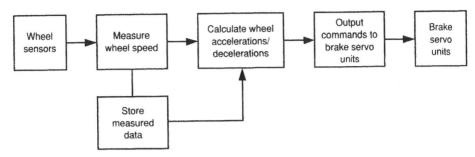

Figure 4.6   Functional view of the anti-skid system.

- How the software is designed is up to the software engineer, but it *must* provide the required functionality.
- A good understanding of system structure and operation is needed in order to produce a dependable software design.

Currently three distinct methodologies are used for software design:

- Functional structuring.
- Object structuring.
- Data flow structuring.

In reality there is a fourth approach, defined by Tom DeMarco as the 'Mugwump School'. It is practised by 'people who believe design is for cissies and that the structure of the system should be whatever occurs to the coder while seated at the terminal'. This has no place in a professional environment; yet all too often real-time software is designed in this way.

(NB: functional and data flow structuring are often considered to be synonymous. Although they have much in common they are *not* the same.)

First consider describing the system and its design using a functionally structured method (Figure 4.6). Here the system structure is expressed in terms of the functional interaction of the different parts. In this case four functions are defined:

- Measure wheel speed.
- Store measured data.
- Calculate vehicle conditions.
- Output commands to brake units.

Using this functional description we could implement the system shown in Figure 4.5a. Equally well we could adopt the method of Figure 4.5b. In contrast, the object-structured method describes the system as a collection of objects (Figure 4.7), not functions.

Communication between objects is carried out using messages, the ones shown here being 'send speed signal' and 'send actuator command'. Object internal actions

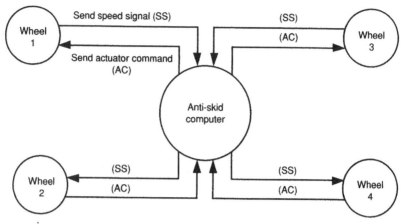

Figure 4.7 | Object-structured view of the anti-skid system.

aren't shown (at this level) in order to hide the 'how' from the 'what'. By using this technique objects can be treated as separate but co-operating entities. This profoundly changes how we view the problem and institute design solutions. Remember that when using a functional approach, speed measurement, computation and actuator control are all linked together. But with object structuring they are quite clearly decoupled. Moreover, each object has clearly defined responsibilities, viz.:

- Wheel 1: Measure wheel speed, store wheel 1 data, generate speed signal.
- Anti-skid computer: Calculate acceleration/deceleration commands for all wheel servos.

These may not seem especially significant – until we change the system. Suppose now that each wheel is to be monitored for tyre pressure, this being linked into a diagnostic computer. Changing the object-structured design to reflect this modification is fairly simple, Figure 4.8.

By contrast the corresponding functionally structured design would require a major re-build. However, this example isn't meant to imply that object structuring is better or easier than functional structuring. It's just a different way of looking at the same problem.

The final method is that of data flow structuring, Figure 4.9. It is based on the following concepts:

- The software is initially treated as a single component part of the overall system (Figure 4.9a).
- Emphasis is placed on establishing the requirements, features and qualities of the overall system (and not merely the software).
- The software is formed as a set of communicating software machines, each having clearly defined functions and responsibilities, Figure 4.9b.

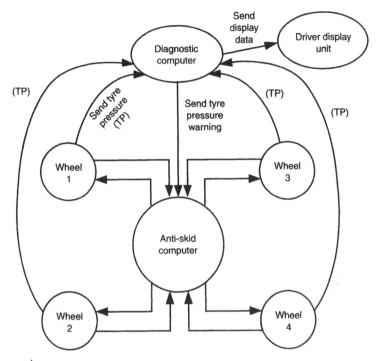

Figure 4.8 ┆ Modified object-structured diagram.

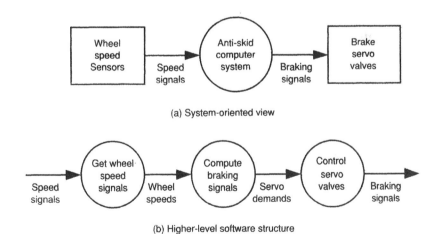

Figure 4.9 ┆ Data flow view of the anti-skid braking system.

There is one essential difference between this technique and an OO approach. Here the model is based on a materials flow one, the 'material' being the data that flows between the machines (or 'processes'). By contrast OO methods assume a client/server relationship between objects. More will be said later concerning this topic when software design processes are described.

Each method described above illustrates one specific way of tackling a design and development problem. But these aren't mutually exclusive; using one doesn't preclude use of the others (shrieks of horror from the OO purists). Each provides a different view of the problem. In practice many solutions use a combination of the methods, picking them as appropriate. Some design methodologies are composites of these, which, at first, can be quite confusing.

4.1.3 How to generate abysmal software – the good kludge guide

There are at least three ways to develop software: unplanned, apparently planned and properly designed. The first is practised by those who don't believe in software design. But, surprisingly, this is also true of the second group. Only it doesn't seem like it at the time. Such people produce plans; and don't use them at the coding stage. Documentation produced for the software is often done *after* coding. It may look impressive; whether it really describes what the code does is another matter.

Lee Harrisberger, in his *Engineermanship, a Philosophy of Design*, describes the production of a 'kludge'. In essence this is a product that, no matter what you do, is always going to be a mess. Producing code without designing the software in the first place results in a kludge. For those who consider design rules to be an infringement on their creativity and individuality, the following good kludge guide is offered. Moreover the rest of the chapter can be skipped.

- Don't plan.
- Don't introduce structure or order into the software.
- Begin coding straight away.
- Be clever.
- Be obscure.
- Don't use standard methods – invent new ones.
- Insist that the source code listing is sufficient to document the software – and use cryptic and meaningless comments.
- Never revise the design.
- Make the software unportable.
- Sacrifice all to code efficiency.

The real reason for giving this guide is that it neatly and concisely highlights why so much software is abysmal. Simply put, good design methods are the direct opposite of these.

4.2 The elements of modular design

4.2.1 Introduction

At this stage the overall concepts of software design should be clear (if they aren't, go back and re-read earlier sections). We can now put them in the context of specific software design methodologies. But before doing so the more important elements and building blocks of the design process need to be explained. Some of these we've already met within the framework of general design procedures. Now their functions as software design elements are examined.

4.2.2 Modules and modularization

It can be seen that a basic feature of 'good' design is the partitioning of systems into smaller chunks. The primary reason is to reduce the total problem into one of manageable proportions (the 'head full of information' limit). In software terms this process is call 'modularization', the elements resulting from this being 'modules'. It is a basic requirement that modules should be fairly simple, thus enabling us to:

- Understand their purpose and structure.
- Verify and validate their correctness.
- Appreciate their interaction with other modules.
- Assess their effect on the overall software structure and operation.

But precisely what is a module? Many definitions are possible; here it is considered to be 'a software unit which has a well-defined function and well-defined interfaces to other program elements'. Clearly, a module can be defined using functional, object or data flow structuring. How it's implemented is – at this stage – not important. Before doing that, the designer must answer one major question: precisely how should a system be modularized?

There isn't a unique solution to this; much depends on the particular application. Even then, significantly different approaches can be used. Consider, for instance, writing software to implement the anti-skid braking and tyre-pressure monitoring systems. One solution is shown in Figure 4.10 (for simplicity only two wheels are automated).

Note the similarity between this and Figure 4.6. This reinforces the fact that software design is just one stream within the total range of design techniques. An alternative solution is that of Figure 4.11.

This might be the one which maps the software onto the hardware in a more logical manner. Then again, it might not. It depends on the decisions which were made when designing the modules (Figure 4.12).

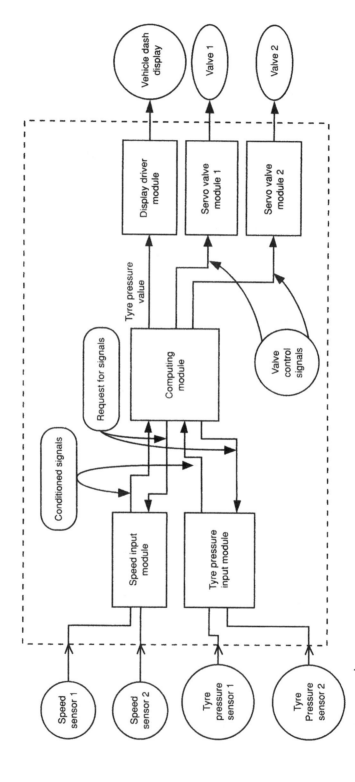

Figure 4.10 Modularization – solution I.

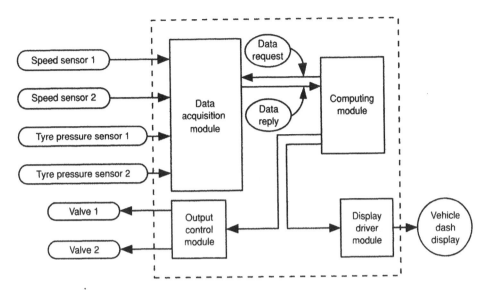

Figure 4.11 ⋮ Modularization – solution 2.

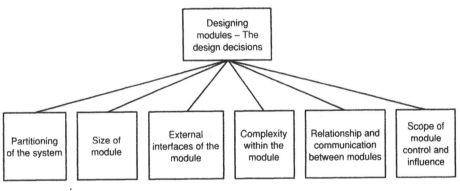

Figure 4.12 ⋮ Modules – design decisions.

These determine the resulting module structure, organization and performance. But how can we decide whether the modularization we've arrived at is a good one or not? The answer (in part, at least) lies in the properties of modules known as coupling and cohesion.

4.2.3 Coupling – a measure of module independence

Modules cannot exist in isolation. Each one is designed to perform part of the total system function; therefore they must communicate with each other. Now, experience has shown that the amount of interaction between modules has a significant effect on software quality. Where modules are well defined, having clear functions and simple interfaces, levels of interaction are low. In other words, modules are relatively independent. Such designs are usually easy to understand; they are also reliable and maintainable when put into service. Moreover, the software exhibits a high degree of stability; changes within a single module don't 'ripple through' the program.

In aiming for low interaction we need to distinguish between information volume and information complexity. Transferring a large amount of data between modules may be a fairly simple task – if we're dealing with simple data types. For instance, moving an array of 500 elements is both straightforward and easy to comprehend. Yet a module which transfers five different data items may be much more difficult to understand, because it has a complex interface, as in:

```
WriteReal (Integrate(Square, a b Smpson, tervals),  15);
```

where Integrate and Square are both function procedures. Consequently, reducing information *complexity* is a primary design aim. But this isn't the only factor which affects module interaction. Information *type* and *communication* methods also strongly influence system behaviour. Thus when evaluating the degree of module independence we need to take all three into account. This is done using a software measure called 'coupling'. Module coupling occurs in a number of ways, as follows:

- Content coupling.
- Common coupling.
- Stamp coupling.
- Data coupling by reference.
- Data coupling by value.

These are discussed in detail later.

When modules communicate, the information content may take various forms, Figure 4.13. In (a), module A sends data to B, just about the simplest contact method

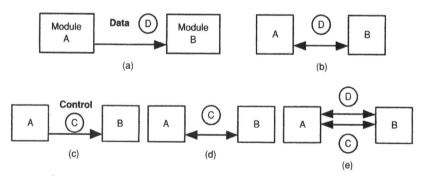

Figure 4.13 | Communication between modules.

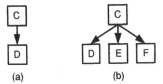

Figure 4.14 | Hierarchical module structure.

(typified by the conditioned speed signals of Figure 4.10). Naturally enough data transfer can be a two-way process, (b). Modules also need to be able to control actions within other modules, leading to the use of control signals, Figure 4.13c ('flags', 'control couples'). Again looking at Figure 4.10, the 'request for signals' can be regarded as a control couple. This increases the interaction between modules; what happens in one depends on decisions made in the other. Control coupling can also be a two-way affair, (d), while the most general case involves two-way data and control couples, (e).

Note that no assumptions have been made about the relationship between modules. They may, for instance, have equal standing in the system. Alternatively there may be a hierarchical structure, involving calling and called modules (Figure 4.14). Two simple examples are shown here. In the first, C invokes D to perform some task; in the second, C first invokes D, then E, and finally F. These invoked modules are activated only by command of the calling module. Operations like these can be implemented quite easily in software, especially when using procedurized high-level languages. However, when modules have the same rank their activation is quite different; fundamentally it is a system (usually a real-time executive, Chapter 5) function. Be warned: much published work on structured design implicitly assumes that modular designs are always hierarchical.

Many early texts on this topic were written from the DP point of view. In such designs control couples can be minimized. But for embedded software they are a natural and commonplace requirement, being essential for event signalling. So although they increase the coupling between modules, they can't be dispensed with. The rule is, use them with care and thought. And, with hierarchical modularization, control flags should only be transferred at a single level. If they pass through a number of levels there is a marked increase in coupling between modules.

Now let's turn to *communication connection* methods, using the output control module of Figure 4.11 as an example. There are two quite distinct methods for transferring information into the module (Figure 4.15). Using the 'normal' (sometimes called 'minimal') method, all information transfer is done via a controlled interface. Assume, for instance, that the computing module wishes to update the valve position command. Information is transferred into the output control module via its interface; setting up the command value is performed by code within the module. This gives secure, reliable and testable module operation. However, if the valve position command information can be loaded directly from outside the module, these

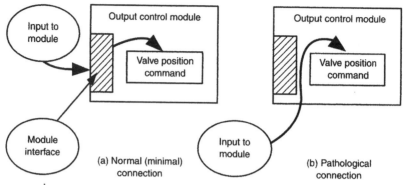

Figure 4.15   Module connection methods.

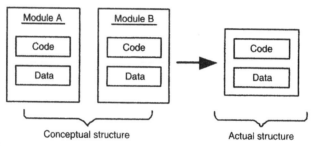

Figure 4.16   Content coupling.

benefits are lost. This is called a 'pathological' connection (yes, I know it's a crazy word but that's computer science for you).

Information complexity and type are highly visible items; hence they are readily controlled. By contrast, *module connection* methods can be quite difficult to manage. There are many ways (deliberately or accidentally) to increase coupling between modules through poor choice of connectivity. Let's begin with the worst possible situation, commonly met in assembly language programming. This, called 'content coupling', is shown in Figure 4.16. Our concept is one of separate modules, each having their own code and data areas. In reality all items can be accessed from anywhere within the program because there isn't a mechanism to prevent this (it depends entirely on the discipline and professionalism of the programmer). Therefore module A can, at any time, make a pathological connection into B (and vice versa). But there is a more subtle (and very undesirable) feature here. Because the code written for A is visible in B, it can be used by B. So, thinks the programmer, if there are identical functions in A and B, why write the code twice? Do it once only and use it in both modules. The result? A saving on memory space (usually insignificant) – and instant tight coupling. Code sharing should *never*

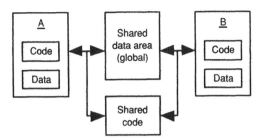

Figure 4.17 Common resource sharing (common coupling).

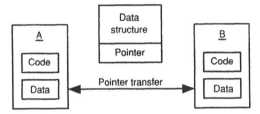

Figure 4.18 Data structure coupling (stamp coupling).

be done unless there are very good reasons for it (discussed later under 'functional decomposition').

Improvements can be made by limiting the amount of code and data which can be accessed globally (Figure 4.17). Here each module has its own private code and data areas. A global data area is used for the sharing of common information, while some code is available for general use. This structure is frequently met in high-level languages, particularly the older ones such as Coral66. Modules are built using program segments; this serves to keep code and data private. Shared resources are normally provided via some form of 'common' attribute of the language.

Limiting resource sharing significantly improves (that is, loosens or weakens) coupling between modules. It is, though, intrinsically unsafe. All global data areas are accessible by all modules; therefore they can also be modified by all modules. Better coupling is attained by defining a specific data structure for holding shared data, then passing pointers to this structure between modules (Figure 4.18). For this to work properly both modules must know how the data area is structured. Moreover, the information within each module must be consistent.

Data structure coupling (called 'stamp coupling') is useful for handling file information. Larger real-time systems frequently use comprehensive file storage systems, including duplicated on-line databases. However, mass storage is rarely incorporated in small embedded systems. Here stamp coupling is most likely to be used for the design of real-time executives or operating systems.

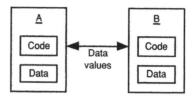

Figure 4.19 | Data coupling – by value.

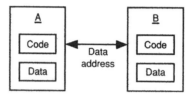

Figure 4.20 | Data coupling – by reference.

In all real-time designs a primary concern is the handling of program data, this being located in normal RAM store. To transfer such information between modules we can use either direct or indirect data coupling. With direct transfer, Figure 4.19, the sending module passes the *value* of the data to the receiving module.

This is a highly secure method – data values can be modified by only one module at a time, the current holder. In many instances transmitted items are copies of the originals. As these originals are held in the sending module the recipient cannot change their state. There may not seem any particular advantage in this – until the receiving module corrupts the data. At least then we can 'roll-back' the program to the point where the data was good, a technique sometimes used in critical systems.

It isn't possible to use direct data transfer for all applications, two particular commonplace examples illustrating this. Consider first where the data includes relatively large arrays of floating-point numbers, each one occupying 8 bytes of RAM space. Making copies of these structures would soon exhaust the data store space of a normal embedded computer. Another situation also negates the use of the direct transfer method. This occurs when the receiver module isn't able to directly pass data back to the original sender – a regular requirement when using hierarchical structuring. To cope with these situations the *address* of the data (not the data itself) is passed between modules (Figure 4.20). Thus the receiving module accesses the data using the address information – access by reference.

Coupling by reference is much more secure than stamp coupling. This security is enhanced by using modern languages which ensure consistency of data structures amongst program modules. It is, though, less secure than coupling by value (for obvious reasons). Taking all factors into account we can draw up a table which shows their influence on module coupling.

| System parameter | Coupling | |
	High coupling (poor)	Low coupling (good)
Information complexity	Complicated/obscure	Simple/clear
Information type	Control	Data
Module connection method	Pathological	Normal
Coupling technique	Content, common, stamp	Data by reference, data by value

In conclusion, the basic aim of the designer is to produce program modules that are as independent as possible – achieved by having low coupling.

4.2.4 Cohesion – a measure of module binding

An ideal module has a single entry and a single exit point (Figure 4.21a). One way to achieve this simple structure is to keep module function and operation very simple. Now, any complete system is made up of a number of modules, interconnected to perform the required function (Figure 4.21b). So far, so good – for a very small design. But adding even a few more modules (Figure 4.21c) makes the connecting link structure fairly complex. As a result it becomes difficult to understand *system* functions and operations. Link complexity can be reduced when the modular structure is hierarchical, but it still remains difficult to grasp system details.

Here is a classic two-way pull situation. Improving factor 1 (module simplicity) degrades factor 2 (system complexity). Is there an easy answer to this problem? Unfortunately, no. The 'right' balance between the number of modules in a system and the size/function of these modules is subjective.

We can reduce system complexity by grouping elementary operations together, these becoming the *elements* of a single module (Figure 4.22). Where elements of a module are very closely related, most module activity is internal. Elements don't need, or want, to 'talk' to other modules. Consequently such designs have low

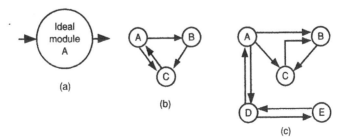

Figure 4.21 : Module interconnection complexity.

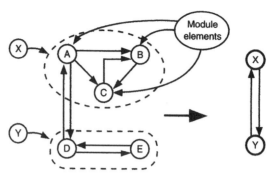

Figure 4.22 Complexity reduction.

module coupling. The parameter which defines how strongly elements are inter-related is called 'cohesion' (the 'glue' factor). High cohesion results from strong relationships. This not only leads to good designs; it also produces maintainable software.

It's one thing to say that a high glue factor is desirable; it's quite another thing to implement it. What the designer needs when modularizing a system is some *measure* of cohesion. One such measure was proposed by Yourdon and Constantine, the seven-level model of Figure 4.23. In reality this is not a discrete scale; it's

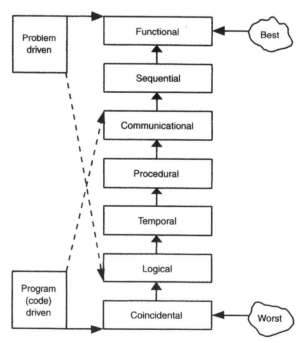

Figure 4.23 The seven-level cohesion model.

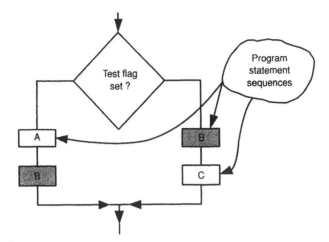

Figure 4.24 : A problem of cohesion.

impossible to draw a clear line between levels. Moreover, these aren't mutually exclusive qualities. For instance, a module may have both sequential and temporal cohesion.

Cohesion can be approached from two points of view, the problem (system) or the solution (program). The results are quite different, as discussed below.

Coincidental cohesion

If the elements of a module are found to be unrelated, then we have zero cohesion. Such modules usually come about because 'somewhere had to be found for the code'. There are, though, underlying reasons for this: inferior design, weak design co-ordination or pressure to produce operational software. It can be difficult to minimize module coupling in such designs.

Another common reason for ending up with minimal cohesion is demonstrated by the flow-chart problem of Figure 4.24. During program design the programmer realizes that instruction sequence B occurs twice. To improve code efficiency he produces a module for B, the individual statements forming the elements of this module. In practice, this method is simple to apply during the initial design stage. Later though, when modifications are made, difficulties arise. It may be, for instance, that the left path B has to be changed, but not the right one. The result? We'll probably have to create an extra (new) module, thus disturbing the original structure of the system.

Logical cohesion

Let's assume that our programmer is writing code for the task shown in Figure 4.14. Further assume that a system requirement calls for each input signal to be filtered.

Ergo, he forms a 'filter' module to perform this function. Into this he inserts the code for each channel filter (the elements), these being related by their logical functioning (logical cohesion).

Now, the code could be written so that each time the module is activated all input signals are filtered. But this might not be necessary (or desirable); some inputs may need servicing more frequently than others. The solution is to process selected signals only, by using a general module activating call accompanied by a selector tag. The tag identifies which inputs are to be filtered. Furthermore, it is commonplace to use a single body of code to perform the program function. Unfortunately, the result is that it then becomes difficult to modify any individual filter function without affecting the others.

These problems are inherent in modules which house logically related elements. The reason is simple; such modules do not carry out a single function only. 'Filter' isn't a single action. It is, in fact, a collection of separate functions grouped together for our convenience.

In the example here the make-up of the 'filter' module was driven by system requirements. Quite frequently such designs make good sense in embedded systems. The resulting modules often exhibit much better cohesion than groupings derived from program code functions. However, when used without care it promotes tight coupling, leading especially to maintenance problems.

Temporal (time) cohesion

When elements of a module are related by time then we have 'temporal cohesion', i.e. time is the glue. A frequently quoted example is that of an initialization routine to set up the hardware of a processor system. All such set-up operations have to take place within a particular period of time. Therefore it makes good sense to group these together in one module, then execute them all at once. But, once again, care and common sense must be used in the program design. When temporal grouping is used, unrelated parts of the system may be located within the resulting module. This, like logical grouping, may well lead to maintenance problems.

Procedural cohesion

Module elements have procedural cohesion when each one is part of a well-defined operation – the procedure. All elements of a procedure *must* be present if it's to perform its desired function. Therefore the binding of elements is good. Procedural cohesion usually results in low coupling – but then again it may not. It hinges very much on how the procedure was devised in the first place. Where, for instance, it performs a clearly defined mathematical operation (say computing the sine of an angle), cohesion and coupling are good. But frequently procedures are used to implement subtasks of larger tasks. The resulting module coupling depends very much on the initial partitioning of the overall system.

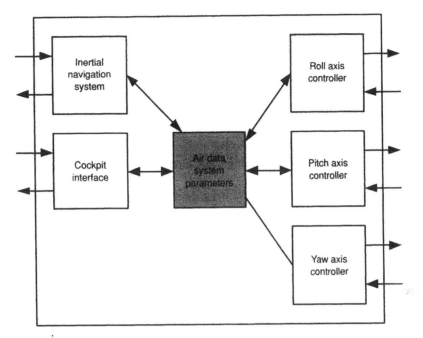

Figure 4.25 Communicational cohesion.

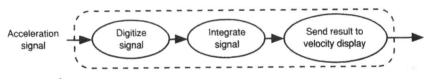

Figure 4.26 Sequential cohesion.

Communicational cohesion

A module has communicational cohesion when its elements act on common data. The actions performed on the data generate the connecting links between the elements, typical instances being shown in Figure 4.25.

Sequential cohesion

Here the elements are organized as a sequence of operations, Figure 4.26. Observe that the output from one element acts as the input to the next one. Sequential structures can be formed starting from the code point of view (a flow-chart approach). But much better function groupings occur when designs are tackled from a system point of view. Any module designed in this way may contain only one function. On the other hand it may hold either part of a particular function or a number of related functions. It fits in naturally with the data flow approach to designing software structures.

Functional cohesion

In general terms a functional module is one that performs a single function. Such structures have the highest level of cohesion because all elements are essential to the operation of the module; none is redundant.

Thus the concept of functional binding seems clear enough – until we try to define it. One definition could be that, for functional cohesion, each element in the module is an essential part of that module. From an abstract point of view this excludes all other forms of cohesion. Therefore each element must perform a single function. Is this recursive, I ask myself? Yourdon and Constantine give a precise but negative form of definition. That is, 'functional cohesion is whatever is *not* sequential, communicational, . . . etc.'. Even they admit this isn't very helpful, by saying that 'any truly adequate definition of function is a structural defect in the theory through which camels and Mack trucks could readily pass'. And, when taking a system point of view, designers often disagree on what makes up a single function.

There's no doubt that good modular designs have high module cohesiveness. And high-strength modules have far fewer faults than low-strength ones. How then does a designer arrive at a 'good' final structure? One approach is to produce an initial design, assess it using the rules given above, refine it, re-assess it, and so on. But it's stretching imagination (and credibility) to think that, in a commercial environment, such practices exist. Moreover, it isn't a case of using a simple design template for cohesion; many modules exhibit a number of cohesion qualities. For instance, a plant sequence controller may have a performance specification which reads (in part):

At time = T + 10
Shut nitrogen and hydrogen valves
Open vent valve
Run purge motor

Thus the items are time-related. The cohesion is quite strong because all activities must be done in this particular time slot. At the same time there is a strong functional relationship between these operations, from a system point of view. This module has an extremely high glue strength.

Sensibly, then, the only workable design methods are those which *inherently* produce high cohesiveness. Can we define such methods? The answer lies in Figure 4.23. Observe: module structures derived from the system (problem) point of view have the highest glue factor. In other words, if we start in the right way, we'll end up with the right results.

4.2.5   Size and complexity

What is the ideal size for a module? One general – but not very helpful – rule can be laid down: don't make it too large. As a result, the amount of information given at any one time is limited. This enables the reader to see the module code as a whole, making it easier for him to absorb and understand it. Smaller modules usually have very clearly defined (and usually simple) functions. Unfortunately, when using small modules, it then becomes difficult to absorb the overall functioning of the system. So, ultimately, the minimum size of a module is determined by our ability to digest information.

One figure frequently quoted is to limit program size to between 30 and 50 executable statements. The number of lines of source code corresponding to this depends on the programming language and environment. But, using a high-level language, one would expect to see a listing of (roughly) between 60 and 100 lines. This equates to two pages of source code per program module.

Using the number of statements as a guide to module size is really only a rough and ready guide. A second factor is the complexity of the language constructs used in the module. Compare, for instance, a program consisting of only sequential statements with one using highly nested combinations of iteration and selection operations. Obviously it's going to take much more mental effort to understand the second one, even if both have the same print-out length. Much work has been done to develop models of software complexity – software metrics. A number of different rules have been developed.

One technique is based on counting the number of operators and operands in the program code. Furthermore, it takes into account the number of distinct items as well as the totals. Program complexity is deduced from a count value computed using these values. This method gives a better guide than a simple count of instructions; more complex instructions give a higher count value.

A second method uses a count of the number of independent paths through a program as a measure of complexity (McCabe's cyclomatic number). This approach has its roots in graph theory. Extensions to this work have been done taking data (program variable) references into account.

It seems, however, that any pronouncement on module size is likely to be challenged. Moreover, a distinction must be made between library (service) modules and application modules (discussed later). But personal experience has shown that limiting module size to only a few pages of print-out is a good rule. It seems to produce little benefit in the initial design stage; error rates are relatively unaffected. The difference shows later on, though. Such code is quickly comprehensible, making updating and modification work a relatively easy task (especially if you didn't write the code in the first place). Limiting size has another advantage. It becomes much easier to perform static analysis of the code during the software test phase.

This topic – that of software metrics – is covered in more detail in Chapter 11.

4.2.6   Some general comments on modules

Why modularize programs?

- The 'divide and conquer' approach produces programs which are easy to manage, understand and test.

- Program development can be done on an incremental basis ('a bit at a time').

- Errors are easier to track down and correct.

- Modifications are usually localized, so maintaining high program stability.

- Portability can be increased by burying machine-specific features within designated modules. Thus, when moving to other target systems, only these modules need changing.

- Libraries of useful functions can be built up (especially true of complex maths functions), so leading to software re-use.

- It is easier to attack the problems of slow code and memory inefficiency when using modular construction (the 'code optimization' requirement).

- In a large system, development times can be pruned by using a team of designers working in parallel. Although various work-sharing methods could be used, allocating work on a module basis has two particular advantages. First, it enables programmers to work independently; second, it simplifies integration of the resulting code.

What are the ideal characteristics of 'good' modules?

- Each module has a clearly defined task.

- There is a one-to-one relationship between system function and module function – functional cohesion.

- There isn't a need to see the internals of a module to understand its function.

- Modules can be combined to form 'super' modules – without regard to their internal implementation details.

- It is possible to test a module in isolation from other modules.

- Module functional connections are defined by their functional relationships with other modules.

- Module control connections are defined by their code. Each module should have a single program entry point and a corresponding single exit point (though see 'exceptions').

- Data connections are made with the lowest form of coupling – parameter-passing mechanisms.

What are the disadvantages of modularization?

- Much greater effort has to be put in at the initial design stages.
- Much greater project management is required (even if, in a small job, it's self-management).
- Much more time is spent designing (as opposed to coding). Thus productivity, measured in a very narrow way over a limited part of the job, decreases.
- Program run-times usually lengthen.
- More memory is required (most noticeably RAM).

4.3 Program control structures – the influence of structured programming

4.3.1 Introductory comments

The first real step away from undisciplined program methods was made in the late 1960s by a group of academics. Their proposals, summarized as *Structured Programming* (SP), were typified in a 1969 article by Edsgar Dijkstra. SP is a methodology used for translating module descriptions and specifications into program source code. Its primary objective is to reduce software complexity, so:

- Reducing the number of mistakes made in the first place.
- Reducing the time and effort taken to correct such mistakes.
- Improving overall reliability, correctness and safety.

As defined by Wirth, SP 'is the formulation of programs as hierarchical, nested structures of statements and objects of computation'. Over the years its original ideas were modified. Nowadays we generally consider the basic rules of SP to be that:

- Programs are designed in a top-down manner.
- Programs are constructed as hierarchical modules.
- The program control structures are limited.
- Program correctness can be proved.

Until recently, structured design and structured programming were regarded as being synonymous. However, this link has been weakened as design structures may now be either functional, object or data-flow oriented. Nonetheless, in all cases, the rules concerning control structures and program correctness still apply. These are the items which go right to the heart of good programming.

4.3.2 Fundamental control structures

Is it possible to define a minimum set of program control structures from which *any* program can be built? And why should we want to do this in the first place?

Much of the heat generated by arguments concerning the first question results from ignorance of the reasons behind the second one. The primary reason for restricting control structures is so that we can prove that programs are correct. Consider, for example, the program operations described in Figure 4.27. In (a) the variable X is operated on by the program statement S1 to give Xi. Now, provided we can define the range of values taken on by X (called a pre-condition), then we can define those of Xi (post-condition). This can be considered to be an elementary step; we're dealing with a single statement which produces a single transformation. For Figure 4.27a, suppose that:

TRANSFORMATION S1:   Xi := X/2;
PRE-CONDITION: $0 \leq Xi \leq 10$
Then POST-CONDITION is $0 \leq Xi \leq 5$

If the statement S1 (as actually implemented in code) generates a result which violates this assertion, then clearly the program is incorrect.

Figure 4.27b is again quite straightforward, as is (c) (although proving its correctness is rather more difficult). But what about the case of Figure 4.28? Here the effects produced by individual statements are easy to check out. Unfortunately, as their

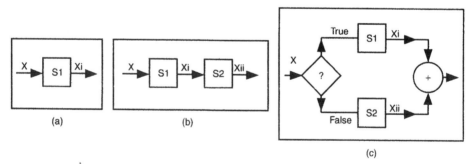

(a)   (b)   (c)

Figure 4.27 Simple transformation actions.

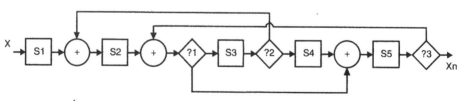

Figure 4.28 Complex transformation action.

interaction is quite complex, this isn't a great deal of help. It can be seen that the current output depends on:

- the current input and
- previous inputs.

In other words, the transformation has memory. In this case trying to prove the relationship between X and Xn is a fairly daunting task. Yet flow structures like these can easily be generated, especially when programming at a low level (such as assembly language operation). Frankly, with such designs, it is highly unlikely that their correctness is ever verified because:

- They're too complex to analyse in the time available.
- It would cost too much to prove it.
- Programmers just wouldn't do it because of the tedium of the job.

The groundwork in tackling this problem was done by G. Jacopini and further refined by others, notably Wirth, Dijkstra and Hoare. Jacopini showed that only three basic flow control structures were needed to form any program: sequence, selection and iteration (Figure 4.29). Note that the two iteration structures can always be implemented using either the pre-check or post-check operation; thus only one is needed (Figure 4.30). These basic forms were later augmented by variations on the multiple select operation, the 'Else-If' and 'Case' (see programming languages, Chapter 9).

A second (very important) point is that each structure has one entry point and one exit point. From these simple beginnings any program can be built up. Moreover, when using such building blocks, the program always consists of the basic control structures (Figure 4.31), no matter what level it's looked at. Therefore, given a program formed like this, we can first prove the correctness of the individual building blocks. Then, by extending this to larger groupings, the proving process encompasses larger and larger program sections. Ultimately it takes in the complete program.

In informal (non-mathematical) terms, program correctness is checked as follows:

Sequential operation

- Are all statements listed in correct order?
- Are these executed *once* only?
- Are sequence groups executed from a single entry to a single exit point?
- Do the statements represent the solution to this problem?
- Does the order of execution produce the required result?

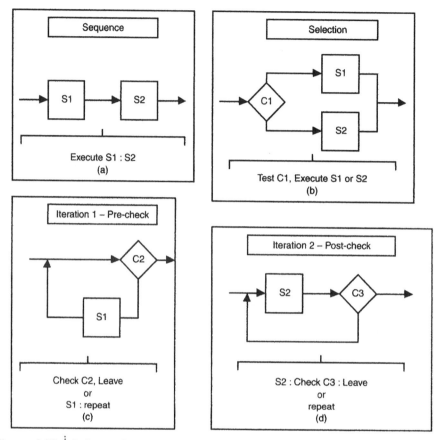

Figure 4.29 Basic control structures of structured programming.

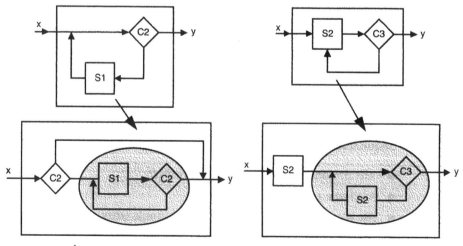

Figure 4.30 Equivalence of iteration structures.

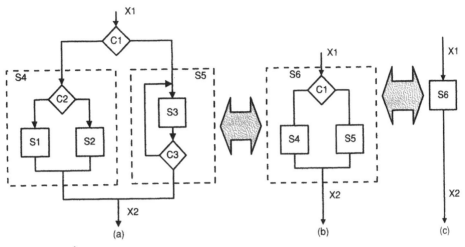

Figure 4.31 : Composition of a structured program.

Iteration operation

- Are the controlled statements executed at least once (post-check)?
- Can control pass through the operation without ever executing the controlled statements (pre-check)?
- Is iteration guaranteed to finish (that is, are the loop termination conditions correct)?
- Is the correct number of iterations carried out?
- Is the control variable altered within the loop itself?
- What is the state of program variables on exit from an iteration?

Selection operation

- Are all alternative courses of action explicitly taken into account (including answers that don't fit the question)?
- Are the alternative statements constructed using the basic structures of SP?
- Have the questions relating to sequential operations (and, where appropriate, iteration) been considered?

That's fine. But, you may well argue, few programmers are actually ever going to carry out a correctness check on their code. It's enough effort to produce it in the first place. Does this diminish the value of the control structures of structured programming? The answer, emphatically, is *no*. Programs built using these rules are much more likely to be reliable, robust and trustworthy.

Modern high-level languages directly support these aims, in many cases building in extra controls. For instance, several languages prevent statements within a loop changing the loop control variable. Consequently, when good design practices are combined with high-level language programming, the result should be quality software.

4.3.3 Uncontrolled branching of control – the great GOTO debate

Most languages enable a programmer to branch without constraint using a 'GOTO' statement (the destination being either a line number or label). In assembly-level programming this is done using a 'jump' instruction. As this construct is not allowed in SP it became a controversial issue, fuelled by Dijkstra's famous letter 'Go To statement considered harmful'. More heat than light was generated in the resulting arguments, most combatants losing sight of the underlying arguments behind this conclusion.

Is the GOTO statement by itself a problem? No, of course not. When used with care and attention, particularly when confined by conditional expressions, there aren't any particular difficulties. The problems come about because of the 'creative' aspects of GOTO programming. Consider the program fragment shown in Figure 4.32. Here the resulting control flow is perfectly well controlled and structured, even though the GOTO is used. Now look at that in Figure 4.33. In this the use of the GOTOs is controlled – but not very well. The result is a complex interactive control flow structure – produced from only a few lines of code. What then is the likely outcome if program jumps are made without *any* form of control?

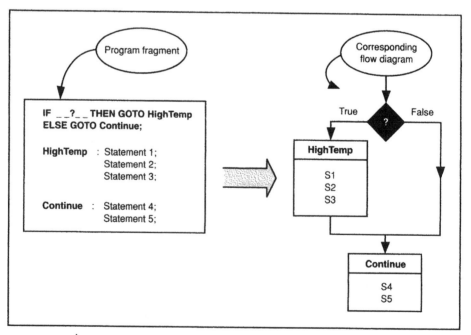

Figure 4.32 | Well-controlled use of the GOTO statement.

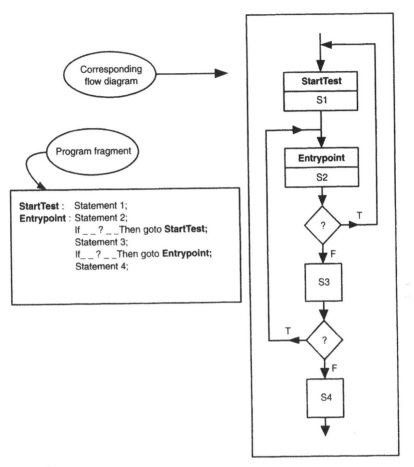

Figure 4.33   Poorly controlled GOTO statements.

It is clear that the GOTO statement provides a means for writing poor, unprovable programs. What Dijkstra observed was that where the GOTO was used extensively, programs were complex – and difficult to verify. Generally, good programs contained few GOTOs (note, though, that the absence of GOTOs doesn't necessarily mean that a program is a good one).

Is it possible to eliminate the GOTO statement (or its equivalent) from real-time programming? In theory it is possible to write any program without having unconditional transfers of control. But this involves a time (and complexity) overhead which may cause problems for time-critical applications. For example, suppose that during program execution an exception occurs which requires prompt attention. Further, the only way to handle this is to branch instantly to the exception handler. But that requires an unconditional transfer of control. So in reality, we can't throw away the GOTO or its equivalent; but it should be used *only* in very exceptional conditions.

4.4 Functional structuring of software designs

4.4.1 Background

Software structures can be derived in many ways, each one having its supporters and critics. But how does one make sense of the various claims and counter-claims? Well, the real test of any method is to see how well it works in practice. Judged against this, techniques based on functional structuring of programs rate highly.

'Functional structuring' is here used as a general characteristic (generic) term, covering a number of design methodologies. It belongs firmly in the Yourdon–Constantine–Myers–Meiler–Ward–Mellor–DeMarco school of design, its premise being that a program takes it shape from the functions carried out by the system. The overall design approach is based on many of the ideas and concepts discussed earlier in this chapter. However, it is important, when reading through the following sections, that the method is very *program* oriented.

We start by defining system functions, Figure 4.34. Then, from these, the modular structure of the program is devised using a set of 'transform' rules. These use a top-down, stepwise refinement decomposition method, resulting in a set of abstract machines. Structured programming is an inherent (and sometimes implicit) part of this process. Once the program structure has been obtained the program source code can be written. And once again the rules of SP are applied, in this case to the flow control constructs.

System functions can be defined using one of two methods. In the first designers use an 'informal' style, based on their own experiences. Alternatively they may choose to use a prescribed technique. Functions, for instance, may be described in terms of system data flow, data transformations, and connections between transformations (see later for detail). Here, though, we aren't particularly concerned with how we derive system functions. The important point is how we devise program structures to implement these functions.

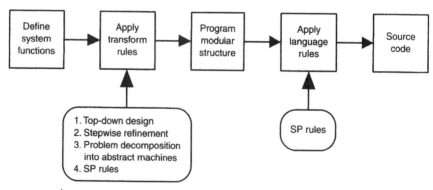

Figure 4.34 | Functional structured design.

4.4.2 Problem decomposition using abstract machines

Programs devised using functional structuring are based on the concept of abstract machines organized in layers (Figure 4.35). Taking a simple view, an abstract machine corresponds to a module. In (a), computing machine M1 invokes machine M2 to perform a specific task. When the task is complete, control is returned to M1, together with relevant data and status information. In (b), M1 invokes both M2 and M3. Unfortunately there isn't any indication as to whether M2 runs before M3 or vice versa. Here, to avoid confusion, all sequences run from left to right (thus, M2, then M3). In (c) M1 invokes M2, thus transferring program control to this machine. M2 in turn activates M4 and M5; on completion of their tasks it returns control to M1, which then starts up M3. This is shown in more concrete terms in Figure 4.36 when used as part of the anti-skid system of Figure 4.5.

When using abstract ('virtual') machines it is important to focus on the service they provide, not how they do it. Ideally it is best to completely ignore the 'how' until fine details have to be worked out. This may seem a pretty abstract point,

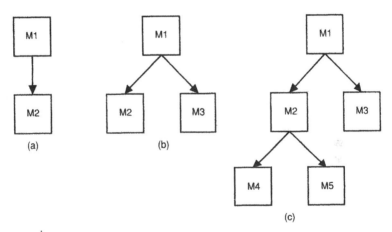

Figure 4.35 The layered abstract machine concept.

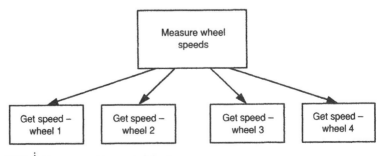

Figure 4.36 Abstract machines – task level.

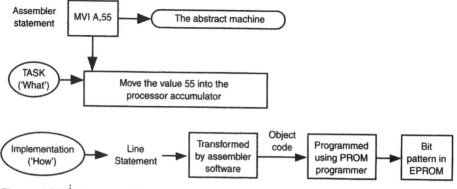

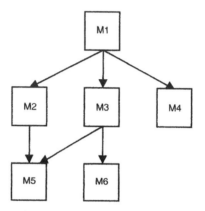

Figure 4.37 Abstract machines — program level.

Figure 4.38 Hierarchical decomposition — general form.

removed from the reality of program design. If so, look at how we regularly use abstract machines at the program level, without even realizing it (Figure 4.37). Here a line statement in assembly language can be considered to be an abstract machine. We invoke it to perform a particular task, completely ignoring how it's translated into code or how it works at the processor level. Moreover, we assume that the operation always works correctly when the code is installed in the target computer. If this isn't an example of abstract operations, what is?

The process of building up the complete program structure is one of hierarchical decomposition, Figure 4.38. Note that in this example both M2 and M3 invoke the same machine (module), M5. In other words, a low-level module is shared by a number of higher-level ones. Now this is undesirable as it can lead to complex and unforeseen interaction between modules. Ideally, hierarchical decomposition should result in a pure tree structure, Figure 4.39. In this case a module at any level can be invoked directly by only one higher-level module; sharing is banned. Thus higher-level modules have sole control over the modules they call. Further, the

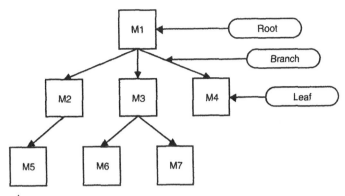

Figure 4.39 Hierarchical decomposition – pure tree structure.

branches of the tree are fully decoupled from each other (data coupling is needed to achieve this). The final result is a highly controllable, visible and stable structure.

A tree structure, taken to its logical conclusion, results in each and every module having its own code. This *could* be done but it would be very inefficient (and perhaps costly). Because, within all computer systems, there are 'building brick' functions which are used repeatedly (e.g. standard maths functions, terminal handling, real-world interfacing), the idea of writing separate code every time we use one of these functions is unrealistic. The sensible way to implement them is to use standard procedures (subroutines), calling them as required in the program.

Now this presents us with the need to handle a second form of problem decomposition, based around the building bricks. Traditionally it has been called 'functional decomposition' (which is confusing); for convenience the term 'service decomposition' is used here. When such decomposition is used the pure tree structure degenerates into the more general hierarchical structure. Therefore it is vital that modules designed as program building bricks must be fully tested and totally predictable in operation. Where appropriate, formal correctness testing should be carried out. Once this is done such service modules may be used as single objects ('primitives') in the program structure. But even so the programmer must always be aware of the effects of service decomposition. Sloppy use of this destroys the in-built qualities of functionally decomposed programs. Hence the design and use of service modules must be rigorously controlled. Where possible they should be placed in a library, with access to the source code being a privileged operation.

When designing any system we need to identify the main program first and then (later) the service subprograms. The main program is designed as described earlier, but *must* have a pure tree structure. Service subprograms are produced to carry out common tasks defined by service modules. Modules within the main program may invoke service modules, but these service modules don't appear explicitly in the structure. Also, they can be invoked by modules at *any* level in the pure tree structure of the main program.

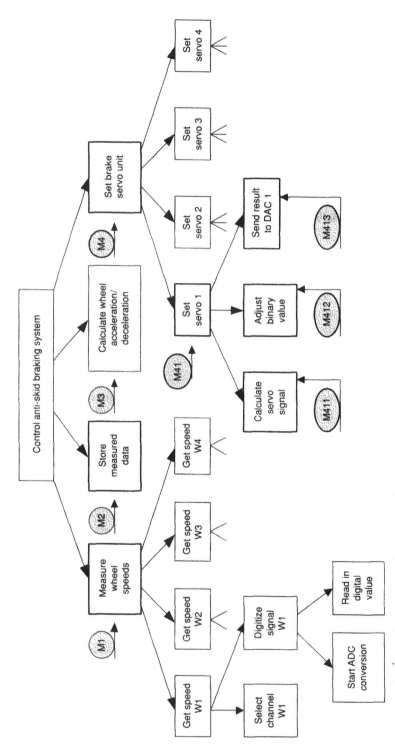

Figure 4.40 Functional structure of the anti-skid braking system (part).

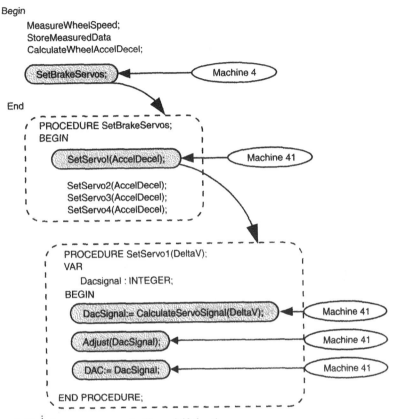

```
Begin
    MeasureWheelSpeed;
    StoreMeasuredData
    CalculateWheelAccelDecel;

    SetBrakeServos;                          Machine 4

End
    PROCEDURE SetBrakeServos;
    BEGIN
        SetServo1(AccelDecel);               Machine 41

        SetServo2(AccelDecel);
        SetServo3(AccelDecel);
        SetServo4(AccelDecel);


    PROCEDURE SetServo1(DeltaV);
    VAR
        Dacsignal : INTEGER;
    BEGIN
        DacSignal:= CalculateServoSignal(DeltaV);   Machine 41

        Adjust(DacSignal);                           Machine 41

        DAC:= DacSignal;                             Machine 41

    END PROCEDURE;
```

Figure 4.41 Program structure for Figure 4.40 (part).

4.4.3 Example implementation

Let's tackle the task of implementing the anti-skid braking system of Figure 4.5. There isn't a unique answer to this (or any other) problem; one possible solution is shown in Figure 4.40. For simplicity only part of the design is given. This is pretty well self-explanatory, the partitioning used leading automatically to low coupling and high cohesion. Many diagramming methods are available to describe program structures obtained using hierarchical decomposition; these shouldn't be confused with the underlying principles of the method.

From this information the program source code can be produced, typified (in part) by that in Figure 4.41. Observe that at the highest level – machines M1 to M4 – simplicity is the keynote. Each machine is implemented using a parameterless procedure. At the next level down the procedures become more complex. Note also that the 'SetServo1' machine (M41) communicates with the ones below it via parameters. Consequently machines M411, M412 and M413 use only local parameters in their computation. Also, it's impossible for them to communicate with each other; they haven't the means to do this. Consequently, these modules affect only a very small, localized part of the total program; they are said to have localized scope of reference.

Tree structuring of designs makes it especially easy to develop programs in an incremental way. For instance, assume that hierarchical decomposition has been carried out on the braking system problem. Figure 4.40 has been produced, and coding now begins. Using incremental methods, machines M1 to M4 would be coded first – a fairly simple (but not trivial) action. Now the modules stemming from M1 can be implemented, while all other second-level modules are coded as dummy stubs. Frequently these contain simple text messages, printing up 'module not yet implemented' or something similar. Once the first set of modules is coded and working, the next set can be tackled, then the next set, and so on until programming is finished. In my experience this is the quickest, easiest and least frustrating way to develop reliable software. But it really does require coupling and cohesion to be right for it to work effectively.

4.5   Object-oriented design

4.5.1   An introduction

It has already been shown in Section 4.1 that designs may be structured as sets of interconnected objects. In the example given (Figure 4.7) the computing objects were clearly linked with physical items. Generally, though, objects don't have such a clear-cut relationship. Mostly they are abstract items which represent computing processes within the system. In formal terms an object, as far as object-oriented design (OOD) is concerned, may be defined as:

> 'A software machine which has a number of defined operational states and a defined means to access and change these states'.

A change of state is achieved by passing a message into an object, as shown conceptually in Figure 4.42a. So, in simple terms, an object-structured program executes as a set of interacting machines (Figure 4.42b), communicating using messages. These objects, acting together, determine the function and behaviour of the overall software system.

A more complete definition would point out that objects usually contain data and operations (discussed later). However, the definition used here emphasizes the key features of OOD from a system perspective (as opposed to a program viewpoint).

At this point it is timely to ask 'why use an OO approach to software design?' Because, for many real-world applications, software objects map quite naturally onto system models. Moreover, in such systems many events occur simultaneously (concurrently). This concurrency can be shown simply and clearly using OOD. In

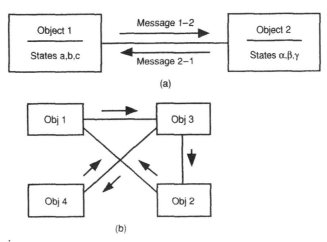

Figure 4.42 Fundamental concept of object-oriented design.

contrast, functional structuring is geared towards a sequential view of life. One consequence of this is that we find ourselves redefining our problem to suit the design method. (It is worth repeating that the computer is merely one component in the overall system. It and its processing activities form part of a totally integrated activity. Some software techniques give the impression that the important actions take place only within the computer, the outside world being a minor irritating side-issue.)

There are a number of major steps involved in producing an OO design, as follows:

- Identify the objects and their features.
- Identify the relationships between objects.
- Define the communication (messaging) between objects.
- Define the interface of each object.
- Implement the objects.

These points are discussed in the following sections.

4.5.2 Object-oriented design – the identification process

From a program point of view an object must have specific qualities. It should, for instance, be:

- Able to represent system functions properly.
- Easy to build.
- Simple to integrate into the overall system.

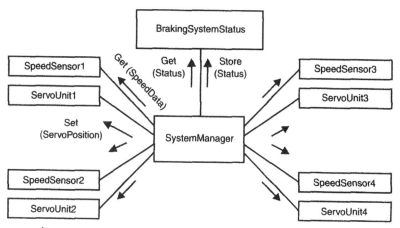

Figure 4.43 Object-oriented design of the anti-skid braking system (I).

- Amenable to testing and debugging as a separate unit.
- Straightforward to maintain.

This looks very much like the specification for a module. In fact, at the source-code level, a module and its equivalent object may be virtually identical (this, to some extent, depends on the programming language). Therefore the ideas of cohesion, coupling, abstraction and data hiding all apply.

How does one go about identifying and implementing objects? Well, consider again the system requirements of the anti-skid braking system. What would an OO design look like here? One possible solution is shown in Figure 4.43. This has been derived by first clearly defining the problem structure and then mapping objects onto this. It can be seen that three mappings have been used:

- Object to physical device (SpeedSensor, ServoUnit).
- Object to abstract device (the data store 'BrakingSystemStatus').
- Object to system function (SystemManager).

Observe that the message names imply a client–server (client–provider) relationship between the SystemManager and the other objects. In fact, for many OO design techniques, *all* relationships are based on this client–server model It is an essential (but usually implicit) feature of the design process. Unfortunately this doesn't always fit in well with many real-time applications, especially embedded systems. More of this later.

An alternative OOD solution is shown in Figure 4.44. Here each wheel unit object encapsulates the features of both a speed sensor and a servo unit. In fact, this provides us with a way of implementing top-down design and problem decomposition, the 'parent–child' structure (Figure 4.45). This, in OO terms, is a form of

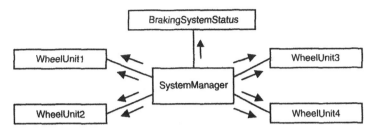

Figure 4.44 : Object-oriented design of the anti-skid braking system (2).

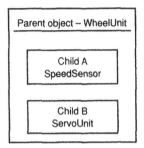

Figure 4.45 : Object structuring — parent–child organization.

'aggregation'. In broad terms, aggregation describes a situation where an object has a number of component parts. For example, a fax machine object consists (or contains) a telephone object, a printer object, a scanner object and so on.

The design diagrams need to be augmented by text definitions of the objects and their essential features (in practice this is likely to be done in an incremental fashion; see the section on class, responsibility and collaboration (CRC) techniques). To illustrate this there follows an outline definition of the SpeedSensor object:

```
0 ject:  SpeedSensor

Function:            Provide wheel speed data in binary form
0 peration performed:  Smple speed transducer
0 peration demanded:   Povide speed data
Data held:           Wheel speed.
```

The 'operation performed' can be viewed as a response to a system requirement. In contrast, 'operation demanded' is a response to a message from some other object. At this level of design there must be correspondence between the two operations. After all, it doesn't make sense to do something which isn't needed. And obviously, one can't demand an item which doesn't exist.

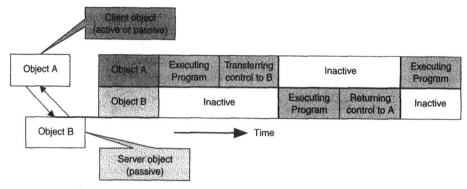

Figure 4.46 | Passive object behaviour.

4.5.3 Relationships and communication between objects

The first (identification) stage of design defines the broad relationships of the objects and the messages sent between them. The second stage firms up on these items, specifying them precisely and totally. It also identifies passive, active and interrupt-driven objects (see following text), together with exception-handling issues.

Assume a client object demands an action by another object (Figure 4.46), transfers control to this object, and the demand is then immediately serviced. On completion of the demanded action, control is returned to the calling object. In this case the receiving object is said to be a 'passive' one. Note that with a passive object structure, one, and only one, object is 'alive' at any one time.

By contrast, 'active' objects may be working simultaneously, Figure 4.47. With such arrangements the receiving object may or may not react instantly; it depends on its current situation (Figure 4.47).

Interrupt-driven objects should be shown so that they stand out from normal objects (Figure 4.48). In all cases the reasons for generating such interrupts should be made clear. It may be necessary to use *ad hoc* notation to illustrate these points; some modelling languages do not support such features. Generally, if the receiving object cannot perform its task, it should raise an exception signal.

Conceptually, an interrupt-driven object is an active one.

Communication between objects is, as pointed out earlier, implemented by messages. Such messages consist of either data and/or commands (in this context the operations Read(Data) and Store(Data) are essentially data-transfer messages). Where passive objects are used, there is an in-built hierarchy in the structure. Moreover, communication takes place using a call–return protocol. Active objects, though, are regarded as independent items operating as concurrent communicating processes. The techniques used to implement communication between such processes are described in Chapter 5.

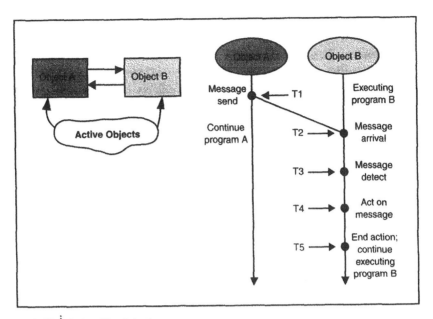

Figure 4.47 Active object behaviour.

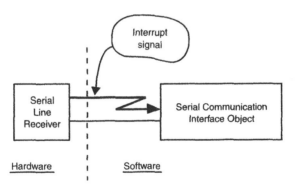

Figure 4.48 Interrupt-driven object.

At a system level the difference between active and passive objects may not seem significant. They are, in fact, profoundly different. When designs use active objects they need the support of a real-time operating system (RTOS). By contrast, passive objects can be built using standard code structures, viz.:

- With OO languages, the class.
- With non-OO languages, subprograms (functions, procedures) having associated (bound) data items.

A second important point concerns system and software performance, i.e. respons- iveness and throughput. Software designers, when using OO techniques, tend to produce designs that consist of many objects. This may well result in implementa- tions that work correctly; unfortunately they may also work very slowly. The reason is simple; as the number of active objects increases, the operating system (OS) overheads also rise.

One way to reduce the OS loading problem is to use passive objects wherever possible. Two workable approaches are:

● Top-down: decompose each major (active) object into a set of subordinate passive objects.

● Bottom-up: group sets of objects together into single active super-objects.

In practice both top-down and bottom-up methods are likely to be used.

4.5.4 Object interfaces

One of the primary aims in object-oriented design is to hide as much information as possible. It's a variant on the 'need to know' principle: what you don't know about can't hurt you. We do this by separating an object into two parts: the visible and hidden sections, Figure 4.49. The visible section (the interface) describes essentially the services it provides. In the outside world of software only the inter- face details can be seen. The body itself implements the required functions of the object. How these are achieved is hidden within the body, being of no concern to the user. In fact, it is imperative that internal operations and data cannot be accessed directly by external objects. As shown here, for example, the object contains three operations and one unit of internal data. Operations 1 and 2 are made available for use by other objects (*clients*) as they are listed in the interface section. Hence they are considered to be public items. By contrast, the internal operation and the data unit remain hidden – they are private to the object.

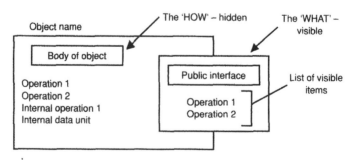

Figure 4.49 | Global view of an object.

Modern mainstream diagramming methods don't usually show interface or implementation aspects on the *object* diagram (e.g. Figure 4.42b). These aspects will be discussed shortly.

4.5.5   Object-oriented design – implementation-related issues

Up to this point most of our discussion has related to system-level analysis and design aspects. In particular it has focused on how we can generate – by toil, sweat, rigour, persistence and creativity – a successful OO design. However, the issues covered here are much more related to implementation factors, such as:

- How to produce effective and efficient code-level designs.
- How to describe in diagram form the source-code structures and relationships of OO designs.

In the next section we'll look at how to:

- Incorporate software reuse techniques in our work, supported by appropriate diagramming methods.
- Implement software so that it can readily adapt – in a dynamic way – to changing run-time demands.

Earlier the concept of the abstract software machine was introduced, see Figure 4.40. Part of this figure is reproduced in Figure 4.50, which concentrates on the machine 'Set Brake Servo Unit'. To explain a fundamental point, take the very simple analogy between a software application and an automobile system, Figure 4.50a. If a software machine is considered to be equivalent to an actual vehicle, then its declaration code is equivalent to vehicle manufacturing plans. Thus the source code (here a procedure declaration) acts as the plan or template for the machine, Figure 4.50b. Putting this another way, *the work done by a software system is actually performed by software machines, but the machine features themselves are defined by their 'template' code.*

An object can also be viewed as a software machine, though clearly it differs from the structured model. *The* major difference is that the object encapsulates both operations and data; further, its operations are bound to its data. With this in mind, the OO equivalent of Figure 4.50 is shown in Figure 4.51. Here the software template from which objects are created is called the *class*. Note this most carefully (imprint it on your brain – it will help you deal with the dross regularly found in OO articles). Thus the class (essentially a source-code declaration) defines the form, content and behaviour of objects. The symbol used for the class is given in Figure 4.52, a rectangular box having three compartments. The name of the class is shown in the first (upper) section. Its attributes (qualities) are listed in the middle section, whilst

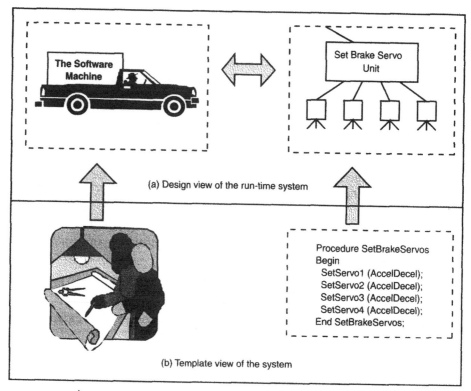

(a) Design view of the run-time system

(b) Template view of the system

Figure 4.50 The software machine and its template — structured techniques.

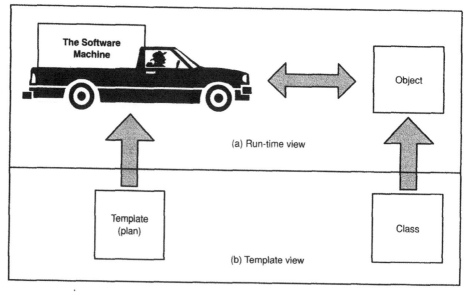

(a) Run-time view

(b) Template view

Figure 4.51 The software machine and its template — OO techniques.

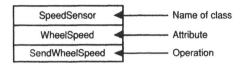

Figure 4.52 Class symbol.

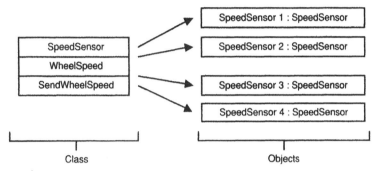

Figure 4.53 Class and object notation.

its *visible* operations appear in the bottom section. Note that at the program level, attributes become data items; operations are implemented by subprograms (procedures or functions).

From a diagramming point of view, how do we represent classes and their related objects? One standard notation is that given in Figure 4.53. Here each object is represented by a rectangle, being identified as follows:

```
0 bjectName : ClassName
```

Two important points are illustrated here. First, class attributes (i.e. WheelSpeed) and operations (SendWheelSpeed) are not included in the object figure. Second, you cannot deduce from a class diagram how many objects will be created (this has extremely important consequences, as you will see later).

Using the newly introduced notation, let us update the OO design originally given in Figure 4.43 (see Figure 4.54). The object notation is self-explanatory, following the syntax defined in Figure 4.53. Note, however, some new terminology; the connections between objects are defined to be 'links'. Note also that message names have been redefined to relate more clearly to the provided operations of the objects. Thus what we have in front of us is a design description of the actual object structure of the software system – the 'things' that, by working together, produce the required functionality of the software system. This diagram is commonly called an 'object collaboration' diagram.

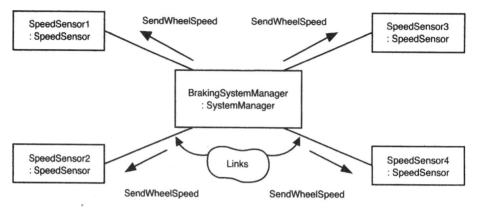

Figure 4.54 Updated OOD of the anti-skid braking system (I) — PART.

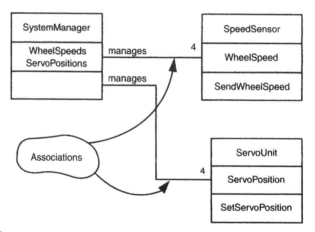

Figure 4.55 Class diagram (simplified) of the anti-skid braking system (I).

We saw a moment ago in Figure 4.53, for a single class, how the class and object diagrams relate. But what of the situation of Figure 4.43, which contains objects belonging to three classes? How do we show the template for this in class diagram form? The answer is given in Figure 4.55. This, it can be seen, shows both the classes and their interrelationships. In this case the relationships are deemed to be 'associations'; the naming used ('manages') denotes the nature of the relationship between the *objects*.

The specific nature (i.e. syntax and semantics) of class diagrams will be covered later. For the moment the following interpretation of Figure 4.55 is sufficient:

● If we create one SystemManager object, then we must also create four SpeedSensor and four ServoUnit objects.

● The SystemManager object is the client in a client–server relationship.

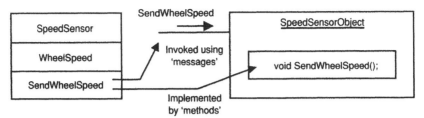

Figure 4.56   Concept – methods and messages.

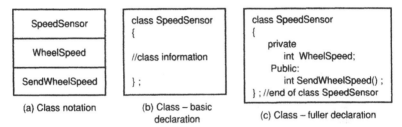

Figure 4.57   The class – diagram to code.

- The SystemManager object manages the other objects. It does this by sending messages to these objects. However, no information is provided as to the nature of the messages.

The object collaboration diagram allows us to show the messaging between objects. From Figure 4.56 it is clear that a SpeedSensor object would expect an incoming message invoking the operation SendWheelSpeed (if possible, the naming of the message should be identical to that of the operation). The implementation of the operation is called a 'method'. However, we cannot deduce anything concerning outgoing messages generated by SpeedSensor objects.

Next for consideration is the translation of the class diagram into code. The example given here (Figure 4.57) is loosely based on a C++ implementation. It is not intended to act as a language tutorial; rather it sets out to illustrate general principles (an Ada 95 code example would look significantly different but would still conceptually be the same). Figure 4.57a is the class diagram, whilst (b) shows the basic code template relating to this. Figure 4.57c is a fuller form, which includes the declaration of the attribute WheelSpeed and the method SendWheelSpeed. Note that the attribute is hidden from the outside world by being declared to be private. In contrast, the method is made available to external bodies as it is denoted to be public.

Let us now see how the class diagram of Figure 4.55 might be translated to code. For the present we'll concentrate on defining the classes as shown in Figure 4.58. For demonstration purposes, each class has been placed in separate program units. These

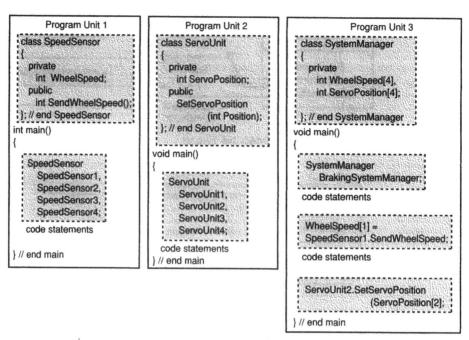

Figure 4.58 OO class design — key program-level details.

may be compiled separately. Within the individual units, objects of each class are created as and when required. For simplicity we will ignore the mechanisms by which objects in the different program units communicate (a most important topic, discussed in later chapters).

Two important points are illustrated here. First, all data items (e.g. WheelSpeed, ServoPosition, etc.) are localized to, and hidden within, the program units; there are no global items. Second, message passing is accomplished by a client making a call to a supplier (server), as in program unit 3:

```
SpeedSensor1.SendWheelSpeed;
```

and

```
ServoUnit2.SetServoPosition (ServoPosition[2]);
```

The general syntax is:

```
ServerObjectName.OperationProvidedByServer [Parameters];
```

4.5.6 Reuse and run-time flexibility issues

Reuse of software applies to two areas of work: design and implementation. Take the case of program unit 1 of Figure 4.58. Here, each time an object of class SpeedSensor is declared (i.e. created) we, in effect, reuse the class source code (reuse the template). Now, each object will contain an integer data item called WheelSpeed; thus memory storage must be provided for each individual item. However, the situation concerning the operation SendWheelSpeed is quite different. When the class code is compiled, object code is produced for the operation. More correctly, one piece of code is generated, this being (re)used by *each* and every SpeedSensor object.

Reuse of this type has been with us for many years, starting with subroutines at assembly language level. The technique tackles reuse at two levels: designer productivity (fewer source code items, hence less design effort) and storage requirements (fewer object code items, hence reduced memory needs). Both are important, but here we'll concentrate on aspects relating to design productivity.

Our aim is to produce as little source code as possible. One way to achieve this goal is to minimize the number of classes in a system. How, though, can we do this? Let us consider the object design shown in Figure 4.59a. We *could* produce a class (a template) for each object. Much more sensible, though, is to see if there

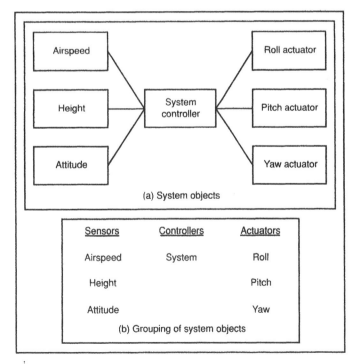

(a) System objects

(b) Grouping of system objects

Figure 4.59 Classifying items.

are natural groupings of objects and produce a class for each group. One such group-ing solution (a 'classification' of objects) is given in Figure 4.59b, decisions being based on commonality of:

- Function and behaviour (related to operations).
- Qualities (attributes).

As shown here there are three classes: Sensors, Controllers and Actuators. In a per-fect world all objects within *each* class would be identical; hence these could be produced from just one unit of source code. As a result the system of Figure 4.59 could be built using just three classes.

Unfortunately, reality is rarely so obliging. It is likely that the initial classification exercise will collect together objects that are similar *but not identical*. In our ex-ample the various sensors are (it turns out) really quite different at the detailed level. Thus a single class cannot act as the template for all objects which naturally belong to that class. It might, at this point, seem that we are back to square one, needing a class for each object. However, object-oriented programming offers us a way out of the problem: the use of inheritance. Central to this as a design technique is the concept of class structuring, Figure 4.60. We have made a design decision that the actuator objects can be built from a single template: one class only is needed. As there is just one controller object, classification is not an issue. However, the sensor aspects lead to a different form of class structure, one involving subclasses and super-classes. These, it can be seen, are organized in a hierarchical manner. At the top there is the super-class 'Sensor' class. Below this are the three subclasses 'Speed', 'Height' and 'Attitude' which in turn have a number of subclasses.

The super-class Sensor gives the most abstract definition (in terms of attributes and/or operations) of a sensor object. A subclass adds detail to the super-class definition

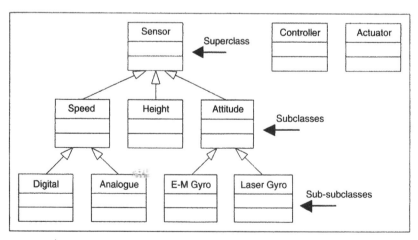

Figure 4.60 Class structuring – subclasses and super-classes.

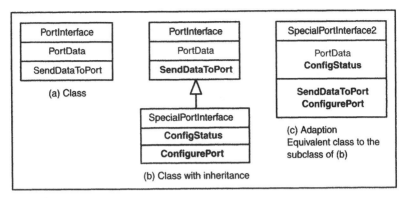

Figure 4.61 : Inheritance — what it does.

which is specific to that individual subclass. However, it also automatically acquires the properties of its parents, this being known as inheritance. Thus, moving down the hierarchy, classes become progressively more specialized. But now for a most important point. *What we have here is essentially a class-cataloguing exercise; we aren't decomposing objects.* Thus a Laser Gyro class is a specialized form of an Attitude class; in turn this is a specialized form of a Sensor class.

Note: some terminology. A super-class is also known as a parent or base class, while a subclass is often called an extended or derived class.

Producing such inheritance diagrams may be intellectually stimulating; but how does it help to raise software productivity? This is where the inheritance features of OO languages come into play. Let us see what they can do for us by looking at the example of Figure 4.61. First we define a class PortInterface, Figure 4.61a. It has an attribute PortData and an operation SendDataToPort. We later decide to produce a specialized version of this, SpecialPortInterface, Figure 4.61b. This adds another attribute, ConfigStatus, and another operation, ConfigurePort. As a result of inheritance, SpecialPortInterface is equivalent to the class of Figure 4.61c, SpecialPortInterface2. However, there is a significant difference between the two *from a source-code point of view*. Without inheritance we would have to produce two separate classes. As each one *has* to be complete in its own right, there will be duplication of source code. But with inheritance, there is no need to reproduce the super-class material in the subclass. It is automatically inherited (and thus reused) by applying appropriate programming constructs.

The benefits obtained by using inheritance are quite limited in designs structured *à la* Figure 4.61. However, if we now take Figure 4.62 the reuse benefits are more obvious. Another factor to take into account is how changes made to the parent class(es) affect the design. Such changes are, in fact, automatically propagated on code recompilation to their subclasses. This can profoundly improve productivity *vis-à-vis* maintenance efforts, software configuration control and program version

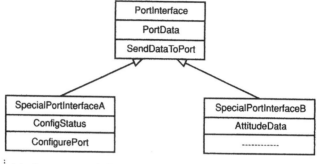

Figure 4.62 | Inheritance – example 2.

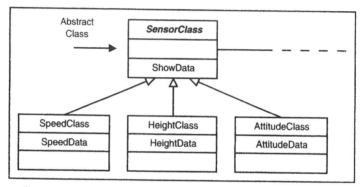

Figure 4.63 | The use of an abstract class.

control. But a word of warning concerning inheritance. You don't inherit only the good things; you also get the dross. Please: use inheritance carefully.

Now let us look at a second major use of inheritance, the provision and control of interfaces. Take the example of Figure 4.63, where the super-class has been marked as being 'abstract'. This means that we never intend to build SensorClass objects. Our aim is to create objects of the subclass type: SpeedClass, HeightClass and AttitudeClass (hence these are termed 'concrete' classes, object creation, also known as *instantiation*). At first sight it may seem that the base class is used merely to define the root point in the inheritance structure (actually a commonplace application of abstract classes). In fact *the* key aspect here is the operation ShowData, which is inherited by all subclasses. The result is that all objects generated using this template end up with identical interfaces. This approach, in effect, provides for reuse of the interface. Hence, should we add a TemperatureClass subclass, then its objects would also present the same ShowData interface.

What are the benefits of having a standard, consistent interface? Twofold. First, interfaces usually become simpler and cleaner, making overall object testing simpler.

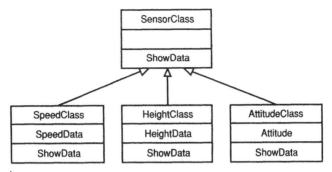

Figure 4.64 Overriding operations.

Second, integration testing also becomes more straightforward as a result of the consistency and clarity of interfaces.

We could achieve the same aims without using an inheritance structure. So why use inheritance? Well, there are two particular advantages. To start with, it guarantees that as new subclasses are added their interfaces will, by default, be correct. The inheritance process takes care of that. Another way of looking at it is that policing of the interface standard is enforced automatically; it doesn't require manual checking (although never underestimate the creativity of programmers).

The second advantage is quite different, one related to flexibility issues. It gives us a simple yet powerful way of leaving decisions concerning code execution to *run-time*. To understand what happens, and to see the advantages of the approach, take the following example, Figure 4.64. The scenario is that we wish:

(a) To provide a consistent interface for all objects – the operation ShowData.

(b) To call on this operation as and when required.

(c) To allow, when required, the run-time code to select which ShowData operation should be called.

Unfortunately, it turns out that the detailed actions within ShowData vary from subclass to subclass. Thus each one must have its own version of the operation. What we then need is a way of making a 'general' ShowData call and have the correct operation invoked. This is known as *polymorphism*.

The first step is to denote on the class diagram that each subclass has a ShowData operation. This indicates that the operation in the super-class is to be replaced (overridden) by that in the subclass. Suppose we have the following part declaration:

```
SpeedClass    TrueAirspeed;
HeightClass   RadarAltimeter;
AttitudeClass Angle0 fAttack;
```

Then the following message–operation relationships would be true:

Message	Resulting operation
TrueAirspeed.ShowData	ShowData (from SpeedClass)
Angle0 fAttackShowData	ShowData (from AttitudeClass)
RadarAltimeter.ShowData	ShowData (from HeightClass)

Such statements would be placed in the program source code; as such the choice of ShowData operations is made at compile time. Here we have a case of *static polymorphism*.

Although this is very useful in simplifying source code, it doesn't meet the requirement of point (c) above. It is here, however, that the power of OO languages excels. We can use a source code statement like

```
Some0 ject.ShowData;
```

and have the run-time software work out which particular operation should be called (*dynamic polymorphism*). Precise details are language-dependent but the general principles are as follows:

● Because of the way Some0 ject is declared, the compiler knows that the *actual* object called at run-time is undefined.

● However, it also knows that it will belong to one of the following: SpeedClass, HeightClass or AttitudeClass.

● At some stage of program execution, Some0 ject is replaced by the actual object identifier.

Thus, when the statement Some0 ject.ShowData; is reached, the run-time code works out which specific operation should be invoked (typically using a look-up table technique).

Two points to note here:

● There is a run-time time overhead incurred in deciding which method to invoke.

● It is impossible to statically verify the code.

4.5.7 Composite objects – aggregation

Up to now we have seen the object or class as a single entity. It is possible, though, for an object to consist of various parts. The concept is shown in Figure 4.65a. This, from a high-level view, contains one object only: the Generating set. In fact the generating set consists of two major components, a Power unit and a Generating unit. Each of these in turn is made up of further components. Thus the generating set is said to be an *aggregate* object; it is a combination of its parts.

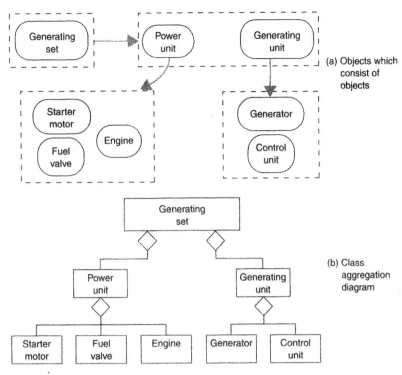

Figure 4.65 Object aggregation.

Now let us look at this from a class point of view. The naming used in Figure 4.65a is generic; i.e. 'Generating set', not 'Generating set serial no. 3568'. Thus it is clear that we can also define aggregation relationships at the class level, as shown in Figure 4.65b. Here the diamond symbol is used to denote aggregation (compare with the use of an arrow for inheritance). If we use this as the template for our **object** diagram, then the top-level object Generating set is defined to be a *parent*. The contained objects Power unit and Generating unit are *children* of this parent. They in turn act as parents to their child objects.

4.5.8 Devising the object model – a responsibility-based technique

The core components of an OO design are shown in Figure 4.66. As part of the design process, all items, together with their interrelationships, have to be identified and defined. But faced with a blank sheet of paper, where does one start? The answer, according to 'classical' OO techniques, is to first develop the class model, placing great emphasis on class attributes. Such approaches are based on information modelling techniques, having their roots in database systems and the like.

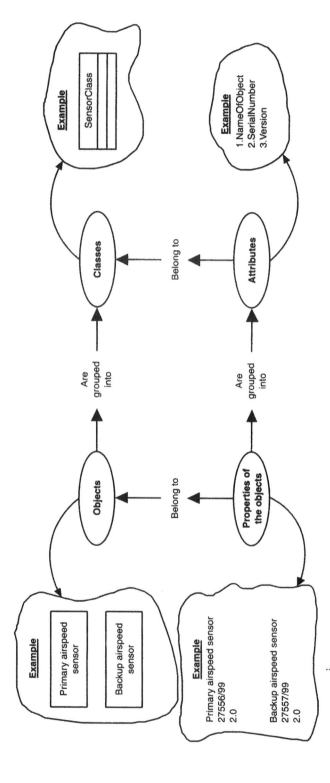

Figure 4.66 : Core components of OO designs.

However, the majority of real-time systems are *not* data-driven; the central issue is that of system dynamic behaviour. In short, it relates to:

- What a system does.
- How it does it.
- Why it does it.
- When it does it.

Even real-time systems that contain large amounts of data (e.g. machinery monitoring, command and control, etc.) are shaped primarily by their dynamics and functionality. More generally, all real-time designs are heavily influenced by two factors: reaction to events in the outside world and dynamic processing within the software.

Clearly, successful design techniques must naturally fit in with this view of systems. But how can we – without experience – gauge the usefulness of different design methods? To answer this, let us pose a different, apparently unrelated, question. What actually does the work in a software system? The answer, obvious in hindsight, is 'the software machines' (objects), acting both individually and collectively. In other words, the dynamic and functional behaviour of a software system is determined by the *object* structure; not, you will note, the class structure. Thus a successful design method must start from this point of view. And that is exactly the route proposed by responsibility-driven methods. Their root concepts can be simply and easily outlined using a non-computer example, Figure 4.67.

Here we have a main battle tank and its crew: driver, gunner, loader and commander (the objects). Each object has a specific job to carry out. However, for the tank to function properly, all need to work together in a defined, organized manner. Now, suppose we had to:

- Produce a job description for the crew members and
- Show the collaboration structure of the crew as a whole.

The (simplified) results might be something like that shown in Figures 4.67b and c.

Let us return to the job specifications, specifically for the commander. Looking at these in more detail, it can be seen that they are based on three factors:

- What the object knows – information or knowledge (vehicle control, battle tactics).
- What the object does – service (controls tank operation).
- Who the object works with – collaboration (driver, gunner, loader).

Knowledge and service will, for convenience, be grouped together as *responsibilities*.

Implicit in this model is that the objects collaborate by sending messages to each other. Note also that such collaborations can be described using a client–server model, where any object can be a client, a server or both. Thus the total system can be

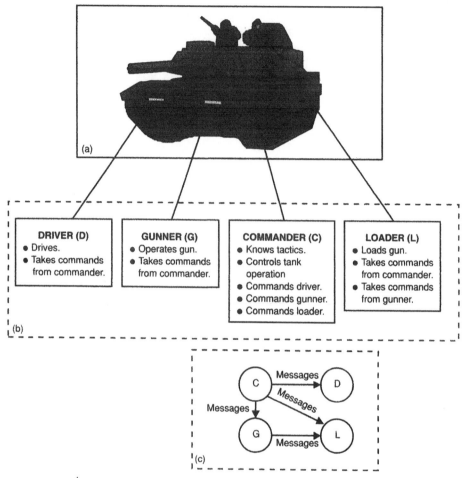

Figure 4.67 Collaborating objects.

described in terms of objects (and/or classes), responsibilities and collaborations – CRC.

The CRC method has its roots in the teaching of object-oriented techniques, being devised by Kent Beck and Ward Cunningham. However, experience has shown it to be very effective for developing the initial designs of real-time OO systems. As such it is a essentially a front-end method, being applied as follows:

● Identify potential objects using existing information (e.g. requirements documents, operational information, domain knowledge, etc.).

● For each object define its responsibilities (its knowledge and the service it provides).

- For each object specify its collaborators. These are defined to be *other* objects, which send messages to or receive messages from this object.
- Repeat until satisfied.
- Classify the objects to form an appropriate set of classes.

However, to produce a sound design, you need to:

- Clearly understand the problem to be solved.
- Emphasize what the objects are responsible for, what they do, when they do it and what information they exchange.
- De-emphasize what they have (their attributes).

A minor aside at this point. If you feel confused by the use of the term CRC when mostly we've discussed objects, I wouldn't be surprised (a much better name for the method would be ORC). Perhaps the words of Beck and Cunningham will clarify the matter: 'We settled on three dimensions which identify the role of an *object* in a design: class name, responsibilities and collaborators'.

Developing a design using CRC techniques is a step-by-step process, gradually building up a complete solution. In general it proceeds as follows:

Step 1: Make a preliminary list of potential, suitable objects.

Step 2: Use a single physical card to represent each object, its layout being similar to that shown in Figure 4.68a. Each card is identified with the class (object) name; on it is listed the responsibilities and collaborators, as in Figure 4.68b for example.

Step 3: List the major operational scenarios of the system into which the software is to be embedded (use cases are especially helpful here). For each one specify:

- What causes the scenario to start.
- When the scenario finishes.
- Precisely what happens between these two points.

Step 4: Form a small team to develop the design. Give each person a card (or cards; it will depend on the number of objects and the size of the team).

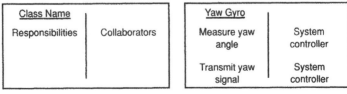

(a) General form   (b) Example

Figure 4.68 CRC cards – structure and content.

Step 5: Pick one of the operational scenarios and 'walk' your way through it, bringing in the objects as required. During this the team members play the roles of the objects, seeking to establish:

- What their responsibilities are.
- Who they collaborate with.
- What messages they pass to each other.
- If the design actually works.
- If more objects are needed.
- If any of the existing objects are redundant.

As responsibilities and collaborations emerge from the role playing, note these on the appropriate cards. When (if) new responsibilities are identified, these can be allocated to the existing objects. Alternatively, new objects can be created to deal with them. During the exercise, if objects become complex, consider splitting them into a number of simpler objects.

Step 6: Repeat step 5 for all other scenarios until the design is satisfactory.

The result of applying steps 1 and 2 to the system described in Figure 4.59 is shown in Figure 4.69. Steps 3–6 can now be applied in an iterative way to bring the high-level design to completion.

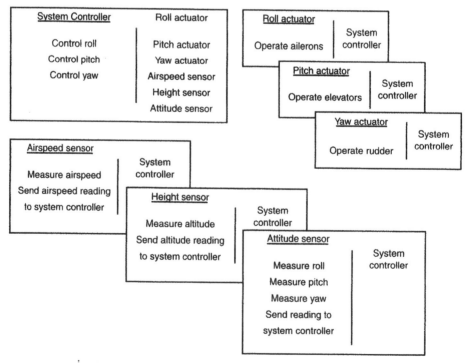

Figure 4.69 CRC cards for the system of Figure 4.59.

4.6 Data flow design

4.6.1 Structured design and the structure chart – limitations

Visualize the situation where you have been appointed software manager of the anti-skid braking system project. You have never worked on this project or even have any previous knowledge of the design. So, on day one, you set out to get an in-depth knowledge of the system and its software. Assume that the project documentation held by the software team consists of:

● A structure chart(s) as per Figure 4.40.

● Source code modules for the application, at varying stages of completion.

The question is, how helpful is this material, especially the structure chart? Well, it would certainly give you a very clear guide as to how the software should be structured. Moreover, it would allow you to do a code walk-through to check compliance of the code (the implementation) with its design specification (the structure chart). But there are many things that you *can't* deduce from the current information, such as:

● Precisely what each processing function sets out to achieve.

● What specific data is used when calculating wheel accelerations and decelerations.

● What the qualities (attributes and attribute values) of the input and output signals are as seen in the real world.

● Co-ordination and timing aspects of the system.

You may even have some questions of your own to add to these.

The lesson here is clear. The structure chart, as a means of specifying software structures, is an excellent technique. Unfortunately it says little concerning the system-related features of the design. In the scenario outlined above you would have to go further afield for the relevant system documentation. Now suppose that your searches throw up a diagram similar to Figure 4.10, together with fully descriptive text support information. How useful would this be to you? Very much so, I suggest.

Why then don't we have diagrams like this specifically aimed at supporting software development? The short answer is, we do: the data flow diagram (DFD). Briefly, the DFD and its related text:

● Enable us to graphically depict the required software processing from a system perspective.

● Provide extensive information concerning processing, signals, interfaces, etc.

● Act as a design specification for the generation of related structure charts.

● Allow us to develop designs in a top-down modularized fashion.

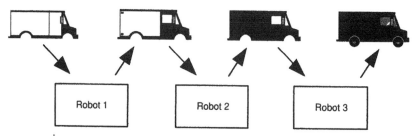

Figure 4.70 : A simple example of a materials flow model.

4.6.2 The materials flow model of software processing

The underlying processing model of the DFD is that of materials flow, a well-established technique in the world of engineering and science. Using appropriate diagramming methods, it allows us to model the function, structure and operation of real systems. It has been effectively employed to describe many and varied engineering systems; these include manufacturing and production operations, control applications, digital electronic devices, etc.

A simple example of a production line operated by robots (Figure 4.70) demonstrates the fundamental ideas. This is a very simplistic view of a vehicle assembly line, where the robots perform a variety of welding and assembly operations. A basic body shell enters the production line (left) and moves down the line, eventually emerging ready for final testing. At each individual stage it is worked on by a robot which carries out a set of pre-defined actions. As you can see, the overall operation is clear and easy to understand. But more importantly, it contains the key elements of data flow design methods, viz.:

- Each robot is completely independent. It knows exactly what to do and how to do it. Arrival of a vehicle on the line provides the stimulus to begin operations.

- The robots are entirely concurrent in operation.

- Provided that material (the vehicles) is available on the production line, all robots may be working simultaneously (and may possibly work at different rates).

- Without synchronization of activities material may be produced faster than it can be accepted (or vice versa). In such cases methods are needed to either prevent or else handle a build-up of material on the line.

- In the more general case some synchronization of the robots may be required, say, for example, on line start-up.

In computer systems we find similar structures in pipelined multiprocessor designs, each processor being equivalent to a robot. For example, in a tactical shipborne weapons system, the incoming material could be a sonar signal. As this passes through the system, Figure 4.71, it is 'worked-on' by the various processors, e.g. processor

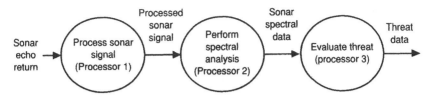

Figure 4.71   Simple DFD example – multiprocessor support.

Figure 4.72   Materials flow model – single work resource example.

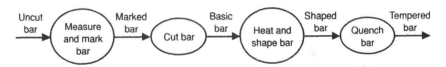

Figure 4.73   DFD example (part) – single work resource.

('robot') 1 for front-end signal processing, processor 2 for spectral analysis, processor 3 for threat-analysis, etc.

The DFD model is also an effective way to show the structure and operation of multitasking designs, see Chapter 5. And, of course, it isn't just limited to the simple linear production line situation; more complex interactions can be dealt with.

Now let us turn to a materials flow situation where we have only one 'robot' capable of doing work, Figure 4.72. Here, for example, the objective is to turn the input raw material (a bar of steel) into an art deco product. We can represent the processing involved using a DFD, as shown in Figure 4.73.

There is one most important point here which, unfortunately, cannot be deduced from the diagram. That is, one, and only one, process can be active at any one time. In computer terms this is similar to carrying out a set of actions within a single sequential program. Our operator mimics the action of the processor itself.

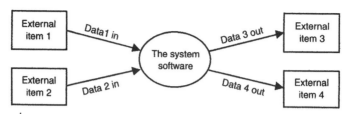

Figure 4.74 DFD design – the context diagram.

Observe how alike Figures 4.73 and 4.71 are, yet the underlying computer mechanisms are entirely different. Thus the DFD can show the abstract (ideal) software structure of a system without concern for implementation details.

At this point you should have a good understanding of the fundamentals of DFD techniques. Hence we can now proceed to look at data flow design principles in more depth.

4.6.3 Software design using data flow design techniques

Fundamental to data flow design techniques are the basic ideas of:

- Top-down design.
- Hierarchical structuring.
- Stepwise refinement.

The highest-level design diagram – the 'context' diagram, Figure 4.74 – is totally system-oriented. What it does is show the complete system in its simplest form: a set of external items connected to a software 'black box'. It contains:

- A single processing unit (a 'data transformation', DT) representing the complete software system.
- The external items which this software interfaces to.
- Data flows into and out of the software.

The result of applying these ideas to the anti-skid braking system is shown in Figure 4.75. The context diagram serves a number of purposes, but *the* crucial points are implicit, not explicit. First, it makes us focus on system, not software, aspects of the design. Second, it emphasizes that in embedded applications, the computer is just one component in the complete system.

We can now begin to develop the software design for the system defined in the context diagram. This is done by using a DFD to define the functions to be carried out by the software. The process, called 'levelling', results in a diagram – the *first-level DFD* – having the form of Figure 4.76. Each 'bubble' represents a piece of software processing, a 'software robot' if you will. In data flow terminology these are

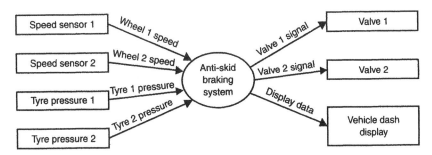

Figure 4.75 Context diagram – anti-skid braking system.

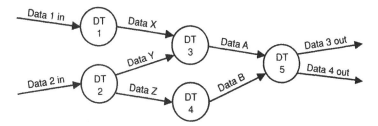

Figure 4.76 First-level DFD – general form.

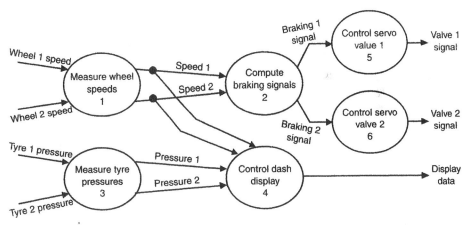

Figure 4.77 First-level DFD – anti-skid braking system.

also called 'data transformations'. However, it is strongly recommended you treat these as clearly identifiable software machines; further, this approach should be carried forward into the implementation stage.

For the anti-skid braking system, the levelled form of the data transformation of the context diagram ('Anti-skid braking system') is shown in Figure 4.77. The diagram should be self-explanatory, otherwise there is something lacking in our appreciation of the design objectives. Some points to note:

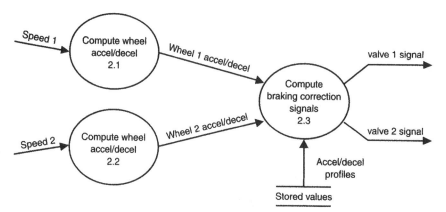

Figure 4.78 | Second-level DFD — levelled form of the DT 'Compute braking signals'.

- The number of DTs, and their functions, are determined by the designer.
- DT names are assigned by the designer.
- Usually DTs are numbered as well as named. This may be done automatically by your CASE tool.
- External entities aren't usually shown at this level (though this is a convention and doesn't need to be adhered to rigidly; however, some CASE tools automatically include entities on lower-level diagrams).
- All external data flows on both diagrams are totally consistent – they are said to *balance*.

The DFD Figure 4.76 is said to be the 'child' of the context diagram. Not surprisingly, the context diagram is considered to be the 'parent' of the first-level DFD.

If desired, we can level each individual DT to show its function in more detail. For example, the DT 'Compute braking signals' may be elaborated as shown in Figure 4.78. This is the child of Figure 4.77; thus Figure 4.77 is its parent. As before, the diagrams must balance. From a conceptual point of view, each DT in the child diagram should also be viewed as a software machine. The build technique should match this view of the software.

A new symbol has appeared on this diagram, that for a data store. It is denoted by a pair of parallel lines, similar to that used on electrical diagrams for capacitance. It can be seen that in this case it:

- Holds deceleration profiles for the vehicle.
- Is used as a read-only store.

More generally stores are read/write structures.

In graphical terms the result of applying data flow design techniques to a problem is a multilevel diagram showing, in layered form (Figure 4.79), the:

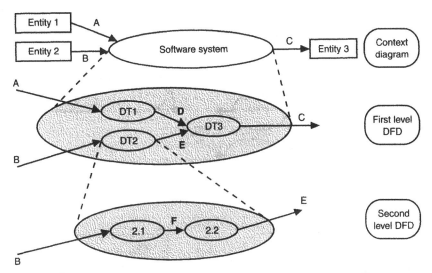

Figure 4.79 Levelling and balancing in DFD design.

- Function of the software, as a set of data transformations.
- Interactions of the DTs.
- Data flows, both external and internal, of the software system.

If we wished we could level any (or all) of the other DTs of the first-level DFD. This may, if desired, be repeated at the second level, third level, etc. There comes a point, though, when the work done by a DT is relatively simple; hence further levelling achieves little. These lowest-level DTs are called 'primitive' or 'atomic' processes.

4.6.4 Using the control flow diagram to organize DT execution

The data flow diagrams, as they stand, show exactly what processing is to be carried out. Unfortunately they don't explain *when* or *why* the individual data transformations are executed. This comes about because the ideal DFD model assumes that a DT:

- Will run as soon as all its data inputs are present and
- Can run simultaneously (concurrently) with all other DTs.

For this to work in practice each DT would need its own computer – not exactly a practical proposition. So, for the moment, assume that all the DTs of Figure 4.77 are hosted on a single computer. Thus one, and only one, DT can be active at any one time. And that brings us back to the questions of when and why.

Can we deduce this information from the current DFD? Well, in part we can. For example, in Figure 4.77 it seems logical that DT1 must operate before DT2; in turn

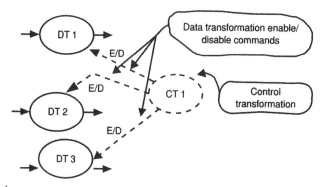

Figure 4.80 | Combining data and control transformations.

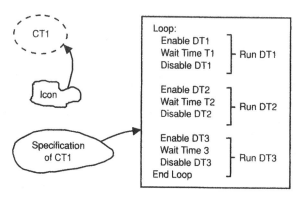

Figure 4.81 | Control transformation – icon and specification.

DT3 must run before DT4 is activated. But we have no idea whether DT1 is run before or after DT3, DT2 before DT4, and so on. One way of dealing with this situation is to use a new construct, the control transformation (CT), Figure 4.80. Here the CT, drawn as a dotted bubble, is shown interacting with the DTs via enable/disable commands (called 'enable/disable prompts'). We interpret this to mean that the DTs are executed in accordance with some set of rules; the rules themselves are defined by the specification of the control transformation, Figure 4.81. Strictly speaking the dotted bubble is the CT icon; its definition is the CT specification.

As shown the specification is defined using structured English, similar in form to that of a program design language (PDL). Sensibly, as long as the specification is clear, precise, unambiguous and testable, then any suitable technique can be used (later, however, we will see the use of state transition diagrams for this role). A more complex specification is given in Figure 4.82. Even so, its logic can be clearly understood.

All control-related features are identified using dotted lines; these form the control flow diagram. However, for real-time systems, both diagrams are always combined

```
Set loop counter to 0
Loop:
    If loop counter = 0 then
        Run DT1
    Else if loop counter = 1 then
        Run DT1
        Run DT2
    Else if loop counter = 2 then
        Run DT2
        Run DT3
    Increment Loop Counter by one
    When Loop Counter = 3 reset to 0
End Loop;
```

Figure 4.82 A more complex control transformation.

into a single diagram, the 'real-time data flow diagram'. This topic will be covered later in depth when data flow methods are used to implement a real-time design.

4.6.5 Data flow design using graphical techniques

With this approach, designers use interactive graphics to produce a design based on a block-diagram style approach. This, of course, is fundamentally a materials flow (data flow) model of the software process. There is no defined standard notation or process; features are vendor-specific. However, the fundamentals are pretty similar in most tools, although detail and implementation aspects may be quite different. It is up to the software developer to decide which tool best suits the needs of the project (see for example HP VEE lab, MATLAB and LabVIEW).

To reiterate: the ideas underlying the conceptual model development are based on data flow techniques. Nevertheless, differences show when it comes to designing and implementating this conceptual model.

From a *design* perspective the difference between them is twofold:

- The diagramming syntax (icons).
- The design process.

From an *implementation* aspect, the differences are quite radical in nature. Tool facilities often include:

- True automatic run-time embedded code generation.
- Support for a (specified) range of hardware boards, instruments, etc.
- Provision of an operating system (see Chapters 5 and 6).
- Debugging development tools (see Chapter 12).

What these tools offer is essentially a real-time *integrated development environment*, see Chapter 12.

It takes experience to fully appreciate the features of these graphical design and programming environments. However, many relevant aspects are discussed in Chapter 5, 6, 10 and 12.

Review

The various design methods described in this chapter should not be seen as mutually exclusive techniques (a statement which may cause OO purists to froth at the mouth). All have strong and weak points, and, in many instances, are complementary. Both functional and data flow methods can be (in fact, have been) used as a way of forming structures *within* objects. In other applications the overall system structure has been initially defined using data flow methods; these have subsequently been translated into object models. It's also been the experience from Matra Space [MAT89] that a hierarchically structured OO design approach works well. But no matter what methods are used, the fundamentals of good design always apply.

If you have absorbed the lessons of this chapter you should now:

- Understand the basics of functional, object-oriented and data flow design methods.
- Appreciate that for all of them the key issues are those of problem abstraction, problem structuring and software modularization.
- Know what the terms top-down, middle-out and bottom-up mean when applied to the design process.
- See how the use of a limited, well-defined set of program constructs can help in producing quality software.
- See how coupling and cohesion can be used as indicators of the quality of a software design.
- Realize that the software of a real-time system can be grouped into two layers: application and service.
- Know what these two layers are, what they do, what benefits are obtained by using this approach and how to implement them.
- Understand what is meant by hierarchical structuring, and see how it may be applied as part of software design.
- Know what is meant by the terms object, class, method, message, subclass, superclass, inheritance.
- Feel confident to apply CRC techniques to the object identification process.
- Realize that the data flow model of software presents a materials flow view of the process.
- Be competent to assess real designs that are based on DFD methods.
- See the need for, and use of, control flow diagrams.

Exercises

1. Produce a functional design solution for the software of the system described below:

   The primary function of the attitude sensor system is to measure the degree of tilt ('slant angle') and the magnetic bearing ('slant angle bearing') of an oil well logging tool. Basic measurements are made by triaxial accelerometer and magnetometer assemblies. From these the actual slant angle (SA) and slant angle bearing (SAB) values are computed. Temperature monitoring of the sensor mounts is carried out so that errors caused by dimensional changes due to the high operating temperatures can be corrected for. These are called 'misalignment errors'. The order of processing the input accelerometer signals is as follows:

   (a) Correct raw signals for static misalignment errors.

   (b) Apply temperature compensation to the results.

   (c) Compute the SA and SAB values using appropriate trigonometric formulae.

   Attitude data is transmitted to the surface on a serial transmission system that uses a carrier encoding scheme. The sensor unit is required to interface to the line modem using standard logic level signals.

   A secondary function of the unit is to provide support for field maintenance of the equipment. It enables an operator to perform a series of tests using a laptop computer linked to the unit via an RS232 serial communication link. These features include:

   ● System calibration.

   ● Input signal validity check.

   ● Display of all input and computed values.

   ● Operator help information.

2. Produce an object-oriented design solution for the attitude sensor system.

3. Produce a data flow design solution for the attitude sensor system.

4. Compare and contrast the three solutions. Determine the advantages and disadvantages of the various techniques. Evaluate the degree of modularization inherent in the three approaches. Compare the coupling and cohesion of the various approaches. Evaluate the impact of the methods on the later development, integration and testing of the software.

References and further reading

[BOE66] *Turing machines and languages with only two formation rules*, C. Bohm and G. Jacopini, Communications of the ACM, Vol. 9, No. 5, pp 366–371, May 1966.

[BOO94] *Object oriented analysis and design with applications*, 2nd edition, G. Booch, Benjamin/Cummings, ISBN 0-8053-5340-2, 1994.

[DIJ69a] *Structured programming (in software engineering techniques)*, E.W. Dijkstra, Nato Science Committee (Eds. J.N. Buxton and B. Randell), pp 99–93, Rome, 1969.

[DIJ69b] *Go To statement considered harmful*, E.W. Dijkstra, Communications of the ACM, Vol. 11, No. 3, pp 147–148, March 1969.

[ELL94] *Objectifying real-time systems*, J.R. Ellis, SIGS books, New York, ISBN 0-962-7477-8-5, 1994.

[GOL93] *A practical guide to real-time systems development*, S. Goldsmith, Prentice Hall, ISBN 0-137-18503-0, 1993.

[HAR66] *Engineermanship, a philosophy of design*, L. Harrisberger, Brooks/Cole, ISBN 0-8185-0441-2, 1966.

[HAT88] *Strategies for real-time system specification*, D. Hatley and E. Pirbhai, Dorset Publishing House, ISBN 0-932653-04-8, 1988.

[HPV01] *Graphical programming for DAQ and GPIP using HP VEE Lab*, Adept Scientific plc, www.adeptscience.co.uk, 2001.

[JAC75] *Principles of program design*, M.A. Jackson, Academic Press, ISBN 0-123-79050-6, 1975.

[LAB01] *LabVIEW graphical programming, 3rd edition*, G.W. Johnson and R. Jennings, McGraw-Hill, ISBN 0071370013, 2001.

[LOC96] *Succeeding with the Booch and OMT methods*, Lockheed Martin Advanced Concepts Centre, Addison-Wesley, ISBN 0-8053-2279-5, 1996.

[MAT00] *An engineer's guide to Matlab*, E.B. Magrab *et al.*, Prentice Hall, ISBN 0-130-11335-2, 2000.

[MAT89] *Hierarchical object oriented design*, Matra Aerospace, HOOD manual, prepared by CISI Ingenierie, CRI A/S and Matra Aerospace for the European Space Agency, Issue 3, 1989.

[PRE00] *Software engineering, a practitioner's approach, 5th edition*, R.S. Pressman, McGraw-Hill, ISBN 0-07-709677-0, 2000.

[PRI96] *Practical object-oriented design*, M. Priestley, McGraw-Hill, ISBN 0-07-709176-0, 1996.

[RUM91] *Object-oriented modelling and design*, J. Rumbaugh *et al.*, Prentice Hall, ISBN 0-13-630054-5, 1991.

[SOM96] *Software engineering, 5th edition*, I. Sommerville, Addison-Wesley, ISBN 0-201-42765-6, 1996.

[WAR85] *Structured development for real-time systems*, P.T. Ward and S.J. Mellor, Vols. 1, 2, 3, Prentice Hall, ISBNs 0-13-854787-4, 0-13-854795-5 and 0-13-854803-X, 1985.

[WIL95] *Using CRC Cards*, N.M. Wilkinson, SIGS Books, ISBN 1-884842-07-0, 1995.

[YOU89] *Modern structured analysis*, E. Yourdon, Prentice Hall, ISBN 0-13-598632-X, 1989.

Operating Systems for Real-Time Applications

In the world of large computers, operating systems (OSs) have been with us for quite some time. In fact the elementary ones go back to the 1950s. Major steps were made in the 1960s, and by the mid-1970s their concepts, structures, functions and interfaces were well established.

The micro arrived about 1970. It would seem logical that operating systems would find rapid application in microprocessor-based installations. Yet by the mid-1980s few such implementations used what could be described as formally designed OSs. True, CP/M was released in 1975, and was later put into silicon by Intel. But it made little impact on the real-time system field. There were two factors working here, one relating to machine limits, the other to the design culture surrounding the micro.

The early micros were quite limited in their computing capabilities, speed of operation and memory capacity. Trying to impose an operating system structure on this base wouldn't work. Another (major) factor was that microprocessor programmers generally didn't have the background or knowledge to implement an OS. During the last few years, however, there have been major strides in both areas. As a result, operating systems have now become an important topic in real-time applications.

The purpose of this chapter is to describe the basics of real-time OSs (RTOSs), setting out to show:

- What, in general terms, an RTOS does.
- Why we use real-time operating systems.
- How they work, in detailed terms:
  - The tasking model of software
  - Scheduling principles
  - Shared resources and resource contention issues
  - Inter-task communication features
  - Memory management aspects
  - RTOS use in distributed systems
  - In-depth review of scheduling policies
- The benefits and drawbacks of using RTOSs.

5.1 Why use an operating system?

Embedded microcomputer systems have now been around for many years. The majority don't use operating systems as understood by, say, mainframe designers. Therefore it seems reasonable to conclude that we don't need these in embedded applications. True. But what isn't apparent (at first sight) are the profound effects produced by using operating systems. Specifically, OS support has a major impact on software dependability, productivity and maintainability.

Consider the small, relatively simple, real-time system of Figure 5.1. Here the requirement is to measure temperature using a sensing probe, digitize the sensor output and display the results on a portable meter. This is a straightforward and well-defined task. In such a case how would the software be designed? Most likely

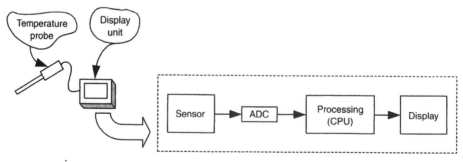

Figure 5.1 A simple processor-based real-time system.

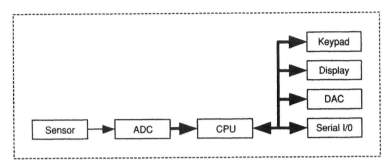

Figure 5.2 A more complex example.

we'd see a 'single thread' program, that is, a single contiguous set of instructions running as a continuous loop. This doesn't, of course, preclude the use of sub-routines or procedures. It would include both general (high-level) program operations and machine/device-specific ones (low-level programming). There aren't any real timing constraints (provided results are produced fairly quickly), thus simplifying the program design. After all, if the program cycle time varies from run to run (say due to the use of conditional constructs), who cares? Therefore, this is a perfectly reasonable way of designing programs for small applications. But can it be improved?

In the main, low-level operations are concerned with system hardware and related activities. Even if a high-level language is used, the programmer must have expert knowledge of the machine hardware and functioning. And that highlights one of the issues related to conventional programming of micros: the hardware/software expertise needed to achieve good designs. Even for this simple example the programmer needs a considerable degree of hardware *and* software skills.

Now examine a similar but more complex system, Figure 5.2, typical of many small-to-medium applications. Its primary function is to control the temperature in an engine jet pipe. This temperature is measured using the sensor, the resulting analogue signal is digitized, an error signal is calculated internally in the computer, and a correcting signal is output to the fuel valves via the DAC. The unit, however, is also required to perform several secondary tasks. First, the pilots need to have access to all system information via the keypad/display unit. Second, the flight recorder must be able to acquire the same information using a serial data link.

Given these requirements how do we go about writing the program? The simplest approach would be to use the single-thread method. But, given the operational requirements above, such a solution is unlikely to be satisfactory. The problem stems from the inherent 'asynchronous parallelism' of the tasks. What this means is that we have a number of distinct tasks, which, in the real world:

● May have to be serviced at random (and not preset) times – the asynchronous aspect.

● May have to be processed simultaneously, i.e. in parallel.

These aspects are normally handled by using interrupt-driven programs. In such designs, each interrupt routine can be regarded as a separate task. All aspects of task handling (e.g. safety, security, timing, etc.) are thus the responsibility of the programmer.

The central function of the operating system is to remove this burden from the code writer (all other OS features follow from this). It screens the complexities of the computer from the programmer, leaving him to concentrate on the job in hand. Detailed knowledge of interrupts, timers, analogue-to-digital converters, etc. are no longer needed. As a result, the computer can be treated as a 'virtual' machine, providing facilities for safe, correct, efficient and timely operation. In other words, it makes life easy (or at least easier).

5.2 Basic features of real-time operating systems

5.2.1 System requirements

Taking into account the factors discussed above, our hardware and operating system software must support:

- Task structuring of programs.
- Parallelism (concurrency) of operations.
- Use of system resources at predetermined times.
- Use of system resources at random times.
- Task implementation with minimal hardware knowledge.
- Task implementations as logically separate units (task abstraction).

These apply to all operating systems; but that doesn't mean that all OSs are designed in the same way or with the same objectives.

In all computer applications, two major benefits stem from using commercial operating systems: reduced costs and increased reliability. Nevertheless, the way in which machines are used has a profound effect on the design philosophy of their OSs. For instance, a mainframe environment is quite volatile. The number, complexity and size of tasks handled at any one time are probably unknown (once it's been in service for a while, that is). In such cases a primary requirement is to increase throughput. On the other hand, in embedded applications, tasks are very clearly defined. The processor *must* be capable of handling the total computer loading within quite specific timescales (if it doesn't, the system is in real trouble). Therefore, although the OS must be efficient, we are more concerned with predictability of performance. Moreover, reliability of operation is paramount.

Now let's take a more detailed view of the problem. Consider Figure 5.3, which shows the processes to be executed by the jet pipe temperature (JPT) controller of

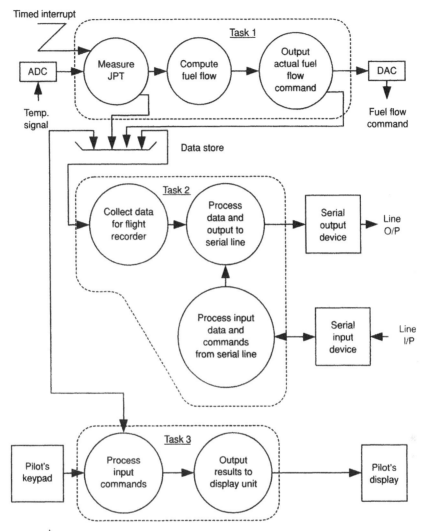

Figure 5.3 | Simplified process structure diagram of Figure 5.2.

Figure 5.2. There are three major tasks: JPT control, flight recorder interfacing and pilot interfacing. Each one *could* be run on a separate processor, i.e. multiprocessing. In such a small system this would be extremely expensive, very complex and a massive technical overkill. Therefore one processor only is used. This, in fact, is the situation in most embedded systems.

It is impossible to have true concurrency in a single-processor system; after all, only one task can run at any one time. Task executions are said to be 'quasi-concurrent'. In this text, single-processor multitask designs are called 'multitasking' systems, to distinguish them from multiprocessing techniques (this definition isn't quite correct, but fits in with common use).

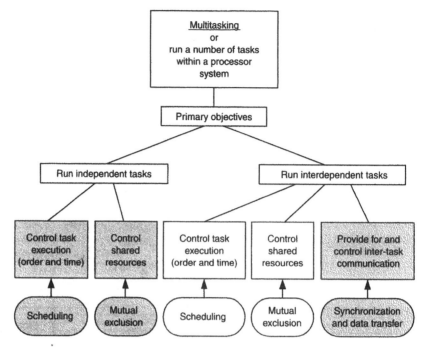

Figure 5.4 | Objectives of multitasking software.

What we have then are three separate but interdependent tasks. This raises a number of interesting problems, the solutions being provided by the multitasking software of the operating system (Figure 5.4). First, we have to decide *when* and *why* tasks should run – 'task scheduling'. Then we have to police the use of resources shared between tasks, to prevent damage or corruption to such resources – 'mutual exclusion'. Finally, as tasks (in this example) must be able to 'speak' to each other, communication facilities are needed – 'synchronization and data transfer'.

In a multitasking system it is possible to have tasks which are functionally independent. For instance, one can implement several separate control channels on a single-board digital controller. These tasks proceed about their business without any need to communicate with each other. In fact, each task acts as if it has sole use of the computer. But that doesn't necessarily mean that each task has its own resources; there may still be a need to share system facilities. For instance, each control loop may have to report its status regularly to a remote computer over one common digital link. So we still have to include mutual exclusion features in such designs.

5.2.2 Executives, kernels and operating systems

We haven't yet said what an OS is. One starting point is the *Oxford Dictionary of Computing* definition as an OS being 'the set of software products that jointly

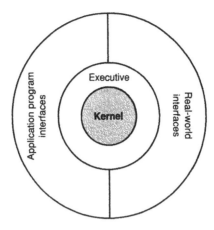

Figure 5.5 Overall operating system structure.

controls the system resources and the processes using these resources on a computer'. Nevertheless, trying to define precisely what an OS is and how it is constructed is more difficult. Many have the same overall structure but differ, often considerably, in detail [DEI84]. Embedded operating systems are smaller and simpler than work-station/mainframe types. The structure shown in Figure 5.5 is typical of modern designs, formed from a relatively small software set. Note that it consists of a series of well-defined but distinct functions.

First consider the middle ring, the 'executive'. This is where control functions are concentrated, the executive being the overall controller of all computer programs. User tasks (programs) interface with other system activities (including other tasks) via the executive. This is quite different from single-thread designs where task actions are distributed throughout the program. Here each task is written separately, call-ing on system resources via the executive. The executive itself directly controls all scheduling, mutual exclusion, data transfer and synchronization activities. To do this it calls on detailed facilities provided by the inner ring, the kernel. In a sense, the executive behaves as the manager, the kernel as the executor. At this stage the detailed functions of the executive/kernel combination won't be spelt out; instead they will be developed as we go along.

One part of the outer ring, labelled 'application program interfaces' is self-explanatory. The other, 'real-world interfaces', consists of software which handles the hardware of the system. Such hardware, which varies from design to design, is driven by standard software routines. This typically includes programmable timers, configurable I/O ports, serial communication devices, ADCs, DACs, keyboard con-trollers, and the like. Tasks do not usually access I/O devices directly; instead they go via OS-provided routines.

In summary then, each task may be written as if it is the sole user of the system. The programmer appears to have complete access to, and control of, system resources. If communication with other tasks is required, this can be implemented using clear and simple methods. All system functions can be accessed using standard techniques (as developed for that system); no knowledge of hardware or low-level programming is needed. Finally, the programmer doesn't have to resort to defensive programming methods to ensure safe system operation.

How well we achieve these goals depends entirely on the design of the executive and kernel.

5.3 Scheduling – concepts

5.3.1 Introduction

This section deals with the underlying concepts of scheduling, using an analogy to a real-world non-computer task. Let's make one restriction: it applies to single CPU systems only.

The problem is a simple (perhaps unrealistic) one. Assume that a firm has only one truck (the CPU), but has a number of drivers (tasks or processes). Only one driver can use the truck at any one time. Further, each driver is specialized in one, and only one, job. In these circumstances, what is the 'best' way for the transport manager to organize the delivery schedules (the 'scheduling' problem)?

5.3.2 Cyclic scheduling

One of the simplest solutions is that shown in Figure 5.6, the 'cyclic scheduler'. First, a queue of drivers is formed. The 'head of queue' is then given full use of the truck until he completes his job. It is then passed on to the next driver in the queue, who carries out his work, who then passes it on, and so on. All changeover activities are controlled by the scheduler/dispatcher (part of the executive); he does not,

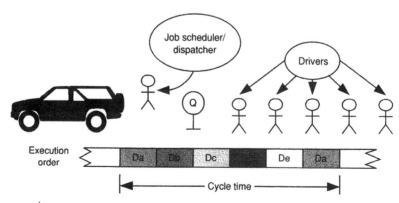

Figure 5.6 Cyclic scheduling.

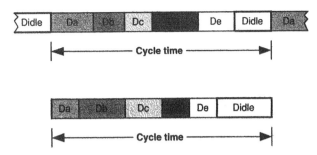

Figure 5.7 Timed cyclic scheduling.

Figure 5.8 Interleaving of jobs.

though, control task activities themselves. This method, described as first-in first-out (FIFO) scheduling, could be used to implement the measurement and display tasks of Figure 5.1. Certainly it would work where tasks are independent, as, for instance, running two control loops using a single control processor.

Notice that time plays no part in FIFO scheduling. Yet many tasks must be executed at predetermined and accurate time intervals. To achieve this we need to add a timing unit *and* another task: the 'idle' one (Figure 5.7). This acts as a buffer, absorbing any variations ('jitter') in task execution times.

If we use this simple scheduling scheme we're likely to meet some very real problems. First, consider what happens if a driver fails to return the truck (i.e. a task gets stuck). In the basic cyclic scheduler the system instantly grinds to a halt. When timing control is used the situation is different, but just as serious. Here the dispatcher always retrieves the truck from a stuck task, thus restarting the cycle. Thus, each timed cycle begins correctly. But tasks only execute until the 'stuck' one is reached; following ones are never activated.

Second, system performance is affected mostly by long, not short, tasks. No matter how short tasks are, they still have to wait for their designated slot. Yet it might be that one short job could be done many times within the time slot of the long jobs. It might even be satisfactory to interleave the long job with multiple executions of the short one (Figure 5.8). This usually makes better use of system resources (i.e. the truck or CPU). Unfortunately, there isn't any way this can be done using FIFO scheduling.

Third, a new driver (task) joining the system goes to the end of the queue. Accordingly, there could be a long delay before that job is carried out. In other words, the organization reacts slowly for requests to run new tasks.

These limitations are unacceptable for most systems, especially where fast responses are needed. One improvement is to set timing constraints on task execution, the 'time slicing' approach.

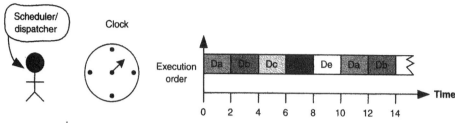

Figure 5.9 Time slicing of tasks.

5.3.3 Time slicing

Here the scheduler/dispatcher is given a clock for the timing of jobs and the means to recall trucks (Figure 5.9). Tasks are still carried out on a first-in first-out basis. Now, though, each driver is allocated a fixed time for use of the truck, the 'time slice'. When time is up, the truck *must* be passed on to the next user (task), even if the current task hasn't finished. This task is resumed at its next allotted time slot, exactly from where it left off. It is then run for a preset period of time, put into suspension, and so on. Note: the basic unit of time is called the 'tick'. Such a process is called 'pre-emptive' scheduling. That is, the running task is replaced (pre-empted) by the next-to-run task. More generally, this applies whenever the resource (the CPU) can be taken away from the current user. Now this raises a problem not found in simple cyclic (non-pre-emptive) operations. With non-pre-emptive designs tasks run to completion. But in pre-emptive systems tasks don't necessarily finish in a single time slot; a number are needed. Stopping and restarting must be done without these being apparent to the user (i.e. 'transparent'). The only way to do this is to restart using precisely the conditions pertaining at shutdown. And, to achieve this, we must do two things. First, save all task information at the time of pre-emption. Second, restore this at the restart time.

So, whenever a task is pre-empted, two extra operations take place. Initially, current information is stored away for later retrieval, then information relating to the new task is retrieved from *its* store. This is called 'context switching', the related time being the 'context switch time'. Context switching is an important factor in real-time operations because it takes up processor time. Consequently it reduces the available computing time, becoming a system overhead.

This scheduling, where tasks are dispatched FIFO for preset time slots, is also called 'round-robin' scheduling. Its advantages are improved responsiveness and better use of shared resources. But in practice it needs to be modified because tasks:

● Vary in importance.

● Don't always run at regular intervals.

● May only run when specified conditions are met.

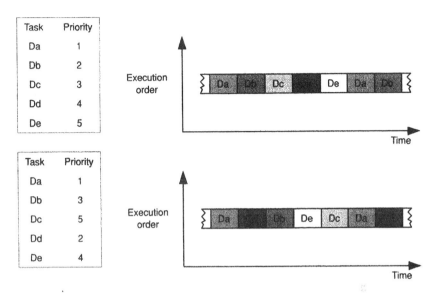

Figure 5.10 Setting task priorities.

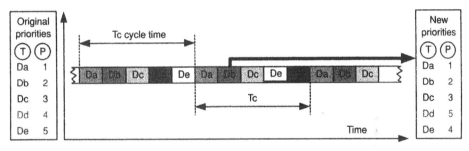

Figure 5.11 Dynamically changing priorities.

5.3.4 Task priorities

So far we have assumed that all tasks have equal status or priority. Hence the execution sequence is arbitrary, depending on how the system was set up in the first place. In reality a particular execution order may be required, and so tasks are allocated priorities (Figure 5.10). Here the lower the number, the higher the priority. If this order remains fixed then we have a *static* priority scheme. If it can be changed during program execution then it is said to be *dynamic*. Priorities can be changed either by some external event or by a running task. Suppose, for instance, that during one run of task Db it changes the original priority order, setting De higher than Dd (Figure 5.11). This doesn't produce an immediate effect; its consequences can be seen later on in the execution time sequence. Such implementations are defined as 'priority scheduling algorithms'.

The reason for using dynamic priority schemes is to improve flexibility and responsiveness. For example, when using cyclic scheduling, priorities may be changed where:

- In specific situations a task needs to very quickly act on the output of the running task, but isn't scheduled to run next.

- Systems have mode changes (e.g. from surveillance mode to tracking mode to engage target), each mode having specific schedules.

It is, however, more complex and also imposes a greater time overhead. Further, it has an in-built danger, that of blocking out tasks for long time periods. Observe that, when priorities are changed, the queue order is shuffled. And the task which next runs at the end of each time slice is that having the highest priority. Hence, if priorities continually change as programs run, low-priority tasks *could* be blocked out. Not permanently, of course. They will eventually run at some time. But the responsiveness of such tasks may be pretty awful.

5.3.5 Using queues

So far only one queue has been used, consisting of all drivers, ready to perform their tasks when called upon. This we'll define to be the *ready* queue. In reality the situation is more complex because tasks aren't always ready to run. They may, for instance, have to wait until specific conditions are met before joining the ready queue. While 'not-ready' they are said to be in the *blocked* or *suspended* state, and are held in the waiting queue (Figure 5.12). This is still a simplified situation because, in practice, it is necessary to use a number of suspended queues (Figure 5.13). First there are task requests which must be serviced very quickly, a 'fast service' operation. An example of this in the JPT system (Figure 5.3) is the need to respond rapidly to incoming signals on the serial line.

Second, some tasks are suspended until specific events occur. Consider the keyboard handling task of the JPT system. This would normally be left blocked until a key is pressed (the 'event').

Next there are tasks which have to be run at regular, predetermined intervals, that is, timetabled jobs. Measuring the sensor input signal, for instance, is something which would be done in this way.

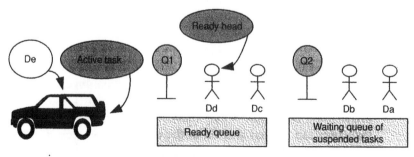

Figure 5.12 Ready and suspended task states.

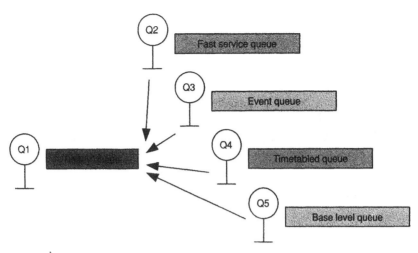

Figure 5.13 Types of queue.

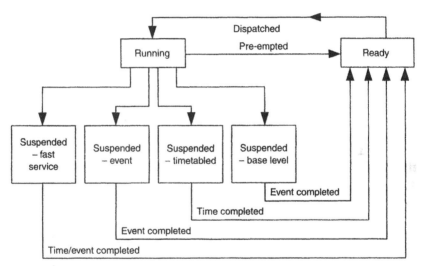

Figure 5.14 Task states.

Finally, jobs which don't fall into any of these categories are done only when free time is available. These are defined to be 'base level' tasks (frequently these are always ready to run). Updating the display could very well operate like this.

The state transitions which occur during task scheduling are given in Figure 5.14. This is self-explanatory. It can be seen that tasks are readied from the suspended state when particular conditions occur. These include the completion of some event, elapse of a specific time interval, or some combination of event and time.

When a task goes into the suspended state it 'releases' the CPU for use by other tasks (Figure 5.15). Release is either self-induced or externally effected. Self-release can be initiated by the running task itself, in two ways. First, it may have completed

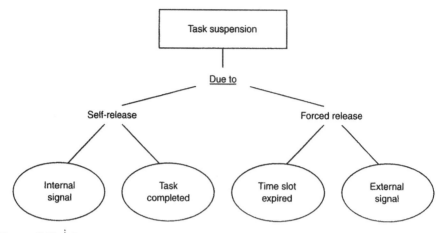

Figure 5.15 | Reasons for task suspension.

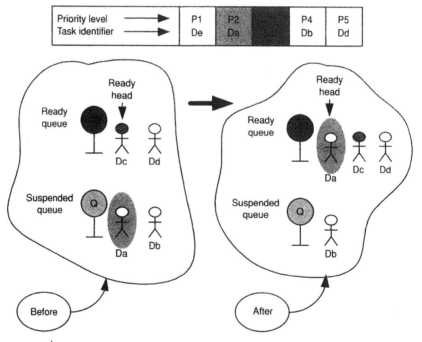

Figure 5.16 | Effect of priorities on queue states – task awakening.

the required operation and so gives up the CPU. Second, it may relinquish control as a result of signals generated within its own program (internal events). Otherwise it must be forced to give up the resource (pre-empted).

When tasks are given priorities, operations become even more complex. A simple instance is given in Figure 5.16, showing how priorities determine task positions in both ready and suspended queues. It also shows how the ready queue changes as new tasks are readied.

5.4 Scheduling – implementation

5.4.1 Implementing queues – the task control block

The basic item used for constructing queues is a task description unit or 'task control block' (TCB). Information held in the TCB enables the executive to control all scheduling activities. Note, however, that TCBs carry task status and control information; they don't hold the program (task) code itself.

There isn't a unique design of TCB. Nevertheless, certain features have to be included, Figure 5.17. Within the TCB are a number of elements or 'fields'. These are used as follows:

- 1 – Identifies the task.
- 2 – Shows whether the task is ready to run or is suspended.
- 3 – Defines the priority of the task within the system.
- 4 – Gives the identifier of the task which follows (this applies to ready queues, suspended queues, and any other queues which may be implemented in the system). The task identifier field is used only when task queues are organized using linked list constructs. Queues ('lists') are formed by linking individual TCBs together using pointers. For instance, the ready list (Figure 5.18) consists of task X followed by Y, then A, finally terminating in the Idle task. The Idle task, usually needed in embedded work, shows that it is the end point by pointing to 'nil'.

Suspended lists can be formed in much the same way, Figure 5.19. The operating system may use one or more suspended list constructs; this depends entirely on individual designs. Task order within individual lists can be changed using one simple mechanism: the pointer construct. Reordering of tasks, moving tasks between lists, adding new tasks to the system – all can be achieved merely by altering pointer values.

1	Task identifier
2	Status
3	Priority
4	Next task

Figure 5.17 Task control block structure.

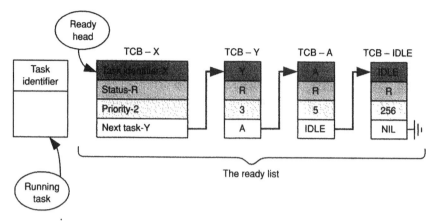

Figure 5.18 Ready list organization.

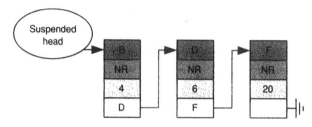

Figure 5.19 Suspended list organization.

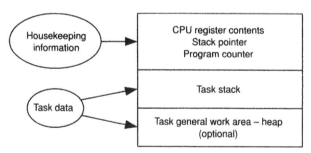

Figure 5.20 Process descriptor structure.

The task identifier field may be used to fulfil an extra role: a pointer to the so-called 'process descriptor' (PD). Dynamic information concerning the state of the process (task) is held in the PD, Figure 5.20. Each task has its own private PD and, in some designs, the descriptors may be located within the TCB itself.

One important point concerning the TCB and the PD is that both contain dynamic information. Thus they have to be located in read–write memory, usually RAM.

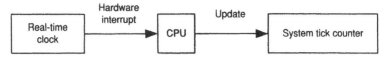

Figure 5.21 | Updating the tick.

5.4.2   The tick

The tick is an elapsed-time counter, updated by interrupts from the system real-time clock (Figure 5.21). It is often implemented as a time-of-day (TOD) counter, supporting four major functions:

- Scheduling timing.
- Polling control (related to scheduling).
- Time delay generation (related to scheduling).
- Calendar time recording.

Scheduling timing

Here the real-time clock sets the time slot for scheduling. It would normally be used to underpin a pre-emptive round-robin scheduling algorithm.

Polling control

Where tasks are event-driven, how is the processor made to respond to the event? One common solution, especially for time-critical events, is to use interrupts. But for many applications, interrupt-driven solutions aren't right; polling for status information is preferred. This solution could, for instance, be used with the keypad handling task of the JPT system, Figure 5.2. Here the keyboard status is scanned ('polled') at regular intervals, set by the tick. If a key is pressed the keyboard handler task is activated; otherwise it remains suspended. With this approach the executive never loses control of the system, which may happen when using interrupts.

Time delay generation

This feature is needed in most real-time systems, especially for process control work. Moreover, many applications use multiple time delays, with significant variations in the timing requirements. For instance, a combustion controller may wait for 250 milliseconds while checking flame conditions after generating an ignition command. On the other hand, a temperature controller may wait for one hour between turning a heater on and running the control loop. These diverse demands can be met, fairly painlessly, by using the tick.

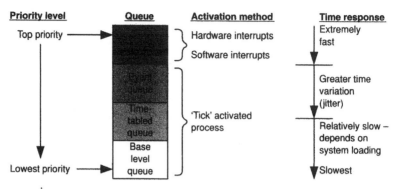

Figure 5.22 System responsiveness.

Calendar time recording

In specific instances, system activation, control and status recording must be tied to the normal calendar clock. A count of hours, minutes and seconds – a 24-hour clock – can be implemented using the tick counter. The tick could also be used for months, days, etc. But remember, when processor power is switched off, everything stops (including the tick). Therefore, for embedded applications, it is better to use special battery-backed TOD clocks for long-term timing.

5.4.3 System responsiveness

How quickly does a task get service in a multitasking environment? Unfortunately there isn't a simple answer – it's interlinked with task priorities (Figure 5.22). High-priority tasks of the 'fast service queue' type are only readied when service is required, using interrupt signalling. But the reaction time ('interrupt latency') is small, typically in the range 1–100 microseconds. This assumes, though, that the task is allowed to run (a higher priority one may be executing at the time of interrupt).

When task execution is interlinked with the tick, some time variation or 'jitter' is experienced. This is small for the higher-priority jobs, getting larger as priorities reduce. Only tasks which can tolerate quite slow responses are implemented at the lowest (base) level. Further, the use of priorities may be abandoned down here. Instead, round-robin scheduling is likely to be used.

From what has been said, the tick period has a significant effect on system responsiveness. The issue isn't clear-cut, however, being interlinked with scheduling strategies. For real-time working it is a primary design requirement that *all* tasks be completed within an alloted time period. So CPU performance is the limiting factor here. In cases like this there seems little point in pre-empting important tasks, i.e. a task, once activated, should run to completion. This is a reasonable approach provided the current task has highest priority, any waiting (ready) tasks being of lower priority. But now suppose that a task is readied having a higher priority than the running one. In this instance a task swap takes place. The running task is returned to the head-of-queue position, its place being taken by the new task.

To support this strategy each task is given a specific priority; all tasks above the base level must have individual, different, priority setting. Base-level tasks may have the same priority level, being executed in round-robin fashion.

Assume that a currently executing task reaches completion. It then stops, indicating a 'not-ready' status; only at the next 'tick' does the executive regain control of the system. To minimize this 'wasted' time it makes sense to have a short tick period. Yet this may cause problems. The tick, remember, is updated on an interrupt from the real-time clock. This results in the current task being replaced by the tick handler (a 'context switch'). All current information must be saved before this handler is loaded up and set going, which not only takes time, but contributes nothing to processing performance. So, as the tick period is reduced, the available task processing time also falls. Ultimately, for very high rates, tasks would never be executed; the processor would spend its time just servicing the tick (a ridiculous situation, of course).

Choosing the timing rate of the system isn't easy. It is determined by both response requirements *and* scheduling methods. For fast real-time applications it usually lies in the range 1–100 milliseconds.

5.4.4 By-passing the scheduler

Under most circumstances all tasking control is handled by the scheduler. For instance, when an interrupt occurs, the interrupt handler only readies the appropriate task; it doesn't activate it – that is the responsibility of the scheduler. So far, so good. But this could lead to an unacceptable delay between requesting service and getting it. And unfortunately there are situations where this cannot be tolerated, e.g. system exceptions. To cope with these we completely by-pass the operating system and go directly to a special interrupt handling routine. What this routine does depends on the system application, design and the exception condition which invoked it in the first place. But great care and thought need to be put into its construction.

5.4.5 Code sharing and re-entrancy

The most widely used building blocks of modern programs are the subprogram (for high-level languages) and the subroutine (assembly language programming). These are invoked as and when required by running tasks. Now, in a multitasking system, each application process (task) is written separately and the object code loaded into separate sections of ROM. As a result tasks may appear to be independent, but this isn't true. They are interlinked via their common program building blocks, the subprograms (procedures or functions) or subroutines.

Consider the following scenario. A general procedure (e.g. one that is available for use by all tasks) uses a specified set of RAM locations. It is invoked by task 1, which begins to manipulate data in the RAM locations. Task 1 is pre-empted by task 2, which then also calls the same procedure and operates on the same data locations. Some time later task 1 resumes, being totally unaware that the RAM data has been altered – and chaos ensues. To avoid this problem each task (process) is allocated its own private stack and workspace. All subprogram parameters are normally kept on the stack, all local variables residing in the workspace. Now shared code can be used with safety because each task keeps its own data to itself. Such code is said to be 're-entrant'.

5.5 Control of shared resources – mutual exclusion

5.5.1 The problem of using shared resources

In a single CPU system the processor is a shared resource. Now there aren't contention problems when sharing it between the various processes; everything is controlled by the scheduler. But this isn't true for the rest of the system. Different tasks may well want to use the same hardware or store area simultaneously. Without controlling access to these common resources, contention problems soon arise. Consider, for instance, what can happen in the following situation. Here a control algorithm is executed at regular intervals, interrupt-driven by a timer process (Figure 5.23). Part of the data used comes from the coefficient's data pool. The

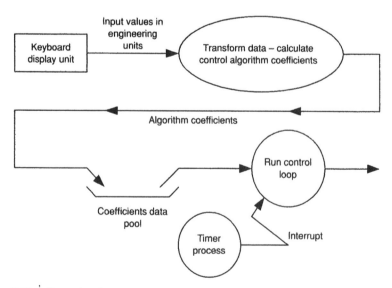

Figure 5.23 Shared data between processes.

coefficient values are derived from engineering units input from a keyboard-display unit. Now, the problem here is a simple one. What would be the result if the control loop was activated while the coefficients were being updated? Up to 8 bytes may be used for each coefficient; yet it might be that only one or two can be changed at a time. Therefore a value might only be part-updated when a task switch takes place. If this happened the results could well be disastrous.

How can we tackle this problem? In very general terms the solution is clear. Make sure that a shared resource can be accessed by one, and only one, process at any one time. That is, implement a 'mutual exclusion' strategy. The difficulties come, however, when we try to institute specific methods.

5.5.2 Flawed solutions to the mutual exclusion question

Flawed solutions are those which:

● Appear to work, but fail under certain circumstances.

● Are very restrictive in operation.

● Are highly inefficient or extremely difficult to implement.

Such offerings are not acceptable for real-time systems.

It may seem a negative (or even pointless) exercise to discuss techniques which aren't used. Not so. By understanding these methods and their drawbacks it is easier to appreciate what structures *do* work.

In the following sections the use of flags and control variables for mutual exclusion are covered. Concepts only are discussed; no programs are given. However, implementations in pseudocode form can be seen in Deitel [DEI84] and Leigh [LEI88].

The single-flag approach

Imagine that, to control access to a shared (or 'common') item, we put it in a special room (Figure 5.24). A gatehouse is provided for each task wishing to use the

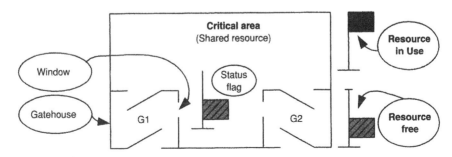

Figure 5.24 | The single-flag approach.

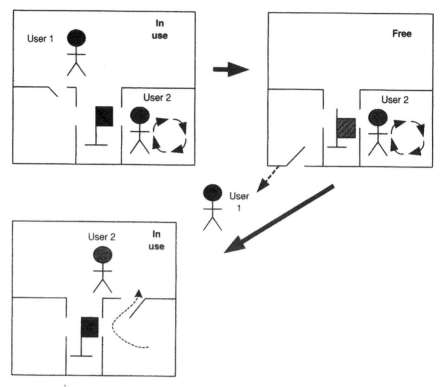

Figure 5.25 | Mutual exclusion in action (single-flag method).

resource; this is its means of access. An indicator flag is used to show whether or not a task is in the room (in the 'critical area'). The flag can only be seen, raised or lowered from within a gatehouse (any gatehouse, in fact).

Assume initially that the critical area is empty, the flag being down. User 1, who wishes to use the resource, enters his gatehouse. He first checks the flag status. Finding it down, he knows that the resource is free for use. Now, as a separate, distinct, activity, he raises it, and then enters the critical area. At this point user 2 arrives on the scene, also wanting access to the shared item (Figure 5.25). He enters his gatehouse and checks the flag. As it is up (resource in use), he waits here, constantly rechecking the flag status. Eventually user 1 leaves, his last job being to lower the flag, indicating 'resource available'. When user 2 next checks the resource status, he finds it free. Consequently he raises the flag and enters the critical area, now being its sole owner.

This all looks pretty good. Mutual exclusion has been successfully achieved using a fairly simple mechanism. Or has it? Consider the following scenario. The resource is free when user 1 enters gatehouse 1. He checks the flag. Finding it down, he turns to raise it. Just at this moment user 2 enters his gatehouse and checks the flag; he also finds it down. So, as far as he is concerned, his way is clear to enter the critical area. What he doesn't realize is that user 1 is also doing the same thing. Clash!

Here protection breaks down because there is a time lapse between user 1 checking the flag and then changing its status. In computing terms, for a single-processor system, this is equivalent to:

- Loading a variable into a processor register.
- Checking its status.
- If the variable says 'free' then change to 'not free', else recheck.

During this sequence, user 1 (i.e. task 1) could very well be pre-empted. If that happens *after* loading up the variable but *before* changing its status, then we may have problems (assuming the status is 'free'). Suppose that the pre-empting task is user 2. It checks the flag status, finds the resource free, and enters the critical area. When task 1 resumes, it also finds that the resource is free, enters the critical area – and so the mutual exclusion mechanism has failed. Failures are much more likely in multiprocessor systems as such designs have true task concurrency.

A safe, single-flag mutual exclusion technique – the turn-flag

Let's see if a modified flag operation can achieve safe mutual exclusion. The flag, instead of showing resource free/in-use, now indicates which task can *next* use the resource (Figure 5.26). It retains this number until the task designated by NEXT has finished with the resource. Only then is it changed. Consider the situation shown in Figure 5.26. Assume initially that the turn-flag shows '1', i.e. task 1 has been given the right to use the shared resource. Task 2 enters its gatehouse, finds the resource unavailable, and waits. Periodically it checks the turn-flag condition. At some later point, task 1, now wanting to use the resource, also enters its gatehouse. It sees the turn-flag set to '1', and therefore proceeds into the critical area. When it has finished it leaves this area, returning to the gatehouse. It then sets the turn-flag to '2', and leaves the area entirely. Task 2, on checking the flag status, finds that it is now authorized to use the shared resource. It therefore enters its critical area. If, by any chance, task 1 returns during this interval, it is blocked out as the turn-flag shows '2'. Ergo, mutual exclusion has been achieved.

Unfortunately there is a price to be paid for this. In the first place, tasks must go in strict alternate sequence (the 'lock-step synchronization' problem). This is usually inefficient, becoming a major problem as the number of tasks increases (like the cyclic scheduling problem). Second, each task may spend considerable time merely checking flag status. During this time no useful work is done, a very inefficient system. Finally, if a task halts within its critical section, it completely blocks access to the shared resource.

So the single-flag solution is unacceptable on the grounds of security or efficiency. The inefficiency of the single turn-flag solution is due to use of a *single common* variable. Perhaps a two-variable (two-flag) solution will work?

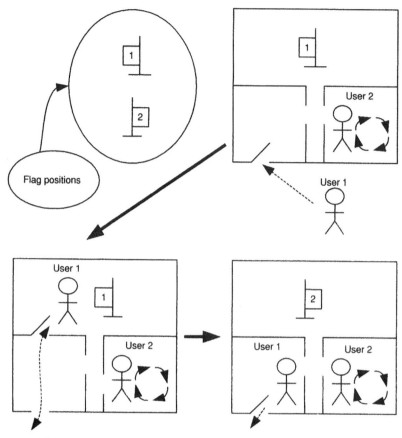

Figure 5.26 | The turn-flag solution.

The basic two-flag solution

In this approach, each user is given his own flag, located in the appropriate gatehouse. It is used to show access requests for the shared facility ('request to enter the critical area → flag up, no request → flag down'), Figure 5.27. Assume the critical area is free; both flags are down. User 1 enters his gatehouse and *first* raises his flag. He then checks the status of the user 2 flag. Finding this down, he enters the critical area and proceeds to use the resource. When finished he leaves via the gatehouse, lowering the flag as he goes. After this user 2 may access the critical area; alternatively, user 1 may return to re-use the resource.

Assume now that, when user 1 is inside the critical area, user 2 wishes to access the shared resource. He first enters his gatehouse and raises his flag. Next he checks the user 1 flag; and finds it up. User 2 now waits in the gatehouse, constantly rechecking the user 1 flag status. When flag 1 is lowered he knows that it is safe to enter

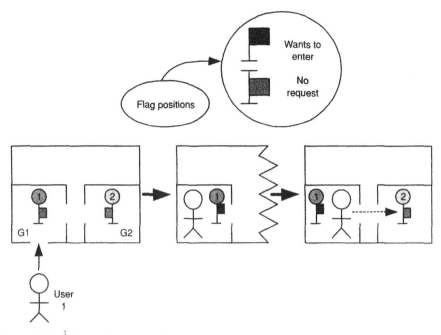

Figure 5.27 : The basic two-flag solution.

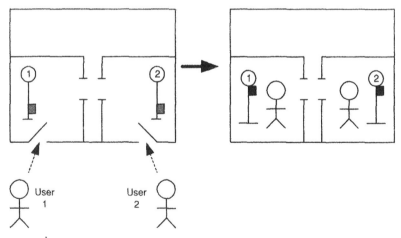

Figure 5.28 : Deadlock in a two-flag system.

his critical area. User 1, should he return, will find flag 2 raised; therefore he will wait his turn.

This seems very straightforward. Unfortunately it has a subtle flaw, a problem of deadlock (Figure 5.28). Assume that user 1 enters his gatehouse and raises flag 1. Before he has time to check flag 2, user 2 enters *his* gatehouse and raises his flag.

Both users check the flag conditions, find the resource unavailable, and go into a permanent wait condition. The system is now deadlocked and comes to a permanent halt.

One way out of this is to make each user periodically lower his flag, wait a short period of time, and then raise it again. This provides an 'access time window' for the other user, thus eliminating permanent deadlock. Flag checking is only carried out by an individual user while he has his own flag raised. It works as follows: suppose that both users are waiting (flags up) in their gatehouses. User 1 lowers his flag; user 2 happens to check during the same period. He sees that the resource is accessible, and so enters it. From this point on, operations are as described above.

Unfortunately, in solving one problem, we've introduced another one. Both users 1 and 2, while in their gatehouses, may operate at exactly the same speed, doing exactly the same things. Thus the lowering, raising and checking of flags are done in synchronism. Consequently, every time a flag check is carried out, both flags are up. Therefore neither user can get into the critical area!

This problem is called 'indefinite postponement', 'lockout' or 'starvation'. In practice it wouldn't continue forever; some timing jitter will always take the tasks out of step. What it *will* do is introduce an unpredictably long delay which, in critical real-time use, is not acceptable.

Deadlock and lockout avoidance – Dekker's algorithm

A solution to the deadlock and lockout problems is achieved by adding an extra flag to the system, the 'priority' flag (Figure 5.29). This is called Dekker's algorithm, in recognition of its designer. The priority flag is used *only* if there are simultaneous requests for access to the shared resource, its function being to resolve the contention issue. Otherwise operations are as described for the basic two-flag method.

Now examine what happens when both users make simultaneous requests using Dekker's algorithm. The two flags are raised at the same time (Figure 5.29a), each user then checking the status of the other request flag. Each user, on finding a raised flag, now checks the status of the priority flag (Figure 5.29b). Assume the priority flag shows '2', thus giving task 2 priority. While user 2 enters the critical area (Figure 5.29c) user 1 lowers his request flag. User 1 then continually checks the status of the priority flag, waiting for it to change to '1'.

When user 2 has finished with the resource he returns to his gatehouse, changing the priority flag setting on the way (Figure 5.29d). User 1, on the next check of the priority flag, finds it set to '1'. He first raises his flag, then checks the user 2 request flag status (Figure 5.29e). As it is still raised user 1 enters a wait-and-check state regarding flag 2. User 2 lowers the request flag (as described earlier) just before exiting the gatehouse (Figure 5.29f). Then, and only then, can user 1 enter the critical area. The contention problem has been eliminated.

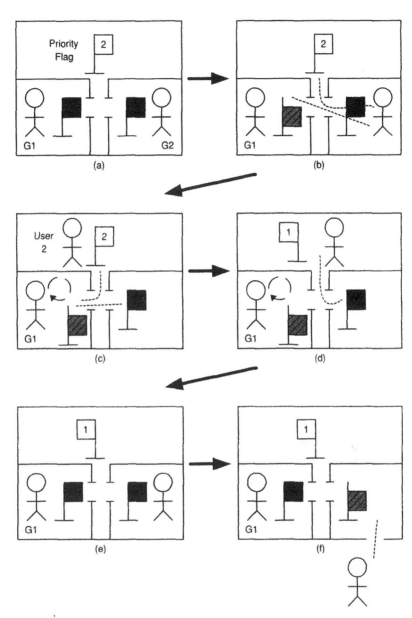

Figure 5.29 Deadlock and lockout avoidance using request and priority flags.

Dekker's algorithm provides a safe and secure mutual exclusion mechanism. Unfortunately the method becomes unwieldy as the number of tasks increases. Therefore it isn't usually used in such cases, especially for real-time systems. So, we still have to design a safe, secure and *efficient* mutual exclusion mechanism.

5.5.3 The semaphore

All flag methods considered so far fail for one reason. That is, while one user is testing a flag status, the other may come along and change it *without* the first user seeing this change. How can we prevent this happening? The solution, fairly clearly, is to make testing and setting of flags an indivisible operation.

This problem was tackled by Dijkstra [DIJ65], who developed the concept of the 'semaphore'. In very simple terms, this is a program data item which is used to decide whether task execution can proceed or should be suspended. There are two semaphore types, the 'binary' and the 'general' or 'counting' semaphore. Both work on the same principles.

The binary semaphore

The binary semaphore is used extensively as a control mechanism within programs. As described here it functions as a mutual exclusion (contention elimination) device, one semaphore being allocated to each shared resource. It can also be used for other functions, as will be seen later.

The concept of the semaphore is shown in Figure 5.30. The shared resource – in this case a single parking space – is housed in a protected area, with access through a single entry point. Located at this point is an access control interface which consists of a:

- 'Request' pushbutton. A user presses this to signal the car park attendant that entry is required to the car park.
- 'Finish' pushbutton. The user presses this on exit to inform the attendant that the car park is once again free.
- Loudspeaker. The car park attendant uses this to answer the customer's request.

The purpose of the access control mechanism is to ensure that one, and only one, user can enter the parking area at any one time. A binary semaphore is the software equivalent of this access control mechanism; and for 'user' read 'task'.

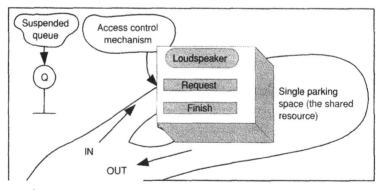

Figure 5.30 The binary semaphore concept.

Assume initially that the car park – the resource – is free. The first operation is to provide the attendant with this status information (assume that the parking space cannot be seen from the control room). Its software counterpart is the initialization of the semaphore. Similarly, the 'attendant' functions are provided as part of the OS software.

When a user wants to use the resource he approaches the barrier and presses the button. In semaphore terminology this is defined to be a 'wait on the semaphore', the WAIT operation. As the resource is free the attendant answers 'pass'; the user then enters the protected area.

At some point the user will leave and so vacate the parking space. On exit he signals this to the access control mechanism by pressing the 'finish' button. This is defined to be the SIGNAL operation. The result is to update the attendant's status information to show that the car park is once more vacant.

Now examine the case where the resource is being used when an access request is made. In response to WAIT? the requesting user is made to wait (corresponding to a task *suspension*). Once the current user has finished with the resource he leaves the area, generating a SIGNAL as he goes. As a result the control mechanism records that the resource is free. But now, subsequent events follow a different pattern. Instead of updating the attendant's status information, a 'pass' message is issued to the waiting user (equivalent to one task waking up another one). This authorizes the user to enter the protected area; from this point on events proceed as described earlier.

In normal circumstances the waiting task would be the one to be activated. Unfortunately, it is possible for another – higher priority – task to arrive before the resource becomes free. This would then pre-empt the waiting (suspended) task, further delaying its execution. To prevent this:

- A resource queue is provided.
- Tasks wishing to access a semaphore currently in use are suspended and queued (usually on a first-come, first-served basis).
- The exiting task reactivates the task at the head of the queue.

Only when the suspended queue is empty is direct entry available to other tasks (Figure 5.31).

Now for some very important points:

- Creating a semaphore and associating it with a specific resource are – conceptually – two quite different operations. However, it is essential to correctly pair these up. In practice this would be done as part of the creation/initialization procedures.
- In the operation described so far there is no concept of 'seeing' the state of the semaphore. What the requester really does is to ask 'can I use the resource?' (and if the answer is no, then the requesting task is *automatically* suspended).

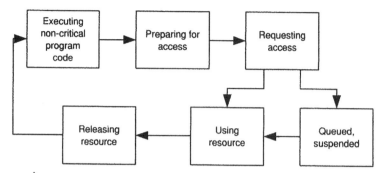

Figure 5.31 Task states when using semaphores.

- A suspended user never repeats the request, but gets woken up automatically by the system (compare this with the use of flags to check on resource availability).

- WAIT and SIGNAL operations form a pair. Regrettably the basic mechanism *does not* enforce this pairing. Not only that, but nothing prevents SIGNAL being called before WAIT (which can lead to very unusual behaviour). Note these points well.

- Just because a resource has a semaphore associated with it does *not* guarantee protection. Safeguards can be by-passed if there is a 'back-door' route into the protected area (using a resource which is declared to be global to the program, for example).

As stated earlier, an individual semaphore is developed for each individual controlled resource. To identify the resource in question its name is given (conceptually) as a parameter of the semaphore operations. For instance, assuming the resource contains the set of control coefficients referred to earlier, we have:

- WAIT (coefficients)
- SIGNAL (coefficients)

A binary semaphore has two values only, '0' or '1'. An '0' shows that the resource is in use, the '1' indicating that it is free. In its original form, the semaphore operations are:

```
(*Part of Procedure 'WAIT' on semaphore 'Coefficients'*)
 IF (Coefficients=1) THEN
   Coefficients:=0;
 ELSE Suspend Task;
 END
(*Part of Procedure 'SIGNAL' on semaphore 'Coefficients'*)
 IF (Task Waiting) THEN
   Wakeup Task;
 ELSE Coefficients:=1;
 END
```

Within a program these would be used as and when needed, as follows:

```
BEGIN
  ProgramStatements;
  WAIT (Coefficients);
  UseSharedResource;
  SIGNAL (Coefficients);
  ProgramStatements;
END
```

WAIT and SIGNAL operations are defined to be 'primitive' types, i.e. each one is indivisible. In other words, once the WAIT (SIGNAL) process is started, the sequence of machine instructions cannot be interrupted. This is essential, otherwise we'll just end up with the problems of the single-flag exclusion mechanism. Providing indivisibility isn't an easy task; it may pose real implementation difficulties. But they *have* to be overcome for the semaphore to work. Further, these operations must be protected by the operating system, not the programmer.

In practice the binary semaphore can be implemented as a single byte or even a bit within a byte. Some processors support this construct by having a single 'set-and-test bit' instruction. Without this, indivisible ('atomic') operation is attained typically by disabling interrupts before carrying out semaphore actions. In multiprocessor systems this isn't sufficient; a hardware lockout mechanism is needed.

Note in passing that WAIT and SIGNAL are also called P and V, derived from the Dutch *Passeren* (to pass) and *Vrygeven* (to release).

The general or counting semaphore

Suppose that our single shared resource is restructured so that it now consists of a number of items. Each item is identical, providing a specific service. For instance, it could be a set of data stores, used to store objects for later collection by other users. Given this arrangement it is safe to let more than one user into the controlled area, provided they don't access the *same* store. To support this the semaphore construct is altered so that:

- It has a range of values (say 0 to 5); initially it is set to the maximum value (5).

- Each value corresponds to a specific instance of the provided resource, zero indicating all devices in use.

- When a user wants to access the store it first checks that the resource is available (not a zero value). If access is granted it decrements the semaphore value by 1 (one), and proceeds to use the resource facilities.

- When the user has finished, it increments the semaphore value by 1 and exits the store.

```
(*Part of Procedure 'WAIT on CAN queue'*)
 IF (Q ueue > 0) THEN
   Q ueue := (Q ueue 1);
 ELSE SuspendTask;
 END;

(*Part of Procedure 'SIGNAL on CAN queue'*)
 IF (TaskWaiting) THEN
   WakeupTask;
 ELSE Q ueue := (Q ueue + 1);
 END;
```

The value of Q ueuecontrols access to the resource and defines the item which can be used; it is never allowed to go negative.

5.5.4   The monitor

The binary semaphore has been widely used to enforce mutual exclusion policies. It is easy to understand, simple to use and straightforward to implement. Fine. But it has one particular weakness, more to do with its use rather than its construction. Most programs which use semaphores implement them as and when they are needed. Consequently they tend to be scattered around the code, often proving to be difficult to find. Moreover, with the semaphore, there isn't a concept of ownership – P and V aren't encapsulated. In effect, P can be done by one task, V by another (which, of course, may well be exactly what you want to do).

In a small design this isn't too much of a problem, but the same can't be said of large ones. As a result, the designer *must* keep track of all mutual exclusion activities. Later on, in the maintenance phase, scattered mutual exclusion constructs can make life very difficult indeed. In such circumstances, 'simple' program modifications can produce some strange side-effects.

What we want then is a replacement for the binary semaphore which, in program terms:

- Provides protection for critical regions of code.
- Encapsulates data *together* with operations applicable to this data.
- Is highly visible.
- Is easy to use.
- Is difficult to misuse.
- Simplifies the task of proving the correctness of a program.

The most important and widely used construct meeting these criteria is the *monitor*. This owes its origins to Dijkstra [DIJ71], then Brinch Hansen [BRI72], the

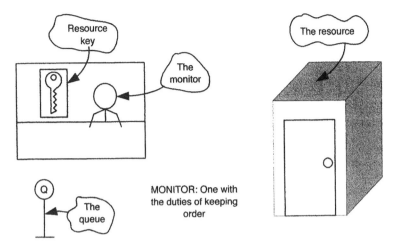

Figure 5.32 Essential elements of the monitor.

final definitive paper coming from Hoare [HOA74]. Fundamentally it functions as a system policeman, keeping order in the use of shared resources. Contact between program processes and shared resources isn't done directly; instead it goes through the monitor. This, as we'll see, allows us to meet the criteria laid out above.

Let's start by looking at the concepts and implementation of the monitor, using a very simple analogy. The essential elements of the construct are shown in Figure 5.32. First we have the resource which is to be shared out. This can be used only by the holder of the resource 'door key'; the key itself is managed by the monitor. By having one key, only one user can access the resource at any one time. This, fundamentally, is how mutual exclusion is imposed. Requests to use the resource are made via monitor-provided access functions; no *direct* use can be made of the resource itself. The function of the queue will become clear later.

A change of situation: the resource is free (depicted by 'key in', Figure 5.33) and a process wishes to use it. The user requests access to the resource from the monitor; this responds by giving him the resource key. He now enters the resource, knowing there will be no interference from other users (it can be seen that the resource is busy because the key is out). When the user finishes he returns the key to the monitor – who hangs it up – and then vacates the area.

Now visualize the case where a requester (user 2) arrives when user 1 is using the resource (Figure 5.34). The monitor checks the key status. Finding it out, he instructs user 2 to WAIT at the queue sign (this is called the 'external' queue). No further action occurs until user 1 returns the key, releasing the resource. With the key 'in', the monitor SIGNALs user 2 to take it and enter the resource. Thus user 2 gains the key, knowing that the monitor will handle resource contention problems. Any further requesters arriving during this period are lined up in the external queue, generally being serviced on a first-in first-out basis.

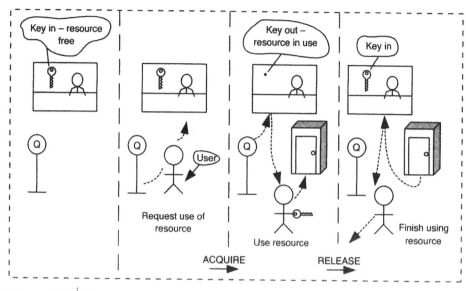

Figure 5.33 | Resource access via the monitor.

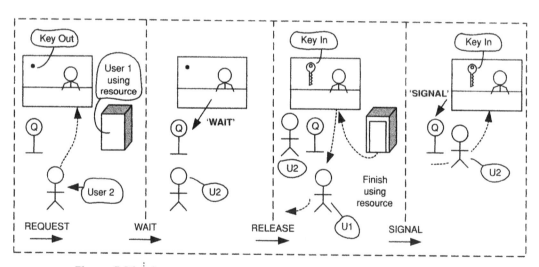

Figure 5.34 | Access request – resource in use.

So far, so good. What we've described are the basics of the monitor, incorporating a single resource. But practical systems contain more than just one shared item. In such cases, separate monitors may be provided for each distinct facility (effective in small systems). A second approach is to use a single monitor to control all shared facilities. A final option is to allocate one monitor to each logically related group of functions. Access to the resource bank is made through the appropriate

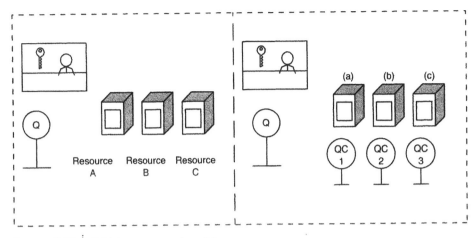

Figure 5.35 Multiple resources and condition queues.

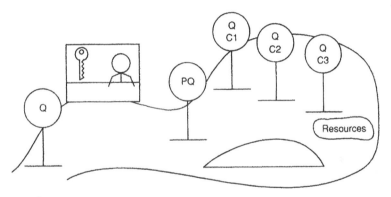

Figure 5.36 Condition and priority queues.

monitor (Figure 5.35), so ensuring visibility and security of operation. Now this raises an interesting point. Suppose a user goes into the controlled area but then finds that the resource isn't available. What should he do? If he waits for it to come free he blocks all other users during the waiting period. This clearly is inefficient, though on some applications it may be acceptable. Hoare's solution is to have a set of queues in the controlled area (loosely, 'inside the monitor'), one for each individual resource. These are called 'condition' queues (Figure 5.35). It also turns out that another queue is needed inside the resource area, the 'priority' queue, PQ (Figure 5.36). How does all this work (and please bear in mind that only one user is allowed to be active at any one time)? Suppose, for instance, user 1 gets the key and accesses resource A, Figure 5.37. He then finds that, for some reason, the resource cannot be used. To free the system he first returns the key and then joins the appropriate condition queue. Now, as the key is 'in', any other user may be granted access to

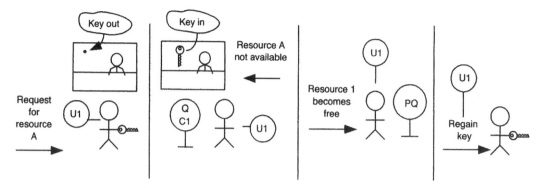

Figure 5.37 | Use of condition and priority queues.

the controlled resource area. A number of outcomes are possible, depending on the following conditions:

- No additional request.
- A new external request.
- Two users waiting on conditions.

No additional request

Assume that no other user arrives begging service from the monitor. User 1 remains in his queue while resource A is tied up. When it eventually becomes free he moves to the priority queue, at its head. From here he can request reuse of the resource from the monitor, which, as the key is in, the monitor will grant. User 1 then regains the key and carries on with his task.

A new external request

Suppose a second user (user 2) arrives while 1 is waiting in his condition queue. This user wishes to enter resource B, not A. User 1 isn't active at this moment, so the monitor gives the key to 2, who now proceeds to use the resource. During this period, 1 continues to check the status of resource A. Once it becomes available, user 1 goes to the priority queue (as before). It then signals the monitor that it is ready to resume its task. However, as the key is out, the monitor merely notes the signal; no action is carried out. What does result, though, is a change in the consequential behaviour of the system. When user 2 vacates the controlled area the monitor doesn't check the external queue; it gives the key directly to user 1. That is, the internal queue is given priority over the external one (hence its name). This arrangement guarantees that tasks waiting inside cannot be blocked out by the arrival of new requests.

Two users waiting on conditions

It still isn't obvious why we need a priority queue. But consider what happens if two users end up waiting inside the monitor (in different condition queues, of course). Let's further suppose that both resources become free while a third user has the key. How is the monitor supposed to decide which of the waiting users should next receive the key? This question is resolved by the priority queue. Users move into the queue as resources become available; they are then served in the order in which they arrived.

Clearly the monitor is more complex than the semaphore. In practice it would normally be implemented using a number of core subprograms, as follows:

```
/* Allow a task to gain control of the monitor*/
GetKey;
/* Define that a task has finished with the shared resource*/
ReturnKey;
/* Control operation of the condition and priority queues*/
WaitInMo nito r(Monitor Shared Resource,
                            Monitor Signal SignalName);
SignalTo Moino r(Monitor Shared Resource,
                            MonitorSignal SignalName);
```

Note that it is assumed that mechanisms are available for creating and initializing each monitor object (these are very much language-dependent).

Let us look at a simple outline example of the use of a monitor. Here is the (pseudocode) implementation of a pool, designed to store a single data item.

```
Class PoolMonitor {
private
/* Data structure for the pool */
/* Private functions GetKey,
        ReleaseKey, etc.*/
public
  PutInPool (TheData);
  GetFromPool(TheData);
}; /* end Class PoolMonitor */
```

The PutInPool and GetFromPool functions would have the following form:

```
PutInPool (TheData) {
  GetKey;
  /* TransferData*/
  ReturnKey;
}
```

```
GetFromPool (TheData) {
  GetKey;
  /* TransferData*/
  ReturnKey;
}

GetKey{
/* KeyOut is a Boolean */
  if (KeyOut) ben
    SuspendTaskInMonitorEntryQueue;
  Else
    KeyOut = True;
}

void ReturnKey{
  KeyOut = False;
  AwakenTaskInMonitorEntryQueue;
}
```

Objects of PoolMonitor class are declared in a conventional manner, e.g.:

```
PoolMonitor ControlCoefficients;
```

Then to send data to or get data from the pool, the following constructs would be used:

```
ControlCoefficients.PutInPool (SetPointValue);
ControlCoefficients.GetFromPool (SetPointValue);
```

This example should make it clear that the key can be released *only* by the user who got it in the first place. In other words, once a task acquires a monitor object, it has exclusive ownership of it. Thus even if there are multiple Put and Get calls spread across a number of tasks, mutual exclusion is always maintained.

5.5.5 Resource contention – the deadlock problem in detail

In this section we'll look at deadlocks in more detail, first by reviewing why and how they occur. Once this is understood then it is only a small step to work out how to deal with the problem. A number of solutions are possible, some complex, some simple. You will see, however, that only a few are suitable for use in real-time (and especially fast and/or critical) systems.

Let us begin by considering the structure of a typical small control system of Figure 5.38. Here we have:

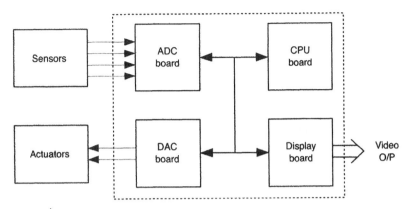

Figure 5.38 Small control system – hardware structure.

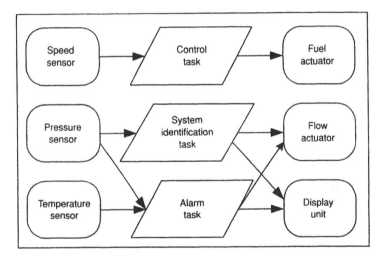

Figure 5.39 Small control system – basic software task structure.

- A set of sensor signals fed in via a single multichannel ADC board.
- A set of actuator control signals fed out via a single multichannel DAC board.
- All display information generated by a video display board.

The software in this system is designed to provide multitasking operation. In its simplest form, the relationship between the system devices and the software tasks is shown in Figure 5.39. Here there are three tasks: Control, System Identification (SI) and Alarm. The control task is a commonplace closed-loop one. It reads in speed sensor data, computes a control signal and sends this out to the fuel actuator. The role of the system identification task is to mathematically identify some part

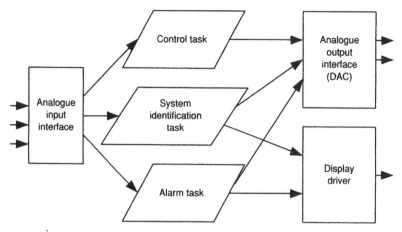

Figure 5.40 | Small control system — complete task-level software structure.

of the physical system. This it does by generating an output signal to stimulate the system via the flow actuator, 'simultaneously' reading the response via a pressure sensor. The alarm task is self-explanatory. From this diagram it can be seen that the control task is functionally independent of the other two. It is tempting also to think that these are independent from the software point of view. However, a more complete diagram of the software structure, Figure 5.40, shows this isn't the case. Before running through its operation, however, let us introduce a new tasking model feature: the passive software machine (denoted by a rectangle). This is *not* a schedulable item; it is used primarily to house shared software facilities. In effect these items become available to all tasks, which call on them as and when required. From a practical point of view they could be implemented as a Java package, a C++ object, a C file, etc. Figure 5.40 contains three passive objects, Analogue Input Interface, Analogue Output Interface and Display Driver.

Now let us review the operation of the Control and SI tasks. The Control task, when activated, first selects the speed input channel of the ADC board. It then starts conversion, selects the fuel actuator output channel, reads the digitized input, computes the output signal and writes it to the DAC. When the SI task is started it first selects the flow actuator output channel, then selects the pressure input channel of the ADC. At this point it generates a stimulus signal and sends it to the DAC. It then starts conversion and, when completed, reads in and stores the input value. After N reads it computes the system identification polynomial.

Note well: tasks which are functionally independent (e.g. Control and System Identification) may be coupled together by software functions or resources (here the passive objects). For safe operation mutual exclusion is normally provided within the access mechanisms of shared resources. Such resources are said to be 'non-preemptive'.

Using non-pre-emption, however, has a number of consequences, some quite cata-strophic. Let us start by looking at a normal error-free situation, Figure 5.41. This demonstrates the acquisition and release of shared non-pre-emptive resources. It also shows what happens when a task tries to access a resource already held by another (suspended) task. Given the right set of circumstances the system could run for long periods without faults appearing. We could, given the natural optimism of engineers, believe that all is well with the design. But look at the situation depicted in Figure 5.42. The sequence of events is that:

- At t_1 the Control task acquires the ADC.

- Shortly afterwards there is a task switch; the SI task begins to run.

- At t_2 the SI task acquires the DAC.

- At t_3 the SI task tries to acquire the ADC. As this is held by the Control task, the request fails. The SI task is now suspended and the Control task reawakened.

- At t_4 the Control task tries to acquire the DAC. As this is held by the SI task, the request fails. The Control task is now suspended.

- These two tasks are now deadlocked – neither can proceed.

Note that the other tasks in the system could function perfectly well provided they don't want to use either the ADC or the DAC. This, in fact, illustrates one more important aspect of multitasking, especially in complex, large systems. It may be some time before we realize that a deadlock situation exists; its presence is masked by the amount of ongoing activity.

The sequence of events given in Figure 5.42 can be shown in a different way, Figure 5.43, demonstrating clearly how deadlock has been produced. Here a task may hold onto a resource while it waits to acquire a second one (logically enough called a 'hold and wait' situation). Note how resource sharing results in a simple form of circular dependency. It is quite easy to see here how the dependency circle gets formed.

In larger systems dependency circles can arise in a slightly different fashion, Figure 5.44. In Figure 5.44a there is no dependency between tasks (based on resource sharing, that is). In (b) there is dependency, best illustrated in Figure 5.44c.

Suppose that the tasks are run round-robin fashion, starting with task T_1. At some stage of program execution this task acquires resource R_1. Whilst it is holding R_1 a task swap takes place; T_1 is suspended and T_2 activated. This starts executing and, in doing so, acquires R_2. It later tries to use R_1 but this, unfortunately, is locked out. As a result the task suspends, being replaced by T_3. If the same pattern of operation is repeated T_3 will fail to get resource R_2, and will therefore suspend. It will be replaced by T_1. At some point the task will eventually finish with resource R_1, thus enabling T_2 to execute correctly. Once T_2 has released the locked resource T_3 can be executed.

The result of this dependency is reduced performance, but at least there is no deadlock. Now consider that (for some reason) T_1 needs to use resource R_3. The resulting dependency relationship is shown in Figure 5.44d. It is clear that given the right set of circumstances, deadlock will occur.

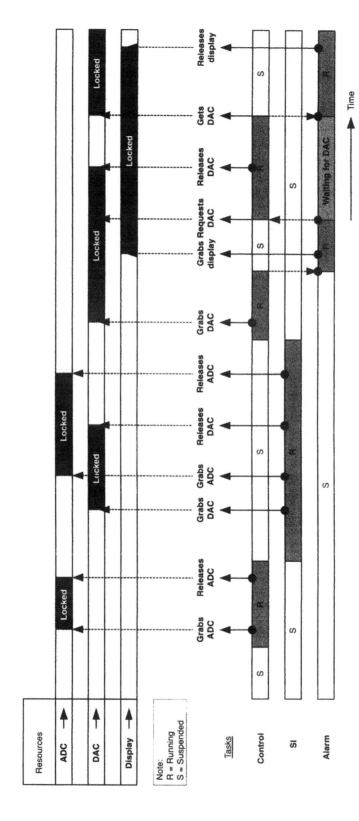

Figure 5.41 Task interaction — error-free situation.

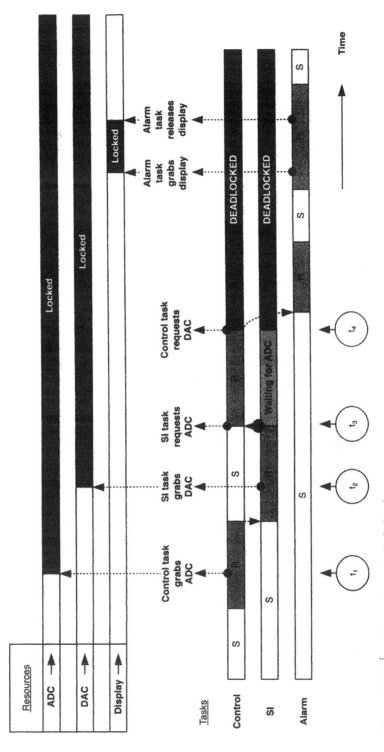

Figure 5.42 Task interaction – deadlock situation.

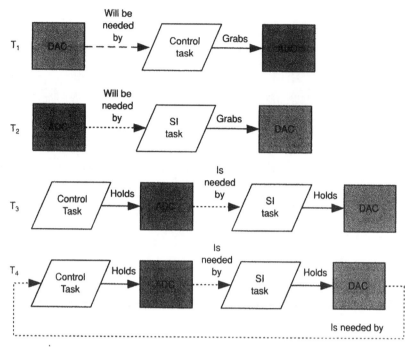

Figure 5.43 | Simple circular dependency due to resource hold and wait.

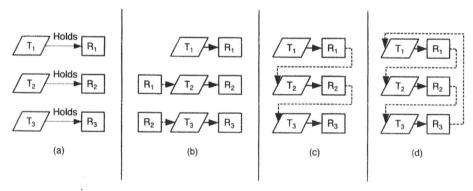

Figure 5.44 | Showing circular dependency developing.

A dependency circle may occur only in rare situations; moreover the dependency may not be obvious from the design diagrams. This should tell you that it makes good sense to limit the number of tasks in a multitasking system.

The key question here is 'what conditions are *necessary* before deadlock can occur?' These are listed in Figure 5.45. But note that these by themselves are not *sufficient* for deadlock to arise.

CONDITION	NAME
A task has exclusive use of resources	Mutual exclusion
A task can hold on to a resource(s) whilst waiting for another resource	Hold and wait
A circular dependency of tasks and resources is set up	Circular waiting
A task never releases a resource until it is completely finished with it	No resource pre-emption
Once deadlocked, the situation is non-recoverable	Non-recovery

Figure 5.45 Deadlock – necessary pre-conditions.

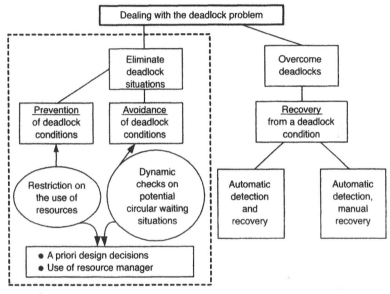

Figure 5.46 Strategies for dealing with deadlocks.

Summarizing: deadlock can occur only if all four conditions are satisfied simultaneously. However, even in the best of designs we cannot guarantee that, over the life of a system, deadlocks *won't* occur (poorly implemented modifications may destroy the quality of the original work). In some situations deadlocks cannot be easily or simply broken; the processor may enter a permanent deadlock state. Hence, without a recovery mechanism, we can lose control of part or all of the processor system. Therefore, for critical systems, some form of error-recovery action *must* be implemented. Which recovery strategies are applied will depend on the application – the most commonly used measures are discussed below

5.5.6 Dealing with deadlocks

There are two basic ways to handle the deadlock problem, Figure 5.46. First, make sure that it just isn't possible to get into a deadlock situation. Use prevention or avoidance methods. Second, accept that deadlocks may occur but take steps to overcome the problem.

To prevent deadlocks, we must ensure that at least *one* of the conditions listed in Figure 5.45 cannot arise. This requires that we make *a priori* design decisions concerning the use of resources. For complex systems we may have to provide a software resource manager (which could be implemented as a monitor).

Avoidance is based primarily on controlling what happens at run-time. The key is to guarantee that the run-time behaviour doesn't lead to circular dependencies. Central to this is a knowledge of:

- Resource/task relationships.
- Resources claimed and in use.
- Resources allocated to tasks but not yet claimed ('preclaimed').
- Resources available for use.

Some form of resource manager will be needed to assess system status and take appropriate action. Such operations must, of course, be performed dynamically as the code executes. For fast systems with frequent task switches the associated run-time overhead is likely to be substantial (and probably unacceptable). As a result deadlock avoidance is rarely used in real-time systems.

Overcoming deadlocks with the assistance of manual recovery techniques may be applicable to desktop computing operations. It is not, though, a serious contender for use in fast and/or embedded applications. Needed here are fully automatic detection and recovery mechanisms. For hard–fast systems this will normally involve watchdog timer activated methods (a topic covered in the section on critical systems). In general deadlock recovery should be seen as a last resort action, a 'get out of trouble' provision. Thus to handle deadlocks we usually rely on prevention as the primary mechanism, with recovery as a last line of defence.

Now to look specifically at deadlock prevention. We can apply a number of policies (Figure 5.47):

- Allow simultaneous resource sharing.
- Permit resource pre-emption.
- Control resource allocation to tasks.

These may be applied individually or in concert. Let us consider each in turn.

Allow simultaneous sharing of resources

With simultaneous sharing, tasks are allowed to access resources whenever they want to; there is no mutual exclusion. This, whilst simplicity itself, is generally unacceptable in any form of critical system; the dangers of unwanted task interference speak for themselves. There is, though, another way of dealing with the access problem: make tasks queue up in order to use the resource. This technique

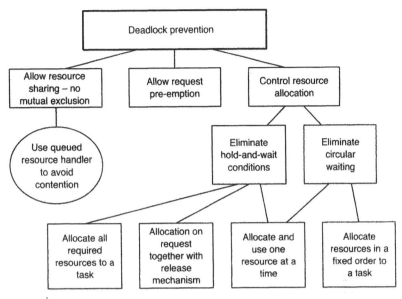

Figure 5.47 Prevention of deadlocks.

is frequently used with, for example, shared printers, plotters, network interfaces and the like. It is normally implemented by means of a queued resource handler. From the tasks' point of view such sharing is – or appears to be – simultaneous (though from the job perspective it is entirely sequential).

Implicit in the approach is that time is not especially pressing.

Permit resource pre-emption

With resource pre-emption a resource held (locked) by a suspended task can be retrieved for use by the running task. Clearly this approach, like simultaneous sharing, can lead to dangerous situations and must be used carefully. However, there are situations where it *can* work effectively and safely. This is useful, for instance, when looking at the contents of shared data stores or checking the status of I/O devices. The following scenario demonstrates the technique in action. Task A makes a read access to a data store and locks it. Some time later it suspends, being replaced by task B. During execution B finds that it wishes to read the contents of the data store. Even though this resource is locked the OS permits the read to be carried out. In effect the resource is temporarily reallocated. However, should B try to *write* to the data store, the rules are changed (write access to a locked resource has the potential for generating chaos; thus it is disallowed). Task B finds the resource locked and so suspends on a wait condition.

From this description we can see that a resource manager is needed to make the technique work. Consequently the method imposes a complexity and time overhead which may cause problems in small and/or fast systems.

Control resource allocation

By controlling the allocation of resources it is possible to eliminate two problems: hold-and-wait and circular waiting. A number of techniques can be used; one which solves both problems is for a task to acquire and use only one resource at a time. This, though very secure, has a drawback when a task uses a number of resources; it may be impossible to accurately predict execution times. For example, when the Control task executes, its operational cycle is:

- Acquire ADC resource, process input signal, release ADC.
- Compute algorithm.
- Acquire DAC resource, write to output, release DAC.

Unfortunately, if the Control task cannot acquire a resource when it needs it, then unpredictable delays can occur. To minimize this problem resource holding times should be as short as possible (in other words, get in, carry out the job and get out as quickly as possible).

Other resource allocation techniques are applicable to *specific* situations, as detailed below.

Hold-and-wait prevention

Two methods can be used to ensure that tasks cannot hold onto a resource whilst waiting to acquire another one. The first – *allocation of all required resources* – simply allows a task to grab all needed resources simultaneously; there is no waiting for other resources. The method is simple, safe and effective; the downside is that it may significantly degrade the overall performance of the system.

A second method is *allocation on request*. Here a task requests the use of resources as it executes, gradually acquiring the required items. However, should it ask for a resource which happens to be locked, it suspends; at the same time it releases all resources currently in its possession. When next activated it tries to re-acquire the required set of resources.

Clearly this is a complex procedure having quite unpredictable timing behaviour. As such it is very unlikely to be used in real-time systems, especially in fast and/or critical applications.

Circular wait prevention – fixed-order allocation

It can be very useful – especially in large systems – to show the resource requirements of tasks in a table form. One example is that of Figure 5.48. From this it can be seen that task A needs (N) the Display and the UART, task B the ADC and the DAC, etc. The underlying principle of the *fixed-order allocation strategy* is that:

Task / Resource	Task A	Task B	Task C
4. ADC		Needed	Needed
3. DAC		Needed	Needed
2. Display	Needed		Needed
1. UART	Needed		

Figure 5.48 Example task–resource relationship.

Task / Resource	Task A			Task B			Task C		
	N	C	A	N	C	A	N	C	A
4. ADC				Y	Y	Y	Y		
3. DAC				Y	Y	Y	Y	Y	No
2. Display	Y						Y	Y	Y
1. UART	Y								

Key: N = Needed C = Claimed A = Allocated

Figure 5.49 Example of claim by order in action – I.

- A task, when activated, requests each resource individually when it requires it (a 'claim').
- If the resource is free it is allocated to the task.
- There is a defined claim order for resources.
- If a second resource is required, a second claim is issued (and so on for further resources). If at any time the first resource is completely finished with, it may be released.

Let us see how this works in practice, Figure 5.49.

As shown here the resources have been numbered 1–4. A task must start its claim operation beginning with the lowest number in its own set. Thus task A, when executing, will first claim (C) the UART; if it is free the resource is allocated (A). Likewise, task B's first claim is for the DAC, whilst task C's first request is for the Display.

Task \ Resource	Task A			Task B			Task C		
	N	C	A	N	C	A	N	C	A
4. ADC				Y	Y	Y	Y		
3. DAC				Y	Y	Y	Y		
2. Display	Y	Y	Y				Y		
1. UART	Y	Y	Y						

Figure 5.50 | Example of claim by order in action – 2.

The reason for ordering resources – an essential aspect of this method – becomes clear when a number of tasks compete for resources. Assume that task B is running and has acquired both the DAC and the ADC. At this point a task swap is made to C, which, at some later stage, acquires the Display. It then requests use of the DAC. However, this is locked by task B; the request fails. As a result task C *must* give up all resources it is holding; it then suspends. When next activated it once more tries to acquire the required set of resources.

From this description it can be seen that it is impossible for:

● Task B to hold the ADC whilst waiting to acquire the DAC, and simultaneously
● Task C to hold the DAC whilst waiting for the ADC.

Ergo, circular waiting has been prevented.

A different scenario is shown in Figure 5.50. Here both A and B are runnable; in this case both can execute concurrently without problem as there is no resource contention.

Some important points can be gleaned from the foregoing scenarios. First, the information contained in the task–resource table shows us which tasks can *always* execute concurrently. Second, it shows where resource contention *may* occur, resulting in task blocking. Now, these have important performance (timing) implications. When a task cannot acquire a resource it is forced to suspend and to give up any resources already allocated. Fine. But, given a multitasking shared-resource environment, *can* we predict when it will be able to acquire all its resources? This is difficult enough where the table is static (doesn't change with time). However, if tasks are created dynamically then things are much more complex; timing predictions may be filed under 'fiction'. Whilst fixed resource allocation may be effective in soft and/or slow systems, it is quite unsuitable for hard–fast applications.

5.5.7 The priority inversion problem – task blocking

Deadlock prevention is an essential factor in the design of real-time systems. Unfortunately, even when secure exclusion techniques are included, this may not be the end of our difficulties. In solving one problem – deadlock – we may introduce another one – *priority inversion*.

The basics of priority inversion can be explained easily by looking at the behaviour of a simple two-task (A and B) system. Suppose task A is using a locked resource when the scheduler decides to do a task swap. Assume also that the new task B wishes to use the resource held by A. On checking the access mechanism, it finds the resource unavailable, and will thus suspend. Mutual exclusion is working as planned. But what if B's priority is greater than A's? This makes no difference; B still gets blocked. The result is that the low-priority task A blocks the higher-priority one; B cannot proceed until A allows it to. The system behaves as if the priorities have reversed, a *priority inversion*. However, this behaviour is exactly what one would expect when mutual exclusion is used; there is nothing abnormal about it.

In a two-task system the performance deterioration is unlikely to be a great problem. But look at the following situation, Figure 5.51. Here is a four-task system, comprised (in order of priority) of tasks A, B, C, and D. The system also includes two shared resources, W and X. The following assumptions are made in order to simplify the explanation of system behaviour:

● Context switching (rescheduling) takes place only at tick time.

● Tasks can suspend at any time.

● Tasks can be readied at any time.

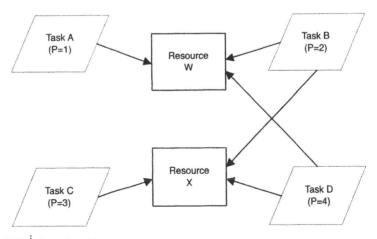

Figure 5.51 Example tasking structure.

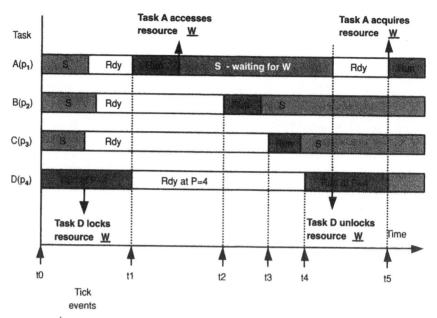

Figure 5.52 The priority inversion problem.

At time t_0 in Figure 5.52, task D is executing; all other tasks are suspended. Before the next tick occurs (at time t_1) D locks resource W. Note also that (by coincidence) all other tasks have been readied. At t_1 task A pre-empts D; D goes to a ready (waiting to run) state. Shortly afterwards A tries to use resource W but finds it locked; it therefore self-suspends. When t_2 is reached task B is made active, runs to completion, and then suspends. This is repeated for C at t_3; then at t_4, D is set executing once more. Only when it releases the lock can A replace it (time t_5).

In this design A was given the highest priority because it is an important task. Yet it has been forced to wait for *all* other tasks to execute because of the mutual exclusion locks. Clearly this sort of performance cannot be accepted. How, though, can we prevent priority inversion occurring?

The problem can be tackled in two ways, both involving a temporary increase in task priorities. In the first the priority of a runnable task may be raised to a value determined by other tasks. In the second, priorities are first assigned to shared resources; then the priority of a running task may be raised to a value set by the resource priority. These two approaches are considered to be subsets of the *Priority Ceiling Protocol* [SHA90, CHE90].

When using the first technique (or subprotocol), a running task can inherit the priority of a suspended task (*priority inheritance*). This applies only when a low-priority task blocks a higher-priority one (as shown in Figure 5.53). Operation proceeds as in the previous case until task A suspends (tries to access the locked resource W). At this point the priority of D is raised to equal that of A (i.e. 1). Thus,

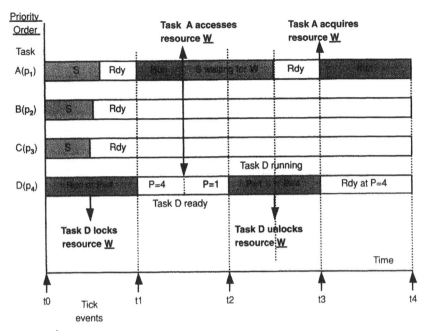

Figure 5.53 Priority inheritance protocol in use – I.

at reschedule time t_2, task D is once more set executing. Slightly later it unlocks resource W (which readies task A), with the result that its priority is returned to normal (4). Consequently, at tick time t_3, it is pre-empted by task A, which now begins executing. Thus task A only had to wait while D was using the shared resource before it could restart.

A second scenario is given in Figure 5.54. You should be able to follow this through by yourself (please do so, it is important to understand this topic). One very important point is demonstrated in this diagram; the (perhaps) unpredictable effect of task interactions on system performance. If task 4 *hadn't* locked resource X then it is possible that task C would have finished executing by time t_2; as shown it is still running after time t_4.

As an alternative to priority inheritance we can use the priority ceiling protocol (a better and less confusing name would be *priority ceiling locking*). With this method each resource has a defined priority ceiling – set to that of the highest-priority task which uses the resource. Thus resource W has a ceiling priority of 1 while that of X is 2. Any task using a resource executes at its own priority – until a second task attempts to acquire the resource. At this point it has its priority raised to the ceiling value, so preventing suspension. It can, however, be suspended by tasks which have a priority higher than that of the ceiling. By definition such tasks do not share the resource in question; hence there isn't a priority inversion problem. These points are demonstrated in the situation depicted in Figure 5.55. Between

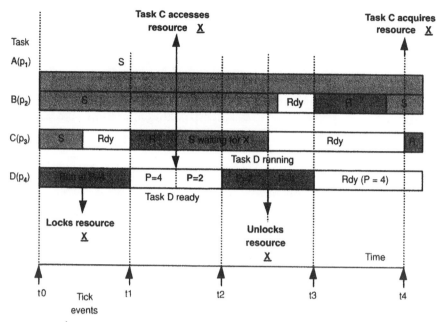

Figure 5.54 Priority inheritance protocol in use – 2.

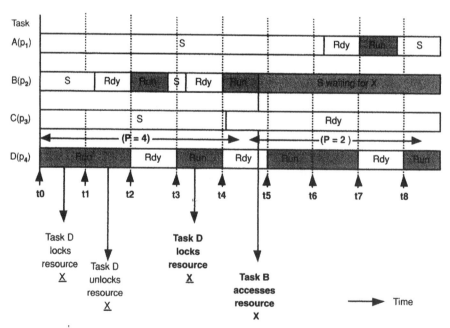

Figure 5.55 The priority ceiling protocol in use.

times t_0 and t_4 task D executes at priority 4. This doesn't change even though the task acquires and then releases resource X. During this period task B becomes ready, pre-empting D at time t_2 (which goes to the ready state). Task B completes execution before t_3 is reached and thus suspends. Task D resumes at t_3, shortly afterwards acquiring (locking) resource X. Task B once again becomes ready, thus pre-empting D at time t_4. It then tries to acquire resource X but, finding it locked, suspends. At this point D has its priority raised to the resource ceiling, 2. By chance task C also becomes ready during this same time interval. Thus, when the tick occurs at t_5, D – not C – is set running at priority level 2. Task C enters a ready state. Hence priority inversion is avoided.

Some time after t_6 task A becomes ready; this pre-empts D at t_7 (as it has a priority of 1). It completes before t_8, going into suspension. At t_8, D resumes execution at priority 2. Later, when it unlocks X, its priority reverts to 4.

These techniques have been used in a number of operating systems and language task models (for example, the protected object of Ada 95 incorporates the priority ceiling protocol). It should, though, be clear that there is an overhead incurred. The system must:

- Keep track of all task suspensions (a task suspension list).

- Keep track of all locked/unlocked resources.

- Dynamically change the priority of a suspended task which currently holds (locks) a resource(s) each time a second task attempts to acquire the resource(s).

- Reset task priorities when a resource is unlocked.

All this takes time, which may well pose problems for hard–fast systems.

5.5.8 Deadlock prevention and performance issues

Deadlock prevention is an essential factor in the design of real-time systems. Avoiding priority inversion – though not essential – is highly desirable. For soft and/or slow applications a number of techniques are available which combine security with good performance. In hard–fast systems, by contrast, our choices are very limited. The simplest approach is to inhibit context switching whilst tasks are using shared resources, usually by disabling interrupts (this is essentially a form of priority inheritance, conceptually raising the running task to the highest possible level). The method is safe, effective and easy to implement. As a result it is widely used. But it is vital that the time spent with interrupts disabled is kept to a minimum.

It can be seen how task interaction may produce significant variation in the time performance of multitasking systems. Such indeterminate behaviour may well result in systems failing to meet their specifications. Worse still, they may work correctly most of the time but fail at the worst possible moments. Once again the message here is to limit the number of tasks in a multitasking system.

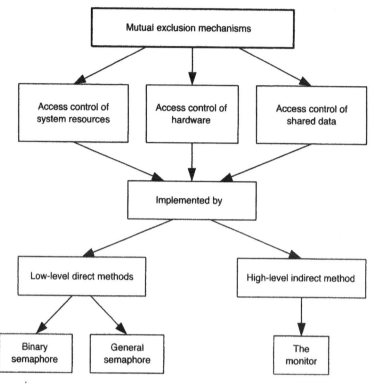

Figure 5.56 | Practical mutual exclusion mechanisms.

5.5.9 Mutual exclusion – a comment on practical solutions

The primary purpose of mutual exclusion mechanisms is to control access to shared resources, including both hardware and software (data areas), Figure 5.56. Many solutions to resource contention have been proposed; few are used in practice. For small programs, or those with little parallelism, low-level direct methods are quite suitable. This also applies to designs which don't use formal operating systems (typical of most small embedded functions). In real-time systems, access control of hardware is usually done via the binary semaphore, the general semaphore being less widely used. There is nothing fundamental about this. It's just that, for the monitoring and control of external devices, the binary semaphore does the job quite well. Even so, semaphores have features which can make them unsafe in use, especially where:

- Programs are large.
- The software is structured as a number of co-operating parallel tasks.

In such instances the monitor should be used.

5.6 Inter-task communication

5.6.1 Introduction

Where a design functions as a set of concurrent co-operating activities we need to support inter-task communication, for three reasons. First, tasks may need to synchronize or co-ordinate their activities. Consider, for instance, the JPT system of Figure 5.3. Here data might be sent to the serial output line *only* when a command is received from the serial input handling task. No data exchange takes place, merely event signalling.

Second, tasks may have to exchange data but without needing to synchronize operations. In the JPT example, crew information is controlled by a display output task, the data being obtained from other tasks. Now there is no reason why these should all work in synchronism. They can very well proceed as asynchronous functions, merely transferring data as required.

Third, tasks may have to exchange data, but at carefully synchronized times. For example, the output from the measurement task is also the input to the computation task – a data transfer requirement. But it is also important that the computation task acts only on the latest information. Thus it works in step with the measurement process – task synchronization.

Separate mechanisms have been developed for each of the three functions – summarized in Figure 5.57 – to provide safe and efficient operation. Their details are given in the following sections.

5.6.2 Task interaction without data transfer

Synchronization and co-ordination requirements (Figure 5.58a) generally occur where tasks are linked by events (or event-sequences), not data. Such events include time-related factors such as time delays, elapsed time and calendar time.

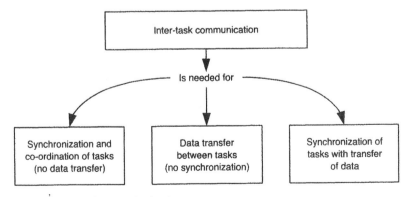

Figure 5.57 ┆ Inter-task communication features.

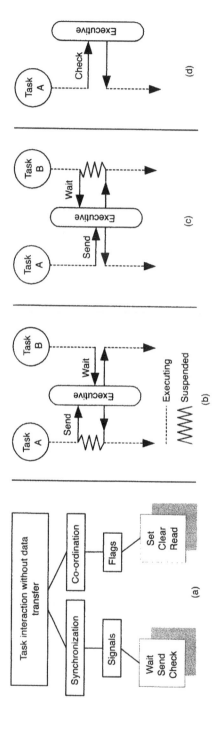

Figure 5.58 : Task interaction without data transfer.

Task synchronization

Synchronization is achieved by using signals, these being 'wait', 'send' and 'check' (Figure 5.58a). Signalling activities are the responsibility of the executive; to the user such operations (described below) are transparent.

First consider the 'send' action (Figure 5.58b). Here task A executes its program and reaches a point where it sends a signal (effectively to the executive). At that instant no tasks are waiting to receive this signal; consequently task A is suspended. Some time later task B generates a wait request for the signal sent by A. It (task B) picks up the signal and carries on executing. The wait request also restarts task A.

What happens if B generates the wait before A has sent the signal (Figure 5.58c)? The result is that task B is suspended until A sends the signal. Task A never suspends since it finds a task waiting for its signal. B resumes task execution on receipt of the signal.

In many instances a task may wish to invoke suspension as a conditional feature. That is, it maintains synchronization, but either suspends or continues depending on the signal check (Figure 5.58d). The check surveys the status of the signal but does not, in itself, halt task execution. Such decisions are taken by the checking task. Conditional checking can be used very effectively for polling operations.

In practice, signals are usually realized using procedures, as follows:

```
PROCEDURE Send (VAR SyncSignal :Signal);
(*Sends a signal. Suspends if no tasks are waiting for the signal*)
PROCEDURE Wait (VAR SyncSignal :Signal);
(*Waits for a signal. If the signal is not present when the request is
generated, be task suspends. O therwise be sender is reactivated and the
system rescheduled*)
PROCEDURE Check(VAR SyncSignal :Signal):BOO EAN;
(*Checks to see if a task is waiting to send a signal. Returns TRUE if a
signal is present*)
```

Two important points should be noted. First, there isn't a one-to-one link between senders and waiters; recipients are not specified in these constructs (which makes it easy to implement a broadcast function – one sender, many receivers). Second, signals look remarkably like binary semaphores, something which causes great confusion. In fact their implementations are very similar. The fundamental difference is in *how* they are used, *not* their construction. Semaphores are generally used as mutual exclusion mechanisms, signals for synchronization. Note, however, that semaphores may be used to create signals. In such cases a single signal must consist of two semaphores (one for each direction of signalling).

Task co-ordination without data transfer

There is a somewhat fine line at times between task synchronization and task co-ordination. Fundamentally, though, the difference is simple: co-ordination sets out to make sure that tasks run:

- In the correct order and/or
- When specific conditions are met.

Thus there is no inherent requirement for either a sender or a receiver to enter a waiting or suspended mode, awaiting synchronization.

We have already covered various applications of flags; the basic ideas are straightforward enough. Let us here, however, look at the use of event flag groups, Figure 5.59a. Here we logically group together a set of flags into a single unit, which, as shown, supports simple task-to-task signalling. Quite frequently the flag group is a single word, each flag being a bit within the word. (A word of caution here: do not base your normal flags on such structures. One simple programming mistake can wreak havoc in your system. We'll leave you to work out why.) There are two widespread applications of event flag groups:

- A task waiting on a set of events (Figure 5.59b) and
- A task broadcasting an event (Figure 5.59c).

5.6.3 Data transfer without task synchronization or co-ordination

There are many occasions when tasks exchange information, either randomly or periodically, without any need for synchronization or co-ordination. This can be supported by using a straightforward data store which incorporates mutual exclusion features. In practice, two data storage mechanisms are used, 'pools' and 'buffers' (Figure 5.60a), the buffer being constructed as a 'channel'.

Pools

Pools (Figure 5.60b) hold items which are common to a number of processes, such as coefficient values, system tables, alarm settings, etc. The notation used here shows tasks A and C depositing data into the pool, with B reading information out. This is not a destructive read-out, i.e. information within the pool is unchanged by the read action. The pools consist of sections of read–write memory, usually RAM (or for read-mostly operations, flash memory).

In practical systems it makes sense to use numerous pools, as and when desired. This restricts access to information, so avoiding problems related to using global data. Even so, it is still essential to control pool usage via a mutual exclusion mechanism like the monitor. Note that the monitor is used to support data transfer activities; it is not *itself* a communication mechanism.

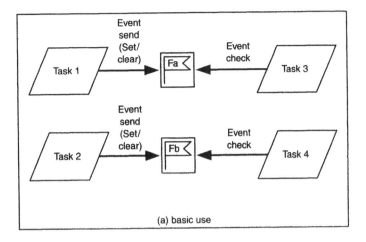

(a) basic use

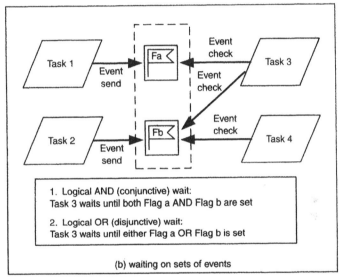

1. Logical AND (conjunctive) wait:
Task 3 waits until both Flag a AND Flag b are set

2. Logical OR (disjunctive) wait:
Task 3 waits until either Flag a OR Flag b is set

(b) waiting on sets of events

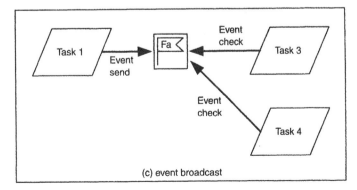

(c) event broadcast

Figure 5.59 Task co-ordination — event flag groups.

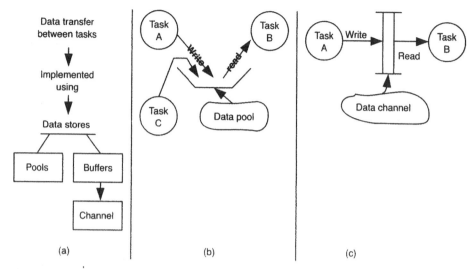

Figure 5.60 Transferring data between tasks.

Channels

Channels are used as communication pipes between processes, normally on a one-to-one basis (Figure 5.60c). Here, task A deposits information into the channel, task B extracting it in first-in first-out style. The channel is usually made large enough to carry a number of data words, not just a single data item. As such it acts as a buffer or temporary storage device, providing elasticity in the pipe. Its advantage is that insertion and extraction functions can proceed asynchronously (as long as the pipe does not fill up). It is implemented in RAM. The information passed between processes may be the data itself; in other cases it could be a pointer to the data. Pointers are normally used for handling large amounts of data where RAM store is limited.

Two techniques are used to implement channels, the queue and the circular buffer. Queue structures have been discussed under scheduling; no further description is needed. The main advantage of the queue concerns its size. This is not fixed, but can be expanded or contracted as desired. Further, very large queues can be built, limited only by the available memory space. Yet for embedded systems these are not particular benefits. First, if RAM is limited, it is impossible to construct large queues at all. Second, large queues organized as FIFO stores have a long transport delay from data-in to data-out. The resulting performance may be too slow for many real-time applications.

A circular buffer is normally assembled using a fixed amount of memory space (Figure 5.61a), being designed to hold multiple data units. Buffer size is defined at creation time, but is fixed thereafter. Under normal circumstances tasks A and B proceed asynchronously, inserting and removing data from the channel as required. Task suspension only occurs under two conditions, channel full and channel

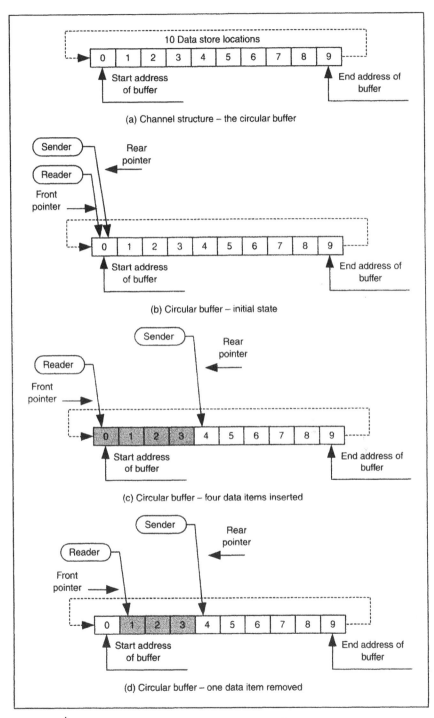

(a) Channel structure – the circular buffer

(b) Circular buffer – initial state

(c) Circular buffer – four data items inserted

(d) Circular buffer – one data item removed

Figure 5.61 The circular buffer – cyclic storage for the channel.

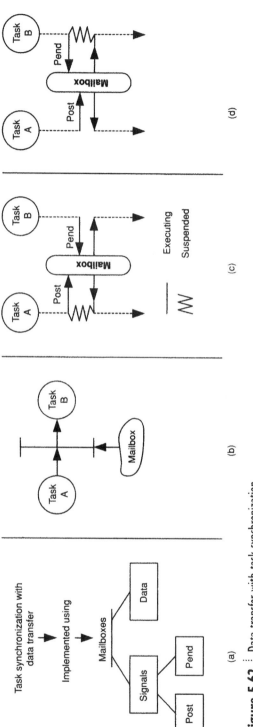

Figure 5.62 Data transfer with task synchronization.

empty. Should the channel fill up *and* task A tries to load another data unit then A is suspended. Alternatively, if the channel empties and task B tries to remove a data unit, then B is suspended.

Figure 5.61 shows how the data is stored in a cyclic manner. The basic concept (Figure 5.61a) defines the physical and logical constructs of circular buffers. Figure 5.61b shows how pointers are used to identify the start and finish locations of the stored data ('Reader' and 'Sender'). By using these we do not have to shift data through the buffer. Inserted data units always stay in the same memory locations; only the pointers change value, as explained in Figures 5.61c,d. These pointers can also be used to define the 'channel full' and 'channel empty' conditions – they become equal.

There is a conceptual difference between the pool and the channel. In the first, reading of data does not affect the contents. In the second, though, channel data is 'consumed' by a read operation.

5.6.4   Task synchronization with data transfer

As shown earlier, situations arise where tasks not only wait for events, but also use data associated with those events. To support this we need both a synchronization mechanism and a data storage area. The structure used is the 'mailbox', this unit incorporating signals for synchronization and storage for data (Figure 5.62). When a task wishes to send information to another one it 'posts' the data to the mailbox. Correspondingly, when a task looks for data in the mailbox it 'pends' on it. In reality, post and pend are signals. Moreover, the data itself is not normally passed through the mailbox; a data pointer is used. Even so, no matter how large the data contents are, the data is treated as a single unit. Thus, conceptually, we have a single-store item. Task synchronization is achieved by suspending or halting tasks until the required conditions are met (Figures 5.62c,d). Any task posting to a mailbox which has not got a pending task gets suspended. It resumes when the receiver pends for the information. Conversely, should pending take place first, the task suspends until the post operation occurs.

Frequently the mailbox is used as a many-to-many communication pipe. This is much less secure than a one-to-one structure, and may be undesirable in critical applications.

5.7   Memory management

5.7.1   Memory aspects – conceptual and physical

Let us start by looking at how memory devices relate to the basic elements of a real-time operating system, Figure 5.63. The major items are tasks, communications components and global data. Strictly speaking you could argue that global data *is*

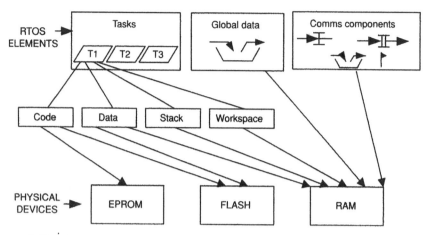

Figure 5.63 Typical memory usage in a multitasking system.

a communications component; it does provide a means for sections of software to 'speak' to each other. However, it is not normally viewed as being a comms component *per se* (note: in this context 'comms' means 'task comms'). Even so the most appropriate model for global data is a pool.

The elements making up a task are its code, data, stack and general working area. Code is normally held in EPROM or flash memory. Flash – a specific type of non-volatilve ROM (NVROM) – is now very widely used for the storage of both program code and data. With regard to data, it is used mainly to store important items, in particular ones that need retaining on power-down. More commonly data is stored in RAM, as are the comms components and global data (a point: for brevity NVROM includes EPROM, flash, FRAM and battery-backed RAM).

Now consider the conceptual processor-oriented view of a multitasking system given in Figure 5.64. In this model we pretend that each task has its own processor, the task 'virtual' processor. In its simplest form a virtual processor consists of the 'register set' in the task process descriptor. It becomes an actual processor when a task is switched into context, interacting with both private and shared memory areas of NVROM and RAM. Private memory houses information which is specific to a task; this includes both data and code items. Other tasks have no need to access this material. Shared memory is generally used for global data, comms components and shared code.

It is important to be able to reconcile these two views in the context of memory usage and devices, Figure 5.65. This memory structure is typical of those found in smaller systems. It consists of two 64 kByte memory chips, one EPROM (or flash) and one RAM. Observe that these devices are mapped into specific positions in the processor memory address space. Each memory address is unique – device addresses cannot overlap. The RTOS elements shown earlier are mapped (located) at specific locations within the address space of each device.

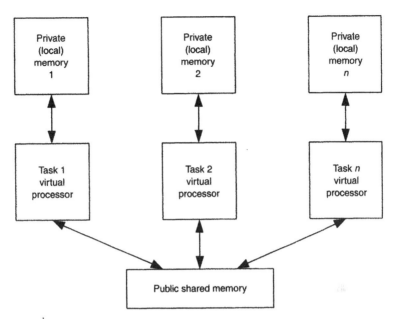

Figure 5.64 : Conceptual view of a multitasking structure.

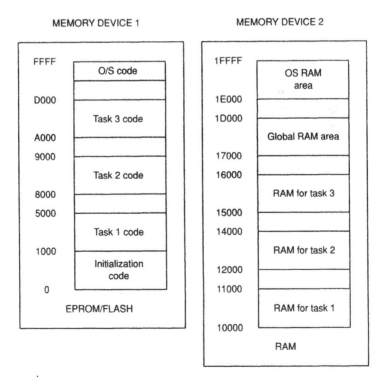

Figure 5.65 : Example memory usage – small system.

5.7.2 Inter-task interference – problem and remedy

A number of important points can be deduced from the detail of Figure 5.65. The first is possibly one of the most important. With this physical structure, the distinction between private and shared (public) memory is merely conceptual. There is absolutely no reason why task 1, for instance, cannot access the private memory of tasks 2 and 3. Perhaps even worse it could interfere with the operating system itself. This points up the need for some form of protection mechanism. As a result a number of processors provide a 'firewall' to allow (at the very least) separation between the operating system and the application tasks (e.g. protected modes of operation). Unfortunately this still leaves us with the danger that tasks may illegally interfere with each other. One simple technique to counter this is shown in Figure 5.66. When a task accesses memory, the address bounds are loaded into two registers. Each memory address produced by the processor is compared with these; any violation leads to the generation of an error signal (usually an interrupt).

While the idea isn't complex, it does have some drawbacks. The first (and fairly obvious) one is that it takes time to load the registers and to carry out comparisons. There is also the difficulty of getting the bounds information in the first place (this will depend on the memory allocation method being used). These problems can be minimized by using hardware to provide the necessary protection, Figure 5.67. Here a hardware device called a memory management unit (MMU) acts as an interface between the CPU and the memory devices. This is programmed as and when required with the relevant task address information; any violation of address bounds causes an error signal to be produced. It is recommended that, where possible, hardware designs intended to support multitasking operation should include

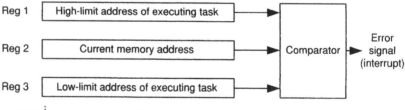

Figure 5.66 Preventing task interference – a simple protection scheme.

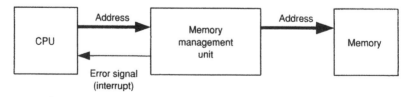

Figure 5.67 Preventing task interference – hardware (MMU) protection.

MMU facilities (many processors now provide an MMU as part of the on-chip circuitry). However, it isn't by itself capable of working out address bounds; these still have to be obtained from program (or compiler) information. And this leads into the topic of memory allocation strategies.

5.7.3 Memory allocation, fragmentation and leakage

The issue of memory allocation together with its related problems of fragmentation and leakage apply mainly to RAM (although similar problems may arise with the use of flash memory). Moreover, these issues may also apply – though less critically – to designs which do *not* use multitasking.

As pointed out earlier, tasks require RAM space for a variety of reasons. The most elementary problem is how to provide this space. A simple, effective and clean technique is to define – as part of the task creation – the amount and location of RAM provided for each task. This allocation can be explicit; that is, the details are defined in source code by the programmer. Alternatively such decisions can be left to the compiler. Either way, the allocation is a static one; once made it remains unchanged during the lifetime of the task. Thus at the beginning of a program in a small system, the RAM usage could be as shown in Figure 5.68a. Observe that we have 'chunks' of allocated memory.

In many small systems the allocation would never change (of course the amount of RAM actually in use will vary). Unfortunately there are situations where this approach causes difficulties. Consider, for instance, a data monitoring system which periodically (say once per minute) measures, processes and displays system information. This operation may use a large amount of RAM store; yet it is needed

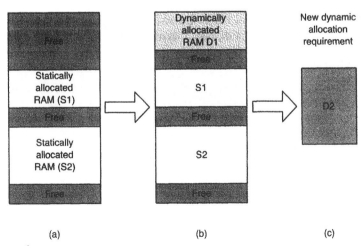

(a)   (b)   (c)

Figure 5.68 Memory allocation, fragmentation and its consequences.

only for a short period of time. It is wasteful to tie up permanently a resource which is used only intermittently. A much more efficient way is for the system to allocate RAM only when it is needed; on completion of the required activities it is retrieved for future use ('deallocated'). That is, allocation and deallocation are dynamic in operation, Figure 5.68b.

All is fine with this strategy as long as the chunks of free RAM space are large enough to meet our needs. Unfortunately, if memory allocation and deallocation aren't carefully controlled, the system will almost certainly fail. Some day a task will request an allocation of memory greater than any of the free areas, Figure 5.68c. It might take months of operation before the problem surfaces, but when it does the failure can be deadly. This can happen even when the total amount of free memory is sufficient to meet our needs.

The problem has arisen because the allocated memory is not nicely, compactly organized; instead it is fragmented throughout the available memory space. This points up the need to have a well-defined, organized and controlled memory allocation technique. Slow or soft systems don't present a major problem; there is usually plenty of time to rearrange (shuffle) existing allocations under the control of a background task. By contrast, hard–fast implementations are much more challenging; techniques must be used which avoid memory fragmentation in the first place, such as:

● Fixed block size allocation.

● Partitioning and sizing of allocated memory.

● Identifiers to track allocated memory.

● Protected and isolated segments, etc.

Now let us look at a second problem, that of memory leakage, Figure 5.69.

Figure 5.69a shows a situation where a static memory allocation has been made for two tasks, T1 and T2. Task 1 uses memory area S1, task 2 using area S2. At some later stage, Figure 5.69b, task 1 dynamically acquires extra memory space, D1. Later still it decides that it no longer requires the extra amount; conceptually it reverts to using S1 only. Unfortunately, owing to a programmer mistake say, it doesn't deallocate D1. As a result the amount of free memory is now permanently reduced for the duration of the program. We have 'leaked' memory from the available pool. A single leak is unlikely to be a problem; the same cannot be said for multiple occurrences.

Leakage is not merely a tasking issue; it applies anytime where memory can be dynamically allocated and deallocated. In particular it is a well-known source of angst in C and C++ programs resulting from 'dangling pointers'. There are two basic techniques to deal with this: OS activated (implicit) or programmer controlled (explicit).

When the OS retrieves allocated but unreferenced memory it is said to perform 'garbage collection'. It carries this out with the aid of a task called the garbage

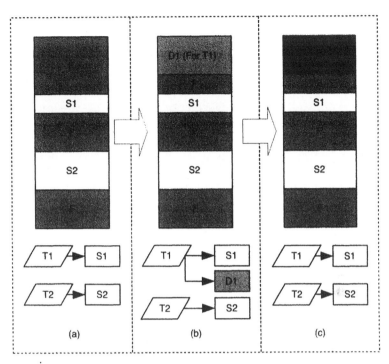

Figure 5.69 Memory leakage problem.

collector. This has the job of keeping track of all the memory items (objects) and references to such items. If it sees that an object is no longer referenced, it retrieves the memory space for future use. While this method is safe, secure and simple to use, it has one major drawback. The garbage collector task itself introduces uncertainty into the timing performance of the system. In designs where the garbage is collected in one go, the effect can be substantial. Such methods are totally unacceptable for hard–fast systems. The problem can be minimized by collecting the garbage incrementally – 'a bit at a time'.

Explicit memory management has been a standard programming feature for many years. The problems associated with allocating and then failing to deallocate memory (the dangling pointer) are well known. It is strongly recommended that – even if performance suffers somewhat – you take a safe and secure approach in your programs. One proven, practical technique is to encapsulate matching allocation and deallocation operations within a subprogram. Failing that check your programs using a run-time analysis tool designed to catch memory leaks (thought for the day: why is it that such tools have been commercially produced only since the advent of C?).

A final word: dynamic memory manipulation should be avoided wherever possible in real-time systems. It should *never* be used in critical applications.

5.7.4 Memory management and disk-based systems

In disk-based systems tasks run from RAM-based primary store. The task programs themselves are held on disk (the backing store), being switched into primary store for execution. Therefore, when a task is switched in, its code may replace that of a task which has been switched out ('overlaying'). Switching control is handled by the executive. The executive also implements 'policing' functions to prevent tasks making accesses outside their allotted memory space. In the past the majority of embedded systems didn't use disk storage; hence this aspect was relatively unimportant. And even those that did include disks normally used them only for the storage of information, not programs.

This is still true for the majority of embedded systems, including:

- Small cost-sensitive systems.

- Ruggedized systems designed for operation in adverse environments.

- Fast systems.

- Critical (especially safety-critical) systems.

However, what is becoming a feature of many operating systems is the use of flash memory to mimic a disk, the 'Ramdisk', Figure 5.70. It is normally provided as a subsystem within a full embedded file system structure. Here application tasks interface to the individual storage subsystems (e.g. hard disk, floppy disk, PCMCIA device) via a file system server. Each subsystem has its own individual file manager, thus effectively becoming a 'plug-in' component. More will be said on this topic in the next chapter.

On a closing point, be careful with the use of flash memory. This, like EEPROM, 'wears out' as a result of changing its stored data (i.e. write operations). A typical

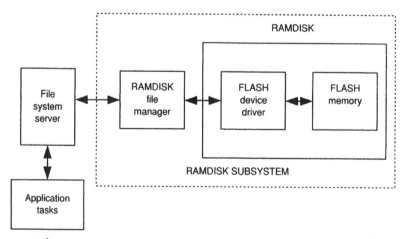

Figure 5.70 | Embedded file system – ramdisk storage.

figure is 100,000 write cycles. When it is used as a 'read-mostly' memory, this is unlikely to be a problem. However in ramdisk applications, writing is much more common-place; wearout is a real issue. The file managers often incorporate special algorithms to spread out the wear across the device(s) memory locations. Even so it introduces a potential lurking problem which could jump out and bite when you least expect it. Be warned.

5.8 Distributed systems

5.8.1 Geographically distributed systems

Up to now we have dealt with real-time operating systems applied to single-processor designs. How, though, do we deal with distributed systems which contain a number of processors – true concurrency? Do the concepts, structures and implementation features of multitasking carry across to multiprocessing? Easily? With difficulty? With sweat and toil? To answer that let us start by looking at a realistic problem: the development of a computer-based controller for the system of Figure 5.71a (a simplified version of a marine propulsion system).

Here a single propulsion engine – a gas turbine (GT) – drives two propeller shafts via a gearbox. The propellers are of the variable pitch type, being operated by individual propeller units. The function of the controller is to control three items: GT fuel flow, port propeller pitch and starboard propeller pitch. These are set in response to bridge commands using the parameter profile information of Figure 5.71b.

Initially a single, centralized computer scheme is proposed (stay with us; the reason for going down this route will shortly become clear). After studying the problem a first-cut multitasking (seven-task) design scheme is produced, Figure 5.72. For clarity comms components have been excluded from the tasking diagram.

It is now decided that a distributed networked arrangement would be a better solution to the problem. The resulting design is that of Figure 5.73. The next point may sound too obvious to need making (but that won't stop us). From a *propulsion system* point of view, the function, behaviour and performance of both solutions should be identical.

We review our previous design work and conclude that the overall software structuring of Figure 5.72 is an optimal one. That is, it not only does the job; it is the best solution taking *all* factors into account. This can now be treated as an abstract software model which has to be distributed across the system. The outcome is shown in Figure 5.74, which initially deals only with the tasks of the abstract model.

Naturally enough, the inter-task communication defined in Figure 5.71 must be maintained in the new design. However, some of this now goes across the network, shown as the dashed lines of Figure 5.74. From this it is clear that, because the system is distributed, we need support for:

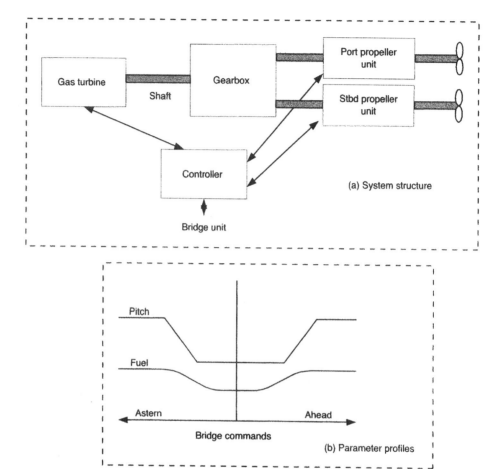

Figure 5.71 | Example system — marine propulsion.

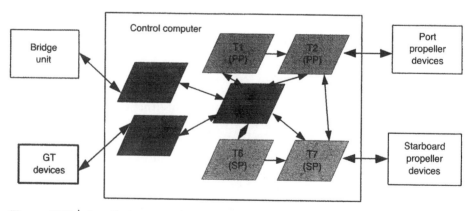

Figure 5.72 | Centralized control — simplified tasking structure.

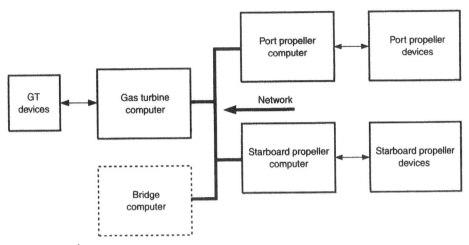

Figure 5.73 | Distributed control – computer structure.

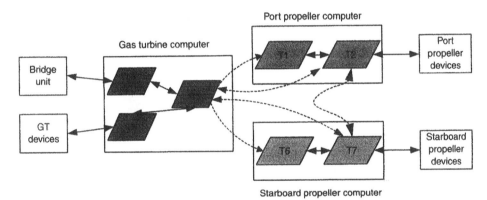

Figure 5.74 | Distributed system – task allocation.

- Network message handling (physical and protocol aspects).
- Message routing across the network.
- Message routing within each computer.
- Co-ordination and timing of computer activities.

There are a number of ways to deal with these issues. The approach taken here is a very practical one. Moreover, it has proved to be highly successful in the implementation of real-time embedded distributed systems. It hinges on the following:

- All inter-processor communication is based on message-passing techniques.
- Communication is essentially asynchronous; any synchronization requirements must be explicitly designed into the software (precluding, for instance, the use of remote procedure calls).

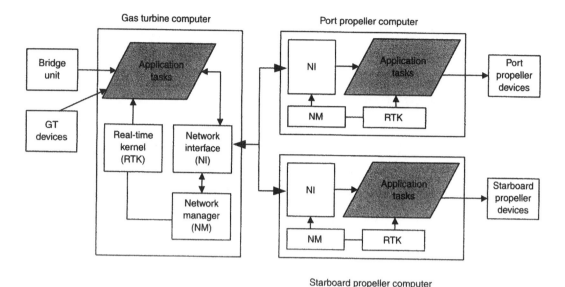

Figure 5.75 | Distributed system – overall system and software structure.

- For hard and/or critical systems the location of software functions is pre-defined (no dynamic redistribution is allowed at run-time).

- The software within individual computers is organized as desired (e.g. multitasking, interrupt-driven, etc.).

- If timing is critical, then a system-wide time reference signal ('global time') must be provided.

By taking these factors into account the basic design of Figure 5.74 becomes the practical one of Figure 5.75. Here, within each computer, the application tasks are – as before – run under the control of the real-time kernel. A network interface section deals with message-handling aspects whilst a network manager deals with message routing. This design can be implemented in many ways, ranging from DIY solutions to complete reliance on operating system facilities. The first is hard, time consuming, and requires much skill and knowledge. However, it gives full visibility and control of the design, together with a complete understanding of timing aspects. The second, which (relatively speaking) is easy and fast, shields the designer from all low-level computer and network details. A key feature of this approach is the provision of transparent network support, the so-called 'virtual circuit'. One technique based on this is the 'virtual connection, Figure 5.76a. In this example tasks 4 and 7, each on a different computer, need to communicate with each other. The OS provides mechanisms to connect the two together, the connection channel being invisible to the programmer. When task 4 wishes to speak to task 7 (a 'remote' task) it merely includes the identifier of task 7 in the message

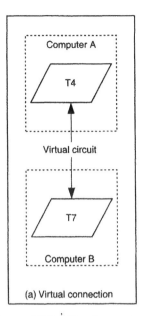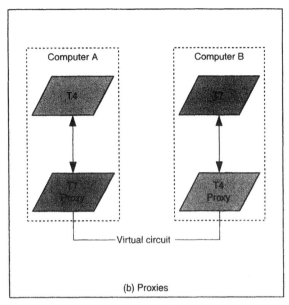

Figure 5.76 | Virtual connections and proxies.

call. All location and routing details are handled by the operating system network manager.

An alternative method is based on the use of 'proxies', Figure 5.76b (although this is normally met in OO designs as proxy objects, not tasks). Proxy, *OED*: 'A person authorised to act for another'.

With this arrangement, extra tasks – the proxy tasks – are created to simplify the programming of the communication software. On computer A, for instance, task 4 talks to the proxy of task 7 (a 'local' task). As far as task 4 is concerned task 7 lives on the same machine; thus standard (non-distributed) task communication features can be used. Task 7 proxy carries information about the real task 7 so that it can forward all messages from task 4 to it. A similar situation applies in computer B, except that we now have a proxy of task 4.

This is a very powerful technique and can be of great value in large systems. Implementation is very much simplified by using standard software ('middleware') to build the proxies and the virtual circuits. Unfortunately, you now lose sight of what precisely happens at run-time. Thus it can be quite difficult (if not impossible) to guarantee timing performance. Further, the behaviour of the system under fault conditions may not be predictable (in particular from a time point of view).

The example used here, although highly simplified, does point up the extra difficulty met in designing distributed systems. Moreover, it shows that the fundamental issue is one of *system and software* design, not just task scheduling. The route to producing successful designs for distributed systems is to:

- Define the system architecture.
- Develop an abstract software model which meets all functional and timing requirements.
- Partition the software across the processors of the system.
- Design the networking and multitasking software within each processor.
- Check that the design still meets its requirements. If not, go round the loop again.

To use a cliché, this is easier said than done. But it is the path most likely to bring rewards.

5.8.2 Functionally distributed systems – multiprocessors

The great majority of multiprocessor systems come in two flavours, Figure 5.77: loosely coupled (a) and closely coupled (b). In both cases each board is equipped with a real-time OS. The difference, however, lies with the communication mechanisms. Conceptually the loosely coupled structure is the same as the geographically distributed system of Figure 5.75: for 'parallel bus' read 'LAN'. Thus standard LAN techniques can be used to provide inter-processor communication facilities.

The situation is somewhat different with closely coupled systems. Here, as speed requirements are paramount, processors communicate via shared memory. From a design perspective this looks more like a distributed *task* structure, tasks

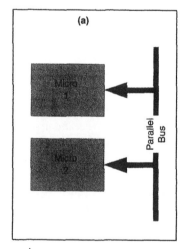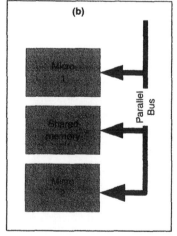

Figure 5.77 Multiprocessor structures.

communicating via flags, mailboxes, etc. Where communicating tasks sit on different processors their common communication components reside physically in the shared memory. This, of course, raises two very interesting questions:

- Who creates the necessary components?
- How are the various tasks made aware of such details?

One practical solution is to designate one of the kernels as the 'master'. It has the job of setting up all tasking information in the shared memory. Other kernels then obtain this information from (or via) the master.

5.9 Analysis and review of scheduling policies

5.9.1 Overview

Earlier we looked at some basic ideas of scheduling and scheduling rules ('policies'). The objective here is to introduce the broader range of scheduling policies which are – or may be – used in real-time systems. Many different techniques are available, yet relatively few are widely applied. By the end of the section it will become clear why this is so. First, though, a general overview, Figure 5.78. This, it should be said, shows one way of categorizing the various scheduling policies; other classification schemes are possible.

For brevity those methods which don't use priority mechanisms are called 'simple' schemes. We have already met the first-come, first-served policy as a FIFO one. Also, simple round-robin scheduling has been covered in depth. A discussion on co-operative scheduling will be deferred for the moment, so allowing us to move on to the priority-based schemes. These, it can be seen, are collected into 'non-pre-emptive' and 'pre-emptive' groups. The pre-emptive category is in turn divided into two major sets, 'static' and 'dynamic'. Here the word static is used to denote schemes where task priorities are assigned at compile time (these are also called *a priori* or 'off-line' scheduling). By contrast, dynamic policies set priorities as the software executes, changing them to respond to operational conditions. This implies that there must be pre-defined, mechanized rules for adjusting such priorities 'on-line'.

With off-line scheduling it is the responsibility of the programmer to define task priorities. This raises a most important – and difficult – question. How does a designer deduce the best (optimal?) task schedule for a particular application? Two approaches are in general use. The first, an objective method, relies on task time information to define what the various priorities should be. The second is subjective; that is, the selected schedule depends mainly on the opinion of the designer. Here this is called 'heuristic' scheduling.

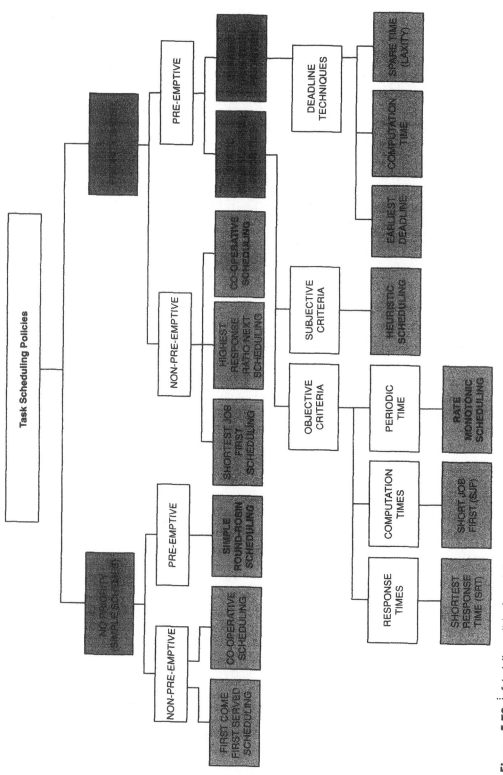

Figure 5.78 :::: Scheduling policies for real-time systems.

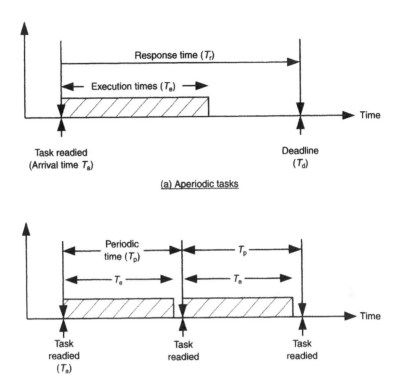

Figure 5.79 Task timings – some basic definitions.

The various policies will be discussed in detail after some basic timing definitions have been given, Figure 5.79.

Figure 5.79a, which applies to aperiodic tasks, identifies four important items:

- Task arrival time (T_a): the time at which a task is put into the ready-to-run state.

- Task deadline (T_d): the time by which the task *must* deliver its result.

- Response time (T_r): The time allowed for a task to carry out its function (note: if timing is done on a relative, not absolute, scale, then response time and deadline have the same value).

- Execution time (T_e): The actual execution time of the task.

For periodic tasks, Figure 5.79b, the time between successive invocations of a task is called the periodic time (T_p).

A last point: static scheduling does *not* imply fixed priorities. It may – depending on the design of the kernel – be possible to change a task's priority during program execution. However, such changes are normally invoked as a result of decisions made by the application program, not by the operating system itself. With dynamic scheduling, priority settings are:

- Usually determined by the rules of the OS.
- Likely to change during program execution.

It is also possible to have scheduling policies which combine both static and dynamic techniques.

5.9.2 Priority-based non-pre-emptive scheduling policies

The schemes considered here are those of Shortest Job First (SJF), Highest Response Ratio Next (HRRN) and co-operative scheduling. In these an executing task cannot be pre-empted no matter how low its priority. Either they run to completion or else voluntarily make way for another task. However, the *position* of tasks in the ready queue is determined by their priorities. Both SJF and co-operative scheduling are static schemes; the HRRN algorithm used here is a combination of both static and dynamic methods.

SJF scheduling

In essence this is a priority-based version of FCFS scheduling. Each task has its priority (P) calculated as follows:

$$P = \frac{1}{T_e}$$

The order of tasks in the ready queue is determined by their priorities; that with the highest is placed at the front of the queue.

Compared with the simple schemes, SJF scheduling generally produces a better average response time. The operative word here is *average*. There may well be significant variation in *actual* response values obtained during program execution. There is a further complication when a system contains a mix of short and long tasks. Those having long execution times have low priorities. As a result their response times are likely to be adversely affected by the presence of short (higher-priority) tasks. Hence this technique is not suitable for use as the core scheduling policy in real-time systems. It may, though, be effectively incorporated within one of the priority-based schemes (e.g. to run base-level tasks).

HRRN scheduling

This improves on SJF (in terms of task responsiveness) by taking into account the time tasks have been waiting in the ready queue (T_w). T_w is used dynamically in the calculation of the priority index, one algorithm being:

$$P = \frac{1 + T_w}{T_e}$$

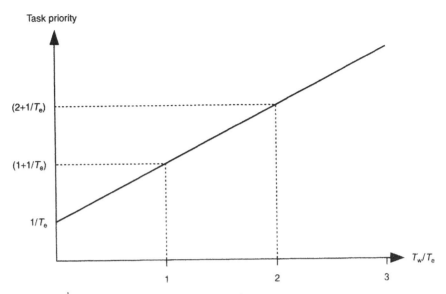

Figure 5.80 HRRN task priority profile – normalized.

Note: Rewrite this as:

$$P = \frac{1}{T_e} + \frac{T_w}{T_e}$$

From this it is clear that the first component can be calculated off-line ('static') whilst the second must be computed at run-time ('dynamic').

The normalized priority profile produced by this calculation is shown in Figure 5.80. Observe that the 'time' scale is a normalized one, T_w/T_e. Consequently each and every task has this same profile. Actual (as opposed to normalized) priority values depend of course on actual execution and waiting times. This is illustrated in Figure 5.81 for two tasks which have different execution times. It can be seen that as a task waits in the ready queue its priority is gradually raised (e.g. task 2 reaches the initial priority value of task 1 after it has been waiting for 1 second). This ensures that tasks which have long execution times (and thus begin with low-priority ratings) get better service than that provided by SJF scheduling.

HRRN is unlikely to be used in fast real-time systems. However, it provides a simple way to introduce three important points:

- The *a priori* setting of initial task priorities – a static schedule.
- The adjustment of these priorities as the system runs – a dynamic schedule.
- Priority profiles.

These are further discussed in the topic of deadline techniques.

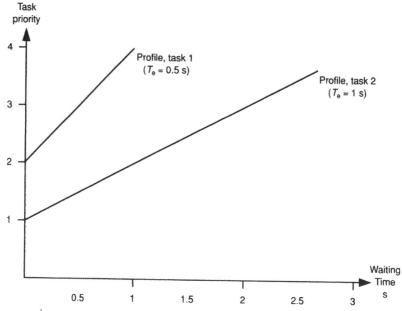

Figure 5.81 Example HRRN task priority profiles.

Co-operative scheduling

With co-operative scheduling the decision to allow a context switch is made by the running task itself. Moreover, such switches are made *at very specific program points*. In doing so the executing task may:

(i)   Designate the next task to be set running, or

(ii) Return control to the scheduler, or

(iii) Return control to the scheduler together with task synchronization information (typically using signals).

Both (i) and (ii) are very easy to implement if your programming language supports coroutines. Coroutine structures have been applied to good effect in soft real-time systems. They have also been used as sub-policies within pre-emptive schedulers. One feature of this technique is that system behaviour is much more predictable, particularly when all tasks are periodic ones. As such the policy may, when applied with care, be especially suitable for use in critical systems (even in hard–fast ones). However, without this language feature it may be easier to apply other methods.

Situations sometimes arise which require high throughputs together with high processor utilization. Where other policies fail to deliver the required performance, approach (ii) may be used. An essential aspect here is to eliminate the need to save task information at context switch time. Clearly this calls for some 'hand-crafting' of the source code, paying *great* attention to detail. Normally this method would only be used as a last resort; upgrading the processor hardware is likely to be much more cost-effective. Unfortunately this isn't always possible. The good news is that impressive performance improvements have been achieved using this technique (personal correspondence).

5.9.3 Priority-based pre-emptive static scheduling policies – general

In static priority scheduling schemes, task priorities are set at compilation time. It therefore is the responsibility of the programmer/designer to establish and define such priorities. Once set, these are not usually changed at run-time.

Four criteria may be used to arrive at priority settings. Three are objective, the fourth being subjective. The objective criteria, all based on time, are:

- Response times – shortest response time, SRT, gives highest priority (SRT scheduling).
- Computation times – shortest time gives highest priority (shortest job first; SJF scheduling).
- Periodic execution times (periodicity) – shortest period gives highest priority (rate monotonic scheduling)

By contrast, designers often devise task schedules based mainly on experience and judgement. This subjective *heuristic* approach normally takes into account timing and criticality factors.

Let us see how the objective criteria work when applied to an example task set, Figure 5.82. The resulting task schedules are shown in Figure 5.83.

Task	Type	Response time (milliseconds)	Computation time (milliseconds)	Period (milliseconds)
1	Periodic	20	10	100
2	Periodic	18	15	120
3	Aperiodic	110 – Deadline	5	–
4	Aperiodic	5 – Deadline	2	–

Figure 5.82 Static priority pre-emptive scheduling – example task attributes.

Scheduling policy →	Response time (SRT)	Computation time (SJF)	Periodic time (Rate monotonic)
Task ordering → (priority listing, highest to lowest)	4 – Highest	4 – Highest	1 – Highest
	2	3	2
	1	1	?
	3	2	?

Figure 5.83 Static priority pre-emptive scheduling – example task schedules.

Priority as a function of response times

With SRT, the shortest task is given highest priority, calculated by:

$$P = \frac{1}{T_r}$$

While this criterion is easy to apply it is, in practice, less objective than it seems. Required response times are often a matter of opinion, especially in the area of man–machine interfacing.

Priority as a function of computation time

This scheduling policy, in essence, is that of shortest-job-first used in a pre-emptive mode (also called shortest remaining time – SRT – scheduling [DEI84]). Priorities are calculated as:

$$P = \frac{1}{T_e}$$

One major problem with this scheme is being able to define computation times accurately. This is especially true in the early development stages of a project.

Priority as a function of periodicity

With this technique, tasks having high repetition frequencies (low periodic times) are assigned high priorities. The theoretical groundwork for this was done by Liu and Layland [LIU73], where the policy was defined to be 'rate-monotonic priority assignment'. Unfortunately, we are unable to assign priorities to tasks 3 and 4 using the basic method – they are not periodic. More of this in a moment.

It is frequently claimed that rate monotonic scheduling offers superior performance. Moreover it is also supported by various vendors (e.g. Aonix), provided as a component within their design environments. As such it is important enough to warrant a section to itself.

5.9.4 Priority-based pre-emptive static scheduling – rate monotonic scheduling (RMS)

First, a recap. Rate monotonic scheduling (also known as rate monotonic analysis, RMA) sets task priorities according to their periodicity, as follows:

$$P = \frac{1}{T_p}$$

The task with the shortest period (thus highest priority) is placed at the front of the ready queue. Next in line is the task having the second shortest period;

following this is the one with the third shortest period, and so on to the end of the queue. Thus as we go down the queue task periods always increase – a monotonic sequence. Central to RMS scheduling theory are the following assumptions:

- All tasks are periodic.
- A task's deadline is the same as its period.
- Tasks may be pre-empted.
- All tasks are equally important – criticality doesn't enter the equation.
- Tasks are independent of each other.
- The worst-case execution time of a task is constant.

A fundamental question in scheduling is 'is the given task schedule feasible?' That is, will the system meet its requirements within the specified time frame(s)? Clearly a heavily loaded processor – one having high utilization – is less likely to succeed than one which is lightly loaded. Before discussing this further we need to be careful with the use of the word *utilization* (U). In basic RMS it is defined as the percentage of available processor time spent executing tasks, Figure 5.84. Here task 1 has an execution time of 30 milliseconds; its period is 100 milliseconds. Task 2 has an execution time of 20 milliseconds and a period of 200 milliseconds. The relevant utilization factors are:

- Task 1 only scheduled – $U = 0.3$.
- Task 2 only scheduled – $U = 0.1$.
- Both tasks scheduled – $U = 0.4$.

A second term which needs explaining is 'full utilization' of the processor. This, you might think, is when the processor is fully occupied executing software, having no spare capacity (i.e. $U = 1.0$). Not so (at least where RMS is concerned). Here it describes a very specific situation: where a given task schedule is feasible but *any* increase in execution times will lead to failure. We might, for instance, find that only 80% of the processor time is spent executing tasks; yet any attempt to use the spare capacity will cause task(s) to miss deadlines. Take it on trust that for a given processor having:

- a fixed set of tasks and
- a fixed total computation time for all tasks

the 'full utilization' figure is *not* a fixed value. It depends on the individual task timings and the relative activation time of tasks. Liu and Leyland showed that the lowest figure for n tasks is:

$$U = n(2^{1/n} - 1)$$

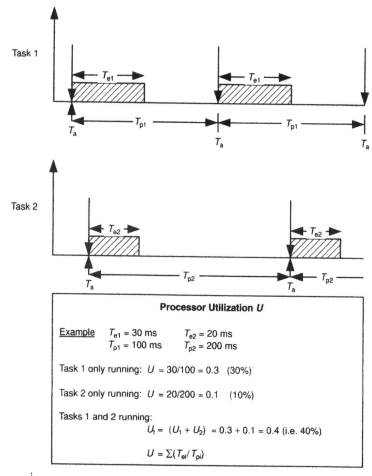

Figure 5.84 Rate monotonic scheduling – definition of processor utilization.

As n increases the value of U decreases, eventually having a value of 0.693 when n is infinite. This means that if more than 69.3% of the processor time is spent executing tasks, we may not meet our deadlines (i.e. there is no guarantee that the schedule is feasible). More usefully put: a task set scheduled using RMS is guaranteed to be feasible provided its utilization does not exceed 0.693.

This seems fine; unfortunately it contains three major weaknesses where real-time systems are concerned. These are:

- It cannot deal with aperiodic tasks.
- Task deadline and period are considered to be synonymous.
- Tasks are independent, i.e. non-interacting.

Let us take these items in turn.

Task	Type	Response time (milliseconds)	Computation time (milliseconds)	Period (milliseconds)
1	Periodic	20	10	100
2	Periodic	18	15	120
3	'Periodic'	110	5	**150**
4	'Periodic'	5	2	**250**

Figure 5.85 Rate monotonic scheduling – example task attributes.

1			2			3		
For aperiodic tasks: **Period** set by **Interval time** **Priority** set by **Period**			For aperiodic tasks: **Period** set by **Response time** **Priority** set by **Period**			For aperiodic tasks: **Period** set by **Interval time** **Priority** set by **Deadline**		
Task $\rightarrow$	Period	Task priority	Task $\rightarrow$	Period	Task priority	Task $\rightarrow$	Period	Task priority
T1 $\rightarrow$	100 ms	1	T1 $\rightarrow$	100 ms	2	T1 $\rightarrow$	100 ms	2
T2 $\rightarrow$	120 ms	2	T2 $\rightarrow$	120 ms	4	T2 $\rightarrow$	120 ms	4
T3 $\rightarrow$	150 ms	3	T3 $\rightarrow$	110 ms ($T_d = 110$ ms)	3	T3 $\rightarrow$	150 ms ($T_d = 110$)	3
T4 $\rightarrow$	250 ms	4	T4 $\rightarrow$	5 ms ($T_d = 5$ ms)	1	T4 $\rightarrow$	250 ms ($T_d = 5$ ms)	1

Figure 5.86 Rate monotonic scheduling – handling aperiodic tasks.

Aperiodic tasks are present

There are two ways to handle aperiodic tasks. First, turn them into periodic tasks by using polling techniques. Second, provide computing resources to deal with the random arrival of an aperiodic task *within a pre-defined period*. This is called an 'aperiodic server' [SHA90].

Let us return to the example set of tasks of Figure 5.82. and modify it to show all tasks as periodic ones, Figure 5.85. This has assumed that task 3 might be re-readied, in the worst case, every 150 milliseconds. This 'interval time' between (possible) task executions is chosen to be its periodic time.

For task 4, 250 milliseconds has been used.

Of course we still have to decide on the priorities of the aperiodic tasks. The simplest way is to use the interval time to calculate priorities, as shown in Figure 5.86, column 1. If we set all tasks ready at time t_0, then task 3 will complete at ($t_0 + 30$) milliseconds – well within its deadline. Unfortunately task 4 won't finish until ($t_0 + 32$) milliseconds, much too late. This can be alleviated by using a different set of rules in defining the 'period' of an aperiodic task; use the task response time (or deadline – they're the same in this case) as the period (column 2, Figure 5.86). In this particular case the schedule will work, even though task 4 is activated every 5 milliseconds. Unfortunately such high-rate operation dramatically increases processor utilization; furthermore, in many cases it may generate infeasible schedules.

A technique developed to overcome this drawback is the *deadline monotonic* scheduling policy. With this, aperiodic tasks are treated as periodic tasks, periods being based on interval times (Figure 5.86, column 3). However, priorities are based on deadlines (for periodic tasks, remember, period and deadline are the same thing). As a result task 4 gets activated only every 250 milliseconds, but when it does it takes on highest priority. As a result it is guaranteed to run to completion without being pre-empted.

Polling, as a technique to handle random inputs, has a number of drawbacks:

- Excessive overheads – polling whether or not an event occurs.

- Staleness of acquired data – time between an event occurring and it being recognized by the software.

- Skew between input signals – simultaneous event signals may, as a result of the polling action, have significantly different time stamps.

The periodic server attempts to alleviate these problems by not polling; instead it builds time into the schedule to handle random inputs *should they occur*. One technique allocates a fixed amount of processing time in a pre-defined time slot for the aperiodic tasks. Once this is used up no further aperiodic processing can be done until the beginning of the next time slot.

Task deadline and period are not necessarily synonymous

In practice it is unlikely that the execution time of a task is constant from run to run; a number of factors are likely to produce variations (e.g. conditional actions, task synchronization, contention for shared resources, etc.). For many applications this isn't a problem. Take the case of actively refreshing an alphanumeric display panel. Provided a sensible update period is chosen, significant variation of actual updating times can be tolerated (remember they are always bounded by the period of the task). However, in other systems such variations may lead to performance degradation (for example, jitter in closed-loop control systems). Most crucially, in some cases (e.g. manufacturing processes) they may lead to system malfunction or even total failure. Thus, in situations where timing is critical, other scheduling methods may have to be used.

Tasks are frequently interdependent

In general tasks are likely to be interdependent rather than independent. Interactions take place for three reasons:

- Synchronization of operations.

- Communication of information.

- Access to shared resources.

All can lead to so-called blocking conditions. The first two items are quite difficult to deal with theoretically; this is especially true when aperiodic tasks are involved. Mathematical analysis of such interactions tends to be limited to somewhat simplistic situations (perhaps realistic structures are too difficult to analyse?).

Where tasks share resources, blocking may be produced by the activation of protection (mutual exclusion) mechanisms. Rate monotonic theory has been extended to cover this situation where a ceiling priority protocol is used [SHA90]. In such cases a high-priority task has to wait at most for only one lower-priority task to finish using a protected resource. If the maximum time that such blocking can occur is T_b (i.e. when the low-priority task has locked the resource), then the modified RMS algorithm is:

$$\sum_{i=1}^{n} \left[\left(\frac{T_{ei}}{T_{pi}} + \frac{T_{bi}}{T_{pi}} \right) \le n(2^{1/n} - 1) \right]$$

5.9.5 Priority-based pre-emptive static scheduling – combining task priority and criticality: a heuristic approach

The methods described earlier have one major weakness: they ignore the criticality of tasks. Consider tasks having the timing attributes defined in Figure 5.87. Using the criteria of time, task 1 is always assigned the highest priority. Thus if both tasks get readied at the same time, task 2 will be blocked out until task 1 has executed. But what of the precise nature of the tasks? We have said nothing about this. Consider that both tasks are part of a flight control system. The function of task 1 is to remove data from a data comms (serial line) buffer. Task 2 is part of a protection system within the terrain-following subsystem. It is activated if there is a failure of the altitude sensor – its function is to the put the aircraft into a safe mode. Using an adapted RMS algorithm based on deadlines, task 1 will be given the highest priority. Which is the more important task? In this situation we have a clear-cut case – task 2. However, if both tasks get readied at the same instant then task 2 will go late. An even worse situation can arise if the control system happens to have a number of messages streaming in from various other systems. If this leads to degradation of performance (or worse, physical damage) the situation is unacceptable. Task 2 *must* be assigned the highest priority.

Task	Type	Response time (milliseconds)	Computation time (milliseconds)
1	Aperiodic	5	4
2	Aperiodic	8	6

Figure 5.87 Task priority and criticality – example task attributes.

In practical systems the issues are rarely so clear-cut. It takes experience and judgement to arrive at a sensible priority scheme, backed up by historical real-time performance data information. But even then the *actual* performance may well differ from the predicted one.

5.9.6 Priority-based pre-emptive dynamic scheduling policies – general

These dynamic scheduling policies have one simple objective: to maximize performance by making scheduling decisions based on the actual (current) system state. Priorities are assigned:

- In accordance with criteria based on time factors and
- On the fly, as tasks are executed.

The approaches used are also categorized as 'deadline scheduling'. Here the programmer does not specify task priorities. Instead, when tasks are created, specific attributes are defined in the source code. These are subsequently used by the scheduler to dynamically adjust priorities.

There are a number of different approaches, discussed in detail later. All take into account – in some shape or form – the following timing information (see Figure 5.88):

- Task execution (or computation) time, T_e – a pre-defined value.
- Required response time, T_r – a pre-defined value. This is also called the 'due time'.
- Spare time, T_s – a computed value (also called the 'laxity').
- Required completion time (deadline), T_d – a computed value.
- Task activation (arrival) time, T_a.

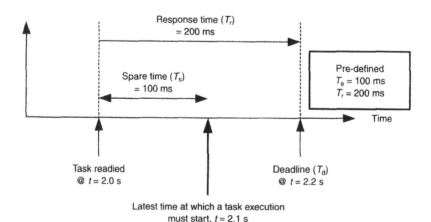

Figure 5.88 Definition of timings in deadline scheduling – I.

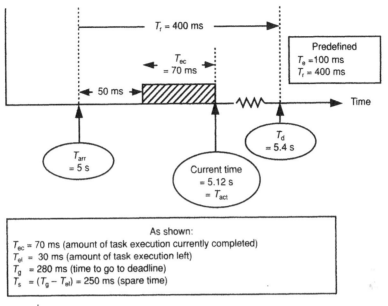

Figure 5.89 Definition of timings in deadline scheduling – 2.

As shown in Figure 5.88 a task is readied at time $T_a = 2.0$ s. It has a required response time T_r of 200 ms. Thus its deadline T_d falls at $t = 2.2$ s. Its pre-defined computation time T_e is 100 ms; consequently we have 100 ms of spare processing time T_s before the deadline expires. When a task has been partly executed, additional timing data is of interest; all are computed values (Figure 5.89):

- Amount of task execution currently completed, T_{ec} – a computed value.
- Amount of task execution left, T_{el} – a computed value $[T_{el} = (T_e - T_{ec})]$.
- Time to go to deadline, T_g – a computed value.

In Figure 5.89 the example task also has a predefined computation time of 100 ms and a required response time of 400 ms. At time = 5.0 s it was readied. The current time is 5.12 s. As shown, it has been executing for 70 ms (T_{ec}), performed after an initial delay of 50 ms. Thus the time to go to its deadline (T_g) is 280 ms, while the remaining spare time (T_s) is 250 ms.

Notes:

- When a task is readied ('activated') $T_d = (T_{actual} + T_r) = (T_a + T_r) T_g = (T_d - T_{actual})$.
- T_{ec} is also called the *accumulated execution time*.
- T_s is also called the *residual time*, calculated as $(T_g - T_{el})$.

More strictly, we can define a task's deadline as the 'time at which the due-time expires'.

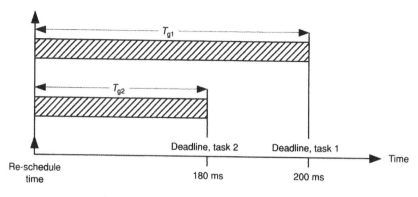

Priority (task 2) > Priority (task 1)

Figure 5.90 Priority as a function of due time.

The decision to re-schedule tasks can be based on numerous factors, three important ones· being:

- The nearness of the deadlines (earliest deadline scheduling).
- The amount of computation still to be done (computation time).
- The amount of spare time remaining before we *have* to run the task (laxity).

These are discussed below.

5.9.7 Priority-based pre-emptive dynamic scheduling – earliest deadline scheduling

Assume that at re-schedule time we have the situation shown in Figure 5.90. Here two tasks are ready to be run – therefore we must decide which one. Using earliest deadline scheduling, the task which has the smallest (shortest) due time is run (in this case, task 2). That is:

$$P_{max} \Rightarrow \text{Task}(\min T_g)$$

This policy is also called the earliest due date. The priority profiles of both the running and the ready tasks depend on the scheduling algorithm being used. For example, the algorithm

$$P = \frac{1}{T_g} \leq P_{max} \qquad (P_{max} \text{ is a pre-defined value})$$

generates the profile shown in Figure 5.91. Applying this to task 1 of Figure 5.90 results in the actual profile of Figure 5.92. Observe that P_{max} has been set to 15 (an arbitrary choice).

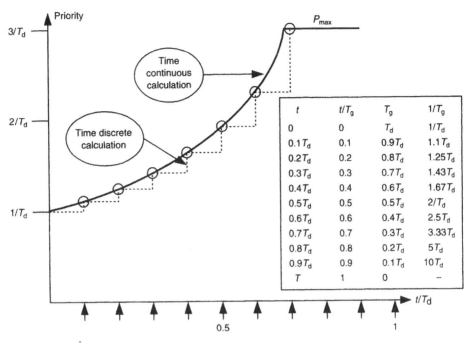

Figure 5.91 Earliest deadline scheduling, task priority profile — normalized.

t	t/T_g	T_g	$1/T_g$
0	0	T_d	$1/T_d$
$0.1T_d$	0.1	$0.9T_d$	$1.1T_d$
$0.2T_d$	0.2	$0.8T_d$	$1.25T_d$
$0.3T_d$	0.3	$0.7T_d$	$1.43T_d$
$0.4T_d$	0.4	$0.6T_d$	$1.67T_d$
$0.5T_d$	0.5	$0.5T_d$	$2/T_d$
$0.6T_d$	0.6	$0.4T_d$	$2.5T_d$
$0.7T_d$	0.7	$0.3T_d$	$3.33T_d$
$0.8T_d$	0.8	$0.2T_d$	$5T_d$
$0.9T_d$	0.9	$0.1T_d$	$10T_d$
T	1	0	–

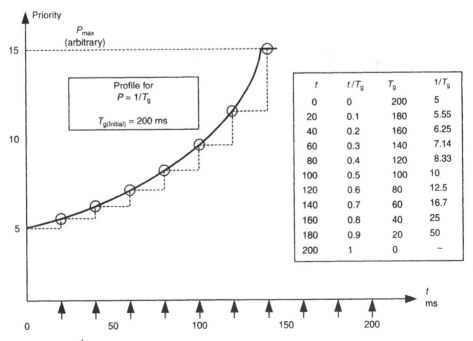

Figure 5.92 Example EDS task priority profile.

t	t/T_g	T_g	$1/T_g$
0	0	200	5
20	0.1	180	5.55
40	0.2	160	6.25
60	0.3	140	7.14
80	0.4	120	8.33
100	0.5	100	10
120	0.6	80	12.5
140	0.7	60	16.7
160	0.8	40	25
180	0.9	20	50
200	1	0	–

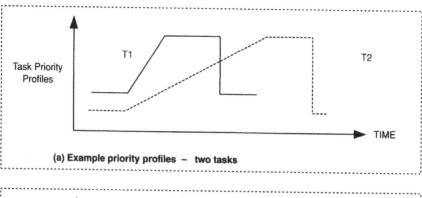

(a) Example priority profiles – two tasks

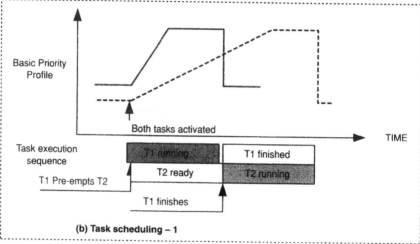

(b) Task scheduling – 1

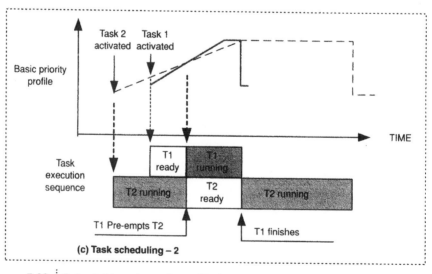

(c) Task scheduling – 2

Figure 5.93 Task priorities and execution profiles in deadline scheduling – example.

A further simple illustration of the use of earliest deadline scheduling is given in Figure 5.93. This describes the behaviour of a two-task system whose individual priority profiles are shown in Figure 5.93a. Figure 5.93b shows what happens if both are readied at the same time, a fairly straightforward case. In Figure 5.93c task 2 is readied first and then set running. At a later point task 1 is activated but, as it has a lower priority, remains in the ready queue. There comes a time, however, when its priority exceeds that of task 2. As a result task 2 is swapped out, being replaced by task 1. In this instance it will run to completion; only then will task 2 resume execution.

5.9.8 Priority-based pre-emptive dynamic scheduling policies – computation time scheduling

The scenario given in Figure 5.94 is the same as the one described in Figure 5.90. Here, though, priority is set depending on the amount of computation still to be carried out within the tasks (T_{el}). As shown, task 1 needs 70 ms to complete, whilst task 2 requires 100 ms. We assign highest priority to the task which needs the *least* computation time to finish – in this case task 1. Therefore:

$$P_{max} \Rightarrow Task(\min T_{el})$$

A workable algorithm is:

$$P = \frac{1}{T_{el}} \leq P_{max} \qquad (P_{max} \text{ is a pre-defined value})$$

It can be seen that this is a dynamic version of the (non-pre-emptive) shortest job first policy.

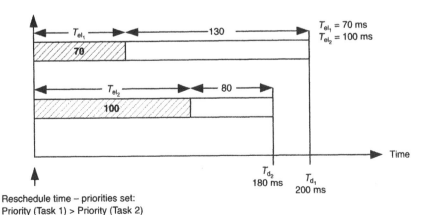

Figure 5.94 | Priority as a function of time to complete task.

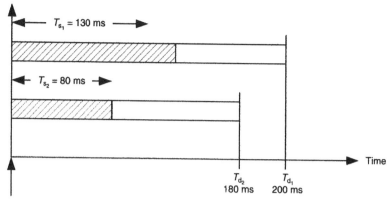

Reschedule time – priorities set at this time:
Priority (task 2) > Priority (task 1)

Figure 5.95 | Priority as a function of task laxity (spare time).

5.9.9 Priority-based pre-emptive dynamic scheduling policies – spare time (laxity) scheduling

Laxity is the amount of time which can 'wasted' between activating a task and having it deliver its result. It is defined as:

$$T_s = T_r - T_{el} - t$$

where t is the elapsed time from the task being activated.

$$P_{max} \Rightarrow \text{Task(min } T_s)$$

P may be computed as follows:

$$P = \frac{1}{T_s} \leq P_{max} \qquad (P_{max} \text{ is a pre-defined value})$$

Figure 5.95 is a redrawn version of Figure 5.94, emphasizing the spare time (the laxity) of each task (T_s). In this instance task 2 has the lowest (least) laxity. Thus it is assigned highest priority.

This scheduling method is also called the 'least laxity first' (LLF) policy.

5.9.10 Improving processor utilization – forming rate groups

It has been pointed out in earlier work that multitasking carries with it a penalty in terms of processor overhead. In some cases this may significantly reduce the processing time available to the application tasks. However, by minimizing the number of tasks in a system, processor efficiency can be improved. To do this we need to combine two or more tasks into an equivalent single task (the combined

Task no.	Period (ms)	Run time (ms)
1	20	8
2	39	8
3	81	4

Figure 5.96 Example task set.

Task no.	Period (ms)	Run time (ms)
1	20	8
2	40	8
3	80	4

Figure 5.97 Modified task set.

code is organized as a single sequential program). The resultant design must, of course, meet system objectives in terms of time and functionality. Let us look at how this can be done.

Suppose that an existing multitasking design consists of three periodic tasks, their details being given in Figure 5.96. In order to meet this requirement the tick timer must have a resolution of 1 ms. That is, it must interrupt at a 1 ms rate. Clearly the resulting processor overhead is considerable, and may significantly degrade system performance. One technique which, in some circumstances, can reduce processor loading takes the following approach:

● All task periods are set so that they have a simple numerical relationship to each other.

● Periodic tasks are executed at their correct periods and run to completion at each activation.

● Processor loading is spread evenly over time. This generally gives best performance in the presence of aperiodic tasks.

Consider the effect of changing task periods so that their timing relationship is a simple one, Figure 5.97. Task 2 now has a period which is twice as long as that of task 1. For task 3, the ratio is four. With this arrangement the tick resolution can be changed to 20 milliseconds.

What has been done is to organize processor execution as a series of minor cycle time slots. Each one has the same duration: that of the shortest period (in this case 20 milliseconds). Tasks are allocated to specific time slots, resulting in the run-time scheduling of Figure 5.98a. The point at which the allocation pattern repeats defines the duration of the major cycle time, here being 80 ms. You can see that a group of tasks are *launched* into execution within each time slot (leading to the expression *rate groups*). With this arrangement the code for all tasks is collected into one module, organized as a sequential program. At each tick time the scheduler control software merely decides which section of the code to execute.

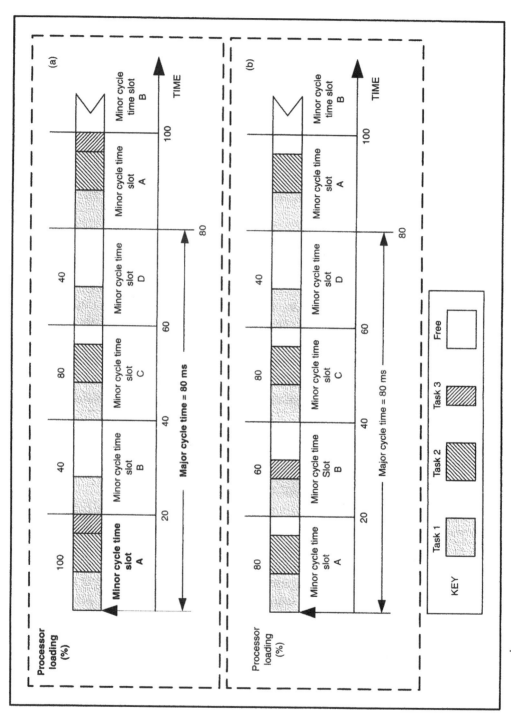

Figure 5.98 : Run-time scheduling of tasks.

One potential weakness with the schedule of Figure 5.98a is that the processor loading is very uneven (ranging from 40% to 100%). As a result there could be problems if an aperiodic task arrives during a heavily loaded period. It may produce considerable disturbance, causing a number of tasks to go late. One way to alleviate this is to 'spread' the periodic tasks so as to even out loading variations, Figure 5.98b. Of course the effectiveness of the schedule depends very much on the nature of the aperiodic tasks. Unfortunately these, by their very nature, are not deterministic; they must be described in statistical terms.

5.9.11 Scheduling strategy – a final comment

Many scheduling strategies have been devised and put into service [DEI84]. But in the main these have been designed for commercial applications, being quite unsuited for real-time systems. The constraints and features of real-time applications are well covered by Allworth [ALL81] and Leigh [LEI88]. Taking these into account, the most widely used successful scheduling strategies follow a particular pattern (Figure 5.99). First, tasks above base level are set in priority order. Once such a task is set running it goes to completion unless pre-empted by a higher-priority task. It is resumed at the first opportunity.

These tasks, when in possession of the CPU resource, can lose it to the executive in two ways. In the first case it voluntarily gives up the CPU because it no longer

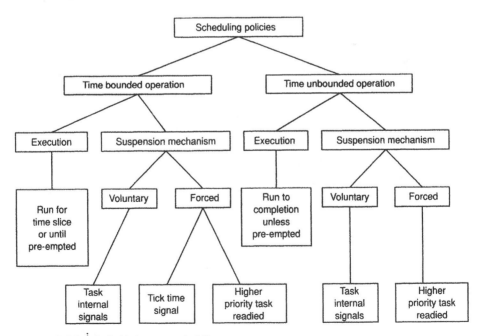

Figure 5.99 | Embedded systems scheduling strategy.

wants or needs it – 'self-release'. This arises, for instance, where a process cannot proceed any further until some event occurs. It also happens where the task is completed and the process has no further need for the CPU. The second reason for losing the CPU is a 'forced release' action. Usually this results from the readying of a higher-priority task, forcing the current task to give up the processor on the next tick count.

Base-level tasks are normally run round-robin, at equal priority settings. Both self- and forced release mechanisms are used as described above, together with a third forced release mode. Each task is forced to give up the CPU (even if it hasn't finished) when its allocated time slot expires.

5.9.12   Scheduling timing diagrams – list of symbols

- (T_a) Task arrival (activation) time: the time at which a task is put into the ready-to-run state.
- (T_b) Resource blocking time.
- (T_d) Task deadline: the time by which the task *must* deliver its result.
- (T_e) Execution time: the actual execution time of the task.
- (T_{ec}) Amount of task execution currently completed: a computed value.
- (T_{el}) Amount of task execution left: a computed value $[T_{el} = T_e - T_{ec}]$.
- (T_g) Time to go to deadline: a computed value.
- (T_p) Task period.
- (T_r) Response time: the time allowed for a task to carry out its function (note: if timing is done on a relative, not absolute, scale, then response time and deadline have the same value). This is also called 'due time'.
- (T_s) Spare time: a computed value $[(T_r - T_{el}) - t]$.
- (T_w) Waiting time.

Review

In this chapter you have seen how the nature of software design changes when we use multitasking techniques. If you have taken these lessons to heart you will now:

- Have a good grasp of the basics of real-time operating systems, in particular the tasking model of software.
- Understand why they are used, what advantages they have for the designer, and what their accompanying disadvantages are.
- Know the format, content and use of the tasking diagram.
- Understand the roles and interrelationships of the OS scheduler and dispatcher.

- Appreciate the role of scheduling in the operation of an RTOS. Have a good grasp of both the theoretical and practical aspects of scheduling policies.

- Recognize that many scheduling techniques can be used, each having pro's and con's.

- Know why, in practical multitasking systems, resource sharing always takes place.

- Realize what problems arise from using shared resources: contention, performance, data corruption, deadlocks, livelocks and priority inversion.

- See how and why flags, semaphores and monitors are used as protection mechanisms for shared resources.

- Understand the need for task communication, co-ordination and synchronization, together with the role of the various supporting components: flags, pools, channels and mailboxes.

- Be aware of the need to manage memory use and allocation, in particular issues of protection, fragmentation and leakage.

- See clearly the difference between RTOS use in single processor and distributed (multiprocessor and multiple computer) systems. Recognize that distributed systems are much more complex than single-processor implementations.

Exercises

1. Figure 5.100 is typical of many small-to-medium applications. Its primary function is to control the temperature in an engine jet pipe. This temperature is measured using the sensor, the resulting analogue signal is digitized, an error signal is calculated internally in the computer, and a correcting signal is output to the fuel valves via the DAC. The unit, however, is also required to perform several secondary tasks. First, the pilots need to have access to all system information via the keypad/display unit. Second, the flight recorder must be able to acquire the same information using a serial data link.

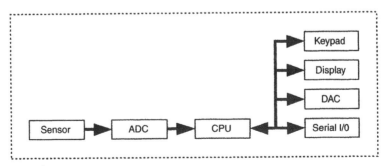

Figure 5.100 Exercise 1 – small-to-medium complexity control system.

(a)

1. Evaluate the timing requirements of the system.
2. Define the major software functions to be carried out by the system as a set of software subsystems.
3. Show all information flow, both between subsystems and to/from I/O devices.
4. How would you design the software if all the code had to be contained within a single sequential program? Explain your design decisions.

(b)

Redesign the software assuming that interrupt-driven activities are permitted. Again, explain your design decisions.

2.   An embedded system contains the following independent software tasks:

● Alarm monitoring: A set of 10 alarm sensors are connected to the processor via a slow-speed serial link. Each individual monitoring transaction (per alarm point) takes 10 milliseconds. It is assumed that all points are scanned in sequence.

● Display driving: A standard monitor is used to display system status to an operator. The display subsystem has a dedicated graphics board. It takes a maximum of 10 milliseconds to update the display information.

● Control: The system performs multi-axis closed-loop control of a robot. Loop processing takes 10 milliseconds.

● System identification: A processing algorithm is used to mathematically identify the robot system. This takes 500 milliseconds to execute.

(a)   When using simple cyclic scheduling, what is:

(1)   The worst-case delay (latency) between a sensor going into alarm and the processor system recognizing this condition?
(2)   The control loop update rate?

(b)   Reorganize your schedule using round-robin techniques to meet the following requirements:

● Control loop: A 10 Hz update rate.
● Alarm scanning: An alarm scanning cycle of 1 second.
● Display: Five updates per second.
● System identification: Do your best.

3.   A single CPU system consists of three independent control loops, each having a single analogue input and single analogue output signal. In terms of hardware, this is implemented as a single processor board, a single data-acquisition board and a single analogue output board. Each individual output channel has an independent data latch; thus each one can be written to individually. However, on the input

board, a single ADC is shared between the data channels. The normal sequence of events to acquire a signal is as follows:

- Select required channel.
- Start conversion.
- Check conversion completed.
- Read in data.

For noise rejection purposes, an integrating ADC is used, this having a conversion time of 20 milliseconds. The ADC and DAC software items are designed to be 'passive' objects which can be used by any task in the sysem.

(a) Produce a suitable software design to meet these requirements, incorporating semaphores as you see fit.

(b) Produce the source code for the semaphore(s).

(c) Show how these would be integrated into the task source code.

4. Produce a code solution showing how a semaphore may be used to enable two tasks to synchronize their activities.

References and further reading

[ALL81] *Introduction to real-time software design*, S.T. Allworth, Macmillan, London, ISBN 0-333-27137-8, 1981.

[BRI72] *Structured multiprogramming*, P. Brinch Hansen, Communications of the ACM, Vol. 15, No. 7, pp 574–577, 1972.

[CHE90] *Dynamic priority ceilings: A concurrency control protocol for real-time systems*, M.I. Chen and K.J. Lin, International Journal of Time-Critical Computer Systems, Vol. 2, No. 4, pp 325–345, 1990.

[DEI84] *An introduction to operating systems*, H.M. Deitel, Addison-Wesley, ISBN 0-201-14502-2, 1984.

[DIJ65] *Cooperating sequential processes*, E.W. Dijkstra, Technological University, Eindhoven, The Netherlands, 1965 (reprinted in *Programming languages*, ed. F. Genuys, Academic Press, New York, 1968).

[DIJ71] *Hierarchical ordering of sequential processes*, E.W. Dijkstra, Acta Informatica, Vol 1, pp 115–138, 1971.

[HOA74] *Monitors: An operating system structuring concept*, C.A.R. Hoare, Communications of the ACM, Vol 17, No. 10, pp 549–557, 1974.

[LEI88] *Real time software for small systems*, A.W. Leigh, Sigma Press, Wilmslow, Cheshire, ISBN 0-905104-98-6, 1988.

[LIU73] *Scheduling algorithms for multi programming in a hand real-time environment*, C.L. Lin and J.W. Layland, Journal of the ACM, Vol. 20, No. 1, pp 46–61, 1973.

[SHA90] *Real-time scheduling theory and Ada*, L. Sha and J.B. Goodenough, IEEE Computer, Vol. 23, No. 4, pp 53–63, 1990.

part II

Designing and Developing Real-Time Software

chapter 6

Practical Aspects of Real-Time Operating Systems

The previous chapter should have given you a good grasp of RTOS fundamentals. Its objective was to set the groundwork for the topic, creating firm foundations for future work. You are now in a position to apply these ideas in real, practical situations. Broadly speaking there are two choices. First, you may choose to develop your own operating system, the DIY method. Alternatively, a standard off-the-shelf commercial real-time operating system could be used. Whichever route is chosen, you will find the gap between theory and practice a large and challenging one.

The purpose of this chapter is to help you cross that gap. It is written primarily from the point of view of building applications on top of commercial RTOSs. However, all the lessons are equally applicable to the home-grown variety. They are intended to shed light on aspects such as:

- Why operating systems are structured in particular ways.
- What features are provided as part of the OS itself and which are essentially 'bolt-on' items.
- How OS performance is measured (and, for that matter, how it is defined in the first place).

- The time overheads incurred by using an RTOS.
- Features needed to support distributed systems.
- Practical file management requirements.
- Graphics-based user interface development within RTOS environments.
- Tools, methods and methodologies for developing practical applications.
- Portability of operating systems, with special reference to POSIX.

There isn't, unfortunately, a clear-cut division between theory and practice. However, the material included in this chapter has been selected using a rough-and-ready guide; the detail is likely to change as software technology advances over the next few years.

6.1 Operating systems – basic structures and features

6.1.1 Setting the scene

There is no such thing as a 'standard' real-time operating system; they come in a whole variety of shapes and sizes. Commercial offerings vary in code size from about 1 kByte to a few megabytes; RAM requirements are equally variable. Their functionality ranges from basic kernel operations through to full-blown Internet compatibility. And cost variations are equally bewildering.

In the light of this you can be forgiven for being confused; after all, how can such diverse products satisfy the multitasking needs of embedded systems? However, a moment's thought will show that you are asking the wrong question. It should be 'which product is best suited to *my* embedded system?'

Embedded systems are extremely diverse; moreover they tend to be shaped very much by their areas of application, Figure 6.1. Further, both technical and commercial factors determine the form, function and capabilities of real-time systems.

In this section we'll look at the need for and use of operating systems for the support of such architectures. Not surprisingly the 'one size fits all' RTOS approach is a somewhat poor engineering solution. For instance, with small, cost-sensitive units (e.g. automobile applications) an RTOS must be small. Fortunately such systems are likely to need only limited functionality; thus a small OS should be sufficient. By contrast, applying the same RTOS to a complex control system – *and* expecting it to deliver the required performance – is rather optimistic (the words 'plug and pray' spring to mind). To help choose the best solution to our multitasking requirements we need to define the:

- Core functionality provided by an RTOS.
- Additional functionality needed to support more complex architectures.

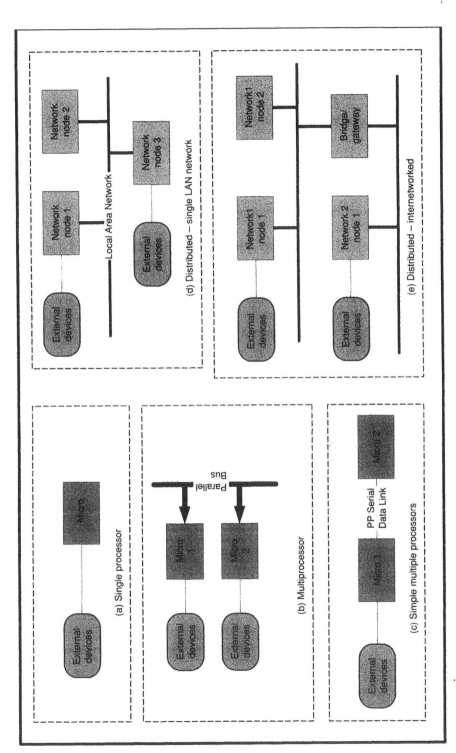

Figure 6.1 ┊ Embedded systems — some common architectures.

- Component parts of both core and extended RTOSs.
- Structuring and interconnection of the various RTOS components.

Let us begin by seeing how a simple non-RTOS control system design might be implemented. The reasons for doing this are threefold:

- To identify key sections of the program code.
- To show how these sections relate to each other.
- To set a baseline for further work.

6.1.2   Simple multitasking via interrupts

Assume that we are tasked with providing the software for a digital controller – a two-loop design – having the hardware structure of Figure 6.1a. The code for each control loop may be considered a task (in a multitasking sense, that is) needing to be executed at quite accurate intervals. One simple way to achieve this is to first write each 'application task' as an interrupt routine; then use hardware timers to generate the necessary interrupt signals. However, for this to work, the micro must be brought to a fully operational condition: that is, correctly and fully initialized. Thus the complete code for the system is likely to be organized as in Figure 6.2.

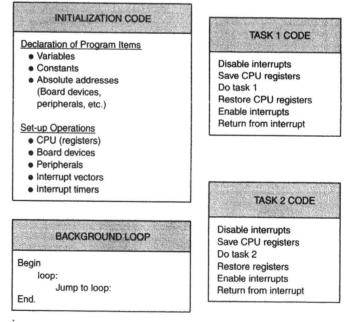

Figure 6.2   Code organization – simple single-processor application.

This, it can be seen, consists of three major groups: initialization code, background processing and application code. Consider each in turn.

Initialization code

The purpose of initialization code is to bring the processor to a state where useful work can be done. There are two main sections: declarations and set-up operations. A key aspect of declarations is to define all items used within the program (strictly this is for use by the compiler). It is also essential to specify, where needed, the absolute address locations of such items. For simplicity, processor-related components such as timers, counters, etc. are here called board devices. Components which interface to the outside world are denoted as peripheral devices.

Following this, forming part of the executable code, are the set-up operations. These ensure that the CPU, devices, peripherals, etc. (i.e. those requiring programming) are correctly initialized and readied for use by the application software. In particular they must set up and activate the interrupt system.

Background processing

In this example the background loop is simply a continuous loop which does nothing. It would be a perfectly reasonable design decision to omit this altogether; merely terminate the code after initialization. However, most embedded designs do use a background loop, even if only for calculating processor utilization (in such cases the background loop is considered to be another application task). What *is* important is to recognize that the background loop runs at a lower priority than the interrupt-driven application tasks.

Application tasks

There are, as already described, two application tasks, each having similar code structures (Figure 6.2). From this it can be seen that, in each case, the basic task code is surrounded by interrupt-specific code. Depending on the design it may also be necessary to include timer-related programming. To keep things clean, simple and maintainable, operations 'Do Task 1' and 'Do Task 2' would be calls to subprograms 'Task 1' and 'Task 2'. Both tasks will have different priorities – it is up to the designer to define the ordering in the initialization code (e.g. by appropriate set-up of a programmable interrupt controller). Designs like this tend to be tackled to some extent in an *ad hoc* programmer-dependent manner. Moreover, the resulting code tends to conceal the underlying conceptual model of the structure, Figure 6.3.

Three points should be noted. First, control of hardware items – both for initialization and normal operation – is performed by the following software subsystems:

- Interrupt service routines, ISRs (for handling interrupts).
- Interfacing code, board devices (for control of standard on-board devices).

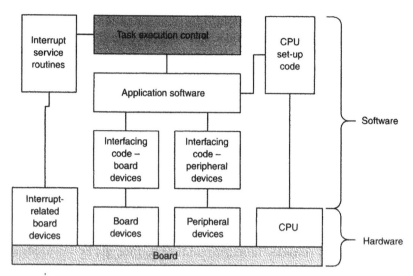

Figure 6.3 Conceptual model – simple single-processor hardware–software structure.

- Interfacing code, peripheral devices (for use with peripheral devices – usually non-standard or special-to-application).
- CPU set-up code (for manipulation of the CPU facilities).

Second, the application software interacts with the hardware via the interfacing code layer; in turn this runs under the control of the task execution control code. Third, task activation is carried out by ISRs, these being triggered by hardware-generated signals.

6.1.3 The nanokernel

It is only one small jump from an interrupt-driven home-grown 'tasking' design to the smallest type of RTOS, the nanokernel (more properly this should be described as a real-time executive). Furthermore, the word nanokernel isn't standardized; variations, sometimes quite major, can be found in practical designs. However, in this text it will be taken to mean a software component which provides a minimal set of OS services, namely:

- Task creation.
- Task management – scheduling and dispatching.
- Timing and interrupt management.

The conceptual model of a nanokernel-based system, Figure 6.4, demonstrates two important features.

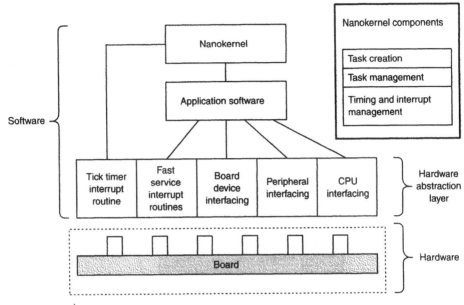

Figure 6.4 Conceptual model – nanokernel-based system.

First, all application tasks – *except time-critical ones* – are controlled by the kernel. Critical tasks require the fastest of responses, and cannot tolerate delays introduced by the OS. They are activated by the fast service interrupt routines which invoke immediate task dispatch (thus by-passing the kernel). A separate interrupt routine is provided for the tick timer, this providing the basic timing mechanism of the nanokernel.

Second, the layer of software which interfaces directly to the hardware:

● Is intended to provide an abstract interface to the application software and the kernel itself.

● Should encapsulate all code needed for the set-up and operation of the board hardware.

● Depends on the nature of the computer hardware.

● Is usually produced by the programmer as a special-purpose design.

This software is sometimes called the Hardware Abstraction Layer, HAL (to some extent a fashionable name).

The design of the HAL is entirely the responsibility of the programmer. A good design will provide strong encapsulation of this service software (so called as it provides a service to the application) together with the hiding of implementation details. The application programmer should merely have to call on these services without needing to know anything of their innards. Unfortunately, there

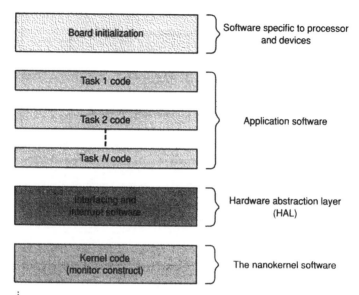

Figure 6.5 Code organization – nanokernel-based system.

is no guarantee that the software will be designed in this way; you may well find detailed service code *within* the application code.

An examination of the code organization (Figure 6.5) shows that requirements for timing and interrupt handling have apparently disappeared. In fact they are contained within the kernel. The kernel code is usually composed as a set of sub-programs encapsulated within some software container, often a monitor (which also provides safe operation as a result of its inherent mutual exclusion mechanism). Typically these enable us to:

- Initialize the OS.
- Create a task.
- Delete a task.
- Delay a task.
- Control the tick (start time-slicing, set the time slice duration).
- Start the OS.
- Set the clock time.
- Get the clock time.

6.1.4 The microkernel

The next step up the OS ladder brings us to the microkernel. Its code is often organized in a manner similar to that of Figure 6.6. There are two significant

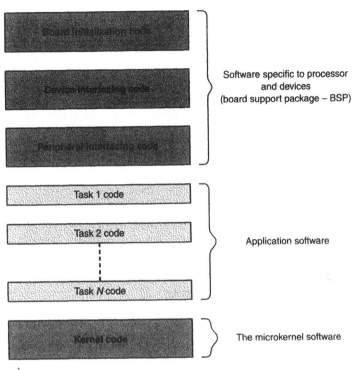

Figure 6.6 Code organization – microkernel-based system.

improvements over the nanokernel: increased kernel functionality and the use of a board support package (BSP). Let us turn first to the BSP.

This, the BSP, is provided as part of the microkernel package to support both custom and standard hardware designs. Its purpose is to minimize the efforts involved in developing interfacing software for new designs. Board initialization, device interfacing and peripheral interfacing code are all contained in the BSP (which normally includes interrupt handling operations). Though features vary from RTOS to RTOS the following facilities are found in many packages:

- Board-specific functions, including general initialization, RTOS initialization and interrupt configuration.

- Device-specific driver software, supplied in template form. This is board-independent and therefore needs configuration by the programmer.

- Detailed low-level code used by the device drivers, but applicable to specific devices (e.g. Intel 82527 communications controller).

- Support for the development of special-purpose BSP functions.

The kernel itself has many more features (compared with the nanokernel, that is). Whether one is designed in-house or bought-in, it should provide a set of operations (or 'primitives') relating to:

(a) System set-up and special functions

- Initialize the OS (if not part of the BSP).
- Set up all special (non-kernel) interrupt functions.
- Start execution of the application programs.

(b) Process (task) scheduling and control

- Declare a task.
- Start a task.
- Stop a task.
- Destroy a task.
- Set task priorities.
- Lock-out task (make it non-pre-emptive).
- Unlock a task.
- Delay a task.
- Resume a task.
- Control the real-time clock (tick, relative time and absolute time functions).
- Control use of interrupts.

(c) Mutual exclusion

- Gain control using semaphores (entry to critical region).
- Release control using semaphores (exit from critical region).
- Gain control using monitors.
- Release control using monitors.
- Wait in a monitor.

(d) Synchronization functions – no data transfer

- Initialize a signal/flag.
- Send a signal/flag (with and without timeouts).
- Wait for a signal/flag (with and without timeouts).
- Check for a signal/flag.

(e) Data transfer without synchronization

- Initialize a channel/pool.
- Send to a channel/write to a pool (with and without timeouts).
- Receive from a channel/read from a pool (with and without timeouts).
- Check channel state (full/empty).

(f) Synchronization with data transfer

- Set up a mailbox.
- Post to a mailbox (with and without timeouts).
- Pend to a mailbox (with and without timeouts).
- Check on a mailbox.

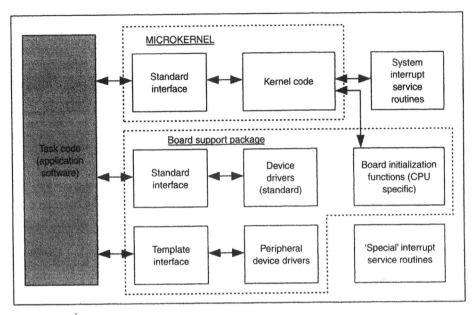

Figure 6.7 | Software conceptual model – small microkernel-based system.

(g) Dynamic memory allocation

- Allocate a block of memory.
- Deallocate a block of memory.

In conceptual terms, the software of a typical microkernel-based system may be modelled as in Figure 6.7.

6.1.5 A general-purpose embedded RTOS

Figure 6.8 illustrates the hardware structure and software functions typically found in larger general-purpose embedded systems. From the figure it should be clear how the software functions relate to the hardware items. Note the following significant new features:

- Industrial networking, including standard systems (e.g. CAN, fieldbus, etc.) and special-purpose designs.
- General-purpose networking, with emphasis on Internet applications (e.g. Ethernet, ATM, etc.). Many embedded systems now have the ability to act as mini-Web servers, so providing remote access facilities.
- Graphics-based user interfaces (PC-based GUIs and specialist designs).
- Long-term persistent storage (disks and semiconductors).

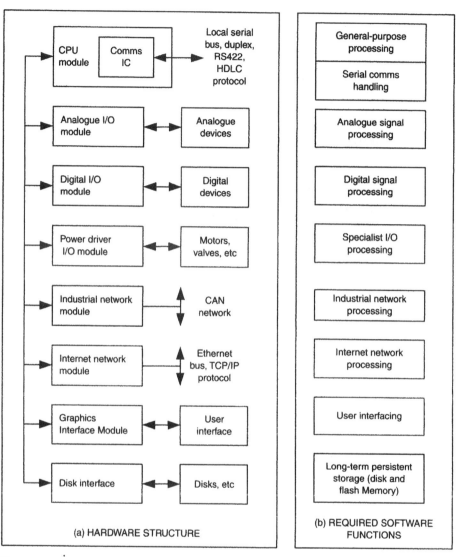

Figure 6.8 Typical large general-purpose embedded system – hardware structure and software functions.

The software conceptual model of Figure 6.9 is characteristic of these larger systems. At its core is the microkernel, which acts as the overall orchestrator of events. Individual software packages are provided for network, device/peripheral, file and graphics handling. Application software is isolated from the microkernel via a memory management and protection layer. In its simplest form this supports two modes of operation: kernel (protected) and other (non-protected). Critical systems use more secure techniques, adding an isolation barrier between the individual tasks.

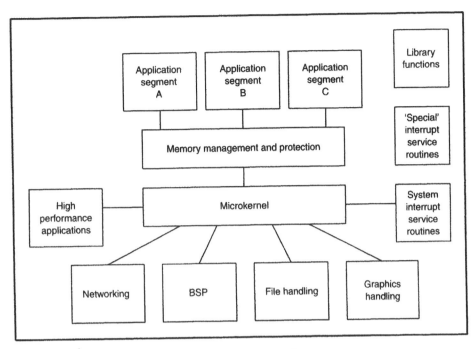

Figure 6.9 ┊ Software conceptual model – typical large general-purpose system.

System interrupt routines are those which interact with the kernel itself (e.g. tick timer, peripheral devices, etc.). In contrast, special interrupt-driven routines are allowed to completely override kernel operations. These are normally reserved for use by highly time-critical functions. Applications which are less time critical but still must deliver high performance often interface directly to the kernel.

A major support facility is that of a set of library functions, usually based on standard C and C++ facilities. However, to be able to use these safely in embedded systems, full re-entrancy is *essential* (some OS vendors have developed fully re-entrant versions of the standard libraries just to meet this requirement).

6.2 Inter-processor communication

6.2.1 General aspects

Where a system contains more than one processor they, the processors, usually need to talk to each other. For many years software support for inter-processor communication has tended to be a bolt-on feature, quite independent of the OS. Standards, if used, were applied mainly in two areas. The first is the task of managing communication over the data link itself, called Medium Access Control

1. Multiprocessor (Figure 6.1b).

- Backplane connection (parallel, typically 32 to 128 bits wide).
- Fast data rates (100 MBytes/s).
- Messaging supported by custom protocols.
- Device drivers – custom or standard (e.g. PCI).

2. Simple multiple processors (Figure 6.1c).

- Serial link connection, simplex or duplex.
- Slow-to-medium data rates (9.6 kbaud to 1 Mbits/s).
- Message flow control – custom or standard (e.g. Xon, Xoff, etc.).
- Device drivers – specific to chip (use BSP facilities).

3. Distributed – single LAN network (Figure 6.1d).

- Standard LAN connections (e.g. CAN, Profibus, Ethernet, etc.).
- Medium-to-high-speed data rates (1 to 100 Mbits/s).
- Medium access control protocol.
- Logical link control protocol.
- Device driver specific to LAN chips (e.g. CAN 2.0 interfacing via a Siemens C505c device).

4. Distributed – internetworked (Figure 6.1e).

- Based on interconnected subnets.
- Medium-to-high-speed data rates (1 to 100 Mbits/s).
- Device drivers specific to network interfaces (e.g. CAN, Ethernet, etc.).
- Medium access control protocol.
- Logical link control protocol.
- Routing control protocol (delivery service).
- End-to-end message handling protocol.

Figure 6.10 Inter-processor communication features.

(MAC). Typical examples of MAC protocols are those of Ethernet and Token Ring. The second, Logical Link Control (LLC), deals with a number of aspects including:

- Assembly/disassembly of link messages.
- Addressing and code checking (error detection) facilities.
- The provision of software interfaces to users of the LLC.

One widely used link control protocol is HDLC (High-level Data Link Control).

In recent years the use of multiprocessor, multiple-processor and distributed networked systems in embedded applications has increased significantly. Figures 6.1b–e illustrate the type of architectures commonly found in modern systems; the corresponding communication requirements are listed in Figure 6.10. Frequently, large systems consist of combinations of such architectures.

From this it can be seen that the communication requirements are very wide-ranging in terms of:

- Network media and topologies.
- Data rates.
- Protocols.

In essence, the communication functions are an integral part of the total system [STA97]. To meet these needs many RTOS vendors provide a suite of network facilities as part of a complete package. As a result the distinction between operating systems and communication functions has become blurred.

6.2.2 Communication protocols and related models

The purpose of this section is to give an overview of the fundamentals of networking protocols. It is *not* a detailed implementation guide. By understanding this you will be in a position to assess the impact of such features on OS size and performance (in fact networking aspects often become the dominant factor, greatly bloating the size of the RTOS). A good place to start is to look at some models of communication protocols, Figure 6.11. Here four models are shown, including the OSI seven-layer one. This is included to act as a reference for the others; it is doubtful if a true OSI protocol has been applied in an embedded application.

A very brief definition of the OSI model layers follows.

1. Physical: defines aspects relating to the transmission of bits over a physical link – example: RS422.
2. Data link: provides for reliable transfer of data across the link, incorporating the features of the MAC and LLC protocols (already described) – example: Token bus.

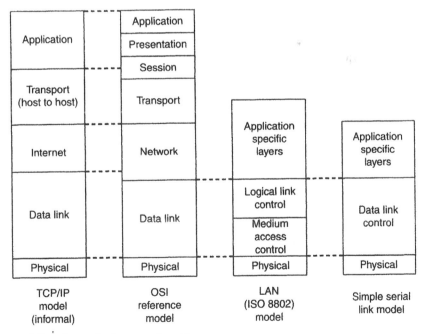

Figure 6.11 Communication protocol models.

3. Network: responsible for control of all connections and end-to-end data transfer (including routing) on the *network* – example: X25 packet level protocol.

4. Transport: enables data to be transferred reliably and transparently between endpoints, supported as required by flow control mechanisms.

5. Session: controls the end-to-end dialogue between interacting *applications*.

6. Presentation: acts as an interface between the OSI environment and the various applications using techniques such as data transformation, encryption, compression, etc.

7. Application: provides methods by which applications can *access* the OSI environment.

The facilities provided by the other three models (of practical communication systems) can now be cross-referred to the seven-layer model. Of these the most basic is that representing the protocols of a simple serial link connection, Figure 6.1c. This is typical of the support needed to implement a point-to-point duplex link using, for instance, an on-chip UART (Universal Asynchronous Receiver Transmitter). It is possible that many of the MAC functions are carried out in hardware.

The local area network (LAN) model – typified by Figure 6.1d – is slightly more complex, this incorporating LLC functions. Many industrial networks conform to this model, including the widely used Controller Area Network (CAN). In this model, applications 'speak' to the LLC layer via standard interfaces called service access points (SAPs). Most (if not all) LANs used for fast and/or critical real-time systems are of this type.

For general-purpose networking, Figure 6.1e, the *de facto* standard is that of TCP/IP (transmission control protocol/Internet protocol, [WIL93]). This suite of protocols has now become a dominant one, in part due to the almost universal use of the Internet. From Figure 6.11 it can be seen that it aligns broadly with the OSI model. Here the IP layer performs functions similar to that of the OSI network layer. Sitting above this is the transport layer, TCP, providing end-to-end transfer of information between host machines. At the highest level is the application layer, providing communication between application processes hosted on different machines. These points are illustrated in Figure 6.12, its abbreviations being defined below.

At the lowest level, software protocols (network access protocols) are supplied so that higher-level functions can access the network itself. A number are in common use, including PPP. These implement the LLC and MAC aspects of network interfacing (note that the combination of the Internet and Network Access level functions are often lumped together as the 'Network Layer Protocols').

The IP protocols are concerned with network operation, typical functions being:

● Datagram delivery (a datagram is the basic data transfer unit of the Internet).

● Routing functions (routing information and algorithms).

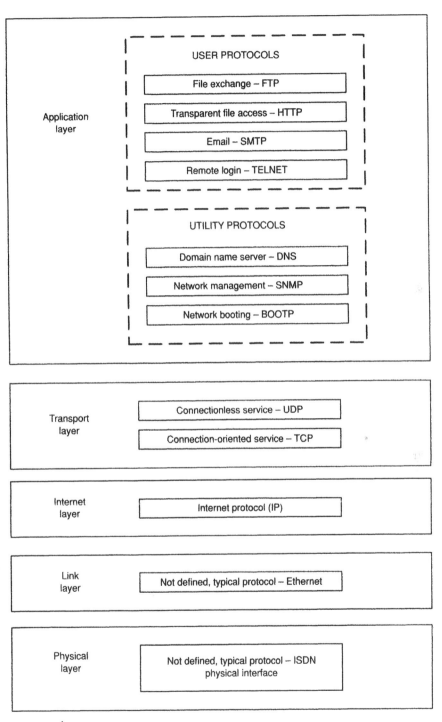

Figure 6.12 Typical TCP/IP protocols – usage and relationships.

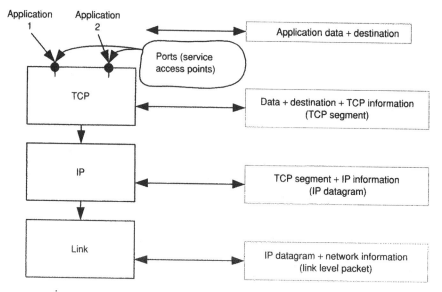

Figure 6.13 | TCP/IP – message structure and content.

A variety of applications are supported by the TCP/IP protocols, major ones being:

● The transfer of files between systems – file exchange.

● Client–server operations involving hypertext – transparent file access.

● Electronic mail.

● Attaching remote terminals to a computer – remote login.

Thus to send email, for instance, the application program first accesses the TCP layer via a SAP or 'port', Figure 6.13. A SAP is the address of the application within the host computer. What it does is give the message plus destination address details to the TCP layer. Control information is added at this point. The sum total – called the *TCP segment* – is then handed to the IP layer, using the UDP protocol. UDP now attaches addressing and control information to the TCP segment, forming the IP datagram. In turn this is passed to the link layer which constructs a Link Level Data Packet. The related Protocol Data Units (PDUs) are shown in Figure 6.14. At each stage approximately 20 bytes are added to the existing data. Thus each transmitted packet carries an overhead in the order of 62 bytes.

The reason for looking into TCP/IP in some detail (as an OS-related topic, that is) is threefold. First, embedded systems are now often required to interface to higher-level functions such as management reporting, statistics collection, remote supervision and the like. This involves interfacing to other networks, which nowadays are likely to be based on TCP/IP. Second, the software to implement such interfaces is both large and complex; it is best to construct these using standard, vendor-supplied, network protocols. Third, its complexity, speed, size and inherent features make it unsuitable where speed and safety are paramount.

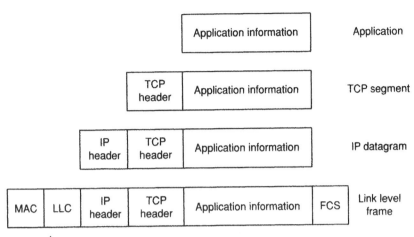

Figure 6.14 TCP/IP – protocol data units.

At this point some definitions are in order:

- Protocol: the rules to be followed when setting up and sending network messages.

- Protocol architecture: the extent and structuring of the protocols as specified by individual communication standards, e.g. OSI, ISO 8802, etc.

- Protocol stack: a *specific* set of protocols used in a *particular* application.

Many systems connected to TCP/IP networks are UNIX-based. As a result, modern operating systems often include the UNIX-specific communication facilities of sockets and streams. Sockets connect processes (tasks), a pair of sockets forming a bi-directional data pipe or channel (Figure 6.15). Each socket is the end-point

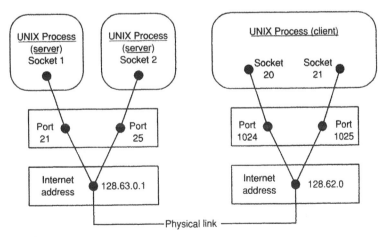

Figure 6.15 Inter-processor communication of UNIX-based systems.

of the communications channel (ports are defined to be the connection between a machine and the outside world). Hence data can be written to or read from a socket.

Streams are also a form of pipe, but are used to connect processes to I/O devices.

6.3   File handling

6.3.1   Setting the scene

The development in recent years of high-density low-cost data storage devices has had a major impact in embedded systems. More and more, designers are using the features and facilities of such devices to enhance equipment capabilities. Personal organizers, smart projectors, network configuration tools: just a few examples where mass storage devices are both an intrinsic and essential part of the equipment. Typical of those used in real-time applications are:

● Floppy disks

● Hard disks

● RAMdisks

● CD-ROMs

● Remote (nework-accessible) disk stores.

For simplicity, these are considered to be 'disk subsystems'.

Here we concentrate on interactions between the application tasks and the disk subsystems: that is, program-generated activities. The issue, conceptually, is one of transferring information between a task and a data store, Figure 6.16. Such information is transferred in file form (File, *OED*: 'information held on backing store . . . which may hold data, programs, text or any other information'). More commonly we regard a file as being an entity which contains information.

From the program's point of view it shouldn't matter which type of device is being used. Hard disk, floppy disk, RAM disk, etc.; these should appear to be essentially the same (apart from differences in functionality, of course). This 'abstraction' is attained by the use of a file management system, FMS. By providing an abstract interface(s) to the program, the FMS hides the details of specific devices.

A slightly different view of file handling concepts is shown in Figure 6.17. This highlights the role of the FMS.

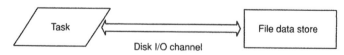

Figure 6.16 | File data I/O – a conceptual view.

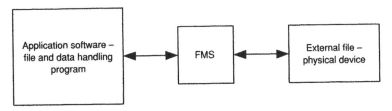

Figure 6.17 File handling concept.

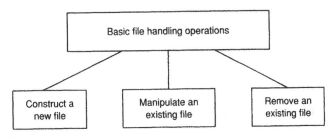

Figure 6.18 File handling — basic operations.

6.3.2 File management systems

Basic file operations consist of (Figure 6.18):

- Constructing a file in the first place, and defining its attributes (create).
- Manipulating an existing file (open, close, rename, write data, read data).
- Removing a file when it is no longer needed (delete).

These are often called the CRUD functions – Create, Read, Update, Delete.

However, these need to be augmented by further management functions, as for example:

- Device initialization.
- File system (bad media) recovery.
- File locking.
- Construction and manipulation of directory structures (a file organization function).
- Disk partitioning.
- Volume mounting and dismounting (a volume is a generic term meaning *a removable unit of any data storage medium*).

Details, of course, may vary from system to system.

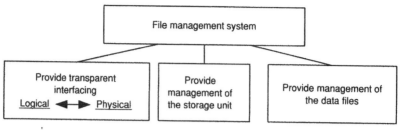

Figure 6.19 File management system – overall requirements.

Thus in general terms, the requirements of a file management system are those shown in Figure 6.19. Simply put, the FMS provides a set of services which simplify the use of mass storage in embedded systems. It can also be an advantage if file handling facilities support standard file features and systems such as:

- UNIX and Linux
- DOS
- Win 32
- ISO 9660 CD-ROM file system
- Client and server for NFS (network file service)
- C and C++ streams.

6.4 Graphical user interfaces in embedded systems

6.4.1 Introduction

This section should really be called 'user interfaces' as it relates to the use, by people, of computer-based systems. However, as so many modern applications use visual interfaces, including 'graphical' in the title seemed appropriate. And, of course, the expression 'graphical user interface', GUI, is now a very well-established one.

Graphical displays have been in use in embedded systems for many years now. In earlier times two distinct groups predominated: low-cost simple alphanumeric types and relatively expensive CRT-based colour ones. Typical of the more expensive applications are:

- Flight-deck instrumentation on civil aircraft (the 'glass' cockpit).
- Operator displays for sector-scan sonar systems.
- Control room displays for SCADA (Supervisory Control And Data Acquisition) systems.

These require the presentation of complex real-time information having fast update rates. The corresponding software workloads are quite demanding, often

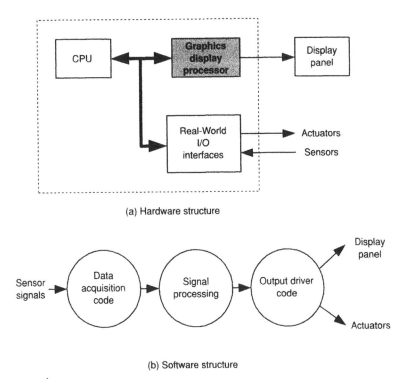

(a) Hardware structure

(b) Software structure

Figure 6.20   Traditional embedded graphical interface – hardware and software features.

exceeding the capabilities of the main processor. As a result, specialist graphics display processors (GDPs) were developed to control the display subsystems, acting as
peripherals to the main processor (Figure 6.20a). In many cases the primary signals
to the graphical system (e.g. engine speed, inlet pressure, exhaust gas temperature,
etc.) are provided by devices, not people. Figure 6.20b gives a simple view of the
related software processing, typical of that used for processing engine data, say.

A major problem with this approach is that the GDP software is intermingled
with that of the core application itself. Such software is both detailed and complex.
Developers need to be both highly proficient *and* have a very good understanding
of GDP programming. These factors, taken together, may adversely affect:

● Cost
● Reliability
● Timescales
● Skill levels.

To attack these problems, software development had to be simplified. This resulted
in the basic software structuring model of Figure 6.21. The central point here is the
distinct separation of graphical interface (GDP-specific) code from that of the core

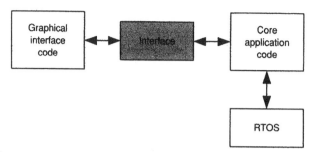

Figure 6.21 Embedded graphics system — basic software structuring model.

application itself. In elegant designs the graphics code is encapsulated in a set of libraries, these having simple clean interfaces. As a result, development of the core application is decoupled from that of the graphics software itself.

6.4.2 Modern developments in user interfaces

In recent years there has been a tremendous upsurge in the use of graphics-based user interfaces for embedded systems (with emphasis on user *interaction* with the computer system itself). Examples include:

- Mobile phones
- Personal digital assistants
- Electronic test equipment
- In-car navigation systems.

As a result a better view of software and device relationships is that shown in Figure 6.22. Here the overall application code is split into two parts (as before): core application code and graphical interface code. Interfacing to real-world devices (e.g. sensors, actuators, etc.) is carried out by the core application code. The graphical section is responsible for handling all graphics-related input and output devices. But be aware; this may or may not reflect reality. In simpler, smaller systems it may be necessary to access such devices via core application code. A much better solution is to provide specific support for graphics interfacing and device handling within the operating system. An added bonus is that the software may be readily produced using some form of GUI tool builder.

What can be achieved in practice depends to a large extent on the hardware platform in use, Figure 6.23. Consider two extremes. At one end we might have Windows NT running on a PC; at the other a 'home-grown' OS running on bespoke hardware. In the first case the OS is aware of all standard user interface devices attached to the PC hardware. Thus a PC-specific GUI builder (such as Visual Basic or Delphi)

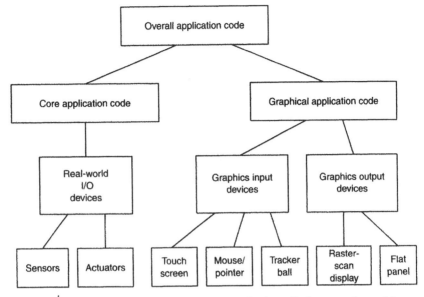

Figure 6.22 : Modern embedded graphics system – overall software/device structuring model.

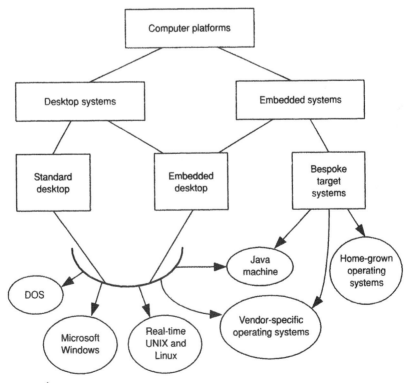

Figure 6.23 : Hardware platforms and their related operating systems.

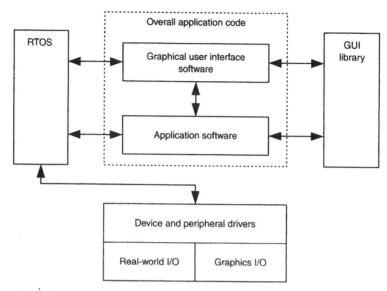

Figure 6.24 | Software components of a modern graphics-based embedded system.

can provide all the necessary software 'hooks' to these devices. This approach allows a developer to build a user interface which (say):

- Incorporates mouse-activated buttons.
- Associates these with the relevant interrupts.
- Links to the underlying source code for handling related input/processing/ output activities.

For the second case, the OS will probably know nothing of the interface devices; code must be specially developed to handle these. Moreover, the relationship between the graphical and application software is likely to be similar to that depicted in Figure 6.21.

Most commercial and research embedded operating systems lie somewhere between these two extremes. And the question then is 'how easy (or difficult) is it to develop GUIs when using these OSs?' The answer? It all depends on the support features of each specific operating system. Before looking into this in more detail, let us re-assess the software structuring of a modern graphics-based embedded system (Figure 6.24). Note that the overall application code components are now organized as two distinct groups: 'GUI software' and 'Application software' (fits in with terms in common use).

Both the GUI and the application software interface to the RTOS; observe also that the GUI software also interfaces directly to the application software. From the GUI point of view these interfaces are of major interest, Figure 6.25. It is assumed here that the RTOS has a board support package which houses all required I/O drivers.

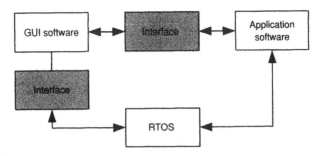

Figure 6.25 : Key graphics software interfaces.

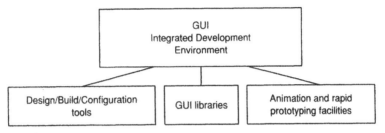

Figure 6.26 : Basic features of a GUI IDE.

Thus both software components interface to the I/O subsystem via the RTOS. Hence the GUI software has the capability to access the graphics I/O devices independently of the application software. Whether it does depends on circumstances. Take the case where user interaction takes place via the display and a set of softkeys (say). Here the GUI software is likely to access related I/O devices via the RTOS. Now consider a much different requirement: the need to show aircraft air data information on an electronic display (e.g. an artificial horizon). In this instance external signals will probably interface to the GUI via the application software.

6.4.3 GUI integrated development environments

Three particular issues are important when developing graphical interfaces:

- The range of graphics which can be produced.
- Techniques for designing and building GUIs.
- Methods for testing, evaluating and demonstrating GUIs.

A comprehensive integrated development environment (IDE, Figure 6.26) should take all three into account, providing appropriate tools and libraries. IDEs should also be assessed in terms of their ability to support the development of graphical interfaces which are:

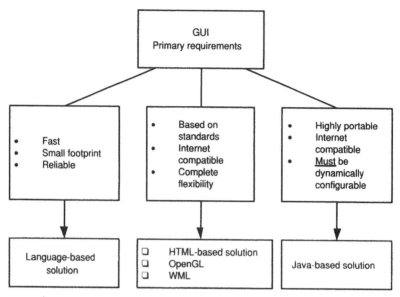

Figure 6.27 Building embedded GUIs – mainstream techniques.

- Reliable
- Portable
- Scalable
- Configurable
- Network compatible (especially TCP/IP)
- Able to interface to a wide range of devices.

It is also important to assess the memory requirements ('footprint') of GUIs when using different development techniques (Figure 6.27). Those shown here are representative of three distinct approaches. First, where speed, size and reliability are paramount, a language-based solution gives best results. Normally both the GUI and the application software are developed using the same language (e.g. C++); interfacing is essentially performed by linking the various source files. The method is flexible, scalable and can be portable (it is possible to interface to more than one operating system). However, it *is* tied to a specific language, which somewhat limits its portability. Note that as the object code is produced using a compile/link/locate process, it cannot be reconfigured at run-time (i.e. a static configuration).

The second approach is to build on a 'standard' programming language that provides Internet compatibility yet retains flexibility. To this end some GUI development tools enable coding to be carried out using the hypertext mark-up language (HTML). HTML coding is used for the development of the user interface itself; however, mechanisms must also be provided to link this to the application software. As these may be vendor-specific, portability could be a problem. Furthermore, the type of implementation determines whether or not the interface can be dynamically configured. Several domain-specific standards are emerging, including the OpenGL [OPE02] and WAP Wireless Markup Language (WML) [WML02] specifications.

Finally, for high portability, Internet compatibility and dynamic configurability, a Java-based solution can be adopted. Details may vary from vendor to vendor, but the overall concepts are likely to be similar: a Java machine (doing the GUI work) sitting on top of an RTOS. In turn this interfaces to the application software, which may be coded in C, C++, Ada 95, etc. (especially in fast, hard systems). This approach may, of course, change as Java's embedded performance improves.

6.5 Performance and benchmarking of RTOSs

6.5.1 Introduction

This may sound like a mantra, but it's still worth repeating. *Computers in real-time systems must deliver the right answers in the right order and at the right time.* And lest you should ever forget, these are determined by system, not computer, requirements.

To meet these objectives software must have deterministic behaviour. That is, we must guarantee what it will do both in terms of function (*functional correctness*) and time (*temporal correctness*). The use of real-time operating systems has significantly simplified the task of implementing large, complex software systems. In particular they have made it easier to produce designs which are functionally correct. Unfortunately, the same cannot be said for timing correctness; if anything the reverse is true. And that can raise serious problems for the designer of embedded systems, especially the hard–fast ones.

The core mechanism in a multitasking structure is the RTOS. Where time behaviour is critical, we would dearly love to employ one whose performance is fully predictable (from here on, 'performance' is shorthand for 'time performance'). And this leads to the following questions:

- What information do we need?
- From where can this be obtained?
- How can we use such information in defining the performance of the system?

To answer these a good starting point is information produced by the RTOS vendors themselves. The best provide comprehensive material containing all important timing details. Unfortunately these may be less helpful than you might think, for a variety of reasons:

- Comparison problems.
- Hidden overheads.
- Timing methods.
- System architectures.

Let us take these in turn.

1. If we wish to compare products, then it's essential that we compare like for like. This may not be as straightforward as it should be, on two counts. First, different vendors may use the same word to mean different things. One example is 'context switch'. This seems straightforward enough. But does it include a rescheduling decision or not? Second, the items measured may not in fact be directly comparable (as from two vendors, 'Interrupt Latency' and 'Interrupt Dispatch Time').

2. The operations defined are in fact only part of the whole story, thus misleading the reader. For example, to use a particular kernel function, it may first be necessary to perform some 'prologue'. To do this, extra source code must be added to the application program. No mention is made of this in the vendor's timing data.

3. Timing measurements can be carried out in a number of ways. Some are less precise than others, leading to greater error margins. It is unusual to find vendors explaining, in detail, how their timing information is gathered.

4. Most data sheets specify the CPU type (and clock speed) to which the timings apply. However, the architecture of the processor system can also affect timings. Regrettably, details of the test environment are rarely provided with the performance information.

Having said this, however, we have to live with reality. In most cases timing data can be found only in documentation produced by RTOS suppliers. What *we* need, therefore, is the knowledge to allow us to interpret, assess and use such data.

6.5.2 Measuring computer performance – benchmarking

Benchmarking is a technique used to derive the performance of a computer system. In benchmark tests a system is required to carry out a set of defined tasks; the time taken to do these is then used as a measure of its performance. We say that the system has been *benchmarked*.

Two major areas of computer performance are of interest to the designer: computation performance and OS performance, Figure 6.28. Benchmarks relating to computing functions are well established, having been used for many years. In contrast those concerned with OS performance are much newer and are not widely applied. However, they provide a good base from which we can build our own assessment frameworks. First, though, let us have a brief look at computation performance benchmarks to see their relevance to real-time computing.

Computation performance benchmarks

Computation benchmarks fall into three categories: synthetic, kernel and application programs. They were originally devised for general-purpose systems, to provide

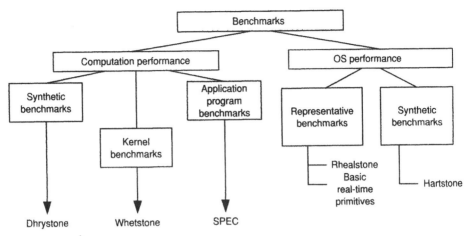

Figure 6.28 Some performance measures of computer systems.

a measure of the performance of specific computer architectures. The results obtained are heavily dependent on system features such as the CPU, maths coprocessors, cache organization, memory structure, etc. The basic testing mechanism for all three is similar. Systems execute a standard set of programs, timing data being collected during the testing. The collective data set is then used to calculate a single performance index for the computer system.

The first, *synthetic*, is obtained by executing a set of artificial programs which are representative of real computing needs (in other words the programs don't do anything useful). For the second, *kernel* (a confusing term), the tests are based on simple but real representative programs. The third one uses test programs derived from real application areas. Many specific measures have been devised, some of the best-known ones being Dhrystone [WEI84], Whetstone [CUR76] and SPEC (System Performance Evaluation Cooperative [GIL95]).

Dhrystone benchmarking is intended to provide performance metrics which can be applied to systems programming. Performance figures depend on two factors: hardware platform and programming language. Exercises involve data and data types, assignments, control statements, procedure and function calls and the like. The rate at which the test suite executes – measured as *Dhrystones per second* – is used to generate the widely used MIPS figure (millions of instructions per second). This benchmark does not use floating-point operations.

Whetstone has its roots in scientific numerical computing. It is geared to measuring floating-point (FP) performance, programs being typical of those found in real FP applications (e.g. matrix inversion, tree searching, etc.). As with Dhrystone, test results are used to provide a performance metric, in this case Mflops (mega floating-point operations per second).

SPEC measures were established to overcome the perceived narrowness of the Dhrystone and Whetstone test suites. Tests are derived from real applications (e.g.

circuit design with Spice2g6, simulation with Doduc, etc.), and results are used to establish the throughput of the system. The benchmarks are specified in terms of a geometric mean based on the average of all individual test times (a normalized figure).

Now for a most important point. These figures are normally used to provide a *comparative* measure of performance, not an absolute one. In spite of their limitations they can be of help in choosing a processor. Unfortunately they don't give much idea as to how well your specific application will perform. Moreover, nothing is said *vis-à-vis* the OS.

OS performance

From earlier work it should be clear that many factors determine RTOS performance other than pure computation times. Examples include scheduling techniques, interrupt handling, context switch times, task dispatching, etc. As a result any useful benchmark test must exercise these features, either directly or indirectly.

OS benchmarks fall into two broad categories: representative and synthetic. In simplistic terms they can be considered as low-level and high-level tests. Representative benchmarking sets out to provide performance figures for specific RTOS functions such as:

- Task management calls (create task, suspend task, lock scheduling, for example).
- Memory management calls (e.g. get a memory block, extend a memory partition, etc.).
- Inter-process communication calls (post to mailbox, send to channel and the like).

This sort of material is usually provided by RTOS vendors, though test methods are product-specific. Several standards have also been proposed, including the Rhealstone and Basic Real-Time Primitive benchmarks. More will be said on these shortly.

Synthetic benchmarks, in contrast, set out to obtain a measure of RTOS responsiveness and throughput. This is done by varying the workload on the system by changing, for example:

- Task numbers and types.
- Task qualities.
- Scheduling algorithms.
- Run-time mix of tasks.

Proposed methods include the Hartstone benchmark, discussed later.

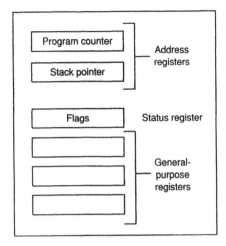

Figure 6.29 Register structure – simple microcontroller.

6.5.3 Time overheads in processor systems

This section could be loosely retitled 'Where does all the time go to?' To answer that you need some understanding of what happens within the processor system as it executes code. You could, of course, argue there is little value in having such information; as an application designer you have no control over these activities. Now, it is true that you cannot change detailed activities. However, the *way* in which these are used in a multitasking design may *significantly* impact on performance. To appreciate this only a broad – essentially conceptual – understanding of certain basic operations is required.

A good starting point is the register structure of a simple microcontroller (very simple indeed, Figure 6.29). Here memory and I/O address details are handled within the address register set. Processor status is maintained by the flags register, whilst a set of general-purpose registers supports all remaining functions.

The program counter (PC) – an essential part of any CPU – contains the address of the *next* instruction to be executed. It is fundamental to, and forms an integral part of, the Von Neumann computer architecture. A second essential register is the stack pointer, SP. This holds the address of the top of the stack (a memory store area, organized on a last-in first-out basis, and located in RAM). Note that register naming varies between processor types.

We are now in a position to look at the problem of program overheads. To start with, consider assembly-level programming, the lowest practical source code level. A tiny sequential program which executes all of its statements is unlikely to incur an overhead. However, as soon as subroutines are used, this is no longer the case. Take the situation shown in Figure 6.30a. Here the code of the processor main

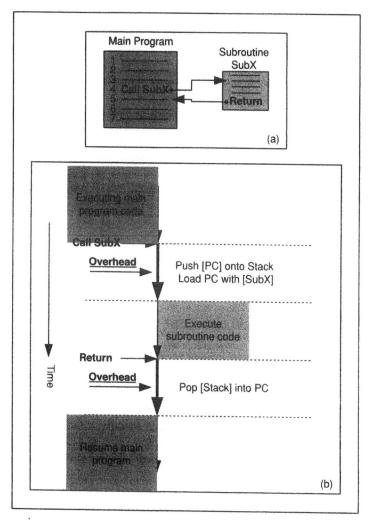

Figure 6.30 | Subroutine call — assembly-level operation.

program has within it a call to a subroutine SubX. For the processor to be able to branch to the subroutine (and to begin executing it correctly), it must be supplied with the address of its first instruction. The Call SubX provides this information: it also initiates transfer from the main program to the subroutine itself. The processor must also have information as to when the subroutine finishes; this is provided by some form of return instruction.

As shown in Figure 6.30a, the call instruction is located at line 4 of the source code. Once the processor has loaded the instruction the PC will automatically increment; it now shows the address of the instruction defined in line 5. Operations then proceed as follows, Figure 6.30b:

- The contents of the PC (i.e. the address of the next executable instruction of the main program) are stored on the top of the stack.

- The PC is loaded with the address of the first instruction of the subroutine.

- Execution of the subroutine commences, finishing when the return instruction is met.

- The contents of the top of stack are loaded into the PC.

- Execution of the main program resumes with the instruction specified by the PC.

It can be seen that by using a subroutine the processor has been forced to carry out extra operations. These, as far as the application is concerned, don't perform any useful work; they do, though, consume processor time.

A more complex situation arises when the subroutine is required to act on data 'passed' to it by the main program (these data items are the subroutine 'parameters'). The most general-purpose technique uses the stack as the communication mechanism, illustrated in Figure 6.31. Here, prior to making the call, parameter information is pushed onto the stack (overhead 1); on starting the subroutine the

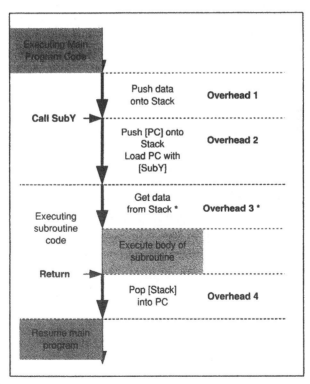

Figure 6.31 : Subroutine call with parameters.

first action is to retrieve this same data, overhead 3 (note that this overhead isn't always present – many processors can work directly with stack data). Quite clearly these operations form yet more overheads.

How important is this extra loading? This is a difficult question to answer; much depends on the processor type. However, in time-critical applications, it is always worth developing general guidelines for use by programmers. For instance, in the example above, the following metric was produced for one widely used 8 bit microcontroller:

- Overhead – basic subroutine: 1.0 unit of time.
- Overhead – parameter passing operation, one data byte: 1.5 units.
- Overhead – basic subroutine with one data byte parameter: 2.5 units.

At this point you may be wondering what this has to do with RTOS work. Well, many (if not most) kernel operations are based on subroutines which use parameter passing techniques. Thus the number of parameters and their data types have a significant effect on system overheads (hence pass-by-value generally produces much greater overheads than pass-by-reference). Moreover, composite data types (arrays, for example) often consist of a large number of individual data items. Finally, some prologue code has to be written to set up the parameter information prior to calling the subroutine. Depending on the application the overhead may be significant. If the times quoted by a vendor do not include these factors, your performance estimates could be rather wide of the mark.

Although assembly language is used for RTOS applications, this tends nowadays to be restricted to handling detailed (CPU-level) functions. In general the majority of commercial designs provide high-level language interfaces to the OS features. Unfortunately, from a performance point of view, programmers aren't always conscious of the accompanying overheads. For example, consider the use of a simple function call (ComputeSpeed), Figure 6.32. Unlike assembly language operation, the source code gives no indication of its associated overheads. However, the similarity between the overheads shown here and those of Figure 6.30 are clear enough. Should the function have parameters, then extra overheads are incurred (Figure 6.33) like those illustrated in Figure 6.31.

Now to turn to another important component of real-time operating systems: the interrupt. Interrupts are used for various reasons, two major functions being to:

- Enable the processor to deal with external aperiodic events.
- Provide accurate timing for system operation.

We'll look at both of these, with emphasis on the overhead baggage associated with such operations. The first, for clarity and simplicity, will not involve any operating system facilities. Assume that the processor is executing a background loop when an external device signals a (hardware-generated) interrupt, Figure 6.34. Assume also that interrupts are enabled. When the processor receives an interrupt signal it

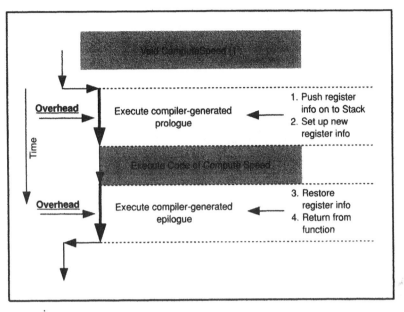

Figure 6.32 Function call – HLL operation.

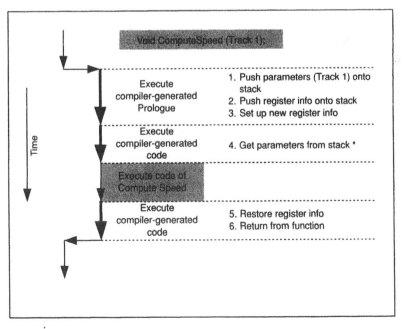

Figure 6.33 Function call with parameters.

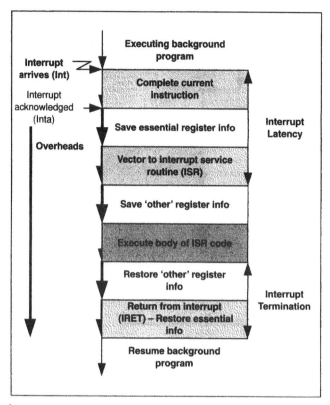

Figure 6.34 Interrupt-driven operation.

continues normal processing until its current instruction is completed. At that point it acknowledges the interrupt (a hardware signal), and begins to save essential register information to the stack. It now obtains information identifying the interrupt type, then branches ('vectors') to the related interrupt service routine (ISR). Note: the time between receipt of an interrupt and subsequent branching to the ISR is called the *interrupt latency*. This is the best guide to just how quickly a system can respond to external events.

One of the first statements in the ISR saves the contents of other registers (normally this means saving the contents of *all* other registers unless there is a very clever compiler at work). Following this the body of the ISR is executed, this leading into an interrupt termination stage. First, all 'other' register information is restored. Second, a 'return from interrupt' instruction causes the processor to retrieve the essential register information from the stack; it then resumes execution of the background program.

Figure 6.34 identifies all the overheads related to this operation. Comparing these with a function call, Figure 6.32, it can be seen that these differ in two ways: interrupt vectoring and the saving of register data. Both are important issues.

The time taken to vector to an ISR can range from the insignificant to something quite substantial. Where, for example, a processor has a *set* of interrupts, each interrupt signal forces a branch to a specified address. As the ISR will (should) have been placed there by the compiler, vectoring takes a trivial amount of time. The other extreme is met where systems use a single interrupt line which can be activated by various I/O modules. Extra time is needed to identify the interrupting source and to transfer control to the appropriate handling routine.

Saving of register data may appear to carry similar overheads to that of the function call. However, one factor makes a significant difference: the amount of control the programmer has over program execution. In normal sequential programming, the programmer decides what function to use and *when* to use it. As such, the compiler will ensure that only minimal register information need be saved. By contrast, with interrupts, the programmer has no idea when they are going to appear. The interrupted program could be doing anything; in the worst case all registers could contain essential information. As a result all register data must be saved (and, of course, subsequently restored). Which, it might be added, can take a significant amount of time.

Please note that these comments apply to mainstream microprocessors and microcontrollers. There *are* types designed to minimize switching overheads by using extra sets of registers to hold system context. Each set is allocated to an interrupt vector, and 'shadows' the structure of the CPU registers. When an interrupt occurs, the general-purpose register set of the CPU is switched out, being replaced by the shadow set. At the end of the ISR, system context is retained in the shadow register set. This arrangement leads to a massive speed-up in context switch times.

One important use of interrupts is to act as the tick time signal. Assume that tasks are executed round-robin fashion, with rescheduling decisions made at tick-time (Figure 6.35). Two outcomes are possible at each tick. In the first no rescheduling is needed; the current task is reinstalled (Figure 6.35a). In the second a reschedule takes place, and the current task is suspended, being replaced by a different one (Figure 6.35b). This incurs extra overheads, specifically time to:

- Save the context information (which may involve more than merely register data) of the current task.
- Reorder the task schedule.
- Restore the context information of the new task.

The most flattering performance figures can be obtained by doing a context switch which doesn't involve rescheduling operations. Be aware of this.

Another measure sometimes used is called 'interrupt dispatch latency'. To explain this, let us revisit Figure 6.35b. It can be seen that the second-last operation is to return from the interrupt. This is necessary in order to restore essential register information. However, the operation can also be provided as an integral part of the context-restore action. In such cases the time which elapses between 'Check if

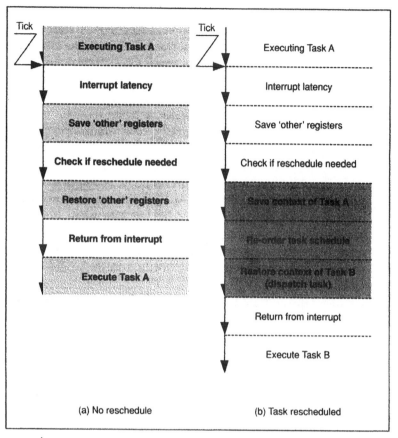

Figure 6.35 Tick-driven scheduling.

reschedule needed' and 'execute Task B' is an important measure; it shows how quickly a new task can be set running after completing the body of the ISR. This is the interrupt dispatch latency (but be aware; there doesn't seem to be a standard definition for the completion point of the ISR code).

Some RTOSs use the interrupt mechanism to provoke a context switch. Others embed the kernel functions within a monitor (say), and rely on function calls to achieve the same ends. Clearly this gives a much faster response than interrupt-driven methods. The time taken for task switching in such circumstances is sometimes called the 'task switch latency'.

6.5.4 OS performance and representative benchmarks

As stated earlier, representative benchmarks provide performance figures for specific functions. Unfortunately, there is one major (and I do mean *major*) problem here.

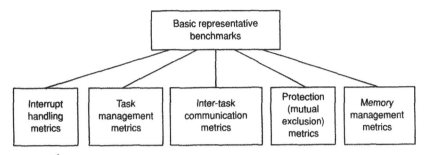

Figure 6.36 : Representative benchmark metrics – basic set.

Unless all benchmarking is carried out on a uniform, well-defined, hardware platform, cross-comparison of figures may be meaningless. Having said that, it is rare to find such information available (one notable exception is that produced by Martin Timmermann for Windows NT and CE [TIM98]). In reality our options are quite limited. First, though, recognize that if accurate figures *are* required, RTOS testing must be done in the application environment. But that is likely to be done *after* an RTOS has been acquired. Prior to this the main (and perhaps only) source of OS performance data is that produced by the vendors themselves. Such information can be used only as a general guide. Even so, provided it is very carefully scrutinized and evaluated, it can be quite useful.

The basic set of representative benchmarks is that shown in Figure 6.36. Specific data relating to these can be presented in many ways, usually being RTOS dependent. However, some standard tests have been proposed for this benchmarking purpose, including the:

● Basic real-time primitives benchmark [DIG97] and

● Rhealstone real-time benchmark [KAR89, KAR90].

The factors taken into account by these benchmarks are given in Figure 6.37. Although these tests haven't been widely used, they provide a good basis for the development of company-specific benchmarking techniques. A brief description follows.

(a) Interrupt response latency: is the elapsed time from when the kernel receives an interrupt until execution of the first instruction of the ISR. Results are given as *min, max* and *average*.

(b) Process dispatch latency: is the time needed for the system to respond to an external interrupt (event) and produce a task reschedule. It assumes that:

 ● A task is suspended, waiting for the event to arrive.

 ● The processor is executing a task which has lower priority than the suspended one.

 ● In response to the interrupt, the suspended task is awoken, replacing the lower-priority one.

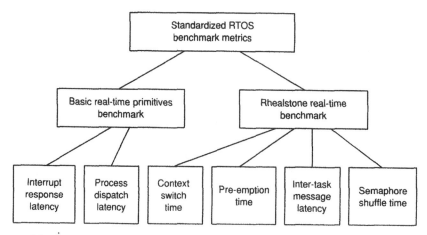

Figure 6.37   Standardized benchmark metrics.

More precisely, it is the time between an interrupt arriving and the execution of the first instruction of the suspended task. Results are given as min, max and average.

(c) Context switch time: is the *average* time to switch between two tasks of *equal* priority.

(d) Pre-emption time: is the average time for a high-priority task to pre-empt a running low-priority task.

(e) Inter-task message latency: is the average latency within the kernel when a data message is sent from one task to another.

(f) Semaphore shuffle time: is the average time delay between a task asking for a semaphore and it actually receiving it. It is assumed that, at request time, the semaphore is currently held by another task. The shuffle time *excludes* the run-time of the holding task.

One application example is an evaluation by DEC of VxWorks running on various Alpha-based platforms [DIG97].

Establishing metrics for your OS is to be heartily recommended. It does, however, require proper test facilities, personnel, time and money. What do you do though if you don't have such luxuries? There is little choice but to rely on data provided by the RTOS vendor. And the next question is how best to use this information.

Frankly, it is most unlikely that a product would be selected on the single criterion of speed; other factors such as cost, pedigree, technical support, etc. are also very important. Thus performance information is probably most useful when deciding *which* OS features to use and *when* to use them. Following on here are a set of performance figures for a mainstream microprocessor, measured as part of a research program. All times have been normalized, the context switch time being

TASK MANAGEMENT METRICS	
Do context switch	Normalized – 1
Create a task	3
Delete (kill) a task	2.7
Suspend a task	0.9
Resume a task	0.84
Delay a task	1.4
Change priority	1.14
Get task status	0.48

Figure 6.38 Task management overheads.

INTERTASK COMMUNICATION METRICS	
Mailbox – Post (no rescheduling)	0.42
Mailbox – Post (rescheduling)	1.28
Mailbox – Pend (no rescheduling)	0.38
Mailbox – Pend (rescheduling)	1.72
Channel – Send (no rescheduling)	0.44
Channel – Send (rescheduling)	1.54
Channel – Get (no rescheduling)	0.5
Channel – Get (rescheduling)	1.54

Figure 6.39 Inter-task communication overheads.

given the value of 1 (one). Why pick on this as the reference measure, you may ask. The reason is that many inexperienced developers seize on this as *the* measure of kernel performance. This, it will become clear, is somewhat naive.

To begin with, take some task management metrics, Figure 6.38. The first thing that stands out here is the extremely long time taken to create and delete tasks. This should tell you that in fast systems the use of dynamic tasks (i.e. ones that come and go) is going to lead to substantial overheads. By contrast, where tasks are static, creation is a once-only activity; moreover it normally takes place during initialization. Observe next the amount of time taken to delay a task. If you think about what actually happens this shouldn't surprise you. Also, changing a task's priority is no trivial matter. Moreover, it is possible that a number of tasks may have their priorities changed at the same time.

A second set of extremely important metrics (from a performance point of view, that is) concerns inter-task communication, Figure 6.39. These figures are based on the time taken to transfer a single data pointer through the relevant component.

Two points stand out here. First, inter-task communication times are not something to be ignored when doing performance calculations. Second, when rescheduling takes place as a result of task-interaction, the overheads are quite significant.

Similar comments can be made regarding the use of semaphores, Figure 6.40.

PROTECTION (MUTUAL EXCLUSION) METRICS	
Semaphore – Create	0.42
Semaphore – Delete	0.44
Semaphore – Check	0.38
Semaphore – Wait (no rescheduling)	0.48
Semaphore – Wait (rescheduling)	1.62

Figure 6.40 Mutual exclusion overheads.

MEMORY MANAGEMENT METRICS	
Get a block	0.48
Create a partition	0.96
Extend a partition	0.9
Return a block	0.58

Figure 6.41 Memory handling overheads.

Finally, activities related to the dynamic handling of processor memory (Figure 6.41) are also important sources of overhead.

It should now be clear to you why performance degrades rapidly as more tasks are added to a design. As the number of context switches increases, the overhead rises at a linear rate. Worse still, the need for extra communication and protection facilities leads to geometric-like increases in the overheads. You have been warned.

The preceding data, useful as it is, can be used only as a guide to performance. Figure 6.42, typical of ISR latency test results, shows exactly why this is the case. It can be seen that there is wide range of latency times, the worst being approximately twice are long as the best. Figures for the other metrics can also have a wide spread in value. For example, a set of measurements was produced for the MicroC/OS operating system running on an Intel MCS251 processor [LAB97]. These showed that semaphore and mailbox operations had maximum/minimum time ratios in the order of 7:1. What all this means is clear: it is impossible to predict precisely the *actual* performance of a multitasking (OS) based design.

Where do we go from here concerning the performance issue? A pragmatic approach is needed, based on data we *can* obtain. Recommendations are as follows:

- Soft–slow systems: OS performance isn't usually a significant factor. Average times are sufficient if performance prediction is required.
- Hard–slow systems: Similar comments apply.
- Soft–fast systems: Average times are satisfactory. Variations between actual and predicted performance are unlikely to be upsetting.
- Fast–hard systems: For these, worst-case maximum timings *must* be used (essential for critical applications).

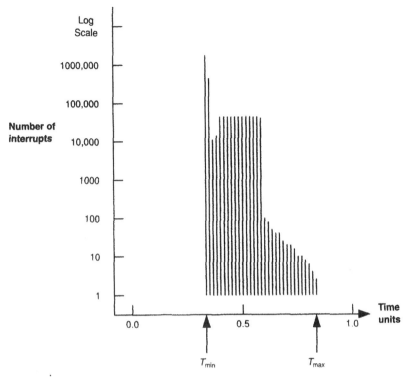

Figure 6.42 | ISR latency test results.

There is a fast–hard subcategory which can tolerate occasional failures to meet dead-lines (sometimes referred to as 'firm deadlines'). How you handle these depends on specific applications.

6.5.5 OS performance and synthetic benchmarks

The information provided by representative benchmarks is best used as a design guide; it helps us to produce efficient, effective and high-performance multitasking systems. Unfortunately the very specific nature of the data involved limits the use-fulness of the benchmarks. What we have is a set of individual, isolated measures relating to individual RTOS features. But real systems use combinations of these, their interactions being multiple and varied. Remember, the fundamental question facing us is 'will the system meet its deadlines?' That is, will the combination of task code and RTOS functions execute sufficiently fast for our needs? There is only one way to truly answer that: build and test the product. The drawback with this method is that all information is gathered as a post-mortem activity. By the time

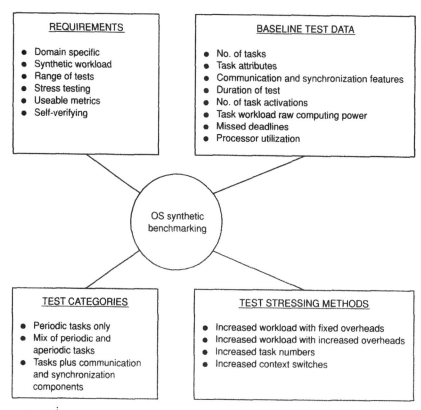

Figure 6.43 | Key components of RTOS synthetic testing.

we've found out that the system has a dog-like performance, it's a little bit late in the day. What is needed is a predictive benchmark which:

- Is not application-specific.

- Gives general guidance on the structuring of multitasking designs.

- Helps identify time-critical operations.

- Indicates, for a specific kernel, ways to achieve optimum performance.

One important step in developing such benchmarks was *Hartstone: Synthetic Benchmark Requirements for Hard Real-Time Applications* [WEI89]. Although it hasn't been widely used, the basic ideas are sound and well thought out. They are promoted here as a way of generating company-specific guidelines for developing multitasking designs.

The Hartstone technique is based on four key components (Figure 6.43):

- Basic requirements.

- Test categories.

- Baseline (reference) test data.
- Test stressing methods.

Let us take each of these in turn and examine them in more detail.

Basic requirements

(a) Domain specific: All testing must be relevant to the application domain. For real-time (especially embedded) systems this includes exercising:

- Both periodic and aperiodic task execution.
- Interrupt-driven actions.
- Task synchronization and mutual exclusion features.

(b) Synthetic workload: The chosen workload should be typical of that found in the application domain.

(c) Range of tests: Tests used must range from simple to complex, exercising an appropriate set of functions.

(d) Stress testing: It must be possible to stress the performance of the system to identify its limits (expressed in terms of missed deadlines).

(e) Useable metrics: Figures obtained should be able to distinguish between useful work and OS overhead. These should provide a base from which performance estimates can be developed.

(f) Self-verifying: Each test should be complete in its own right, generating values for all result parameters.

Test categories

This section defines in general terms the nature of a set of tests applicable to real-time systems. These are intended to show how specific multitasking features impact on system performance. However, in most cases relevant information can be gleaned only by cross-comparing two or more tests (one of the reasons for using a suite of tests). Test categories (based on, but not exactly the same as, Hartstone) include:

- Periodic tasks (harmonic frequencies).
- Periodic tasks (non-harmonic frequencies).
- Aperiodic and periodic tasks.
- Communication and synchronization involving periodic tasks.
- Communication and synchronization involving aperiodic and periodic tasks.

(a) Periodic tasks (harmonic frequencies): Here tasks are periodic, their repetition rates, i.e. frequencies, having a whole number (integral) relationship. This could be simple (e.g. 10 Hz, 20 Hz, 30 Hz, etc.) or logarithmic (1 Hz, 2 Hz, 4 Hz, for example). A good reason for using this as the starting point is that such task arrangements:

- Are the easiest to schedule (typically using a simple cyclic scheduler) and
- Produce good performance figures.

As a result designers frequently use this as a design criterion in the tasking structure. Results from this test category are just about the best that can be obtained for any particular RTOS.

(b) Periodic tasks (non-harmonic frequencies): While a harmonic task relationship is desirable, real-world requirements often dictate otherwise. For example, sample rates in closed-loop control systems are related to issues such as bandwidth, responsiveness and stability.

Where tasks end up being non-harmonic, a more complex scheduler – one carrying extra overheads – must be used. In practice such scheduling is much more commonplace than the simple cyclic technique. Consequently the results generated by this test group are useful as a practical best performance baseline.

(c) Aperiodic and periodic tasks: Where fast responsiveness with low overheads is required, interrupt-driven aperiodic tasking must be employed. Such tasks can be described in statistical terms only, but frequently have to meet specific response times. These tests highlight the interference effects – in terms of missed deadlines – of random inputs on pre-defined schedules. As such they give a good guide to the percentage of processing time which may be safely allocated to periodic tasking.

(d) Communication and synchronization involving periodic tasks: Both factors lead to a degradation of performance, especially if priority inversion comes into play. Their impact is more easily seen when evaluated in the context of a set of periodic tasks (by comparing the results with those of test group (a)). The tests also allow the designer to evaluate various alternatives for task communication and synchronization.

(e) Communication and synchronization involving aperiodic and periodic tasks: These tests bring into play all the features already covered, thus thoroughly exercising the RTOS functions. With only a small amount of tailoring they can be used for the testing of actual real systems.

Baseline (reference) test data

For *each* set of tests a baseline must be established, to be used as a reference point for stress testing. The following items are relevant to the baseline configuration:

- Number of tasks, their attributes and task loading of the processor.
- Communication and synchronization features.

Baseline test: Periodic tasks (harmonic frequencies only). Test duration: 1 second. Raw computing power: 1500 KWIPS.			
Task	Frequency	Task load	Task total load/s
Task 1	80 Hz	1 KWI	80 KWIPS
Task 2	40 Hz	1	40
Task 3	20 Hz	20	400
Task 4	10 Hz	10	100
Total task loading/s = (80 + 40 + 400 + 100) = 620 KWIPS Processor utilization = 620/1500 = 0.413 = 41.3%			

Figure 6.44 Specimen data – RTOS synthetic test.

- Test duration, number of task activations, processor utilization and missed deadlines.
- Raw computing power.

The last item, raw computing power, is a measure of system throughput when using simple sequential processing (i.e. without multitasking). In the Hartstone suite this is measured in KiloWhetstone Instructions Per Second (KWIPS). Each task load can be expressed in KWI per task run. To calculate the total loading per task simply multiply this figure by the task frequency. Summing the results for all tasks gives the total loading on the processor. From this the processor utilization can be calculated. For example, consider the following data collected (Figure 6.44) from one specific test. It makes sense that in the baseline tests all tasks should meet their deadlines. Stress testing can then be applied to see the conditions which lead to deadlines being missed.

Test stressing methods

Test stressing sets out to see what changes in the baseline test conditions take a system to its limits (this is defined to be the point at which tasks begin to miss deadlines). The methods outlined here set out to assess the sensitivity of a design to increases in:

- Workload.
- Overheads (i.e. overheads incurred during the test run).
- Task numbers.
- Context switch rates.

Wherever possible only one parameter is varied, the others being kept constant (in some cases this just isn't possible – results have to be assessed with this in mind).

In all cases the most important result is the processor utilization (U) when deadlines are missed. The collective set of U values can be combined to give an overall performance metric.

(a) Increased workload with fixed overheads.
The purpose of this test is to see how the system responds to increases in task workload only.
Constants: Number of tasks; task periods.
Variables: Task load (all tasks) – gradually increased from the baseline value.

(b) Increased workload with increased overheads.
The objective here is to assess how OS overheads impact on system performance. This can be deduced by comparing the results obtained with those of (a).
Constants: Number of tasks; task loads.
Variables: Task frequencies (all tasks) – gradually increased from the baseline value.

(c) Increased task numbers.
This test also sets out to see how OS overheads affect system performance. However, compared with (b), it seeks to answer two further questions. First, are context switch times dependent on task numbers? Second, how sensitive is the system to increases in synchronization and communication functions?
Constants: Task frequencies; baseline task loads.
Variables: Number of tasks; synchronization and communication components – gradually increased from the baseline value.

(d) Increased context switch rates.
This is an attempt to examine the effects of high context switching rates on system performance. As such it increases the overhead while leaving the workload constant.
Constants: Number of tasks; task loads; all task periods except the test task.
Variables: Test task frequency – gradually increased from the baseline value.
The simple technique used here does lead to an increase in workload, but only a relatively small one. It is essential to allocate a very low load (say < 1% of task total) to the highest frequency baseline task.

Obviously the detail will depend on the nature and scope of the baseline tests.

6.6 Development support

Developing multitasking software is a much more challenging task than that of producing code for sequential programs. For real-time systems the objectives can be summarized as delivering software which is:

- Functionally correct ('producing the right results').
- Temporally correct ('producing results at the right time').

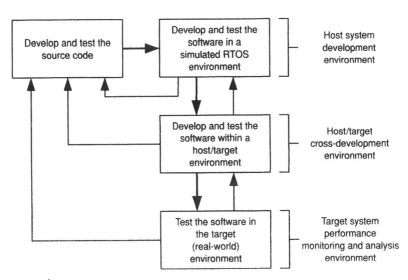

Figure 6.45 : Real-time multitasking software development process.

- On schedule.
- Within budget.

The combined pressures of cost, time and reliability have produced a market requirement for RTOS-specific design and development tools (which RTOS vendors are delighted to fill). Multitasking software development, when using one of the more comprehensive toolsets, usually follows the process outlined in Figure 6.45. Implicit here is that system and software design (to task-level) has been completed. Now the goals are to:

- Produce, compile and test the source code for each sequential program unit (e.g. task, ISR, passive object, etc.). This is carried out on the host development machine.
- Validate multitasking operation in a host-based simulated RTOS environment (please note: relatively few vendors offer this facility). As before, this work is done on the host.
- Incrementally transfer the software into the target system, developing any new software as and when required. Testing is carried out to ensure that each increment works correctly. Both host and target software facilities are needed to achieve these aims.
- Test the real-world behaviour of the software when it runs in the target system. Here the host facilities are used mainly for performance monitoring and analysis.

Linking all the component parts of the development process is the RTOS integrated development environment, Figure 6.46. In practice the designer normally interacts

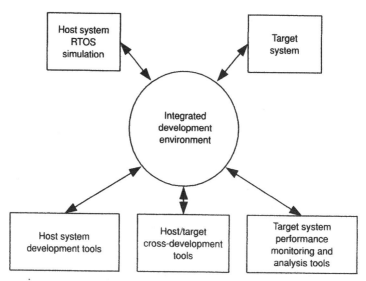

Figure 6.46 | A multitasking software integrated development environment.

with the development facilities using familiar multiwindow displays (usually PC or UNIX-based). Three sets of development tools are provided within the IDE:

- Those which use host system facilities only (host system development tools).
- Those which use both host and target system facilities (cross-development tools).
- Those for performance monitoring and analysis of the target system (these use both host and target facilities).

Turning first to the host system development tool suite, Figure 6.47, these tools fall into two major subgroups: source code development and run-time analysis.

Source code development has two component parts: code production and code testing. The first requires the use of assemblers, compilers and editors (which may, of course, be part of a mini-IDE). Code testing, the second, is usually supported by source code debuggers and browsers. Facilities may also be provided for object code disassembly; much depends on individual packages.

Run-time analysis is normally carried out at two levels. The first (and easiest) is evaluation of the sequential code of each task (there isn't really a clear split between this activity and that of source code testing; it depends on testing strategies). At this stage both code and test coverage analysis can be applied. The second level of analysis takes place at the task level, and includes debugging and performance monitoring. How much can be achieved in practice depends heavily on the quality of the RTOS simulator. A good simulator should include most of the monitoring and interaction features listed in Figure 6.48.

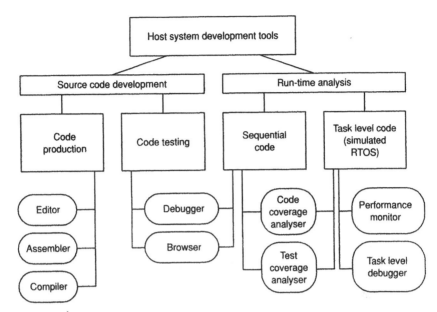

Figure 6.47   Host system development tool suite.

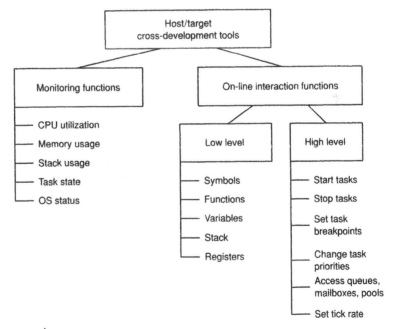

Figure 6.48   Host/target cross-development features.

Here the monitoring functions allow the developer to view in depth:

- The behaviour of the target system as a whole.
- Execution of the application code.
- Resource usage (e.g. CPU utilization, memory, etc.).
- OS activities.

For debugging and test purposes a set of on-line interaction functions is supplied. The low-level ones apply to detailed items within the source code and the processor itself. Thus it is clear that the cross-development tools must be configurable; they need to take into account the programming language (and compiler) and CPU type used for the project.

High-level facilities enable the designer to develop and debug the application at the multitasking level; the points noted in Figure 6.48 speak for themselves.

The final stage of development concerns the test of the target system within its real-world environment. Its primary purpose is to ensure that the system really does meet its design aims when deployed into the field. From a practical point of view such testing will probably start with a laboratory mimic of the real-world system. During this the host and target systems are interconnected, data from the target being uploaded to the host (a monitoring function). Information can be displayed live or stored for later processing. It can be seen from Figure 6.49 that two distinct issues need to be addressed: RTOS behaviour and application performance. These are two separate but interrelated factors: changes to one are likely to impact on the

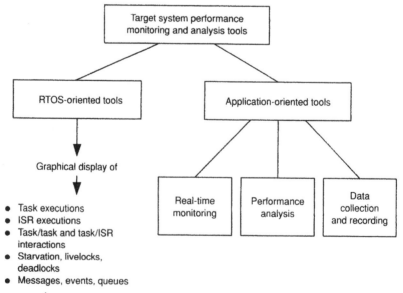

Figure 6.49 Evaluating target system behaviour.

other. Thus it is essential to evaluate them in an integrated way and not as separate, isolated topics.

RTOS-oriented tools are fairly commonplace, information usually being displayed in graphical form (with text support, naturally). This shows the behaviour of the system from the perspective of the tasking model, focusing on:

- Timing behaviour of tasks and ISRs.

- Effects caused by task/task and task/ISR interactions (e.g. synchronization, pre-emption, etc.).

- Problems related to resource protection features (e.g. priority inversion, livelocks, etc.).

- Overheads and delays due to inter-task communication.

A self-evident comment: if the RTOS performance is poor, then the application software is very unlikely to be satisfactory. However, the converse isn't necessarily true; good RTOS performance doesn't guarantee that the application(s) will perform correctly. This is where application-oriented tools come into play.

Sensible designers, when assessing system performance, normally start at the macro level. That is, the computer is treated as a black box, performance figures being derived from real-world activities. Now, if the target system meets all its requirements, why carry out *internal* (white-box) testing? It really does depend on the application. One reason could be to obtain specific information (detailed algorithmic behaviour, for example). Another could be the collection of long-term data to help form statistical models of the application. But the most likely reason to resort to internal testing is that the target performance *isn't* satisfactory.

The basic functions of application-oriented tools are shown in Figure 6.49. In simple terms these allow us to probe the target with a very powerful, flexible 'logic analyser'. Thus all digitized real-time information is (potentially) available for display and analysis. There are many ways in which this can be used; two have already been outlined earlier. In the end all will be determined by the aims of the designer and the capabilities of the tools.

What has been described so far might be called the 'core toolset'. Others are available, supporting functions such as:

- Project management

- Configuration control

- Third-party interfacing

- Class and object browsing

and the like. However, these tend to be quite vendor-specific and hence will not be discussed further here.

6.7 POSIX – Portable Operating System Interface

6.7.1 POSIX – what and why?

The word 'POSIX' features heavily in the literature produced by many RTOS providers; clearly it is perceived (at least by marketeers) to be an important topic. But what exactly is POSIX? It is, in fact, the name given to a set or suite of operating system *standards* produced by the IEEE [IEEE1003]. However, the name is usually taken to refer to the POSIX System *Interface* Standards: other component parts are *Shell and Utility*, *System Administration* and *Test Methods*. We are concerned with the interface standards only; henceforth POSIX will be used as shorthand for POSIX System Interface Standards

Why has POSIX been produced? Basically to improve the portability, maintenance and reuse of application code which relies on operating system services. These should lead to better, more reliable software, together with reduced costs (that's the theory, at least). How does it aim to achieve this? The idea is that when an application uses an OS facility, it accesses it in a pre-defined, standard way. This should not depend in any way on the OS type, nor the machine on which it is hosted. For example, the function call posix-fork should invoke exactly the same response from *any* operating system. However, to guarantee this, the OS must comply with the POSIX standard; it is then said to be POSIX compliant. Hence the burden of producing compliant interfaces falls on the shoulders of the RTOS designer.

Let us look at just one example where such compliance can be useful. You have an existing application which runs on a POSIX compliant OS. For a new project it is essential to use a much newer processor, one which doesn't support your current OS. However, an OS *is* available which provides POSIX interfaces. In this case porting the application to the new design – from the point of view of interfacing to the operating system – is (ideally) straightforward. Contrast this with a different situation. A company has an old C-based (legacy) application which originally ran under the RMX OS. It now decides to upgrade to Windows CE, using the same hardware. The basic application code will compile correctly, which is fine. Unfortunately all the hooks into the OS are different. Thus new ones have to be created and tested, followed by full testing of tasking operations. The resulting development and test work is likely to be extensive, time-consuming and expensive.

It should be added, however, that many OS vendors do provide interfacing software that offers POSIX-like features.

6.7.2 Basic features and real-time extensions

POSIX is based on UNIX, mainly because it was (almost) a standardized, manufacturer-independent operating system. Unfortunately, a number of different (and not quite compatible) versions of UNIX exist. As a result the POSIX standards were devised to provide interfaces compatible with the major flavours of UNIX. These include application calls related to:

- Process functions.
- Time functions.
- Files and directories.
- I/O facilities.
- Error management.
- System information.

However, it must be borne in mind that UNIX was mainly intended to support program operations in a soft-time environment. The scheduling model is very simple, and cannot be regarded as deterministic in the hard real-time sense. Thus to make POSIX suitable for real-time applications, many extensions have been made to the basic model. Logically enough these are called the *real-time extensions*, and include:

- Priority-based pre-emptive task scheduling.
- High-resolution timing.
- Asynchronous I/O.
- Message handling.
- Memory management.
- Task synchronization.
- Mutual exclusion.

6.7.3 Using POSIX – some issues

Three particular factors to be kept in mind when using POSIX features are:

- Overhead penalties.
- Language dependencies.
- Portability aspects.

First, most RTOSs which offer POSIX real-time facilities tend to be on the large size (0.5 MBytes and upwards – the split of ROM and RAM varies considerably). If you are working with smaller microcontrollers such store overheads are likely to be unacceptable. Much also depends on the structure of the OS. Where component parts can be included/excluded as desired, overheads can be minimized.

A second factor concerns the use of programming languages for the development of the application software. POSIX calls are embedded within the application code; clearly they must be compilable. As UNIX was developed in C, it is no surprise that the initial standard offers C language interfaces. However, to enable programmers using other languages to interface to POSIX compliant OSs, language bindings have been specified. These are defined for Ada, Fortran and Fortran90.

The third point of concern is that of portability. That is, if POSIX functions have been used to develop an application, can you guarantee that porting can be done without problem? The answer is 'maybe'; it hinges on the replies to three questions:

- What does 'RTOS conformance to the standard' mean?
- What does 'Application conformance to the standard' mean?
- How can you tell that a product actually conforms to POSIX standards?

Consider the first question. An RTOS may fall into one of two categories. It may:

- Not conform to POSIX standards or
- Be a *conforming implementation*: meets the requirements laid down within the standards to be able to claim conformance.

Concerning application conformance, the *application* code may be:

- Only a partially conforming (or even non-conforming) implementation.
- A *strictly conforming application*: means it is limited to the language plus the POSIX functions.
- An *ISO conforming application*: extra functions, based on ISO standards, are provided for applications programming.
- A *national standards conforming application*: extra functions, based on ISO and national standards, are provided for applications programming.
- A *conforming application with extensions*: any extensions are allowed as long as their use is documented.

Concerning RTOS conformance, the Portable Applications Standards Committee POSIX description states 'Test methods have been defined in POSIX standards, these increase the confidence that a product that claims conformance, does conform. There are capabilities required by the standard which cannot be tested . . . so comprehensive testing is not possible.'

The only sensible advice is to tread carefully if you are really interested in portability and reusability. Best results will be obtained by designing your application software to be strictly conforming.

Review

If you have taken the lessons of this chapter to heart you should now:

- Appreciate the general conceptual model of the hardware and software structures of embedded processor systems.
- Realize that interrupt-driven designs provide a simple form of multitasking.
- Understand the concepts and code organization of nanokernels and microkernels.
- Understand the role of MMUs and BSPs within these kernels.
- Appreciate the overheads (time and storage) associated with operating systems.
- See that distributed systems must incorporate a safe, secure and flexible communications infrastructure.
- Know the OSI seven-layer communication reference model, and see how the following models relate to this: simple serial link, ISO 8802 LAN and TCP/IP.
- Realize why TCP/IP is the single most important general-purpose network for use in networked systems.
- Understand its features, organization and message structures.
- See how Unix ports and sockets relate to TCP/IP communications.
- Understand the need for and use of files and file management systems in embedded applications.
- Realize that graphics-based user interfaces have become increasingly important in embedded systems and see how they impact on the overall system structuring.
- Recognize that the application software, when using GUIs, consists of two major component parts – core application code and graphical application code.
- Appreciate how GUIs may be built, and understand the various development methods available to the designer.
- Know how RTOS performance may be expressed, measured and benchmarked.
- Understand in detail the factors which produce RTOS time overheads and recognize their relative importance.
- Have sufficient knowledge to set up a benchmarking programme.
- Understand the overall process for the development of multitasking software.
- Appreciate the role of the RTOS integrated development environment in this process.
- Understand the features and use of host, host/target and target-based development tools.
- Appreciate the fundamentals of POSIX and see how it might be applicable to your own work.

References and further reading

[CUR76] *A synthetic benchmark*, H.J. Curnow and B.A. Wichmann, Computer Journal, Vol. 19, No. 1, pp 43–49, 1976.

[DIG97] Technical Report: Performance evaluation of VxWorks for Alpha, Digital Equipment Corporation, Digital Systems Engineering and Characterization Group, July 1997.

[GIL95] *SPEC as a performance evaluation measure*, R. Giladi and N. Ahituv, IEEE Computer, Vol. 28, No. 8, pp 33–42, 1995.

[IEEE1003] IEEE Std 1003.0-1994: Guide to the POSIX Open System Environment.

[KAR89] *RHEALSTONE, A real-time benchmarking proposal*, R.P. Kar and K. Porter, Dr. Dobbs Journal, Vol. 14, No. 2, pp 14–24, 1989.

[KAR90] *Implementing the Rhealstone real-time benchmark*, R.P. Kar, Dr. Dobbs Journal, pp 46–102, 1990.

[LAB97] *Comparing the 251 and the XA: A kernel's perspective*, J.J. Labrosse, Embedded Systems Programming, pp 56–69, 1997.

[OPE02] OpenGL – the 3-D standard, www.opengl.org.

[STA97] *Data and computer communications, 5th edition*, W. Stallings, Prentice Hall, ISBN 0-13-571274-2, 1997.

[TIM98] *RTOS evaluation project – latest news*, M. Timmermann, Real-Time Magazine, No. 98-4, pp 6–8, 1998.

[WEI84] *Dhrystone: A synthetic system programming benchmark*, R.P. Weicker, Computing Practices, Vol. 27, No. 10, pp 1013–1030, 1984.

[WEI89] *Hartstone: synthetic benchmark requirements for hard real-time applications*, N. Weiderman, Technical Report, Software Engineering Institute, Carnegie Mellon University CMU/SEI-89-TR-23, June 1989.

[WIL93] *A guide to the TCP/IP protocol suite*, F. Wilder, Artech House, ISBN 0-89006-693-0, 1993.

[WML02] WAP Wireless Markup Language Specification, www.wapforum.org.

chapter 7

Diagramming — An Introduction

In the early days of computers, diagramming didn't figure as an important topic in the design process. Further, the only pictorial method used was that of the flow-chart. At that time there was little distinction between programming and design (nor, for that matter, between programmers and designers). The design and development process usually went something as follows:

- Programmers thought about the problem to be solved.

- They wrote lines of code to solve it.

- The code was tested and modified until it was correct (or appeared to be so).

- This source code was released as the system documentation.

Sometimes, in a token gesture to appease senior management (or the customer), a system flow-chart was produced. Whether it represented what went on in the program is another matter.

In recent years a revolution has taken place concerning the use of diagramming for software. Practically all modern software tools use diagrams as an integral part of the design and development process. The driving force for this has come from commerce and industry, not academia. Underlying this has been the need to produce reliable software which is delivered on time at the right price. Although these changes have their roots in large system developments they are making a major impact in the microprocessor field. We are also seeing the arrival of tools specifically produced for use in embedded systems.

This chapter sets out to:

- Show why diagrams are used as part of the modern software toolset.

- Describe, in general terms, what they achieve.

- Define the requirements and attributes of software diagrams.

7.1 Diagrams – why?

7.1.1 Introduction

Why do we use diagrams? Not 'why do we use software diagrams?', but why do we use diagrams at all? We couldn't imagine civil, mechanical or electrical engineers working without diagrams. And, at a much simpler level, try putting together self-assembly furniture using only written instructions (no pictures).

This takes us into the area of psychology. Our experiences show us that pictures must convey information in a different way from words: and in a way which is clearer and easier to understand. T.R.G. Green [GRE82] describes this in terms of temporal processes, dealing with many aspects of the problem, including:

- Recognition – is the process familiar?
- Modularity – what chunks can the description be broken into?
- Tractability – how can a modification be made?
- Sequence – in what order do the events happen?
- Circumstance – if such-and-such happens, what does it mean?

So, assuming that pictures really do help us, where can we sensibly use them in the software world? There are four main areas in which diagramming can be applied (Figure 7.1). In the following sections these are discussed in general terms; specific techniques are covered in Chapter 8. But note that here we are mainly concerned with the *effects* produced by using diagrams, not *how* they are used in detail.

Before looking at how diagrams fit into the development process, consider two basic questions:

- Are the correct diagrams being used?
- Are the diagrams really usable?

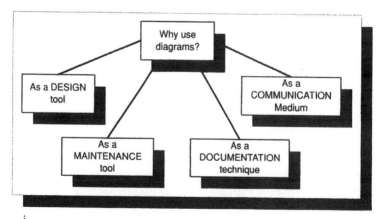

Figure 7.1 The role of diagrams in software development.

The first point is to do with the matching of diagrams to what they represent (rather grandiosely, their domain of application). What a diagram does is to abstract reality from a particular domain into a model. But the model has to be the right one for the domain. This point is very well demonstrated in Figure 7.2 giving two views of

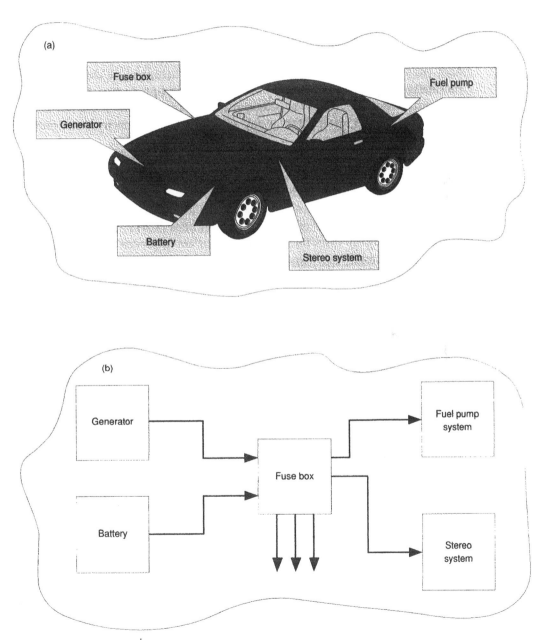

Figure 7.2 Domain-specific views.

part of an auto electrical system. Figure 7.2a represents the system from the point of view of the repair mechanic (the maintenance domain). In contrast, Figure 7.2b shows its electrical structure (the design domain). Same system, different views. Therefore it should be no surprise to find that we meet exactly the same issues in software development.

The second point is concerned with how much information a diagram should contain. Put simply, just how complex can a diagram be before it becomes unusable? This issue was investigated as a psychological problem in the 1950s by George Miller. His paper, *The magical number seven, plus or minus two*, is a landmark one – I recommend it to you [MIL56]. The conclusions are clear. Too much information (especially the complex variety) is counter-productive. It merely confuses rather than enlightens. The reason is that people can only effectively handle a limited amount of information at any one time. Thus simplicity is the order of the day.

Perhaps you can now begin to see the difficulty we face when using diagrams. On the one hand, there is a need to keep them simple and clear. On the other, the system we are dealing with is likely to be complex. The only sensible way to deal with this mismatch is to use *sets* of diagrams. Those produced first aim to give a large-scale (high-level) view of the system; later ones provide detailed (low-level) information. In many cases these later diagrams are 'exploded' versions of earlier ones, as, for example, the maps of Figure 7.3. In such situations, there must be complete consistency across levels.

7.1.2   Diagrams as a design tool

Consider an electronic engineer carrying out power-circuit design. One of the first things he does is to sketch the circuit diagram (Figure 7.4). Very quickly this is followed up by a series of calculations to verify the performance of the design. It *would* be possible to describe the design using words only. In one sense this is how computer-aided design tools for printed circuit board layouts work. Yet no engineer would adopt such an approach at the initial design stage. Why not?

First, the exercise of producing the diagram requires an explicit action. Implicit relationships cannot exist. Thus, even to draw a diagram requires a clear understanding of the problem. But when we just think about designs we often carry implicit information in our minds.

Next, if we work to an agreed set of drawing rules we introduce formality and design rigour into the process (Figure 7.5). This means that it is possible for others to view, assess and discuss the design. It also eliminates ambiguity and ambivalence. For instance, in Figure 7.5, a dot indicates a connection; but why is one arrangement satisfactory and the other not so? Because in one format there is no confusion between crossing lines and connecting lines should the draftsman omit a dot.

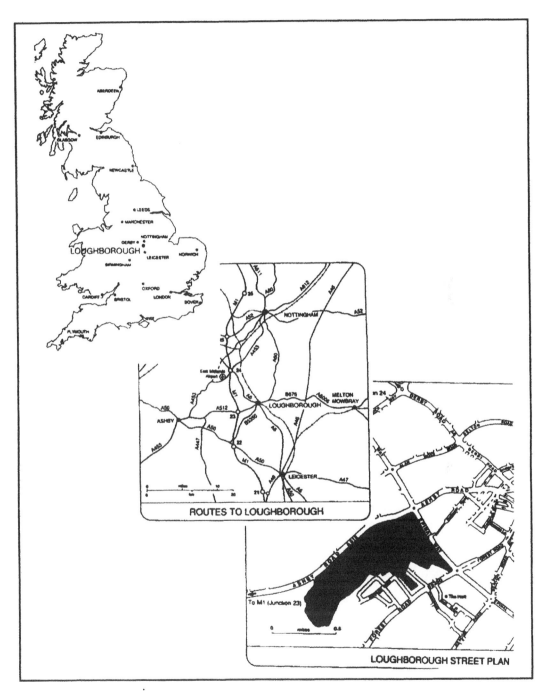

Figure 7.3 High-level and low-level views.

Figure 7.4 | Initial design.

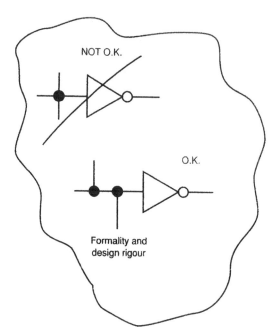

Figure 7.5 | Drawing rules.

Finally, the design as a whole can be reviewed and analysed, and the performance assessed. At this stage many incorrect or illogical design features come to light (Figure 7.6). These can be corrected at a very early stage, saving time, effort and money (and embarrassment for the designer).

All of this is directly applicable to software. After all, at this stage of the design we are still working with concepts and ideas, so it should work for software as well as hardware.

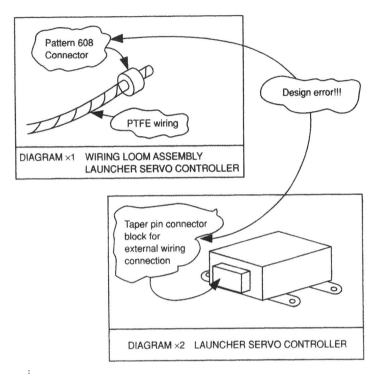

Figure 7.6 Design review.

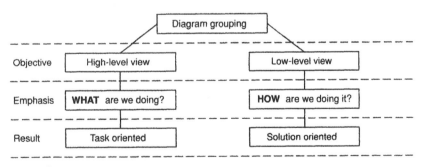

Figure 7.7 Diagrams for documentation.

7.1.3 Diagrams for design documentation

Diagrams are a powerful means of documenting the design task (preferable to a mass of source code listings). But a moment's thought shows that a single type of drawing is very unlikely to meet all our needs. Two groups of diagrams are needed (Figure 7.7). The first gives us a high-level view of the problem, showing what we've set out to do. The second, low-level, one concentrates on how we're going about solving the design problem. Each one is oriented towards a different aspect of the same problem. For any particular system, high-level diagrams:

● Are task oriented.
● Show the overall system structure together with its major subsystems.
● Describe the overall functioning of the design.
● Show the interaction of the system with its environment.
● Describe the functions and interactions of the various subsystems.

Low-level diagrams:

● Are solution oriented.
● Concentrate on detail.
● Emphasize system internal information.

Consider the attributes of such diagrams when applied, at a functional block level, to a mythical weapon control system (Figure 7.8). The high-level view concentrates on the overall task; its object is to ensure that we tackle the right problem. We can see from this figure how the main building blocks of the system fit together. Questions like 'Is the launcher compatible with the servo controller? Will the servo be powerful enough? Should we use hydraulics instead of electrics?' are considered at this level. In contrast, the low-level diagram tells us how the design task has been solved. It gives much information about the system internals, together with the interaction of such internals. It deals with questions like 'What's the best type of power amplifier?'

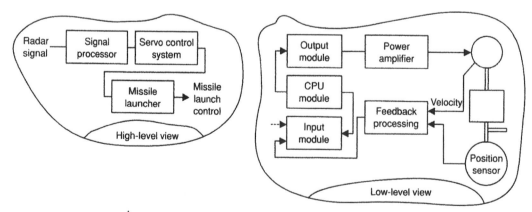

Figure 7.8 | High-level vs. low-level views.

Good high-level diagrams are simple and clear, bringing out the essential major features of a system. Using these it is relatively easy to see the effects on system behaviour when making modifications. On the other hand, low-level diagrams tend to be cluttered and complex. This is inherent in their nature; it isn't a criticism of such drawings. But, although their structure helps us to answer the question 'are we doing the job correctly?' they aren't very good when we ask 'are we doing the right job?'

These ideas can be directly translated to software engineering. We gain all the benefits outlined above by using pictures in the design process. What it also shows is that whatever diagramming method is used, it must be able to give both high- and low-level views.

7.1.4   Diagrams for maintenance

Post-design maintenance is done for two reasons: either to correct faults or to upgrade equipment. Ideally, this would be done by the original designers. But, in reality, once some years have passed, few of the original designers are still around. So, software maintenance is usually carried out by workers who:

- Weren't involved in the development in the first place.

- Have only a limited understanding of the overall task.

- Have to learn a lot very quickly to perform even small design changes.

- Wouldn't have written the code like that in any case.

It is not surprising that maintenance is unpopular. It may be an obscure and difficult job but somebody has to do it. And the better the original documentation the easier it can be. Therefore, design information must support the maintenance process by being complete, correct, clear and consistent (Figure 7.9).

System documentation needs to give both an overview as well as detailed information. It is very easy to be swamped by an excess of paper, typified by many technical manuals. As an example of such overkill, Rothon [ROT79] reported that 'the recent specification for the software for an American fighter plane occupied more than 26 thick volumes of text. It is hardly surprising that developers faced with such bulky documentation are unable to perceive the nature of the software . . . .' By using overview information it is much easier to see the overall picture. For instance, questions such as 'Where and how can changes be made? What are the knock-on effects of these on the complete program?' can be much more easily answered. However, we still need detailed information, relating specifically to the source code itself. Once again there is a clear need for a two-level documentation system.

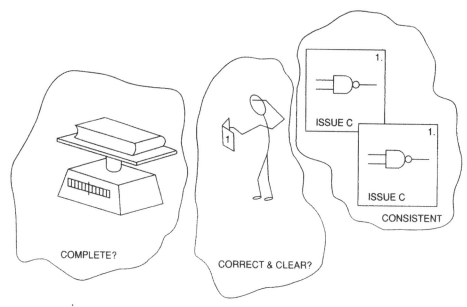

Figure 7.9 Document requirements.

7.1.5 Diagrams for communication

It's already been shown that written and spoken words can be ambiguous, ambivalent or even totally confusing. We've also seen that by using sketches, pictures, etc., many such problems are eliminated. Therefore, design diagrams can be used to help communications between members of the software and system project teams.

Who are likely to be the main users of such diagrams? They are: the system users (or procurement agency), the system designers and the post-design support group (maintainers). Figure 7.10 shows the general lines of communication between these groups. It also shows at which periods of the design these take place.

What questions do diagrams aim to answer? Consider first the user–designer interaction, Figure 7.11. Read through this and see how there are two matching aspects ('two sides of a coin') of each individual question.

Let's now turn to designer–designer communication. Even in a small job involving only one designer there are still 'chiefs' to be talked to (Figure 7.12). Ideally, such discussions should be clear, understandable and not open to individual interpretation. Pictures can help considerably in such cases.

In the post-design phase the requirements of the user tend to reduce in quantity. Unfortunately for the maintainer, these requirements are usually highly demanding ones (Figure 7.13).

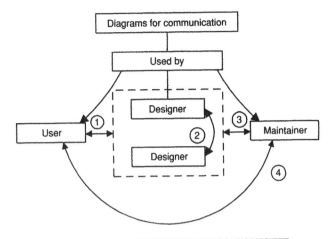

Figure 7.10 Communication aspects of diagrams.

Dialogue	Main use
1	During tendering, design and system acceptance.
2	During the design phase
3	On completion of design
4	Post-design service phase

User	Designer
Does **he** understand what I want?	Has the job been properly specified in the first place?
Am I getting what I want?	Am I doing the right job?
How is the job going?	How is the job going?

Figure 7.11 User–designer dialogue.

Chief Designer	Designer
This is the overall plan.	I understand the task.
This is how the job is split up.	Here is the detailed design response.
These are **your** responsibilities.	
This is the development plan.	Here is a progress document.
These are the timescales.	
These are the task interfaces.	Here is a record of the design.
I want a record of progress.	

Figure 7.12 Designer–designer interaction.

User	Maintainer
Fix my problem (now!).	Can this problem even be fixed?
How much to fix my problem?	
What happens if . . . ?	How does the system really work?
Modify my system.	
How much for modification?	Can it be modified successfully?
How long?	How long, how much?

Figure 7.13 | User–maintainer interaction.

7.2 The essentials of software diagrams

7.2.1 Fundamentals

What is the fundamental purpose of software design diagrams? In a very simple way they can be seen as a way to bridge the gap between what is wanted (the problem) and what is provided (the solution), Figure 7.14. In fact, the total design process can be viewed as a two-stage activity (Figure 7.15). The diagram sits in the middle of this, serving two groups of people. From the point of view of problem translation, diagrams *must* meet the needs of the user. That is, the design approach must be stated in terms of the problem not its solution; the diagrams must be easy for the users to understand. In most cases they won't be software engineers, so there's not much point in sending them a pile of computer print-outs. Finally, it must be easy to produce and modify such diagrams to encourage their use in the translation stage.

The information shown by the diagram is then used as an input to the program production process. But unless diagramming methods support program design

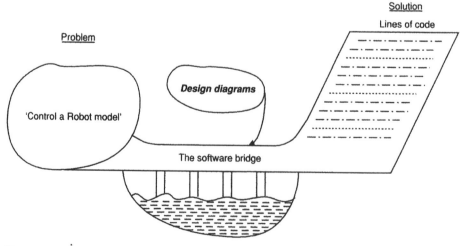

Figure 7.14 | Bridging the gap.

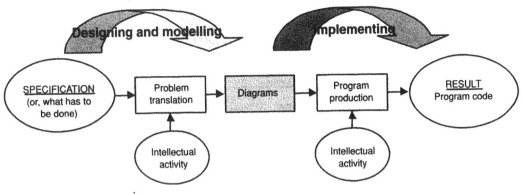

Figure 7.15 | The two-stage design process.

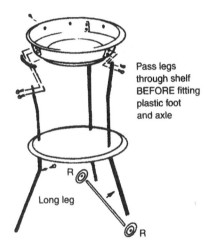

Figure 7.16 | Kit assembly diagram.

techniques (e.g. top-down design), programmers won't find them very helpful. In such cases all that happens is that yet another translation stage is used in the design process. It is also essential that the diagramming method relates strongly to modern program design methods. Ideally the diagram constructs should mirror those of the more widely used programming languages.

7.2.2 Basic qualities

Consider the assembly instruction diagram of Figure 7.16. This has taken time and money to produce; yet its manufacturer considers this a worthwhile investment. This isn't done through a sense of altruism, it's just good business practice. It conveys considerable information to the user in a simple, direct way. But it succeeds in this only if it has specific basic qualities (Figure 7.17). Let's look at each point in turn, putting it in terms of software production.

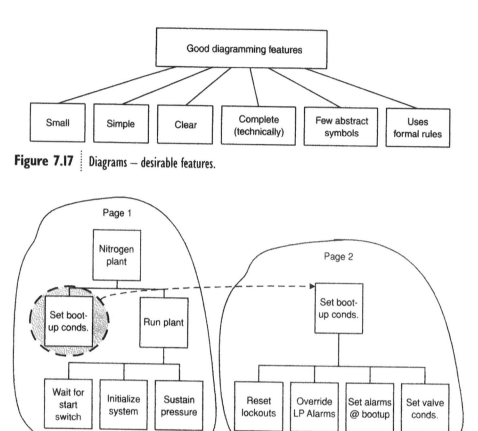

Figure 7.17 ⋮ Diagrams — desirable features.

Figure 7.18 ⋮ A top-down diagramming method.

Small

Here, small means sizes between A2 and A4. One major reason for limiting diagram size is to avoid overloading the reader with information. Good pictorial methods use a top-down method in presenting such information, as in Figure 7.18. There are, however, some mundane grounds for keeping to these sizes. In the first case they can be produced easily on low-cost plotters and printers. Moreover, these are usually widely available; there's no need to invest in expensive plotters. Second, such diagrams usually form part of a main design document; thus it must be easy to integrate these with the rest of the documentation. Large diagrams cause problems here.

Simple and clear

Diagrams are supposed to help our understanding, not act as intellectual puzzles. When diagrams are simple and clear they are quickly understood and assimilated.

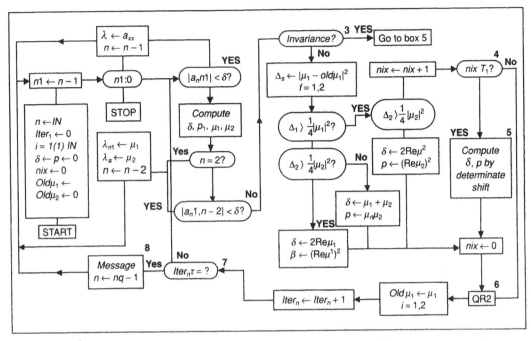

Figure 7.19 A confusing diagram (reproduced from [GRE82] with kind permission from Taylor & Francis Ltd., http://www.tandf.co.uk/journals).

This may seem a statement of the obvious, yet many diagrams break these rules. The resulting consequences may be disastrous. Some years ago a military transport plane crashed on take-off, killing 50 passengers. The fault was caused by the reverse fitting of a non-return fuel control valve. But the factor which led to this was a poor, ambiguous fitting diagram which didn't show clearly the flow direction through the valve.

An example of a diagram which breaks all the rules is given in Figure 7.19.

Complete

This means that information should not be missing from the diagram. Now this shouldn't be confused with the use of extra pictures to show all the facts. That, for software documentation, is the rule rather than the exception. What it does mean is that omissions of data which leave the information incomplete are taboo.

Few abstract symbols

It is impossible to construct software design diagrams without using abstract symbols. Unfortunately, abstract symbols can be a problem in themselves, especially if complex constructs are used. In such cases it may be quite difficult to see what message the picture is trying to convey. So the fewer symbols used the better. And keep them simple.

Uses formal rules

All notation used in diagramming should be done in accordance with a set of rules. These rules should be defined, clear and consistent. Without this we can never be sure that we understand what the diagrams mean.

7.2.3 Real-time systems diagramming – matching ends to needs

No single diagram type can meet all the needs of the software designer. Over the years many different types have been proposed; most have fallen by the wayside. Only those which are genuinely useful have survived the test of time. Remember, diagrams are not an end in themselves; they are intended to fulfil some purpose. And on that point, we can begin to look at what we really need from our diagrams, Figure 7.20 [FOX99]. Please note that the emphasis in these sections is on design, *not* requirements.

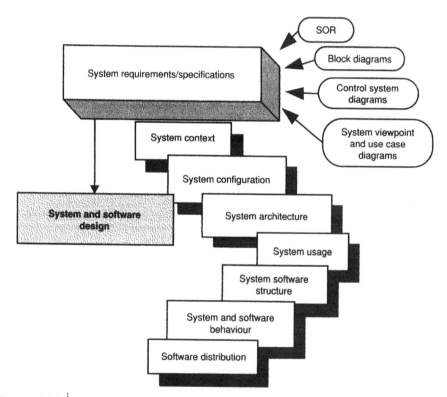

Figure 7.20 | Overall diagram set for real-time systems.

System context

Let us start by looking at the opening stages of work. It is important at this point to define:

- All external entities (e.g. devices, users, network interfaces, etc.).
- Entity attributes (e.g. sensor parameter, range, accuracy, etc.).
- The relationship of external entities with the software system.

This defines the *context* of the software within the complete system.

System configuration

Another major activity which starts early in the design cycle is a definition of the system *configuration*. This is the identification and specification of the major physical components of the system (e.g. display consoles, operator stations, electronic cubicles, etc.) together with their interconnection method(s). This work tends to run side by side with the other activities over the duration of the design phase.

System architecture

Models of the system architecture are further key aspects of this work. It is important to remember that the system architectural model is driven mainly by system, not software, aspects. In fact, for many (if not most) projects, architectural-related decisions are made during the project proposal phases.

System usage

A central aspect of real-time systems work is that the design is driven by the needs of the system itself. Thus it is essential to produce descriptions of the way in which the system is used by (or provides services to) external items.

System software structure

Running in parallel with the architectural design is the development of the system software model. This model represents an abstract, ideal, software solution to the system requirements, being independent of implementation techniques. It consists of a (packaged) set of software machines – objects, entities, what you will – which, working together, provided the desired system functionality.

System and software behaviour – interactions and dynamics

While it (the system software model) is an essential part of the design, it has limitations; the view it presents is a static one only. Just as important are the behavioural aspects of the software, described in terms of:

- Interactions between software components and the outside world.
- Internal interactions between the software components.
- Dynamical behaviour of the overall software structure.
- Dynamical behaviour of individual software components.

Such interactions are based on the use of message-passing techniques.

Software distribution

The next step in the design process is to map the software onto the system hardware, taking into account:

- Operational and performance requirements, including system responsiveness, safety, degradation and failure modes, test, commissioning and maintenance functions.
- Information concerning the execution times of individual software entities (objects).
- Timing data for inter-object communication activities.
- Network timing performance.

It should now be crystal clear why we need a range of diagrams; a single type couldn't possibly illustrate the many and varied requirements outlined above. Which is fine – except that we still need to specify exactly which diagrams *are* needed. These aspects we'll leave for later chapters. For the moment, provided you understand:

- What diagrams are used
- What the objectives of the various diagrams are and
- Why we use these diagrams

then you'll have achieved a great deal.

7.2.4 Practical diagramming techniques – a general comment

From the previous section we've seen that a range of diagrams may be used when designing real-time systems. But it is important to realize that, in any particular job, not all types may be necessary. It depends very much on the size and complexity of the task in hand. For instance, a single-processor non-multitasking design requires few diagrams. Even more minimalist – when developing service software, only program structure diagrams may be needed.

Life can be further complicated by diagramming techniques that are intimately bound to specific design methods. And even more frustrating, your CASE tool may ultimately determine the nature of the design diagramming set. But more of that in later chapters.

Review

Having completed this chapter you should:

- Appreciate the importance of diagramming as a core design tool.
- See how diagrams bring rigour, clarity and formality to the design process.
- Perceive the power of diagrams as an aid to communication.
- Understand that these objectives cannot be achieved unless the syntax and semantics of diagrams are well defined.
- Realize that diagrams are used for a variety of purposes: analysis, design, documentation and maintenance.
- See how diagrams fit into the overall software design process.
- Know what qualities to look for in diagrams and their associated methods.
- Recognize that many diagrams are needed to fully define large systems.
- Be able to define a basic range of diagrams that would support the development of real-time systems.

Exercises

1. The source code of a high-level programming language is much more formal than its natural language equivalent. Yet most people, at some time, have developed programs which fail to behave as expected at run-time. Why should this occur? How can diagrams and diagramming help us to produce predictable, reliable programs?

2. Which diagrams would you generate when doing a stand-alone single-processor non-tasking design? Explain your reasoning.

3. Until recently, relatively few software projects have used diagramming as a design technique. With this in mind, explain why there is much truth in the following claim: 'during the maintenance phase, approximately 50% of the cost is incurred merely in trying to work out what the existing system is supposed to do'.

References and further reading

[FOX99] *Integrated design approach for real-time embedded systems*, A.M. Fox, J.E. Cooling & N.S. Cooling, IEE Proc.-Software, Vol. 146, No. 2, pp 75–85, 1999.

[GRE82] *Pictures of programs and other processes, or how to do things with lines*, T.R.G. Green, Behaviour and Information Technology, Vol. 1, No. 1, pp 3–36, 1982.

[MIL56] *The magical number seven, plus or minus two*, G.A. Miller, Psychological Review, Vol. 63, No. 2, pp 81–87, 1956.

[ROT79] *Design structure diagrams: A new standard in flow diagrams*, N.M. Rothon, Computer Bulletin, series 2, No. 19, pp 4–6, 1979.

chapter 8

Practical Diagramming Methods

Chapter 7 laid the groundwork for the use of diagrams as a software design tool. In general it described the basic ideas of the subject in a fairly abstract way. These now need to be related to practical methods. In this chapter the work is extended to show:

- The general role of diagrams as a design and modelling tool/language.

- How these fit in with structured/data flow and object-oriented design techniques.

- What information they contain.

- Why extensions and modifications of basic diagram types are needed in certain real-time applications.

- The general syntax and semantics of commonly used notations (specifically Yourdon and the Unified Modelling Language).

- That different techniques have been developed to solve the same problem.

- That methods which differ in detail are often based upon the same structural concepts.

How we use these diagrams when developing real systems is the topic of a later chapter.

8.1 Introduction

At this point it wouldn't be surprising if you are wondering:

- Why the topic has been left until now when we've been using diagrams for the past seven chapters?
- Are you faced with learning the details of yet another set of diagrams?

Dealing with the first point: diagrams were introduced – in a very informal way – only as and when needed (in other words, used in a relevant context). The reasons for doing this are threefold. First, it demonstrated the power of diagramming techniques. Second, it implicitly made a good case for using diagrams as a design tool (they aren't just a set of 'pretty pictures'). Third, it (hopefully) made the task of learning the syntax and semantics of a wide range of diagrams a fairly painless process. Now, though, we can deal with diagramming in a more formal manner. And, to take the second question: yes, we will meet some new diagrams along the way. But there won't be a need to redo the material of earlier chapters. Most of the software diagrams used so far are based on the methods discussed in this chapter (note: to save cross-referencing and make the text easier to read, some material from previous sections is reproduced here).

It is easy to confuse diagramming methods and design methods. This happens because some diagramming methods form an integral part of specific design processes. One can end up believing that design and diagramming are inseparable. This isn't so. Diagramming methods *can* be used without adopting the associated design principles.

The reference point for this chapter is the diagram of Figure 7.20, 'Overall diagram set for real-time systems'. What we wish to do is to show how specific diagrams which:

- Are in common use
- Form part of accepted design methods and
- Are always supported by CASE tools

match up to the needs outlined in Figure 7.20. For sound practical reasons the topic is set in the context of two major design techniques:

- Structured/data flow methods (for brevity: *structured*).
- Object-oriented methods.

The reason for grouping things in this way is that most CASE tools are organized in a similar fashion.

Although a number of structured methods are in widespread use, CASE tool support is greatest for the Yourdon [WAR85] and SDL (Specification and Description Language, [SDL88]) approaches. Therefore the example diagrams given here are based mainly on those techniques. For object-oriented work the industry *de facto* standard is the Unified Modelling Language, UML [UML99]. However, none of these provide *all* the features needed for the development of real-time systems. Hence you will find that designers frequently use extensions or variations of these standard techniques. Some may be company-specific (i.e. bespoke) while others may be provided by CASE tool vendors. The following diagrams are covered in this chapter:

(a) Structured designs

    (i)   Context diagrams.
    (ii)   Entity relationship diagrams.
    (iii)   State transition diagrams and state transition tables.
    (iv)   Real-time data flow diagrams.
    (v)   Message sequence charts.
    (vi)   Structure charts and program description languages (PDLs).
    (vii)   SDL process diagrams.
    (viii) Event–response lists.

(b) Object-oriented designs

    (i)   Use case diagrams.
    (ii)   Deployment diagrams.
    (iii)   Packages.
    (iv)   Class diagrams.
    (v)   Object and object collaboration diagrams.
    (vi)   Statechart diagrams.
    (vii)   Sequence diagrams.
    (viii) Activity diagrams.
    (ix)   Component diagrams.

(c) Extensions and variations of the standard diagram sets

    (i)   System configuration diagrams.
    (ii)   System architecture diagrams.
    (iii)   System scope diagrams.
    (iv)   Node architecture diagrams.
    (v)   Processor architecture diagrams.
    (vi)   Tasking diagrams.
    (vii)   Memory map diagrams.

8.2 Diagrams for structured and data flow designs

8.2.1 Context diagrams

The purpose of a context diagram is to show the relationship of the system software with its environment. It portrays the complete system in its simplest form: a set of external items connected to a software 'black box', Figure 8.1a.

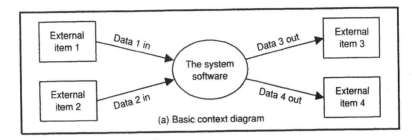

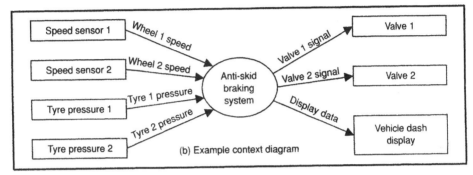

Figure 8.1 Context diagram.

It contains:

- A single processing unit (the 'bubble') representing the complete software system.
- The external items which this software interfaces to.
- Data flows into and out of the software.

The result of applying these ideas to the anti-skid braking system of Chapter 4 is shown in Figure 8.1b. This would be used in concert with the system operational description contained in the SOR document. Details concerning system behaviour, signal levels, required response rates, etc. are normally tied in with the context diagram documentation.

8.2.2 Entity relationship diagrams

Any real system consists of a set of individual 'things' or 'entities'. However, these don't exist in a vacuum; somehow they are related to each other. In some circumstances it may be important to capture and show such information. To do this diagrammatically we use an entity relationship diagram (ERD), an example being that of Figure 8.2. This shows the distinct items – and their relationship with each other – of a cockpit climate control system.

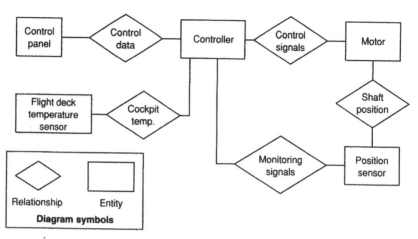

Figure 8.2 Entity relationship diagram.

In practice ERDs have limited application in embedded systems, being used mainly in database design work.

8.2.3 State transition diagrams and state transition tables

A finite-state machine (FSM) is a device for modelling the behaviour of a system in time. Specifically it represents this behaviour as a set of discrete, mutually exclusive and finite states. Events cause the system to change state; these changes are assumed to take place instantly. Such events, which may be periodic or aperiodic, usually provoke some sort of response from the system. The behaviour of finite state machines may be shown using state transition diagrams, Figure 8.3a. Each state is denoted using a rectangle, the connecting lines being transition arcs or simply transitions. When defining dynamic behaviour, four items are relevant. These are:

- The current state.
- The next state.
- The event (or events) which causes the transition from the current to the next state.
- The action (or actions) which the event (or events) produces.

As shown here the system has two states and two transitions. Assume it to be in state 1. Should event 1 occur then the system will change state to state 2; it will also react by producing a response (response 1). Transition from state 2 to state 1 takes place in a similar manner. This particular form of FSM is called a 'Mealy' machine.

A somewhat more concrete example, that for a motorized conveyor belt, is shown in Figure 8.3b.

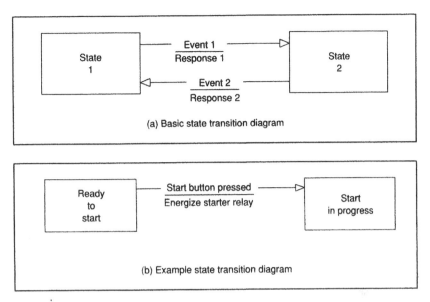

(a) Basic state transition diagram

(b) Example state transition diagram

Figure 8.3 State transition diagram (part).

Current state	Event	Response	Next state
Ready to start	Start button pressed	Energize starter relay	Start in progress
Start in progress	Idling speed reached	'System active' sign illuminated	System active

Figure 8.4 State transition table.

We can also show FSM details using tables such as the state transition table (STT) of Figure 8.4. These have the advantage of being compact; much information can be presented in just one piece of paper. However, the disadvantage is that it is much harder to see the overall picture; as a result it is easier to misread the information and make mistakes.

8.2.4 Real-time data flow diagrams

Fundamentally, the purpose of data flow diagrams (DFDs) is to depict the processing carried out by the software. The underlying model is that of materials flow, as depicted in Figure 8.5a. Here, for 'materials flow', read 'data flow'. Each bubble represents a processing machine or data transformation (DT), processing input data to produce an output result. Good naming can make the diagrams self-explanatory (Figure 8.5b).

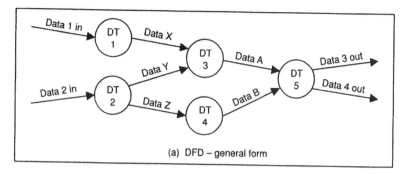

(a) DFD – general form

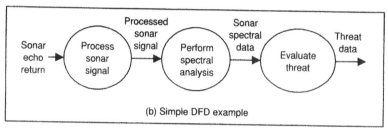

(b) Simple DFD example

Figure 8.5 | Basic data flow diagram.

The data flow diagrams, as they stand, show exactly what processing is to be carried out. Unfortunately they don't explain *when* or *why* the individual data transformations are executed. This comes about because the ideal DFD model assumes that a DT:

- Will run as soon as all its data inputs are present and
- Can run simultaneously (concurrently) with all other DTs.

However, for sequential programs, one, and only one, DT can be active at any one time. And that brings us back to the questions of when and why. One way of dealing with this situation is to use a new construct, the control transformation (CT), Figure 8.6. Here the CT, drawn as a dotted bubble, is shown interacting with the DTs via enable/disable commands (called 'enable/disable prompts'). We interpret this to mean that the DTs are executed in accordance with some set of rules; the rules themselves are defined by the specification of the control transformation.

As shown here communication between the CT and the DTs is a one-way process. However, DTs may, in fact, send signals to CTs, so modifying the logical behaviour of the control transformations. Moreover, the activation/deactivation of data transformations may also be determined by external events, as shown in Figure 8.7. Here external commands 'Manual selected' and 'Auto selected' are fed to the CT. This (the CT) determines the operational mode of the data transformation in accordance with the logic of its specification. In this example the behaviour of the control transformation is defined using a state transition diagram.

A more detailed description of data flow diagrams is given in Chapter 4.

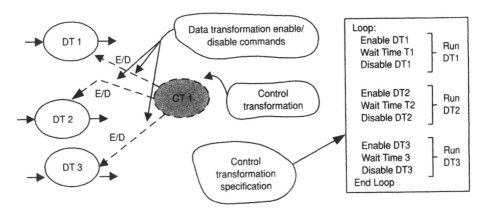

Figure 8.6 Combining data and control transformations – the real-time data flow diagram.

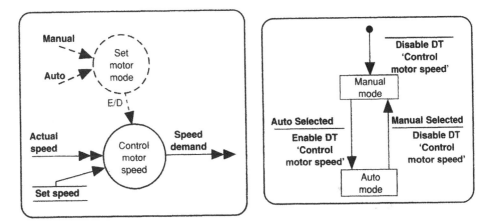

Figure 8.7 Reacting to external events.

8.2.5 Message sequence diagrams

Systems based on multiple computers, multiprocessors or multitasking structures have one important common feature. They contain 'things' which may be (usually are) concurrently active and operational. These component parts (the 'things') have to work together in a correct manner if the complete system is also to work correctly. Thus they need to communicate with each other.

The most widely used technique to support such communication is that of message passing. From a behavioural point of view we need to know:

● What messages are sent.

● When messages are sent.

● Who the sender and receivers are.

● How much time elapses during the various message transactions.

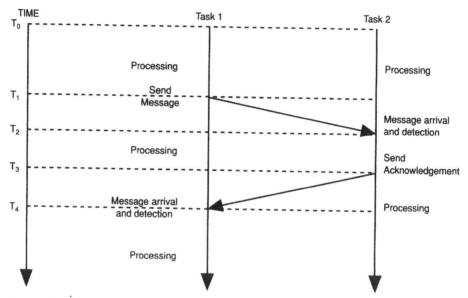

Figure 8.8 | Message sequence diagram.

This information can be shown in a message sequence diagram, Figure 8.8. This simple example illustrates messaging between two tasks of a multitasking system over a particular period of time. Each task has its own time line or trace, where time runs from top to bottom of the diagram. When task 1 sends a message to task 2, an arrowed line is drawn from 1 to 2. Here, for instance, task 1 sends a message to task 2 at time T_1. This is detected by task 2 at time T_2. In turn, task 2 sends a message at time T_3 to task 1, which is detected at time T_4.

The timescale may be absolute or relative; it depends entirely on the application. Note that these diagrams are also known as message sequence charts, MSC.

8.2.6 Structure charts and program description languages

Structure charts and program description languages have essentially one function. They provide the link between the problem specification and the production of source code. To do this effectively they must satisfy a number of criteria:

(a) Support for design techniques.
   - Modular structure
   - Top-down design
   - Stepwise refinement
   - Module relationships
   - Execution logic

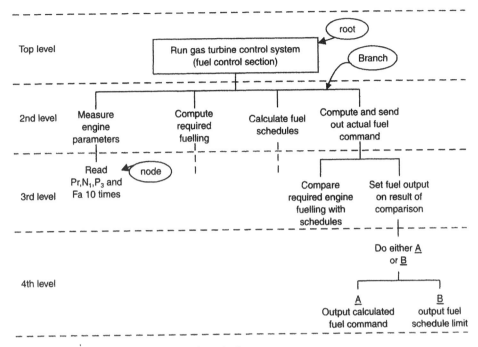

Figure 8.9 | Top-to-bottom decomposition – basic structure.

(b)   Support for programming constructs.

- Sequence
- Selection
- Iteration

Program description languages are, in this context, the text counterpart of structure charts.

Structured programs are designed as a layered set of operations (Figure 8.9) following the concepts of top-down design.

This example defines part of the program for a gas turbine control system. At the top there is a single root module or root operation. This is decomposed using a tree structure to interconnect lower-level operations. This is the basis of two widely used structure charts, those of Jackson [JAC75] and Yourdon [YOU78].

Jackson structure charts

Jackson diagrams can be used to show both program and data structures. However, here we will use them only for the structuring of programs. Program behaviour is described using the three basic operations of sequence, selection and iteration, Figure 8.10. In this example the **Sequence** construct shows that Alpha is composed of w, x, y, z; they are executed in the order shown. Next, Alpha involves a choice,

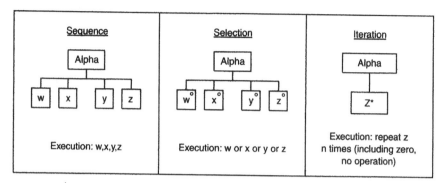

Figure 8.10 | Jackson structure charts — basic constructs.

that is, **Selection**. Thus, either w or x or y or z is executed; these choices are mutually exclusive. The diagram, in its basic form, doesn't show the test condition for the selection action. Finally we come to **Iteration**. This construct defines that:

- There is an operation, Alpha, which has an iteration (loop) structure.
- Alpha is actually implemented by the execution of z.
- More precisely, z is the iterated component. It may be executed once, twice or as often as specified by some control condition.
- z, in some cases, may never be executed, the zero loop.

Note that the diagram doesn't distinguish between pre-check and post-check loops. The Jackson diagram corresponding to Figure 8.9 is shown in Figure 8.11.

One fundamental point concerns code generation. In the original Jackson method, code is produced which directly relates to the bottom-most nodes (also called 'terminal points' or 'elementary components'). Code is never produced for higher-level operations. Looked at in another way, a high-level component is the 'sum' of its lower-level parts; it doesn't have an independent existence. However, experience has shown that allowing code to be produced for any 'box' has significant advantages. In such cases extra notation is needed to denote this fact [COO97].

Yourdon structure charts

Yourdon structure charts are, at first sight, apparently very similar to Jackson diagrams. In fact, their information content is quite different in many ways.

The fundamental building blocks of these charts are mainly rectangular boxes. These are interconnected using data and control flow arrows, Figure 8.12. Each box describes a software process, known as a module. In Yourdon design a module is implemented as a sequence of program instructions having a single entry and single exit point. These, in practice, are usually built using the procedure or function construct.

Where a process (A) needs to be split into a number of parts (step-wise refinement) it is broken down into lower-level processes (B, C). Lowest-level modules are

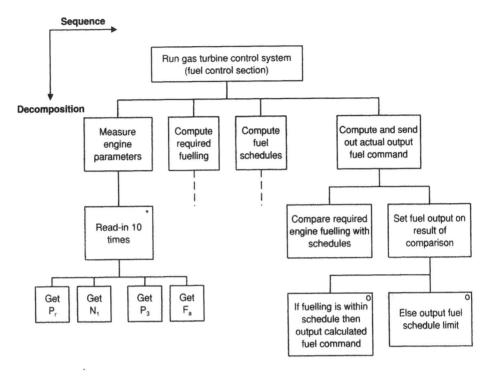

Figure 8.11 : Jackson structure chart – gas turbine example.

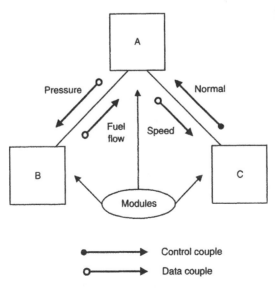

Figure 8.12 : Yourdon structure chart – basic layout and components.

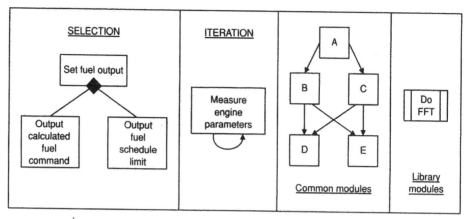

Figure 8.13 Yourdon structure chart – additional components.

known as 'leafs'. The structure chart shows this hierarchical relationship between modules. Arrowed lines are used to show the connection between modules.

The arrowed line connection does more than just show the connection between modules. It also specifies that, at execution time, control passes from the higher-level (or 'parent') module to the lower-level 'child' module. That is, the parent module calls the child. In doing so it may well pass information to it; at the end it may receive data back. This flow of information is called a 'data couple'. In many cases the response required from the called or 'invoked' module is not data, but information to be used for the control of the program. For example, the module might have to evaluate if the speed of a unit is in the normal range. The reply would be a simple YES/NO, which can't really be considered to be data. It is, in fact, defined to be a control couple or 'flag'. Note that a called module always returns control to the calling module.

This diagram, as it stands, does not show sequence, selection and iteration control structures. Unfortunately a Yourdon diagram does not specify the order in which modules are executed. However, selection and iteration are defined by using extra notation, as shown in Figure 8.13.

Selection or decision making is denoted using a diamond symbol, often called a 'transaction centre' (the centre, by the way, is the diamond, not the module). Iteration of a module is indicated by the curved arrowed line. Where any particular module can be called by more than one higher-level module it is called a common module (observe that the use of common modules changes tree-structured diagrams to mesh ones). Library modules – which carry out pre-defined tasks – form the elementary 'bricks' of program construction. Normally one would expect a library module to be a leaf.

The Yourdon diagram for the example gas turbine control system is shown in Figure 8.14. Note that the diagram has been arranged to reinforce the point that the diagram does not give sequence information.

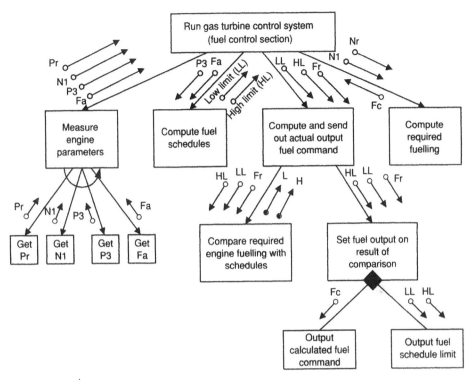

Figure 8.14 Yourdon structure chart – gas turbine example.

Program description languages – structured text

Structured text is designed to express program operation using either structured English or pseudocode (these words are often used interchangeably). It describes program operations using the fundamental control structures of structured programming, thus bringing formality to the process. These descriptions are extended – and made more understandable – by defining program objects and decision-making operations using everyday language.

There isn't a single definitive method in general use. Techniques range from structured but casual English notation to rigorously defined layout methods. Whichever is used, the following rules should be followed if they are going to be of any use:

- Descriptions should be easy to understand.
- They should use a hierarchical structure.
- This structure should be obvious from the text layout.
- The structures of sequence, selection and iteration must be supported.
- Keywords should be used to identify these structures.
- Keywords should be used to identify logical operations.
- Comments to be inserted in the source code should be clearly marked.

An example is given in Figure 8.15.

```
SEQUENCE Outer
        Measure engine parameters
                ITERATION Alpha
                        REPEAT 10 times
                                Get Pr
                                Get N1
                                Get P3
                                Get Fa
                        END ITERATION Alpha
        Compute required fuelling
        Calculate fuel schedules
        Compute and send out actual output fuel command
                SEQUENCE Beta
                        Compare required engine fuelling with schedules
                        Set fuel output on results of comparison
                                SELECTION Gamma
                                        IF fuelling is within schedule THEN
                                                Output calculated fuel command
                                        ELSE
                                                Output fuel schedule limit
                                        END IF
                                END SELECTION Gamma
                END SEQUENCE Beta
END SEQUENCE Outer
```

Figure 8.15 Structured text — gas turbine example.

8.2.7 SDL (Specification and Description Language) process diagrams

SDL was designed to specify and describe the functional behaviour of telecommunication systems. Those wishing to use the full features of the method are advised to consult [SDL88] and the web site at [SDL88/tutorial]. We will limit ourselves to one particular aspect: the use of processes. The reason for doing so is because the ideas (and notation) have been used in the design of many embedded systems. These are especially useful when dealing with concurrency and task design.

In simple terms a process is equivalent to the task of a multitasking system (Chapter 5); thus it is a unit of sequential code. A process diagram is used to show both the dynamics and the data processing of such program units. Hence each process has its own individual diagram, formed from the basic set of symbols shown in Figure 8.16.

To lead into the use, syntax and semantics of such diagrams, first consider the behaviour of two interacting processes, Figure 8.17. Here the external behaviour of the processes is modelled using a message sequence chart. All process interaction takes place using messages, these, in SDL terminology, being defined to be 'signals'. By definition, an incoming signal produces a state change in the receiving process

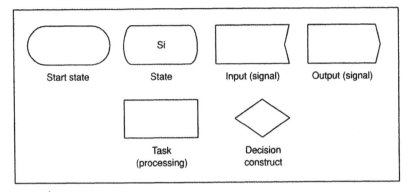

Figure 8.16   SDL process diagram constructs.

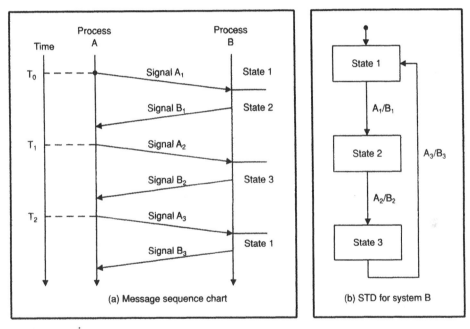

Figure 8.17   Modelling the behaviour of interacting processes.

(for clarity, this is shown only for process B in Figure 8.17a). Hence the dynamic behaviour of individual processes can be expressed using a state transition diagram, Figure 8.17b. The SDL process diagram expresses this same information, and more, as demonstrated in Figure 8.18. Here process B goes from the start state into state 1, and waits for incoming signals. When signal A_1 arrives:

● Some processing (computation) is carried out, then
● Signal B_1 is generated, and
● A transition is made to state 2.

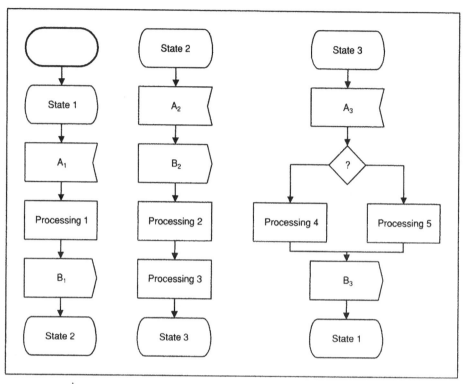

Figure 8.18 SDL process diagrams for process B of Figure 8.17.

In state 2 the processes respond to signal A_2 only, by:

● Generating an outgoing signal B_2, then
● Performing computation (processing 2 followed by processing 3) and then
● Making a transition to state 3.

In this state the system reacts only to signal A_3. On receipt of this signal:

● It is examined to determine its value, then
● Either processing 4 or processing 5 is carried out, depending on A_3's value
● Signal B_3 is generated and
● The process moves back into state 1 (from where the whole procedure can be repeated).

Thus it can be seen that fundamentally we have a combination of state diagrams and flow-charts.

Source	Input event	Processing	Output response	Destination
Cruise select switch	Cruise control set 'on'	Control vehicle speed	Modulate fuel settings	Engine management unit

Figure 8.19 Specimen event–response list.

8.2.8 Event–response lists

Event–response lists are used to show how items respond to external actions. Such items can be sections of code, individual tasks, network nodes or complete systems. There is no standard format for these lists, but most contain the following information:

- Source
- Input event
- Processing carried out
- Output response
- Destination.

An example is given in Figure 8.19, describing operations at the system level for a car (auto) cruise control system.

8.3 UML diagrams for object-oriented designs

8.3.1 Use case diagrams

A use case *model*, Figure 8.20, consists of actors, use cases and use case descriptions. Its purpose, in simple terms, is to show why systems are used and who uses them.

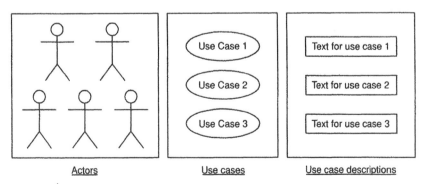

Figure 8.20 The components of the use case model.

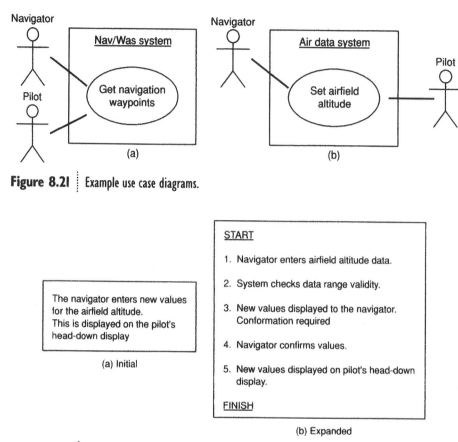

Figure 8.21 Example use case diagrams.

Figure 8.22 Text description – initial and expanded versions.

Each system has its own model, with actors depicting users (more correctly, roles performed by users). The reasons why these actors are using the system are shown as a set of use cases within the system boundary. Two simple examples are given in Figure 8.21. Each system is drawn as a rectangular box, with the relevant use cases shown as ellipses inside them (the box, representing the system boundary, is optional). Outside the system boundary are the actors, connected via lines to the use cases. In (a), both the navigator actor and the pilot actor interact with the NAV/WAS system in the same way; they use it to find out what the navigation waypoints are. Information flow is a two-way process. In (b), the navigator uses the air data system to set airfield altitude: again a two-way process. However, in this case the pilot receives only output (information) from the system; the role played by the actor is thus a 'passive' one.

Now let us look into the use case text descriptions in more detail. The first version should be short, clear and use ordinary language, Figure 8.22a. A structured, formalized version can be used to expand on this at a later stage, Figure 8.22b.

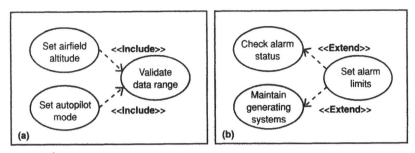

Figure 8.23 : Comparing the includes and extends relationships.

Applying these ideas leads to what might be called a 'flat' set of use case descriptions – each one exists at the same level. This, in large systems, can be a problem. Without structuring, text documents soon become complex, difficult to read, difficult to understand. Two particular relationships can be used to help here: 'include', and 'extend', Figure 8.23.

● Include use cases collect in one place behaviour which is:
  – Repeated within one use case and/or
  – Common to a number of use cases (Figure 8.23a).
● Extend use cases show variations on a theme (Figure 8.23b).

We read the use case relationship in the direction of the arrows. For instance, in Figure 8.23a, the use case 'set airfield altitude' – defined to be a 'base' use case – *includes* the use case 'validate data range' (likewise, the base use case 'set autopilot mode' includes 'set airfield altitude'). By contrast, the use case 'set alarm limits' in Figure 8.23b *extends* the base use cases 'check alarm status' and 'maintain generating systems'.

A fuller description is given in Chapter 3, whilst detailed coverage can be found in Booch *et al.*'s book [UML99].

8.3.2 Deployment diagrams

Deployment diagrams are used to model the physical aspects of systems. They consist primarily of nodes, node relationships and components. In UML-speak, a node is 'a run-time physical object that represents a processing resource . . . Nodes include computing devices but also human resources or mechanical processing resources.' The UML definition of deployment diagrams and nodes is somewhat esoteric (clarity is not its strongest point). However, we will use them for a very specific purpose: to model the physical architecture of systems.

A simple example of a one-node embedded system is shown in Figure 8.24. The node itself is shown as a three-dimensional cube, while devices external to the node have been depicted using appropriate symbols. This device representation method

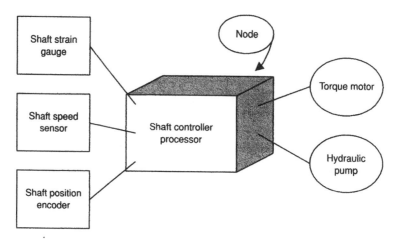

Figure 8.24 Deployment diagram – single-node embedded system.

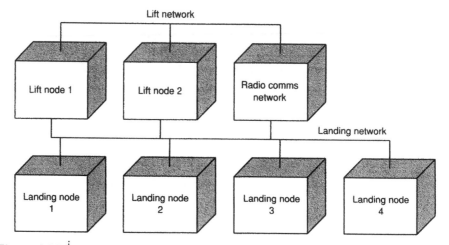

Figure 8.25 Deployment diagram – networked embedded system.

is not specified in the UML standard; it has in fact been suggested by Booch *et al.* [UML99]. A more complex example, that of a distributed networked system, is shown in Figure 8.25. Strictly speaking this is a modification of the standard deployment diagram (mainly because UML is rather weak in this area).

8.3.3 Packages and package diagrams

One of the simplest features of UML – yet an extremely useful one – is the *package*. In simple terms this is nothing more than a holder or container for other items. You use it to group things together in a sensible manner for sensible reasons (best

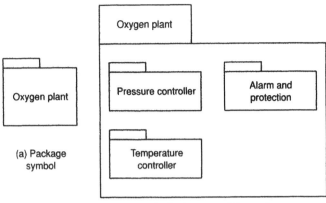

Figure 8.26 | Basic package diagrams.

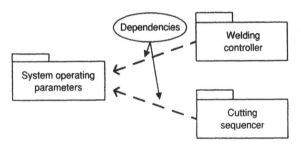

Figure 8.27 | Package dependencies.

illustrated by example; see later chapters). These 'things' can be classes, objects, packages, subsystems, what you will. Thus we can have packages of classes, packages of objects (but not packages of classes *and* objects). The basics of the package diagram are shown in Figure 8.26, which is pretty-well self-explanatory. Figure 8.26a shows the symbol for the package, a 'tabbed' rectangle or folder. The name of the package is written within the main area. In Figure 8.26b the package 'Oxygen plant' itself contains three packages. Observe that the name has been written within the tab (not mandatory but usual).

At this time the only other aspect worth covering is that of 'dependencies', Figure 8.27. The dotted-arrowed lines show that packages 'Welding controller' and 'Cutting sequencer' somehow depend on the package 'System operating parameters' (note the direction of the arrow). It may be, for instance, that the values of the operating parameters are used by the dependent packages. Thus changes to these parameters may affect the operational behaviour of the welding and cutting units.

What we have here is an example of an 'import' dependency. A second dependency form is 'access', which indicates that access permission is required to use packaged items.

Showing such dependencies explicitly is an important part of the configuration control of software.

8.3.4 Class diagrams

General details and association relationships

By 'class diagrams' *we* mean diagrams which show the classes of a system and their relationships. If this sounds somewhat pedantic, you need to know that the UML specification says (amongst other things) 'a "class" diagram may also contain interfaces, packages, relationships, and even instances, such as objects and links'.

As pointed out earlier (Chapter 4) the work done by a software system is actually performed by objects. These encapsulate both operations and data, where operations are bound to their associated data. By contrast, the class is a software template from which objects are created. Thus the class (essentially a source-code declaration) defines the form, content and behaviour of objects. Its notation is that of Figure 8.28, a rectangular box having three compartments. The name of the class is shown in the first (upper, name) section. Its attributes (qualities) are listed in the middle section, whilst its *visible* operations appear in the bottom section. Only the name section need be shown on a class diagram; the others are optional.

Classes, of course, do not exist in isolation; real systems consist of many classes. These, and their relationships, are shown using the class diagram, Figure 8.29. Here the relationships are deemed to be 'associations', the naming used ('manages') denoting the nature of the relationship between the *objects*. A class diagram also

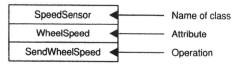

Figure 8.28 Class symbol.

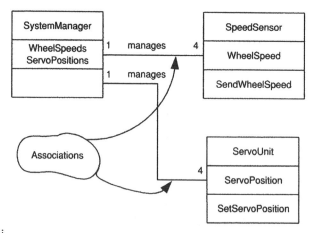

Figure 8.29 Class diagram (simplified) of an anti-skid braking system.

defines how many objects may be generated for a particular relationship. We do this by putting a 'multiplicity' symbol at each end of the association line, the general notation being:

lower_bound .. upper_bound

Note that a star symbol can be used for the upper bound; this denotes that there is no limit to the upper bound (a bit iffy for real systems). Examples are:

0 .. 2 – a minimum of no (zero) objects, a maximum of two objects.
1 .. 3 – a minimum of one, maximum of three objects.
1   – precisely one object
2 .. * – a minimum of two objects, the maximum being unlimited.

Thus from Figure 8.29 we can see that:

- If we create one SystemManager object, then we must also create four SpeedSensor and four ServoUnit objects.

- If we create a SpeedSensor object then we must also create a SystemManager object. This, in turn, requires that we create the ServoUnit objects.

- If we create a ServoUnit object then we must also create a SystemManager object. This, in turn, requires that we create the SpeedSensor objects.

Inheritance and inheritance relationships

The topic here is essentially one of specialization and generalization. This leads to a different form of class structure, one involving subclasses and superclasses, as illustrated in Figure 8.30. These, it can be seen, are organized in a hierarchical manner. At the top there is the superclass 'Sensor'. Below this are the three subclasses 'Speed', 'Height' and 'Attitude' which in turn have a number of subclasses.

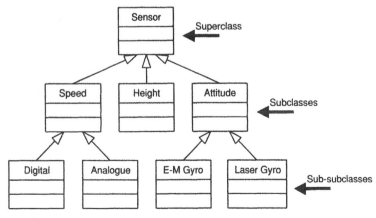

Figure 8.30 | Class structuring – subclasses and superclasses.

The superclass 'Sensor' gives the most abstract definition (in terms of attributes and/or operations) of a sensor object. A subclass adds detail to the superclass definition which is specific to that individual subclass. However, it also automatically acquires the properties of its parents, this being known as inheritance. Thus, moving down the hierarchy, classes become progressively more specialized.

Note: some terminology. A superclass is also known as a parent or base class, while a subclass is often called an extended or derived class.

Aggregation and aggregation relationships

Time and experience have shown that building systems in a modular fashion is a very powerful technique. Such ideas can be implemented by having groups of objects which are:

● Intended to work together very closely and

● Are essentially components of a larger unit.

Thus we form an 'aggregation' of objects. To define such object designs we use the class aggregate association (or simply aggregation), Figure 8.31. Here the diamond symbol is used to denote aggregation, specifically *composite* aggregation. Compare this with the use of an arrow for inheritance. If we use this as the template for our *object* diagram, then the top-level object (of class GeneratingSet) is here defined to be a *parent*. The contained objects (of classes PowerUnit and GeneratingUnit) are *children* of this parent. They in turn act as parents to *their* child objects. Putting it another way, a generating set is made up of a power unit and a generating unit. A power unit has (or consists) of a starter motor, a fuel valve and an engine. A generating unit consists of a generator and a control unit.

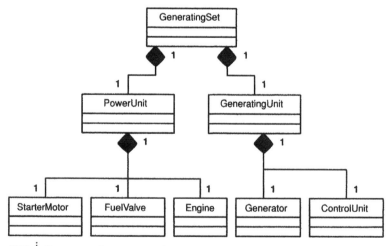

Figure 8.31 Class structuring – aggregation.

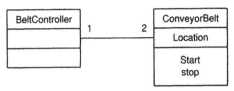

(a) Class diagram - conveyor belt system

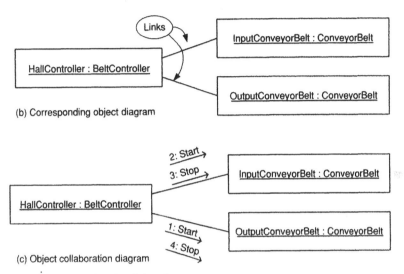

(b) Corresponding object diagram

(c) Object collaboration diagram

Figure 8.32 Objects and their collaborations.

8.3.5 Object and object collaboration diagrams

The purpose of an object diagram is to show the objects of a system and their relationships. An object collaboration diagram is basically an object diagram which also shows the interaction(s) between the objects.

A simple example of a conveyor belt system is given in Figure 8.32, where the class structure is defined in (a). The object diagram, Figure 8.32b, shows that the system as built consists of a hall controller and two conveyor belts. Here the connection between objects is defined to be a link.

Each conveyor belt object has two operations that can be invoked (called on) by other objects: Start and Stop. These externally visible operations are activated by passing messages to the objects, as shown in Figure 8.32c, the object collaboration diagram. Here the messages have, for clarity, been given the same name as the operations. Moreover, we can define the time ordering of messages by attaching numbers to them. Thus in this example the first message is 'Start', sent to the output conveyor belt. The next one starts the input conveyor belt, the third one stops the output belt, etc.

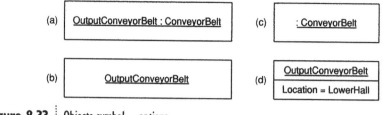

Figure 8.33 Objects symbol – options.

Objects can be depicted in a number of ways, Figure 8.33. The naming options are:

(a) The name of the object and its class are specified.

(b) Only the name of the object is given.

(c) Only the name of the class is used (this gives us a nameless or anonymous object).

In addition to this, the attribute value can also be included if desired, as shown in Figure 8.33d.

A last point: there are a number of variations on the arrowhead, but for details see [UML/OMG].

8.3.6 Statecharts

Introduction

Statecharts, devised by David Harel, are state transition diagrams. These are based on, but substantially extend, the Mealy machine. More importantly (from the point of view of this text), the dynamic model of UML stems from the statechart model. Moreover, the diagramming notations are very similar. Therefore it is desirable to understand statechart concepts and notation.

Figure 8.34 illustrates the basic notation of the diagram. Shown here is a two-state machine with a single transition from state 1 to state 2. The notation used for events and actions is similar to that of the Mealy machine. However, an additional factor is introduced – the idea of a condition or guard (G) on the transition. The reading of the diagram is that 'if event E occurs, then the system will transfer to State 2 provided condition G is true' *at that time*.

What is given here is a one-level or *flat* state diagram. A major difficulty with such diagrams (discussed earlier) is that they can rapidly become cluttered and complex. Statecharts tackle these drawbacks by providing both refinement and depth, using substates, Figure 8.35. Here the top-level diagram is a three-state one: Standby, Starting and Running. Analysis of Starting shows that it actually consists

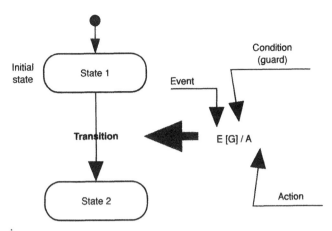

Figure 8.34 Statechart – basic notation.

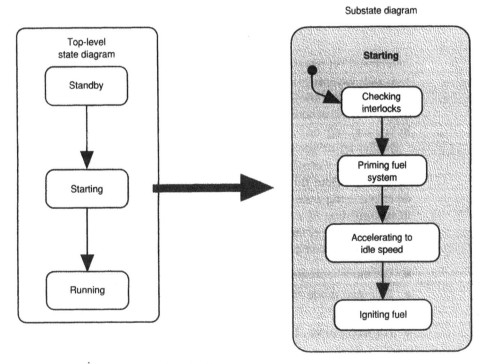

Figure 8.35 Refinement (depth) and substates.

of a number of localized states – the *substates*. Including this information on the top-level diagram would transform it from a three-state to a six-state description (which shows how quickly flat state diagrams can 'explode' as more detail is added). Refining the state information into a separate child diagram allows detail to be

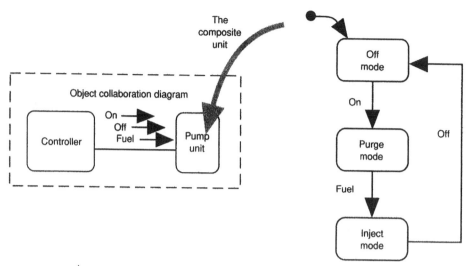

Figure 8.36 | Collaboration and state diagrams for a composite unit.

hidden and yet remain accessible. Thus refinement is a top-down concept, each top-level state encapsulating a set of substates. Please note that a high-level state is really an abstraction of the substates. Consider, for example, when the system is in Starting mode. It must actually be in one of the designated substates. To be more precise, in one and *only* one substate.

Finally, let us see how statecharts can portray concurrent behaviour within a single object. Consider the object collaboration diagram and state diagrams of Figure 8.36. Here the pump unit is treated as a single unit, its behaviour being described using a single state diagram. However, the unit is actually a composite item, consisting of a fuel–air mixer valve and a fuel pump – two separate, concurrently operating components. Thus each has its own mode of behaviour, given in Figure 8.37. By comparing Figures 8.36 and 8.37 it can be seen that:

- Off mode corresponds to the valve being isolated and the pump stopped.
- In purge mode the valve goes to the air feed state while the pump begins running.
- For inject mode, the valve is in the fuel feed state and the pump is running.

Observe that Figure 8.37 provides information relating to:

- Independence of component states.
- Synchronization between component states.

Here Fuel changes the state of the fuel–air valve only. It has no effect on the fuel pump – *independence* of behaviour. In contrast 0 ffand 0 rcause a simultaneous state change in both components – *synchronization*.

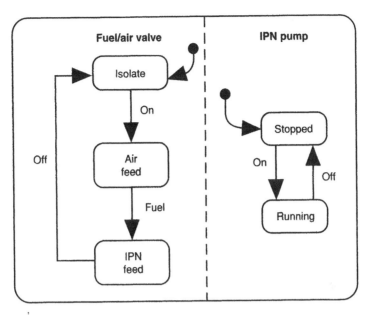

Figure 8.37   Concurrent states.

UML notation

The UML statechart is based on Harel's work. However, it extends this by also using concepts from the Moore machine, where responses are associated with states. Figures 8.38 and 8.39 contain the constructs which are most likely to be used in practice. Figure 8.38a(i) shows the fundamental state/event/guard/action notation of the UML state diagram. On a small but important point, UML defines actions as *atomic and non-interruptible* operations. Be careful with this; it has got nothing to do with interrupt-driven operations. What it means is that once an action starts it will run to completion irrespective of system events.

Initial states are illustrated in a(ii), whilst final states are defined in a(iii). Figure 8.38b shows how attributes of events can be added to state diagrams. Here an object has two states, Ready to Weigh and Computing Cost. A state change takes place when the event Load on Bridge occurs. Associated with this event is the attribute Weight.

Up to this point, the notation is essentially that of a Mealy machine. Now we have aspects of the Moore machine, where operations are associated with states. Such operations are grouped into four categories, depending on the operations performed:

- On entry to a state.
- Within the state.
- On exit from the state.
- During a self-transition (i.e. transition back to the original state).

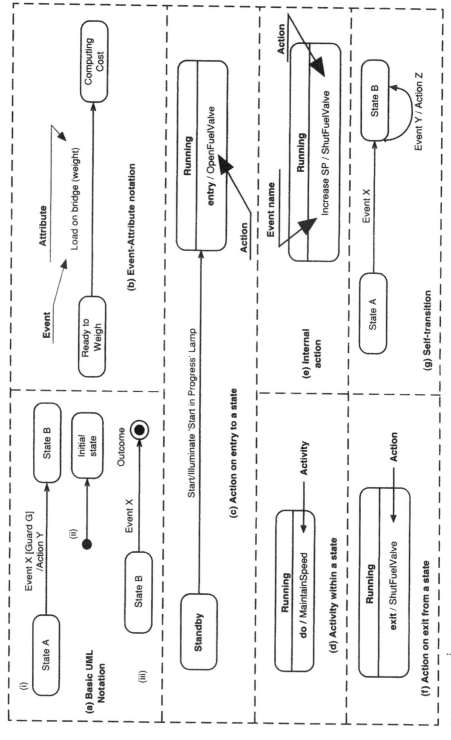

Figure 8.38 UML notation for statecharts (I).

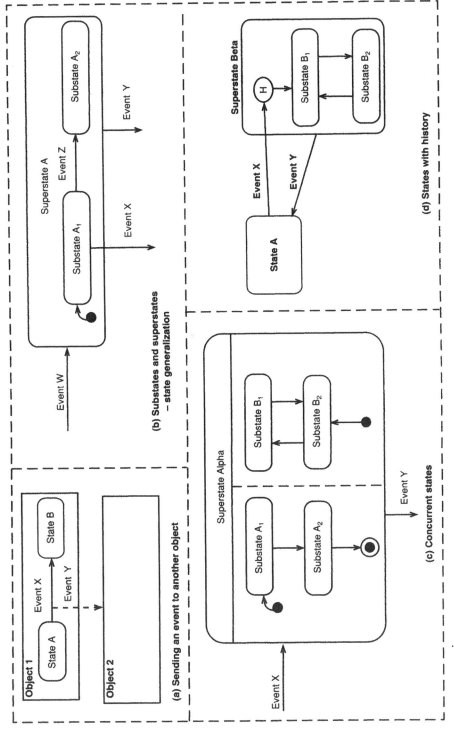

Figure 8.39 UML notation for statecharts (2).

Entry to a state is shown in Figure 8.38c. Here, when event Start arrives, the action Illuminate 'start-in-progress' Lamp is performed. The system now enters the Running state. On entry the operation O pen Fuel Valves conducted (note well; this is defined to be an *action*). The identifier *entry/* is used to denote such actions.

Once the entry action(s) has been executed, the system proceeds into what might be called a steady-state condition. It remains in the state, performing a required set of operations called *activities*. An activity is defined to be an operation that takes time to complete. Figure 8.38d indicates that the operation Maintain Speed is an activity by the keyword **do**. Whilst in a state, events may arrive which – although they generate *internal* actions – do not cause a state change. Figure 8.38e illustrates the notation used, which is of the form **Event Name/Action Generated**.

When a state is exited, exit operations are effected. These are identified using **exit**, Figure 8.38f.

The self-transition (see state B of Figure 8.38g) is slightly unusual. When an event (Y) arrives it produces an action (Z), but there is no resulting state change. More strictly, we consider that a transition is made out of a state and then back into the same state. This might perhaps seem a pedantic point. Not with UML, though; here it is an extremely important aspect: because, when a self-transition occurs, all exit and entry actions are performed. Note this well.

Entry and exit actions are *always* completed. This, however, is not necessarily true of activities. For instance, an event which generates a state change may arrive during the execution of an activity. The result is that the activity is terminated, and then the exit actions performed.

The notation of Figure 8.39a is used to show the sending of events to other objects.

Substates and superstates, Figure 8.39b, are illustrated much like the statechart method. Here a transition is made into superstate A when event W occurs. What actually happens is that substate A_1 becomes active. Should event Z arrive, the system moves into substate A_2. But, if event X is generated instead, the system will move out of substate A_1 (and thus out of the superstate). Event Y causes an immediate transition out of the superstate, irrespective of the substate conditions.

Concurrent states are identified using the notation of Figure 8.39c. Here a superstate Alpha consists of two concurrent substates, A and B. The superstate is activated by event X: this causes the system to enter sub-substates A_1 and B_2. As shown, substate A could reach a termination condition whilst the superstate is active. Substate B denotes cyclic operation. Irrespective of the actual situation, transition out of Alpha takes place when event Y arrives.

Finally, let us look at the idea of giving states a memory or 'history' feature, Figure 8.39d. From this it can be seen that superstate Beta is made up of two substates, B_1 and B_2. If the system is in either of these and event Y occurs, then a transition is made to state A. However, the system remembers which substate it was in (say B_2, for example). Now the next time event X arrives the transition is back to the substate B_2. In other words, the state machine has a memory (history), indicated by the H symbol.

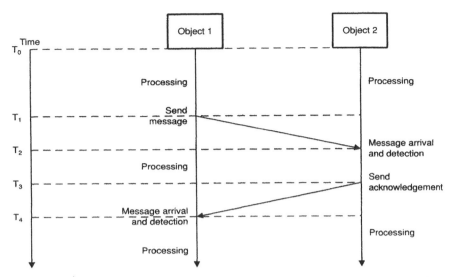

Figure 8.40 Sequence diagram showing object interactions.

Now this raises a small but important point: how do we show which substate goes active on the *first* transition into Beta? This is denoted in a simple fashion, by connecting the H symbol, via a transition, to that particular substate. Thus, in Figure 8.39d, on the first transition to state Beta, substate B_1 becomes active.

8.3.7   Sequence diagrams

The fundamental purpose of sequence diagrams is to show interactions between items (usually objects) as time elapses. The basic concept for a two-object system is shown in Figure 8.40. As you can see this is essentially the same as the message sequence chart of Figure 8.8. In essence it shows:

● What messages are sent.

● When messages are sent.

● Who the sender and receivers are.

● How much time elapses during the various message transactions.

However, UML extends the notational aspects of MSCs in a number of ways. It:

● Distinguishes between concurrent and sequential program operations and

● Uses a number of different arrows to denote different forms of messaging.

Note that the vertical lines are called *lifelines* in UML.

Before giving examples of sequence diagrams it is necessary to understand a little more of the basic semantics and syntax used.

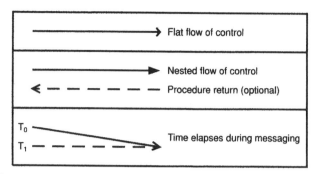

Figure 8.41 | UML message or stimulus notation.

- Focus of control: the period of time that an object spends performing an action is called its *focus of control*. This is represented by showing the object lifeline as a tall, thin rectangle whilst the action is being carried out. The top of the rectangle denotes the start of the action, the bottom being the completion time. Otherwise a lifeline is drawn as a dashed line.

- Message or stimulus: UML defines the communication between objects as a stimulus, shown as a horizontal arrow between the object lifelines, Figure 8.41.

- Flat flow of control: denoted using an open arrowhead.

- Nested flow of control: denoted using a solid arrowhead.

- Procedure return: a procedure return is shown as a dashed arrow shaft and an open arrowhead.

- Message transfer time: defined by using slanted arrows bounded by the sending and receiving times.

One further point: a focus of control is also called an *activation*. Two simple examples of sequence diagrams are given here. The first applies to concurrent operations (Figure 8.42), the second to sequential ones (more specifically, operations that are implemented in sequential code), Figure 8.43. Figure 8.42 shows a set of interactions between two objects in a particular time period. The objects are assumed to be alive continuously as long as the processor is powered up. It can be seen that the first message in the sequence is 'StartMeasurements'. This is generated by object 1, being sent to object 2. Some time later 2 sends the message 'StoreData' to 1.

The next message, 'PrepareForRun', is also sent as a flat flow of control from 1 to 2. Following this is the message 'OpenHatch', sent from 1 to 2. In this case object 1 chooses to enter a suspended state until it receives a reply from object 2. When this – the message 'ElevateMissile' – is received, object 1 is reactivated and resumes execution.

Now let us deal with sequential operations, but first, two points for your consideration.

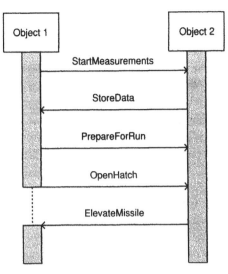

Figure 8.42 UML sequence diagram — concurrent operations.

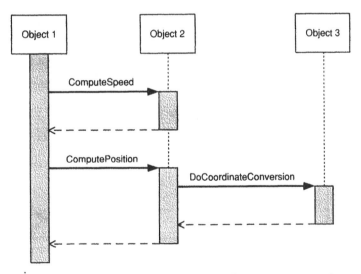

Figure 8.43 UML sequence diagram — procedural (sequential) operations.

- Point 1: *In an object-based sequential program, one, and only one, object can be active at any one time.* This may seem too obvious to be worth mentioning; yet many designers appear to be oblivious to this truism.
- Point 2: The more complete definition of focus of control is that it shows the period during which an object is performing an action *either directly or through a subordinate procedure.* This is highly relevant to sequential operations, as shown in Figure 8.43.

Assume that object 1 is a form of control object, responsible for the running of the system. Initially it is the one which is active. Now, as this is a procedural program, objects 2 and 3 *must* therefore be inactive.

At some time later object 1 sends the message 'ComputeSpeed' to object 2, so activating it. The message is, of course, really a procedure or function call; thus it must be a synchronous (blocking) one. Program control is thus transferred from object 1 to object 2, which, on completion of its work, returns control to object 1.

During this latter period, although object 1 was *actually* inactive, it was still shown as having a focus of control. This, in line with the full definition of focus of control, is correct; its action was being performed indirectly through the subordinate, object 2.

The next set of interactions demonstrates this feature in more detail. The message 'ComputePosition' activates object 2, which, some time later, sends the message 'DoCoordinateConversion' to object 3. Whilst object 3 is computing, object 2 still has a focus of control (as, of course, does object 1).

8.3.8 Activity diagrams

Activity diagrams are defined to be a combination of flow-charts and state machines (though at heart they are really dressed-up flow-charts). The main symbols of activity diagrams are shown in Figure 8.44. Their use is shown in Figure 8.45.

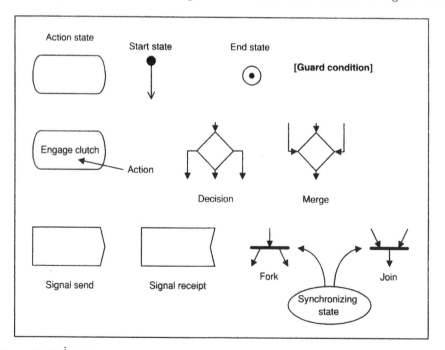

Figure 8.44 Activity diagram constructs.

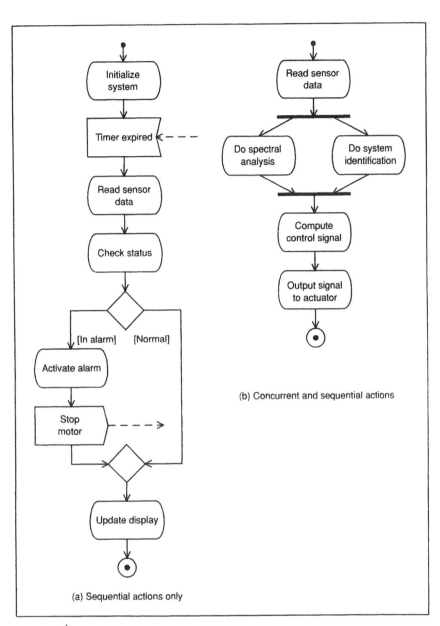

Figure 8.45 | Example activity diagrams.

Figure 8.45a shows how a diagram is used to portray the sequential processing carried out by an object say (a personal view: this is probably the best use for sequence diagrams, especially as they seem to be a close cousin of SDL process diagrams). It can be seen that after starting up, the object enters a state where it initializes the system. The expression 'initialize system' defines the action which is carried out; it is not a state name (there is no naming of states in activity diagrams). Once the processing is completed, the system makes a transition into a state in which it waits for an incoming signal. 'timer expired'. On its arrival it moves to the next state where it reads the sensor data. After checking the data, future progress depends on its status. A decision is made as to whether the data is normal or in alarm. The guards on the outgoing transitions of the decision define which route is taken. If the system is in alarm, then the alarm is activated and a signal ('stop motor') is transmitted.

The two routes come together at the merge; thus the final action is that of updating the display.

Figure 8.45b illustrates both concurrent and sequential actions. Here, after the data is read, two activities are performed simultaneously: 'do spectral analysis' and 'do system identification'. The split takes place at the *fork* point. The bar indicates that synchronizing of transitions (in this case, outgoing ones) takes place so that the actions start at the same time. On completion of each action, a transition is made to a *join* synchronizing state. Both actions must be completed before the system moves into the next state where it computes the control signal.

In practice the processing could be carried out within a multiprocessor or a multitasking structure (or some combination of these). The diagram, as it stands, doesn't help here. However, if we were concerned with highlighting the concurrency in the system, then we can use the 'swimlane' construct, Figure 8.46. Here the overall activity diagram of Figure 8.45 has been split into three parallel areas or *swimlanes* (don't blame me, I didn't invent the names). In this example the swimlanes are 'data acquisition processor', 'spectral analysis processor' and 'system identification processor'. Activities have been allocated to the individual swimlanes, these showing the work done by the separate processors.

8.3.9 Component diagrams

The purpose of component diagrams is to show the structure of the code of the system. This includes both the software components themselves and their dependencies. There are numerous software component *types*, including:

- Source code files.
- Binary code files.
- Data files.
- Executable (.exe-type) files.
- Dynamic link libraries.
- Middleware (e.g. OO to relational database interface components).

Irrespective of the type involved, the same symbol is used, Figure 8.47a. As you can see, the name of the component is written inside the symbol.

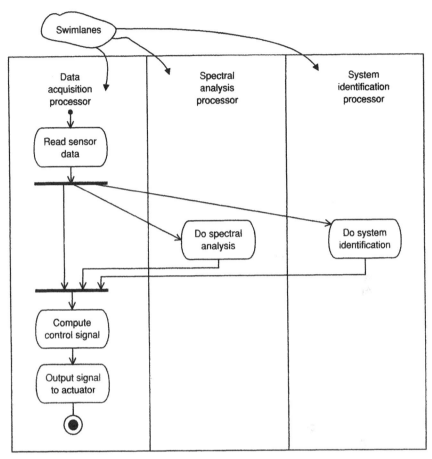

Figure 8.46 | Activity diagram swimlanes.

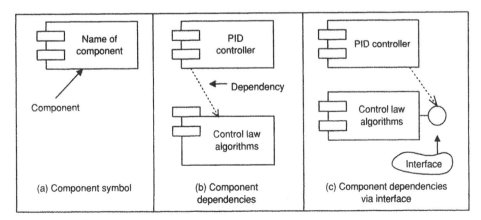

Figure 8.47 | Component diagram.

In many circumstances components depend on other components. For instance, for a PID controller to work correctly, it may depend on the operation of a control law algorithms component, Figure 8.47b. This relationship is shown as a dotted, arrowed line, the direction showing which component is the dependent one. Very often – especially when dealing with libraries – a component interacts with another component via its interfaces, Figure 8.47c. In fact, the interface may be treated as a component in its own right.

8.4 Extensions, variations and project-specific diagrams

The diagram sets considered so far, especially UML, are wide-ranging and comprehensive. However, for the development of real (and in particular, embedded) systems, they aren't sufficient. It may be, for instance, that:

- Notation just isn't provided to show particular items or areas of concern or

- The diagram models provided are inadequate and need to be expanded or adapted or

- Diagrams must be provided to meet specific (e.g. defence) standards which use quite a different notational method.

What follows is essentially a 'broad-brush' look at the issue, giving some examples of extensions, variations and project-specific diagrams. By definition there cannot be a standard (in terms of semantics and syntax) for these, although common factors can certainly be identified.

System configuration diagrams

In real-time embedded systems it is necessary to show how the computer hardware relates physically with the overall system. This can be done using a system configuration diagram, an example being that of Figure 8.48. These diagrams specify the major physical components of a system together with their interconnections.

System architecture diagrams

These diagrams describe the structure and interconnection of the major functional units within systems. In particular, they provide a good overview of the interconnection architecture of complex distributed systems, Figure 8.49. This is especially useful in systems that use a combination of interconnection techniques (e.g. CAN networks, RS422 dedicated links and hard-wiring).

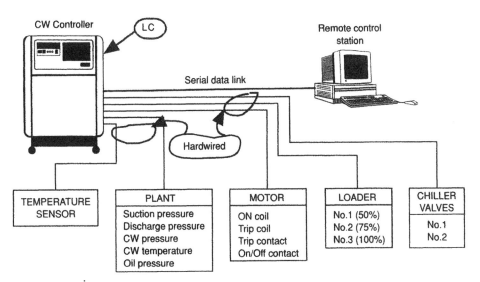

Figure 8.48 System configuration diagram.

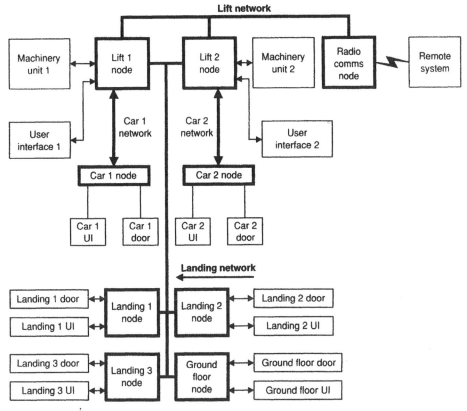

Figure 8.49 System architecture diagram.

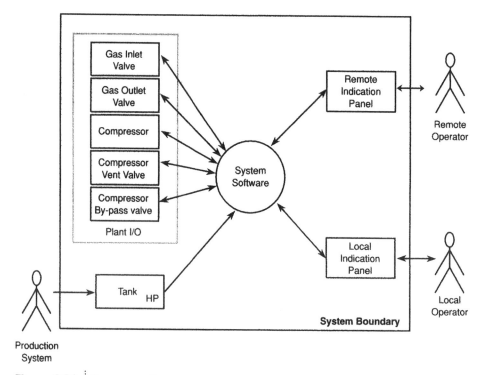

Figure 8.50 | System scope diagram.

System scope diagrams

These are based on the context diagram but extended to show users of the system, Figure 8.50. They also allow us to differentiate clearly between the system boundary and the software boundary.

Node architecture diagrams

These show the major computing and communication elements of a node, together with appropriate interconnection information, as in Figure 8.51. A node architecture diagram would normally be produced only where nodes are complex. In simpler cases a processor architecture diagram can illustrate these features.

In some cases it may be appropriate to produce node configuration diagrams to show the physical structure of the node itself.

Processor architecture diagrams

The purpose of these diagrams is to show, in precise detail, the hardware make-up of each processor unit. An example is given in Figure 8.52.

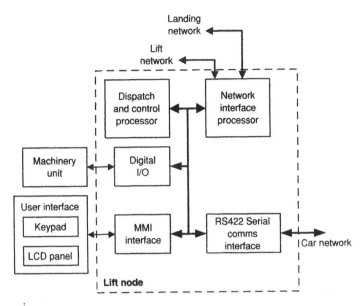

Figure 8.5I Node architecture diagram.

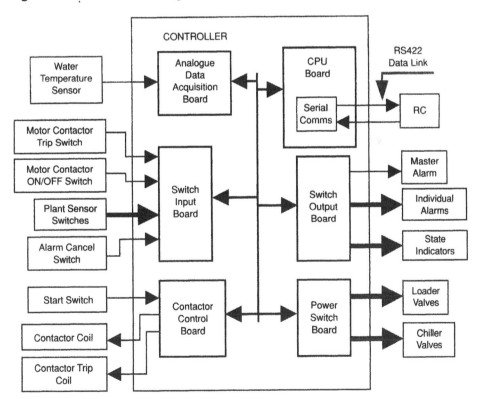

Figure 8.52 Processor architecture diagram.

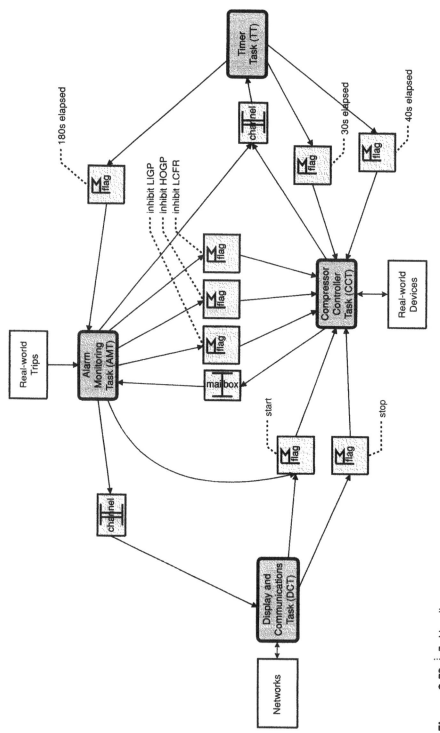

Figure 8.53 Tasking diagram.

Tasking diagrams

These are used in multitasking systems to show the task structure of the software, together with all intercommunication components, Figure 8.53.

Memory map diagrams

In embedded applications we normally specify where the software should be located within the target system. There are two major reasons for performing this location or mapping operation (i.e. mapping into the processor address space), as follows:

● Embedded computers generally use a combination of memory storage devices (e.g. EPROM, RAM, flash memory, FRAM, etc.), each housing specific software components. Such components must be placed at ('mapped' into) their correct locations.

● All physical devices (e.g. timers, ADCs, etc.) are located at specific memory addresses ('absolute' addresses).

One way of keeping track of this information is to use a memory map diagram, such as that of Figure 8.54.

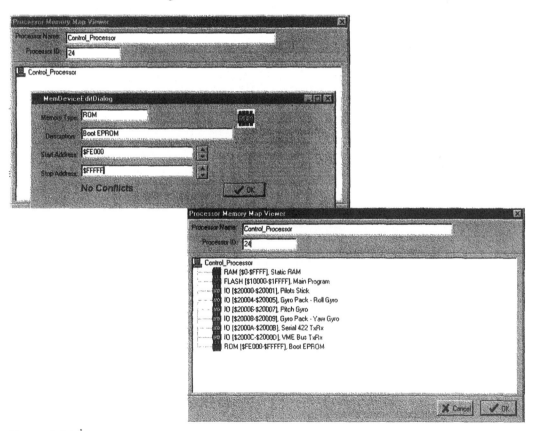

Figure 8.54 Memory map diagram.

8.5 Diagrams and the design process

We have covered a great deal of ground in this chapter concerning the syntax and semantics of diagrams. Now, though, is the time to step back and take a look at the larger picture: the use of these diagrams within the software design process. Here our process model is based on implementing a large system consisting of: network, node, processor and task-level design. The diagrams listed have been defined in general or generic terms only; detailed syntax and semantics are not specified. Now, in practice, we're likely to implement a design using either standard structured/data flow methods or OO techniques. So, how well do these support the diagramming needs outlined in Figure 7.20? The answer to this is given in Figures 8.55–8.58. You will see from these that extensions or bespoke diagramming methods are frequently used to augment the standard ones.

Now for two small but important points:

● The process expounded here *assumes that the system under design is a distributed (networked) one*. Many applications, however, are based on the use of a single processor. In cases like this the diagrams specified in Figure 8.57 for processor level design will not be sufficient. Additional ones (such as context, use case, system STDs, etc.) will be needed. The choice is left to you, the designer.

DESIGN TECHNIQUE → DIAGRAM TYPE ↓	Standard structured/data flow methods (Yourdon/SDL diagramming)	Standard object-oriented methods (UML diagramming)	Extensions or bespoke methods
System context	Context diagrams	Use case diagrams Deployment diagrams	Yes
Topology (system configuration)	–	Deployment diagrams	Yes
Structure (system architecture)	–	Deployment diagrams	Yes
System usage	Event/response lists	Use case diagrams	Yes
System software structure	Data flow diagrams	Object diagrams Component diagrams	Sometimes
Communication (message sequence)	Message sequence diagrams	Sequence diagrams Collaboration diagrams	–
Dynamics – system and software (state transition)	State transition diagrams State transition tables	State diagrams	–
System software distribution (node software packaging)	–	Component diagrams	Yes

Figure 8.55 Diagrams and network level design.

DESIGN TECHNIQUE → DIAGRAM TYPE ↓	Standard structured/data flow methods (Yourdon/SDL diagramming)	Standard object-oriented methods (UML diagramming)	Extensions or bespoke methods
Node architecture	–	Deployment diagrams	Yes
Topology (node configuration)	–	Deployment diagrams	Yes
Node usage	Event/response lists	Use case diagrams	Yes
Node software structure	Data flow diagrams	Object diagrams Component diagrams	Sometimes
Communication (message sequence)	Message sequence diagrams	Sequence diagrams Collaboration diagrams	–
Dynamics – system and software (state transition)	State transition diagrams State transition tables	State diagrams	–
Node software distribution (processor software packaging)	–	Component diagrams	Yes

Figure 8.56 Diagrams and node level design.

DESIGN TECHNIQUE → DIAGRAM TYPE ↓	Standard structured/data flow methods (Yourdon/SDL diagramming)	Standard object-oriented methods (UML diagramming)	Extensions or bespoke methods
Configuration (topology) and architecture	–	Deployment diagrams	Yes
Processor usage	Event/response lists	Use case diagrams Sequence diagrams	Yes
Processor software structure	Data flow diagrams	Object diagrams Component diagrams	Sometimes
Processor tasking structure (tasking diagram)	Data flow diagrams	Object diagrams Collaboration diagrams	Yes
Communication (message sequence)	Message sequence diagrams	Sequence diagrams	–
Dynamics – software (state transition)	State transition diagrams State transition tables	State diagrams	–
Processor software distribution (task software packaging)	–	Component diagrams	Yes

Figure 8.57 Diagrams and processor level design.

DESIGN TECHNIQUE → DIAGRAM TYPE ↓	Standard structured/data flow methods (Yourdon/SDL diagramming)	Standard object-oriented methods (UML diagramming)	Extensions or bespoke methods
Program structure diagrams	Data flow diagrams Structure charts PDLs SDL process diagrams	Activity diagrams PDLs	Yes

Figure 8.58 : Diagrams and task level design.

- The approach used is essentially descriptive, not prescriptive. You should (and are encouraged to) adapt it to your own way of working.

Review

At this point you should:

- Appreciate that diagrams are an important part of the software design process.
- Understand why, in practice, a range of diagrams is required.
- Know what basic modelling features (e.g. system dynamics, messaging, structure, etc.) need to be supported by diagrams.
- Know when, why and how to apply the various modelling techniques outlined in this chapter.
- Be able to select the diagram set which best meets your own needs.
- Recognize the distinction between design processes and diagramming (modelling) techniques.
- Have knowledge of the diagrams used when designing using both structured and OO methods.
- Realize that these, in many cases, are not sufficient; extensions or additions may be needed.
- Realize that there isn't a uniquely 'right' diagramming method.

Exercises

1. Select an appropriate set of diagrams for use in the following situations:

    (a) Development of a service or library module (component).

    (b) The design of the software for a small controller where operations are mainly interrupt-driven.

(c) Development of a larger multitasking software system (single-processor structure).

(d) Development of a pipe-lined multiprocessor system.

2. Choose diagram(s) for use in modelling the following aspects of systems and software:

(a) Concurrent (multitasking) structures.

(b) Logical software subsystems.

(c) The interaction of software and its environment.

(d) Overall system structure and related physical devices.

3. You can use a meta-CASE tool to produce diagrams of your own choosing. What are the advantages and disadvantages in going down this route?

4. Compare and contrast the features of the following diagrams:

(a) Use case and event/response lists.

(b) SDL process diagrams, UML activity diagrams and structure charts.

(c) Sequence and collaboration diagrams.

(d) Data flow and object diagrams.

References and further reading

[COO97] *Real-time software systems – an introduction to structured and object-oriented design*, J.E. Cooling, PWS Publishing Company, ISBN 1-85032-274-0, 1997.

[JAC75] *Principles of program design*, M.A. Jackson, Academic Press, ISBN 0-123-79050-6, 1975.

[SDL88] CCITT Recommendation Z.100: Specification and Description Language SDL, Annexes A-F to Z.100, ITU, Geneva, 1988.

[SDL88/tutorial] http://sdl_forum_org/sdl88tutorial.

[UML99] *The Unified Modelling Language user guide*, G. Booch, J. Rumbaugh and I. Jacobson, Addison-Wesley, ISBN 0-201-57168-4, 1999.

[UML/OMG] *OMG Unified Modelling Language Specification*, www.omg.org.

[WAR85] *Structured development for real-time systems*, P.T. Ward and S.J. Mellor, Yourdon Press, ISBN 0-13-854803-X, 1985.

[YOU78] *Structured Design*, E. Yourdon and L. Constantine. Yourdon Press, ISBN 0-1385-44719, 1978.

chapter 9

Designing and Constructing Software — Code-Related Issues

There comes a point in every project when the software design must be turned into a working product. Central to this are the:

- Development of the application-level source code.
- Organization and packaging of this code into sets of program units.
- Development of low-level (service software) source code.
- Organization and packaging of this code into appropriate program units.
- Integration of these various program units.
- Incorporation and integration of library units (especially commercial off-the-shelf (COTS)) software components.
- Documenting the work in an organized, useful, understandable and maintainable manner.

How well we handle this depends on many factors; here we will limit ourselves to code development issues.

This chapter sets out to show:

- The fundamental approaches that can be used in the design and construction of software.
- How the choice of technique has a major impact on the development process.

- The concept and use of component technology in software development.
- How the availability and use of programming language features significantly affect the quality of software.
- The programming requirements of embedded systems.
- How current mainstream languages meet these requirements, in particular Ada 95, C, C++, EC++ and Java.
- Documentation of code-related work using UML constructs and notation.

9.1 Fundamental design and construction methods

9.1.1 Introduction

Software design techniques can be split into three major groups – monolithic, independent and modular. These, in reality, are not mutually exclusive. Many programmers use combinations of these when writing source code – which probably says more about the rigour and discipline of software design as practised rather than preached. The concepts behind these methods can be grasped fairly easily by looking at a simple DIY task, design and build of a kit-car.

Method 1, 'monolithic', is illustrated in Figure 9.1. Work begins by producing an all-embracing design plan. That is, the problem is considered as consisting of a single design task. Once the design is complete the car can be built to the plan's specifications and instructions.

Method 2, 'modular', tackles the problem in a different way at the design stage (Figure 9.2). An overall design plan is produced together with individual designs for major subsystems such as chassis, wheels, etc. The complete design may be carried out by one individual, as in method 1. Alternatively it may be performed by a number of designers, who can then work simultaneously on the various subsystems. When design work is finished, the various subsystem designs are integrated to produce a manufacturing work-plan. Manufacture takes place as in method 1.

Note a significant difference between these two methods. In the first one, as the design is monolithic, all information relating to the system is implicitly available at all times. However, in the second method this may not be the case. Some information just doesn't need sharing; it's private or 'local' to that particular design activity. However, other information does have to be made generally available. For instance, both the wheel and the suspension system designers need to know the wheel/drive shaft coupling arrangement. Otherwise there's no guarantee that the items will fit together correctly. Question. How are these details made known throughout the design team? Simply by explicitly defining design data which is to be made available to all parties, the so-called 'global' information.

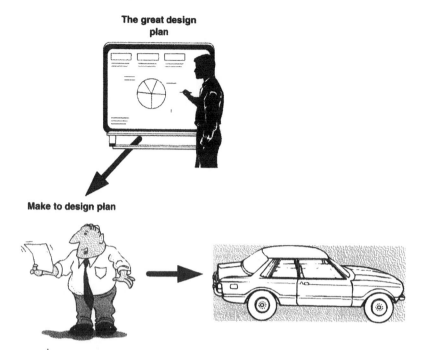

Figure 9.1 | Monolithic design and make.

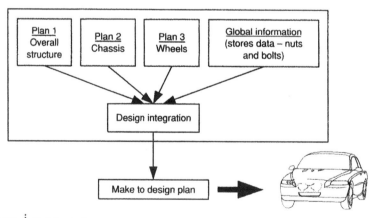

Figure 9.2 | Modular design.

In the third design method the idea of splitting the total task into a number of 'independent' subtasks is taken one stage further. Not only is the design compartmentalized; the same ideas are applied to manufacturing as well (Figure 9.3). It is at the final production stage that all parts come together in what is basically an assembly operation. Only the interfacing details of the subsystems are important, assuming, of course, that the design itself is satisfactory.

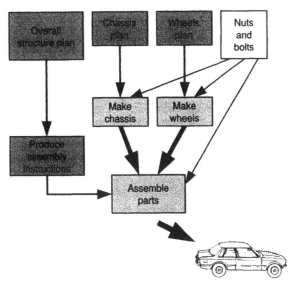

Figure 9.3 ⋮ Independent design.

Note also that the final assembly is essentially divorced from the detailed design process. This means that we can develop optional designs and choose the most appropriate one at assembly stage (compare this with selecting either a 1.3 or 1.6 litre engine in a standard production car).

9.1.2 An evaluation of design and construction methods

Monolithic operation

The monolithic method will clearly work best where one person only is concerned with the design and build programme. For simple tasks it works quite well. As the project becomes more complex, though, the design document itself becomes equally complex. In the end only one person may be capable of understanding it, the original designer. Further, the technique inherently makes it very difficult to split the job amongst a number of designers.

Now consider what happens when a revision to the operation of a unit is requested. The complete design plan has to be assessed in the light of any changes, a time-consuming and costly effort. Once changes are made a full rebuild is necessary before we can even begin to evaluate the change effects. And this is where many problems really start. In a complex system the introduction of just a single revision may very well produce a 'knock-on' effect, leading to totally undesirable (and unpredicted) side-effects. As a result it can be extremely difficult to maintain such designs once they are in service.

Modular operation

By breaking the complete problem into a series of smaller ones even quite complex designs can be managed comfortably. Moreover, individual subtasks may be handled simultaneously by different designers. This assumes, of course, that the job is properly co-ordinated. As a result, designs become more understandable and can be completed more quickly.

What about introducing modifications to an existing program? Here significant advantages have been gained over the monolithic approach. Individual changes are likely to be quite localized, possibly affecting only one subtask. Hence the effects of such changes can be quickly evaluated. Further, they are far less likely to lead to unwanted side-effects. The disadvantage, though, is that a complete rebuild is needed to carry out any change in a production unit.

Apart from this last point, does the modular approach have any other major drawback? Unfortunately, yes. Global information, by definition, is available to all design sections. Consequently it may also be modified by any individual as work progresses. Where only one designer is involved this probably won't be a problem. Where the design is a team effort global information falls into the category of 'accidents waiting to happen'. Without rigorous project control, changes to the global values (especially undocumented ones) can produce design chaos.

Independent operation

This sets out to minimize the shortcomings of the modular method of working. All of the advantages gained at the design stage are retained but are now extended into manufacture as well. This has a tremendous impact on product development and maintenance. For instance, suppose a fault shows up in a gearbox which calls for redesign action. Now we can limit the design and build operations to the gearbox and its interfacing components (Figure 9.4). This minimizes the time taken to implement and test the change. It also reduces the likelihood of side-effects.

What about global information? Clearly, when designs are carried out as described here, information has to be passed between individual subtasks – which

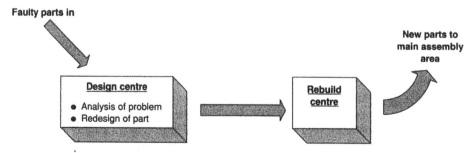

Figure 9.4   Design modification procedure – independent operation.

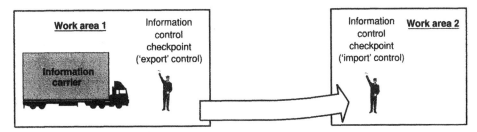

Figure 9.5 Controlling information flow.

brings us back to the use of a 'global bin' of information. The only way to prevent (in reality, minimize) errors caused by the abuse of global values is *not* to use globals. This means that information interchange must be handled in a more controlled (and probably more complex) way, Figure 9.5.

9.2 Code development and packaging

9.2.1 Code development and the physical software model

What we have to do during the code development process is to translate the logical design model of the software into its physical counterpart, Figure 9.6. From this it can be seen that the physical software model consists of two parts, constructs and components. Software constructs are the things (elements) which go to make up the source program itself. These include, for example, classes, objects, functions, data items and program statements. Components, in contrast, show the

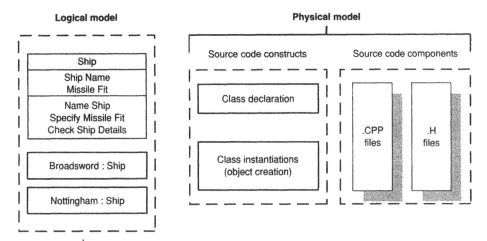

Figure 9.6 Logical and physical models of software.

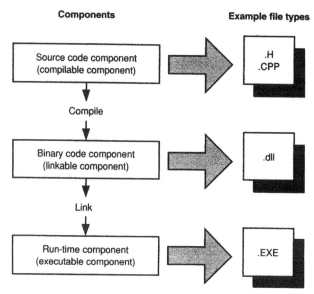

Components   **Example file types**

Figure 9.7 | UML component types.

organization of the code itself (UML uses the word *structure*). Within the definition of UML, software code components have a very specific meaning. They are 'distributable' items, typically files, which are either (Figure 9.7):

● Compilable or

● Linkable or

● Executable.

Thus source code files are compilable components. These may be compiled to produce binary code (linkable) components. In turn these may be linked to form run-time code (executable) components.

Well, all this is fine. But exactly *how do* we do the translation from the logical model to the software components?

9.2.2 Software construction methods – general

From the previous section you should have grasped the basic concepts of the three different constructional methods. Now let's put them in the context of software development, specifically:

● The structuring of source code and

● The production of object (executable) code as a compilation/linkage process.

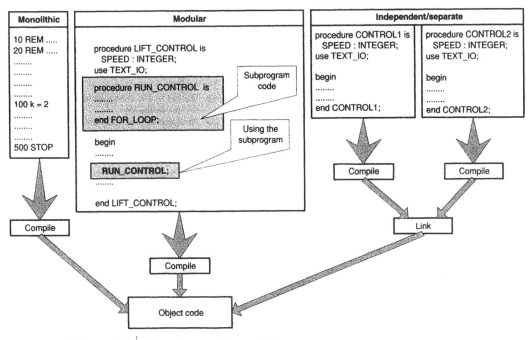

Figure 9.8 | Alternative compilation methods.

Broadly speaking we can organize source code in one of three forms:

- Monolithic code units.
- Modular code units.
- Sets of combined (but individually compiled) code units.

Monolithic program development is simple and straightforward. Here the source program is written out in its entirety as a series of successive statements, i.e. one large block. Compilation to object code may then be carried out, Figure 9.8. Modular methods allow us to use a 'building-block' approach in the design of the software. The blocks are realized as a series of subtasks (or subprograms) based on the use of procedures and functions. But compilation of the source code is, as in monolithic designs, still carried out on the complete program.

With the third approach the fundamental program building block is a separately compilable program 'unit' (module, file, package; it all depends on the programming language). Individual units are written and compiled as complete but separate items. These come together only at the final stage of 'linkage'. Bennett [BEN88] defines two compilation methods which support this approach, 'independent' and 'separate'. These differ in their compilation and linkage operations. For instance, suppose that a function in unit 1 references a function held in unit 2. When 'independent' compilation is used, no cross-checks are made between the function call

Structuring method	For	Against
Monolithic program structures	• Simple to use. • Suitable for small programs.	• Large programs are difficult to handle. • Program document soon becomes complex. • Difficult for more than one designer to work on the job. • Revisions can be costly and time consuming. • Unwanted effects may easily be inserted when doing changes.
Modular program structures	• Overall structure can be made highly 'visible' using modularity of design. • Design can be split among a number of programmers, giving faster program development. • Changes are easier to implement. • Side effects are reduced. • Standard program building blocks can be developed (e.g. I/O to console).	• Any changes mean a complete program recompilation. • Global variables are a source of potential danger.
Independent and separate program structures	• As for the modular method. • Global data items are minimized. • When modifying a program, only the affected items need recompiling.	• More complex cross-referencing needed.

Figure 9.9 Comparison of program structuring and compilation methods.

and the function format. Thus it would be possible to use an incorrect format – wrong number of parameters, for instance – and still compile correctly. We rely on the linker to find such mistakes. On the other hand, 'separate' compilation methods do not allow this problem to arise in the first place. They demand that the compiler be given specific information concerning external code at compile time.

Figure 9.9 compares the advantages and weaknesses of the three methods discussed above. Here both 'independent' and 'separate' methods are grouped together as they both require similar control mechanisms. For error-free code production tight cross-checking must always be done, either at compilation or linkage time

Independent or separate compilation is recommended for high-quality work (note: some authors, most confusingly, use 'independent' to mean the same as 'modular').

9.2.3 Introduction to component technology

The concept of a software component has already been introduced in earlier sections. There, however, the emphasis was mainly on what a component is and what it contains (especially within the context of UML). Here we take a much broader view, looking at some of the underlying ideas of component-based software engineering.

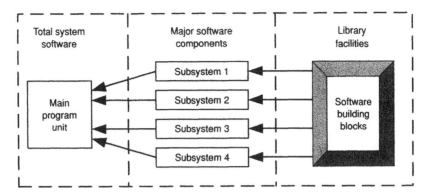

Figure 9.10 ⋮ Typical structure of a large program.

For teaching and learning purposes programs often consist of single program units. But this is not the way that real, practical software is constructed, even for small systems. And for large systems? Well, such projects consist of many program units, built by a team (or teams) of programmers. For a single-processor system the software would typically be structured as shown in Figure 9.10; distributed systems would naturally be more complex. The program structure of Figure 9.10 arises from the use of good, modern software design principles. Here the total problem is formed as a set of smaller, manageable units using two techniques: application level and service level software.

The purpose of the application level software is to provide the functionality, behaviour and performance required of the system. Here the overall system software is structured as a set of collaborating subsystems. How the subsystems are formed and how they interact depend on the design method used in the project (see, for instance, the design examples of Chapter 10).

By contrast, service level software is essentially application-independent, e.g. device drivers, control algorithms, file handling software, etc. They provide a 'service' to the application; as such they can be viewed as the standard software 'building bricks' of our programs (the software equivalent of integrated circuits). They may be industry-standard (e.g. an Ethernet interface on a PCI bus) or bespoke designs (e.g. adaptive compression of speech signals). It is commonplace to refer to them as 'library' items.

How does all this relate to components and component technology? Well, begin by substituting 'component' for 'unit' and we have a good beginning. A good starting point, but there is much more to components than this [KOZ98].

9.2.4 Code packaging and components

Components are intended to be the major building blocks in the construction of software systems. Fundamentally they act as a 'holder' for software facilities. Such facilities consist of:

- Design-time items – classes, objects, functions, etc.
- Compose-time items – items intended to be assembled together at link (construction) time.
- Run-time items – items intended to be linked together dynamically as the program runs.

However, providing a distinct, clearly identifiable component is only one part of the story. Facilities are needed to allow components to be assembled in a safe, simple and secure manner. To support these aims there must be strict control on the access to and usage of components, viz.:

- Components must be able to explicitly control what they show to the outside world (use an export interface on the component).
- A user of a component (client or importer) must be told precisely how to obtain and use the component (use an import interface in the client).
- Clients must be prevented from interfering with the internal workings of the component (use information hiding techniques in the component).

The concepts underlying these features are discussed below, once more using the kit-car analogy.

Note: generally you'd expect clients to also be components.

Component interfaces and information hiding

Each individual component consists of two distinct parts, an interface (or specification) and a body (or implementation), Figure 9.11. The interface defines what the component does and what it provides. The body describes how it achieves its objectives.

At first sight this may not appear to be exactly a radical move. In fact, the separation of specification and implementation is one of the most important features of modern software design.

The relationship between a component and its client may conceptually be described as in Figure 9.12. Here a client unit 'Make wheel' makes use of the facilities provided by the component 'Wheel manufacture'. This diagram brings out the basic function of the specification – to act as the component interface. To use the features provided by the component the client only needs to know how to interface to it. Its internal workings are of no concern provided it does the job correctly. Here we have a prime example of 'information hiding'. The designer makes only essential information visible to the client in the specification or 'public' part of the component. The rest – the implementation – is hidden away in the body.

So far we've seen that the component provides us with a 'software building block' for program construction. It also presents us with a means to hide information. But that's not all it does. By using this construct we can have different implementations for one specification. That is, it allows us to implement the same function in

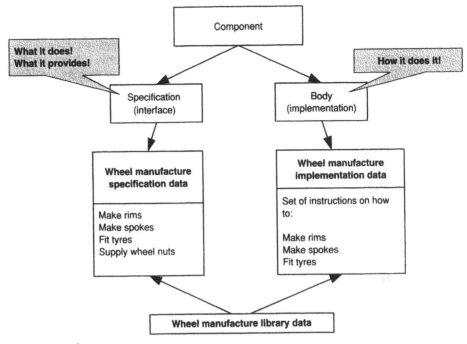

Figure 9.11 Concept — component interface and implementation.

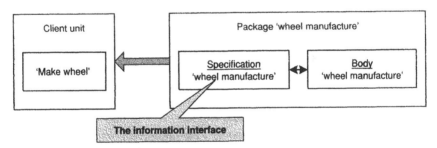

Figure 9.12 Components and their clients.

quite different computing environments. This has an important bearing on program portability.

Components – collaboration and dependencies

Any practical program will contain several components. Moreover, these normally have to exchange information. This could be done using global variables; but, as pointed out earlier, this is a potentially dangerous method. How then can we provide a communication method which is well defined and controlled, yet avoids global information?

```
┌─────────────────────────────────────────┐
│  WHEEL MANUFACTURING COMPONENT           │
│                                          │
│  What do I need? ................. IMPORT │
│  What will I supply? ............. EXPORT │
└─────────────────────────────────────────┘
```

Figure 9.13 | Components – the import–export concept.

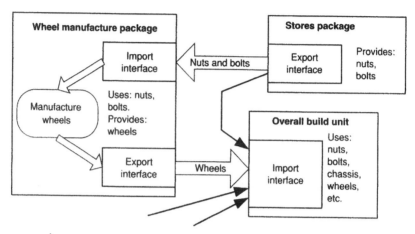

Figure 9.14 | Use of imports and exports.

Let's go back to our kit-car again. Consider the manufacture of a wheel followed by the overall assembly operation. Nuts and bolts are just two of the items needed by the Wheel manufacture component for the construction of a wheel. These items can be considered to be 'imported' into the component. On completion of wheel manufacture the finished unit is sent off to the final assembly stage, that is it is 'exported' to the overall build module. This import–export feature (Figure 9.13) is an essential aspect of component operation.

Now let's turn to (part of) the complete manufacture and assembly process, Figure 9.14. The overall build unit imports wheels from the Wheel manufacture component. But it also imports nuts and bolts from the Stores component to fix units together. Nuts and bolts come from the stores package, forming export items. This simple example thus illustrates the concept of import only, export only, and both import and export.

So far, so good. But how do we control the exchange of the parts (information) flow to minimize unwanted changes to this information? Simply by *defining* what is to be imported or exported, the rules being:

● Items are made available by using an explicit listing.

● A component can only use items located in another component by importing that component in the first place (frequently implemented via a 'uses' clause).

A further point worth noting is that, strictly speaking, we use component contents, not the component itself.

Summarizing, a component:

● Is part of a system that carries out some specific, well-defined function.

● Is treated as a single unit.

● Has a clear, well-defined interface.

● Is accessed via its interface.

Clearly there are similarities between classes/objects and components. However, objects are much smaller and simpler than components, tending to be used in very specific ways. Components are much, much larger-grained items. To use an analogy: objects are similar to small-scale integrated circuits; components are like very large-scale ICs.

We can model these features in part using UML component diagrams, Figure 9.15. Figure 9.15a gives the syntax for a component. Figure 9.15b shows two independent components; Figure 9.15c contains the same two components but now indicates that:

● There is collaboration between them.

● The relationship is a client–server one.

● The component 'PID controller' – the client – accesses the 'Control law algorithms' component.

Figure 9.15d basically has the same information but now shows that the client accesses the server via the server interface.

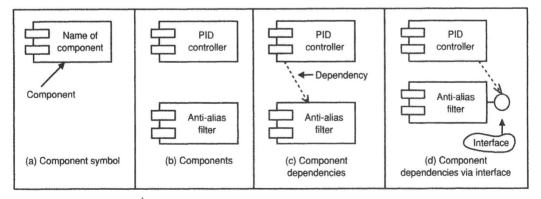

Figure 9.15 ⋮ UML modelling of components and component relationships.

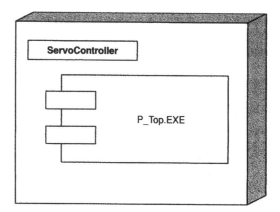

Figure 9.16 | UML deployment diagram – node containing a run-time component.

We can also show the location of run-time components in our system using a deployment diagram, Figure 9.16.

9.2.5 Classes, packages and components

Scenario: suppose during development we need to make changes to the class (logical) model. Assume for simplicity that only one class is affected. Finding and modifying the class in the design model is unlikely to be a problem. However, we now need to consider a most important question: will the design change impact on clients of the class? Can we evaluate the change effects? Answering these is not necessarily easy but isn't usually a major problem. But what about clients of the clients? And their clients? Now it's beginning to look a much more formidable issue.

The message here is that when systems have a large number of classes, design maintenance isn't trivial. Relying on tools to help you out is a little like putting up scaffolding on an unsound building. What we need to do is to build it correctly in the first place; use an organized, structured approach in the development of the class model. This is where the package diagram can be useful. By packaging together classes which logically belong together we should (with good design) find (Figure 9.17):

- Most of the class interactions occur within the package (intra-package associations).

- Few class interactions take place between packages (inter-package associations).

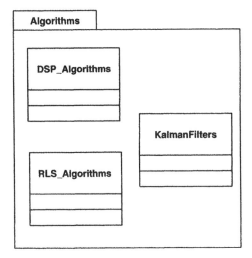

Figure 9.17 Packaging classes.

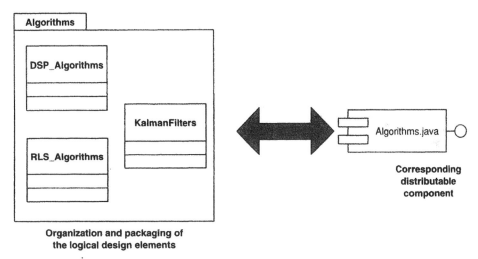

Figure 9.18 A package and its corresponding component.

Following this, it makes good sense to simplify the relationship between the class and component diagrams. Thus we should aim for package designs which map directly on a one-to-one basis to components, Figure 9.18. By attacking the design in this way it is much easier to keep track of both the class and component design, Figure 9.19.

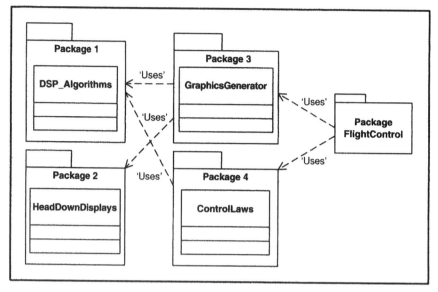

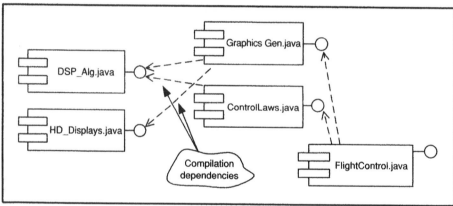

Figure 9.19 | Relating packages, components and dependencies.

9.3 | Important features of programming languages

9.3.1 Introduction

There are two quite different views on how to choose a programming language. The first is held (usually) by academics, compiler writers and standards committees. Here, language features are carefully listed, defined and assessed; then languages are compared on a point-by-point basis using an unbiased, objective approach. The second method, used by most practising software designers, assesses languages within the context of their own work. Evaluation is supposedly objective. In fact it tends to be highly subjective, prejudiced and emotional, opinions being held with a form of religious fervour. Rational arguments rarely change religious beliefs.

Even accepting that exponents of new languages might be given a fair hearing, there are other, significant, factors to be considered. Many have nothing to do with languages; instead they are tied up with commercial pressures of cost, manpower availability and customer preference. Without a doubt, these are major concerns for any company; their influence on engineering decisions should never be underestimated. Technically brilliant languages can fail purely on commercial grounds. So, in reality, a pragmatic approach is needed.

The following sections set out to show:

- The requirements of languages for use in real-time systems.

- The importance of design, compilation and readability factors.

- Modern high-level language constructs involving variables, data typing, program flow control, exception handling and low-level features.

- Interfacing to and use of 'foreign' high-level languages and assembler coding.

- The current language situation together with a comparison of Ada, Ada 95, C, C++, EC++, and Java.

The approach used is to discuss language features which are considered to be 'good'. These features are then used as a template against which modern languages are assessed. Although this is reasonably straightforward, the problem comes in defining their *relative* importance. This is left to the reader although guidance is given (based on a set of personal prejudiced views). Readers unfamiliar with compilation and assembly operations are recommended to consult Chapter 11, *Development tools*.

9.3.2   Choosing a programming language – the real questions

In choosing a programming language, the starting point is to show what is important in embedded software code writing. Consider the following scenario. A highly enthusiastic academic is trying to persuade an overworked, slightly cynical and less-than-enthusiastic software engineer to adopt a new programming language. The questions posed by the engineer highlight what, to him, are important.

Let's start with costs and effort, Figure 9.20.

Q. We've got a major investment in our current software. Do we have to throw it all away and start afresh? Or can we include source files already written in other languages with this particular language?

Q. If we use this language, will our staff need special training (or can they easily build on their current knowledge)?

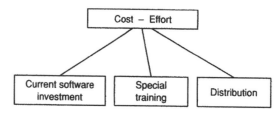

Figure 9.20 : Resource implications.

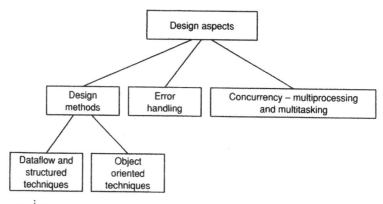

Figure 9.21 : Design implications.

Q. How much time and effort is it going to take to distribute this information through the company and to set up the new development environments?

Moving on to design aspects, Figure 9.21.

Q. We seem to design software systems by bending reality to suit our languages and design methods. How well do *these* language constructs mirror the real world?

Q. How well does the language let me, as a designer, express my ideas?

Q. Does the language help us avoid making mistakes when writing programs in the first place?

Q. Our designs use diagramming methods. Do the language constructs provide support for such techniques?

Q. How easy is it to write multitasking software using this language?

Now what about the higher-level aspects of software development, Figure 9.22.

Q. Quite often our design timescales are short, so we have to split the work between a number of programmers. How easily can this be done using the proposed language? Is integration of code difficult?

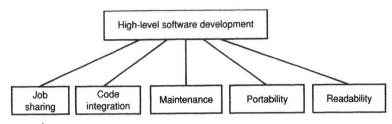

Figure 9.22 High-level software development aspects.

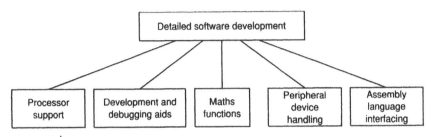

Figure 9.23 Detailed software development features.

Q. One difficulty we constantly face is updating software without introducing new (and usually unforeseen) mistakes into it. How will this language help us here?

Q. How portable are programs produced using this language?

Q. Is the language sufficiently flexible to let us devise text layout styles so that it's easier to use, read, change, test?

Q. As a project leader I'm often called on when problems come up. Inevitably this means checking out source code. Will the document be easy to read? Does it take up many pages? Will it be easy to grasp the meaning of the program? How easy will it be for me to *misunderstand* it?

And at a more detailed level, Figure 9.23.

Q. We use a number of different processors in our hardware. How extensive is the current range of compilers which produce ROMable code? How portable is the code between compilers? Is there support for in-target debugging? How good is this?

Q. What about mathematical operations? What features are available as standard? What number types and sizes are included? Are there in-built safety factors concerning maths working?

Q. In our embedded designs we have a large and diverse range of peripheral devices. Can I access this hardware – easily?

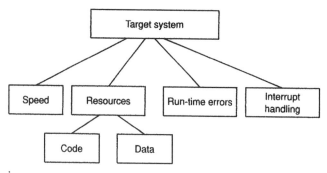

Figure 9.24 Target system considerations.

Finally, in the target system, Figure 9.24.

Q. How fast is the object code produced by this language?

Q. If we find it's too slow can we write time-critical sections in assembly language and then integrate this with the high-level code?

Q. We often have to work with a limited amount of memory. Will the object code produced from this source language fit into my available space?

Q. Are there features in the language for handling run-time errors?

Q. How easy is it to handle interrupts?

From these it is clear that a language can't be assessed in isolation from its development environment. Software engineers frequently produce very good designs even when using a poor language – given the support of a comprehensive software toolset. Conversely, some rubbish has been produced using the best of programming languages. But this is beyond the control of the language designer.

9.3.3 High-level languages – general requirements

The questions above state basically what the user wants. More formally these requirements can be grouped as:

- Acceptable initial cost, effort and disruption.
- Easy integration within current design practices.
- Language flexibility.
- Portability.
- Program readability.
- Execution speed and memory requirements (efficiency).
- Security at compile time.
- Security at run-time.

The first two items listed vary considerably from company to company. Thus they can't easily be tackled by the language designer; therefore emphasis is placed on the other objectives. Language features which help to meet these include:

- Program syntax and layout rules.
- Modularity, encapsulation and information hiding.
- Variable usage – scope, visibility, lifetime and declaration.
- Abstract data typing.
- Program flow control structures.
- Low-level facilities.
- Exception handling.
- Interfaces to assembly language routines.
- Interfaces to other high-level languages.
- Multitasking constructs.

Note that there isn't a one-to-one relationship between the questions raised earlier and the items of the requirements list. Similarly there isn't a one-to-one correspondence between the requirements and language features lists. In general, individual program constructs usually provide solutions to a number of requirements.

9.3.4   Modularity, encapsulation and information hiding

Modularity, encapsulation, information hiding. Years of experience have shown these to be central to the development of dependable software. They impact on all stages of software design. However, in this section we concentrate on one specific part of the design process: the code development stage. Three important questions to be asked of any programming language are:

- Is modularity an integral feature of the language (and if not, what are the consequences)?
- What encapsulation mechanisms are provided?
- How effective are the information hiding features?

These three factors tend to be highly interrelated and usually can't be considered in isolation. However, before assessing language facilities we first need to be clear what our objectives are. Two extreme cases:

- Are we concerned with the building of the executable software (the run-time machine)? Or
- Are we primarily interested in the organization and management of the source code units?

In the first case the issues of modularity, etc. apply to the elements of the run-time machine, i.e. the individual 'software machines'. This topic has been covered in some detail in Chapter 4; suffice it to say that the two major code constructs used here are the subprogram (procedure, function) and class.

The issues relating to the second case have been discussed earlier in this chapter. From this it should be clear that (ideally) some 'packaging' construct should be provided as part of the language. A package should have:

- A formally specified structure.
- The ability to encapsulate any program construct.
- Facilities to hide encapsulated items.
- Features to control access to such items.
- Pre-defined import/export features.

These, however, are really only the minimum requirements. For the production of quality software there should be extensive compiler-generated checks on the use of package contents (e.g. checking actual–formal parameter matching when using functions imported from other packages).

But what if your chosen programming language doesn't intrinsically provide decent packaging features? Then, if you are in the business of developing dependable software, you have a problem. The best thing to do is to resort to tools which will check out your code, a strategy expounded eloquently by Les Hatton [HAT94].

9.3.5 Program syntax and layout rules – the readability factor

We can write readable programs only if the language syntax and layout rules allow us to. A number of factors affect this, including:

- Case sensitivity and mixing.
- Identification of words reserved for specific program usage.
- Constraints on naming identifiers.
- Clarity of program maths symbols.
- Format rules.

Case sensitivity and mixing

Examine the following small section of a program:

```
IF O LTYPE = 'A' THEN WRITESTRING ('O L IS SAE 20'); WRITELN;
ELSE WRITESTRING ('BAD ENTRY'); WRITELN;
```

Now consider a rewritten form:

```
IF 0 iltype = 'A' THEN Writestring ('0 il i$AE 20'); Writeln;
ELSE Writestring ('Bad Entry'); Writeln;
```

An important point, not obvious in a small example, is that lower-case text is generally easier to read than upper case. Why this should be so is a question of psychology – but the effect is well known in the printing industry. Second, case mixing within a word makes for readability. It also allows the use of alternatives in writing identifier names, as in:

```
HIGHTEMPALARM --> HIGH_TEMP_ALARM --> High_Temp_Alarm --> HighTempAlarm
```

Identifying reserved words

All languages use defined constructs as part of their structure, e.g. repetition, selection, logical operations, etc. Specific words are reserved to implement such features and may not be used for any other purpose. These reserved words act like signposts, guiding the reader through the program, indicating what it does and how it does it. Therefore it is important to be able to find these easily within the program text. Three general approaches are used, shown here for the word 'procedure'.

● Case not considered: PROCEDURE or procedure. Here the reserved word is written in the same case as the rest of the text.

● Case ignored, but special identifying marks used: 'PROCEDURE' or 'procedure'.

● Case defined and the language is case sensitive: PROCEDURE or procedure, but only one of these is correct.

The first method is poor because the program writer has to find some way of making reserved words stand out. In the second, reserved words are more easily found, especially if lower case is used elsewhere in the text. The third method works well *provided* the rest of the program is written predominantly in a different form.

Some languages allow only one case to be used. Others don't worry whether text is written in upper or lower case (as long as reserved words are done correctly). That is, they are case insensitive. Others, though, *are* case sensitive. Consequently, in such a language,

```
HIGHTEMPALARM ----> HighTempAlarm ----> Hightempalarm
```

are regarded as three different words.

Naming identifiers

Identifiers are symbolic names used to represent items within a program. If a programmer uses meaningful names, programs instantly become readable. Compare for instance the following as alternatives in naming a program variable:

```
x ----> HITEMP ---> High_Gearbox_Temp ----> HighGearboxTemp
```

Names become more meaningful, recognizable (hence readable) as they look more like the real-world values they represent. Therefore the greater the number of letters and digits that can be used in any one identifier, the better. Some older languages aren't very flexible, six characters being a typical maximum. In some instances the number is unlimited but only the first few are analysed by the compiler. In such cases, for instance, HITEMP and HITEMPALARM are the same variable as far as the compiler is concerned.

Clear, meaningful and simple names make a program easy to read and understand. Even so, it's easy to go to extremes when there's no restraint on the number of characters used.

Clarity of program maths symbols

For maths working in particular, it is essential to understand two factors: the meaning of program symbols and their precedence. This applies to both conventional arithmetic and logic functions. Software engineers should have a good basic grounding in maths; therefore program rules and notation which mirror conventional mathematics work best. For instance, compare an algebraic expression with its program counterpart:

```
Y = 2C + BD + 5 ----------> Y:= 2*C+B*D+5;
```

This is easy to follow because the symbols are similar to conventional ones. And, provided operator precedence follows familiar rules, the equation form can be quickly checked for correctness.

Therefore a good language will support all basic arithmetic functions, using rules closely related to conventional maths. It is extremely useful if a maths library package comes as part of the language, again using recognizable symbols, e.g. 'sin' for sine, etc.

Format rules

Most languages give the programmer a good deal of flexibility in laying out text. Some, the 'free format' ones, impose hardly any restrictions. This, unfortunately, is a two-edged sword. When used sensibly, text layout can be standardized in a highly readable form. When used without thought, programs can become quite difficult to follow, as in:

```
REPEAT WriteString('input data');ReadReal(x1);WriteLn;x2:=x2+x1;
WriteString('the value of x2 is');WriteReal(x2, 15);WriteLn;UNTILx1>100.0;
```

Not too difficult over two lines, but difficult when dealing with page upon page of code.

9.3.6   Variable usage – scope, visibility, lifetime and declaration

Visibility and scope

Modern software engineering methods demand the use of techniques which:

● Develop programs from sets of building blocks.

● Allow a number of programmers to work simultaneously on a project.

● Hide information.

● Provide program stability.

The first two items have little to do with the use of program variables (well, not directly). But, once we decide on a building-block approach, the way variables are used *does* become important. Information hiding and program stability are profoundly affected by this factor. Further, when program development is split between designers, variable usage must be carefully controlled.

What are the advantages of using local variables? The major one is that it helps us to produce reliable, maintainable programs. An identifier is bound to its function or package, etc.; therefore it cannot be accessed from other parts of the program. By limiting scope, identifiers become easily visible and hence controllable. Accidental access to, and modification of, such items is eliminated. Moreover, the same names can be used for different variables provided their scopes don't overlap. In large projects this minimizes the number of global names, making it easier for programmers to spot name clashes.

The area of a program in which an identifier is *potentially* visible is called its 'scope'. Within these areas it can be accessed and, if required, changed. If it is visible in all areas of a program it is said to be 'global'. Conversely, if it can be seen in only one part of the program, it is 'local' to that section. Various methods are used to enforce locality such as the class, package, file, module and subprogram.

Mixing global and local variables

Given the right language then, in theory, global variables don't need to be used (for variables, also read constants in this context). In practice this tends to become

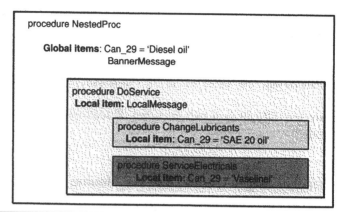

Item	Where visible	Scope
Can_29 = 'Diesel oil'	Everywhere except the two innermost procedures	Everywhere
BannerMessage	Everywhere	Everywhere
LocalMessage	Within all three inner procedures	Within all three inner procedures
Can_29 = 'SAE 20 oil'	Procedure ChangeLubricants	Procedure ChangeLubricants
Can_29 = 'Vaseline'	Procedure ServiceElectricals	Procedure ServiceElectricals

Figure 9.25   Scope and visibility within modules and procedures.

clumsy; hence global variables are always used. The question is, how do we decide whether items should be global or local? One proven method is to declare as global objects which reside at defined locations in the processor system (either memory or I/O). All other items become local. But this rule can't be applied in a simple go/no-go manner; much depends on the language being used.

So what are the rules for handling the combination of local *and* global items? There are minor variations between languages, but most follow the general concepts of Figure 9.25.

The lifetime of variables

Assume our program has 100 variables. Does that mean that 100 RAM store locations have to be permanently allocated for these? Well, it depends. Certain variables exist (are 'alive') for as long as a program runs. These are defined to be 'static'. Others are activated and then disposed of as determined by the program, the 'dynamic' ones. All programs *need* static variables; this isn't so for dynamic ones. In fact, the idea of dynamic variables is generally unknown in assembly language programming. So why use them? The answer is, they save on RAM space. As far as variables are concerned, storage is needed only for the maximum number active at any one time, not the total number used in the program.

Normally program or global variables are static, procedure variables being dynamic. But, if procedure variables *are* static, the demands on RAM store may limit the use of procedurization as a design technique.

Declarations

Any object (constants and variables) used in a program must be 'declared' to the compiler. The primary reasons are twofold. It allows the compiler to build up a list of all program symbols (a symbol table) required by the compilation process. Further, it provides information regarding the storage space needed for these objects.

Two different declaration techniques are used. In one, declaration is an implicit process. Here the programmer chooses a name for an object and uses it as required in the program. When the program is compiled the first use of the name acts as its declaration. In the other case declarations are explicit; that is, the programmer must list the objects outside the executable part of the program. Explicit declarations are the preferred method. Using information from the symbol table the compiler can check that such items are used correctly in the program. In contrast, implicit declarations are extremely unsafe, for two reasons. First, any single, simple spelling mistake creates a new object which will be accepted as valid by the compiler. The mistake shows only at run-time, the most difficult point to track down errors. Second, object types (e.g. integer, real, etc.) have to be extracted automatically by the compiler. One well-known method used for this relates object type to the first letter of its name. For example, if the first letters are I to N then it's an integer. The opportunities for making mistakes in this situation are immense.

9.3.7 Data types – concepts and uses

Background

The use of data types is an abstraction process, being a fundamental instrument of high-level language working. Before looking into this in detail it is worth considering the problems that typing can eliminate. These are most troublesome in assembly language work, where typing is pretty primitive. Let's assume that the only types available to us are defined to be bytes, words (16 bits) and double words (32 bits). Now:

- Is it possible to examine the contents of a data store and define its meaning? Well, only as a binary number.

- What happens if you try to store a data word in the wrong location? The system will do exactly what you tell it to do, within type constraints (and sometimes not even then).

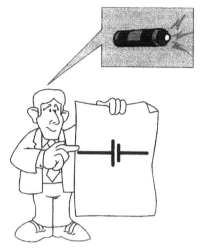

Figure 9.26 | The basic idea of abstraction.

- If you mistakenly add two different quantities together, what happens? They usually get added together.

- By examining detailed operations carried out on the data can you deduce the program function? Only if the text is littered with comments and you have a good understanding of the processor instruction set.

It isn't surprising that mistakes are made at this level, the most serious ones being algorithmic and logical. This situation arises because we concentrate mainly on machine details and data-handling features, not on the problem itself. Data typing, however, helps us to focus on what we're trying to do (that is, solve a particular problem) instead of getting trapped in the finer points of machine detail.

Abstraction and data types

Show Figure 9.26 to an electronic engineer and ask him what electrical component is shown here. The answer is likely to be 'a battery', although in reality it's nothing more than marks on a piece of paper. What he means is that it 'represents' a battery in his mind. Not that it has a particular shape and size, etc., but that it has the electrical circuit properties of a battery. Now this is an important point; it demonstrates our ability to separate concepts from implementations – *abstraction*. Moreover, once we work in abstract terms, the same physical item can be viewed in quite different ways, Figure 9.27.

In terms of languages a data type is also a conceptual idea. Each type defined within a programming language has two attributes:

(a) A set of values.

(b) A set of operations which can be carried out on these values.

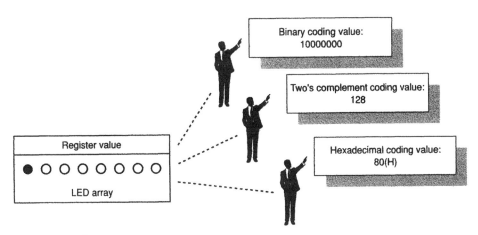

Figure 9.27 Reality and concepts.

Consider, for instance, type integer. This has a set of values consisting of whole numbers usually lying in the range –32,768 to +32,767, the step size being 1 (one). Some of the operations which may be carried out on these values include addition, subtraction, multiplication, etc. Note that we haven't said anything about how integer values are held within the machine itself. Thus at the programming level we work with an abstract concept; particular implementations only become important when used in target machines.

Most modern languages are designed to be 'strongly typed', that is, subject to the following rules:

● Every data object must belong to one (unique) type.

● Associated with each type is a set of values and operations.

● Every operator used with a data type must belong to the set defined for that type.

● Where assignments are carried out, data objects must be of the same type (unless actively overridden).

It is fundamental to high-level language design that data objects should be named and not accessed using memory addresses. This can't hold in all situations, though, a point covered in low-level programming.

Typing has a strong bearing on program design and maintenance, its objective being to enhance program reliability. By using type information the compiler can pick up many errors which otherwise would go through to the run-time code. Weakly typed languages do little to enforce type rules. Therefore it is recommended that strongly typed languages should be used for real-time systems programming.

```
VAR
        NewValue,TotalValue,AverageValue,Num:INTEGER;
        ................................................................
        TotalValue := 0;
        FOR Num := 1 TO 4 DO
                ReadInt(NewValue); WriteLn;
                TotalValue:=TotalValue + NewValue;
        END; (* end of for *)

        AverageValue := TotalValue DIV 4;
        WriteString('The average value is');
        WriteInt(AverageValue,5); WriteLn;
```

Figure 9.28 | Example listing 1.

Inventing your own data types

All languages have a pre-defined set of data types, such as integer, real, character, etc. In some cases user-defined types may be added to this set. Now, why should we want to devise new data types in the first place? This feature isn't available on older languages, including many used successfully in real-time systems.

The reason stems from the fact that the number of pre-defined types is relatively small. As a result any individual type (e.g. integer) may represent a wide range of variables which, logically, are incompatible (from the programmer's point of view). Now, the compiler can look for type incompatibility; logical compatibility checking is beyond its powers. Consider the following simple example (Figure 9.28) for computing the average of four analogue measurements.

If for any reason the programmer had written

```
TotalValue := TotalValue + Num;
```

the compiler would accept it as a perfectly valid statement; yet logically it is completely wrong. What can be done to help the compiler stop us implementing such code? It can't possibly spot flaws in program logic; after all each program is unique. The answer is, first invent new data types, then use these to distinguish between logically different items. In effect, force the compiler to check for name equivalence instead of structural compatibility. This isn't foolproof – but it does significantly improve the situation.

Defining new types – enumerated types

Types which can be defined by the programmer are usually enumerated ones. That is, we have to list the values of the type, the ordinality of the values being given

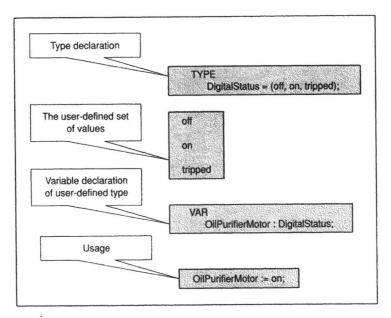

Figure 9.29 User-defined enumerated type.

```
TYPE    Digital1Status = (off, on, tripped);
        Digital2Status = (low high);
VAR
        OilPurifierMotor, CPPpumpmotor :Digital1Status;
        BearingTemp, SealTemp          :Digital2Status;

BEGIN
        CPPpumpmotor     := on;
        OilPurifierMotor := tripped;
        BearingTemp      := high;
END.
```

Figure 9.30 Example listing 2.

by the listing order. For example, we could invent a type DigitalStatus, to represent the possible states of a motor controller (Figure 9.29). How do we benefit from using programmer-defined types?

Look at the program abstract of Figure 9.30. First, for the two user-defined types (Digital1Status, Digital2Status) we've clearly and unambiguously spelt out all possible conditions. The reader doesn't have to interpret the meaning of the source code. Second, the names used are logically associated with the type attributes. This

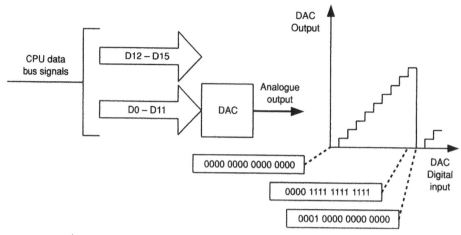

Figure 9.31 | Working with subranges of a value.

makes the program easier to read, understand and maintain. Third, we've built in extra safety factors. Consider that, by accident, we write:

```
BearingTemp:=off;
```

When the program is compiled a 'type incompatibility' error message will be flashed up. For the small number of variables shown here such a mistake is unlikely. In large systems, where the number of program objects runs into thousands, this is a definite hazard.

Subrange types

There are situations where the range of a variable needs to be limited ('constrained'), often for reasons of safety. Let's look at a specific example (Figure 9.31). Assume a number is represented in a processor using 16 bits, counting in straight binary. The program uses this value to set the output of a 12 bit digital-to-analogue (DAC) converter. Because the DAC is a 12 bit type, the four most significant bits are irrelevant; that is, it uses only a subrange of the total number range. When decimal 4095 (binary 0000_111111111111) is fed to the DAC it produces full range output; for zero (0000_000000000000) it produces its minimum value. Unfortunately it does the same for 4096 (0001_000000000000). Visualize this device being used to set the blade pitch of a ship's propeller. For a 4095 output maximum ahead pitch is set, giving full pitch ahead. If the output is incremented just by 1 (giving 4096) the DAC signal will go from full ahead to full astern pitch. At the very best this would result in an embarrassing situation.

In many languages the only way to avert this is to positively check for out-of-range conditions. That puts the responsibility entirely onto the programmer; no

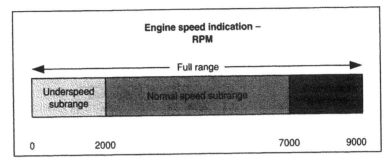

Figure 9.32 Subrange concept.

support is given by the language. As a result, one single 'mistake' in a syntactically correct program could produce catastrophe. But if the language includes subrange constructs, such mistakes can be minimized.

A subrange is defined as a contiguous subset of a given data type (Figure 9.32). For the DAC example the declaration section defines the subrange, as follows:

```
CONST
  BladeAngleMax = 4096;

TYPE
  DacRange = [0 .. 4095];
VAR
  DAC1 : DacRange;
```

Consequently, should mistakes such as

```
IF (PowerDemand = FullAhead) THEN DAC1 := BladeAngleMax;
```

be made in the source code, the compiler would flag up an error.

Subranges may also be used with enumerated types (Figure 9.33). This could be used, for example, in the part program of (Figure 9.34). Here an enumerated type Digital1Status is first defined. Following this is the declaration of a subrange of it, PartDigital1Status, its lower bound being off, the upper one, standby. As a result the oil purifier motor can be defined to be in one of five conditions, but the CPP pump motor in only three.

Subranges may not give protection against out-of-range values at run-time. It is possible that values lying outside the defined subrange *could* be computed. If run-time checks aren't performed on numerical values these will be accepted as valid, with the attendant consequences. Even when such checks *are* done, serious thought must be given to the resultant responses (see Section 9.3.10, *Exception handling*).

Subranges are most useful when developing programs, mainly to identify mistakes of logic. They also make it easier to read and understand programs.

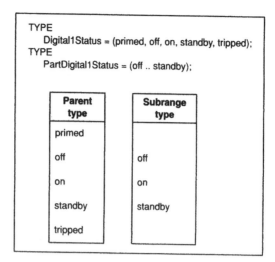

Figure 9.33 | Enumerated types and subranges.

```
TYPE Digital1Status = (primed, off, on, standby, tripped);
        PartDigital1Status = [off..standby];
VAR
        OilPurifierMotor : Digital1Status;
        CPPpumpmotor : PartDigital1Status;

BEGIN
        CPPpumpmotor : = on;
        OilPurifierMotor : = standby;
END.
```

Figure 9.34 | Example listing 3.

Derived types

Derived types are those invented by the programmer, usually being based on stand-ard language ones. The reasons for their use are to minimize errors and to make the program more readable – not necessarily at the same time. For example, the declaration

```
TYPE
  NavWeaponsSystem :REAL;
  EngineDataSystem :REAL;

VAR
  Groundspeed, Altitude : NavWeaponsSystem;
  Airspeed, JetPipeTemp: EngineDataSystem;
```

```
TYPE
        Distance:REAL;
        Velocity:REAL;
        Time:REAL;
VAR
        Waypoint0, Waypoint1, Waypoint2: Distance;
        Time0, Time1, Time2: Time;
        Velocity0to1, Velocity1to2: Velocity;

BEGIN
        Velocity0to1: = (Waypoint1 - Waypoint0)/(Time1 - Time0);
END.
```

Figure 9.35 Example listing 4.

creates derived types NavWeaponsSystem and EngineDataSystem, both having a parent type REAL. In a strongly typed language it isn't possible to mix variables of different types (without explicit type overriding). Thus the statement

```
Groundspeed  : = Airspeed;
```

would be flagged up as an error by the compiler.

In a weakly typed language this would be taken as valid, because the parent types are the same. But, even here, derived types can be used for reasons of program readability, as in Figure 9.35.

We rely on the programmer to pick up logical errors such as:

```
Velocity1to2  : = (Waypoint1 - Waypoint0)/(Time1 - Time0);
```

With weak typing, to spot illogical and incorrect operations, it is important to use types correctly and consistently.

Procedure types

If a language lets us treat procedures as variables then it is possible to perform operations on them as an entity. One particular feature, the assignment operation, is important, as it allows us to:

● Change the functionality of a procedure without changing its name.

● Use a named procedure in place of a standard one.

We can make a program much more readable and understandable using this approach (after all, that's why we use names for identifiers).

```
TYPE
        CartesianCalculation = PROCEDURE(REAL):REAL;
VAR
        Radius, Theta, A, jB :REAL;
        RealPart, ImaginaryPart :CartesianCalculation;
BEGIN
        RealPart: = sin;
        ImaginaryPart: = cos;
        A: = Radius * RealPart(Theta);
        JB: = Radius * ImaginaryPart(theta);
END.
```

Figure 9.36 Example listing 5.

As an example, suppose that we have to take in a complex number in polar form (i.e. $R \angle\theta$) and calculate its Cartesian values $A + jB$. The basic mathematical relationships are:

$A = R(\cos \theta)$ – the real part

$B = R(\sin \theta)$ – the imaginary part.

Frequently these operations are mistakenly interchanged (i.e. $A = R(\sin \theta)$). Such mistakes can be eliminated by replacing the standard sine and cosine calculation procedures with well-named user-defined procedures. First, the procedure type must be established, Figure 9.36. Then procedure variable names are declared. Finally, assignment of procedures to these variables is done in the body of the program. Note that these new procedures do exactly the same job as the ones they replace; therefore they must have exactly the same structure.

Structured types

Structured types allow the programmer to work collectively with groupings of data items (which generally relate to each other). The basic requirements of such a data structure are that:

- It must allow data objects to be grouped together. This includes objects of the same type ('homogeneous') and those of different types ('heterogeneous').
- It must let us handle individual objects within the group as well as manipulating the group (or parts of the group) as a single entity.
- Where appropriate it must enable single items to be accessed at random. In other situations it should allow us to work with large quantities of data using sequential accessing methods.
- Accessing information should be both simple and efficient.

To meet these requirements a number of different data structures have been produced:

- Arrays
- Sets
- Records
- Dynamic structures.

Each has particular features and uses.

Arrays

The array structure is provided in virtually all high-level languages, being used with homogeneous data objects. Only its main features need be noted as it should be a familiar construct to all software engineers. It is a data type which:

- Holds a related set of individual items ('elements').
- Allows the whole set of elements to be handled as a single variable.
- Enables each element to be manipulated separately.
- Is easy to manage.

Modern languages offer features for:

- Multidimensional array structures.
- Forming new types from array structures.
- Using user-defined enumerated types as array bounds.
- Using undefined array sizes as formal parameters of procedures ('open arrays').

The array is extremely powerful in supporting complex or large mathematical operations such as matrix manipulation. Its disadvantage is that it is relatively inflexible for general-purpose work, as all elements must be the same type.

Sets

Sets are similar to arrays in many ways. First, individual elements of a set belong to some base type. Second, all elements are of the same base type ('homogeneous'). Third, elements can be accessed directly, i.e. it is a direct access method. Now for the differences. The maximum number of elements contained within a set is defined at declaration time; however, the actual number present at any time can be changed by the program. As such the contents can range from an empty set (null set) through to a full one (all components present). Further, set elements are constants. Thus it is impossible to alter their values. All that can be done is to check whether a set element is present, add elements to the set, or delete elements as required.

Operators used with set variables				
Operator	Name	Logical	Example	Result
+	Union	OR	X + Y	The resulting set has elements which occur in X or Y or both.
*	Intersection	AND	X * Y	The resulting set has elements belonging to both X and Y.
~	Difference	DIFF	X ~ Y	The resulting set has elements which occur in X and are not in Y.
/	Symmetric difference	EX-OR	X / Y	The resulting set has elements which occur in either X or Y, but not in both.

Figure 9.37 Operators used with set variables.

Set relational operators			
=	Equality	X = Y	Boolean result, true if X = Y.
< >	Inequality	X <> Y	Boolean, true if X and Y are not equal.
< =	Inclusion (set is contained in)	X < = Y	Boolean, true if set X is contained in set Y.
> =	Inclusion (set contains)	X > = Y	Boolean, true if set X contains set Y.
IN	Membership	X IN Y	Boolean, true if ELEMENT X is contained in SET Y.

Figure 9.38 Set relational operators.

Various operators can be used on set variables, those in Figure 9.37 being representative. The results of such operations are evaluated using relational operators such as those of Figure 9.38. Sets are used mainly for:

● Mathematical operations.

● Validity testing.

● Control of individual bits within computer words.

Bit management is probably the most important application for the embedded systems programmer. Using this construct single bits of a processor word can be handled quickly and easily. Yet this can be written at a high level, providing visibility, clarity and security.

One last point concerning sets is their size, that is, the number of elements within the set. Practical systems considerably limit set sizes (16 elements is not unusual). Further, sizes vary between different computers or compilers. Therefore set operations tend to be highly unportable features of programs.

Records

As shown previously, all data elements within array and set structures are the same type. This is sufficient to satisfy most engineering and scientific needs. Unfortunately these constructs are unsuited for handling large amounts of data, especially data involving different types. Data structures are needed which allow different types to be mixed together. Further, it is desirable to manipulate the contents of these structures both collectively and individually. And it must be possible to work with large quantities of data.

The type which meets these requirements is the record, this being defined as a direct access, heterogeneous, fixed-size data structure. It has the following features:

- It allows a mix of data types.
- The complete data structure can be handled as if it is a single object.
- Each component (element) within the structure can be accessed and manipulated individually.
- Names are used to identify the complete structure and its elements.

When building a record, four items have to be declared to the compiler:

- The name of the record structure.
- The fact that it is a record.
- The individual components of the record.
- The type of each component.

Consider the requirements to form a record for a control loop (Figure 9.39). The declaration format is typically:

```
type ControlLoop is
  record
    Alarm : Boolean;
    InputSignal : Float;
    O utputCommand : Integer;
end record;
```

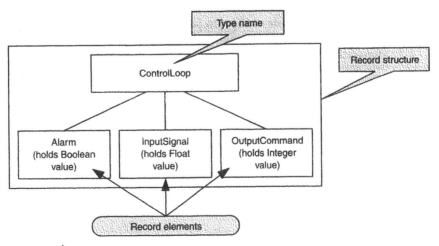

Figure 9.39 : Structure of record type.

Variables belonging to this record type are declared in the usual way:

```
PortEngineController, StbdEngineController : ControlLoop;
```

Thus each variable has a set of individual components, these being Alarm, InputSignal and OutputCommand When used in a program they are accessed by name, as in:

```
PortEngineController.InputSignal
StbdEngineController.InputSignal
PortEngineController.Alarm
```

The record structure simplifies many data-handling tasks, even in small programs.

Dynamic data structures and pointers

There are occasions when systems must handle large amounts of data, placing considerable demands on computer storage space. Data like this is usually dynamic, i.e. in a constant state of change. Consequently, during a program run, the amount of storage space needed at any particular time can vary considerably.

All structures discussed so far have one common feature: their sizes are fixed by program constructs. When sizing them, a worst-case approach must be used, i.e. cater for the maximum needed. But where data is dynamic this clearly is inefficient. In fact small systems may not have enough RAM space to cope with such demands. What's the best way to deal with this?

To meet such needs dynamic data structures have been devised. These structures are created and then disposed of as required; during use they expand and contract as store requirements change. In practice this has led to the use of sequential data storage techniques for dealing with dynamic variables. Variables stored within a dynamic structure do not have individual names, only data values and locations. Consequently, access to such variables is done using address (pointer) information, not names.

Dynamic data types are usually organized as lists or trees, but unlike arrays, etc. are not explicitly defined as such. Instead they are built up using the pointer type, one declaration format being:

```
TYPE
  LogPointer = POINTER TO RunningHours;
  RunningHours = [0..9000];

VAR
  Log :LogPointer;
```

Thus, LogPointer is a pointer type, by type definition. It points to another type, in this case RunningHours. The variable Log is of type LogPointer.

One important use of pointers in embedded systems is for building up operating system constructs. Without this, code would have to be written in assembly language. So even though pointer operations are inherently insecure, they should be provided as part of a modern language.

9.3.8 Program flow control

General

It may seem simplistic to say that all programs can be written using only the three structures outlined in Chapter 4. Yet, with one exception, this really is the case with well-designed software. The exception occurs only when special steps need to be taken to get out of extreme difficulties – which should be a rare event in embedded systems. Even here recovery techniques should be precisely formed and controlled.

The three structures of sequence, selection and iteration form the basic syntax for structured programming techniques; all programs can be constructed using just these. Most languages allow the programmer to transfer program control unconditionally, usually by using the GOTO function. Modern software design practice avoids GOTO constructs as their use can result in badly structured programs. However, for embedded applications, the GOTO or its equivalent is essential for handling dangerous exception conditions.

Simple selection

There are a number of variations on the simple selection construct, these being (Figure 9.40):

- The IF-THEN statement.
- The IF-THEN-ELSE statement.
- NESTED-IF statements.

IF-THEN is the simplest version of the selection statement, having the structure of Figure 9.40a.

More generally, though, we want to carry out alternative actions as a result of the evaluation, one set for true, the other for false. The IF-THEN-ELSE control structure is designed for this, Figure 9.40b.

In some situations, to arrive at an answer, a series of decisions have to be made. Using the IF statement this can be done, as follows:

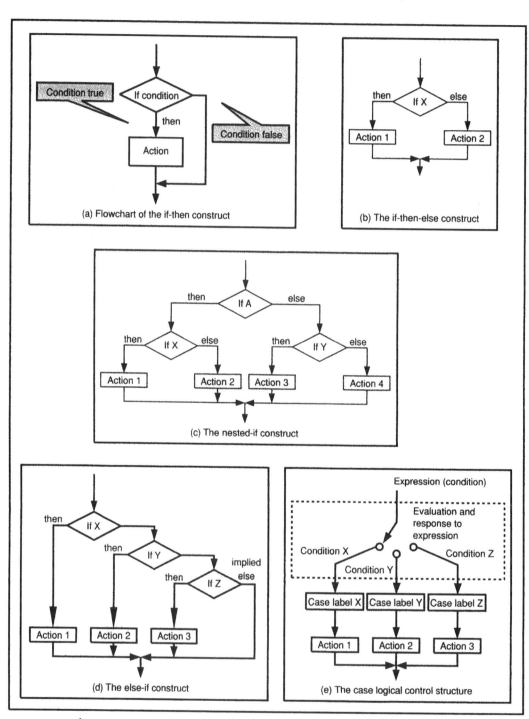

Figure 9.40 Selection constructs.

```
IF < condition A > THEN
  If < condition X > THEN < action 1 > ELSE < action 2 >
ELSE
  If < condition Y > THEN < action 3 > ELSE < action 4 >
END
```

This is described as the NESTED-IF operation (Figure 9.40c).

Multiple selections – ELSE-IF and CASE statements

Often we are faced with having to select one path only from many options. This requirement *could* be handled by using either a sequence of IF-THEN statements, as in

```
IF <X> THEN < action 1 >;
IF <Y> THEN < action 2 >;
etc.
```

or a series of IF-THEN-ELSE actions. The first case, although it will work, does not by itself ensure that the operations are mutually exclusive. A little bit of creative programming will soon put an end to such good intentions. The second, using multiple IF-THEN-ELSE's, results in a complicated program structure which is difficult to read and understand. Two methods of dealing with situations such as these are provided in some modern languages, the ELSE-IF and CASE functions.

ELSE-IF

This selection operation allows a single choice to be made in a straightforward manner, as in:

```
IF        <X> THEN < action 1 >
ELSE-IF   <Y> THEN < action 2 >
ELSE-IF   <Z> THEN < action 3 >
END
```

The flow of operations is shown in Figure 9.40d.

CASE or Switc h

An easier way of handling multiple-choice problems is the selector switch construct, usually called the CASE or Switch statement. Here the switch (Figure 9.40e) selects one course of action from a number of choices.

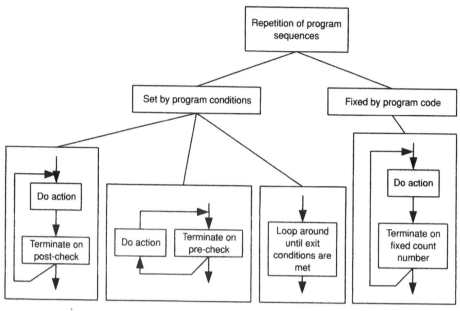

Figure 9.41 Repetition constructs.

The CASE syntax usually has the form:

```
CASE Condition IS
<X>: <Action 1>
<Y>: <Action 2>
<Z>: <Action 3>
END
```

The route selected for use is determined by the value of Condition.

Repetition or 'loop control'

Very broadly, repetitive constructs can be split into two groups (Figure 9.41). Within the first set, repetition depends upon program conditions, the number of loops set by the state of some control variable. This also includes the case where the program never loops. In contrast, repetitive actions may be defined quite precisely by the program code itself; termination takes place only after the correct number of iterations has been carried out.

Thus the four basic iteration control structures are (Figure 9.42):

- Post-check loop (the REPEAT-UNTIL construct).
- Pre-check loop (WHILE-DO construct).
- Check within loop (the LOO Pconstruct).
- Fixed looping conditions (the FOR-TO construct).

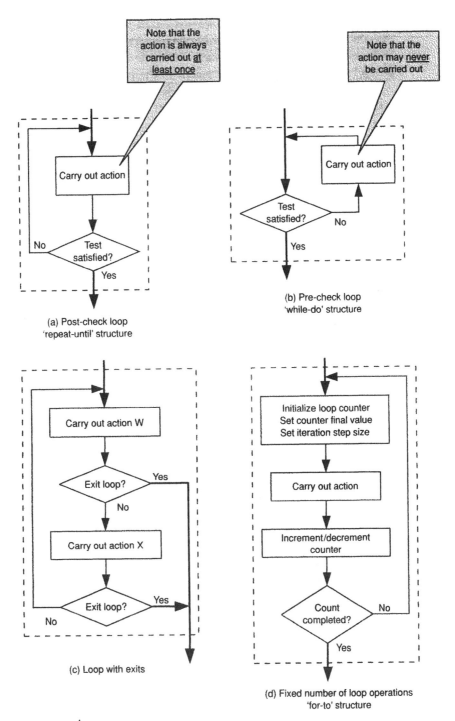

Figure 9.42 | Iteration control structures.

With the REPEAT-UNTIL operation we first do the required action and then check the test condition (Figure 9.42a). If this condition isn't satisfied then the action is repeated and a further test carried out. Finally when the test conditions are fulfilled control passes to the next sequential statement in the program.

When using the WHILE-DO statement the test condition is evaluated before the action is carried out (Figure 9.42b). Depending on the result, two outcomes are possible. One is that no action is performed and control passes on to the next program statement. Otherwise the defined action is implemented and the test condition is once more evaluated.

The LOO PEXIT construct (Figure 9.42c) is extremely useful because it:

- Can result in more readable code.
- Minimizes the need for GOTO operations.
- Enables the programmer to implement multiple terminating conditions in a simple fashion.

When the number of iterations can be defined in the program code, the FOR-TO construct is usually used (Figure 9.42d).

The importance of flow control constructs

It isn't often realized that *all* flow control constructs can be devised using just two operations: the combination of IF-THEN-ELSE and GOTO (this, though, requires that the language uses either line numbering or labels). Unfortunately, with such an approach, it becomes difficult to see exactly which operation is being carried out. In contrast, highly readable code results by using program statements which relate directly to specific control structures. Therefore, a good modern programming language should provide a full range of control structures.

9.3.9 Interfacing to other languages

Assembly language interfacing

For professional work it is a primary requirement to work whenever possible with high-level languages. These are easy to understand, straightforward to maintain, and much less likely to hold unwitting mistakes. Nevertheless, there will be occasions when the high-level approach fails. Therefore we must be able to integrate assembly language into the high-level code.

This is a fundamental requirement for all high-level languages. Two methods are commonplace, using either code inserts or linked assembly routines (Figure 9.43). Code inserts ('inline code') are program statements which are placed directly in the high-level source code. Either assembler mnemonics or machine instruction

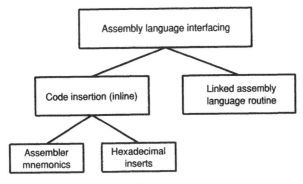

Figure 9.43 Using assembly language with HLLs.

hexadecimal values can be used. To use assembly statements the compiler first generates intermediate code; it then submits this to an assembler process. This is a highly flexible programming method; unluckily, few compilers offer this feature. The second method doesn't involve an assembler and has the advantage of producing fast and small code. It also allows the programmer to manipulate processor registers, etc. knowing that unforeseen effects won't be generated by the compiler. This method, when combined with a good high-level language, eliminates the need for separate assembly language routines. But, to use it, the programmer must have an expert knowledge of microprocessor machine language.

The most common method of assembly language interfacing is to first write assembler operations as separate routines, then link these in with the compiled code of the high-level language. One highly desirable feature is the ability to reference high-level designators (e.g. variables) from assembly code (and vice versa). For professional work this should be mandatory. The degree of cross-checking performed by the linker on the high-level and assembler routines (e.g. version numbers) is important.

High-level language interfacing

From a technical point of view there isn't a need to interface to other high-level languages. However, should a company decide to use a new language it can't afford to throw away its existing software investment. It must be possible to integrate existing work with new developments. Unless a language provides this facility it may well be rejected on commercial grounds. The important factors here are the:

● Range of language interfaces available.

● Ease of interfacing.

● Degree of cross-checking of 'foreign' language routines.

Note that these features are frequently compiler, not language, dependent.

9.3.10   Exception handling

Exceptions are 'errors or fault conditions which make further execution of a program meaningless' (*Dictionary of Computing*). For embedded systems this definition should have the words 'and/or dangerous' added. When errors do occur, the usual response is to invoke an exception handler routine; this decides what action should be carried out. It can be seen that there are three distinct issues here:

- What errors should be detected?
- Who provides the error detection mechanism?
- What should be done once the exception is identified?

The final item is application-dependent; thus it is beyond the scope of the language (although it's probably the most difficult question to answer). In a data processing environment it may be sufficient to halt the program; for embedded working this may be even more dangerous than the original error condition.

The first two items *are* language related, these being another contentious issue. The questions are, how much should be built into the language itself, and how much should the programmer handle explicitly? Now, certain errors may occur on any processor system. Others, though, are specific to system and hardware design. It is recommended that:

- Languages should provide certain basic automatic error detection facilities at run-time, especially for maths handling. These include number overflow, divide by zero, array bound violations, etc.
- The programmer should be able to switch off these checks if required to speed up execution times.
- Ideally languages should provide exception-handling mechanisms by which programmers can detect errors and invoke appropriate responses.

Doing it this way removes a significant burden from the programmer; he doesn't have to include code to check for *all* possible error conditions. This also keeps the source text clear; automatic checks require no program code. Moreover, the use of exception constructs highlights those error checks which the programmer *does* insert. And finally, by grouping error-handling routines together, it is easier to assess system safety.

9.3.11   Accessing processor hardware – low-level facilities

Introduction – the need for device access

Do we need to manipulate hardware at the chip level? Well, it depends in the first place whether we're developing application software or board support (low-level) functions. For application-level work the crucial factor is the support of a comprehensive RTOS. In such cases we'd normally interface to devices using the OS board support facilities. However, many small computer-based real-time engineering functions don't use operating systems. Software tends to be tailor-made for the task in hand, with little or no distinction between systems and application software. In fact, software in these smaller embedded systems is considered to be 'applications' only, interacting directly with the computer hardware. This, of course, is exactly the situation that those developing board support facilities find themselves in.

With a standard hardware platform (e.g. a PC) it may be possible to develop generic templates to simplify low-level programming. Unfortunately embedded designs vary considerably in terms of:

- Use of memory space for code, data, heap and stack.
- Amount of code in read-only store.
- Amount of read/write store.
- Special store provisions, such as non-volatile devices.
- Address locations of these devices.
- Location, size and activating methods for interrupt-driven programs.
- Use of processor on-chip programmable devices.

Facilities needed to access devices

Access facilities can be grouped roughly into four areas:

- Memory accesses, for the control of code, data, heap and stack operations.
- Peripheral device interfacing and control.
- Interrupt handling.
- Support of special machine operations.

Memory operations

Memory chips are mapped into the processor address space, their locations being determined mainly by processor characteristics. For instance, ROM must be mapped at the bottom of memory in some processors (Figure 9.44). This comes about because, on power-up, program execution begins at location 0H. Others, however, restart with their instruction pointer pointing elsewhere in memory, e.g. almost at the top of the address space. For this processor ROM must be located at the top of memory.

Thus the software engineer must take into account the mapping scheme in use when compiling the program (as it's rather difficult to write information into EPROM).

In some situations we have to access information residing at specific memory locations (absolute addresses). Here the need is to specify precisely the addresses of these memory locations. Such features should be standard within the language.

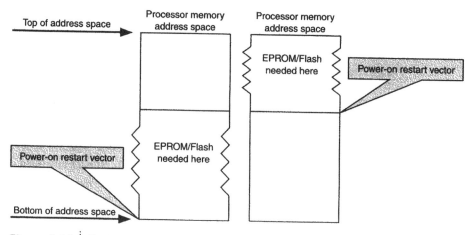

Figure 9.44 Mapping of memory devices.

Management of peripheral devices

Virtually everything except processor and memory devices come into this category. Included are items such as programmable timers, interrupt controllers, serial I/O controllers, maths chips, analogue-to-digital converters, etc.; the list is immense. Generally, though, they have three factors in common:

- They are mapped at specific absolute addresses.
- Both read and write operations are performed on them.
- Individual bits within a data word have specific meanings.

Where peripherals are mapped into memory then, to the processor, they look like RAM. Thus addressing and read/write operations need no further discussion. However, bit management is a different matter. This facility is required for two main reasons. We may, in the first instance, want to establish the status of the device being accessed. In the second we may wish to change its operational mode. Both status and control information is handled using word (in smaller systems, byte) data transfers. For such applications the information carried by the word is set by individual bits within the word. Therefore, when interacting with peripherals, we must be able to examine and modify data words bit by bit. And for the sake of clarity and reliability, bit-handling should be supported within the high-level language itself.

Interrupt handling

The role of interrupts has been discussed elsewhere. But no matter how these are implemented, we always end up using absolute addressing methods. Two alternative techniques are shown here (Figure 9.45). In the first one the interrupt program is located at a defined absolute address in memory; the processor is then 'vectored' to this when the interrupt is activated.

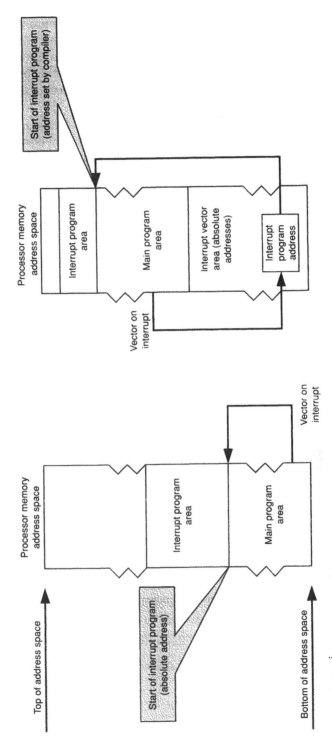

Figure 9.45 Interrupt operations.

Alternatively, the compiler fixes the program location; we then 'plant' the necessary reference to this at an absolutely defined address in the interrupt vector area. When an interrupt occurs, program control is initially transferred to the appropriate location in the vector area. The program residing here is usually quite short. Normally it performs limited housekeeping functions and then transfers program execution to its interrupt program.

Interrupt handling obviously is machine specific. This causes great difficulty in trying to standardize such operations in any general-purpose high-level language. To avoid using assembly language, two features should be provided. The language should provide constructs which allow the programmer to implement interrupts in his own fashion. It should also provide an interrupt-handling mechanism which is non-standard but supplied as part of the compiler.

Special machine instructions

Occasionally processors provide facilities which are unique to their design. For instance, on Intel processors, data can be transferred quickly and efficiently using IN and 0 U instructions. Peripheral devices which respond to these are mapped into the so-called I/O space. Clearly such instructions cannot be included as standard within the language; yet we should still be able to invoke all facilities provided by the processor. It is desirable that such features are included within the language package, as a non-standard extension.

9.3.12 Assembly language programming

For professional programming, assembly language working should be avoided wherever possible. Justification for this is given both explicitly and implicitly in many parts of this book, embracing topics such as:

- Inherent insecurity of the basic coding method.
- Lack of scoping control.
- Extremely weak data typing.
- Limited (or non-existent) flow control mechanisms.
- Difficulty in understanding program intent (readability factor).
- Non-portability of source code to other processors.
- Difficulty in maintaining the software.

But, having said that, there are still occasions when it must or should be used. The reasons include:

- Lack of a high-level language.
- Hardware testing.

- Interrupt handling.
- Peripheral and subsystem interfacing.
- Speed of program execution.
- Program (code) and data size.

HLL availability

When manufacturers release new processors they're always accompanied by an assembler package. C compilers usually – but not always – follow on fairly quickly. Therefore the software writer may have no choice but to use assembly language programming.

Hardware testing

Hardware testing, especially when faults are present, must be very precisely controlled. This can be done most easily, clearly and with confidence by using assembly language instructions. HLLs are totally inappropriate – the tester must have full control of the object test code (compiled code is a problem here).

Interrupt handling

Many HLLs don't give the programmer any means of interacting with interrupts. Yet interrupts are an integral part of most embedded designs (note that, where possible, interrupts are avoided in safety-critical software). Therefore, in such cases, the programmer has little option but to resort to assembly language routines.

Peripheral and subsystem interfacing

There are occasions when interfacing to peripherals and subsystems can be difficult (or even impossible) from an HLL. For instance, it isn't unusual for 8 bit peripherals to be used in a 16 bit system. Here the HLL may not even recognize the existence of data objects smaller than 16 bits; device control has to be done using assembly language. In other cases devices are mapped in the input/output address space of the processor; yet the HLL may not support such operations.

Program performance aspects

Execution times and program store requirements are parameters frequently mentioned in the context of embedded system programming. Two particular areas deserve special attention: high technology (especially defence) and the mass consumer market.

In high-tech areas such as avionics, fighting vehicles and the like, speed and space have always been important. But now, with major improvements in EPROM, flash and RAM packing densities, storage is rarely a problem. Speed of response, though, remains just as important as ever. In the consumer area low cost is a fundamental goal. This means that processor designs use minimum silicon, which means minimal storage. Speed of response isn't usually a major difficulty.

Maximum computer throughput combined with minimum store (both ROM and RAM) *can* be attained using assembly language programming. The operative word is 'can', as many factors affect the outcome. Three points need special note: programmer competence, design methods and compiler performance.

Programmer competence has a profound impact on the performance of the target system. There is a marked difference (in terms of speed and store) between programs produced by good designers and those developed by mediocrities. So, for fast and tight programs it isn't just enough to program in assembler; the right man must be used for the job. In contrast, when HLLs are used, programmer variability is small.

In many applications the space constraint comes about because only a small amount of (static) RAM is available (ROM packing densities and costs are significantly better). And HLL programs usually use much more RAM space than their assembler counterparts.

It should be pointed out that space and speed penalties are not necessarily inherent in HLL working. Often these are caused by the program design methods, not the language itself. Where procedures are used extensively as program building blocks, heavy demands are placed on temporary data storage. The same is true when designs are implemented using tasking (concurrent) structures. Both methods also impose time constraints. Experience has shown that by minimizing procedure nesting, a speed improvement of between 2 and 3 can be attained (this is highly dependent on individual programs). The solutions to these problems lie in the hands of the programmer.

Probably the most important factor affecting target system performance – in terms of code size and execution speed – is the compiler. Different compilers, designed for the same HLL and target processor, produce quite different results; variations of 4:1 have been experienced. A good compiler, when used with a good optimizing suite, will come close to equalling the performance of the best assembly language programmers. Certainly the results will be better than those produced on average from assembler writing.

9.3.13 Miscellaneous items

Macros and macro-processors

A *macro-instruction* ('macro' for short) is an instruction inserted in the source code, representing a sequence of program statements. When the source file is compiled the macro is replaced prior to compilation by the statement set. This is done by a *macro-processor* program. Macros perform much the same task as procedures except that:

- Executable (object) code is generated for each insertion of the macro; in the case of a procedure, code is generated once only.
- Execution times are faster as there isn't any saving or restoring of processor information.

These are powerful mechanisms, particularly when parameters can be used with the macro call (as with procedures). They are especially useful when structured design methods are used. Most implementations of top-down modular structures use procedures as building blocks. But this has one (not so obvious) drawback. That is, as the levels in the structure increase so do the number of nested procedure calls. The save/restore overhead can be substantial in such cases. In contrast, the macro allows the designer to implement top-down designs with minimal effect on run-time. The trade-off for this is code size, faster run-times requiring more object code. Unfortunately there aren't simple rules for calculating the code ratio between macro and procedure implementations. A further complication is that small procedures may have as much code for save/restore instructions as that in the procedure body itself.

A second factor, particularly important for small embedded systems, is the demand placed by nested procedures on RAM space. Each time a procedure is called, processor status must be preserved. Further, variables local to the procedure also need RAM space. Add to this the need to store parameters, especially those copied into the procedure ('value' parameters). With nesting these can mount up dramatically, resulting in the processor running out of RAM space and consequent failure of the program.

Few languages provide the macro facility as standard. Where it isn't available it is recommended that a language-independent pre-processor be used.

Variable initialization

Some languages enable a value to be assigned to a variable at the time of its declaration – 'variable initialization'. The compiler itself generates object code to set the variable to this value; no statements need be made in the program. Variable initialization is also implemented in several OO languages using the constructor method.

Opinions differ concerning the usefulness of this feature. What *is* useful is a compiler check to ensure that variables have values assigned to them before they are used. In many cases it doesn't matter that variables aren't initialized; in others it may be crucial. Without automatic initialization checks, responsibility lies entirely with the programmer.

Constant expressions

In high-level language working all program items should be given names. This includes constant values as well as variable ones. A fairly standard declaration form is:

```
CONST
  pi = 3.14159;
```

where the right-hand side of the equation is defined to be a constant expression. If the language allows this to be treated in the same way as normal expressions then it's possible to build up constructs as:

```
CONST
  pi = 3.14159;
  f = 50;
  omega = 2* pi * f;
```

The readability of the source code can be greatly improved using such methods.

Concurrent constructs

It is important that a general-purpose programming language contains constructs for building concurrent programs (Chapter 5). This allows the programmer to implement the high-level features – scheduling, mutual exclusion and task communication – of operating systems. These can be applied both to single- and multiprocessor systems, being tailored to suit the application.

9.4 Choosing a high-level language for embedded systems

9.4.1 Basic requirements

Before choosing a high-level programming language, four fundamental questions need to be answered. They are: which language features:

- Do we really *need*? – *essential requirements*.
- Are needed to produce high-quality software? – *primary requirements*.
- Would be really *useful*? – *secondary requirements*.
- Would be nice to have? – Flavour of the month (take your pick).

Essential features

Essential features are those needed for the development of application software for loading onto a **'bare-bones' embedded** machine. A minimal set of requirements includes:

- Assembly language and machine code interfacing.

- Absolute addressing.

- Access to and control of hardware.

- Interrupt handling.

- Bit manipulation.

- Processor (or environment) specific extensions to the core language.

- Pointers (for use with dynamic data structures).

- Control of timing and time delay functions.

You *could* argue that the only essential item here is the provision of assembly language and/or machine code interfacing. But this is true only if you intend to program in assembly (and not a high-level) language.

Primary features

Primary features are the underpinnings for the development of correct, reliable and safe programs. They may be regarded as essential for the production of high-quality software, and include:

- A comprehensive and well-defined language standard, including maths facilities.

- Well-defined behaviour.

- Strong data typing.

- Rigorously defined control structures.

- Modular structure with good software encapsulation.

- Separate or independent compilation facilities with full type checking across component boundaries.

- Exception-handling constructs.

- Facilities to develop task structures.

- Facilities to interface to commercial real-time operating systems.

- Memory exhaustion checks.

- A language subset for safety-critical languages.

Secondary features

Secondary features make a significant contribution to productivity, portability, maintainability, flexibility and efficiency (though note that portability and efficiency may be contradictory attributes). They may also enhance correctness, reliability and safety aspects, though that isn't their basic intention. They include:

- Good readability – clear, non-cryptic syntax and layout.

- A comprehensive standard library.

- OOP constructs.

- Multitasking – language and run-time support.

- Interfacing to 'foreign' high-level languages.

Performance aspects

Features which allow us to define and assess run-time performance are highly desirable. Unfortunately most current programming languages do not contain such facilities. You will normally have to look to software development environments for these. Broadly speaking they fall into two groups, related to sequential and multitasking programs, as follows:

- Sequential programs

  - Generation of deterministic code with upper limits on execution times.
  - Facilities to determine execution times statically (from the source code).
  - Ability to measure actual execution times dynamically.

- Multitasking programs

  - Selection of scheduling strategies.
  - Setting of task deadlines.
  - Provision for dealing with task overloading (going late).
  - Ability to extract and analyse task run-time performance.

9.4.2 Assessed languages – background

Over the years many languages have been used for the programming of real-time embedded systems, Figure 9.46. All have been used in real-time systems and some will continue to do so in the future. However, here we'll look only at those which are currently widely used in real-time applications.

The following languages are assessed against the features outlined in the previous section:

- Ada 95

- C

- C++

- EC++

- Java

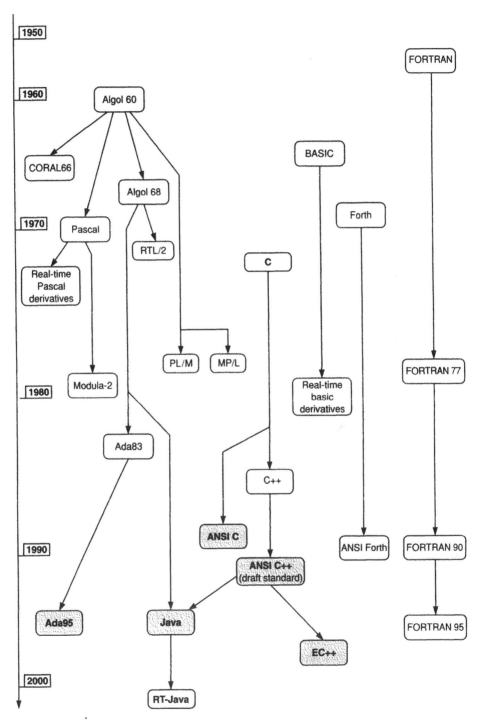

Figure 9.46 Languages for real-time embedded systems.

Ada 95

In the 1970s the US Department of Defense (DoD) found that it had over 300 languages in use. Therefore it set out to bring order to this chaotic situation by commissioning four separate design studies to develop a new language. The result, finalized in 1983, was Ada (now known as Ada 83). This was later formalized as ANSI/MIL-STD 1815.

A major revised version of the language incorporating many OO and other features was released in 1995 (ANSI/ISO/IEC-8652:1995).

Ada is now widely used in defence, aerospace and safety-critical systems (such as railway signalling and train control). A safety-critical subset, Spark-Ada, has been developed.

C

C, designed by Dennis Richie, came from AT&T Bell Research Labs in 1972. Its intention was to provide:

- The flexibility of assembly language programming together with
- The power and productivity of high-level language working and
- High efficiency.

One early major application was in the writing of the UNIX operating system. Only much later, circa the mid-1980s, did it make inroads into real-time embedded applications.

A subset of C, MISRA-C, has been specified for use in safety-related systems.

C++

C++, also a product of Bell Labs, first appeared as 'C with clauses' in 1980, being designed by Bjarne Stroustrup. Its first proper release, V1.0, was in 1985. C++ is on OO language but was based on, and was made compatible with, C. Thus C can be viewed as being a subset of C++ (it is, however, a major mistake to think that C++ is just an extended C).

EC++

Embedded C++ (EC++) is a Japanese-led initiative to develop a C++ subset suitable for embedded applications. To quote the EC++ rationale: 'The ultimate goal of Embedded C++ is to provide embedded systems programmers with a subset of C++ that is easy for the average C programmer to understand and use'. It does not add features specifically for embedded systems, but is a pure subset of ISO/ANSI C++.

Java

Java resulted from the development work done by James Gosling of Sun Microsystems in the early 1990s. His aim was to provide platform-independent software technology for consumer electronics companies. The formal release of Java in 1995 described it as 'a simple, object-oriented, distributed, interpreted, robust, secure, architecture neutral, portable, high performance, multithreaded and dynamic language'. Make what you will of that.

9.4.3 Assessed languages – comparison and comment

A detailed comparison of the five languages is given in Figures 9.47, 9.48 and 9.49. The languages evaluated here represent three distinct strains of development. There is good reason to believe that, over the next few years, all will continue to co-exist. Each will tend to dominate particular sectors of the marketplace (though this is likely to be a very fluid situation). At present the following predictions seem to stand up to examination:

Ada 95

Ada will continue to be dominant in defence, avionics and similar applications in North America and western Europe. It will also have a strong presence in the safety-critical world.

	Ada 95	C	C++	EC++	Java
Assembly language/machine code interfacing	Y	Y	Y	Y	N
Absolute addressing	Y	Y	Y	Y	N
Access to and control of hardware	Y	Y	Y	Y	N
Interrupt handling	Y	Y – but no standard method	As for C	As for C	N
Bit manipulation	Y	Y	Y	Y	N
Processor specific extensions	Y	Y – but compiler-dependent	Y	Y	N
Pointers	Y	Y – very strong feature	As for C	As for C	N – but has the 'reference'
Timing/time delays	Y	Not directly	As for C	As for C	N

Figure 9.47 Language comparison – essential features.

	Ada 95	C	C++	EC++	Java
Comprehensive well-defined language standard	Yes	Yes	Yes	Yes	Yes
Modular structure with good software encapsulation	Excellent	Poor	Good	Good	Excellent
Data typing	Good	Poor	Better than C, weaker than Ada, Java	As for C++	Good
Separate compilation with type checking	Good	Poor	Much better than C, weaker than Ada, Java	As for C++	Good
Behaviour and control structures	Good	Poor	Poor	As for C++	Good
Maths model	Good	Poor, insecure	Weak, but superior to C	As for C++	Similar but superior to C++
Exception handling	Yes	No, but can be devised	Yes	No	Yes
RTOS interfacing	No, but can be devised	As for Ada 95	As for Ada 95	As for Ada 95	As for Ada 95
Memory exhaustion checks	Yes	No, but can be devised	As for C	As for C	Yes, including garbage collection
Subset for safety-critical applications	Yes – SPARK Ada	Yes – MISRA C	No	No	No

Figure 9.48 Language comparison – primary features.

	Ada 95	C	C++	EC++	Java
Readability	Good	Moderate to very poor (highly programmer-dependent)	As for C	As for C	Better than C++ (no pointers) but inferior to Ada
Comprehensive standard library	No – only a basic library	Yes – very good	Yes – very good	Uses a restricted set of C++ libraries	Yes
OOP constructs	Yes	No	Yes	Yes	Yes
Multitasking – language and run-time support	Yes	No	No – compiler-dependent	As for C++	Yes – the Java threading model (but must run on top of a host OS)
Interfaces to 'foreign' HLLs	Yes – but compiler defined	As for Ada 95	As for Ada 95	As for Ada 95	Yes

Figure 9.49 Language comparison – secondary features.

C

Currently C is the most widely used language in embedded systems. It will continue to occupy that position for some time, although inroads will be made by C++, EC++ and Java.

C++

C++ is dominating the workstation and PC world, but has had a relatively slow uptake in the embedded world. Its sheer size and complexity has been off-putting for many developers. However, by carefully using a subset of the language, many problems of complexity and code-bloat can be avoided.

EC++

EC++ aims to eliminate features of C++ which are considered to:

- Generate excessive code.
- Make it difficult to estimate processing times.
- Be difficult to understand and use.
- Be inappropriate for use in embedded systems.

This is a step in the right direction, but it still remains a large and complex language.

Java

It can be seen that Java lacks almost all the features labelled 'essential' to go onto a bare-bones embedded machine. This precludes its use in such applications *unless* a work-around is found. One way is to develop all real-world tasks using another language (C, C++ or Ada, for example) and integrate these with Java via an RTOS.
    Strictly speaking, Java comes in three forms:

- Java (workstations, PCs, etc.).
- PersonalJava (personal digital assistants, advanced mobile phones, etc.) and
- EmbeddedJava (simple mobile phones, printers, etc.).

All place demands on memory space and processor performance which are beyond the capabilities of the smaller (resource constrained, usually low-cost) embedded systems. However, the Java scene is in a constant state of flux; things could well change rapidly. Moreover, work to produce real-time extensions has been under-way for some time now, formalized in December 2001. Details can be found in *The Real-Time Specification for Java* [RTS01]. The success of RT-Java will depend very much on the availability of compilers and development environments; we'll just have to wait and see how things turn out.
    In summary, Java *at present* is unsuitable for use in:

- Fast (especially hard) systems.
- Resource-constrained systems.

Even more important for those in some technology sectors is the following statement (from Sun's licence agreement for the distribution of Java); 'Software is not designed or licensed for use in on-line control of aircraft, air traffic, aircraft navigation or aircraft communications; or in the design, construction, operation or maintenance of any nuclear facility'.

What we are also beginning to see are projects where software has been developed in a number of languages. One (not so new) application is the multiple-redundant flight control system of the A320 Airbus. A more recent example is that of the London Underground Jubilee line metro-type transportation system. Here, for the signalling system, safety-critical software is written in Ada whilst less-critical software is coded in C. Within the same project, C++ is used extensively for the higher (non-critical) overall supervisory level functions.

Review

At this stage you should:

- Know what is meant by the terms monolithic, modular and independent when applied to the development and construction of software.
- Recognize the pros and cons of these different approaches.
- Understand how these relate to the current mainstream embedded programming languages.
- Appreciate why proper packaging of software is important, especially in larger and long-life systems.
- See the benefits of using component technology in modern software systems.
- Appreciate what features are needed in languages to facilitate component design and construction.
- Know how to show class packaging using UML diagrams.
- Know how to show components, component relationships and component deployment using UML notation.
- Be able to model package and component relationships using UML notation.
- Appreciate the range of features normally provided by modern high-level languages.
- Be able to assess the capability of the language(s) in use on your current project against this.
- Be in a better position to assess prospective candidate languages for use in embedded systems.
- Recognize that complexity, obscurity and poorly specified languages are the enemy in the battle to produce dependable software.

```
#define _ -F<00 || --F-OO--;
int F = 00,OO = 00; main () {F_OO();
printf("%1.3f\n",4.*-F/OO/OO);}F_OO()
{
```

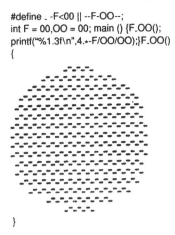

```
}
```

Figure 9.50 C obfuscation example (from *Ada User Journal*, reproduced by permission).

And on that note I leave you with the code in Figure 9.50. Yes, this is a perfectly valid C program which conforms to the ANSI standard. It generates the number 0.25 [HIL91].

References and further reading

[ADA95] *Ada 95 reference manual, International Standard ANSI/ISO/IEC-8652:1995.*

[BAN92] *The C book: featuring the ANSI C standard 2nd edition*, M. Banahan, *et al.*, Addison-Wesley, ISBN 0-201-54433-4, 1992.

[BEN88] *Real-time computer control*, S. Bennett, Prentice Hall, ISBN 0-137-62485-9, 1988.

[C++] ISO/IEC 14882-1998.

[EC++] *Rationale for the Embedded C++ specification*, The Embedded C++ Technical Committee, www.caravan.net/ec2plus, Nov. 1998.

[HAT94] *SAFER C: Developing software for high-integrity and safety-critical systems*, L. Hatton, McGraw-Hill, ISBN 0-07-707640-0, 1994.

[HIL91] *The choice of programming language for highly reliable software – a comparison of C and Ada (part 1)*, A.D. Hill, Ada User, Vol. 12, pp 11–31, 1991.

[JAV00] www.Javasoft.com.

[KER88] *The C programming language, 2nd edition*, B.W. Kernighan and D.M. Richie, Prentice Hall, ISBN 0-131-11036-2, 1988.

[KOZ98] *Component-based software engineering*, W. Kozaczynski and G. Booch (editors), IEEE Software, Vol. 15, No. 5, pp 34–87, 1998.

[MIS98] *MISRA guidelines for the use of the C language in vehicle based software*, The Motor Industry Research Association, ISBN 0-9254-15690, April 1998.

[RTS01] *The Real-Time Specification for Java*, www.rtj.org.

[STR93] *A History of C++: 1979–1991*, ACM SIGPLAN Notices 28, pp 271–297, 1993.

[SZY98] *Component software: beyond object-oriented programming*, C. Szyperski, Addison-Wesley, ISBN 0-201-17888-5, 1998.

chapter 10

Software Analysis and Design — Methods and Methodologies

Finally we've arrived at a state where theory and ideas can be turned into practice. The starting point for this? When a customer arrives on our doorstep, asking us to develop a software system for his application. It finishes when the delivered software runs reliably, correctly and safely in the target system (cynics may argue that by this definition, most jobs are never finished). However, what concerns us here is the piece that fits between the two end states, the design and development phases. Just how do we go about this process? What methods should we use? What tools are available? How can we best use these tools? These, and others, are the questions tackled in the next few chapters.

There are two major steps in the development process. The first involves translating the customer's requirements into source code. The second concerns the transformation of this source code into fully functional target system object code. An ideal software development toolset supports both stages. Unfortunately, this is a rare item, particularly for the support of 'bare-board' original designs. Either tools are intended for front-end use, frequently assuming that the second stage is trivial. Or else they are aimed at the back end of the development, neglecting software design aspects entirely. Chapter 12 deals with development methods and tools designed for use in the second-stage processes. However, in this chapter we look at:

- What the overall specification-to-coding process involves.
- What it means to execute the various steps within this.

- How different techniques achieve the same ends in quite different ways.
- What the unifying themes are within the various techniques.

Specifically, the methods of CORE, Yourdon (Ward–Mellor) and real-time OOD (using UML) are described here.

10.1   The development process

10.1.1   General description

In this chapter the complete development process is viewed as a series of distinct steps, consisting of:

- Requirements analysis.
- Requirements specification.
- Architectural design.
- Physical design.
- Implementation – to source code level.
- Test, integration and debug.

Requirements analysis

Here the purpose is to establish precisely what the system is supposed to do. In small systems it tends to get merged with other parts of the development process; in large systems it is an essential, separate activity.

Requirements specification

This describes what the software must do to meet the customer's requirements. It is based on information obtained during the analysis phase.

Architectural design

This stage is concerned with identifying and modelling the software structure, using information supplied in the requirements specification. It defines the essential software components of the system, how these fit together and how they communicate.

Physical design

Here the architectural structure arrived at in the previous stage is partitioned to fit onto hardware. In a small, simple system this is a trivial task. But, in multiprocessor designs, distributed systems, and designs using 'intelligent' interfacing devices, it is a critical activity.

Implementation

Ultimately the software tasks are expressed as a set of sequential single-thread program structures. The function of the implementation stage is to take these design structures and translate them into source code.

Test, integration and debug

The purpose here is to show that the finished code performs as specified. It involves testing of individual software modules, combined modules (subsystems) and finally the complete system. This topic is covered in Chapters 11 and 12.

10.1.2   Methods, methodologies and tools

Method – a special form of procedure – 'A way of doing something'.
Methodology – an orderly arrangement of ideas.
Tool – thing used in an occupation or pursuit (*Concise Oxford Dictionary*).

In this chapter the following software analysis, design and development techniques are described in some detail:

● Controlled Requirements Expression (CORE).

● Yourdon Structured Method (YSM).

● Object-Oriented Analysis and Design (OOAD).

The purpose is to show what these can do, how they do it, and what the results are. Figure 10.1 shows the methods in question and how they fit into the overall development process.

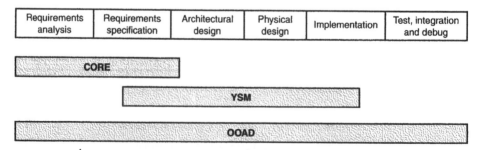

Figure 10.1 | Software techniques – coverage of the development process.

CORE is a systems requirements *analysis* technique only. It is claimed that YSM can be applied successfully to the requirements analysis phase, though this is open to question. However, YSM is widely used in the design and implementation phases. OOAD, when it employs use cases within the process, extends from requirements analysis through to test and integration.

10.2 Requirements analysis using viewpoint techniques – CORE

10.2.1 Introduction

CORE is a practical viewpoint-based method for analysing system requirements. The reasons for describing it are threefold. It:

- Is a requirements analysis tool only (thus avoiding confusion with multipurpose tool implementations).
- Has been applied extensively to the analysis of real-time European avionics and defence projects.
- Is a proven technique.

As a 'front-end' method its role is to:

- Establish the *actual* problem to be solved (as opposed to perceived variations on this).
- Eliminate ambiguities and inconsistencies in customer's requirements.
- Increase knowledge and understanding of the problem.
- Highlight effects produced by changing system specifications.
- Formalize system specifications so that they are understood and agreed by all involved in the project.

But, most importantly, it does not define *how* to solve requirements problems; it attempts to describe *what* has to be solved. In practice it includes, within the functional requirements, design decisions applicable to lower levels of the system. This usually occurs when dealing with very large real-time projects.

10.2.2 CORE fundamentals

CORE is a prescriptive method, consisting of a set of defined steps, for the development of systems requirements models. Information is produced in both text and graphical form, being held in a single database. This 'single-source' approach

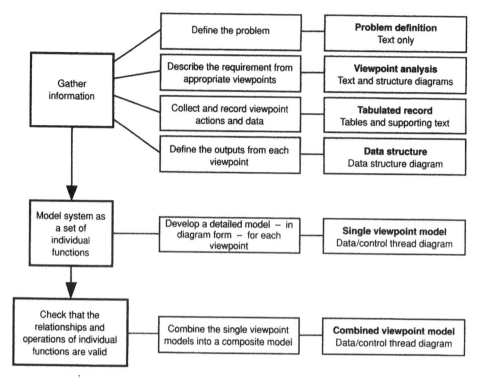

Figure 10.2 : The core analysis method.

ensures documentation consistency, both in the initial analysis phase and, later, when modifications are made.

Central to CORE is the concept of 'viewpoints'. Put simply, they describe the nature and content of the problem as seen from particular points of view. This includes both people and 'things'. Each viewpoint looks at the problem in terms of:

- Information acquired.
- Processing of this information ('actions').
- Generation of output results.

An overview of the CORE analysis method is shown in Figure 10.2. First the analyst collects information and, using this, builds a descriptive model based on the different viewpoints. He then combines the information, picking out loose ends, inconsistencies and conflicts (or, in some cases, unrealistic objectives). This information describes the behaviour of the system (or so we hope); it can then be used as the requirements document for the systems, hardware and software design teams.

Figure 10.2 is self-explanatory except for 'thread' diagrams; they are described later.

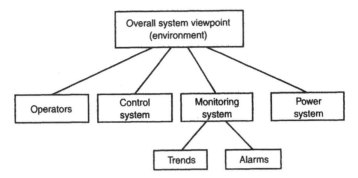

Figure 10.3 Formal viewpoint structure.

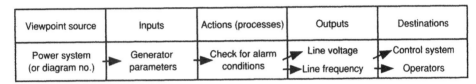

Figure 10.4 Viewpoint diagram (part).

10.2.3 Detailed aspects and notation

One of the first tasks in analysing customer requirements is to form an overall view-point structure model. What this contains varies considerably from system to system; that of Figure 10.3 describes (in simple terms) many real-time avionic and marine applications. For each viewpoint a tabular dataflow diagram is formed ('tabular entries' or 'tabular collections'). Figure 10.4 is typical of these, being developed for the alarm monitoring viewpoint of Figure 10.3. This defines:

- Where input data comes from.
- The input information to a viewpoint.
- What happens within a viewpoint (the actions).
- What information is put out by actions.
- Where output data goes to.

In this particular diagram there is only one level of decomposition; in a large system many levels (typically 3–7) may be required. When all the viewpoint diagrams are produced the complete system can be checked for consistency, loose ends, missing data sources, etc. A more detailed analysis of data structuring may also be done, using data structure diagrams, Figure 10.5. This shows three important factors:

- What data is produced by a viewpoint.
- The order in which data is produced.
- Repeated or optional data groups.

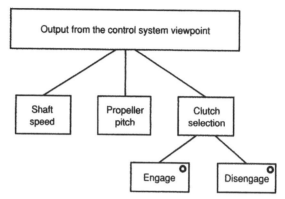

Figure 10.5 | CORE – data structure diagram.

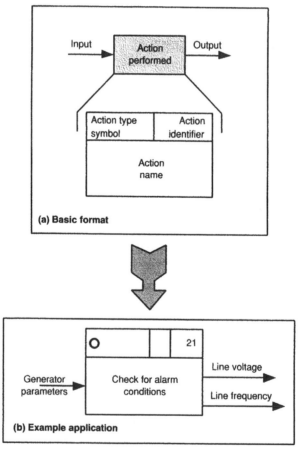

Figure 10.6 | Basic constructs of thread diagrams.

The structure and notation used are similar to those found in Jackson structured diagrams.

Viewpoint tabular diagrams completely describe the dataflow of each viewpoint. They are fairly straightforward to construct; unfortunately they aren't all that easy to use when reviewing system requirements and behaviour. To help us here, dataflows and actions are also shown in diagram form – 'thread' diagrams. The basic constructs of the thread diagram are action boxes and data flowlines (Figure 10.6). Here an input signal is transformed to an output by performing some action on it. Three basic aspects of the action need to be detailed, Figure 10.6a:

- Processing carried out
- Type of action and
- Action identifier.

In Figure 10.6b, for example:

- The processing is 'check for alarm conditions'.
- The type of action is a selection ('if-then' – see later for semantics).
- The action identifier or number is '21'.

Various forms of dataflow can be shown using the notation of Figure 10.7. Actions frequently involve repetition or selection. Such operations are described using the symbols of Figure 10.8. In (a) the label 'Control' controls the extent of the iteration operation. In (b) 'Control' determines whether action A1 or A2 is selected.

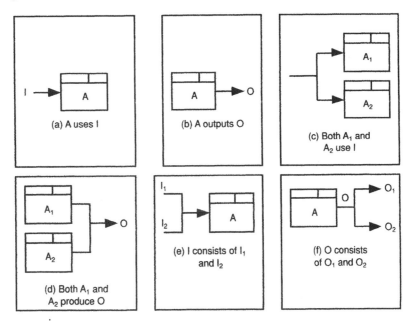

Figure 10.7 Thread diagram – dataflow constructs.

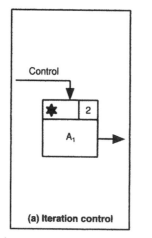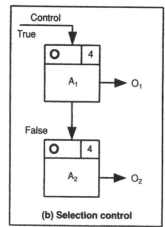

Figure 10.8 Control of iteration and selection.

10.2.4 Design example – steam propulsion system

The purpose of this section is to show how CORE can be used in a practical situation. Clearly, in a text like this, only a small problem can be tackled. It is, though, a realistic one, being based on a control system requirement in a steam propulsion plant.

The starting point, as with all real systems, is the SOR. For this example the relevant parts read as follows:

STATEMENT OF REQUIREMENTS – STEAM PROPULSION SYSTEM

General functional description

The purpose of the steam propulsion system is to provide propeller power using a steam turbine as the mechanical power source. Control of turbine speed and power is achieved by varying the steam feed to the turbine, Figure 10.9, using a steam throttle valve. The valve is motorized, being driven by an electrical actuator. It is fitted with a position sensor. When the valve is closed, steam flow is shut off. With the valve fully open maximum power is delivered by the turbine.

Exhaust steam is fed to a condensing well, where it changes state to water. From here it is pumped out as feed water to the system heat exchanger. Level control of the water is maintained by recirculating some of the output water back into the well, using a motorized water valve (the level control valve). This valve is also fitted with a position sensor.

It is required to automate control of:

- The input steam flow to the turbine.

- The water level in the condenser well.

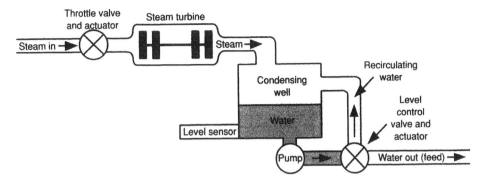

Figure 10.9 ¦ Design example – steam propulsion system.

Steam flow control system

The input steam flow is determined by the position of the throttle valve. This is set by the control system in accordance with the input demand set by the propulsion system power lever. It is required to do this automatically under closed-loop control. Static and dynamic performance requirements are defined elsewhere. Valve position data is to be shown on an operator display.

Level control system

Level is to be controlled to the value set by the operator on a level-setting dial. This is to be done automatically, using a closed-loop control system. Preliminary stability analysis shows that an inner loop is needed to control the position of the level actuator. The input signal for this loop is to be derived from within the level control system. To improve loop dynamics a cross (bias) feed is to be provided by the throttle controller for the level controller. Water level data is to be shown on an operator display.

Special points

Sampling rates

Throttle actuator loop sample rate: 30 Hz.
Level actuator loop sample rate: 30 Hz.
Level loop sample rate: 10 Hz.

Safety

If during system operation the level rises excessively (defined elsewhere) the operator is to immediately close the power lever.

END – STATEMENT OF REQUIREMENTS

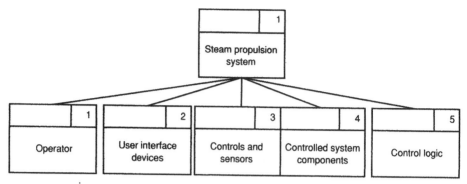

Figure 10.10 Steam propulsion system – viewpoint hierarchy diagram (VPH).

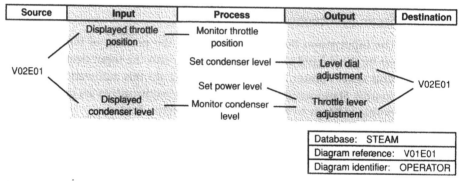

Figure 10.11 Steam propulsion system viewpoint diagram – operator (viewpoint 1).

From this information an overall viewpoint diagram is produced, Figure 10.10. This shows that the total system is described from five viewpoints, labelled 1–5. For each one an individual viewpoint diagram is produced, the following being shown here:

- Figure 10.11, for the operator (reference V01E01).
- Figure 10.12, for the interface devices (reference V02E01).
- Figure 10.13, for the control logic (reference V05E01).

To appreciate these they must be studied carefully; this is left to the reader. Two particular points need stressing. First, across all viewpoint diagrams, there must be a balance between source and destination information. Second, attention must be paid to missing inputs and outputs.

The first point is fairly obvious, but not so the second one. Consider Figure 10.11. On this the action 'monitor-throttle-position' has no output. One may well ask why this function is required at all. From the diagram it appears that the operator monitors the display but does nothing about what he sees. Questioning like this helps us eliminate pointless or redundant operation. However, it isn't always

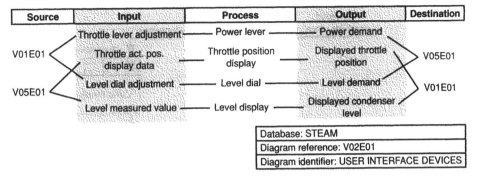

Source	Input	Process	Output	Destination
V01E01	Throttle lever adjustment	Power lever	Power demand	V05E01
	Throttle act. pos. display data	Throttle position display	Displayed throttle position	
V05E01	Level dial adjustment	Level dial	Level demand	V01E01
	Level measured value	Level display	Displayed condenser level	

Database: STEAM
Diagram reference: V02E01
Diagram identifier: USER INTERFACE DEVICES

Figure 10.12 Steam propulsion system viewpoint diagram – user interface devices (viewpoint 2).

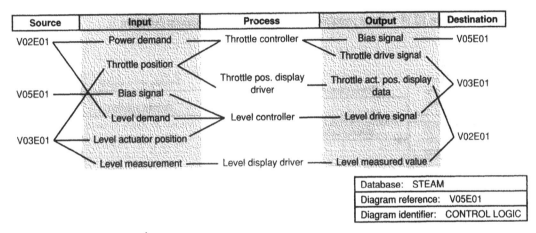

Source	Input	Process	Output	Destination
V02E01	Power demand	Throttle controller	Bias signal	V05E01
	Throttle position		Throttle drive signal	
V05E01	Bias signal	Throttle pos. display driver	Throttle act. pos. display data	V03E01
	Level demand	Level controller	Level drive signal	
V03E01	Level actuator position			V02E01
	Level measurement	Level display driver	Level measured value	

Database: STEAM
Diagram reference: V05E01
Diagram identifier: CONTROL LOGIC

Figure 10.13 Steam propulsion system viewpoint diagram – control logic (viewpoint 5).

obvious when operations *are* redundant. For instance, in the case here, the operator functions may be defined at a higher system level. But at our level we are concerned only with providing information. In this case a no-output action is perfectly valid (similar arguments apply to inputs).

Using this information individual viewpoint thread diagrams are produced. Figure 10.14 is a simple example showing part of the operator viewpoint thread diagram.

In the final stage of analysis – not shown here – the separate thread diagrams are first matched up, then they're combined into composite diagrams. This has two objectives. First, it confirms that the composed system (built from the low-level items) describes the model that we started with. Remember, we began with a top-level view, decomposing as required. Unfortunately, during this process, it's all too easy to make mistakes which don't break decomposition rules – but are logically wrong. Second, it highlights actions which involve many viewpoints. These are usually the most important ones in the system; therefore it's important to identify them early on, before design begins.

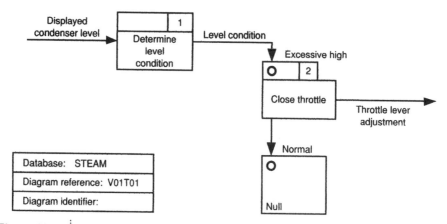

Figure 10.14 Steam propulsion system thread diagram – operator (viewpoint 1).

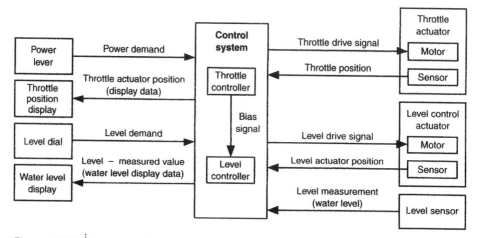

Figure 10.15 Steam propulsion system – block diagram.

The output from the analysis phase forms the specification for the software design phase. Data produced by CORE is likely to be augmented by new – system – information resulting from the analysis process itself, Figures 10.15 and 10.16 for example.

10.2.5 A comment on analysis tools

To do analysis work manually is, at the best, tedious. This is true even of the small example system given here. Moreover, it's very easy to make mistakes with manually controlled methods. In large systems the situation is much worse; errors are likely to be the normal state of affairs. The only practical way to attain high productivity and minimize mistakes is to use automated tools.

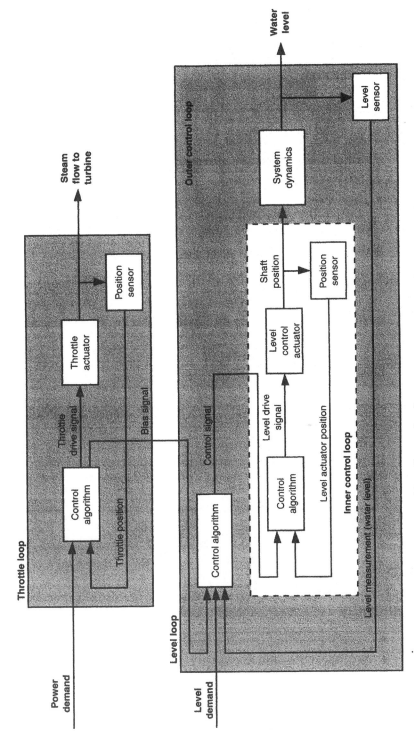

Figure 10.16 Steam propulsion system — control loop diagram (part).

10.3 Yourdon Structured Method

10.3.1 Introduction

The Yourdon Structured Method (YSM) deserves special mention because:

- It is based on quite specific analysis and design methods – functional structuring.
- It has been developed and refined over many years so that it meets the *actual* needs of software designers.
- Two embedded design methodologies which have proved to be very successful – Ward–Mellor [WAR85] and Hatley–Pirbhai [HAT88] – have been derived from the basic Yourdon techniques.
- It is applicable both to small and large projects.
- The basic ideas are used within many design toolsets.

The original ideas were proposed in the mid-1970s. Currently, with the Ward–Mellor extensions, they are widely used in the real-time embedded world.

10.3.2 Design fundamentals

The Yourdon method provides support for the analysis and design of software-based systems (Figure 10.17). Using this the designer first implicitly defines what a system is supposed to do – then implements these requirements. Here, analysis and design are two distinct stages, the output from the analysis stage forming the input to the design phase. In practice, though, they are likely to be used in a cyclic (iterative) manner.

Analysis is concerned with identifying the properties (attributes) of a system and then building a model based on this information. This, in Yourdon terminology, describes the 'essential' model of the system. The essential model itself is composed of two parts, an 'environmental' and a 'behavioural' model; these aren't tied to specific implementations.

Design is concerned with implementing the derived (essential) model on the hardware and software structures available to the designer. In essence it:

- Takes information from the analysis stage.
- Expands and refines this data ('elaboration').
- Maps system structure onto the hardware configuration.
- Identifies task and data aspects.
- Builds program structures for these tasks.

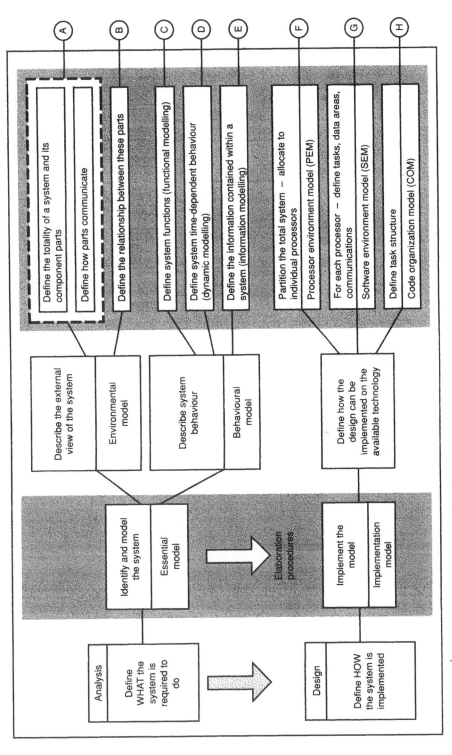

Figure 10.17 ┊ The Yourdon Structured Method (outline).

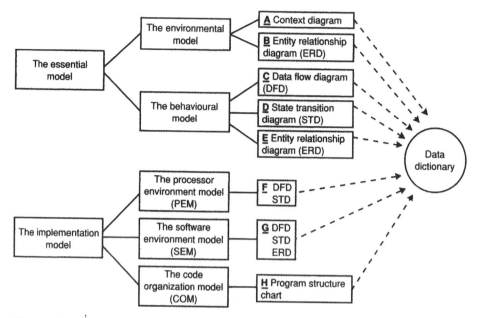

Figure 10.18 Yourdon method – relationship between models and diagrams.

This forms the 'implementation' model, being composed of three separate parts, the 'processor environment' model (PEM), the 'software environment' model (SEM) and the 'code organization' model (COM).

The relationship between the different models, and between the models and the various diagram types, is shown in Figure 10.18. The general structure, content and application of these diagrams were covered in Chapters 7 and 8. Here their usage is described specifically in the context of YSM.

The environmental model

In the analysis phase the system being investigated is described in abstract terms. That is, we set out its functions and operations without considering hardware or software. The first part of this phase consists of forming an external view of the system, using the environmental model. This defines:

● What the system consists of.

● How individual external items communicate with the system.

● How the system responds (relates) to events in the real world.

A context diagram shows the first two aspects, an entity relationship diagram (ERD) the third one.

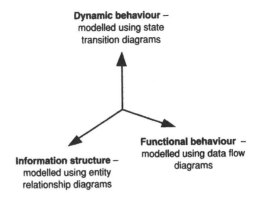

Figure 10.19 | The Yourdon behavioural model.

The behavioural model

System behaviour is described in three ways: functions, dynamics and relationships, Figure 10.19. This is shown in the behavioural model using dataflow, state transition and entity relationship diagrams. Information needed to construct these diagrams is derived from the environmental model.

The processor environment model (PEM)

The highest level design decision concerns the allocation of computing functions to processor hardware. Where more than one processor is used the functions of the essential model have to be spread across these. Precisely how this is done is described using the PEM. The resulting interface connections are also described in this model. This is an elaboration of the required system behaviour; thus it's not surprising that DFDs, STDs and ERDs are used to describe it.

The software environment model (SEM)

Within each processor it is necessary to define the software architecture and its effect on:

- Task allocation.
- Task functions (transforms) and states.
- Interfaces (internal and external).
- Data area structuring.
- Services and resources provided.

This last item includes support for concurrency, task activation and deactivation, task synchronization, and inter-task communication. For that reason an operating system can be viewed as a specific instance of a generalized software architecture.

DFDs, STDs and ERDs are used to build the SEM.

The code organizational model (COM)

The modular structure of each task, built in a functional manner, is described in the code organizational model. Where appropriate the module interfaces are defined. A program structure diagram ('chart') is used to implement the COM.

10.3.3 Design example

The implementation (in part) of the software design for the steam propulsion system using the Yourdon Structured Method is shown below. This concentrates on the essence of the method; for clarity many detailed items are omitted. Figures 10.20–10.26 illustrate the process. In the first place a context diagram is produced (Figure 10.20). Note here the introduction of a 'virtual' terminator named Time. It is necessary to use such a construct to incorporate time-driven events in the system.

There now follows the event list, Figure 10.21, which has been slightly modified to include a list of external responses. Using this information, preliminary design diagrams are produced, Figure 10.22.

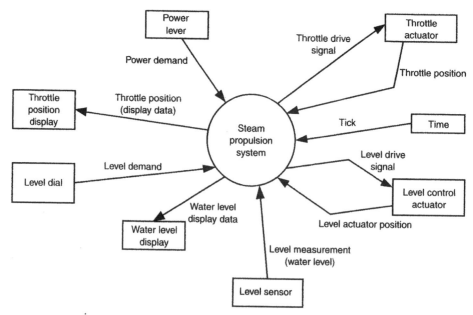

Figure 10.20 Steam propulsion system YSM context diagram.

AGENT	ACTION	SUBJECT	INSTRUMENT	CLASSIFICATION	EXTERNAL RESPONSES
Power level	Sets power demand	Throttle controller	–	Data	Throttle drive signal
Level dial	Sets level	Level controller	–	Data	Level actuator drive signal
Throttle actuator	Gives throttle position information	Throttle and level controllers	–	Data	Throttle position display
Level control actuator	Gives level actuator position information	Level actuator controller	–	Data	–
Level sensor	Gives level information	Level controller	–	Data	Water level display
Time	Activates control loop	Actuator and level controllers	Real-time clock	Control	–

Figure 10.21 : Steam propulsion system YSM event list.

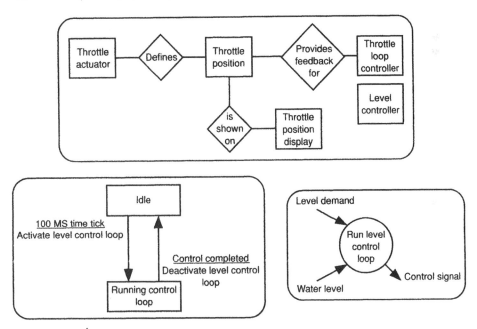

Figure 10.22 : Steam propulsion system YSM preliminary design diagrams (part).

The behavioural model is now developed, its DFD being shown in Figure 10.23. Note that control flows (trigger prompts) have now been introduced to activate the various timed data transformations (processes). These originate in the control transformation 'schedule control loops', responding to the input control flow 'tick'.

At this stage the system is partitioned onto processor hardware as shown in the PEM, Figure 10.24.

Now the SEM is developed for each processor, the relevant DFD for micro 1 being that of Figure 10.25.

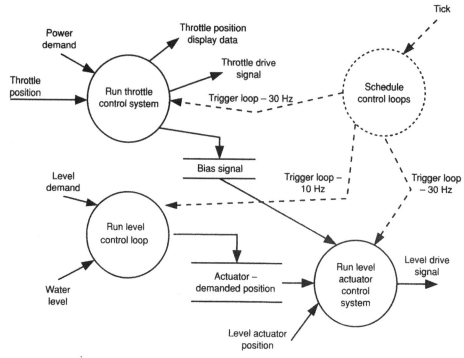

Figure 10.23 Steam propulsion system YSM behavioural model DFD.

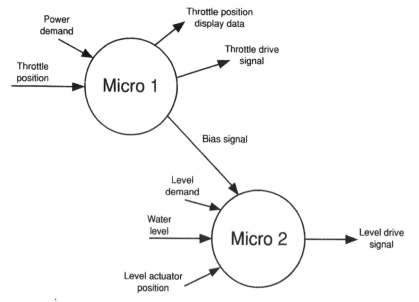

Figure 10.24 Steam propulsion system YSM processor environment model DFD.

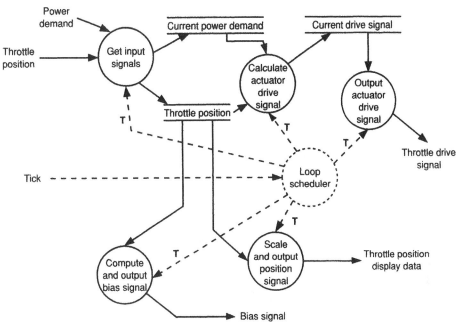

Figure 10.25 | Steam propulsion system YSM software environment model DFD for micro 1.

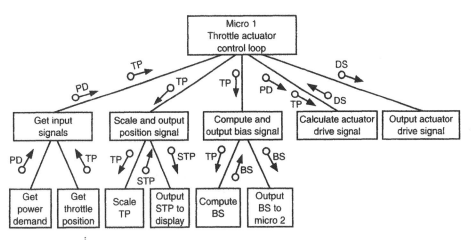

Figure 10.26 | Steam propulsion system YSM code organization model SC for micro 1.

Finally the program structure charts (SCs) are generated. In this case processes are run consecutively – not concurrently – to simplify the design, Figure 10.26.

Handling the documentation for even this relatively simple design is a major task. Thus implementing the Yourdon Structured Method without tool support is daunting; design maintenance even more so.

10.4 Object-oriented analysis and design

10.4.1 Design example – dipmeter wireline logging tool

This example is concerned with the development of software for a wireline oil well logging tool called a dipmeter, Figure 10.27. The purpose of the dipmeter is to extract geological information concerning oil-bearing rock (usually sandstone).

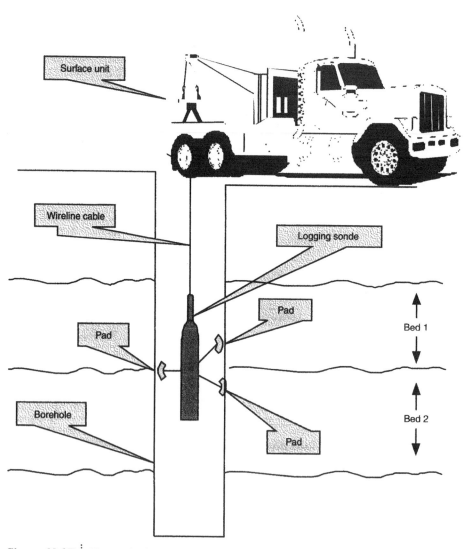

Figure 10.27 Dipmeter logging tool – system configuration diagram.

In particular it seeks to define details of the bedding planes in the subsurface formation, as follows:

- Depth of bedding planes in a borehole.

- Angle of the bedding planes.

- Position of the planes in three dimensions in Earth's coordinates.

This information is gathered by drilling a borehole and then running a dipmeter or logging sonde (housed on the end of a wireline cable) up the hole. During the run a set of electrical sensors ('pads') are held in contact with the borehole wall, measuring wall resistivity. As a pad crosses a bed boundary the formation resistance changes; the resultant change in sensor output identifies the boundary point. These pads are retracted for tool stowage, being extended by a ram when commanded to do so.

At least three pads are needed to identify a plane in space. However, pad measurements are made relative to the logging sonde itself. To develop full attitude information, further data is needed: magnetic bearing, tool tilt ('slant angle') and direction of tilt ('slant angle bearing'). As the sonde must operate at extreme temperatures, e.g. 200°C, temperature corrections must be made to sensor readings.

All downhole measurements ('logging') are carried out under the supervision of a trained operator. Testing, in general, proceeds as follows. The operator initially checks that the dipmeter is working correctly by running a set of self-test routines. If satisfactory, the sonde is lowered into the borehole and the pads extended to contact the wall. At this stage the logging run can begin, all downhole activities being controlled by the sonde computer. On completion of the log, the pads are retracted and the tool removed from the borehole.

The overall system architecture is shown in the deployment diagram of Figure 10.28. It can be seen that this consists of a surface unit, the dipmeter itself, and the

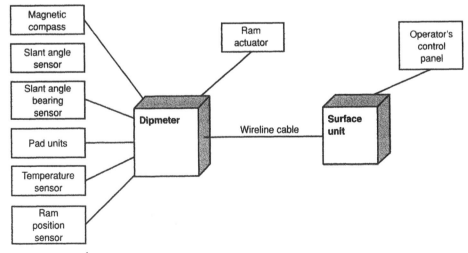

Figure 10.28 Dipmeter system deployment diagram.

connecting wireline cable. The cable is used for a number of purposes, one of which is to provide a full-duplex serial digital communications channel. Owing to the characteristics of the wireline (which may be up to 5 kilometres long), specialized modems are used in this system.

10.4.2 A practical OOAD development process

The basic process model used here is shown in Figure 10.29. Underlying this is the following detailed design strategy:

(a) Establish the real needs of the client. Define the overall architecture early in the project.

(b) Define the outline hardware and software aspects of the system. Set out the system requirements as a set of use cases.

(c) Carry out a detailed analysis of system usage. Formalize this using:

- Use case scenarios using sequence diagrams.
- State machines (statecharts).

(d) Expand these diagrams to show all actor–system interaction (both direct and indirect actors).

(e) Develop an ideal software model in terms of interacting (collaborating) sub-systems. Formalize this using:

- System and subsystem diagrams.
- Sequence diagrams (by extending those produced in the previous stage of work).
- Subsystem collaboration diagrams.

(f) Transform the ideal model into the specification model, this consisting of collaborating active and passive objects. Refine the design as appropriate.

(g) Map the ideal software model onto a practical (multitasking) one. Identify and define the attributes of the various tasks, together with all inter-task messaging.

(h) Develop the program structure models for each (state and algorithmic behavioural features). For UML, use statecharts and/or activity diagrams.

(i) Develop the system static structure models:

- Classes and class diagrams.
- Packages and package diagrams.
- Component and component diagrams.

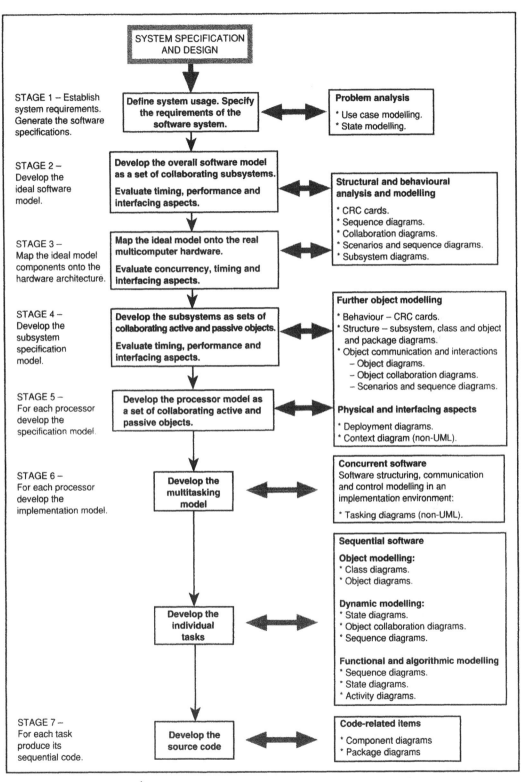

Figure 10.29 : A practical real-time OOAD development process.

10.4.3 Defining system usage

Preliminary analysis results

From an initial analysis of system requirements, overall usage and behavioural aspects can be defined, Figures 10.30 and 10.31.

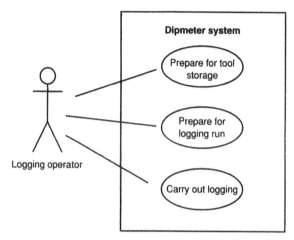

Figure 10.30 Dipmeter system use case diagram.

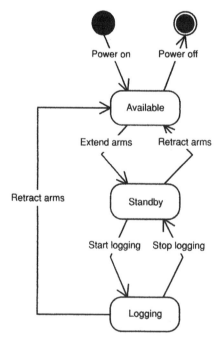

Figure 10.31 Dipmeter system overall state diagram.

Use cases – general description

Use case 1 – Prepare for logging run

Goal: to set up the system so that logging can be carried out.

The operator runs a self-test program and, if passed, extends the dipmeter arms until the pads lie on the borehole wall.

Use case 2 – Carry out logging

Goal: to carry out bedding plane logging of the borehole.

When the dipmeter is in position (not controlled by this system) the operator starts the logging test. This continues under automatic control until halted by the operator. On completion of the logging run the dipmeter is put into the standby mode.

Use case 3 – Prepare for stowage

Goal: to set the dipmeter ready for removal from the borehole.

The operator retracts the dipmeter arms to the stowed position.

Expanded use case descriptions

At this point it is possible to produce a more detailed text description of the use cases. For brevity only one – 'Prepare for logging run' – is given here.

Use case 'Prepare for logging run'

- Goal: to set up the system so that logging can be carried out.
- Pre-conditions: The sonde must be loaded onto the wireline and the system powered up.
- Interaction details:
    1. The system shows that it is available ('operational' mode).
    2. The operator invokes the self-test checks.
    3. The system carries out the self-tests and displays the results to the operator.
    4. IF the tests are successful the operator positions the pads on the borehole wall by extending the ram actuator. The system then displays the ram position (extension).
    5. ELSE if the tests are unsuccessful the operator selects 'dipmeter faulty'. The system stores the failure details and time for later off-line analysis.

Formalizing use case descriptions using sequence diagrams

At this stage the use cases are formalized using sequences diagrams, for two reasons:

- The diagrams provide rigour by removing any ambiguity and/or ambivalence lurking in the text descriptions.
- It acts as a natural stepping-stone into the next stage of software development.

Once again only one use case is described here (Figure 10.32).

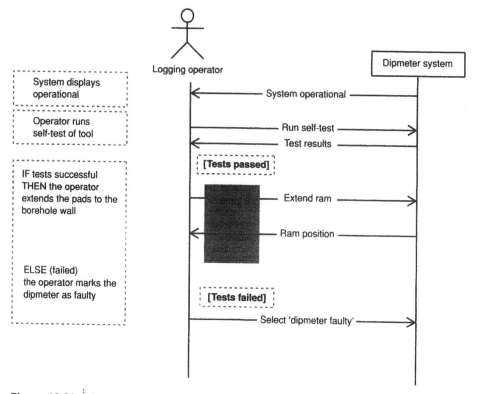

Figure 10.32 Dipmeter system — sequence diagram for use case 'Prepare for logging run'.

Model all direct and indirect actor–system interactions

A (if not *the*) central pillar of the OOAD process described here is one of development by elaboration. Hence the next stage of work is to extend the use case sequence diagrams to include the external devices, Figure 10.33. By comparing Figures 10.32 and 10.33, it can be seen that:

- All external components have been included as 'objects' on the sequence diagram.

- These now become the 'direct' actors.

- These direct actors interact with the system *software*.

- The operator becomes an 'indirect' actor, interacting indirectly with the software via the operator's control panel.

- The system 'bar' or lifeline on Figure 10.32 has now become the system boundary line in Figure 10.33.

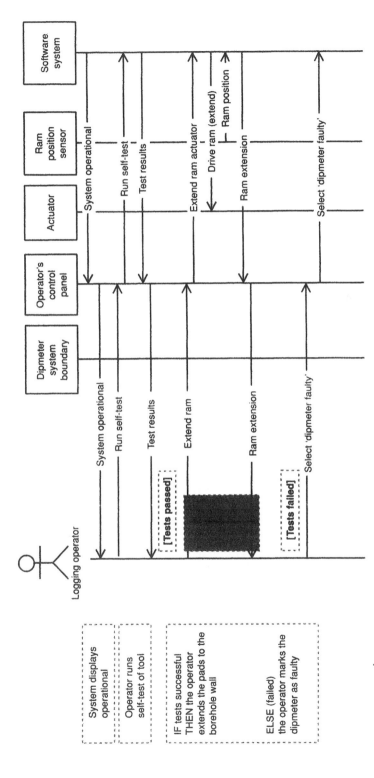

Figure 10.33 Dipmeter system actor–software interaction for the use case 'Prepare for logging run'.

- From the point of view of the operator actor the two diagrams are totally (i.e. 100%) consistent.

This process must be repeated for all use case scenarios.

10.4.4 Developing the subsystem structures

The purpose of this stage is to:

- Design the software system as a set of interacting (collaborating) subsystems.
- Define fully and in detail the *direct* actor interaction with the software subsystems.
- Define the interactions between the subsystems.

One outcome of this work is an overall system diagram, Figure 10.34, which also shows the subsystem organization. These have been devised using CRC techniques (details omitted).

Inter-subsystem communication and interactions are derived during the CRC sessions, being defined formally using sequence diagrams, Figure 10.35. Simultaneously, a subsystem collaboration diagram may be developed, Figure 10.36. This corresponds to the sequence diagram of Figure 10.35.

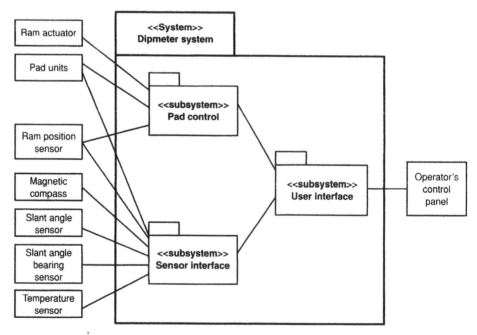

Figure 10.34 Dipmeter system – system and subsystem diagram.

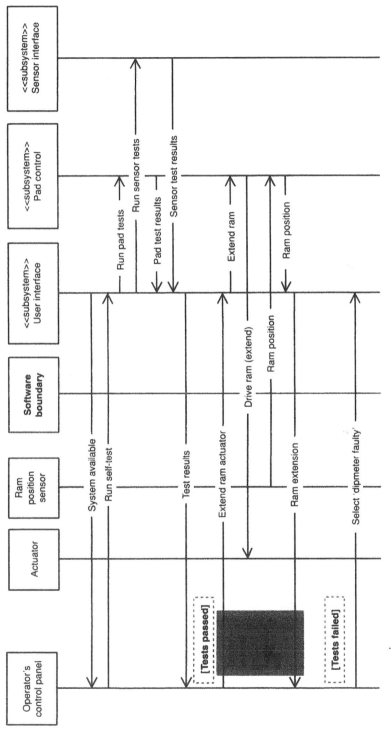

Figure 10.35 Dipmeter system actor–subsystem interaction for the use case 'Prepare for logging run'.

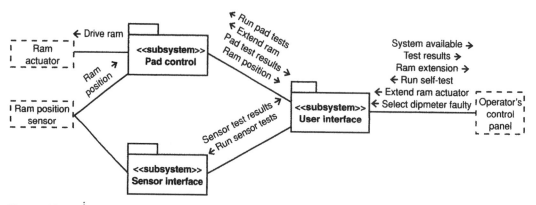

Figure 10.36 Dipmeter system – subsystem collaboration diagram (part).

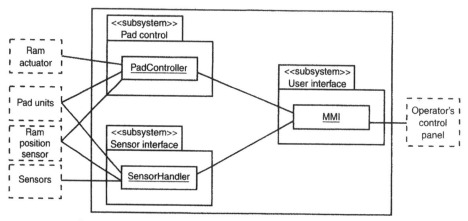

Figure 10.37 Dipmeter system: ideal model – initial object model.

10.4.5 Developing the ideal model object structures

The purpose of this stage is to:

● Design each software subsystem as a set of interacting (collaborating) objects, Figure 10.37.

● Define in detail the *direct* actor interaction with the software objects.

● Define the interactions between the objects.

● Allocate the objects to either the surface unit or the dipmeter (i.e. map the objects to processors), Figure 10.38a.

● Add communications (wireline network interfacing) objects as required, Figure 10.38b.

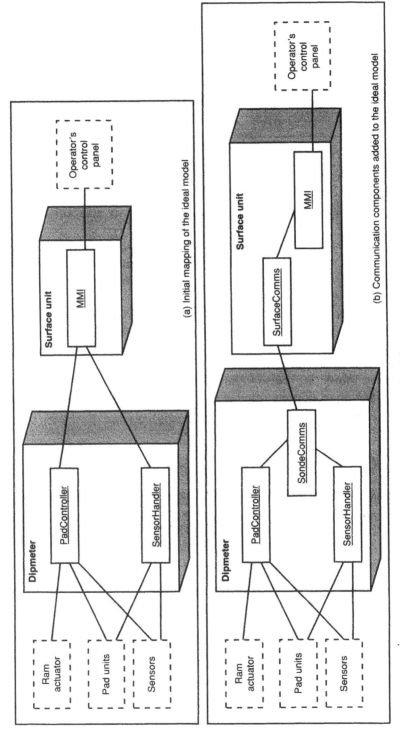

Figure 10.38 ┊ Dipmeter system — mapping of objects to processors (ideal model).

(a) Initial mapping of the ideal model

(b) Communication components added to the ideal model

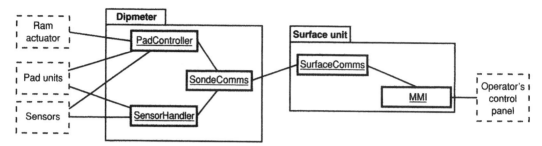

Figure 10.39 Dipmeter system: specification model – object diagram.

10.4.6 Developing the specification model object structures

At this point the objects need to be categorized as being active or passive, Figure 10.39. This structuring makes it easy to map the ideal object model to a practical tasking one. The next step is to extend the object diagram to the object collaboration diagram, Figure 10.40.

Implementing each object from the ideal model as an active object (as done here) is a simple, direct and effective technique. However, in many cases it may be necessary to form each active object as a composition of passive objects.

We are now in a position to develop the class diagram, Figure 10.41. By adopting an 'object-first, class-second' approach, the class diagram is essentially a classification of an existing viable software design. If appropriate the class structure can be further refined.

10.4.7 Developing the individual processor object models

Because the design has been partitioned, work can proceed on a processor-by-processor basis. Here we will look at the development of the *dipmeter* software only. Diagrams are produced as required by the design team, initially using information derived earlier. See, for example, the object collaboration diagram of Figure 10.42.

10.4.8 Developing the multitasking model

The purpose of this stage is to map the specification model into an implementation model. In this case it is assumed that the software will be implemented using multitasking techniques.

The resulting model consists of tasks and all necessary inter-task communication components, Figure 10.43. It can be seen that active objects have been mapped to tasks, the most straightforward approach.

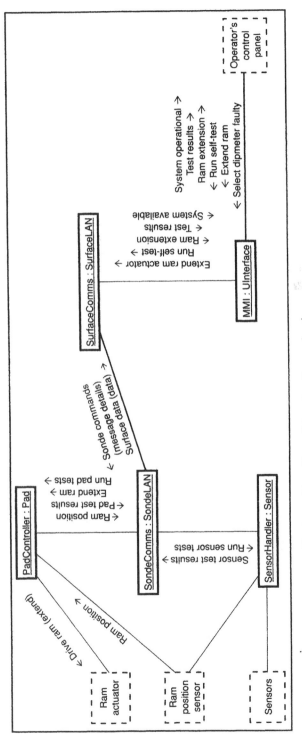

Figure 10.40 Dipmeter system: specification model — object collaboration diagram (part).

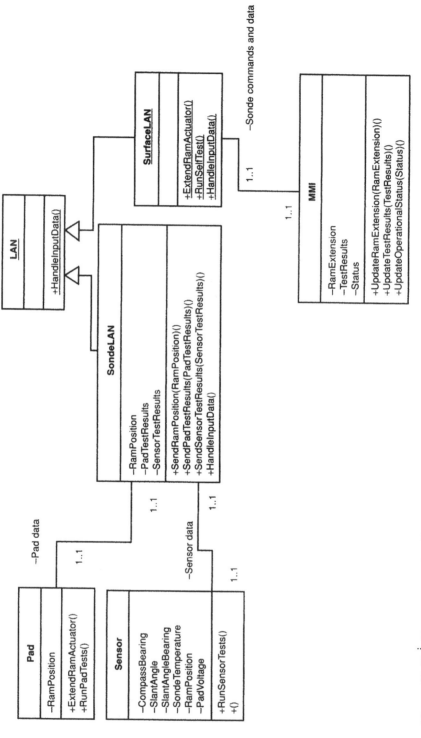

Figure 10.41 Dipmeter system class diagram (initial design).

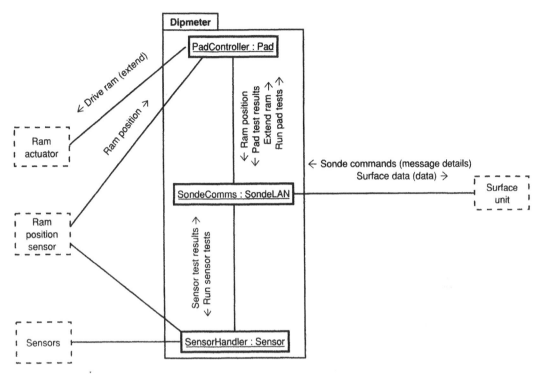

Figure 10.42 | Dipmeter: specification model – object collaboration diagram (part).

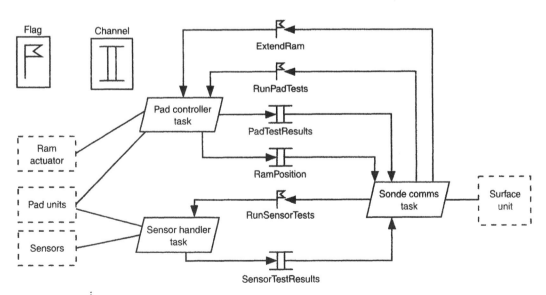

Figure 10.43 | Dipmeter – multitasking diagram (part).

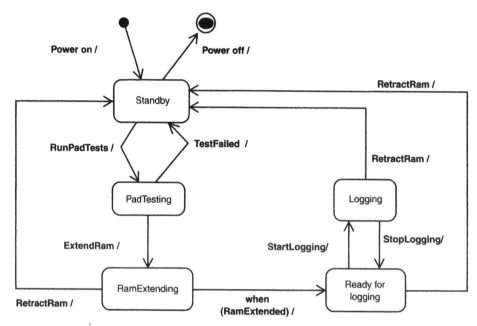

Figure 10.44 Dipmeter – state diagram for the pad controller task.

10.4.9 Developing the individual tasks

This is the final stage before coding the design. A number of techniques can be used at this point; the one demonstrated here is a two-step process:

- Develop the state model for the active object/task (these two are essentially the same given the design approach used here), Figure 10.44.
- Describe the processing carried out in each state using an activity diagram, Figure 10.45.

These, of course, are only part of the full set of state and activity diagrams.

10.4.10 Packaging the software

On completing class development, these 'application-level' classes should be packaged together in a logical manner, Figure 10.46. However, to implement the design fully it will be necessary to use many facilities provided by support – 'service-level' – software. Such software will normally be found in:

- Standard off-the-shelf packages and libraries.
- Company-specific standard packages and libraries.
- Project-specific/bespoke packages and libraries.

If appropriate, component diagrams may now be produced.

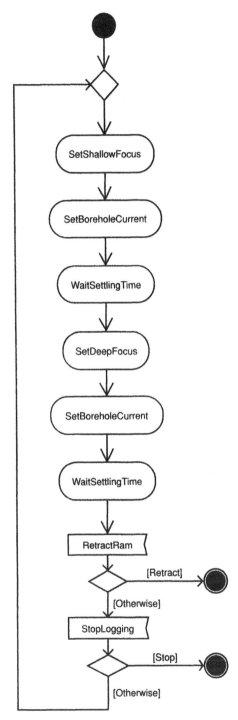

Figure 10.45 Dipmeter – activity diagram for the state 'logging'.

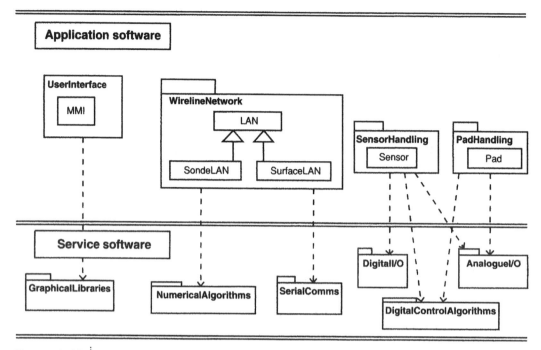

Figure 10.46 Dipmeter system – class packaging diagram.

Review

You should now:

- Understand the underlying concepts involved in translating specifications into practical designs.
- Be able to distinguish clearly between concepts, diagramming and processes when applied to software systems.
- Understand the fundamentals of Yourdon and OO software techniques.
- Have a general understanding of the diagrams used in these two methods.
- Appreciate that while design methods are frequently different their methodologies may be very similar.
- Realize that proper tools are needed to support diagram-based modelling techniques.

The closing message here is that there is only one real way to understand what's involved in the software design process: get out and do it. Taking just one project to completion using just one software tool provides significant insight and understanding – which can never be obtained from trawling through countless chapters like this.

References and further reading

[BOO99] *The Unified Modelling Language user guide*, G. Booch, J. Rumbaugh and I. Jacobson, Addison-Wesley, ISBN 0-201-57168-4, 1999.

[COO97] *Real-time software systems – an introduction to structured and object-oriented design*, J.E. Cooling, ITCP, ISBN 1-85032-274-0, 1997.

[DOU99] *Doing hard time: developing real-time systems with UML*, B.P. Douglass, Addison-Wesley, ISBN 0-201-49837-5, 1999.

[GOA93] *Software design methods for concurrent and real-time systems*, H. Gomaa, Addison-Wesley, ISBN 0-201-52577-1, 1993.

[HAT88] *Strategies for real-time system specification*, D. Hatley and E. Pirbhai, Dorset Publishing House, ISBN 0-932653-04-8, 1988.

[LAP99] *Real-time systems design and analysis – an engineers handbook, 2nd edition*, P.A. Laplante, IEEE Press, ISBN 0-7803-3400-0, 1999.

[SEL94] *Real-time object-oriented modeling*, B. Selic, G. Gullekson and P.T. Ward, Wiley, ISBN 0-471-59917-4, 1994.

[WAR85] *Structured development for real-time systems*, Vols. 1, 2, 3, P.T. Ward and S.J. Mellor, Prentice Hall, ISBNs 0-13-854787-4, 0-13-854795-5 and 0-13-854803-X, 1985.

[YOU89] *Modern structured analysis*, Edward Yourdon, Prentice Hall, ISBN 0-13-598632-X, 1989.

Analysing and Testing Source Code

Analysis is complete. Design is complete. Even more satisfying, coding (and debugging) is complete. So, where do you go from here? The logical step would seem to be to move on to code development in your target system. And that, in practice, is probably what most designers do. Now, this is fine provided the code is of first-class quality, having few errors. But what if that isn't the case? Well then, I'm afraid, you're in for a long, hard slog to:

- First, get the software running.
- Second, get the software running *correctly* – functional correctness.
- Third, get the software running correctly and delivering the required performance – functional *and* temporal (time) correctness.
- Finally, keep the software running properly as corrections and updates are made – stability.

The aims of this chapter are to:

- Explain the underlying concepts related to the software testing of source code.
- Describe the basics of static and dynamic analysis and show how they are used in the testing of software.

- Introduce code complexity metrics, in particular the Halstead and McCabe models.

- Show how complexity metrics are used for the evaluation of code qualities.

- Describe coverage analysis and its use as part of the dynamic analysis process.

- Illustrate test issues specifically related to object-oriented programming constructs.

11.1 Introduction

11.1.1 General concepts

Experienced developers know just how difficult things can be when testing and debugging software in the target system. Anything which makes life easier should be eagerly embraced. And one of the most sensible things you can do is also one of the most obvious (though that hasn't stopped generations of coders from ignoring such moves): simply eliminate problems *before* we go anywhere near the target system. The key to this is to do as much code evaluation and test as we can on the host system. But what precisely should we do and how should we do it? Interestingly enough, the answers can be found using a simple analogy to a normal real-life experience.

Imagine that you've saved enough money to buy a brand new car. Now comes the big decision: what to buy. Initial choices will, of course, depend on what the car is going to be used for – family carrier, farm workhorse, life-style accessory, etc. Most people will then take a long, considered look at the options, assessing the various models, asking questions like:

- How well has it been designed? Teutonic names are reassuring here.

- How well has it been built?

- How good is the material used in its construction (e.g. seat coverings)?

- How reliable is the model?

- How much will it cost to run, service and repair (cost of ownership)?

Most of this information can be found in manufacturers' literature and various motoring magazines.

You've now decided that a particular model is the one for you. Naturally, before you part with your hard-earned money, you'll want a test drive. This will give you a chance to assess:

- How well it lives up to its advertised features and functions (e.g. does it *actually* transport four adults in comfort?).

- How well it drives. What its acceleration, braking and road-holding are like.

- If there are any squeaks, rattles or unpleasant vibrations.

- If things drop off it as it drives along ('oh, there goes that hub-cap again').

Assessment points ▼ ▼ ▼ ▼	Vehicle factors assessed	Software factors assessed
1. Design quality	Design process used	Design process used
2. Build quality	Manufacturing processes	Language – quality and standards Coding – quality and standards
3. Material quality	Quality of raw materials and bought-in components	Language – quality and standards COTS software – quality and standards
4. Reliability	Design and build processes, material quality	Design process used Language – quality and standards Coding – quality and standards COTS software – quality and standards
5. Cost of ownership	Design and build processes, material quality, reliability	Design process used Language – quality and standards Coding – quality and standards COTS software – quality and standards
6. Function	Function	Function (functional correctness)
7. Behaviour	Drive-time behaviour	Run-time behaviour (functional and temporal correctness)
8. Unexpected behaviour	Squeaks, rattles, etc.	Side effects, unexpected software interactions, etc.
9. Unexpected costly and/or dangerous behaviour	Integrity of the vehicle and its component parts	Corruption of data, inconsistent behaviour, program hang-ups, etc.

Figure 11.1 Quality and performance assessment points.

Broadly speaking, the first set of items concerns the quality of the car; the second its behaviour. And we can directly relate these to software (Figure 11.1).

From this it can be seen that 'quality'-related items (points 1–5) can be assessed by analysing the available 'system' (vehicle or software) documentation. By contrast, to establish what a system actually does (points 6–9) we have no choice but to exercise it. Thus software evaluation consists of both analysis and test, as shown in Figure 11.2.

11.1.2 Software evaluation issues

The analysis activities denoted in Figure 11.2 are primarily designed to give us measures of code:

● Correctness

● Reliability

● Maintainability.

The behavioural aspects speak for themselves. Both activities are usually lumped together under the umbrella of 'software testing'. Where there is no confusion the same approach will be used here.

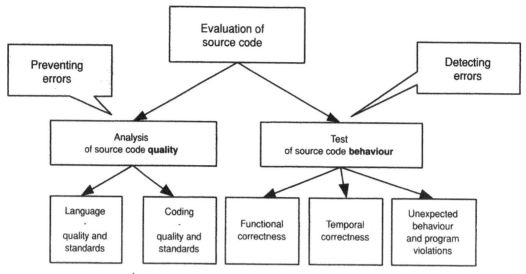

Figure II.2 Evaluation of source code.

Now, to evaluate the source code we need to somehow 'test' the design. And ideally we should be able to put some numbers on the results of these tests, i.e. produce quantitative results or 'metrics'. At the very least testing should show:

- The program fulfils its specification – VERIFICATION.
- The program performs the required task – VALIDATION.
- Modifications to existing good code don't produce errors (i.e. that the quality of the code hasn't regressed) – REGRESSION testing.

Which is fine, but it doesn't tell us:

- What *sort* of tests we should do and
- Having tested, what answers the tests will produce and
- How useful the testing is and
- When to stop testing ('enough is enough').

A moment's thought will show that the behavioural issues are quite different to the quality ones. The essential question raised here is 'does the design work properly?' Well, provided:

- We have a clear specification for the product and
- We test the design fully and correctly

then the answer is clear-cut: *yes, no* or *only partly*. The other points, in contrast, are much more subjective. What, for instance, is a reliable design. What is a maintainable design? Even if we agree on useful definitions (e.g. mean time between failures (MTBF),

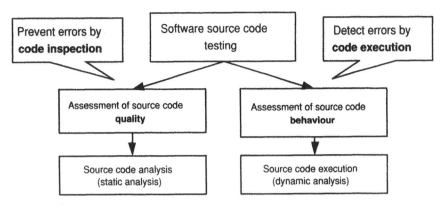

Figure 11.3 Software source code test techniques.

mean time to repair (MTTR)), how do we measure these attributes? Finally, how can we interpret the test results? These aspects are difficult enough when dealing with physical systems; when applied to the nebulous world of software things can verge on the impossible (but we have to do our best).

Software testing sets out to answer these questions using a variety of techniques, Figure 11.3. Quality features can be measured or deduced by inspecting the source code, assessing its features and looking for defects. This inspection technique is called *static analysis*. Second, we can test for defects by actually running the software – *dynamic analysis*.

11.1.3 Software testing – the broader issues

In very small projects the system-level code often consists of a single unit, even though the software may have been developed on a modular basis. In large systems, sizeable chunks of software are developed and coded separately by separate design groups. Integration is the process of combining these separate software units into a single composite item (Figure 11.4).

Individual software units, when tested in isolation, may work correctly. Unfortunately this is no guarantee that the total software package will do the same. Thus the basic function of integration testing is to verify that it does work as planned. Software testing, when applied to such structures, is a general activity which includes:

- Testing of individual software units.
- Integration of these into larger units.
- Debugging at all levels, from the small to the large.

All the techniques discussed earlier are applicable to this activity; it's just that the job is a more difficult one.

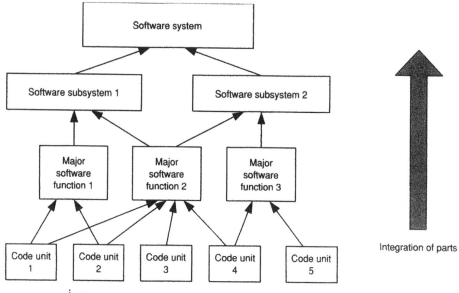

Figure 11.4 | Typical software structure of a real-time project.

11.2 Static analysis

11.2.1 Introduction

It is one thing to say that we need to evaluate code, quite another to decide exactly *what* to evaluate. The issues?

- Which code features *should* be assessed?
- Which code features *can* be assessed?
- What do the test results actually tell us about the quality, reliability, maintainability, etc. of the code?

The testing community generally agrees that the following items contribute to the quality of code:

- Overall program structure.
- Program design techniques.
- Code readability.
- Code complexity.
- Input/output dependencies within programs.
- Data usage within programs.

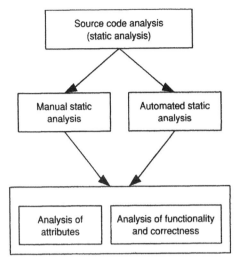

Figure 11.5 Static analysis techniques.

These features can be extracted from the source code itself. But, to properly assess them we also need to take into account the software development process itself.

The following sections deal with techniques that can be applied to most software projects. However, experience has shown that object-oriented programming methods bring with them some quite new problems (compared with procedural languages). These additional OO-specific issues are dealt with separately.

Static analysis as a source code assessment technique has been practised within professional software circles for some time now, Figure 11.5. The principles were adopted early on by the safety-critical real-time software community mainly using manual methods. Typical of these are the techniques described later in Section 11.2.2. However, manual methods have two drawbacks. First, they are time-consuming and manpower-intensive. Second, it may be quite difficult to properly assess the code (in other words, you think you've fully checked it out but in reality you haven't). Clearly automation would be a great help here, automated techniques being described in Section 11.2.3.

11.2.2 Manual static analysis methods

Manual analysis is an informal process. That is, it isn't defined using standard formal sets of rules or mathematical operations. Generally it consists of analysing programs by hand against particular design criteria. The following guidelines are typical of those used in manual static analysis checks. They don't claim to be comprehensive, and will probably need modifying to suit individual applications.

General

- Does the program fulfil (or appear to fulfil) its intended purpose?
- Can the input/output relationships be clearly established?
- Are unwanted relationships present?

Standards check

- Have the overall company design rules been complied with?
- Are the program constructs safe?
- Is the overall structure sensible?
- Are non-standard language features present?
- Have the project naming rules been adhered to?

Program and data structures

- Is all code reachable?
- Are all variables initialized before use?
- Are all declared variables used?
- Are all inputs read as intended?
- Are all outputs written to as intended?

For sequences:

- Are all statements listed in correct order?
- Are these executed *once* only?
- Are sequence groups executed from a single entry to a single exit point?
- Do the statements represent the solution to the problem?
- Does the order of execution produce the required result?

For iterations:

- Are the controlled statements executed at least once (post-check)?
- Can control pass through the operation without ever executing the controlled statements (pre-checks)?
- Is iteration guaranteed to finish (that is, are the loop termination conditions correct)?
- Has the correct number of iterations been carried out?
- Has the control variable been altered within the loop itself?
- What is the state of program variables on exit from an iteration?

For selections:

- Are all alternative courses of action explicitly taken into account (including answers that don't fit the question)?
- Are the alternative statements constructed using the basic structures of SP?
- Have the questions relating to sequential operations (and, where appropriate, iteration) been considered?

One small final point: ideally the analysis should be performed by an experienced designer, preferably one who wasn't involved in the original work.

11.2.3 Automated static analysis methods

Automated analysers attempt to answer the questions set out above but with minimum human intervention. The factors to be analysed can be grouped into two major categories: program attributes and program verification, Figure 11.6.
Program attribute analysers evaluate:

- Program structure (control flow analysis).
- Data usage (dataflow analysis).
- Information flow (information flow analysis).

Data obtained from the analyser may be used to assess the complexity of the program (expressed as a set of complexity metrics).
Verification analysers evaluate:

- Program functional relationships (semantic analysis).
- Program correctness (compliance analysis).

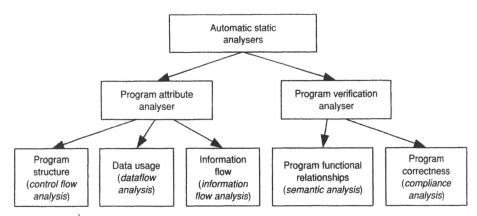

Figure 11.6 Automated static analysis tools.

Control flow analysis

The purpose of this test is to indicate the general quality of the software. It evaluates the control flow through the program, both locally and globally. It also assesses the use (or abuse) of the basic control structures (sequences, loops, selections). Results may be presented in flow-graph form, this being derived by:

- Identifying specific points within the program as nodes.
- Connecting these using arcs or edges.
- Labelling all nodes and arcs.
- Using this information as input to a graph-drawing package.

This is explained more fully in Section 11.3.3.
 The resulting directed flow graph:

- Illustrates program complexity.
- Identifies multiple entries and/or multiple exits from program control constructs.
- Indicates redundant paths or unused code sections.
- Shows unreachable code.
- Identifies dynamic halts in the program (black holes).

The results may also include a call graph display, showing procedure call sequences and structures.

Dataflow analysis

This analysis tool is used to check that data within the program is used correctly. Typically the following items are highlighted:

- Use of undefined variables.
- Uninitialized variables.
- Unused variables.
- Redundant operations (reads and writes).
- Data reads from locations not previously written to.
- Data reads and writes within the directed graph structure.

Information flow analysis

The objective here is to establish the dependencies between input and output variables. The information may be presented as follows:

From Node	To Node	Output Variable	Depends on (Input Variables)
BEGIN	END	StartPump OpenVent	LowOilPressure PumpSelect HighPressureAlarm

It also identifies:

- Unused data.
- Use of undefined data when forming output values.
- Use of incorrect input variables when constructing an output value.
- Specifying an incorrect output variable from specific input variables.

Semantic analysis

The semantic analyser determines the functional relationship between program inputs and outputs. It does this in two stages. First it derives all possible executable paths through the program. Then it applies the full range of input variables to these paths and evaluates the resulting output responses. Thus it is a primary tool for the verification of program code against its specification. It has another particular use – pointing up paths which the programmer may not have been aware of. In many cases such paths exist only for inputs which lie outside their normal range. The programmer should cater for such events using defensive programming techniques. However, if he hasn't, and should out-of-range inputs appear, the software response may be most unexpected (and even catastrophic). But by highlighting these at the analysis stage, disasters can be averted.

Compliance analysis

This is used to verify formally that a program conforms to its specification. Where discrepancies occur the analysis tool should identify the cause of such differences. The basis for the analyser is a comparison between a formal specification of the program and its performance (as deduced from semantic analysis).

The most common technique is to develop a formal specification of the program – typically using VDM, Z or OBJ (Chapter 13). This is input to the compliance analyser together with the output from the semantic analyser. By comparing the two, non-compliances of the program can be identified.

11.3   Source code metrics – code size, content and complexity

11.3.1   General

Software metrics are measures of various features of programs and their development processes. From a practical point of view – based on methods fairly widely used in real projects – measurable software attributes fall into two camps:

- Code size and content.
- Code complexity.

Source code size and content have a large bearing on development effort, object code size and programming time. Code size is probably one of the easiest things to measure, giving rise to 'line count' software metrics, viz.:

- Lines of code.
- Lines of comments.
- Lines of mixed code and comments.
- Lines left blank.

What these really tell you about your software is debatable. However, many companies have nothing else to go on, and use these (especially the lines of code number) to estimate:

- Programmer productivity and
- Number of potential errors present in the code.

Some very crude productivity figures obtained by surveying a number of projects coded in high-level languages are:

- Raw productivity, from initial code design concept to executable code: 50 lines per person per day.
- Overall productivity, high-quality commercial and industrial designs, taken over the complete project: 10–15 lines per person per day.
- Overall productivity, safety-integrity level (SIL) 3 software (see Chapter 13), taken over the complete project: 5–10 lines per person per day.
- Overall productivity, safety-integrity level (SIL) 4 software, taken over the complete project: 2–5 lines per person per day.

Error rates also depend on the nature of the software. Studies by the Carnegie-Mellon Software Engineering Institute indicate that a figure of 5.5 errors per 1000 lines of code is a helpful guide. For high-quality designs this is likely to fall to 2 errors per 1000 lines of code.

However, it is a much more challenging task to estimate:

- How difficult it is to understand code.
- The mental effort needed to code a program.
- The algorithmic complexity of code units.

Such factors form an integral part of Halstead's software metrics [HAL77], discussed in more detail in a moment, Section 11.3.2.

Complexity *per se* is a somewhat different beast. It is known, through practical experience, that bug-laden code is usually complex [WAT96]. Such programs are not only error-prone; they are also hard to understand, hard to test and hard to modify. So, the reasoning goes, if we reduce program complexity we should end up with better programs. In fact, practical experience [WAT96] has shown this to be generally true.

However, to establish a relationship between program quality and its complexity, we first need to define complexity. Many definitions are possible but here we will concentrate on one widely used, practical method; the McCabe cyclomatic complexity metric [MCC76], see Section 11.3.3.

In an ideal world software metrics:

● Could be applied uniformly across projects irrespective of their usage.

● Would be independent of the programming language used for coding.

● Would be independent of code textual layout.

● Would not be affected by the different methods used for the packaging of source code (e.g. Ada package, Java package, C++ file, etc.).

Unfortunately we still have some way to go to achieve this 'open systems' approach.

11.3.2 Halstead software metrics

Halstead's theory of software metrics [HAL77] has its roots in the evaluation of the complexity of low (e.g. assembly) level programs. It sets out to provide an indication of:

● Code creation effort (E).

● Algorithm complexity or intelligence content (I).

● Programming effort – time estimate (T).

● Code comprehension difficulty (D).

● Code comprehension effort (E_c).

● Overall program length (length estimate N_e).

● Number of bits – 'volume' – needed to code an algorithm (V).

● Minimum number of bits needed to code an algorithm (V_{min}).

● The 'inefficiency' or code bloat of a program – program level (L). This, for any given algorithm, is the ratio of the minimum code size required to that actually produced.

All are deduced from the following measurable qualities of the source code:

- Number of distinct program operators (n_1). This includes all control flow constructs, conditional operators and maths operations.

- Number of distinct program operands, i.e. all program variables and constants (n_2).

- Total number of operators used in the code (N_1).

- Total number of operands used in the code (N_2).

Halstead proposed that these be used to predict program features using the following equations:

(a) Length estimate $N_e = n_1 \log_2 n_1 + n_2 \log_2 n_2$

(b) Volume $V = N[\log_2 n]$ where $N = N_1 + N_2$ and $n = n_1 + n_2$

(c) Minimum volume $V_{min} = (2 + n_2^2)\log_2(2 + n_2^2)$

(d) Level $L = V_{min}/V$

(e) Level estimate $L_e = 2n_2/9n_1 N_2$

(f) Code creation effort $E = N_e(\log_2 n)/L$

(g) Code comprehension effort $E_c = N(\log_2 n)/L$

(h) Comprehension difficulty $D = 1/L_e$

(i) Intelligence content $I = L_e V$

(j) Programming time $T = E_c/S$ where S is a discrimination number based on Stroud's psychological theory, taken here to be 18.

The theoretical underpinnings of the Halstead metrics are somewhat suspect. They have, however, proved to be useful in practice, being one of the few techniques applied to real projects (and also supported by commercial tools).

11.3.3 The McCabe cyclomatic complexity metric

McCabe's model for software metrics, the cyclomatic complexity metric, was developed by Tom McCabe in the 1970s [MCC76]. The essential purpose of this metric (symbol $v(G)$) is to determine the complexity of a program unit or module. More precisely, it is a measure of the amount of *decision logic* contained by the module, Figure 11.7. In itself it doesn't identify problems or errors, but can indicate that there may well be some. Experience has shown that there is a strong correlation between $v(G)$ and code errors (see case studies in [WAT96]); thus it is a predictive measure of reliability. Fine. But what exactly *is* cyclomatic complexity?

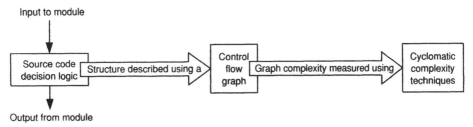

Figure II.7 : Basics of cyclomatic complexity.

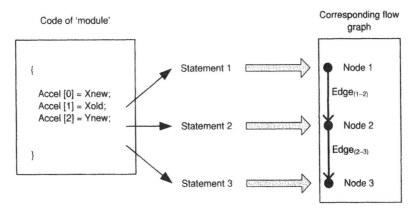

Figure II.8 : Control flow graph – simple sequence structure.

To answer that question we first need to define what a control flow graph is. Consider the code module shown in Figure 11.8. Here the code fragment represents part of a single program module which contains sequential code only (note that in C, for example, a module may be taken to be equivalent to a function). The flow of control through the program can be shown graphically as depicted in the diagram. Here each statement (or expression) maps into a node point in the flow graph. Transfer of control between statements is shown as a line or *edge* connecting the equivalent nodes. The resulting diagram is the control flow graph for that particular module. Please note: an essential requirement is that all such graphs have single entry and single exit points.

Now for the complexity issue. The cyclomatic complexity $v(G)$ is defined to be the number of *independent* paths through the control flow graph. According to McCabe it is calculated as:

$$v(G) = (e - n) + 2$$

where e = no. of edges, and n = no. of nodes. For our simple sequence example:

$$v(G) = (2 - 3) + 2 = 1$$

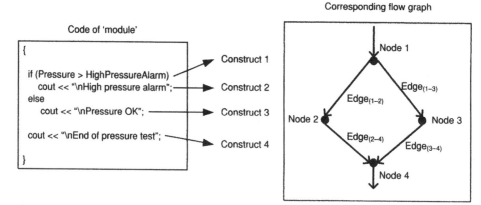

Figure 11.9 Control flow graph – simple selection structure.

In this (trivial) case we could have deduced the answer just by a quick inspection of the control flow graph.

A most important point: observe that the definition states 'independent' paths.

Moving up in complexity we have the simple selection structure of Figure 11.9. For this:

$$v(G) = (4 - 4) + 2 = 2$$

Again this is obvious by inspecting the flow graph (for simplicity the word 'construct' has been used to cover both statements and expressions). Now this example demonstrates a key point: the distinction between the number of independent code paths and the number actually traversed during code execution. Here, on any one run of the program, one, and only one, path can be executed, e.g.:

Run 1: actual test path 1: $N_1 \rightarrow N_2 \rightarrow N_4$
Run 2: actual test path 2: $N_1 \rightarrow N_3 \rightarrow N_4$
etc.

Thus a *single* test case will not fully execute the code; at least two (corresponding to two values of the Boolean test condition) are needed. The full set of independent paths is called the 'basis' set. Thus tests which execute the basis set are guaranteed to execute, at least once, *every* statement in the program. In other words, the basis set exercises all edges.

The third basic structure of structured programming is that of iteration or repetition, Figure 11.10. This particular version, a pre-check one, has a cyclomatic complexity of:

$$v(G) = (5 - 5) + 2 = 2$$

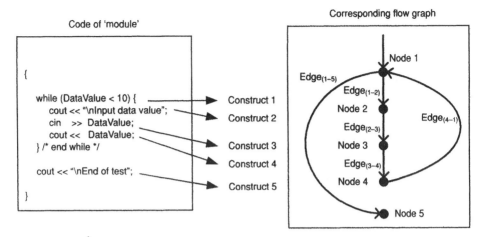

Figure 11.10 Control flow graph – simple iteration structure.

That is, there are just two independent paths. However, when the program executes many different paths could be taken through the program (the *actual* paths), depending on the data values, viz.:

Run 1: actual test path 1: $N_1 \to N_5$
Run 2: actual test path 2: $N_1 \to N_2 \to N_3 \to N_4 \to N_1 \to N_5$
Run 3: actual test path 3: $N_1 \to N_2 \to N_3 \to N_4 \to N_1 \to N_2 \to N_3 \to N_4 \to N_1 \to N_5$
etc.

However, only two tests are needed to execute all statements (correctly chosen, of course); any specific path is a linear combination of the basis paths.

As programs become more complex it is increasingly difficult to do this work manually; automation becomes essential.

Fine, we've measured the program complexity. But how does (or can) it help us? First, it can be used as a guide to program complexity. Second, it specifies the minimum number of tests needed to check out the software (the test coverage). If the number of tests performed is less than $v(G)$, then not all code statements will be executed.

Examples of flow graphs produced for real pieces of code are given in Figures 11.11 and 11.12. The graph of Figure 11.11 has been generated by a program which is long but structurally very simple. In contrast, that of Figure 11.12 has resulted from a relatively short but highly complex piece of code. These have been produced by the McCabe IQ^2 tool [MCC00].

A practical rule of thumb is that the cyclomatic complexity of software units shouldn't exceed 10.

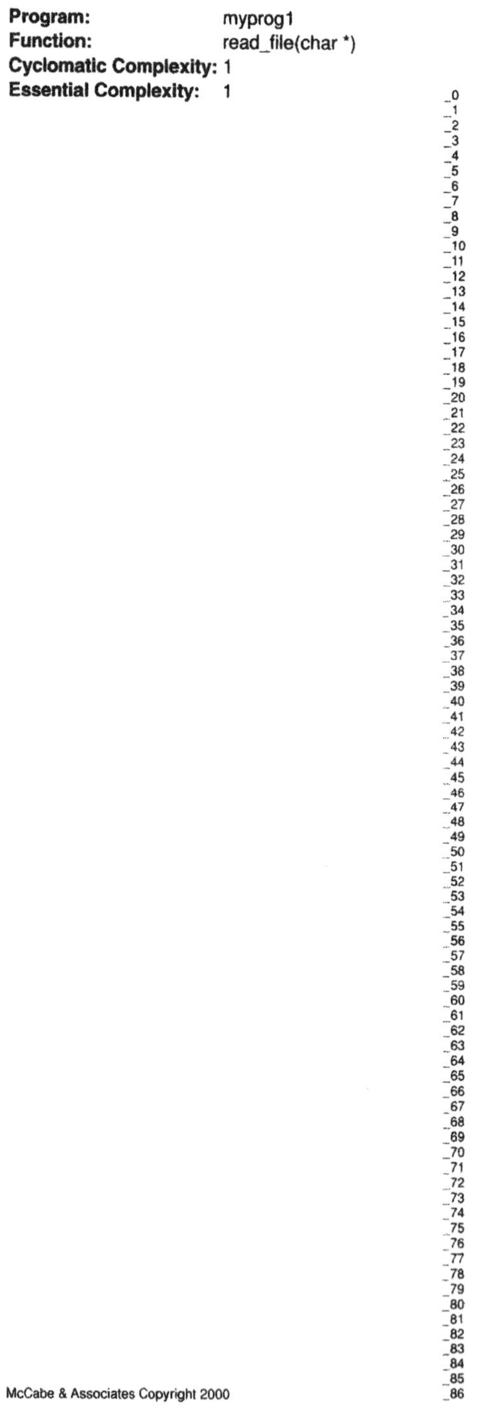

Program: myprog1
Function: read_file(char *)
Cyclomatic Complexity: 1
Essential Complexity: 1

Figure II.II | Control flow graph — simplest structure possible (courtesy of McCabe and Associates UK Ltd.).

Program: myprog1
Function: do_data(int)
Cyclomatic Complexity: 28
Essential Complexity: 1

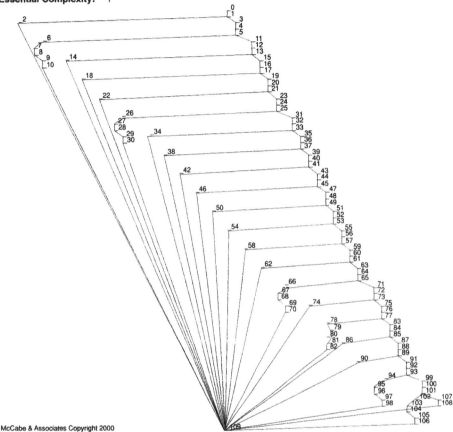

McCabe & Associates Copyright 2000

Figure 11.12 | Control flow graph — highly complex structure (courtesy of McCabe and Associates UK Ltd.).

 ## 11.4   Dynamic analysis – testing and coverage analysis

11.4.1   Overview of dynamic testing

Static analysis is a useful and effective way of producing high-quality code. Unfortunately it can't tell us precisely what the software will do when it's executed. Thus we have no choice but to resort to running the code itself – *dynamic testing*. Here we first look at some of the underlying concepts and practical problems of dynamically testing software. The following section deals with methods used to judge the *completeness* of such testing: *coverage analysis*. The two items taken together –

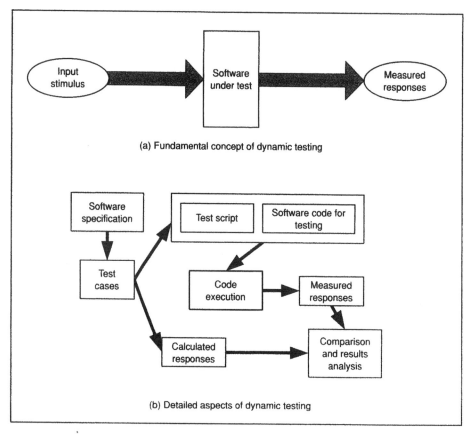

(a) Fundamental concept of dynamic testing

(b) Detailed aspects of dynamic testing

Figure 11.13 | Basis of dynamic testing.

dynamic testing and coverage analysis – are the component parts of dynamic analysis.

In real-time systems dynamic testing is widely used to check the behaviour of run-time software. The basic approach – shown in Figure 11.13a – is to:

- Stimulate the software to be tested and
- Measure the resulting responses.

From this we can at least check that the software actually *does* something and doesn't just fall over (producing, in the process, the really helpful 'this program has performed an illegal operation' message). Even so, we have no idea whether the responses are valid; thus these need to be checked against expected values. To generate such values we need to define the required behaviour of the software. And this can be done only if there is a clear *specification* for the software. Moreover, we may well need to subject the software to a series of tests or 'test cases' to fully exercise the code.

Taking these factors into account, practical dynamic testing consists of the items and processes depicted in Figure 11.3b. We proceed as follows:

(a) From the software specification, decide on the test case(s) needed to exercise the software.

(b) Develop a program – the 'test script' – to exercise the software under test.

(c) From the software specification and the test case information, calculate the expected responses of the software. This, of course, must take into account the input values used in the test.

(d) Run the software under the control of the test script, measure and record relevant responses.

(e) Compare the calculated and measured responses, flagging up errors if they occur.

A very simple example will help in understanding this process.

(i) Get the specification for the software: compute $y = 2x$, for positive numbers only, in the range $0 \le x \le 127$.

(ii) Select the required test cases: as there is only one path through the control flow graph, one test only is needed. The input test data should contain:
  - Valid numbers.
  - Invalid negative numbers.
  - Invalid positive numbers.

(iii) Develop a basic test script:

```
For ( x = -1; x < 129; x++)
  {
  cout << "\n y = " << y << " x = " << x;
  }
```

Now add to this the software to be tested, compile and execute.

(iv) Calculate the *expected* results.

Input value	Expected result
−1	Invalid
0	0
Selected x values	y as calculated
127	254
128	Invalid

(v) Compare actual with expected results.

Dynamic test methods are classified as either specification-based ('black box') or program-based ('white box') [GIL 83]. Two extremes of these groups can be easily defined. At one end, only the function of a program unit is defined; no information is available concerning its internal structure. This is a pure black-box item. Test conditions are thus set to evaluate the function in question. At the other extreme the complete program structure is known. Here white-box tests are devised to exercise both the overall function of the software *and* its internal details. In practice any software unit being tested will usually lie somewhere between these two end-points.

When devising a set of dynamic tests the following questions need to be considered:

- What input stimulus (test data) should be applied?

- What results should be produced (result predictions)?

- How should the actual results be compared with those expected (results analysis)?

- How should discrepancies be reported (fault diagnosis)?

- How effective are the tests (coverage analysis)?

- How do we measure software performance (performance analysis)?

- What sort of environment must be provided to support such testing?

11.4.2 Dynamic testing in a manual environment

Many software developers implement the test procedures manually (apart from executing the software, that is). A typical test document has the following format:

X. GENERAL
    X.1   General description and rationale of tests.
    X.2   Software resources needed.
    X.3   Hardware resources needed.

Y. TEST PLANS
    Y.1   Test 1.
    Y.1.1 Test conditions.
    Y.1.2 Input data.
    Y.1.3 Global data conditions.
    Y.1.4 Expected output data.
    Y.1.5 Expected procedure calls.
    Y.1.6 Expected global data conditions.
    Y.1.7 Special conditions for this test.

    Y.2   Test 2.
etc.

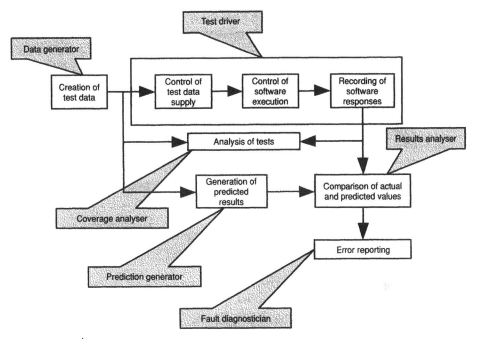

Figure 11.14 Specific aspects of dynamic testing – the test harness.

11.4.3 Dynamic testing in an automated environment

Dynamic testing may be carried out using fully automated test tools. At the core of such tools is a 'test harness', having the features shown in Figure 11.14. Please note: there are variations on this structure and organization.

Tests are carried out as follows. First the test data is created by a test data generator. This is applied via a driver unit to the software under test, subsequent responses being recorded. The input data is also fed to a prediction generator, which outputs a set of predicted responses. These are compared with the actual responses by a results analyser, errors being flagged up. Errors are further analysed by a fault diagnostician, which provides detailed information to help identify likely causes of code defects.

The input and output data, together with details of the test software, are also evaluated by a coverage analyser. Details of coverage analysis follow shortly.

Usually the harness is run on a host machine as part of a more general test tool. Such tools can provide a range of functions as, for example, those given in Figure 11.15. They may also include facilities to emulate target systems. Note that performance analysis done at this level operates on the emulated system. To obtain true performance figures, target system performance analysis tools must be used (Chapter 12).

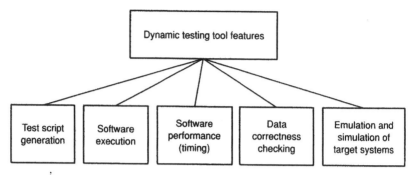

Figure 11.15   Features of general-purpose dynamic testing tools.

There are further advantages in using automated testing tools to record the test scenarios and results, including:

- Documented proof of testing.
- Ability to repeat tests in an identical fashion.
- Ability to (re)use the developed tests elsewhere.

11.4.4   Coverage analysis

You've just finished testing your software and it behaved flawlessly. Excellent. So now we can proceed to download it to the target system? Well, if you truly believe it to be error-free, yes. But how confident can you be that your tests haven't missed anything? Are there lurking bugs within, waiting to strike at the most embarrassing moment? Will particular inputs provoke erratic responses? It takes a brave (or foolhardy) soul to claim any software product to be totally bug-free. From a practical point of view the best we can do is to test it as extensively as possible. But, how extensive is extensive? To gauge this we require some measure of the completeness of our testing. This is where coverage analysis comes in.

The essential aim of coverage analysis is to show just how complete and effective our testing has been. You'll appreciate from Figure 11.14 that dynamic testing is primarily a black-box one. But to judge the extent (*how much*) and quality (*how well*) of these tests we need to look *into* the software. That is, evaluate the white-box aspects. Now, a brief sideways step. Suppose, for a moment, we set out just to perform white-box testing. Well, what testing would we do and why would we do it? Many of the answers can be deduced by reviewing the section on static analysis. It should be no surprise then that the items listed in Figure 11.16 are important ones for coverage analysis. What a coverage analyser sets out to do is really quite simple: to evaluate just how well the black-box tests have also performed white-

Objective of the white box test	Name
To exercise each statement of a program at least once. It is equivalent to traversing a path (or set of paths) through the full control flow graph of the code under test.	Statement testing
To exercise each branch in a program at least once (branching occurs at each decision point).	Decision or branch testing
To exercise all possible paths through the control flow diagram of a program.	Path testing
To exercise all logical conditions within a program.	Condition testing

Figure 11.16 Coverage analysis and white-box testing.

box testing. It does this by analysing the results of the tests and generating sets of coverage statistics. Using this information we can then decide whether the software needs further testing.

Please clear your mind on one important point. Coverage metrics are a *measure* of the effectiveness of testing techniques. They are not in themselves software test methods.

Automation of coverage analysis is essential to make it cost-effective for real projects. Thus it must be easy to automatically collect and analyse the required information. One set of tests that meet this criterion is given in Figure 11.16. Moreover, these particular ones are widely used (and often mandated for use) in critical systems. Observe they are a subset of structural coverage metrics based on control flow analysis. Each one has particular attributes, in particular the degree of the thoroughness of testing (see later).

Note: a mathematical definition of 'coverage': If a test actually executes n items out of a possible maximum of N, then:

Coverage $= n/N$

Statement coverage (Sc)

This is merely a measure of the percentage of statements executed during a test, expressed as:

Sc $= s/S$

where s = number of statements executed at least once and S = total number of statements in the code under test. The results highlight:

● Untested code.
● Unreachable code.
● Code errors not detected by the compiler.

To show some limitations of statement testing, consider the following code fragment:

```
CheckEngineSpeed;
IF HighSpeed THEN
  LimitFuelFlow;
END IF;
DisplayEngineSpeed;
```

If the test case sets HighSpeed to true then all statements would be executed. One test only is required. This, however, is exactly the same as testing:

```
CheckEngineSpeed;
LimitFuelFlow;
DisplayEngineSpeed;
```

No weight is given to the presence (or effect) of the Boolean operator HighSpeed. You could argue that it really makes no difference here. After all, our aim is to execute each code statement, not check the functionality of the program. And that we've achieved at the source code level. Unfortunately, the same may not be true of the object code.

Decision coverage (Dc)

This is a measure of the percentage of decision outcomes evaluated by a test case, expressed as:

$$Dc = d/D$$

where d = number of decision outcomes evaluated at least once and D = total number of possible decision outcomes in the code under test. For the code example above, $Dc = \frac{1}{2}$ (50%) as only one decision outcome was evaluated (HighSpeed is True). To achieve $Dc = 1$ (100%) then a further test case must be used with HighSpeed set to False.

If programs are designed using structured programming principles, then 100% decision coverage will automatically include 100% statement coverage.

Path (branch) coverage (Pc)

This is a measure of the percentage of paths executed by a test case, expressed as:

$$Pc = p/P$$

where p = number of paths executed at least once and P = total number of paths in the code under test.

If the tests execute all paths we can then say that:

- Every statement has been executed and
- Every decision (branch) point has been evaluated for both true and false conditions.

Code which contains multiple, interlinked iterations and selections is likely to contain an extremely large number of paths (see, for example, Figure 11.12). In such cases Pc may not be all that meaningful. Moreover, in practice, there is a high probability that many paths may never be executed ('infeasible' paths). Thus practical path coverage metrics usually consider a restricted – 'feasible path' – set.

Condition coverage (Cc)

This is a measure of the percentage of logical conditions (Boolean expressions) evaluated by a test case, expressed as:

$$Cc = c/C$$

where c = number of logical conditions evaluated at least once by a test case and C = total number of logical conditions in the code under test.

At first sight this might appear to do the same as path testing. However, the following example will show these are **not** the same:

```
IF AlarmInterlocksClear AND StartSelected THEN
  StartEngine;
ELSE
  ShowSystemAvailable;
END IF;
```

Path testing would indicate whether or not both branches had been executed. To achieve full path coverage two tests only are needed. This could be done as follows:

	AlarmInterlocksClear	StartSelected
Test 1	True	True
Test 2	False	True
Alternative test 2	True	False

However, condition coverage calls for all three tests to be performed. Thus the alternative test 2 would then have to be carried out. Clearly, condition testing is more rigorous than path testing.

Strictly speaking, this test evaluates the effects of changing the values of the Boolean operands. Thus it is also known as 'condition operand coverage'.

A more comprehensive test is one which accounts for all possible Boolean operand values, viz.:

	AlarmInterlocksClear	StartSelected
Test 1	True	True
Test 2	False	True
Test 3	True	False
Test 4	False	False

11.4.5 Practical automated dynamic analysis

The purpose of this section is to give an insight into practical techniques for dynamically analysing code. Specifically it shows how one particular tool, Cantata [CAN00], may be used to carry out dynamic testing and analysis of code. It also shows that static analysis can be readily performed by such toolsets. Figures 11.17 to 11.28 have been reproduced from material supplied by IPL Software Products Group.

Please note that other tools such as the McCabe IQ^2 tool can also carry out full automated dynamic analysis.

There are a number of distinct stages involved in the dynamic testing and coverage analysis of software, Figure 11.17. Let us initially deal only with the testing aspects and leave coverage to one side for a moment.

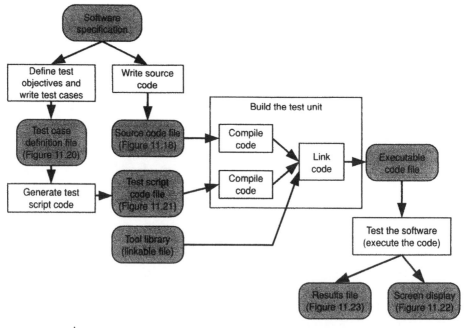

Figure 11.17 Basis of a practical dynamic testing tool.

Dynamic testing

The starting point for the work as a whole is to specify exactly what the software should do. For the example here the problem specification is as follows:

'Produce a C function which converts an integer to a hexadecimal, octal or decimal ASCII string'

From this starting point, two actions follow. First, a program is produced to meet this requirement, the outcome being the C source file Figure 11.18. The program

```
/*****************************************************************/
/* Convert Function
/* Converts integer to string format in DECIMAL, O TAL
   or HEX */
/* File: "CONVERT.C"
/*****************************************************************/

#include <string.h>
#include "convert.h"
#include "range_ok.h"

enum retcodes convert (enum bases type,  int number,  char *output)
{
  enum retcodes ret_val=0 K
  int no_of_digits;
  int base;
  int digit;
  int temp_number;

  char string[16] = {"          "};
/*
 * If number is outside valid range,  eturn error code of RANGE
 */
  ret_val=range_ok(number);
  if (ret_val == 0 K
  {
/*
 * Determine type of conversion to be performed
 */
        switch (type)
        {
          case 0 TAL:
                base=9;
                break;

          case DECIMAL:
                base=10;
                break;

          case HEX:
                base=16;
                break;
```

```
/*
Default case - Illegal conversion type specified
so return error ILLEGALOP
*/
        default:
                ret_val=ILLEGALOP;
                break;
        }
/*
 * If legal conversion type was specified,  do conversion
 */
        if (ret_val==0 )
        {
          temp_number = number;

          no_of_digits = 1;
          do
          {
                digit = temp_number;
                temp_number    /= base;
                digit = digit - ( temp_number * base );

 * Check whether Hex non-numeric character wanted
 */
                if (digit > 9)
                {
                  digit += ('A' - 16);
                }
                else
                {
                  digit += '0';
                }
          string [15-no_of_digits] = (char) digit;
                no_of_digits++;
        }
        while (temp_number != 0);

/*
 * Now output string
 */

        (void) strcpy( output,  (string + (16 - no_of_digits)) );
        }
    }
/*
 * Return error_code
 */

    return ret_val;
}
```

Figure 11.18 Specimen source code file.

Test number	Conversion type	Value	Expected string	Error code
1	Decimal	100	"100"	OK
2	Hex	100	"64"	OK
3	Octal	100	"144"	OK
4	Decimal	32,333	" "	RANGE
5	Invalid	100	" "	ILLEGALOP

Figure 11.19 : Test objectives.

convert is relatively simple but does contain deliberate errors. Second, a range of tests is defined and produced for validating the correctness of the software, Figures 11.19 and 11.20.

It can be seen from Figure 11.19 that five tests are defined. Three should produce valid (error-free) responses whilst two should generate error messages. At this stage it is concluded that these are sufficient to fully exercise the code. Figure 11.20 shows these tests formalized in a test case definition file. Observe that stubbing is used to emulate the external code in the file 'range_ok' (stubbing is frequently needed to emulate both the code and data of external units to permit units to be tested in isolation).

The next stage in the process is to generate the actual software for the testing of the source code. This, produced using the toolset facilities, is the test script code file, Figure 11.21. Shown here is only part of the full script (four pages of ten), showing just how much work is left to automation. Both the source code and test script files are compiled and then linked, together with files from the tool library. This produces an executable file which is run in order to test the software. Results are displayed on the screen of the host computer, Figure 11.22; at the same time a detailed results file is generated, part of which is shown in Figure 11.23.

The screen display is used for a quick check for test failures. Here it can be seen that there is a problem with test 3. The specific details of the problem can be seen in the results file. The expected value from test 3 was 144, but the actual item returned was 121. A check on the source code shows that for case 0 CAL the base was incorrectly set to '9'.

Once this is corrected, a re-run of the tests will produce a successful answer. Now we can move to coverage analysis to check whether our testing really is comprehensive.

Coverage analysis

To be able to do coverage analysis, we need to:

● Define which coverage tests are to be done ('analysis directives') and

● Modify ('instrument') the source code to include operations for performing the coverage work.

```
/*******************************************/
/* Test Cases Definition File For convert.c */
/*******************************************/
%%TEST_CASES 5

/*=============================== TEST 1
================================*/
%%CASE 1
%%COMMENT Decimal Conversion - passing 100

%%CALL convert range_ok#1

%%INPUTS
   convert_type    DECIMAL
   convert_number    100

%%0 UPUTS
   R_convert    O K
%%STCOPY M_convert_output    "100"

/*=============================== TEST 2
================================*/
%%CASE 2
%%COMMENT HEX Conversion - passing 100 -
expect '64'

%%CALL convert range_ok#1

%%INPUTS
   convert_type    HEX
   convert_number    100

%%0 UPUTS
   R_convert    O K
%%STCOPY M_convert_output    "64"

/*=============================== TEST 3
================================*/
%%CASE 3
%%COMMENT O tal Conversion - passing 100 -
expect '144'

%%CALL convert range_ok#1

%%INPUTS
   convert_type    O TAL
   convert_number    100

%%0 UPUTS
   R_convert    O K
%%STCOPY M_convert_output    "144"
```

```
/*=============================== TEST 4
================================*/
□
%%CASE 4
□
%%COMMENT Range Error
□

□
%%CALL convert range_ok#2
□

□
%%INPUTS
□
   convert_type    DECIMAL
□
   convert_number    32333
%%0 UPUTS
   R_convert    RANGE

/*=============================== TEST 5
================================*/
%%CASE 5
%%COMMENT Illegal O peration
%%CALL convert range_ok#1

%%INPUTS
   convert_type    33
   convert_number    100

%%0 UPUTS
   R_convert    ILLEGALOP

/*=============================== STUBS
================================*/

/*----------------- range_ok --------------------*/
%%STUB range_ok

%%ACTION 1              /* 100 passed in  */
%%INPUTS
   range_ok_number    100
%%0 UPUTS
   R_range_ok    O K

%%ACTION 2              /* Range Error  */
%%INPUTS
   range_ok_number    32333
%%0 UPUTS
   R_range_ok    RANGE

/*=========================== END  O F FILE
================================*/
```

Figure II.20 Test case definition file.

```
/*****************************************************************/
/*   IPL Cantata Test Script Generator (CTS) V1.0   */
/*     Copyright (C) 1994; IPL Information Processing Ltd */
/*****************************************************************/
/*      FILE NAME  : convert1.tc                              */
/*****************************************************************/
/*        Preprocessor Declarations                           */
#include <cth.h>
#include <stdio.h>
#include <string.h>
#include <string.h>
#include "convert.h"
#include "range_ok.h"
#define CTH_TOLERANCE 0.0001
#define CTH_MAPSIZE   16
#define CTH_TEMPSIZE   80
#define CTH_INIT(X)   memset((void*)&X,0x55, sizeof(X))
#define CTH_INIT_A(X) memset((void*)X,0x55, sizeof(X))
#define CTH_COPY(X)
        memcpy((void*)&E_##X,(const void*)&X,sizeof(E_##X))
#define CTH_COPY_A(X)
        memcpy((void*)E_##X,(const void*)X,sizeof(E_##X))
#define CTH_STCPY(X,Y) strcpy((char*)X,(const char*)Y)
static enum retcodes R_convert;
static enum bases convert_type;
static int convert_number;
static char *convert_output;
static char M_convert_output[CTH_MAPSIZE];
static enum retcodes R_range_ok;

static enum retcodes E_R_convert;
static char E_M_convert_output[CTH_MAPSIZE];
static int E_range_ok_number;
/*
 * Function Declarations
 */
static void cth_run_tests (void);
static void cth_init_global (void);
static void cth_init_exglobal (void);
static void cth_check_global (void);
/* Function: convert */
extern enum retcodes convert( enum bases type,  int number,  char *output) ;

void main(void)
{
   START_SCRIPT ("convert1",
        5 );
     cth_run_tests();
   END_SCRIPT();
}
/*************************************************************/
/* Tests Section                                            */
/*************************************************************/
void cth_run_tests (void)
{
```

```
/* Start of Test 1 ****************************************/
    START_TEST (1);
      cth_init_global();
    COMMENT( "Decimal Conversion - passing 100" );
      CTH_INIT (convert_type);
      CTH_INIT (convert_number);
      CTH_INIT (convert_output);
      CTH_INIT_A (M_convert_output);
      convert_output = &M_convert_output[0];
      convert_type = DECIMAL;
      convert_number = 100;
      cth_init_exglobal();
      CTH_COPY_A (M_convert_output);
      E_R_convert = 0 K
      CTH_STCPY(E_M_convert_output, "100");

      EXECUTE_BY_REF ( "convert",
              "range_ok#1" );
      R_convert = convert ( convert_type,
                    convert_number,
                    convert_output );
      DONE();
      CHECK_S_INT ( "R_convert",
              R_convert,
              E_R_convert);
      CHECK_MEMORY ( "M_convert_output",
              M_convert_output,
              E_M_convert_output,
              sizeof ( M_convert_output ));
    cth_check_global();
  END_TEST();

/**********************************************************/
/* Stubs Section                                        */
/**********************************************************/
enum retcodes range_ok( int range_ok_number)
{
   START_STUB ("range_ok");
     CTH_INIT (R_range_ok);
     CTH_INIT (E_range_ok_number);
   switch ( ACTION() )
     {
/* Action 1 */
     case 1:
     E_range_ok_number = 100;
     CHECK_S_INT ( "range_ok_number",
             range_ok_number,
             E_range_ok_number);
     R_range_ok = 0 K
     break;

/* Action 2 */
     case 2:
     E_range_ok_number = 32333;
     CHECK_S_INT ( "range_ok_number",
             range_ok_number,
             E_range_ok_number);
```

```
        R_range_ok = RANGE;
        break;
        default:
          ILLEGAL_ACTION ();
        break;
        }
      END_STUB ();

  return (R_range_ok);
  }*****************************************************/
  /* Data Initialisation and Check Functions                    */
  /*****************************************************/
  void cth_init_global (void)
  {
  return;
  }
  void cth_init_exglobal (void)
  {
  return;
  }
  void cth_check_global (void)
  {
  return;
  }
                                                    /* End of Test Script */
```

Figure 11.21 | Automatically generated test script code file (showing only 4 pages out of 10).

```
================================================================================
CTH v3.0          (c) 1993 IPL Information Processing Ltd
--------------------------------------------------------------------------------
Test Results For : convert1
Results File     : convert1.ctr
Tests Run At     : Tue Dec 12 20:36:12 2000
================================================================================
================================================================================
Tests Completed At: 20:36:12
--------------------------------------------------------------------------------
```

Test	Script Errors	Checks Passed	Checks Failed	Checks Warning	Stubs Failed	Paths Failed	Assertions Failed	Status
PTE	0	0	0	0	0	0	0	PASS
001	0	3	0	0	0	0	0	PASS
002	0	3	0	0	0	0	0	PASS
003	0	2	1	0	0	0	0	>> FAIL
004	0	3	0	0	0	0	0	PASS
005	0	3	0	0	0	0	0	PASS
ANS	0	0	0	0	0	0	0	PASS
Total	0	14	1	0	0	0	0	>> FAIL

Figure 11.22 | Screen display of test results.

```
================================================================================
CTH v3.0     (c) 1993 IPL Information Processing Ltd
------------------------------------------------------
Test Results For : convert1
Results File     : convert1.ctr
Tests Run At     : Tue Dec 12 20:36:12 2000
================================================================================
------------------ Start Test 001 ------------------
//Decimal Conversion - passing 100

     EXECUTE_BY_REF: convert,
          Expected calls = 1
        START_STUB : range_ok
        CALL_REF/ACTION: Action 1,  Call 1
        Check PASSED : range_ok_number = 0x00000064 100
        END_STUB : range_ok
DONE : convert
  Check PASSED : R_convert = 0x00000000 0
  Check PASSED : M_convert_output
------------------ End Test 001 ------------------

------------------ Start Test 003 ------------------
//O tal Conversion - passing 100 - expect '144'

     EXECUTE_BY_REF: convert,
          Expected calls = 1

      START_STUB : range_ok
      CALL_REF/ACTION: Action 1,  Call 1
      Check PASSED : range_ok_number = 0x00000064 100
      END_STUB : range_ok

     DONE   : convert
  Check PASSED : R_convert = 0x00000000 0

Chec k FAILED : M_c vent_o upt t>>
Item Address 187F:2D56  Expected Address  187F:2D6A
0 ffset= 0x 0
Expected 31 34 34 00 55 55 55 55 55 55 55 55 55 55 55 55   144?UUUUUUUUUUUU
Item     31 32 31 00 55 55 55 55 55 55 55 55 55 55 55 55   121?UUUUUUUUUUUU
         ^^ ^^                               ^^
16 bytes compared. A total of 2 bytes unequal.
------------------ End Test 003 ------------------
================================================================================
Tests Completed At: 20:36:12
--------------------------------------------------------------------------------
Test  Script  Checks  Checks  Checks   Stubs   Paths   Assertions  Status
      Errors  Passed  Failed  Warning  Failed  Failed  Failed
--------------------------------------------------------------------------------
PTE     0       0       0       0        0       0        0         PASS
001     0       3       0       0        0       0        0         PASS
002     0       3       0       0        0       0        0         PASS
003     0       2       1       0        0       0        0      >> FAIL
004     0       3       0       0        0       0        0         PASS
005     0       3       0       0        0       0        0         PASS
ANS     0       0       0       0        0       0        0         PASS
--------------------------------------------------------------------------------
Total   0      14       1       0        0       0        0      >> FAIL
```

Figure 11.23   Test results file (part).

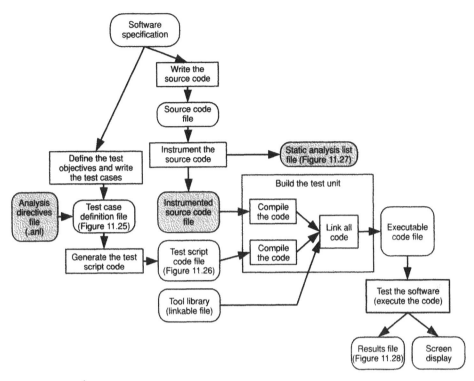

Figure 11.24   Dynamic testing and coverage analysis tool.

```
CHECK_ANALYSIS("Decision coverage",
        GET_ANALYSIS(CTH_FILESUT,
            "DECISION_COVERAGE"),
        95.0,
        100.0);

REPORT_FUNCTION(CTH_FILESUT,
        "ALL_STATISTICS");

CHECK_ANALYSIS("McCabe's Cyclomatic Complexity Measure",
        GET_ANALYSIS(CTH_FILESUT,
            "MCCABE"),
        1.0,
        10.0);
```

Figure 11.25   Analysis directives – dynamic analysis.

The overall change to the tool and process can be seen in Figure 11.24. The details of the required coverage tests are defined in an analysis directives file, Figure 11.25. Reference to this is included in the test case definition file, which is used to generate the test script code file as before, Figure 11.26. The source code is instrumented

```
/*****************************************************************************/
/*          IPL Cantata Test Script Generator (CTS) V1.0                  */
/*          Copyright (C) 1994; IPL Information Processing Ltd            */
/*****************************************************************************/
/*          FILE NAME   : convert3.tc                        */
/*****************************************************************************/


void main(void)
{
  START_SCRIPT ("convert3",
        5 );
  RESET_ANALYSIS();
  START_ANALYSIS();
    cth_run_tests();
  STOP_ANALYSIS();

CHECK_ANALYSIS("Decision coverage",
      GET_ANALYSIS(CTH_FILESUT,
           "DECISION_COVERAGE"),
      95.0,
      100.0);

REPORT_FUNCTION(CTH_FILESUT,
      "ALL_STATISTICS");

CHECK_ANALYSIS("McCabe's Cyclomatic Complexity Measure",
      GET_ANALYSIS(CTH_FILESUT,
           "MCCABE"),
      1.0,
      10.0);
  END_SCRIPT();
}

/*****************************************************************************/
/* Tests Section                                              */
/*****************************************************************************/
void cth_run_tests (void)
{
/* Start of Test 1 ***********************************************************/
```

Figure 11.26 Test script code file – dynamic analysis (part).

using the tool facilities, resulting in an instrumented source code file (detailed instrumentation code aspects are unimportant to the developer). As a quite separate aspect, the instrumented code can readily be statically analysed. Results are provided in a static analysis list file, Figure 11.27.

Having built the test unit the code may be executed. The results of the run are, as before, displayed on the screen and written to a results file. In this particular example the test coverage didn't meet the pre-defined lower limit of 95%, so a failure is flagged up. For brevity, only part of the test report is given here, Figure 11.28. From this it is clear that new (extra) test cases must be devised to raise the coverage level. Once this is done the whole test process must be repeated until results are satisfactory.

11.5 Integration testing

11.5.1 Fundamentals

The basic ideas of software integration and integration testing were spelt out earlier in Section 11.1. Let us return to this issue, to look at the general aspects of the testing of integrated units. The ideas are generally applicable to all the levels and units of software shown in Figure 11.4. In practice a variety of units are likely to be used, including software machines, modules, objects, components and tasks. The one item which stands out as being different is an object *within an inheritance structure*; this is dealt with separately in the section on OO testing. Clearly, test details will depend on the precise nature of the individual software units.

Three integration techniques in general use are the:

- Big-bang approach. All integration and test is done in a single phase.
- Top-down incremental route.
- Bottom-up incremental path.

The big-bang method has been pretty well discredited for many years (but that doesn't stop people using it). In mainstream professional practice, however, integration is usually a mix of some top-down and a lot of bottom-up working.

With hierarchical structures, top-level units (clients) use features of lower-level ones (servers). To allow top-down testing to proceed in an orderly fashion, it is usual, initially, to emulate lower-level units. As mentioned earlier, these are called 'stubs'. The basic design criterion for stubs is quite simple: the client shouldn't be able to tell whether it's using a stub or a real unit. In such cases testing concentrates on the functionality of the client unit and its interactions with the servers. This also ensures that the interfaces (both required and provided) are correct. Valuable as this work is, it is just one step in the overall test process. Until testing is done using real units, the test results can give only limited confidence. In particular, it is only by testing with the full code that we obtain credible performance figures.

```
****************************************************************
* IPL Cantata Instrumenter (CTI) V3.0                    *
* Copyright (C) 1993: IPL Information Processing Ltd
****************************************************************
* Source File  : convert3.c                              *
* List File     : convert3.ctl                            *
* Created At    :
****************************************************************
Instrumented For :

                    Function Entry Points
                    Decision Coverage
                    Boolean Expression Coverage
                    Statement Coverage
                    Call Pair Coverage
                    Dynamic Assertion Coverage
                    Data Coverage Assertions
                    Path Checking
                    Test Code
                    Complexity Metrics

*******************************************
Static Analysis Measures for "convert3.c convert"
SOURCE_LINES                   85
CODE_LINES                     51
COMMENT_LINES                  21
BLANK_LINES                    13

EXPRESSION_STATEMENTS          15
FOR_LOO PSTATEMENTS             0
WHILE_LOO PSTATEMENTS           0
DO_LOO PSTATEMENTS              1
IF_STATEMENTS                   3
SWITCH_STATEMENTS               1
RETURN_STATEMENTS               1
GOTO_STATEMENTS                 0
BREAK_STATEMENTS                4
CONTINUE_STATEMENTS             0
NULL_STATEMENTS                 0
INIT_STATEMENTS                 2

STATEMENTS                     27
DECLARATIONS                    6
COMMENTS                        7

ARITHMETIC_O PRATORS             6
RELATIONAL_O PRATORS             4
LOGICAL_O PRATORS                0
INC_DEC_O PRATORS                1
BITWISE_O PRATORS                0
```

```
ASSIGN_O ERATORS                      15
ADDRESS_O ERATORS                      1
O HER_O ERATORS                        4
TOTAL_O ERATORS                       31

MAXIMUM_NESTING_LEVEL                  4
AVERAGE_NESTING_LEVEL               1.93

CASE_LABELS                            4
GOTO_LABELS                            0
DECISION_O UCOMES                     12
ASSIGNMENTS                           15
FUNCTION_CALLS                         2
SWITCH_STATEMENTS_NO_DEFAULTS          0
UNREACHABLE_CODE                       0

MCCABE                                 8
ESSENTIAL_MCCABE                       1
MYERS_MCCABE_LOWER                     8
MYERS_MCCABE_UPPER                     8

HANSEN_CYCLOMATIC_NUM                  6
HANSEN_O ERATOR_COUNT                 25

HARRISON_SCOPE_RATIO                0.65

HALSTEAD_NUM_UNIQUE_O ERATORS         19
HALSTEAD_TOTAL_NUM_O ERATORS          71
HALSTEAD_NUM_UNIQUE_O ERANDS          26
HALSTEAD_TOTAL_NUM_O ERANDS           52
HALSTEAD_LENGTH                      123
HALSTEAD_VOCABULARY                   45
HALSTEAD_EXPECTED_LENGTH             203
HALSTEAD_PURITY_RATIO               1.65
HALSTEAD_VOLUME                      675
HALSTEAD_ESTIMATED_ERRORS           0.21
HALSTEAD_POTENTIAL_VOLUME          15.51
HALSTEAD_BOUNDARY_VOLUME           25.85
HALSTEAD_LEVEL_O FABSTRACTION       0.02
HALSTEAD_EST_LEVEL_ABSTRACTION      0.05
HALSTEAD_PROGRAM_EFFORT            29420
HALSTEAD_TIME_ESTIMATE             1634
HALSTEAD_DIFFICULTY                43.55
HALSTEAD_LANGUAGE_LEVEL             0.36
HALSTEAD_INTELLIGENCE_CONTENT      35.55

CLASSES                                0
NEW                                    0
DELETE                                 0
THROW                                  0
TRY_CATCH                              0
ANONYMOUS_UNIONS                       0
```

```
PARAMETERS                      3
UNUSED_PARAMETERS               0
AUTOMATICS                      6
STATICS                         0
UNUSED_DATA                     0
LOCAL_TYPES                     0
UNUSED_LOCAL_TYPES              0


== O verall  Measures For  The  File  =======


FILE_SOURCE_LINES             109
FILE_CODE_LINES                52
FILE_COMMENT_LINES             36
FILE_BLANK_LINES               18
FILE_STATEMENTS                27
FILE_DECLARATIONS               7


FILE_COMMENTS                  18
FILE_FUNCTIONS                  1
IGNORED_SEQUENCES               0
USER_METRIC_1          NOT  PRESENT
USER_METRIC_2          NOT  PRESENT
USER_METRIC_3          NOT  PRESENT
USER_METRIC_4          NOT  PRESENT
USER_METRIC_5          NOT  PRESENT
USER_METRIC_6          NOT  PRESENT
USER_METRIC_7          NOT  PRESENT
USER_METRIC_8          NOT  PRESENT
TEST_CODE                       0
FILE_CHECKSUM          1231103581
FILE_CLASSES                    0
FUNCTION_CLASSES                0
FILE_FRIENDS                    0
FUNCTIONS_IN_CLASSES            0
PURE_VIRTUAL_FUNCTIONS          0
NESTED_TYPES                    0
TEMPLATES                       0
O ERLOADED_O ERATORS            0
FUNCTIONS_WITH_THROW            0
FILE_ANONYMOUS_UNIONS           0
GLOBALS                         0
UNUSED_GLOBALS                  0
GLOBAL_TYPES                    0
UNUSED_GLOBAL_TYPES             0
*************************************************
```

Figure II.27 Static analysis list file – dynamic analysis (part).

```
=======================================================
CTH v3.0   (c) 1993 IPL Information Processing Ltd
-----------------------------------------------------
Test Results For  :  convert3
Results File      :  convert3.ctr
Tests Run At      :  Wed Dec 13 10:45:29 2000
=======================================================


   GET_ANALYSIS: convert3.c convert
        DECISION_COVERAGE =    91.67

   CHECK_ANALYSIS: Decision coverage
        >> FAILED
          Lower limit   = 95.00
          Upper limit   = 100.00
          Analysis value = 91.67

   REPORT_FUNCTION: convert3.c convert
        ALL_STATISTICS


+++++++++++++++++++++++++++++++++++++++++++++
   Analysis Report:
Function    convert3.c convert
+++++++++++++++++++++++++++++++++++++++++++++

DECISION STATISTICS REPORT

Decision no Line no Type  No of outcomes Breakdown

   3      69   if     2     TRUE:    3
                            FALSE:   1


   4      83   if     2     TRUE:    0 >> NOT EXECUTED
                            FALSE:   8


Total of decision outcomes = 12
Total outcomes exercised at least once = 11

Decision coverage = 91%
>> WARNING: DECISION COVERAGE INCOMPLETE

STATEMENT STATISTICS REPORT

Statement no   Line no   type        No of executions   Execution profile
   1           26        assignment  5                  ************

   4           39        if          5                  ************
   21          85        expression  0                  >> NOT EXECUTED
   22          89        expression  8                  ********************
```

```
Total of possible statements = 27
Total statements exercised at least once = 26

Statement coverage = 96%
>> WARNING: STATEMENT COVERAGE INCOMPLETE


Boolean Statistics Report not generated - no boolean expressions in function

Assertion Statistics Report not generated - no coverage assertions in function

CALL PAIR STATISTICS REPORT


Call pair no    Line no    No of executions
     1             38       5
     2             100      3


Total number of call pairs = 2
Total number of call pairs executed = 2

Call pair coverage = 100%
++++++++++++++++++++++++++++++++ END O F REPORT

   GET_ANALYSIS: convert3.c convert
         MCCABE =      8.00

   CHECK_ANALYSIS: McCabe's Cyclomatic Complexity Measure
         PASSED
         Lower limit   = 1.00
         Upper limit   = 10.00
         Analysis value = 8.00
```

===
Tests Completed At: 10:45:29

Test	Script Errors	Checks Passed	Checks Failed	Checks Warning	Stubs Failed	Paths Failed	Assertions Failed	Status
PTE	0	0	0	0	0	0	0	PASS
001	0	3	0	0	0	0	0	PASS
002	0	3	0	0	0	0	0	PASS
003	0	3	0	0	0	0	0	PASS
004	0	3	0	0	0	0	0	PASS
005	0	3	0	0	0	0	0	PASS
ANS	0	1	1	0	0	0	0	>> FAIL
Total	0	16	1	0	0	0	0	>> FAIL

===

Figure II.28 Test results file — dynamic analysis (part).

With a bottom-up approach, testing at the lowest levels is concerned with two aspects:

- Program-related (compilation) issues.
- Functionality and performance.

The first point includes items such as correctness of interfaces, exported and imported data types, name clashes, etc. The second aspect is self-explanatory.

One further requirement often met in developing the lower-level units is the need to use stubs. This, at first, might seem surprising – until you implement a practical, structured design. It comes about because units at the same level in the hierarchy ('siblings') may well interact with each other (and with service or library units, of course).

11.5.2 Integration and test strategies (1) – combined module and integration testing

One of the simplest test strategies is *not* to do separate module and integration testing; instead combine the activities. This can be used with bottom-up integration, as illustrated in Figure 11.29. Here, to begin with, test scripts are prepared for each lowest-level unit (e.g. unit A1). Remember that the actual test code is generated from these scripts. In the first phase of testing (Figure 11.29, tests 1(a) and 1(b)), the individual units are analysed and tested as described in earlier sections. When this is completed, we proceed to the second phase of testing, test 2, Figure 11.29. For this a script is produced (and code generated) to test the combination of units A, A1 and A2; that is, when A1 and A2 are being integrated with A.

For test phase 1 the minimum number of tests to be done is:

$T_n = v(A1) + v(A2)$ (the sum of the cyclomatic complexity of the individual units)

For phase 2:

$T_n = v(A1) + v(A2) + v(A)$ (the sum of the cyclomatic complexity of *all* modules being integrated)

The process described here is repeated until all software units are fully integrated.

The advantages of this method are twofold. First, there is no need to produce stubs as with a top-down method. Second, the testing of the high-level unit automatically includes integration testing (with a top-down approach, separate unit and integration testing is required). However, there is a penalty to be paid for using this technique: redundancy of testing activities. As the hierarchy levels increase there is a rapid increase in the amount of testing needed. And unfortunately much of it retreads old ground in the lower-level units.

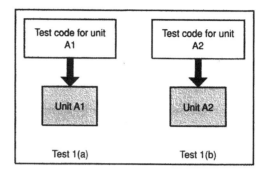

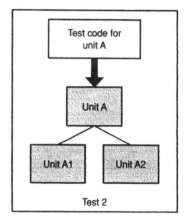

Figure 11.29 Combining unit and integration testing.

11.5.3 Integration and test strategies (2) – integration testing based on unit calls

Having distinct unit and integration testing has one great benefit: integration tests need only concern themselves with interactions *between* the units. Activities within units *not* involved with calls can be eliminated from the unit flow graphs (for integration testing only, of course). The basic idea is to:

(a) Draw the full control flow graph of the unit, then

(b) Produce a reduced control flow graph by removing all control structures which are not concerned with external units.

This results in a simpler or 'reduced' flow graph, a *design reduction* technique. To minimize the work effort, use *this* graph to define the nature and amount of integration testing. An example of reduction applied to a simple problem is that of

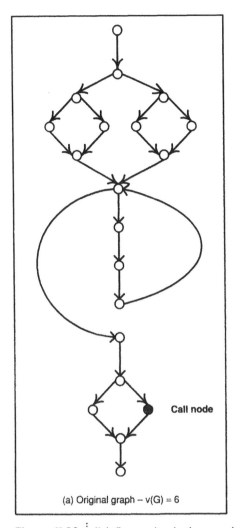

(a) Original graph – v(G) = 6

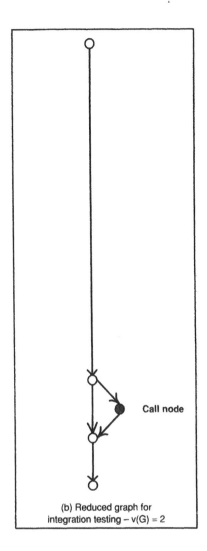

Call node

(b) Reduced graph for
integration testing – v(G) = 2

Figure 11.30 | Unit flow graph reduction example.

Figure 11.30. Note that when an external unit makes a call into this module, it is denoted as a 'call node'.

For details of this technique, and the reduction rules involved, see the paper by Watson and McCabe [WAT96].

These ideas should be supported by integrating units in an incremental fashion. That is, integrate a sensible number of units at any one time. This, of course, is fairly straightforward with well-structured software. Moreover, apply the following golden rule at each integration stage: *test only the interaction between the units being integrated*. As a result previously integrated subunits do not need (re)testing.

11.5.4 Integration complexity

Integration complexity (Si) is the measure of the minimum number of *independent* integration tests required when building a software system. McCabe [MCC89] defines it, for an *n*-unit structure, as:

$$Si = \sum_{j=1}^{j=n} [iv(G_j) - n + 1]$$

where

- *n* is the number of units being integrated
- $iv(G_j)$ is the cyclomatic complexity of the reduced flow graph of unit *j* (*j* lying in the range 1 to *n*).

Probably the best use of this metric is for predicting test effort prior to actual coding. Unfortunately, for the numbers to have any real value, the software design needs to be a well-structured one.

11.6 Metrics for OO designs

11.6.1 General aspects

Experience gained in recent years has shown that OO designs bring new problems to the testing process. As shown in Figure 11.31, whether we're dealing with classes (objects) or systems, three aspects are central to the design: structure, dynamics and function.

From an overall perspective, testing is much the same for all systems structured as sets of software machines – *with one proviso*. If the machines are OO objects *and* inheritance is used, then new, significant factors come into play. Many specific issues are discussed in the following sections.

As portrayed here, system-level testing is akin to integration testing. Here facets such as:

- Coupling between objects
- Responses to messages
- Methods available (which impacts on the first two points)

are going to have a major effect on the amount of testing needed. From such testing we can, as before, establish:

- Overall functional behaviour.
- Overall dynamic behaviour.
- Overall performance.

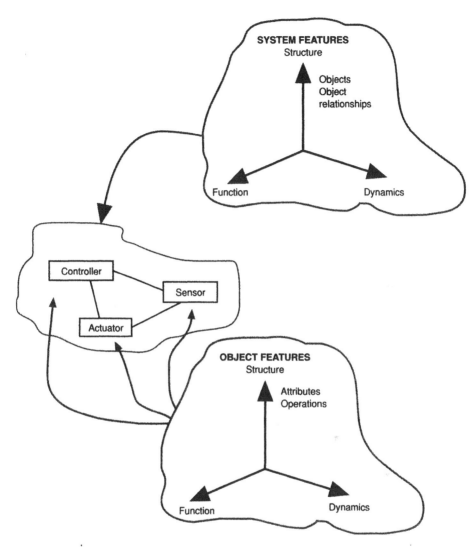

Figure 11.31 System and class (object) features.

It is at the individual class and object level that significant new test requirements (and associated metrics) arise. Amongst the first to publish metrics for OO design were Chidamber and Kemerer [CHI94]. The metric set they devised (now used in many toolsets) comprises:

● Weighed methods per class (WMC).

● Depth of inheritance tree (DIT).

● Number of children (NOC).

● Coupling between objects (CBO).

- Response for a class (RFC).
- Lack of cohesion for methods (LCOM).

WMC

WMC is related to the number of methods in a class and their complexity. The assumption is that the more methods a class contains the more complex it is. Likewise, as methods become more complex, so too do the classes. The 'weight' of the method relates to its complexity.

DIT

DIT, for classes using inheritance, is concerned with the number of levels in the inheritance structure. It is assumed that as the depth increases, so too does the complexity of the classes (as a result of inheriting methods and/or attributes). This is likely to produce a class structure which generates many interfaces, each requiring testing.

NOC

NOC is a measure of the number of *direct* descendants (subclasses or children) of a (super)class. In any inheritance structure, changes made in a superclass affect all subclasses. Therefore, as the number of children increases, so too do the effects of the changes (the re-test effort may be substantial). Thus, it is reasoned, complexity increases in proportion to the number of children.

CBO

CBO is a count of the number of classes to which a given class is coupled (i.e. it is a measure of coupling). As class coupling increases, so too does the complexity of the static structure.

RFC

RFC is a count of the number of methods that could potentially be executed in response to a message (a specially thorny issue where inherited methods are used). As this number increases, so too does the complexity of the class.

LCOM

LCOM is related to the number of *different* methods in a class that share internal data items. Such sharing, it is deduced, reduces method cohesion.

To this list we can add a few simple but useful metrics which are related to code size:

- Lines of code per class (LOC).
- Attributes defined per class (AD).
- Methods defined per class (MD). This may be treated as a simpler version of WMC.

Metrics used to give an indication of the quality of class encapsulation are:

- Method hiding factor (MHF).
- Attribute hiding factor (AHF).

MHF

MFH is a measure of the percentage of class methods which are private. Thus it is an indication of the amount of hidden functionality, i.e. that which cannot be exercised *directly* by black-box testing. This can lead to significant test problems in certain cases, e.g. faults found with service and library classes.

AHF

AHF is a measure of the amount of class data made public. The use of public attributes indicates suspect encapsulation.

In the very broad scheme of things, we can use these metrics for a variety of purposes, as shown in Figure 11.32.

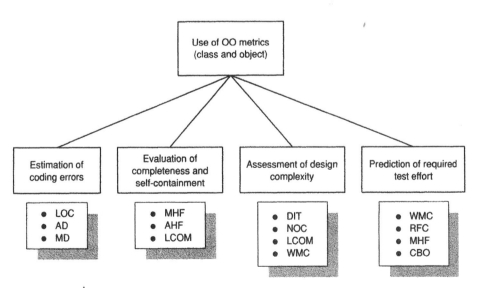

Figure 11.32 Use of OO metrics.

11.6.2 Inheritance, polymorphism and testing issues

The central point here can be explained simply by reference to Figure 11.33. Figure 11.33a depicts a single class, without inheritance. To simplify the explanation, it is shown as having only one public method. When a message is sent to an object of the class, it invokes the method ShowData. The corresponding flow of control in the object may be represented by a simple action (i.e. a single node point on a flow graph). Now look at the class diagram of Figure 11.33b, where inheritance is used. Here the base class is an abstract one, having three subclasses: SpeedClass, HeightClass and AttitudeClass. The base class defines the public interface but the concrete versions are provided by the subclasses. As pointed out in Chapter 4, this is a case of dynamic polymorphism, which involves hidden decision-making. The logic related to the call of SomeObject.ShowData is shown in Figure 11.3b, being generated by the compiler.

In a real system we could have the situation depicted in Figure 11.34 where we have one object for each sensor subclass. How do we go about testing this? A full and comprehensive test strategy requires that *all* calls are exercised, Figure 11.35a. Each client interacts with all sensor objects. This, sometimes called a pessimistic strategy, can be summed up as 'I don't trust *anything*'. Its strength is that you can put complete trust in the results; the downside, however, is the sheer amount of test effort expended.

The minimum acceptable amount of testing is portrayed in Figure 11.35b, where one client interacts with just one sensor object. The basis for this is that 'if it works for one it will work for all'. Its advantage is that it minimizes the test effort. Unfortunately, only limited trust can be placed in the answers obtained.

A compromise strategy, striking a balance between the two, is shown in Figure 11.35c. It may well prove useful to develop another client object purely as a test driver. Whether this compromise solution is satisfactory will depend on individual applications.

Our basic test problem here is due to the use of inheritance, not dynamic polymorphism. Even if we choose to use static polymorphism, it won't help. However, using dynamic polymorphism brings with it an additional problem. The technique is incredibly powerful; it allows us to invoke an operation on an object without explicitly specifying the object. Unfortunately, this produces a problem when we meet a statement of the form SomeObject.ShowData in the source code. Which call should we test? Well, it all depends on the value assigned during execution to SomeObject. As a consequence it is impossible to define, from the source code, which object will be accessed. It is thus no surprise that dynamic polymorphism is *verboten* in safety-critical systems.

Just to round this section off, a couple of points for your consideration. When a fault is found, where should the correction be made – base or child class?

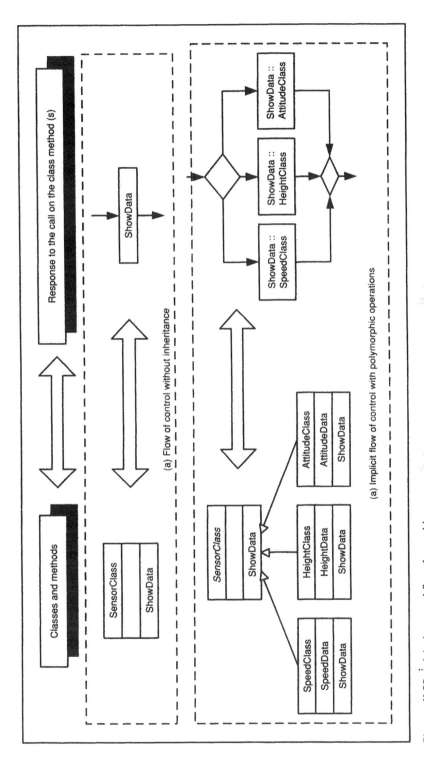

Figure 11.33 Inheritance and flow of control issues.

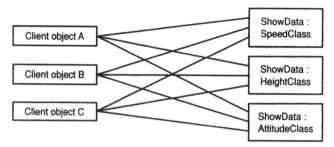

Figure II.34 The testing issue — multiple-client objects using multiple-server objects.

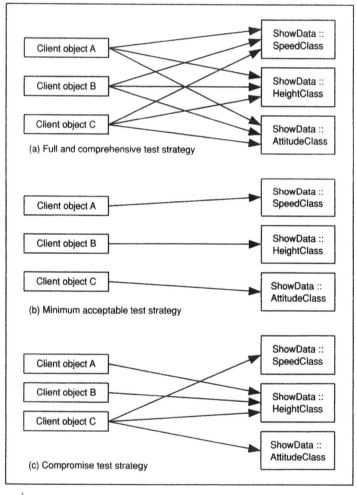

Figure II.35 Alternative test strategies.

(a) In the child class.
     But what if the problem is in the base class? That means that all siblings of the child still inherit the bug.

(b) In the base class.
     But what if the base class is actually OK and our problem is due to how the child is used? Changing the base class is likely to cause problems for the other siblings.

Review

On completing this chapter you should now:

● Be able to explain the underlying concepts of software testing of source code structures.

● Know, when testing software, what the major quality and performance assessment points are.

● Know what static analysis is and how it may be carried out.

● Appreciate the features of automated static analysers.

● Understand what the various analysis techniques are: control flow, dataflow, information flow, semantic and compliance.

● Understand what a control flow graph is and how it is used.

● Appreciate the features and use of Halstead software metrics.

● Appreciate the features and use of the McCabe cyclomatic complexity metric.

● Know what white-box testing, black-box testing and dynamic analysis are.

● Recognize that dynamic analysis includes both testing and coverage analysis.

● Realize why coverage analysis is needed and know what the following coverage features are: statement, path, decision, condition.

● Know how dynamic testing may be carried out in both manual and automated environments.

● Recognize what integration testing is and what it achieves.

● Know what test strategies can be applied to integration testing and how these relate to bottom-up and top-down integration techniques.

● Realize that OO designs bring new problems into the software test arena.

● Recognize that most of these are related to the class/object structure itself.

● Understand the type and range of metrics which may be used with OO designs.

● See why inheritance and polymorphism may make testing especially difficult.

References and further reading

[BSI98] *Software component testing*, BS 7925-2:1998, www.bsi.org.uk/BSIS/home.htm.

[CAN00] *Cantata technical brief*, IPL Software Products Group, Bath, UK, www.iplbath.com/tools, 2000.

[CHI94] *A metrics suite for object-oriented design*, S.R. Chidamber and C.F. Kemerer, IEEE Transactions on Software Engineering, Vol. 21, No. 3, pp 263–265, 1994.

[GIL83] *Software design and development*, P. Gilbert, Science Research Association, ISBN 0-574-21430-5, 1983.

[HAL77] *Elements of software science*, M. Halstead, North-Holland, ISBN 0-137-20384-5, 1977.

[MCC76] *A software complexity measure*, T. McCabe, IEEE Transactions on Software Engineering, Vol. 2, pp 308–320, 1976.

[MCC89] *Design complexity measurement and testing*, T. McCabe and C. Butler, Communications of the ACM, December 1989.

[MCC00] www.McCabe.com, McCabe Associates, High Wycombe, Bucks, UK, 2000.

[WAT96] *Structured testing: A testing methodology using the cyclomatic complexity metric*, A.H. Watson and T.J. McCabe, NIST special publication 500-235, 1996.

chapter 12

Development Tools

The culminating point in embedded system design is the installation of correct, reliable and safe software into the target system. To use a well-known cliché, this is easier said than done. Even assuming that system specifications are clear, precise and agreed, many problems still have to be overcome. The final design and development phase can (no, will) be one of graft, perspiration and frustration. Any help at this stage is gratefully received. The early designers of microprocessor systems soon realized that existing instruments were inadequate. As a result, many tools have been developed over the years specifically to support this task. Such developments have been driven by the needs and demands of the user.

During this time microprocessor software became increasingly more complex. This complexity is mirrored by the facilities of the development support tools. Not surprisingly, the newcomer to the subject can easily be confused by the variety and features of such tools. So, this chapter sets out to show the need for and use of software development tools. Specifically it covers:

- Development environments.
- Host–target debugging facilities.
- Software debuggers.
- Hardware debuggers.
- In-circuit emulators.
- Logic analysers.
- In-target analysis tools.
- Memory device programmers and emulators.
- Integrated development environments (IDEs).

First, a definition: in this chapter a 'bug' is a mistake made in implementing a program, not an error introduced at the requirements or system-design stage.

12.1 The development process

12.1.1 A preamble

Let's be very clear concerning the task of developing software for real-time systems. The end result of this process is to have correct, safe and reliable software running in a target system. In many cases the target will be a 'bare board' unit, having little or no support software. Frequently the board will be a new, untested, hardware design. Mass storage devices such as floppy or hard disks are rarely available for use in the target. True, many embedded systems use such items. However, they are usually integrated into the design only after the processor board itself has been proven. Similar comments apply to display units. Given these conditions, it isn't surprising that the target software cannot be developed on the target itself. Instead we use a separate machine, the 'host' system (usually a PC).

12.1.2 The host–target environment

What facilities should the host provide, and how should it interact with the target? Figure 12.1 lays out the basic software development production cycle which has evolved with time and experience. The process starts with the typing in of the source program itself. Thus keyboard and display facilities are needed, together with text-handling software. Such a software package is called an editor. The source program

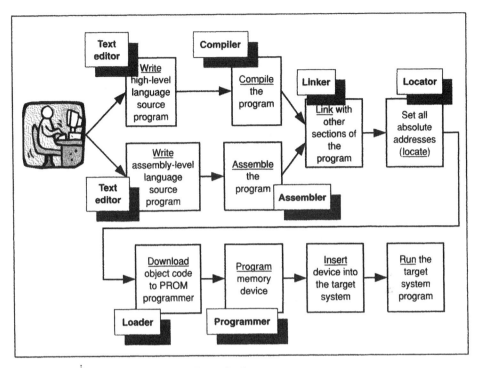

Figure 12.1 A basic microprocessor software development process.

or 'source code' is assembled or compiled into a linkable file. In a small system this would be the complete target program. For most systems, though, we develop software using program building blocks. In their simplest form these are libraries of commonly used functions. The linker software allows us to integrate our program with such libraries. But even more importantly, we don't have to consider the internal details of such programs, only their interfaces. This feature enables us to design programs in a truly modular fashion.

At this stage the complete program is held in storage in the host system. All relative addressing has been sorted out. Next, the actual or 'absolute' addresses have to be set using the locator program. This must be done to allow for differing memory usage of RAM and ROM in target systems. After this the loader software is used to generate a data record file version of the program compatible with the PROM programmer (the most common formats are Intel Hex and Motorola S records). Note that PROM programmers are mainly stand-alone units which communicate with the host using serial and/or parallel interfaces.

The final operation in the host is to download these object files to the programmer unit. Once the EPROM/flash memory device is programmed it is removed from the programmer, inserted into the target board, and the target unit checked out.

This forms the basis of modern, comprehensive microprocessor software development processes, Figure 12.2. Major points of note are that:

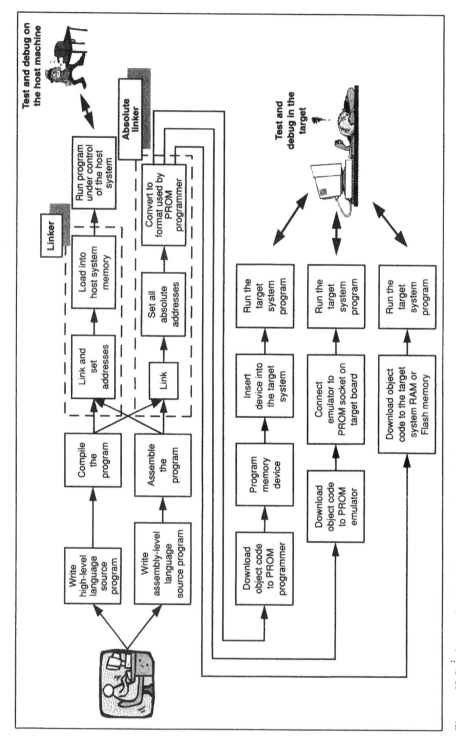

Figure 12.2 A comprehensive microprocessor software development process.

- The link-locate-load actions are usually invoked as a single operation, the so-called 'absolute linker'.

- Target system testing and debugging is usually carried out with the aid of the host machine.

- PROM emulators are often used to eliminate the actual device programming stage.

- The object files (the run-time program) may be downloaded directly to system RAM or flash memory.

- The source program can be executed on the host (but with many limitations, see later).

To repeat, Figure 12.2 describes the *basis* of modern development systems. But many more facilities, both hardware and software, are needed to meet the needs of current microprocessor designs.

12.1.3 Causes and effects of run-time malfunctions

If we could always produce error-free software and hardware then the facilities of Figure 12.2 are all that we need. Unfortunately, this is a mythical situation. New hardware rarely works correctly and almost any target code contains bugs. Tracking down these faults frequently reduces normally sane and balanced engineers to a demented state. And even when software does what it's supposed to do it may run too slowly.

No single tool can analyse and solve these problems. As a result a number of types have been developed (Figure 12.3). System run-time errors are due to both hardware faults and software bugs. Such errors can be made in a number of ways (Figure 12.4), as described in Chapter 2. Notice that certain syntactic mistakes and those due to misunderstandings of system requirements are not included. The reasons for this are that:

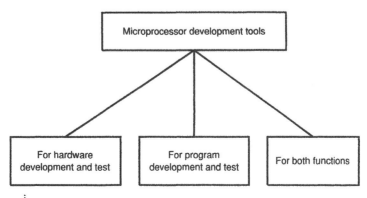

Figure 12.3   Development tool requirements.

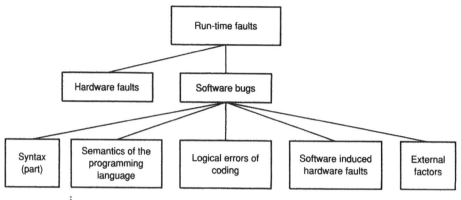

Figure 12.4 Causes of run-time faults.

- Syntax errors which can be picked up by the compiler (or assembler) can't produce run-time faults.

- Misunderstandings of task requirements (task-semantic errors) do not cause run-time faults. Programs will run exactly as designed; unfortunately the designs are wrong. Tools devised as program development aids cannot possibly recognize such mistakes.

What are the effects of software bugs? First (and fairly obviously) target programs won't do what they're supposed to do. The resulting behaviour is wide-ranging and unpredictable. Time and effort spent in tracking down such bugs ('debugging') can seriously affect development timescales. Ultimately these lead to commercial and financial problems such as late delivery and project overspends. As a result, commercial factors have greatly influenced the evolution of development tools. Success comes to those who can deliver good software and systems in the shortest possible time. Never forget that economics is one of the strongest driving forces in our cultural system.

12.1.4 The modern development process

In early microprocessor developments, hardware and software design was treated very much as an integrated activity. Little or no software proving was carried out prior to running it in the target. Most code was written in assembly language, requiring a high level of expertise to analyse and correct mistakes. Further, debugging tools were fairly primitive. Hence coping with simultaneous hardware and software problems was an uphill task. So it's not surprising that it could take a long time to finalize even small programs.

Economic pressures have resulted in a convergence towards a particular development process (Figure 12.5). First, hardware is treated as a separate design and

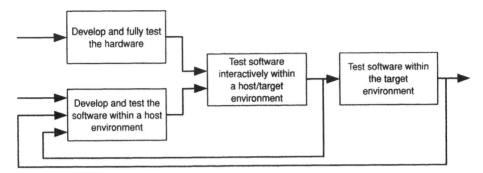

Figure 12.5 : The modern microprocessor development processes.

development action. On new and specialized designs such work is carried out con-current with the software design. The myth that hardware cannot be developed separately from software has been well laid to rest (except, unfortunately, where ASIC and programmable technology is involved). Many designers now use standard hardware such as VME and PCI, installing their own application software as required. The process outlined here has the same purpose: to enable designers to embed their software on fully tested and operational hardware.

If software is checked out by downloading code into EPROM, fitting this into the target, running the system, then re-doing the source code, reloading the target ... debugging becomes a long and tedious task. As a result great emphasis is now placed on tools which enable us to develop and test software on the host machine. Practical experience has shown that major productivity gains are made in this way.

Unfortunately, for a number of reasons, host system testing can validate only part of the complete software task. For instance:

● The hardware configuration (memory, I/O, special devices) of host and target are very unlikely to be the same.

● It is doubtful if real-time interfacing and signalling can be accommodated on the host.

● The host clock rate may not be the same as that of the target.

● It is doubtful whether hardware interrupts specific to the target system can be handled within the host.

The next stage is to test the software when it is actually located in the target. This validates it in its design environment. By doing this *interactively* with the host, how-ever, high productivity levels can be maintained. We have access to and use of all host facilities. These include large-volume disk storage, graphics, hard-copy print-outs, program disassembly and performance monitoring and evaluation.

A number of methods and tools have been developed for such work. In general, they avoid using on-board EPROM during this phase. Sometimes the program runs in the target RAM. Such testing usually involves disturbing the normal operation of the program; hence it cannot be regarded as the ultimate test. More complex tools minimize such restrictions. They provide the memory elements (and sometimes the CPU itself) needed for the task. It is also an advantage to use flash memory with *in situ* programming (instead of EPROMs) in target systems.

However, until programs run entirely within the target system, testing is incomplete. What do we do when bugs are found at this final stage? If we've followed the process described above then the errors are likely to be very subtle ones. At this point there really aren't quick and easy solutions. It's rather like a war of attrition, slogging through the problems one by one. Fortunately, they should be few in number. Experience has shown that, in this situation, tools oriented towards hardware debugging are the most useful. There is now, in fact, quite an overlap between hardware and software debuggers for this level of work.

Microprocessor debugging tools were developed simultaneously from two directions. At one end of the spectrum were the pure hardware items; at the other the host software tools. Initially these were simple and basic. With improvements and refinements they have become complex and extremely powerful (and often very expensive). At the same time the boundaries have blurred between the two areas. The move is towards an integrated workstation which supports all aspects of the development work. This is typified by the modern PC-based microprocessor integrated development environment.

Debugging tools tell us much about the embedded software. But what they don't do is produce information concerning the run-time performance of the code. For instance, how fast does a section of code run? How many times are particular procedures called? True, we can get at such data, but it's not usually an easy process. And, for real-time systems, run-time performance is the bottom line of the design process. In response to these needs, performance analysis tools are being produced for integration within the IDE. These represent the latest stage of software and hardware developments for IDEs.

In the following sections the points discussed above are covered in detail.

12.2 Software debugging – an overview

One point must be clearly understood. Software debugging is concerned with error detection in the software, not in the hardware. We assume that the hardware is fault-free. Hardware faults induced by software are here regarded as software errors; so they are included in the listing of software bugs.

A simplistic view of program execution ('journey into the unknown') is depicted in Figure 12.6. The complete program consists of the instructions and data needed to get from A to B. Along the way many actions are carried out. Data is collected, deposited and modified, output devices activated and input devices interrogated. When B is reached and all actions correctly performed we can be pretty sure that the program is correct.

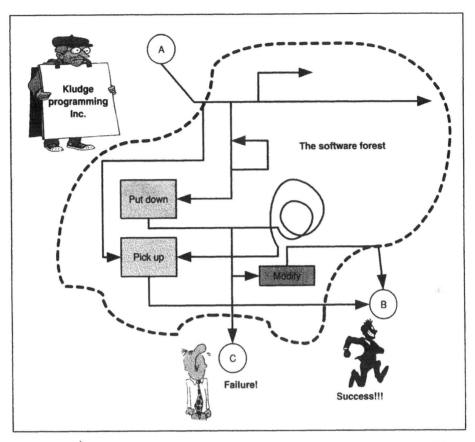

Figure 12.6 The program – journey into the unknown.

Now, how do we test this program? The simplest way is to install it in the target system and run it. In fact, unless special test tools are available, this is our only option. If the program executes as predicted, that's fine. But what if we arrive at C instead of B, carrying the wrong baggage? Or, even more confusing, what if this happens only occasionally, the program running correctly most times? Further, it isn't just enough to arrive at the destination clutching the correct information. All intermediate activities and data changes must also have been done exactly as desired.

Let's assume that errors exist. How can these be tracked down? The most basic method is to print out a source code listing and carefully analyse its operation. This is a time-consuming and tedious task. And it doesn't necessarily provide the answer. For instance, suppose that the mistake is caused by wrongly using an assembler instruction; for some reason we've misunderstood its operation. In this situation no amount of searching through the program listing is going to help. The only option now is to work through the program bit by bit to find the bug. As pointed out

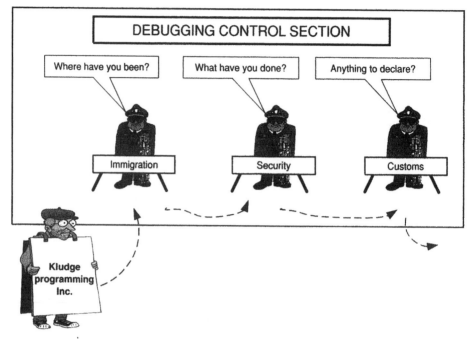

Figure 12.7 | Debriefing a bugged program.

earlier, this is a very lengthy, dispiriting and expensive task. What we really need are tools which allow us to search for bugs much more directly.

What are the primary requirements of such tools? These must be able to elicit three fundamental aspects of the program under test (Figure 12.7):

- What happened within the program as it executed?

- What objects were changed by the program along the way, and how was this done?

- What did the program pick up along the way, and how was this done?

From the debugging point of view it is extremely helpful to use a heuristic approach (i.e. the 'what if'). Thus the ability to change the original program while interrogating it is also a basic requirement.

In response to these needs a wide range of tools has been developed, Figure 12.8; study this figure carefully. Three distinct debugging environments have been identified:

- On the host system only.
- In the target system.
- In host–target combinations.

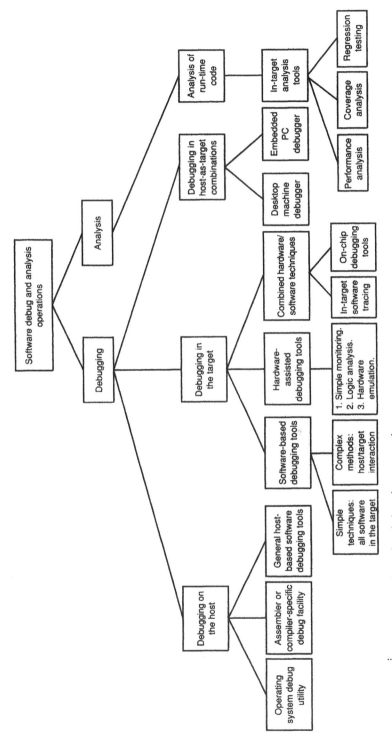

Figure 12.8 Software debugging and analysis tools – an overview.

Host-only debugging

For debugging software in a host environment, the simplest development tool is a utility package specific to the operating system. This is also the cheapest solution of all. However, it normally only supports relatively simple debugging at assembly language level. An alternative at this stage is to use debugging tools supplied as part of a language development package. These allow debugging of both assembler and HLL source code to be carried out (though the great majority are HLL – compiler – oriented). More comprehensive features are available from specialist debugging packages, including, for example, simulation facilities.

In the target

For reasons discussed later, host system software debuggers are unable to test target system software fully. Such software can only be fully validated in its final settings. Three methods can be used in the target: software-based, hardware-assisted or on-chip debugging techniques.

To use software methods some form of target debugger support package must be installed into the target system. In its simplest form it may be an elementary 'home-grown' monitor package. Interaction with the target board is normally done using a PC connected via a serial or parallel communication link. Commercial packages are available which do much the same job; these eliminate the need to produce the DIY variety. The more powerful ones enable the tester to work using high-level language source operations. The result is a much more powerful and comprehensive debugging system. Similar facilities are also provided in some modern compiler packages.

No matter how good software-based tools are, they suffer from one fundamental limitation. Using these methods, debugging is essentially an invasive process. That is, we interfere with the execution of the program. As a result, program behaviour during debugging just isn't the same as that on a normal run. Other restrictions exist (discussed later), but this is the primary one. To overcome this we have to resort to hardware test tools specifically designed for debugging purposes. These allow us to run and observe program execution at full speed with proper isolation between the debugger and target programs. The simpler hardware tools are designed specifically for this purpose. However, more advanced hardware tools such as the In-Circuit Emulator (ICE) do much more than support simple software debugging.

Unfortunately, even the sophisticated tools may have problems in coping with the debugging needs of modern processors (especially highly integrated microcontrollers). As a result new test and debug methods based on the use of on-chip logic have been developed: on-chip debugging (OCD). OCD, to some extent a combination of software and hardware based techniques, is now coming into widespread use.

These various features are described later.

Host–target combinations

Two particular structures dominate here. First is the case where a host machine is also used as the target computer. The second one is where the host and the target, although distinct machines, use the same operating system.

Those in the first group are basically desktop machines, the majority being PCs running Microsoft Windows. However, where greater reliability of service is required, UNIX systems tend to be preferred (and we're now seeing the emergence of Linux-based embedded systems). Note, though, that standard desktop machines are suitable for use only in benign environments. For more demanding applications (e.g. factory floor systems, etc.), ruggedized versions are available. In such applications most developers use standard PCs running PC-specific software. This includes general-purpose software (e.g. spreadsheets) and specialized packages such as control system design, data acquisition and results analysis. Real-world signals are handled by specialist plug-in boards as required (third-party and/or own design). Debugging operations and techniques, because they apply to a host environment, are similar to those described earlier. However, additional test software will usually be needed to debug complex specialized functions (e.g. Mil. Std. 1553 avionic networking). When using commercially available add-on boards, this should be sufficient. For own-design add-ons the same comments apply *provided* such units are guaranteed to work correctly. If not, and problems arise, then extra debugging facilities (such as in-circuit emulators) are probably going to be needed.

The second group, based on the 'computer-on-a-board' design, mainly use PCI, PC-104 and VME hardware (though there are few VME-based hosts). Moreover, it is now very common to base such systems on standard, commercially available boards (including the processor board itself). As a result debugging is much more software-based than in days of yore.

It is tempting to think that, when using proven hardware, hardware-based debugging methods are no longer required. Unfortunately, in real-time systems problems can arise owing to interactions between the real-world and the software world. In such cases we usually have to resort to debugging using hardware-based techniques.

12.3 Software debugging on the host

12.3.1 Example operating system utility – the dynamic debugging tool

Dynamic debugging tools (DDTs) have been around for a long time. Originally they were developed for assembly language operations on mainframe and minicomputers. So it's not surprising that the early desktop microcomputers were equipped with DDT facilities. The general functions provided by such a debugging tool are shown in Figure 12.9. First, it must provide a means to start and stop program execution as and when desired – program execution control. Second, it must

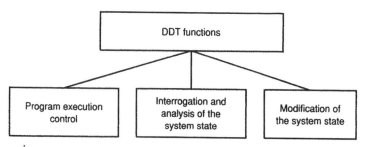

Figure 12.9 DDT – basic functions.

allow us to examine the state of a program before, during and after its execution – interrogation and analysis. Third, it should enable changes ('patches') to be made to the code as required during the debug process – modification. An essential feature of execution control is that of *breakpoints*. These are points in the program where program execution ceases and control returns to the debugger software. Closely related to these are *watchpoints*, being essentially addresses of data items. Typically when a watchpoint is met the value of the data item is shown but control is not returned to the debugger. Such points are, of course, inserted by the tester using the debugging tool. These features are now explained by working through a fragment of a faulty program, Figure 12.10. The purpose of this piece of code is to load information at defined addresses for use by the processor interrupt system. Before starting this, it is important to establish exactly what the correct outcome *should* be. Here, after execution, we should end up with the following data values in memory:

Memory address	0:3E8(H)	0:3E9(H)	0:3EA(H)	0:3EB(H)
Data (contents)	00(H)	00(H)	00(H)	98(H)

Unfortunately, when the software is executed, it fails to work correctly. Finding the reason why now involves a piece of software sleuthing using the debugger facilities. In broad terms, the debugging process involves:

- Presetting the contents of specified memory locations (addresses) (a modification function).
- Running the program to a defined point (control).
- Examining the resulting state of the address contents (interrogation).
- Correcting and re-running the errant program using debugger facilities (modification and control).

Presetting the system

Using the DDT utility functions, the program is first loaded into host RAM and its location is obtained. As a further check, the *actual* program object code together

```
; Listing 12.1
; Filename: Demo.A86
CSEG

; Software interrupt 250 is used to allow transfer of control from the
bootstrap program to the application code.

00FA          StartApplication        EQU 250; interrupt 250
03E8          StartApplicationInterrupt EQU (250*4)

              ; Here are the interrupt vector settings in EPROM. They are
                transferred to RAM during initialization.

0 ß StartApplicationInterrupt

03E8 0000     StartInt0 ffset DW 0H
03EA 0098     StartIntSegment DW 9800H

;**********************************************
;**********************************************

; Here is the start of the bootstrap program.
0 ß 100H;

StartBootstrap:

; Set up the data segment register so that it points to the bottom of the
bootstrap ROM.
0100 B800FE   MOV AX, 0FE00 H
0103 8ED8     MOV DS, AX

; This sets up the jump to the start of the application program
010C 2EA1E803 MOV AX, StartInt0 ffset
0110 26A3E803 MOV ES, StartInt0 ffset,  AX
0114 2EA1EA03 MOV AX, StartIntSegment
0118 26A3EA03 MOV ES, StartIntSegment,  AX

; Set up the data segment register so that it points to the bottom of RAM.
011C B80000   MOV AX, 0H
011F 8ED8     MOV DS, AX
0121 FB       STI
0122 CDFA     Int StartApplication

END 0 FASSEMBLY. NUMBER 0 FERRORS 0.
```

Figure 12.10 Example faulty program fragment.

```
; List command
L3798:100, 11B

3798 : 0100  MOV AX, FE00
3798 : 0103  MOV DS, AX
3798 : 0105  CS: MOV AX, [03E8]
3798 : 0109  ES: MOV [03E8], AX
3798 : 010D  CS: MOV AX, [03EA]
3798 : 0111  ES: MOV [03EA], AX
3798 : 0115  MOV AX, 0000
3798 : 0118  MOV DS, AX
3798 : 011A  STI
3798 : 011B  INT FA
```

Figure 12.11 Example program – listing of program code (assembly language form).

```
; Fill command
F0 : 3E8,  BB, FF
-
; Display command
-D0 : 3E8,  BB
0000 : 03E8 FF FF FF FF  . . . . . . . . . . . .
```

Figure 12.12 Result of filling memory store values.

with its memory location can be listed ('L') in assembly language form (Figure 12.11). Now the contents of memory locations 0:3E8(H) to 0:3EB(H) are set to or filled ('F') with the value FF(H), Figure 12.12. These values (now called the 'vector' values for simplicity) may then be displayed ('D') to ensure that the fill command was performed correctly, Figure 12.12.

Running the program

The program can now be executed at full speed up to the required terminating point, the breakpoint. The command is 'G', Figure 12.13, the breakpoint being at memory address 3798:011B(H).

Examining the results

When the program has been run the vector values may be displayed, Figure 12.13. It can be seen that these values (originally preset to FF(H)) have *not* been changed

```
; Go (run) command
G3798 : 100,  11B
* 3798 : 011B
·
; Display command
-DO : 3E8,  BB
0000 : 03E8 FF FF FF FF ............
```

Figure 12.13   Result of running the program.

```
; Trace command
T3798 : 100, 11A
?
-TS8
```

AX	BX	CX	DX	SP	BP	SI	DI	CS	DS	SS	ES	IP
0000	0000	0000	0000	005C	0000	0000	0000	3798	3798	2C1A	3798	0100

MOV AX, FE00

AX	BX	CX	DX	SP	BP	SI	DI	CS	DS	SS	ES	IP
FE00	0000	0000	0000	005C	0000	0000	0000	FFFF	3798	2C1A	3798	0103

MOV DS, AX

AX	BX	CX	DX	SP	BP	SI	DI	CS	DS	SS	ES	IP
0000	0000	0000	0000	005C	0000	0000	0000	3420	FE00	2C1A	3798	0109

ES: MOV [03E8], AX

AX	BX	CX	DX	SP	BP	SI	DI	CS	DS	SS	ES	IP
0000	0000	0000	0000	005C	0000	0000	0000	3420	FE00	2C1A	3798	010D

CS: MOV AX, [03E8]

AX	BX	CX	DX	SP	BP	SI	DI	CS	DS	SS	ES	IP
9800	0000	0000	0000	005C	0000	0000	0000	3420	FE00	2C1A	3798	0111

ES: MOV [03EA], AX

AX	BX	CX	DX	SP	BP	SI	DI	CS	DS	SS	ES	IP
9800	0000	0000	0000	005C	0000	0000	0000	3420	FE00	2C1A	3798	0115

MOV AX, 0000

AX	BX	CX	DX	SP	BP	SI	DI	CS	DS	SS	ES	IP
0000	0000	0000	0000	005C	0000	0000	0000	3420	FE00	2C1A	3798	0118

MOV DS, AX

AX	BX	CX	DX	SP	BP	SI	DI	CS	DS	SS	ES	IP
0000	0000	0000	0000	005C	0000	0000	0000	3420	0000	2C1A	3798	011B

Figure 12.14   Using the trace facility.

by the program. Quite clearly the program doesn't perform as intended. Therefore we need to establish precisely what happens during program execution. To do this, the program is executed on a step-by-step basis, its state being examined at each step. This is called the trace ('T') facility, illustrated in Figure 12.14. Careful examination shows that the problem lies with the ES register. This, which is used as the segment register in the program, should be initialized to zero. Unfortunately this hasn't been done; it actually has a value (in this run) of 3798(H).

Correcting the program

We could, if we choose to, go back and make changes to the source code. This would, however, also involve re-assembly and reloading. It is quicker if direct corrections can be made to the code within the debug activity. Such modifications are called 'patching', Figure 12.15. In this case new assembly language statements are entered and assembled ('A'), the program executed (G) and the vector values examined, Figure 12.15. It can be seen that the correction has achieved its desired result.

```
; Assemble command
A3798 : FB

3798 : 00FB   MOV AX, 0
3798 : 00FE   MOV ES, AX
3798 : 0100
;------------------------------------
; List command
L3798 : FB,11A

3798 : 00FB   MOV AX, 0000
3798 : 00FE   MOV ES, AX
3798 : 0100   MOV AX, FE00
3798 : 0103   MOV DS, AX
3798 : 0105   CS: MOV AX, [03E8]
3798 : 0109   ES: MOV [03E8], AX
3798 : 010D   CS: MOV AX, [03EA]
3798 : 0111   ES: MOV [03EA], AX
3798 : 0115   MOV AX, 0000
3798 : 0118   MOV DS, AX
3798 : 011A   STI

;------------------------------------
; Go (run) command
G3798 : FB, 11B

*  3798 : 011B

;------------------------------------
; Display command
-D0 : 3E8,  BB

0000 : 03E8 00 00 00 98 .......
```

Figure 12.15 | Details of the corrected program.

Now the source code itself may be modified, re-assembled and then checked out once more.

This is not intended to be a tutorial on DDT. What it does, though, is introduce the basic functions of all software debugging tools. These are to:

- List the program, as loaded for debugging, in assembler mnemonics.
- Execute the program at normal speed under debugger control.
- Single-step through the program.
- Set program breakpoints as required.
- Trace the program as it executes.
- Modify processor and program status during trace and step.
- Modify memory contents.
- Patch the program without the need to re-assemble it.

The above example is only a fragment of a program. When DDTs are applied to code of any sensible size they become awkward to use. Hence operating system utilities are rarely used nowadays for debugging microprocessor-based embedded systems. In the main they have been replaced by powerful and easy-to-use interactive graphics-based debugging tools.

12.3.2 Assembly level language debuggers – specialist packages

Specialist packages have been developed mainly to extend the facilities of DDT. The major primary improvements to DDT at the assembler level fall into four categories (Figure 12.16):

- Symbolic debugging.
- Interactive patching.
- Enhanced trace facilities.
- Improved breakpoint operations.

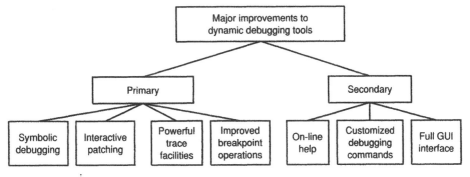

Figure 12.16 Major improvements to DDT at the assembler level.

Symbolic level debugging

Symbolic representation of program items is the norm in modern assembly language programming. Symbolic debugging is the ability to reference such symbols instead of using their absolute addresses. Without this feature debugging is time-consuming, tedious and error-prone.

Interactive patching

This leads directly to the second point, interactive patching. By using program symbols, on-line patching can be carried out without having to worry about absolute addresses. While on-line patching can speed up the debugging process it cannot be recommended as a routine way of working.

Enhanced trace facilities

The debugging process can be greatly speeded up by providing more and better information during the trace operation. Typically debugger facilities include – in addition to that shown in Figure 12.14 – displays of stack, I/O and bus operations, interrupt cycles and data transferred during execution cycles.

Improved breakpoint operations

With DDT, the number of breakpoints is quite limited; further, their locations are specified in absolute address form. That is, each breakpoint is designated as a point within the program code; the effects due to data values or program operations are not taken into account. Such a breakpoint is termed an 'execution' type. But there is also a need for non-execution breakpoints. Modern tools support both execution and non-execution breakpoints, including:

● Unconditional read of memory or I/O.

● Unconditional write to memory or I/O.

● Qualified memory or I/O read or write.

● Complex (multiple) breakpoint sequences.

Other (secondary) improvements are less fundamental in nature. They generally aim to simplify the use of the debugger and improve productivity. That isn't to say that they are less important: far from it. Such enhancements (Figure 12.16) include:

● On-line help, incorporating screen windowing techniques.

● Creation and use of customized debugging commands.

● Data display in clear, understandable form.

Modern debugging techniques and environments are heavily biased towards HLL operation (especially for C and C++). Therefore the points raised here will be discussed within the context of HLL debugging, in the next section.

12.3.3 High-level language debuggers – general

Why should we want to debug at a high-level language source code level? If we do decide to work at this level, what features and facilities are needed? Finally, what tools are available to us? These are the questions we seek to answer in the following sections. Note in passing that 'source level' debugging is generally understood as debugging the high-level source language.

Why debug at a high level?

We can best appreciate HLL debugging by looking at developments in this topic from early days onwards. In the 'dark ages' of microcomputers few real-time high-level languages were around. One which became available quite early on was Coral66, targeted at the Intel 8080. The problems faced by software developers using such languages on minicomputers is well covered by Pierce [PIE74]; the problem was much greater on micros. Figure 12.17 shows the Coral code development sequence for the 8080 system. With this method the only aids to debugging were the source code, assembler and hex listings. Debugging and code analysis using these can be described, at the very best, as primitive. With the arrival of DDT tools an important step forward was made. These could operate on the compiler-generated object code (Figure 12.18), letting the programmer interact directly with his program (as described earlier).

Unfortunately this is not quite as powerful as it first seems. The problems are twofold. First, matching the source statements to the resulting assembler operations must be done manually. Secondly, interrogation of the assembler code is also a manual task. Consider the listing in Figure 12.19a. This relatively small amount of source code is pretty straightforward. Yet the assembler output is much more complex, Figure 12.19b. Further, additional code statements, JMPF, PUSH BP and INT E4, have been added by the compiler. We are certainly going to need the services of a

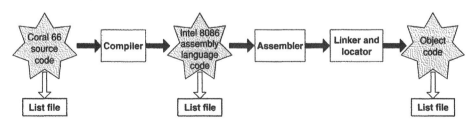

Figure 12.17 Primitive HLL debugging methods.

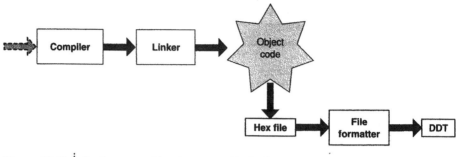

Figure 12.18 The first step – debugging at assembler level.

```
MODULE Test:
VAR
  x,  y  z: INTEGER;

BEGIN
  z := x + y;
END Test.

(a) HLL listing
```

```
3B98: 0100    JMPF  0014:0007
-
3B98: 0147    PUSH  BP
3B98: 0148    MOV   BP,SP
3B98: 014A    NOP
3B98: 014B    NOP
3B98: 014C    NOP
3B98: 014D    NOP
3B98: 014E    NOP
3B98: 014F    CS:   MOV, DS, [0000]
3B98: 0154    MOV   AX, [0000]
3B98: 0157    MOV   AX, [0002]
3B98: 015B    JNO   0161
3B98: 015D    MO V  AL, 24
3B98: 015F    INT   E4
-

(b) Compiler-generated assembly language listing
```

Figure 12.19 Comparing HLL source code with its disassembled object code.

Figure 12.20   Debugging HLLs at the assembler level – the consequences.

proficient assembler programmer to make sense of this. Analysis is going to take time, is a tedious affair (Figure 12.20) and requires much effort. And, in one sense, we spend too much time on the wrong job. That is, effort is concentrated on the symptoms of the problem rather than its causes. Further, the difficulty of handling code generated by an optimizing compiler adds another dimension to this task (due to the problems in debugging such code many designers initially turn off the optimizer; the code produced will certainly be longer but at least it can be analysed).

All these factors produce the same effects: increased time, effort and cost. This, in essence, is the answer to the question posed at the beginning of this section: 'why debug at a high level?'

What features are needed?

Having now decided that HLL source level debugging is highly desirable, what should such debuggers do for us? All the operations used with assembly language debugging are directly relevant. But because of the more complex language structure of HLLs, much more is needed. This is especially true of the latest generation of languages such C++, Java and Ada 95. HLL constructs that are important in debugging sessions include:

- The need to operate with symbols (symbolic debugging).
- The ability to handle and manipulate complex code and data structures such as classes (abstract data types), arrays, records and dynamic data units.

- The ability to work with separately compilable program units.
- The capacity to manipulate both local and global variables.

What tools are available?

Two clear methods have emerged for the provision of HLL debugger tools. In the first, language designers have provided these as part of the total system package ('system resident debuggers'). In the second one, independent software houses have developed general-purpose debuggers to meet market demands. As would be expected these are targeted at the more popular languages, especially C and C++.

12.3.4 Compiler-specific debuggers

It has now become commonplace to provided resident debuggers as part of a compiler package. The example program in Figure 12.21 is included to highlight the use of such debuggers. It uses the C source-level debugger of the Green Hills MULTI 2000 integrated development environment. Note that this is not a tutorial on either the language or the run-time debugger. What it shows is how an HLL debugger helps you to see where you are, where you came from and how your results were

```
double calcIntegral(double Xn,  double K1)
{
   unsigned int i;
   double Yn,  Yo,  Xo;

   Xo = Yo = 0.0;
   for(i = 0; i < 20; ++i)
   {
     Yn = K1 * (Xn + Xo) + Yo;
     Yo = Yn;
     Xo = Xn;
   }

   return Yn;
}

int main()
{
   double Xnew,  Ynew,  K1;
   Xnew = 1.0;
   K1 = 0.05;
   Ynew = calcIntegral(Xnew,  K1);
}
```

Figure 12.21 Example program.

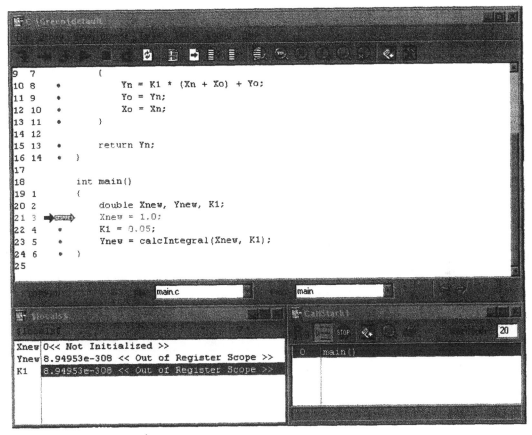

Figure 12.22 Screen display – real-time debugger.

obtained. Consider the example program of Figure 12.21. The first question. 'where are we?' is answered by displaying three items of information in three windows (Figure 12.22):

- The program source code itself.
- The current value of system variables ('locals').
- The function currently being executed ('CallStack').

The data and call information are shown in Figure 12.22. Note that only data declared at the program level is shown (i.e. that local to functions is suppressed). Although this feature is a specific implementation feature it follows the concepts of top-down design. That is, only relevant information is given at any stage; further it invokes the concepts of information hiding, decoupling and cohesion. Observe also the random values of the program variables.

Stepping through the program can be done using the basic methods of single stepping, stepping to breakpoints and stepping to the end. However, two particular

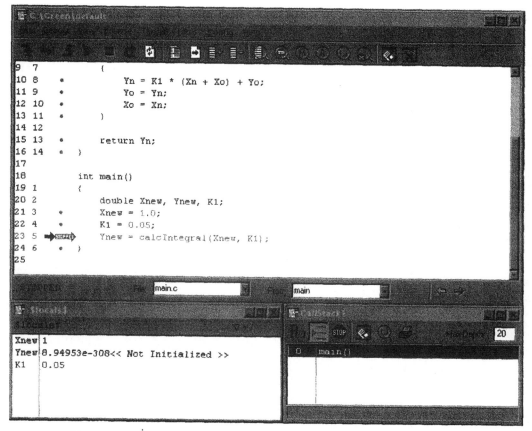

Figure 12.23 Operation: Step to call of function c ac ítegral at line number 23.

features are highly desirable for HLLs. These are, first, stepping on a subprogram
call basis and, second, stepping to breakpoints in different concurrent processes. The
first case is important as subprograms are essential building blocks of many design
techniques. The second is necessary for use with multitasking designs.

Figures 12.23–12.25 illustrate a sequence of operations during the debugging process. Initially (Figure 12.23) we step through main to the point at which the function calcIntegral is called. However, the code at that line hasn't yet been executed;
the call stack window still only shows one function (main) being interrogated. It can
also be seen at this stage that the variables Xnew and K1 have been correctly initialized.
Stepping on into the function (Figure 12.24), we now see that the locals window
shows the values of all relevant program variables. Observe how this allows us to
execute function calls as single program statements; it also shows how the details
of a function may be interrogated. Moreover, it enables us to check parameter-
passing behaviour. Finally, the listing of function calls and current system status can
provide useful information, especially where nested functions are used. In all of this
it is possible to modify program data and so verify particular program operations.

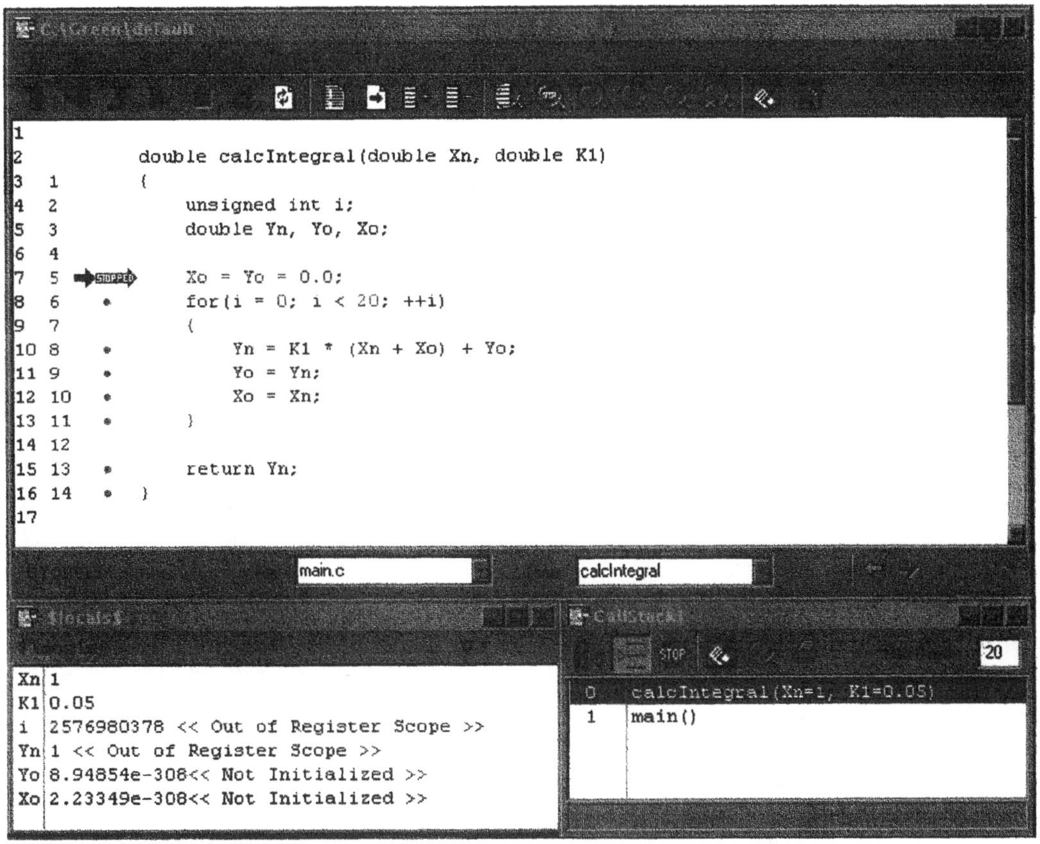

Figure 12.24 : Operation: Step into start of function c àc àtegra1, at line 7.

The final display (Figure 12.25) shows that the program has been stepped to completion and has behaved correctly (as can be seen from the values of the program data items in the locals window).

There are many detailed operations specific to this debugger. Listing these would be pointless. What is important is that this method of interaction allows us to view the program at a symbolic level. Thus we can concentrate on the design and objectives of the software, not its machine operation.

12.3.5 General-purpose debugging packages

A number of software suppliers have developed debugging packages which are general purpose in design. These should have the following hallmarks:

- Support for mixed language development.
- Powerful windows-based user interfaces.
- Session recording, recall and replay facilities.

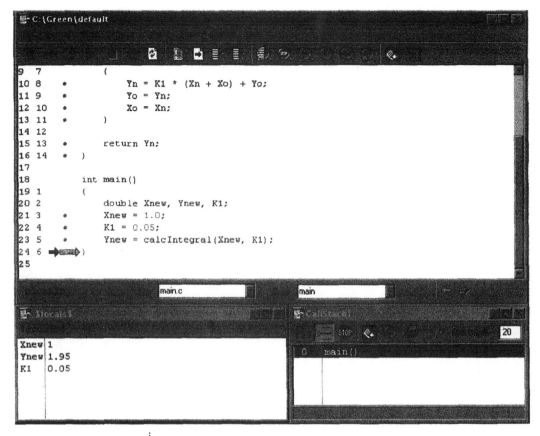

```
9   7                {
10  8   •                Yn = K1 * (Xn + Xo) + Yo;
11  9   •                Yo = Yn;
12  10  •                Xo = Xn;
13  11  •            }
14  12
15  13  •            return Yn;
16  14  •        }
17
18          int main()
19  1            {
20  2                double Xnew, Ynew, K1;
21  3   •            Xnew = 1.0;
22  4   •            K1 = 0.05;
23  5   •            Ynew = calcIntegral(Xnew, K1);
24  6  ➡STOPPED )
25
```

main.c   main

Locals

Xnew	1
Ynew	1.95
K1	0.05

CallStack

STOP   20

0   main()

Figure 12.25 Operation: Program executed to completion, line 24. Note the data values.

- On-line help.
- A library of useful facilities.

They should support a range of high-level languages, together with assembly operation. In contrast the system-resident debuggers operate with one specific high-level language (and the assembler output from this). One important point should be noted at this stage. A debugger may allow the use of a number of HLLs, but it can only test software destined for a specific target processor. Thus, for instance, separate packages would be needed for the Intel embedded 386 and the Motorola powerPC processors.

The four major components of a modern host-based integrated debugging environment are fourfold, Figure 12.26:

- GUI.
- Simulator.
- Compiler.
- Debugger.

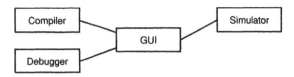

Figure 12.26 ⋮ General-purpose host-based integrated debugging environment.

The GUI is a key part of the environment, providing the user with facilities to access all debugger components. The simulator, however, is what distinguishes an outstanding debugging environment from one that is merely good. Where simulation methods are used, the user has full control over the test environment. It also provides the facility to run a program trace-back (the 'how did we get here?' question) under all modes of operation, including interrupts. Execution control and monitoring can also be very comprehensive. Breakpoint settings can be extended well beyond the basic methods shown earlier. Conditional breakpoints can be incorporated, triggered on memory addressing, reading or writing data, the results of conditional expressions, and *combinations* of these (non-execution breakpoints). Trigger registers are used to set and control such operations.

In selecting a general-purpose debugger it is important to check its real-time capability. A basic one has a simulation model of the processor and memory. Good ones can supply accurate details of program execution times, down to the individual instruction level. Advanced types provide facilities to simulate processor peripherals such as UARTs, programmable I/O devices, display chips, etc. The most powerful enable users to customize their systems in order to simulate design-specific devices.

Figure 12.27 explains the overall organization of a general-purpose system, the detail being mostly self-explanatory.

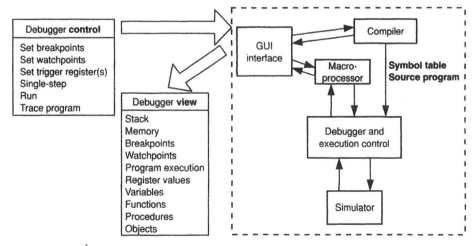

Figure 12.27 ⋮ Integrated debugger organization – host-based system.

One aspect not touched on so far is how we can automate testing to:

- Improve productivity.
- Eliminate tedious tasks.
- Cut costs.

Test sessions may be automated by producing a set of test scripts (using a suitable scripting language) and submitting these to a macro-processor. This in turn generates all commands for the running of tests and the collection of test results.

12.3.6 A closing comment – the pros and cons of host system debugging

Host system debugging has many advantages. With this we can test and debug most of the application program. In some cases this may be as high as 90% of the final product. We can interact directly with the program, seeing exactly how it performs. The effects of changes can be checked almost instantly. We save ourselves the time, cost and effort involved in producing reams of listings. Session recordings can be made, being useful for subsequent analysis. Having information concerning program execution times allows us to evaluate program performance. All this spells high productivity, reduced costs and faster development times.

So far, so good. But as with anything in engineering, there are practical limits to these techniques. These limitations arise as a result of three particular factors:

- Interaction of programs.
- Speed of execution.
- Host–target hardware differences.

Interaction of source and debugger programs

Many debuggers are designed to run in a native environment. In such cases, during the debugging operation, three programs have to be considered. These are:

- The program being debugged.
- The debugger software.
- The host operating system.

These will be partly or completely resident in the host RAM. Hence they are not isolated from each other. It is normal for the operating system to be protected from application programs; this same protection doesn't necessarily extend to the debugger. Thus the test program may alter the debugger itself, producing unexpected results. This interaction may seriously reduce the capability of the debugger.

Speed of operation

One powerful aspect of the debugger is the facility to step through and interrogate the program under test. This means that the program runs at only a fraction of its normal speed. It might appear that we can minimize such problems by running at full speed to preset breakpoints. However, this can only be done with execution breakpoints. Any use on non-execution breakpoints means that the processor needs to stop regularly to check the break conditions. In practice this will result in the test program running quite slowly. In most cases, therefore, it isn't possible to debug at full operating speeds. Unfortunately, a program run slowly may behave very differently compared to its operation at full speed.

Host–target hardware differences

As a general rule target hardware configurations are different from those of the hosts. We've seen that peripheral device simulation goes some way to take into account specific designs. Yet this only scratches the surface of the problem. That is, host system debugging cannot evaluate hardware–software interaction in real time.

In conclusion, a program which has been debugged on the host must give us great confidence in the software design. But until it actually runs on the target hardware it still remains unproven.

12.4 Software debugging in the target – software-based techniques

12.4.1 General

The basic system configuration required for software debugging in the target is shown in Figure 12.28. Here the user interfaces to the target using some form of terminal/display device. This can range from a simple 'dumb' terminal to a UNIX workstation. Communication with the target is usually done using a duplex (two-way) digital serial link. It is still necessary to provide communication and debugging facilities on the target itself. This is done by including a monitor or run-time support program in firmware (EPROM or flash memory) on the target computer. Details of such firmware packages vary from supplier to supplier. However, within reason, it must be possible to locate it anywhere in the processor memory (i.e. be position-independent). This prevents clashes with the program under test. The software to be tested can be resident in either ROM or RAM; the choice has a profound effect on the debugger capability.

This technique, software debugging in the target, implicitly assumes that the target board hardware works properly. The technique *can* be used for hardware

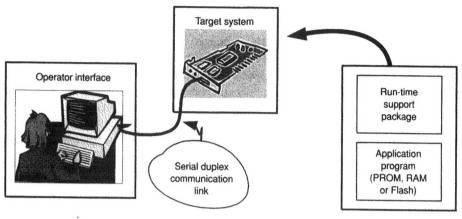

Figure 12.28 Target debugging – basic configuration.

testing when incremental development methods are used. Generally, though, it is meant to support software development only. Once again, please note that the debugger software is located in the target.

12.4.2 A simple monitor program

One of the earlier test/debug packages is the simple monitor program. Its purpose is to supply fairly basic support for target code test and debugging. Interaction with the target occurs at a very low level, typically using absolute addressing and hexadecimal coding. All debugger software resides in the target, the operator interface being a simple 'dumb' terminal. This means that all target code is also located in ROM. Thus, using this debug method, it is impossible to change the program dynamically during the test session.

One would expect to find the following routines implemented as part of the monitor software:

● Display of program (code) memory.
● Display of data memory.
● Display of processor register contents.
● Modification of data memory and register values.
● Single-step control.
● Execute program with or without breakpoints.
● Return to monitor.

Implementing the single-step and breakpoint facilities can be difficult when the program is in ROM. In some cases it may be necessary to add extra hardware to the board design. This can be avoided where processors have a trap-flag facility in the instruction set.

Such monitors have usually been developed by users (not suppliers), especially where development support tools haven't been available.

Slightly more complex monitors have the ability to handle the downloading of object files from development systems. These convert the downloaded files into binary format and load them into system RAM. Program debug is much the same as described above; now, though, it includes the facility to change program code. In this case the simple terminal is replaced by some sort of host system, such as a PC. To support host operations, extra software is required for communication, user interfacing and downloading functions.

12.4.3 In-target source-level debugging

There is one fundamental difference between target source-level debuggers and host-based systems: where the program code is executed. Otherwise the major features are exactly the same. This can be seen from the organizational diagram of Figure 12.29, the target debugger equivalent of Figure 12.27. Observe that the

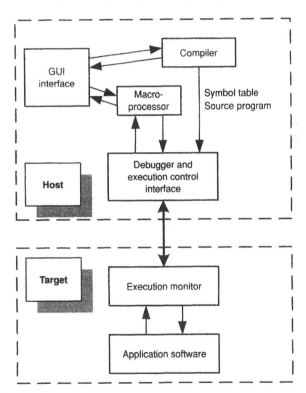

Figure 12.29 | Integrated debugger organization – host–target system.

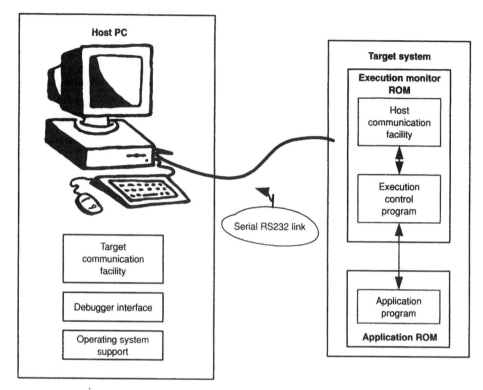

Figure 12.30 Target source-level debugging – typical system configuration.

software simulator has been replaced by an execution monitor. The hardware and software structure needed to support such a package is shown in Figure 12.30. In this case the debugging software consists of two items, a source-level debugging interface and an execution monitor. The interface is located on a host machine while the monitor is fitted to the target. So that these can communicate, extra software is needed. This consists of a target communication facility (in the host) and a host communication facility (in the target). Communication is usually carried out over serial data links, typically RS232 or Ethernet (with PC hosts, the parallel port connection is frequently used).

The arrangement described here has many advantages. First, although debugging is done on the target, all symbol information is held on the host. Thus powerful user interaction and display facilities can be provided at minimal target memory requirements. Typically target run-time support packages occupy less than a few kBytes of code. Second, recording of debugging sessions can be made on disk, useful for post-test analysis. Third, hard copy printout of active and recorded sessions can be obtained. Finally, the only target peripherals needed for debugging are those related to the serial communication system; all others are free for use by the application software.

Target run-time debuggers must be tailored to the target system under test. Pre-configured monitors are sometimes supplied by vendors; in other cases users can create their own for COTS boards using vendor-provided software (as, for example, with the board support library of the SingleStep debugger from WindRiver). In the case of non-standard boards, monitors may be produced by adapting the pre-supplied library software.

A word of caution: hardware interrupts present a particularly difficult problem for target system debuggers. Some make no attempt at all to handle them. Others do provide software support, usually as part of their board support packages. However, to do this, assumptions may be made about the interrupt structure of the target system and its hardware configuration. Always ensure that these assumptions are correct.

12.4.4 Debugging multitasking software

There is a fair degree of overlap between the material in this section and that given in Chapter 6 on RTOS development support. However, that material was presented primarily from the view of designing and developing multitasking software. More-over, it made the assumption that the support tools were produced by the RTOS vendors; as such they will be quite specific to, and highly integrated with, individual operating systems. Here, in contrast, the emphasis is on the debugging of completed software within a target environment. Further, it considers how general-purpose debugging tools can be made to work with a range of OSs.

What distinguishes conventionally written microprocessor programs from multi-tasking software? The answer is that multitasking designs are fundamentally built up as a number of co-operating tasks which run concurrently. Some are interrupt-driven. Some need to respond to interrupt or non-interrupt driven asynchronous external events. Data and signals have to be transferred between tasks, and task execution must be carefully synchronized. And for embedded systems this must be done in a predictable and timely manner. Therefore a multitasking debugger must not only provide all the features discussed so far; it should also have extra facilities to handle the particular requirements of real-time multitasking systems.

Basically what is needed is a tool which is distinct and separate from the system executive. It must be capable of operating in a non-intrusive way in parallel with the native code. That is, it should monitor and control program execution without distorting normal inter-task behaviour. It must allow the user to operate at two levels of debug: the tasking level and the detailed program level. Consider the part-system of Figure 12.31. At the top level it is important to access and control system structures (e.g. tasks, mailboxes, etc.) as logical elements of the multitasking design. Here we are concerned with system status, task status, tasks pending on signals, channel contents and the like. This method should provide a high level of abstraction; the user shouldn't need to know their internal structures to analyse system behaviour.

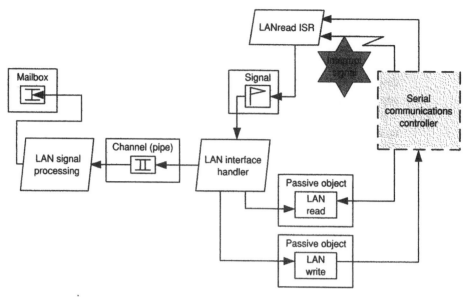

Figure 12.31 | System structure — multitasking design.

These functions are built on the use of register and memory data. Therefore the low-level debug features must let us interrogate and modify these in the usual way. This includes code analysis and disassembly at the task, function and statement levels. In general, most of the debug operations at this level are similar to those met earlier. However, two points need a special mention: breakpointing and register accesses.

It must be possible to set breakpoints as and when desired. This includes an individual task, a number of specified tasks, or all tasks. But this raises a problem where breakpoints are set within code (typically a procedure or function) which is shared by tasks. Using normal methods a break would take place each time the procedure is accessed. In some instances this is exactly what is intended by the debugger. In others we may wish to view the execution path of a specific task, only breaking when the shared procedure is accessed by that task. Therefore we must be able to associate a breakpoint with a task identifier (one further practical issue: it is very important to be able to debug a task and yet leave the others running).

Another significant difference shows in the method by which the debugger interacts with registers. In a conventional debugger the register information available is the current, *actual*, status of the processor. Using this in a multitasking system would be quite limiting. It would be possible to check only the registers of the current executing task. Yet in many instances it is important to see the status of all tasks. So a multitasking debugger must also let the user get at the register contents of the task control blocks.

It is clear that a debugger must be tailored to the individual operating system. In earlier days most multitasking debuggers were, in fact, specific to a product. Nowadays mainstream debuggers are designed to work with a variety of OSs, having what is called 'RTOS or kernel awareness'. This is achieved by having an RTOS interface which can be replaced or adapted as required. The interface has two sections, one in the host and one in the target. The target software is a multitasking version of the execution monitor described earlier. Host software, in its simplest form, provides a general or 'generic' interface for the user. More powerful products allow this interface to be highly customized to individual kernels. In some cases it is possible to adapt the interface to the 'home-grown' (custom-designed) variety of operating systems.

12.4.5   A last comment

Target-based software debuggers are powerful tools, especially where:

- Hardware is proven and fault-free and
- Software is not subject to asynchronous interrupts.

Even then it must be remembered that stepping and breakpoint control usually uses some form of invasive test technique. This disturbs normal program operation, resulting in reduced execution speeds. A program may check out correctly and then fail at full-speed testing. What then? Moreover, the debugger uses a certain amount of target RAM as a workspace. It would therefore be possible for the application program to overwrite this (sloppy programming), causing chaos in the debugger. How do we locate such problems?

From this it can be seen that there is a clear requirement for hardware debuggers; that is the subject of the next section.

12.5   Software debugging in the target – hardware-based methods

12.5.1   Introduction

Most of the tools described in this section were originally designed to tackle hardware problems in microprocessors. Similar items had previously been developed for minis and mainframes, but they weren't widely applied by computer *users*. The real-time microcomputer market is entirely different. Here equipment and system manufacturers predominate, not computer companies. Many, many users, operating in diverse fields, need to get microprocessor systems running correctly and delivered on time. And to do this they need to have the right tools for the job.

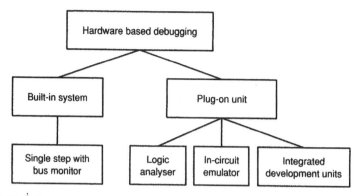

Figure 12.32 | Hardware-based debugging methods.

With time there has been a convergence of hardware and software test methods. As microprocessor software became more complex many hardware-based tools were adapted for use as software analysers. Some problems just couldn't be resolved without using hardware aids. And the difficulties were compounded by the almost exclusive use of assembly language programming in micros. One example which illustrates this point is that of a digital controller which occasionally (and only occasionally) crashed out. The problem was eventually tracked down to an interrupt occurring in the middle of reloading a programmable timer chip. The timer specification gave no warning of such a problem; in fact it seems likely that the chip manufacturer was unaware of such an event. This problem comes into the category of software-induced hardware faults; such problems are virtually impossible to detect using software debugging tools only.

Nowadays many test systems are seen primarily as software development aids. Such tools come in a variety of forms (Figure 12.32), the majority being plug-on units. The role, and effectiveness, of such units is discussed below. Emphasis is placed on their use as software rather than hardware test aids.

12.5.2   A basic test tool – the bus monitor

One of the simplest hardware test methods is to monitor the state of the processor system while stepping through the program (Figure 12.33). This, at the minimum, involves monitoring the address, display and control lines. Stepping can be done in a number of ways: clock cycle, machine cycle or instruction cycle. This depends on the design of both the single-step circuit and the processor itself. The technique is extremely useful for testing the operation of new (untried) peripherals. It is also particularly useful where device programming is complex (such as modern programmable communication controller chips). It has the advantage of being very low cost; thus it can be made readily available within design groups. It also illustrates two basic features of hardware-assisted software testing. First, program control is handled by a device separate from the processor. Secondly, monitoring is non-invasive.

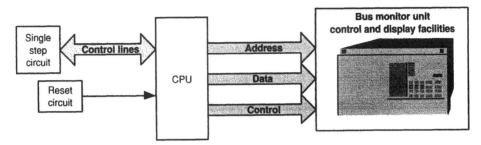

Figure 12.33 Simple hardware/software test method – the bus monitor unit.

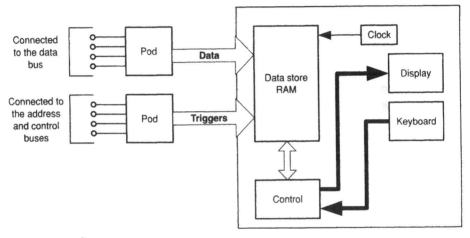

Figure 12.34 Logic analyser structure.

This test configuration enables us to see that the right information appears at the right time. However, its main limitation is that operation is essentially static, i.e. one step and stop. A second problem is that only a fixed number of points are monitored; these are usually set by the design. What do we do then if a program executes correctly on single step but fails at normal run speeds? This problem highlights the need for a dynamic test tool.

12.5.3 The logic analyser

In its basic form the logic analyser is a data acquisition unit (Figure 12.34), gathering information from selected points within the micro system. Control of *when* to record data is determined by the trigger signals. Control of *what* to record is set by the connections into the micro system from the data pod. This includes address, data and control information. The amount of data recorded depends on the size of the RAM store within the analyser. Both *when* and *what* are set by the user via a keyboard interface. Information gathered during a test run is subsequently displayed

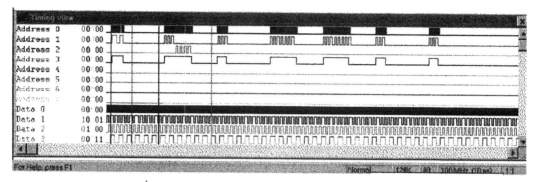

Figure 12.35 Logic analyser timing waveform display.

for user evaluation. Logic analysers may be stand-alone units that contain full control and display facilities. Alternatively they can be integrated with desktop units (usually PCs), users interacting with them via the keyboard, mouse, display, etc.

The logic analyser doesn't control the processor; essentially it records what happens during a program run. Within a recording session the key point is the 'trigger'. This condition is set by the user as a marker for data collection. It may act as the start or finish of the recording session, being activated when the logic inputs on the trigger lines match the preset condition. Triggering may be set to correspond with instruction fetches, specific memory accesses, I/O device operation and such like. Information collected during the run can be displayed in a number of ways including timing waveforms and state information.

Timing waveforms

A typical example of a timing waveform display is shown in Figure 12.35. Although this is mainly used in hardware analysis it has its place in software debugging. For instance, the timer chip problem described earlier was resolved using this display technique.

State diagram

Here the sequence of program operations relative to the trigger condition is displayed. This includes address and data information. Simpler units show these in hexadecimal or binary form (Figure 12.36); more complex types include disassemblers giving assembly language mnemonics as appropriate.

The logic analyser is a powerful tool. In fact, it is usually the second-last resort for analysing really difficult problems (the last line of defence is the oscilloscope). This, combined with single-step control, enables us to get to the bottom of almost all problems, hardware or software. It has one drawback. Analysis using the logic analyser is a time-consuming task, especially when the software is complex. This has led to the development of the in-circuit emulator (ICE).

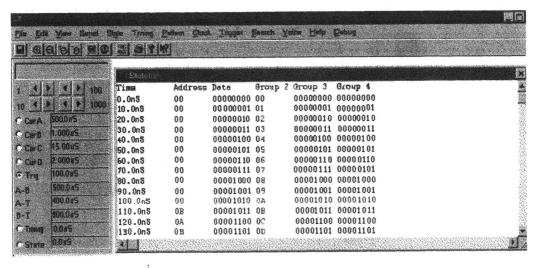

Figure 12.36 Logic analyser state analysis display.

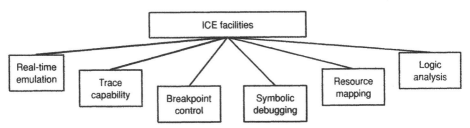

Figure 12.37 In-circuit emulator facilities.

12.5.4 The in-circuit emulator

In-circuit emulation is defined to be 'the replacement of a microprocessor in a prototype by a piece of test equipment intended to provide all the functionality of that microprocessor, along with capabilities to assist in the integration of the hardware and software components of this prototype' [TSE82]. The ICE was originally designed by Intel, primarily to tackle hardware problems. It has now become a major software debugging aid within the embedded systems community.

The facilities provided by ICE are given in Figure 12.37, most of these by now being quite familiar.

Resource mapping is the exception (described below). The important point is that all these features can be used in the target system at target speed of operation.

Many variants of ICE now exist, ranging from general-purpose units to those specific to the manufacturer. However, the basic structure shown in Figure 12.38 is typical of modern designs. It consists of three major components:

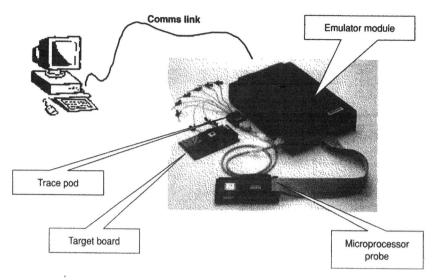

Figure 12.38 | In-circuit emulation – basic set-up.

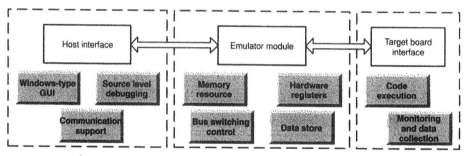

Figure 12.39 | ICE subsystem functions.

● A host interface.

● An emulator module.

● The target board interface – microprocessor probe and trace pod.

Their functions, in broad outline, are shown in Figure 12.39.

The microprocessor probe carries a microprocessor of the same type as the target. During emulation, the target processor is removed and the probe plugged-in in its place. All target software is subsequently executed by the emulation processor. At first sight this may seem odd. Why bother to take out one processor chip and replace it by an identical type? The answer is that the emulation processor can be controlled by the emulation module, something which can't easily be done with the original processor. (Note: it may not always be possible to physically remove the

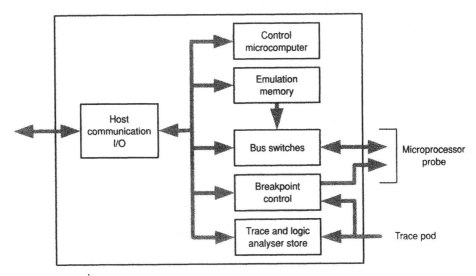

Figure 12.40 Emulator module functional diagram.

target processor. In this case emulation can be carried out provided the target processor can be electrically 'disconnected' from the system.)

The trace probe is used for monitoring target board activities, such as address, data and control signals. Direct control of the target board interface is carried out by the emulator module (Figure 12.40). It also acquires and records data sent to it from the trace pod. This module itself uses a microprocessor, sometimes called the control and interrogation processor. It does not have to be the same type as that in the target. The control processor is responsible for:

● Setting up the emulator module as commanded by the host.

● Uploading data to the host.

● Monitoring and controlling the emulator processor.

● Monitoring the target system for subsequent trace analysis.

Information transfer from the emulator processor to the control processor normally involves direct memory access communication methods.

The trace functions are handled by what, in this context, is best described as a software logic analyser. More powerful ICE units have a large acquisition store and an extensive analysis software suite to support this function. Using the recorded data the analysis software can create a thorough model of the microprocessor system. This includes internal registers, I/O devices and data structures. Such features are augmented by counters and timers which keep track of real-time events. Resource mapping is an important feature of in-circuit emulators. With this the emulator module allows the emulation processor to use its RAM-based emulation memory.

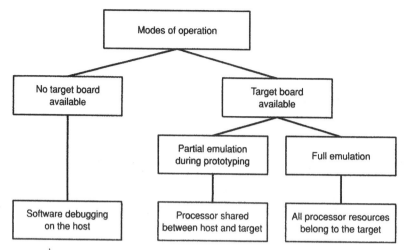

Figure 12.41 | ICE modes of operation.

This is done on a controlled, selective basis. It is thus possible to run an emulation without any components being fitted to the target board. In many systems it is even possible to execute target code without the target board being present. This has given rise to three modes of ICE operation, as shown in Figure 12.41.

It would be impossible to provide an ICE environment without a comprehensive control, display and interface software suite. Earlier systems used dedicated ICE environments. These, unfortunately, were extremely expensive. To meet the demand for lower-cost facilities, one particular configuration has become predominant: the use of a PC host machine. PCs are relatively low-cost items compared with special-purpose ICE tools. And, of course, the PC can be used for other jobs, thus 'sharing' its cost amongst various applications.

ICE is one of the most powerful (and costly) tools of the microprocessor engineer. It lets us analyse software to a very great depth. Yet it still leaves one question unanswered: how good is the performance of our software? More of that later.

12.6 Software debugging in the target – combined hardware/software techniques

12.6.1 Host–target interactive debugging – software tracing

Having a monitor program in the target makes it is possible to debug the target software interactively from the host machine. However, monitor-based methods are intrusive; thus they intrinsically limit the quality and quantity of real-time data that can be gathered in a debugging session. The hardware-based methods described

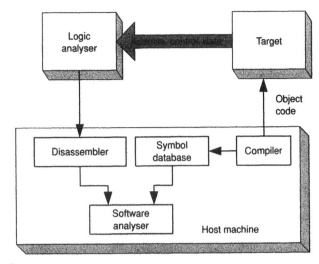

Figure 12.42 ┊ Host–target interactive debugger structure (software trace debugging).

earlier get around this problem. Using these we can obtain run-time information which just couldn't be accessed using a simple monitor. But they don't allow us to *automatically* compare source code aspects with the actual running code. If we could do that, though, we would end up with a greatly improved interactive real-time debugging capability. The only way to achieve such a goal is to combine hardware and software, so forming a *software trace debugger*, Figure 12.42.

The concept is to debug by examining source code that is linked to a real-time trace of the actual run-time code. Here a logic analyser is used to gather real-time information from the target. On disassembly it is forwarded to a software analyser. The data is then cross-referenced to information held in the symbol files or database of the source program. Once the trace information is recorded, it can be displayed in the same programming language as that used for the source code. A complete recording can be stepped through to find out exactly what happened in the target at particular points in time.

Debugging, from the user's perspective, is much the same as host-based techniques. Thus there really isn't much more to say about it, except to point out its drawbacks. While it works very well with simpler and/or older processors, there are problems with more complex designs. Fundamental to the approach is that we can deduce precisely what is happening in the processor from the processor bus status (i.e. the information collected by the logic analyser). Unfortunately, the use of instruction pipelining, on-chip data caches, on-chip memory controllers and other peripherals leads to problems here. Divergence sets in between what happens on the external buses and what takes place in the processor itself. You need to be well aware of your processor's structure and behaviour together with the limitations of your debugger.

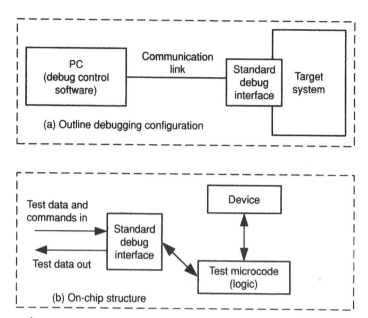

Figure 12.43 | On-chip debugging basics.

12.6.2 On-chip debugging methods

From the previous section, it is clear that debugging modern processors (especially the 32 bit highly integrated microcontrollers) is anything but simple. The problems raised by deep pipelining, on-chip caches, etc. are compounded by high clock speeds. These features increase the performance of the target system. Unfortunately, at the same time they reduce the visibility and quality of debug information. However, the pressures to reduce development time and to improve software quality mean that debugging is still a priority activity. As a result many manufacturers of complex micros provide on-chip logic to support debugging operations. These are generally called on-chip debugging (OCD) systems, Figure 12.43. Figure 12.43a shows the outline system configuration when using OCD methods. It consists of a:

- Host, usually a PC, which houses the software to control running of the debugging session and a

- Target system, which includes the device (microcontroller/processor) under test.

These are connected via a relatively simple serial link. Observe that the target system presents a standard – manufacturer-independent – debug interface to the outside world. The micro itself has test logic included on the chip, Figure 12.43b, this being activated by commands from the host. Such commands are sent via a test access port on the chip. The access port is also used to transmit data collected during a test run to the outside world.

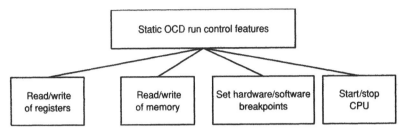

Figure 12.44 : Simple static OCD features.

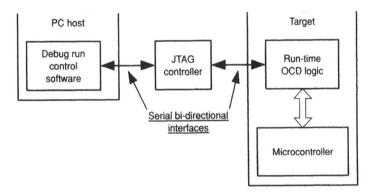

Figure 12.45 : Simple static OCD scheme (JTAG interface).

Fundamentally there are two types of debugging tests: static and dynamic. With static debugging, information cannot be gathered *during* program execution. The CPU must be stopped to allow data to be extracted from the system. In contrast, dynamic debugging enables data to be collected as the CPU runs.

Note that the CPU can execute debug commands only while it is in a specific mode of operation (often called the 'background' mode). This has given rise to the expression 'background debug mode' or BDM.

Simple static on-chip debugging methods

The simplest form of static debugging enables the tester to carry out the operations shown in Figure 12.44. These basic run control features can be implemented using the hardware/software scheme of Figure 12.45. It can be seen that this includes a controller which interfaces to the PC host. This particular arrangement has evolved (for very good practical reasons) from *boundary scan* testing of electronic systems [IEE90]. These techniques were developed so testing could be done without the need to physically probe around circuit boards. A number of manufacturers formed the Joint Test Action Group (JTAG) to develop such test standards. One result was the decision to provide, on-chip, in silicon, a simple serial interface for testing purposes. The JTAG interface has, in fact, been formalized by an IEEE standard (IEEE1149.1).

Thus it was a logical move (for some manufacturers, at least) to use the JTAG interface for OCD purposes. But this brings with it the need to translate standard PC serial I/O signals to JTAG format.

The advantages of this debugging technique are that:

- It is low-cost.

- There is no need to connect probes onto the processor system or to remove the processor from the board for test purposes.

- The communication method and connections are standard, not in any way dependent on processor type, architecture or clock speeds.

- The connection to/from the host is independent of chip packaging methods.

Dynamic OCD schemes

As stated earlier, dynamic methods allow us to perform debugging without having to stop the CPU. Moreover, these can normally be done in a non-invasive (non-intrusive) manner. There are a whole range of static and dynamic debug features, as illustrated in the IEEE-ISTO Nexus 5001 Forum Standard. The most comprehensive ones, corresponding to the highest level in the Nexus standard, are given in Figure 12.46. From previous work it should be clear what these features are used for and what they achieve.

Note that to obtain real-time trace data, it is necessary to extend the basic static scheme, Figure 12.47. The details of the on-chip trace logic vary from manufacturer to manufacturer. Two extremes are:

- Extensive on-chip trace storage combined with moderate-speed transmission of compressed trace data.

- Minimal on-chip storage combined with high-speed transmission of raw trace data.

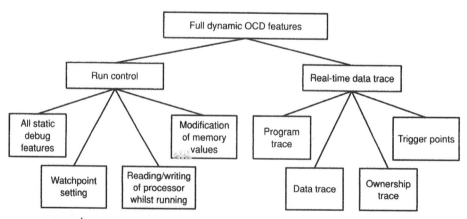

Figure 12.46 Full dynamic OCD features.

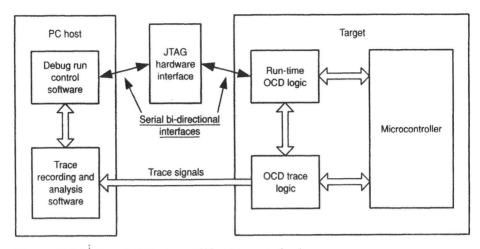

Figure 12.47 Dynamic OCD scheme (JTAG and trace interfaces).

Limitations of the JTAG-based techniques show up when dealing with multiple processors on a chip. Problems arise when trying to:

- Access processors individually.

- Synchronize the starting and stopping of processors.

- Test chips which incorporate a number of processors designed by different vendors (thus needing vendor-specific debugging software).

The reality of the situation, however, is that you'll have to live with whatever the processor manufacturer supplies. For general-purpose applications this should include facilities to carry out RTOS-aware trace and performance analysis.

12.7 Debugging in host-as-target combinations

12.7.1 Background

In this context a host–target combination means one of two things. First, it describes schemes where the target system OS is the same as that of the host. Second, it includes designs where the host itself is used as the target. Both configurations are described below. The first is applicable to target designs which employ operating systems based on standard desktop machines. The second describes the use of the ubiquitous PC as the target machine itself.

The host-as-target idea is not new. One very widely used general-purpose machine in earlier days was the Digital Equipment Corp. (DEC) MicroVAX computer. However, nowadays the PC has become *the de facto* commercial standard.

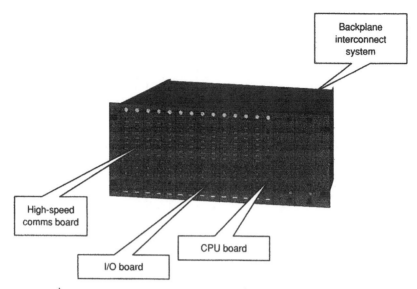

Figure 12.48 Bus-based target system.

And, as pointed out previously, the PC is also penetrating the industrial market, though generally in ruggedized form.

At present the dominating operating systems are Microsoft Windows (usually 98/NT/2000/XP), though Linux is gaining rapid support within the embedded community. Thus the expression 'PC-based' (used below) can be read as 'Windows-based' or 'Linux-based'.

12.7.2   PC-based targets – the embedded PC

PC-based targets range from systems-on-a-chip to bus-based single-board computers (SBCs), Figure 12.48. Typical of these are PC/104 and VME designs. These provide fully operational PC-compatible computer systems. One major advantage of this approach is that (normally) there isn't a need to carry out hardware debugging. Thus efforts can concentrate on:

- Debugging the application software, both in the host and the target.
- Test and development of I/O hardware and device drivers.

The development environment is similar to that of Figure 12.30. Here, though, the original monitor software is replaced by that of the embedded (target) operating system. It thus makes the target system 'look' like a PC. Now both the host and target machines are (from the software point of view) almost identical.

When using this approach there are three distinct development phases:

- Application software debugging on the host.
- Test of target hardware and drivers from the host.
- Application software debugging within the target.

There is nothing new to say about host system debugging. For example, the following features provided by the Microsoft debugger, WinDbg, will be quite familiar:

- Viewing of source code.
- Setting breakpoints.
- Viewing variables (and objects, where applicable).
- Performing stack traces.
- Viewing memory contents.
- Run-time control.

It goes without saying that it is kernel-aware, and may be used to debug multitasking software. It also supports debugging of device drivers. However, more specialized debug packages, such as NuMega SoftICE, are optimized for device driver debugging.

Tools like these are host-oriented and unfortunately fail to meet all the needs of embedded environments. Thus it is necessary to augment their features by hardware-specific debugging software, as for example the VMEbus manager from XYCOM. This is a board support package for Windows NT running in a VME environment. It provides means to access, monitor and test the VME bus system, including features to:

- Read, write, search and fill VMEbus memory.
- Monitor and control VME bus interrupts.
- Read and write values to I/O ports.
- Establish system configuration information.

A short aside: before starting target software debugging one should normally ensure that the hardware does, in fact, actually work. This may be done as follows:

- Set up a control and communications link between the host and the target processor board.
- Issue system-provided test commands from the host machine to exercise the hardware.
- Load specially written hardware test routines into the target RAM, then exercise the hardware.

After this the application software may be downloaded into the target. At this point the application program behaves as if it's running in a PC – though it's actually operating in its native environment. Therefore any implementation problems will quickly show up. Debugging can be done using the usual set of tools, with the added advantage of working within a familiar PC environment.

The software described here is more than just a test/debugger tool. It forms the basis for a complete microprocessor development system.

12.7.3 PC as target

Many of the tools and techniques used with embedded PCs were derived from their desktop counterparts. Moreover, when a PC is used as the target machine one can usually assume that the basic hardware works correctly. Thus debugging is mainly (sometimes entirely) software-based. Why then is there also a demand by developers of PC-based systems for hardware-assisted debugging tools? The answer is that these are invaluable for the development of:

- New hardware, especially plug-in boards.
- Complex software.

The first use is something we'd expect. The second, however, is quite surprising in view of the capabilities of software debuggers. But even in the PC environment, the limitations of software-based tools still apply (discussed earlier). In particular, monitoring and control of program execution while it runs at full speed is a virtual impossibility. And problems which show at that stage are usually the most difficult and obscure ones. The only solution is to use hardware-aided debugging tools. General-purpose in-circuit emulators can, of course, be used for this work. Alternatively, ICE tools optimized for PC work, such as the Periscope debugger, may be a cheaper solution. Tools like these are frequently integrated with software development and debugging tool suites.

12.8 In-target analysis tools

12.8.1 Introduction

What we have been doing so far is verifying the design of our software. That is, does it do what we expect it to (and conversely, does it not do unexpected things)? Let's assume that it has been tested to our satisfaction. Fine. But we still have little explicit data regarding the performance of the program. For instance:

- How long does the complete program take to run?
- How long do component code units (e.g. tasks and subprograms) take to run?
- How often are individual units used?

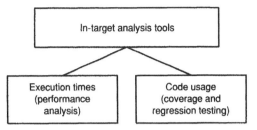

Figure 12.49 ⋮ Use of in-target analysis tools.

- What sort of interaction do we have between the units?
- What is the time latency in the servicing of interrupts?
- If parts of a program are slow, why?
- How heavily is the processor loaded?
- Does the processor get overloaded with work, and if so, what is the impact of the overload on performance?
- Is all the code executed during verification testing?

These questions are not very important for many applications. After all, if a program which runs interactively on a PC is a bit slow, so what? And if it sometimes mysteriously crashes, well, that's not so unusual. For embedded systems such behaviour may be disastrous; hence we do need some (if not all) answers to the above questions. Without the support of analysis aids, finding the answers is a long and laborious job.

In-target analysis tools examine two main program factors, speed (performance) and run-time code usage, Figure 12.49. These frequently come as part of a specific development tool, as in the Hitex DProbe/DBox in-circuit emulators.

12.8.2   Performance analysis tools

To fully evaluate software performance, program analysis must be conducted at various levels, including task, subprogram and statement. Single events must be captured and analysed. Interrupt effects, both in terms of frequency and duration, need recording. Information display needs to be meaningful and clear, with the ability to work at a symbolic level *and* with absolute addresses. And finally, but most importantly, monitoring should be non-intrusive so as not to disturb the normal operation of the program.

Figure 12.50 shows the general functional structure of a performance analysis tool. Address signals are picked up by a measuring probe and fed into a data acquisition section. This is performed 'on the fly'. Selected information, as defined by the control section, is recorded here. The results of this are input to the control section for onward transmission to the host computer. All operator commands are fed in from the host; all results are displayed on this same machine. Precise sampling and

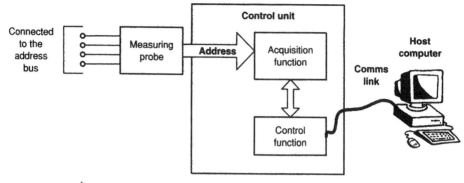

Figure 12.50 | Performance analysis tool (PAT) – overall structure.

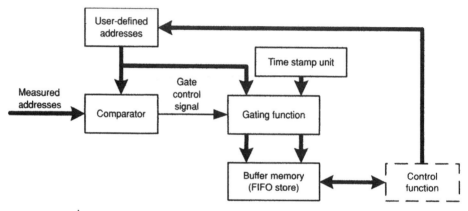

Figure 12.51 | PAT – basic acquisition function.

processing times depend very much on the test tool capabilities and the nature of the software being tested. For example, the Hitex DBox can capture 50 seconds' worth of data before its memory store fills up. Once it uploads this data to the host computer (which takes 5 seconds) it can repeat the data collection exercise. All post-processing and analysis of the data is carried out by the host machine.

The basic operation of the acquisition section is shown in Figure 12.51. Input (measured) addresses are compared with those set by the user. If a correspondence is found, two gates are opened and both the address value and the time of the event are recorded. A serial first-in first-out (FIFO) buffer memory store is used for this; thus all events are stored in sequence. This allows multiple specific address variables to be monitored simultaneously. The time-stamp interval settings typically range from sub-microsecond to hundreds of milliseconds. Analysis of the information is carried out on the host computer by specialized post-processing algorithms.

The overall control and display function (Figure 12.52) enables the operator to communicate with the analysis tool. In a typical session the operator defines (sets) the address accesses which are to be monitored, the processing to be carried out

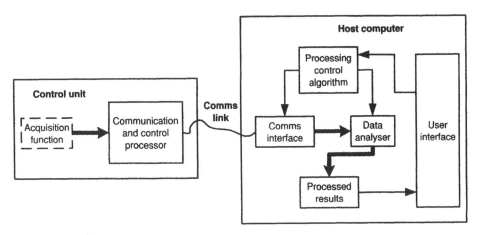

Figure 12.52 : PAT – control and display function.

Eventpair	Procedure	Count	Time	Percent (Absolute)	Time(%)
BACKGROUND	---	---	0us		0%
timer3	timer3_int	3207	386.5ms		10%
AD spd	AD_spd_to_freq	3207	5.775ms		0%
CAN Int	CAN_int	3219	35.12ms		1%
IR to	IR_timeout	380	114us		0%
Trip	trip_period_interrupt	3206	8.686ms		0%
timer1	timer1_int	128625	3.076s		76%
ramp	generate_ramp	3207	55.44ms		1%
implemen	implement_UF	3207	24.64ms		1%
get dema	get_demand_speed	3208	30.32ms		1%
get cont	get_control_parameters	3208	219.5ms		5%
directio	control_direction	3207	10.92ms		0%
Read ADC	read_AD_channel	19252	184.3ms		5%

Figure 12.53 : Time histogram display of software run-times (motor speed controller).

on the resulting recordings, and the form of display to be used for this information. The following figures (12.53 to 12.60) show a specimen set of results generated by a performance analysis tool (this has been provided by Hitex UK, illustrating the use of their in-circuit emulator-analyser ('emulyzer') tools [HIT01]).

The first display (Figure 12.53) is a histogram record of program unit activations within a motor speed control program. Note this includes both subprograms and interrupt-driven programs. This gives a very broad view of program operation, showing how program execution time is consumed by individual procedures. In this case it covers a period or 'record slot' of 4560 ms. This format allows the most time-consuming functions to be quickly identified. The actual CPU loading is indicated by the length of the bar; it is also given numerically in the right-hand column.

More detailed information concerning these procedures can be extracted from the recorded data. For instance, how many times did each procedure run in the record slot? And how much time did a procedure run consume (Figure 12.54)?

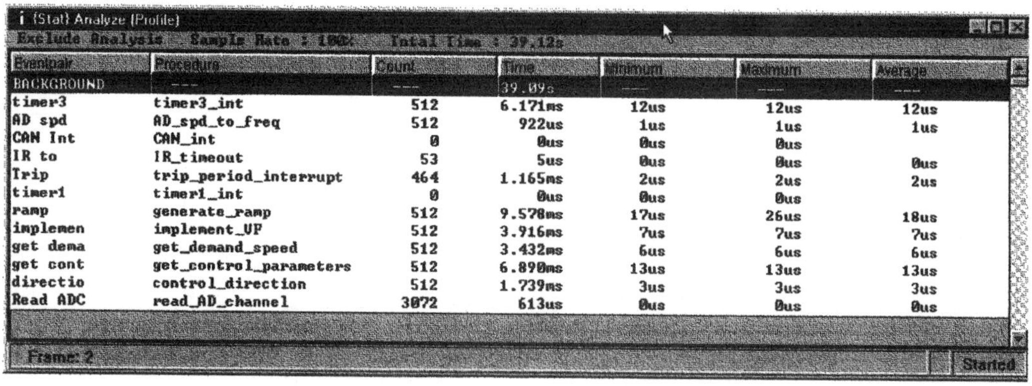

{Stat} Analyze {Profile}

Exclude Analysis   Sample Rate : 100%   Total Time : 39.12s

Eventpair	Procedure	Count	Time	Minimum	Maximum	Average
BACKGROUND	---	---	39.09s	---	---	---
timer3	timer3_int	512	6.171ms	12us	12us	12us
AD spd	AD_spd_to_freq	512	922us	1us	1us	1us
CAN Int	CAN_int	0	0us	0us	0us	
IR to	IR_timeout	53	5us	0us	0us	0us
Trip	trip_period_interrupt	464	1.165ms	2us	2us	2us
timer1	timer1_int	0	0us	0us	0us	
ramp	generate_ramp	512	9.578ms	17us	26us	18us
implemen	implement_UF	512	3.916ms	7us	7us	7us
get dema	get_demand_speed	512	3.432ms	6us	6us	6us
get cont	get_control_parameters	512	6.890ms	13us	13us	13us
directio	control_direction	512	1.739ms	3us	3us	3us
Read ADC	read_AD_channel	3072	613us	0us	0us	0us

Frame: 2   Started

Figure 12.54 Table display of motor speed controller software run-times.

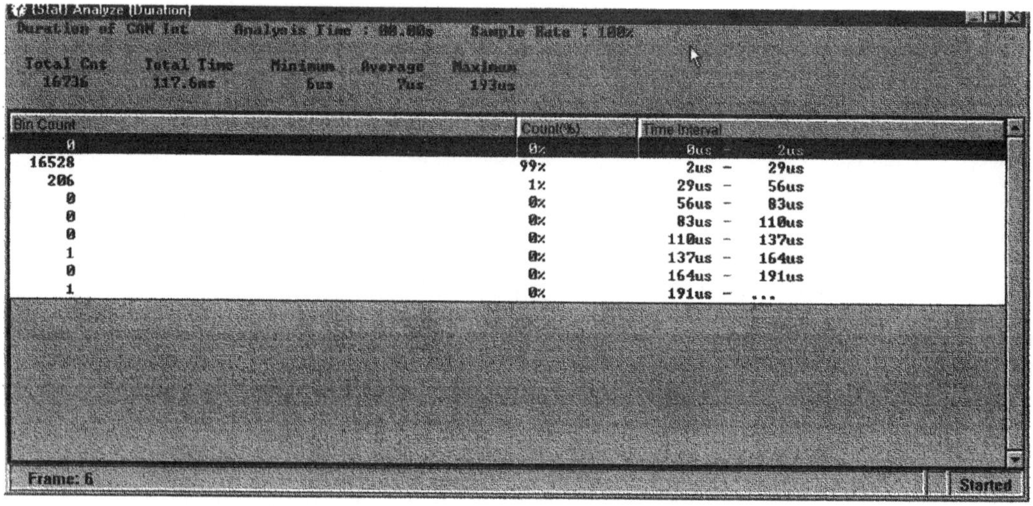

{Stat} Analyze {Duration}

Duration of CAN Int   Sample Rate : 100%

Total Cnt	Total Time	Minimum	Average	Maximum
16736	117.6ms	6us	7us	193us

Bin Count	Count(%)	Time Interval
0	0%	0us - 2us
16528	99%	2us - 29us
206	1%	29us - 56us
0	0%	56us - 83us
0	0%	83us - 110us
0	0%	110us - 137us
1	0%	137us - 164us
0	0%	164us - 191us
1	0%	191us - ...

Frame: 6   Started

Figure 12.55 Duration analysis of motor speed controller software run-times.

Now let's suppose that very specific timing information is needed. For instance, what are the variations in the run-times of program units and are they significant? This is where 'duration times' becomes important (Figure 12.55).

This record shows that the response time of an interrupt designated 'CAN Int' lies in the range 2–29 microseconds for 99% of its activations. However, 206 of its activations (1%) fall into the 29–56 microsecond time slot. But note that one response takes 193 microseconds, something quite significant if deterministic response times are important.

Finally, how can we be sure that all the code is actually exercised? This brings us to the second aspect of in-target analysis tools, coverage analysis.

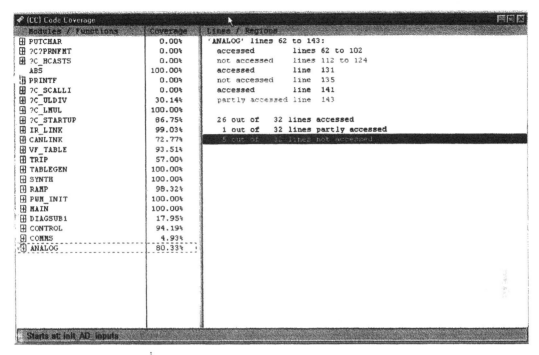

Figure 12.56 ┊ Coverage analysis display of motor speed controller software.

12.8.3 Hardware-based coverage analysis

The basic concepts and practical aspects of coverage analysis were explained in detail in Chapter 11 (Analysing and testing source code). Here, though, our concern is to produce data relating to the software located in the target system itself. Three specific additional factors (over and above those expounded in Chapter 11) need to be taken into account. The testing must be done:

- With the final code.
- On the actual final hardware.
- In real-time.

In these cases we can use a display (the 'coverage' mode, Figure 12.56) to show precisely how well the software was exercised during test. The display gives a list of program units together with general coverage information (and, as shown, detailed information for one program unit ANALOG). However, the program unit of concern for this example is IR_LINK. This holds controller software that allows users to control the motor via a remote serial (infra-red) control link. Initial testing showed that the IR software had not been fully executed, coverage being less than 100%. To pin

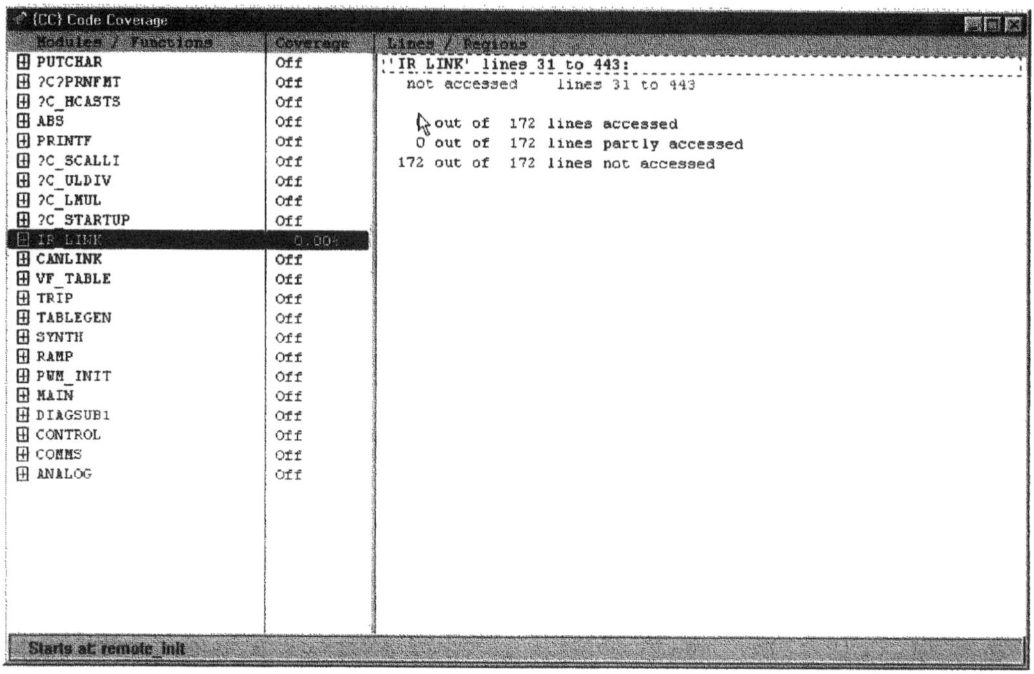

Figure 12.57 Coverage analysis display – detailed function test I.

down the problem, detailed testing of the IR-LINK program unit must be carried out, Figure 12.57. The situation presented here relates to the pre-test stage (testing hasn't yet started), thus the percentage code covered is zero. The program is now set running, initializing the function IR_LINK, Figure 12.58. The coverage analyser shows that only 17 out of 172 lines were fully accessed, these being 'ticked' in the code listing window.

Complete testing requires that a full range of *commands* (both valid and invalid) be sent to the unit. In this case the final coverage results obtained are those shown in Figure 12.59. Observe that lines 399–401 of the source code have not been ticked off. This shows clearly that the code in question hasn't been executed, even though all user-command functions had been exercised.

Deeper investigation revealed that this section of code – designed to deal with error situations – was faultless. In fact a functional test of this particular feature had been carried out, and all appeared to be correct (its aim, by the way, was to prevent the motor speed being set too high). However, there was an undiscovered bug elsewhere in the software. This, unfortunately, had limited the value of the speed increment demand coming from over the serial link. As a result the error-handling code was never invoked.

Finally, where proof of testing is required, a code coverage report may be generated, Figure 12.60.

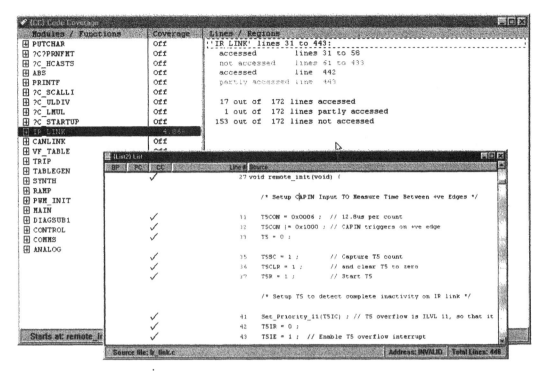

Figure 12.58 Coverage analysis display – detailed function test 2.

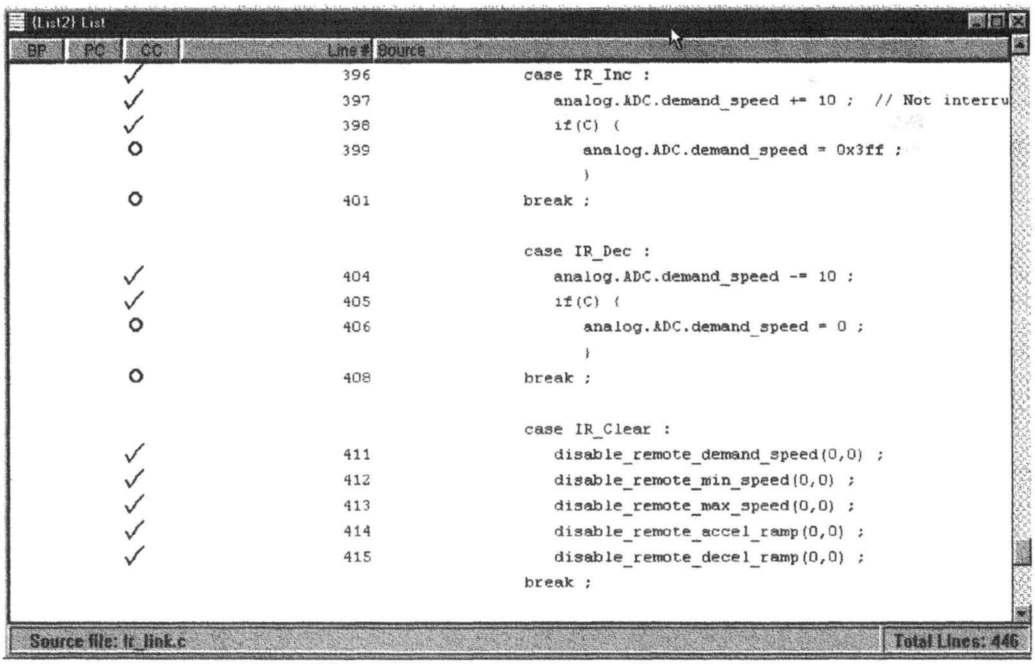

Figure 12.59 Coverage analysis display – detailed function test 3.

```
----- {CC} Code Coverage -----
----- Fri May 19 11:17:35 2000 -----
IR_LINK
99.03%
          'IR_LINK' lines 31 to 443:
            accessed        lines 31 to 398
            not accessed    lines 399 to 401
            accessed        lines 404 to 442
            partly accessed line 443

          168 out of  172 lines accessed
            1 out of  172 lines partly accessed
            2 out of  172 lines not accessed
    remote_init()
    100.00%
          remote_init() lines 31 to 58 in IR_LINK:
            accessed        lines 31 to 58

          16 out of  16 lines accessed
           0 out of  16 lines partly accessed
           0 out of  16 lines not accessed
    IR_int()
98.98%
          IR_int() lines 61 to 433 in IR_LINK:
            accessed        lines 61 to 398
            not accessed    lines 399 to 401
            accessed        lines 404 to 433

          151 out of  153 lines accessed
            0 out of  153 lines partly accessed
            2 out of  153 lines not accessed
    IR_timeout()
    100.00%
          IR_timeout() lines 442 to 443 in IR_LINK:
            accessed        line  442
            partly accessed line  443

            1 out of   2 lines accessed
            1 out of   2 lines partly accessed
            0 out of   2 lines not accessed
```

Figure 12.60 Coverage analysis report.

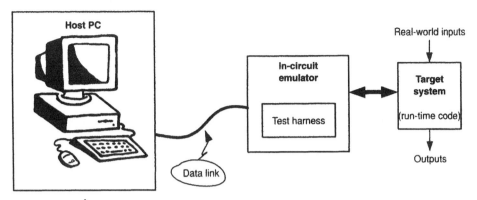

Figure 12.61 Regression testing in target systems.

12.8.4 Hardware-based regression testing

In many applications, especially defence work, systems have long lives, being subject to many modifications. Experience has shown that the testing of modified code (*regression testing*) is much more demanding than testing new software. One major problem is that changes can produce quite unexpected and/or unforeseen behaviour. It may be, for instance, that after a series of changes some code is unused. Or the original test harness fails to check all sections of the 'new' program.

As described earlier, pure software tools are available that contain powerful aids for generating test harnesses. However, always bear in mind that such tools either:

- Run the application in a wholly artificial (host) environment or else
- Alter significantly the conditions under which the software is executed.

The practical structure of a real-time embedded test harness is given in Figure 12.61. Here:

- Test data is downloaded from a PC disk file into an ICE to update a test harness script.
- The ICE values are fed into the parameters of the function to be tested.
- The application is then executed.
- Return values or other outputs are then captured in real-time, non-invasively, by the emulator.
- This data is uploaded to the hard disk for analysis in the usual way.

Over the project lifetime, periodic testing with the same test harness and input data set should always give the same outputs. Any change indicates that the original functionality of the software has been altered (intentionally or otherwise). Clearly, changes of functionality must be tested with revised test harnesses.

There are many aspects of performance analysis which are beyond the scope of this text. However, from preceding sections it can be seen that to perform detailed software analysis, special tools are needed. This approach also has an impact on the use of HLLs. Worries about speed/memory inefficiencies of compilers become less important once we can readily identify problem code areas. Consequently, the bulk of the program can be written in an HLL, limiting assembler code to time-critical sections. As pointed out earlier, this has a major impact on reliability, development times and costs.

12.9 Installing code into the target – non-volatile software (firmware)

12.9.1 Overview

Program environments can be described as volatile or non-volatile. The use of a PC as a target system typifies a volatile setting. Program behaviour in these situations can be broken down into two parts: start-up and application run (Figure 12.62). Here a boot program is carried in a non-volatile store, usually an EPROM. This first performs basic checks and housekeeping tasks, including hardware checks. It then loads part (or all) of the operating system from disk into main, usually RAM-based, memory. To run an application program the user enters appropriate commands at the keyboard. These are interpreted by the operating system, which proceeds to download the user program into main memory and execute the code. Note that the user may be excluded from the process by having an auto-execute feature.

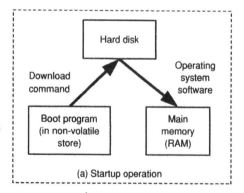
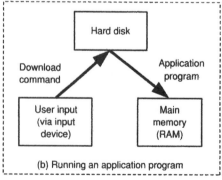

Figure 12.62 Program behaviour in a volatile environment.

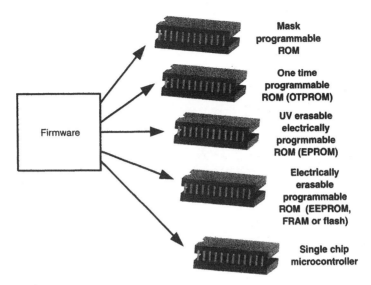

Mask
programmable
ROM

One time
programmable
ROM (OTPROM)

UV erasable
electrically
progrmmable
ROM (EPROM)

Electrically
erasable
programmable
ROM (EEPROM,
FRAM or flash)

Single chip
microcontroller

Firmware

Figure 12.63 Non-volatile software – firmware storage devices.

This configuration is volatile because each time the computer is powered down, all programs in main memory are lost. The system will respond correctly on power-up only if the correct programs are loaded up. Such arrangements *are* used in real-time systems, including, for example:

● In gas, oil and electricity control rooms.

● At the hubs of large distributed systems.

● In portable test equipment.

In the larger applications the control computer is usually a UNIX or NT-based workstation. For stand-alone use standard PCs are employed. However, they are not typical of the wider, more general embedded market. With these the program code is usually held in non-volatile form. Various storage devices (Figure 12.63) are used, having one factor in common: they have to be programmed with the appropriate object code.

Three techniques are used to put code into target systems:

● Memory devices are programmed and then inserted into the target system.

● Target system memory devices are (re)programmed whilst in the target system.

● Target system memory devices are replaced by external units (used for testing only).

In the first case a PROM programmer is used. The second involves bespoke techniques or adapted OCD tools. The third method uses a ROM emulator.

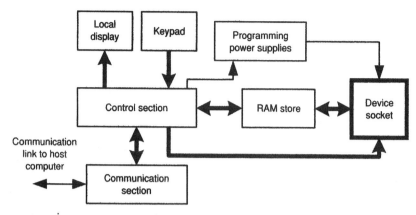

Figure 12.64 | General-purpose PROM programmer structure.

12.9.2 The PROM programmer

The basic requirement of a PROM programmer is that it must:

- Interface to various host development systems.
- Accept object code in specific file formats such as Intel Hex or Motorola S-Record.
- Convert these to pure binary form.
- Program this data into PROM.

Figure 12.64 shows the overall structure of a general-purpose PROM programmer. The final output from a compiler or assembler is an encoded file in, say, Intel Hex form. This contains not only the program code but also information concerning the location of such code in memory. It is downloaded to the PROM programmer over a communication link, typically using an RS232C serial channel. The control section acts on this input; it converts the program code to absolute binary form and loads it into RAM store. Its location within the store is defined in absolute terms by the linker. At this stage, once a device (EPROM, flash or microcomputer) is inserted into its programming socket, programming can begin. The control section handles the programming process, 'copying' each data byte (or word) from RAM into EPROM. This is the only occasion when an EPROM is written to, and requires a relatively high programming voltage. When programming is finished this is indicated on the operator's display. Should the EPROM be faulty and refuse to program correctly this is also shown to the operator.

The local control functions are split into two groups: RAM and EPROM operation. A typical set of operations is listed below; their value can only be appreciated after being heavily involved in program development.

RAM

- Fill a section of memory with a data value.
- Search for a specified data string.
- Replace a data string with a new one.
- Insert and delete RAM values.
- Copy blocks of data within RAM.
- Split the RAM block into two or more sections for set programming (used where the object code is too large to fit into a single EPROM).
- Merge (or shuffle) RAM data (converse of SPLIT).

EPROM/flash/micro

- Check that the PROM is erased correctly (blank check).
- Program the PROM with RAM data.
- Verify that the PROM and RAM contents are the same.
- Store the data from PROM to RAM.
- Erase – for flash devices only.

12.9.3 EPROM emulators

The action of removing, erasing and reprogramming EPROMs is a tedious and time-consuming one. So sensible engineers try to avoid using EPROMs until the final code is ready, testing the code in RAM (as with monitor packages). Unfortunately there are cases where this just isn't possible. For instance, target system debuggers may not be available. Or in a small system it might be impossible to fit all the program code into the available RAM space. This is where the EPROM emulator comes into use, Figure 12.65. By using this, EPROM programming is eliminated, thus speeding up software development. Its similarity to the PROM programmer is obvious. What is different is that the RAM store is connected to a header plug instead of an EPROM socket. This header plug is connected into the EPROM socket on the target board.

The unit has two modes of operation, set-up and emulate. Commands from the host control the settings of the unit. When it is in set-up mode bus switches 'A' are closed, 'B' being open. Object files are downloaded (in their usual format) from the host to the emulator, translated to binary form, and loaded into the emulator RAM. In emulate mode the bus switches change state. These connect the emulator RAM to the header plug and hence to the target processor. Now the target system behaves just as if an EPROM is plugged into the EPROM socket; it will therefore execute the program contained within the RAM.

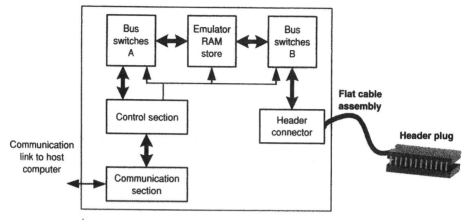

Figure 12.65 | Block diagram of EPROM emulator.

12.9.4   In-circuit programming

When program code is held in flash devices, it is possible to modify such software with the devices left *in situ*. This, however, requires that the target system be equipped with the necessary support hardware and software. Typically data is downloaded to the target via a serial comms channel. All communication, data checking, formatting and device programming is carried out by on-board software (which may be in EPROM or flash). Such facilities may be designed and implemented by the developers of the target system itself. This is the most common method. Alternatively, for highly integrated devices having on-chip memory, such features may be provided by the chip manufacturer. For example, the Motorola 68HC912 microcontroller has 128 kBytes of internal flash memory that can be reprogrammed using its OCD interface.

12.10   Integrated development environments

12.10.1   Back-end toolsets

Modern microprocessors, with their enormous increase in complexity, have brought a new set of problems for the embedded systems engineer. A whole battery of tools and techniques – as described throughout this book – are needed to deal with these. The basis for this is the integrated development toolset, Figure 12.66, usually centred on the ubiquitous PC. Such tools are mainly designed to support the later or 'back-end' development of software, especially in-target work. Good examples are the Green Hills Software [GRE01] and Hitex [HIT01] products. Fundamentally

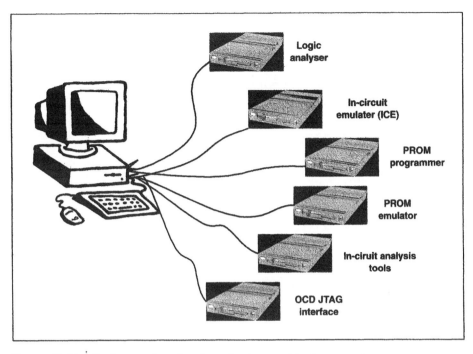

Figure 12.66 Hardware configuration of a modern integrated development toolset.

both toolsets have the same objectives but they achieve them in somewhat different ways.

The overall structure of the Green Hills Software tool MULTI® 2000 IDE, aimed at 32/64 bit processors, is shown in Figure 12.67. This is a very powerful, very comprehensive toolset. However, it has its roots in host-based systems, embedded features being introduced mainly via third-party products. In contrast the Hitex Hitop tool has been strongly driven from the embedded tool end. This, which focuses on 8/16/32 bit systems, is optimized to work with the Hitex tools, including simulators, debuggers, emulators, etc. As a result it can provide very detailed target system information, especially for performance analysis, code coverage and regression testing.

12.10.2 Fully integrated real-time development environments

For many years software engineers have had a wide choice of front-end (design-oriented) and back-end (implementation-oriented) tools. Unfortunately the same cannot be said of *totally* integrated development environments (i.e. those combining real-time design and implementation tools). The nearest to these are the

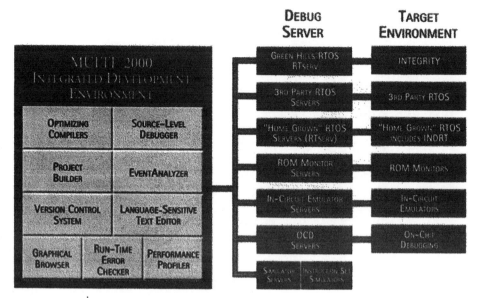

Figure 12.67 : Green Hills Software MULTI 2000 IDE structure.

graphical-based development tools discussed in Chapter 4. However, these tend to be tied to:

- Specific target environments (typically embedded PCs) and
- Specific software design processes.

Such factors significantly limit their range of application.

Fortunately, we are now beginning to see the fruits of co-operation between tool vendors to produce true real-time integrated development environments (RT-IDEs). One recent example is the integration of the Rational Rose RealTime® front-end tool [RAT01] with various back-end tools. The concepts behind such co-operative ventures can be shown using one (very brief) specific example: the interworking of the Rose tool with the MULTI 2000 IDE.

Rose RealTime is a UML-based design tool which, to quote the company, 'addresses the complete lifecycle of a project: from early use case analysis, through to design, implementation, and testing'. It also automatically generates C or C++ code to implement the functions defined by designers in their state diagrams, Figure 12.68. The MULTI IDE, together with Green Hills Software compilers, enable designers to compile, download and debug this code for execution on a target system. Moreover, the MULTI debugger is RTOS-aware, so enabling debugging and tuning to be carried out at the task (implementation model) level. Communication between the two tools is totally transparent to the user. As the program executes on the target the Rose RealTime UML state model animates in step with the code

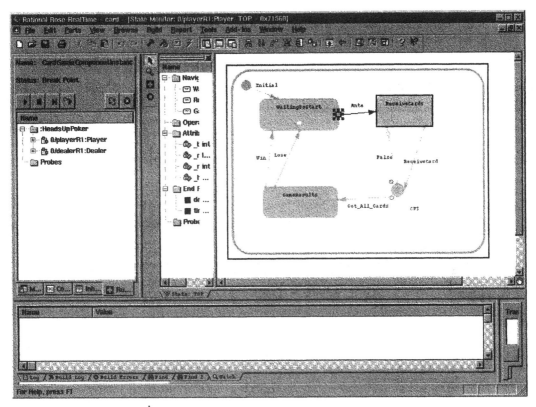

Figure 12.68 ⋮ Rational Rose RealTime example executable state model – screen capture.

(Figure 12.69). As a result the designer can see exactly how the system is behaving at both the model and code levels. This particular example shows one of the tasks within the target application halted at a UML breakpoint (MULTI breakpoints specifically developed for this form of high-level integration).

Review

You should now:

- Recognize that the emphasis here is not on the design of software but on its implementation, test and debug.

- Know the details of the various software development processes.

- Appreciate why real-time software requires a wide range of development tools, both software and hardware.

- Realize that software may be tested and debugged within three major environments: host, target and host-as-target.

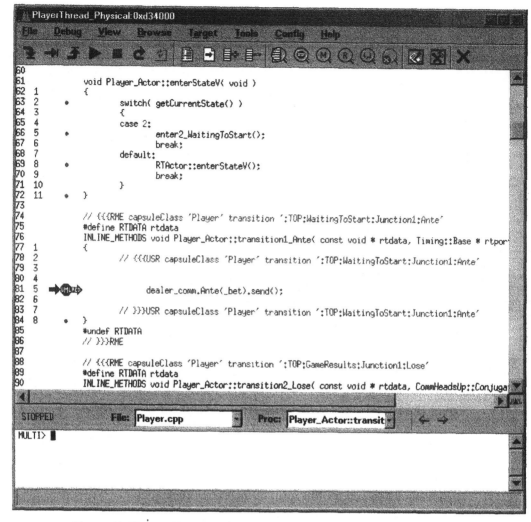

Figure 12.69 MULTI debugger in operation – screen capture.

- Understand the nature, facilities, advantages and drawbacks of the various development environments.
- Appreciate the features, application and outline use of the following:
  - Software debuggers.
  - Hardware debuggers.
  - In-circuit emulators.
  - Logic analysers.
  - OCD tools and techniques.
  - Memory device programmers and emulators.

- Understand how in-target analysis tools can be used for performance analysis, code coverage analysis and code regression testing.
- Know what to expect in modern integrated development environments.

References and further reading

[GRE01] *Software development tools for embedded applications*, Product literature 2001, Green Hills Software Inc., www.ghs.com.

[HIT01] *Using a Hitex emulator for embedded software testing*, Hitex Technical Bulletin, January 2001, www.hitex.co.uk.

[IEE90] *IEEE standard test access port and boundary-scan architecture*, IEEE Std 1149.1-1990.

[NEX99] *IEEE-ISTO 5001 1999, The Nexus 5001 Forum Standard for a global embedded processor debug interface*, IEEE Industry Standards and Technology Organization (IEEE-ISTO): www.ieee.isto.org/Nexus50001.

[NUM01] NuMega SoftICE product literature, 2001, www.numega.com.

[PIE74] *Source language debugging on a small computer*, R.H. Pierce, The Computer Journal, Vol. 17, No. 4, pp 313–317, 1974.

[RAT01] Rational Software, Cupertino, CA 95014, 2001, www.rational.com.

[TSE82] *Microprocessor Development and Development Systems*, V. Tseng, Granada Publishing, ISBN 0-246-11490-8, 1982.

[WIN01] Wind River embedded development tools, 2001, www.windriver.com.

[XYC01] XYCOM Automation product literature 2001, www.xycomautomation.com.

chapter 13

Mission-Critical and Safety-Critical Systems

First, a simple question: should you bother to spend time reading and studying this chapter (I'm sure there are many more exciting things to do)? Well, to answer that, ask yourself another simple but very important question. If your system misbehaves, what are the resulting *consequences*? User irritation, loss of work, loss of money, damage to equipment, injury to people, death? These are just some possible outcomes. So, where is your system on this scale of things? Moreover, apart from the moral issues, what are the legal and financial consequences of such problems?

The purpose of this chapter is to help you to develop a design strategy for critical systems. It does this by:

● Explaining the meaning of critical and fault-tolerant systems.

● Illustrating how systems may be classified in terms of the consequences of their failures.

● Showing the relationship between failure severity levels, failure probabilities, failure rates and areas of application.

- Introducing the use of formal techniques for specifying systems.
- Describing techniques that help produce robust application software.
- Showing the need to explicitly deal with real-world interfacing aspects in critical systems.
- Giving an overview of the desirable qualities of real-time operating systems destined for critical applications.
- Describing many potential problems that can arise from carrying out numerical operations.
- Explaining how, in some circumstances, the effects produced by processor and memory malfunctions can be contained by error-checking software.
- Describing how software faults can be tolerated and overcome by using hardware-based techniques.

13.1 Introduction

13.1.1 Overview of critical systems

Let's start by explaining what we mean by 'critical' systems. A simple definition: ones in which failure(s) may have significant and far-reaching consequences. This, of course, is a very broad view of things, so something more precise is needed. To put things in perspective, consider the following representative real-world examples, Figure 13.1. The first four systems can be categorized as 'safety critical'; the others are 'mission critical'. The essential difference is self-evident.

System type	Consequences of failure
Military aircraft fly-by-wire control systems (unstable aircraft)	Loss of control within 0.5 seconds (errors start to build within 100 ms)
Aero engine advanced variable control systems	Engine blow up (errors begin to develop within 50 ms)
Aircraft autoland systems	If failure occurs above 30 metres and the crew regain control, a safe situation – below this the result may be catastrophic
Airbag deployment systems	Depends on circumstances – ranges from inconvenience to death
Air-sea rescue maritime reconnaissance aircraft – loss of search radar	Inability to complete search mission
Telecommunications switches	Many and varied, depending on the severity of the problem
Financial services on-line transaction processing (OLTP) services	Loss of money – related to the duration of the failure

Figure 13.1 : Typical systems: failures and their consequences.

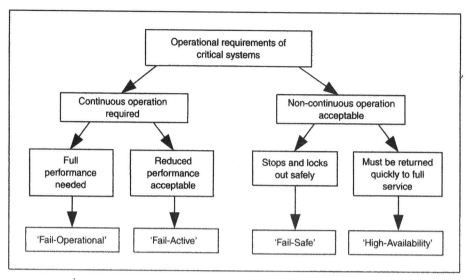

Figure 13.2 | Operational requirements of critical systems.

Assume that your computer forms part of a critical system. What should (or can) you do to put quality into your product? There is no simple answer, it all depends on how systems must operate when faults occur. Very broadly we can group fault-tolerant systems as shown in Figure 13.2. First we have those which *must* carry on working without a break when faults arise, i.e. provide continuous operation. These are defined to be 'fault-tolerant'. Then there are the ones that can go out of action without causing significant problems (or, as in the case with a failure of an autoland system at altitude, a problem that can be dealt with).

There are, in fact, four major subcategories, as follows:

(a) Full performance is required in the presence of faults. In other words, there is no external visible sign that a fault has occurred. This is defined to be a fail-operational (FO) system.

(b) Continuous but reduced performance is acceptable. This behaviour is often described as 'graceful degradation', being defined as a fail-active (FA) system.

(c) The system may cease to work but must go into a safe mode. This is a fail-safe (FS) system. Normally such systems are locked into pre-defined modes and need to be manually reset.

(d) The system may cease to work but must be returned to normal service very quickly. This may involve faulty units being replaced whilst the system is on-line. Such systems are called high-availability (HA) ones.

13.1.2 How critical is critical?

In general it shouldn't be difficult to decide which category your computer system falls into. However, this raises an interesting question: are systems within the same category equally critical? For example, take aircraft fly-by-wire systems. Is the criticality of a Boeing 777 carrying say 200 passengers the same as a single-seat fighter aircraft? Clearly not; the military pilot can at least eject if all else fails. Thus it is necessary to develop quantitative measures for use in critical systems. Two basic metrics are reliability and availability.

Reliability is a measure of how well a system operates correctly. It may be expressed in terms of the time between failures, the *mean time between failures*, MTBF (also called the *mean time to fail*, MTTF). Depending on applications this can range from hours through to years. Using MTBF values we can calculate the associated failure rates, e.g. the number of (potential) failures per hour of operation. For example, an MTBF of 1000 hours (one failure per 1000 hours) gives a failure rate of 10^{-3}. Thus when dealing with highly critical systems reliability is the primary metric.

When it comes to high-availability applications, our concern is the amount of time a system spends out of action (*downtime*). Two factors have to be taken into account. First, how often is it likely to fail, i.e. its MTBF? Second, when it *does* fail, how long will it take to bring the system back into operation? The average repair time or *mean time to repair* (MTTR) is used in availability calculations, as follows:

$$\text{Availability} = \frac{\text{MTBF}}{\text{MTBF} + \text{MTTR}}$$

For example, a system having an MTBF of 1000 hours and an MTTR of 1 hour has an availability of:

$$\text{Availability} = \frac{1000}{1000 + 1} = 0.99900 \text{ (to five decimal places)}$$

Highly critical systems need to be very reliable. But how reliable? To gauge this we must first establish the criticality aspects of systems. Two factors are taken into account when dealing with criticality:

● The severity of any failure.

● The likelihood (probability) of failures occurring.

Typical of severity levels are those shown in Figure 13.3. Various words are used to describe the probability that a failure will arise, such as:

● Extremely improbable.

● Extremely rare.

● Rare.

● Unlikely.

● Reasonably probable.

Severity level	Consequence(s) of failure
Catastrophic	May result in death or major damage (e.g. loss of vehicle)
Critical	May result in injury or extensive damage
Significant	May result in some damage
Minor	Discomfort to people, aborted operation

Figure 13.3 Example classification – severity levels in safety-critical systems.

FAILURE PROBABILITY	ACCEPTABLE FAILURE RATES
Extremely improbable	⇧ 10^{-9}
Extremely rare	⇧ 10^{-7}
Rare	⇧ 10^{-5}
Unlikely	⇧ 10^{-3}
Reasonably probable	⇧

Figure 13.4 Failure probability and associated failure rates.

Severity level	Minor		Significant	Critical	Catastrophic
Probability of failure	Reasonably probable	Unlikely	Rare	Extremely rare	Extremely improbable
Acceptable failure rates	=>	10^{-3} => 10^{-5}	=> 10^{-7}	=> 10^{-9}	=>
Application area	Mission critical			Safety critical	

Figure 13.5 Relating severity levels, failure probabilities, failure rates and application areas.

However, to give these real meaning, we need to put some numbers against them. In the safety-critical world, failure rates (or MTBFs) are used to distinguish the various categories, as shown in Figure 13.4. In practice these are likely to be target design aims (note that specific figures vary from industry to industry).

Putting everything together, you can use the data of Figure 13.5 to decide what your target failure rate should be. Please be aware that different industries (e.g. aerospace, automobile, medical) often use different terminology for safety-critical systems. Also, criticality is often defined in terms of specific applications.

For mission-critical systems, availability is likely to be the dominant factor (many mission-critical applications now demand the so-called 'five nines' availability figure, that is, 0.99999 or 99.999%). In general, failures in high-performance telecommunications and OLTP applications:

- Are usually much less severe in their consequences and
- Are acceptable provided they don't occur too often and repair times are rapid (typical downtimes range from seconds to minutes).

For example, a failure rate of 10^{-4} per hour of operation translates to an MTBF of 10,000 hours, approximately 1 year and 2 months. For many applications such rates are tolerable. Acceptable downtimes depend on individual applications and tend to be domain specific. Moreover, targets are normally set by the client or user; software developers don't necessarily have the background to make such judgements. For instance, what is the acceptable downtime in an electronic broking system which handles $100 million per day? Clearly, for mission-critical systems, availability requirements depend very much on the needs of individual systems.

On a final note: remember, we can *never* guarantee that systems won't fail.

13.1.3 Improving system reliability and availability – general strategies

The most important thing to say here is that quality should (must?) be designed into the product. Trying to add it as a 'bolt-on' feature produces only limited improvements (and may also prove to be rather expensive). However, before looking at how we can improve reliability and availability, we need to understand clearly:

- How and why software systems malfunction.
- Where software remedies can be applied.
- Where hardware solutions can or must be used.
- Where combinations of hardware and software techniques are optimal.

To discuss this it is important to be clear on the meaning of the following terms: fault, error, failure, effect. Unfortunately, these are defined quite differently for software (as, for example, by the IEEE) and for systems (e.g. by the FAA). The words 'utter confusion' spring to mind, especially when dealing with embedded control systems. To simplify matters (and without taking sides), we'll here limit ourselves to the terms and definitions given in Figure 13.6. An *effect* is the visible result of something going wrong inside a computer-based system. That is, it is the end-product of a failure. In software systems, a *failure* is the production of incorrect results (or results not expected by the user) by executing software. *Faults* are errors that lead to software failures. Our design objective is to produce fault-tolerant systems, those which won't malfunction even though they contain faults (though be aware

What the basic cause of the problem was	Exactly why the system failed	What happened – the end result
Software could not handle the number range	Numerical (number) overflow	Loss of control of space vehicle
Wrong value input to the systeme	Wrong number computed	Space vehicle crashed into planet
FAULT (ERROR)	FAILURE	EFFECT

Figure 13.6 Definition of fault, failure and effect.

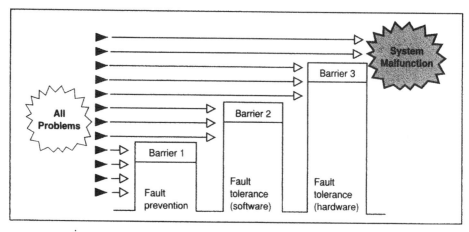

Figure 13.7 Producing fault-tolerant systems.

that failure may occur only under specific operational conditions). This can be done in three ways, Figure 13.7. Visualize, if you will, a whole set of problems which can lead to system malfunction. The first line of defence is to prevent errors arising in the first place by applying *fault prevention* (also known as *fault avoidance*) techniques. The objective is to produce software that is free of faults.

Effective as fault prevention is, it will not (in fact cannot) entirely eliminate faults. Thus a second line of defence is needed to deal with failures which may be generated by such faults. This involves first detecting failures and then taking action to prevent system malfunction. Such designs allow the system to tolerate the presence of faults – *fault tolerance* (strictly speaking, *software fault tolerance*).

Unfortunately some failures may still defeat the fault-tolerance barrier, causing the software to produce incorrect results. Here we have to bring in the third barrier, hardware-based fault tolerance. Its objective is to ensure that the system operates correctly and/or safely even though software failures have occurred.

Problems can come from many different areas, Figure 13.8, especially in real-time embedded systems. These will now be examined in more detail.

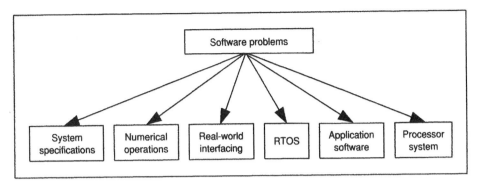

Figure 13.8 Sources of software-related faults.

13.2 System specification aspects

13.2.1 The specification problem – again

The problems encountered in defining system requirements (specifications) have already been well and truly covered. But let us assume that we have managed to produce a complete statement of requirements for a critical system (or so we think). Now, at this point, some very important questions should be asked:

- Are the system specifications clear, understandable and unambiguous?
- Can we be absolutely sure that they are consistent and complete?
- Can we, as the specifiers, be absolutely sure that the software designers correctly and fully understand these requirements?
- Can we review the proposed design to check its correctness (i.e. does it meet its specification)?

Note well this last point, the check for correctness. To do this we compare the program (text) whose syntax is defined formally and precisely with the specification (text) whose syntax is defined – how? The inherent problems of natural language (e.g. ambiguity, redundancy, verbosity) cause difficulties in specifying clearly the true requirements of systems. Using diagramming methods in the specification document can help considerably. But even then, users of the SOR can still end up with different views of the system. Quite often users can agree collectively on the meaning of specifications; yet individuals may interpret them quite differently. This comes about usually because:

- The specification document is not sufficiently precise.
- The specification technique may be inherently ambiguous.

Therefore, if we wish to prove the correctness of a solution, we *must* define system specifications in a formal manner using a formally and precisely defined language. In practice this means that we need to augment the natural language specification with a *formal specification*.

13.2.2 Why mathematics?

Suppose that we are given a specification for a liquid level controller which reads (in part):

> During the first phase of operation, liquid is to be pumped in to raise the level from its initial value to within 100 mm of the required set level at a flow rate Q_1. Now the second phase of operation is invoked. The flow rate is to be gradually reduced until it reaches zero at the set level point. At this stage, phase 3, the heater is . . .

The control system designer, on reading this, will very soon realize that the specification is incomplete and ambiguous. Questions to be answered include:

- What is the initial level, and is it always the same?
- What is the value of the flow rate Q_1? What is the set level?
- During the final phase, is the flow rate reduced in a linear manner?
- When, precisely, is the flow rate to be reduced? That is, at 100 mm below the set level, is pumping done at the original rate or at the new reduced rate?

In such a small section of text, omissions and errors are almost always picked up. But where specifications are large and complex, mistakes frequently go unnoticed right up to system test time.

Let's now add to this specification a mathematical description of the process, as follows:

Phase 1

The level equation is

$h = Q_1 t + h_0$ which is valid in the range $h_0 \le h < (H - 100)$

where h = actual level, h_0 = initial level, Q_1 = initial flow rate, and H = set level.

Phase 2

This is valid in the range

$(H - 100) \le h < H$

giving a level equation of

$h = Q_2 t + (H - 100)$

where Q_2 is the instantaneous flow rate, calculated as follows:

$$Q_2 = \frac{(H - h)}{100} Q_1$$

Phase 3

This occurs when $h \geq H$:

$$Q_3 = 0$$

Observe that the system behaviour has now been specified using a formal language (mathematics), which is rigorous and built on provable rules. So far so good. But what have we gained by using a mathematical specification? Five factors, to be precise:

- Unambiguous communication.
- Consistency of specification.
- Correct specifications.
- Complete specifications.
- Specification clarity.

(a) Unambiguous communication. Mathematics is precise and unambiguous. The statement

$$h = Q_2 t + (H - 100)$$

has only one meaning. Consequently, when using this in a reference document, communication between designers, users, etc. is also unambiguous.

(b) Consistency of specification. All operating conditions must be consistent, as in:

Phase 1: This is valid in the range $h_0 \leq h < (H - 100)$
Phase 2: This is valid in the range $(H - 100) \leq h < H$
Phase 3: This is valid for $h \geq H$

Here the specified conditions cover the total operating range, with subranges being explicit, non-overlapping and consistent.

(c) Correct specifications. The behaviour of the system can be evaluated in all its operating modes using mathematical analysis. Any mistakes made in the specification produce inconsistent results in this evaluation; hence they can be discovered fairly quickly. For instance, the specification above could include the statement 'Tank filling is to be achieved in X seconds'. An analysis of the system equations will soon show whether this can be achieved given the known performance factors. In the example here the filling rate drops rapidly in the final stages, and might be unacceptably low. Consequently the specification could be altered to avoid this by putting a lower limit on the rate, as in:

$$Q_2 = \frac{(H - h)}{100} Q_1 \qquad \text{subject to } Q_{2(min)} = \frac{Q_1}{10}$$

(d) Complete specifications. All system parameters *must* be included in order to form the defining equations correctly. Further, *all* values have to be given to make the equations soluble.

(e) Specification clarity. A mathematical specification can be written fully and correctly only when the specifier:

- Understands the problem correctly.
- Can express it properly and clearly.
- Removes all ambiguous and ambivalent conditions.
- Has full system data, operating conditions, etc. at hand.

Consequently, when formal specification documents are produced they are much more likely to be well thought out, balanced, objective, clear and concise.

Availability of data is a crucial factor in the design of real-time systems. Many projects begin by assuming a great deal about the system to be designed, i.e. uncertainties abound in multitude. So, in such situations it is impossible to satisfy the final requirement listed above. After all, if you don't have the data how can you solve the equations? This factor seems to negate the use of mathematically based specification methods. Surprisingly enough this isn't the case. True, the equations can't be solved until the data is available. But what it does is highlight precisely any missing information from the specification. And this is one of the most valuable items that the developer can have. As system design proceeds the missing bits can be filled in until finally the specification is complete. Some aspects may not even be obtained until system trials are carried out; this doesn't diminish its usefulness.

The example given here uses conventional mathematics to bridge the gap between concept and practice. In reality, formal specification methods are based on discrete mathematics.

13.2.3 Formal methods – general concepts

Formal methods result in verified program code derived from mathematically based system specifications. However, in all systems, statements of requirements are *always* produced using a natural language. Hence the first step along the formal route is to convert these into a formal specification (Figure 13.9). The next step is to validate the correctness of the specification and, once this is done, generate program code from the formal document. The resulting code is then verified, i.e. proved to be correct with respect to its mathematical specification. Often the formal document

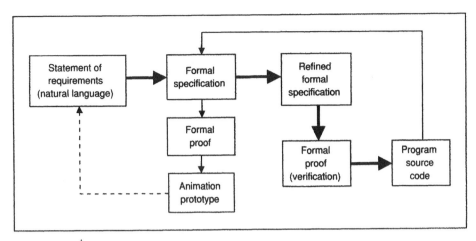

Figure 13.9 Formal specifications within the software design cycle.

goes through a number of refinement stages. The purpose is to get a good match between the specification and the structure of the implementation language. This, in essence, is how formal software methods work. Underlying it is the dependence of each step on the previous step. Now, we can loop around the *'formal specification → verification → code generation'* stages until these are proved to be correct. Unfortunately this doesn't include the SOR. After all, it can't be proved that the system designer has specified what is actually wanted. Mathematics does not help us very much; other methods are needed. One promising solution is that of animation prototyping, using the formal specifications as the input to the animations [COO94]. This sets up an *'SOR → formal specification → animation'* loop which is iteratively refined until the specification is agreed to be correct.

13.2.4 Formal specification languages

The basic requirements of a formal specification language are that it:

● Allows the functions and states of a program to be specified.

● Can be used to prove that the specification statements are logically correct.

The underlying structure is based on discrete mathematics. This is a fairly extensive subject, certainly beyond the bounds of this book. However, for those readers who wish to use formal methods, it is essential to become proficient in the topic. Suitable material can be found in [DEN86].

Many formal specification languages have been developed but few are used in practice. There are two basic categories: model-based and axiom-based. In many respects they are quite similar, using concepts and notation based on set theory.

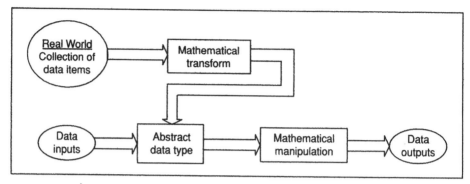

Figure 13.10 | Formal specifications — basic concept.

Typically, data items from the real world are modelled mathematically in terms of abstract data types, Figure 13.10.

Mathematical manipulation of the abstract data type is carried out using discrete mathematics so that, for any set of data inputs, the outputs are correct. In terms of the real-world situation, this describes what the outputs should be for particular input configurations, not how the results are calculated.

Model-based systems are well suited for the specification of sequential operations. These, in practice, have dominated the formal specification scene. Here we build a mathematical model of the state of the system and the operations to be carried out on this. The operations themselves are likely to be broken down into sequences of simpler operations, the so-called decomposition process. Finally the abstract mathematical descriptions are translated to the structures of the programming language. When we can describe the system states and operations completely in terms of the programming language the specification process is complete.

Two particular languages, VDM [ROL92] and Z [LIG91], have been widely used for the specification of critical systems (for example, Rolls-Royce and Associates specified the software requirements of nuclear reactor control systems using VDM). A very brief outline of VDM is given to further explain the ideas underlying formal specification techniques.

13.2.5 An example of formal specification using VDM

VDM stands for Vienna Development Method, first developed at IBM Vienna's laboratories. It is primarily a *notation* for a specification language. However, because of the underlying mathematics it can be used:

- For the design and development of programs and
- To prove that the resulting programs are correct.

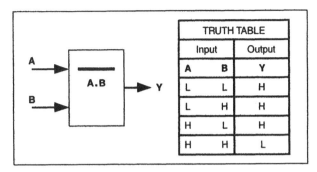

TRUTH TABLE		
Input		Output
A	B	Y
L	L	H
L	H	H
H	L	H
H	H	L

Figure 13.11   The NAND function.

The mathematics behind VDM comprises the theory of sets and logic. Thus it is necessary to understand these topics to write or implement VDM specifications. At first sight this might seem daunting; in fact those with experience of high-level language structures or digital electronic design will quickly grasp the basic ideas. This section is intended to provide an outline of the basics of the language – and a very elementary one at that. But it is sufficient for our purpose.

Never lose sight of the fact that our objective is to specify what a system should do, not how it should do it. Suppose that we are to specify a tiny system (Figure 13.11). This has inputs A and B, producing an output Y. All are Boolean variables. The action performed within the 'box' is that of logic NANDing. Thus we can specify the requirements of this system using a truth table, for instance, as shown in Figure 13.11. Note that this says nothing about how logic inversion is to be implemented. It could be done in hardware or software. Assume that a hardware solution is desired. In such a case the choice of circuitry would be left to the hardware designer. As specifiers we are not concerned with such issues.

What we have here is a set of input conditions, a logical operation, and a set of output conditions. It is, in fact, a mapping of input logical conditions to output logical conditions, a *function*. Let us call the function 'NandGate'. In VDM such functions are written in a very specific way. First there is the 'function signature', having the format:

FunctionName (InParameters : InTypes) OutParameters : OutTypes

In essence, what the signature does is to define a function and specify:

● The set of input values which the function can act on – its domain.

● The set of output values valid for this function – the range.

Therefore the specification must also contain a declaration of the parameter types. For our NAND gate example we define the following type:

Logic : {High, Low}

682 Mission-Critical and Safety-Critical Systems

Following this is the function signature:

NandGate (A : Logic, B : Logic) Y : Logic

Now we are required to specify two logical assertions relating to the function, its pre-condition and its post-condition.

In simple terms the pre-condition says 'if the function is to produce correct answers then the system must be in this particular condition'. For NandGate, the function should operate correctly (*is defined*) provided the inputs are valid. Any combination of highs and lows is permissible. In other words, it is defined for all possible input values. This is denoted by writing the pre-condition as:

Pre true

The post-condition is a statement of the system condition after successful completion of the operation *provided that the pre-condition was met*. For this example we have:

Post (A = High AND B = High AND Y = Low)
  OR
  ((A = Low OR B = Low) AND Y = High)

The format of the simple yet complete VDM specification for NandGate is given in Figure 13.12.

Logic : {High, Low}

NandGate (A : Logic, B : Logic) Y : Logic

Pre true

Post (A = High   AND   B = High   AND   Y = Low)
  OR
  ((A = Low   OR   B = Low)   AND   Y = High)

Figure 13.12 VDM specification for a NAND gate.

As a further example, take the case of the liquid level controller. We will now specify the controller operation using VDM. To do this a new construct, the *operation*, is used. This is similar to a function but with one key difference. An operation may access values that are not listed as parameters. Instead it may read and change the values of items that have an existence outside of the operation (similar to the use of global variables). Here the operation used is called *SetFlow*.

First, a recap:

h = actual level – a read-only value.
h_0 = initial level – a read-only value.
Q_1 = initial flow rate – a read-only value.
H = set level – a read-only value.
flow = instantaneous flow rate – a read–write value.

```
SetFlow

Ext    rd h    : R
       rd h₀   : R
       rd Q₁   : R
       rd H    : R
       wr flow : R

pre     (h > h₀) ∧ (h ≤ H)

post    (h < (H – 100)) ∧ (flow = Q₁)
        ∨
        h > (H – 100) ∧ (h < H) ∧ (flow = CalcReducingFlow)
        ∨
        (h ≥ H) ∧ (flow = 0).
```

Figure 13.13   VDM specification for the flow controller system.

Assume these are held as real numbers external to SetFlow. For simplicity the computation

$$Q_2 = \frac{(H - h)}{100} Q_1$$

is defined within a function *CalcReducingFlow*.

Further definitions:

ext – defines that items are external to the operation.

rd – defines an external item to be read-only.

wr – defines an external item to be read–write.

∨ – means 'or'.

∧ – means 'and'.

Thus the VDM specification for the flow controller is as shown in Figure 13.13.

13.3   Numerical issues

13.3.1   Problems in disguise

Do we really need to understand how mathematical operations are carried out within a computer? Well, consider the situations depicted in Figure 13.14. In (a), we use the calculation $(0 - X)$ to determine if X has a negative value. The next example, (b), shows the output from a shaft angle sensor being fed to a control computer, to provide monitoring data. In (c) a missile aimer measures the angle between a fixed reference point and a target aircraft in order to engage at the optimal launch angle. The final item, (d), is a simple mathematical statement in source code form.

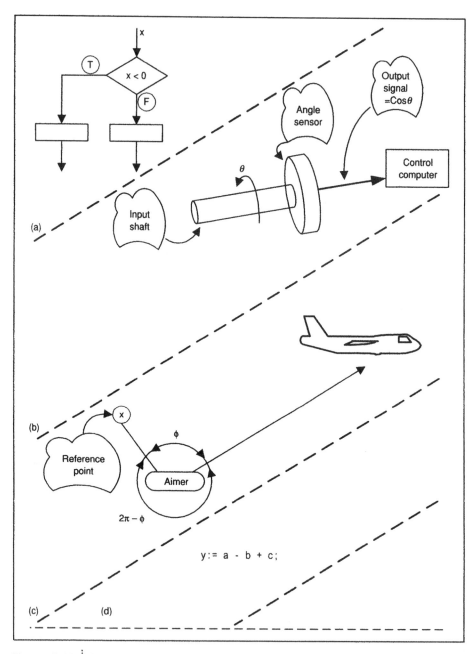

Figure 13.14 | Operations requiring numerical processing.

If you are likely to work with these or similar applications, then you do need to know what happens during the number-crunching process, because there are disguised problems in all these examples. For instance, in (a), the calculation may give a FALSE result (indicating that X is not negative), when it actually is negative. In (b), working with the cosine of the angle may well give different results to those obtained by using the angle itself. With the situation shown in (c), the aimer should be able to use either ϕ or $(2\pi - \phi)$. Yet these may not produce identical results. Finally, for example (d), if the programmer changes the order of calculation (say to $y := a + c - b;$), the computed result may also change. There is a common reason for all these problems: the limits of computers in the handling of numbers. And what disguises the size and nature of this problem? It is that we fail to recognize or remember that computers have these definite limits.

13.3.2 Making measurements

When we make measurements there are two distinct points to consider: measurement type and result representation (Figure 13.15). Measurements that we carry out in the real world fall into two categories, discrete and continuous. Counting the number of students in a class is clearly a case of dealing with discrete values. In contrast, measuring the amount of liquid in a container involves a continuously varying quantity. Now consider how we would show the results of such measurements using written digits. Listing the student total is simple and direct; further, the problem itself defines the number range needed in the calculation. For the second example, writing down the volume isn't a problem. The question is, how

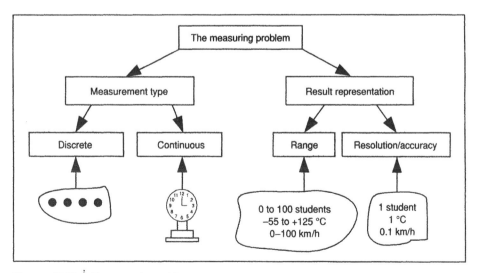

Figure 13.15 | The measuring problem.

many digits should we use? In theory, an infinite number. In practice, a limited amount. Thus the practical answer is less precise than the theoretical one. We say that the theoretical value has infinite precision whilst practical numbers have finite precision.

How, though, is the degree of precision defined? Consider the following:

(a) Number range 0 to 1000 with a step size of 1.
    The precision (or *resolution*) is 1 in 1000 (i.e. 1/1000).

(b) Number range 0 to 10^6 with a step size of 1.
    The precision is 1/1,000,000.

(c) Number range 0.001 to 1.000 with a step size of 0.001.
    The precision is 1/1000.

Now consider the accuracy of measurements and calculations. First, what is accuracy? Second, how do accuracy and precision interact?

Accuracy is defined to be the 'degree of correctness' of the measurement or calculation. In the next section we'll look at accuracy/precision aspects in terms of finite number systems. For the moment, though, consider that we can display a quantity using as many digits as we desire. Suppose that we weigh items using a sensor which, we are told, 'has a range of 0 to 100 kg with an accuracy of 0.1 kg'. Further suppose that the weight display is a six-digit readout. When a sack of potatoes is put on the measuring scales the readout shows 25.7941 kg. The precision of this number is impressive – and can easily fool us into forgetting the accuracy limits of the result. The last digit '1' (the *least significant*) has little meaning; it represents only 0.5% of the total error band of 0.2 kg. We really need to match the number of digits used to the inherent accuracy of the problem. It's pointless using meaningless digits. This leads to the definition of the significant figures of a number – those digits which make a contribution to its value.

In summary, three parameters have to be considered in numerical operations: precision, accuracy and range.

13.3.3 Basic number representation and arithmetic

The basic numeric operations of arithmetic are addition, subtraction, multiplication and division. But how we do the arithmetic is related to the way in which numbers are represented. For us, two particular methods are very important, fixed-point and floating-point representation.

First, though, let us review some basics of number systems, starting with positional notation. Take, for instance, the number '256'. This really means '200 + 50 + 6' – provided we are using decimal values, of course. Thus:

$$256 = 200 + 50 + 6$$
$$\equiv (2 \times 10^2) + (5 \times 10^1) + (6 \times 10^0) = (256)_{10}$$

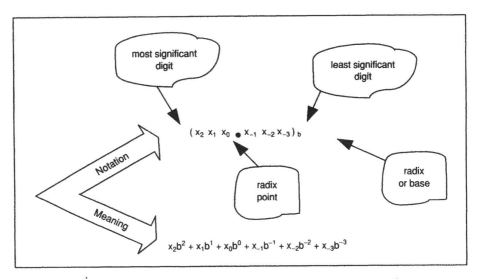

Figure 13.16 Positional number system – definitions.

and

$$0.147 = 0.1 + 0.04 + 0.007$$
$$\equiv (1 \times 10^{-1}) + (4 \times 10^{-2}) + (7 \times 10^{-3}) = (.147)_{10}$$

We can see that these are particular examples of the general rule for positional notation, namely:

$$(X_2\ X_1\ X_0\ .X_{-1}\ X_{-2}\ X_{-3})_{10} \equiv X_2\ 10^2 + X_1\ 10^1 + X_0\ 10^0 + X_{-1}\ 10^{-1} + X_{-2}\ 10^{-2} + X_{-3}\ 10^{-3}$$

Here the X's are the digits of the representation, the leftmost one being the most significant, whilst the rightmost one is the least significant (see also Figure 13.16).

The dot between X_0 and X_{-1} is called the radix point. In this example it is called the decimal point as the number base (or radix) is 10. More generally:

$$(\dots X_2\ X_1\ X_0\ .X_{-1}\ X_{-2}\ X_{-3} \dots)_b \equiv X_2\ b^2 + X_1\ b^1 + X_0\ b^0 + X_{-1}\ b^{-1} + X_{-2}\ b^{-2} + X_{-3}\ b^{-3}$$

When $b = 2$ we have binary notation. Therefore:

$$(\dots X_2\ X_1\ X_0\ .X_{-1}\ X_{-2}\ X_{-3} \dots)_2 \equiv X_2\ 2^2 + X_1\ 2^1 + X_0\ 2^0 + X_{-1}\ 2^{-1} + X_{-2}\ 2^{-2} + X_{-3}\ 2^{-3}$$

The radix point is called the binary point in this instance.

Fixed-point numbers are those expressed using the positional notation outlined above, but subject to certain restrictions. First, a number is represented by a fixed set of digits. Second, the radix point has a predetermined location. Thus 127.5, 0.779, 4095, etc. are examples of four-digit fixed-point numbers. Observe that whole numbers can be considered to be a special case of fixed-point representation – the radix point is at the rightmost part of the number. Extending this idea, we could use representations where the radix point is somewhere to the left or the right of the digits, as in:

Digits ⇒	Representing	Digits ⇒	Representing
1024 ⇒	10,240	1025 ⇒	10,250
1024 ⇒	102,400	1025 ⇒	102,500
1024 ⇒	0.01024	1025 ⇒	0.01025
1024 ⇒	0.001024	1025 ⇒	0.001025

In normal circumstances we wouldn't write numbers down in this format. However, when we have only a limited number of digits available (see later), it can be useful.

At this stage there is little more to be said concerning fixed-point numbers. Everyone should be familiar with their arithmetic operations. They are, after all, the staple diet of elementary school mathematics.

Now let's move on to floating-point numbers. These have the following representation:

$M \times b^e$

M is the mantissa
b is the radix
e is the exponent.

The following are examples of floating-point representation:

Floating-point value	5×10^2	5.4×10^2	$1 \times 10^{2.5}$	$5.4 \times 10^{2.5}$
Fixed-point equivalent	500	540	316.228*	1707.63*

* approximate values

When doing arithmetic on floating-point numbers, the following rules must be followed:

Addition and subtraction

$(M_1 \times b^{e_1}) \pm (M_2 \times b^{e_1}) = (M_1 \pm M_2) \times b^{e_1}$

Note that the exponents must be equal. If they aren't, then the numbers must first be adjusted until they are equal. Only then can addition or subtraction be carried out.

Example

$(5 \times 10^2) + (5.4 \times 10^2) = 10.4 \times 10^2$

$(5 \times 10^2) + (5.4 \times 10^1) = (50 \times 10^1) + (5.4 \times 10^1) = 55.4 \times 10^1$

$\text{OR} = (5 \times 10)^2 + (.54 \times 10^2) = 5.54 \times 10^2$

Multiplication and division

$$(M_1 \times b^{e_1}) \times (M_2 \times b^{e_2}) = (M_1 \times M_2) \times b^{(e_1+e_2)}$$

Example

$$(5 \times 10^2) \times (5.4 \times 10^1) = 27 \times 10^3$$

$$(M_1 \times b^{e_1}) \div (M_2 \times b^{e_2}) = (M_1 \div M_2) \times b^{(e_1-e_2)}$$

Example

$$(5 \times 10^1) \div (8 \times 10^2) = 0.625 \times 10^{-1}$$

Observe that we manipulate only the mantissa and the exponents. The radix itself plays no part in these operations. What it does, though, is allow us to put the radix point in the correct place. For instance:

$$55.4 \times 10^1 = 554.00$$
$$27 \times 10^3 = 27,000.0$$
$$0.625 \times 10^{-1} = 0.0625$$

Floating-point notation is widely applied in scientific and engineering work. It is used mainly for the representation of very large and very small quantities in preference to fixed-point notation. Examples of this include:

- Mean Earth–Sun distance: 1.49×10^8 km;
- Elementary charge: 1.6×10^{-19} C;
- Mass of Earth: 5.98×10^{24} kg.

Do not, however, conclude from this that we use exactly the same reasoning when choosing number representation within computer systems.

13.3.4 The limitations of finite number systems – general points

There are a number of practical reasons for limiting the size of numbers in our calculations. One, as pointed out above, involves the accuracy of information. If we aren't careful we can spend much time producing meaningless results. The second reason concerns the time taken to perform numerical operations. It is generally true to say that bigger numbers result in longer calculation times. Where we want fast calculations we must limit the number of digits used. The drawback, though, is that this limits precision. And we find that many problems arise exactly because of this limited precision.

We need a good understanding of these problems if we are to safely program numerical functions. Moreover, we also need to recognize system limitations if we wish to trade-off time for precision. This is an extremely important factor in hard real-time systems, that is, those with deadlines which must not be missed.

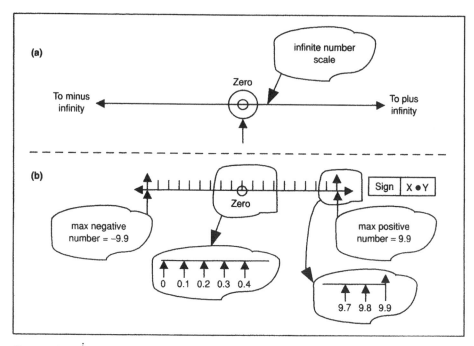

Figure 13.17 Number scale — theoretical and fixed-point values.

13.3.5 Infinite numbers, model numbers and error bounds

Our theoretical number scale is an infinite one, having infinite range and infinite resolution, Figure 13.17a. However, in practical situations, we have to limit the number of digits used. Therefore we can represent only a small portion of this infinite scale. Take, for instance, the situation shown in Figure 13.17b. This is the number scale for the fixed-point format

$$\pm X.Y$$

where X and Y are single decimal digits. The maximum values are 9.9, giving a range of −9.9 to +9.9. The resolution is 0.1. Thus all numbers which fall within this range have to be represented by a number system which has 199 discrete values. So when is the representation error-free? Only if a true value coincides with one of these pre-defined (or *model*) numbers.

An understanding of this topic (model numbers and numeric errors) is extremely important for mathematical computing. Therefore it is worth taking a second look at it in terms of bit representation. Let us suppose that we are restricted to using 3 bits only to represent numbers in our system (totally artificial, of course). Further suppose that the binary–decimal relationship is given by:

Binary value	Decimal value
000	0
001	1
010	2
011	3
100	4
101	5
110	6
111	7

Therefore it is possible to represent only eight specific values in the computer; in other words there are eight model numbers.

Now let us compute first 6/2 and then 5/2. In binary systems, the simplest way to divide by two is to shift the bit pattern one place to the right. Thus:

Decimal value	Binary value	Binary value After division	Decimal value After division
6	110	011	3
5	101	010	2

The first calculation is error-free, as the true value coincides with one of the model numbers. Unfortunately in the second case the true value falls between two model numbers; thus it is impossible to represent it correctly in our given number system. We do the best we can in the circumstances, and accept that computed numbers may well be in error. It should be clear that this is an inherent problem in digital computer systems; errors can be minimized but never eliminated.

In practice we rarely know what values are going to emerge from our calculations. Therefore the only safe approach is to assume that the maximum possible error will always occur. The next question: what is the size of this error? This depends on whether we truncate numbers or round them off. Truncation cuts off the less significant digits of the true number to give us a model number. In contrast, rounding adjusts the true value to be equal to the nearest model number. For example, using the fixed-point representation of Figure 13.17, we could have:

Original number	Operation	True result	Truncated	Rounded
5.8	divide by 5	1.16	1.1	1.2
5.4	divide by 5	1.08	1.0	1.1
5.6	divide by 5	1.12	1.1	1.1
5.75	divide by 5	1.15	1.1	1.2

These points are illustrated in Figure 13.18.

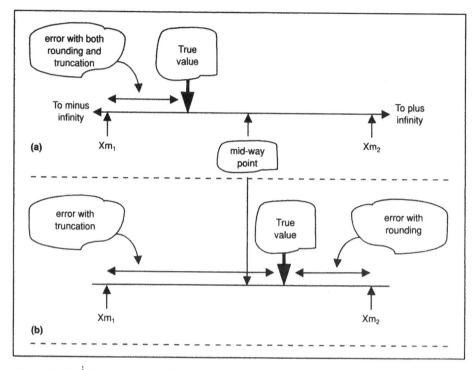

Figure 13.18 Errors due to rounding and truncation.

It should be clear that truncation can generate an error as great (almost) as one least significant digit. For the example above this value is 0.1, giving an error range of 0–0.1. With rounding this maximum is reduced by one half, giving an error range of 0–0.05. Errors can, of course, be negative as well as positive.

Note that if we can control the resolution (the step or *delta*) value then we also control the error size. This example also demonstrates another point: once the resolution is defined the maximum error has a fixed, absolute, value. It is always the same, no matter where we are on our number scale.

Now let's examine floating-point numbers. Take the very simple two-digit representation

$$X \times 10^y$$

where X is a single-digit mantissa and y is a single-digit exponent. Figure 13.19 shows three number scales corresponding to $y = 0$, 1 and -1. Each one has a defined number range with a defined resolution. However, both factors depend on the value of the exponent. The resolution on any one scale is fixed, being proportional to one least significant digit (LSD) of the mantissa. But the absolute value of this depends on the exponent, given by

$$\text{Precision} = (\text{least\_significant\_digit\_value}) \times 10^y$$

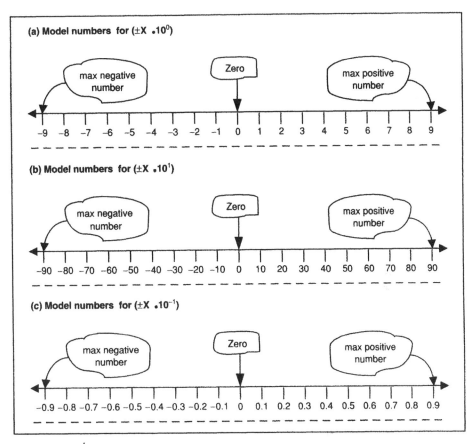

Figure 13.19 Number scale – floating point.

and the maximum error (assuming rounding) is half this value. For the example of Figure 13.19:

Representation	LSD = 1×10^9	Max. error = $\frac{1}{2}$LSD
$X \times 10^0$	$1 \times 10^0 = 1$	±0.5
$X \times 10^1$	$1 \times 10^1 = 10$	±5
$X \times 10^{-1}$	$1 \times 10^{-1} = 0.1$	±0.05

What is the meaning of this in terms of numerical errors? If numbers used in a calculation have equal exponents, the maximum possible error is the same for each number. That is, in relative terms, they are fixed. However, the absolute value of this error depends on the exponent. It can be seen clearly from the above example that the absolute error size increases as the exponent gets larger.

How does this affect us in terms of precision and error bounds? Assume that the number of digits allocated to the mantissa is fixed. Then the model number range is defined by the value of the exponent. If our problem requires a large number range we need to use a large exponent. But the absolute precision reduces as the exponent increases – and the absolute error band increases. So, for floating-point operations, we can have large number ranges and high precision – but not simultaneously.

The essential differences between practical fixed- and floating-point number representations are that:

- Fixed-point arithmetic gives us fixed precision of working. However, it requires many digits to represent both very small and very large numbers. In general, as we increase the degree of precision of computer numbers, calculation times become longer.

- Floating-point arithmetic enables us to express large number ranges using few digits. In such situations calculations can be made considerably faster than the equivalent fixed-point operations. However, the degree of precision obtained varies with the size of the number being manipulated.

13.3.6 Problems in floating-point working

The purpose of this section is to alert the reader to some major issues relating to floating-point arithmetic. It does not set out to give a detailed, mathematically rigorous, description of such issues. That is beyond the scope of this text.

Two particular factors are at the bottom of most floating-point numerical problems: loss of information and violation of basic mathematical laws. These are illustrated in the numeric operations outlined below relating to:

- Changing exponent values.
- Adding and subtracting numbers.
- Multiplying and dividing numbers.

Changing the exponent value

Suppose that our computer allows us to represent floating-point numbers using four digits for the mantissa and one for the exponent. Thus the value 1200 would be represented in written form as:

$$1200 \times 10^0$$

But, within the machine, it would be housed as a two-part value:

| 1200 | 0 |

True value	Computer representation					Computer value
	Mantissa				Exponent	
1200×10^0	1	2	0	0	0	1200
120×10^1	0	1	2	0	1	1200
12×10^2	0	0	1	2	2	1200
1.2×10^3	0	0	0	1	3	1000
0.12×10^4	0	0	0	0	4	0
12000×10^{-1}	2	0	0	0	-1	200

Figure 13.20 Mantissa–exponent relationship.

Now let us see what happens when we change the exponent value. As shown in Figure 13.20, each time we increase the exponent by one we shift the mantissa number one place to the right.

Let us assume that we merely discard the rightmost digit after this shift. In the example here there is no problem until the exponent is increased from 2 to 3. Now the number held in the computer has changed from 1200 to 1000 – a considerable loss of information. But even more dramatic is the last right-shift; the computer internal value drops to zero.

This shows how we can lose information even without performing mathematical calculations. Moreover, in this example, decreasing the exponent (to –1) produces a major error in the number. We lose the most significant digit. By contrast, shifting the mantissa rightwards results in a loss of the least significant digit.

In practice, most computer systems use the same general method for representing floating-point values. The rule used for writing the mantissa is to preset the radix (in this case decimal) point to the extreme left of the mantissa. Thus:

$$1200 = 0.1200 \times 10^4 \quad giving \quad mantissa = 1200, \quad exponent = 4$$

With such representations the mantissa is often called the fractional part of the floating-point number. The following text assumes the use of this notation.

Adding and subtracting numbers

It was pointed out earlier that to add or subtract floating-point numbers, their exponents must be equal (aligned). But, if we have to adjust exponents, should one or both be changed? To simplify computing software or hardware we leave one

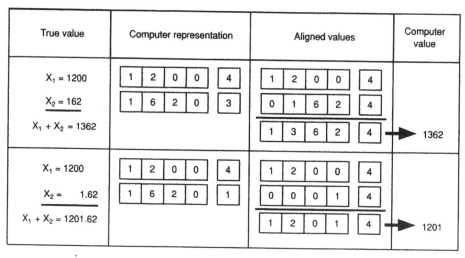

Figure 13.21 Errors in floating-point addition.

True Value	Computer Representation	Computer Value	% Error
$X_1 = 12054$	1 2 0 5 | 5	12050	0.0332
$X_2 = 12040$	1 2 0 4 | 5	12040	0
$(X_1 - X_2) = 14$	0 0 0 1 | 5 →	10	≈ 30%

Figure 13.22 Errors when subtracting similar values.

fixed. The other exponents are aligned with the selected one. But which one? The example above gives the answer to this – the one with the largest exponent. Then, when the other exponents are aligned (increasing their exponents), only least significant digits will be lost. This effect is illustrated in Figure 13.21. In the first part of the example – adding 1200 to 162 – the computed result is correct. However, in the second part, data has been lost due to the rightward shift of the smaller mantissa. This illustrates an important feature of floating-point numbers – error build-up when adding or subtracting very large and very small numbers.

It might seem that we are on safe ground when dealing with similar sized numbers. Unfortunately, no. Major errors can occur when subtracting numbers which are close together, as shown in Figure 13.22. The problem is caused by the limited resolution of the mantissa.

	(a)	(b)
Initial State	(1113 – 1111) + (2.423)	1113 + (– 1111 + 2.423)
Step 1	2 + 2.423	1113 – 1109
Step 2	4.423	4

Figure 13.23 Breakdown of the associative law of arithmetic.

	(a) Fraction Overflow	(b) Number Overflow
X_1	9 0 0 0 8	9 0 0 0 9
X_2	6 0 0 0 8	6 0 0 0 9
$X_1 + X_2$	1 5 0 0 0 8	1 5 0 0 0 9
Normalized	1 5 0 0 9	Overflow (error condition)

Figure 13.24 Overflow during addition.

One of the basic laws of arithmetic is the associative one. This says that, when we perform calculations, the order doesn't matter. For instance:

$$(A - B) + C = (-B + C) + A$$

With limited precision arithmetic this law may break down, as shown in Figure 13.23. This example assumes that only four digits are available to hold the mantissa value, as in the previous cases. In (a), the result is correct. In (b), the first operation, calculating (–1111 + 2.423), produces an error. At this stage it appears to be negligible: 0.423 in 1109, or 0.038%. However, when the next calculation is made, it gives an error of almost 10% in the final result.

When adding numbers together it is possible to produce a result which is too large to be represented, called overflow. Figure 13.24 demonstrates two aspects of this, fraction overflow and number overflow. In (a), the mantissa addition generates an overflow or carry digit. This isn't a problem as the situation can be corrected by adjusting (or normalizing) the exponent. However, part (b) shows addition producing a value which is too large for the defined number system. This overflow must be treated as an error condition.

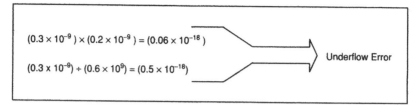

$$(0.3 \times 10^{-9}) \times (0.2 \times 10^{-9}) = (0.06 \times 10^{-18})$$

$$(0.3 \times 10^{-9}) \div (0.6 \times 10^{9}) = (0.5 \times 10^{-18})$$

Underflow Error

Figure 13.25 Underflow during multiplication and division.

Calculation: $(0.3 \times 10^{-9}) \times (0.2 \times 10^{-9}) \times 10^{9} \div 10^{-9} \times 10^{9}$		
Step 1	$(0.06 \times 10^{-18}) \times 10^{9} \div 10^{-9} \times 10^{9}$	$(0) \times 10^{9} \div 10^{-9} \times 10^{9}$
Final Result	$0.06 \times 10^{9} = 6 \times 10^{7}$	0
	Result with infinite precision	Result with limited precision

Figure 13.26 Error due to underflow.

Multiplying and dividing numbers

Multiplication and division are generally easier to deal with than addition and subtraction. We still, though, have to be on our guard for the build-up of errors and the failure of the law of association. The most significant errors are likely to be those of overflow (which we've already dealt with), and underflow, illustrated in Figure 13.25. Here the result of a calculation is too small to be represented within the floating-point number system. Although an underflow value is tiny, its effect can be out of all proportion to its size, as shown in Figure 13.26. This is a rather artificial example. Despite this it does highlight the significance of underflow, especially when it occurs in a chain of calculations. You should now see why this is regarded as a major error, and should be flagged up as such.

13.3.7 Problems in fixed-point working

Many of the potential problems of fixed-point working are similar to those found in floating-point arithmetic. In practice few occur, because fixed-point operations are highly visible. Moreover, if we ourselves define number range and precision – instead of leaving it to specific machines – the situation is further improved. For instance, suppose we define a pressure signal to lie in the range 0–10 bars with a precision of 0.1 bar. From this we can immediately define our model numbers, and, if required, perform error analysis on numerical operations. When we come to carry out calculations we can define the range and precision of the computations to be used. This also allows us to flag up out-of-range results.

13.3.8 Internal representation and binary notation

Binary–decimal equivalence

Numeric processing in computers is usually carried out in binary format. Unfortunately this doesn't fit in well with our normal thinking processes – these are geared to decimal (base 10) notation. So it is useful to develop a feel for the relationship between binary and decimal digits. We can arrive at a rough figure surprisingly easily, as follows. A single decimal digit can represent the values zero to nine. Three binary digits can represent the values zero to seven. Thus it takes between three and four binary digits to replace one decimal digit (the correct figure is 3.32).

Floating-point representation

In floating-point notation a relatively small exponent gives us a very large number range. On the other hand we need as many digits as possible for the mantissa – to increase precision and minimize errors. Two particular number ranges are in common use, defined as single precision and double precision [IEE85]. Single precision uses 23 bits for the mantissa, one for the sign and eight for the exponent. This gives a precision of seven decimal digits or, in fractional terms, seven decimal places. The exponent has the equivalent of two decimal digits, with a range of $10^{\pm38}$. Double precision has a 52 bit mantissa, one sign bit and 11 for the exponent. As a result its precision is 15 decimal digits, with a range of $10^{\pm1023}$.

It was pointed out earlier that in floating-point operations, the binary point normally lies to the left of the mantissa. Suppose that we have four digits available to hold mantissa values. Further suppose that the true value of a binary number is 0.011011×2^3 (i.e. 3.375 decimal). We could put this into floating-point form in a number of ways, including

| 0110 | 3 |

representing decimal 3.0 (error is 0.375), or

| 1101 | 2 |

representing decimal 3.25 (error is 0.125).

Observe that by shifting the mantissa as far left as possible we have achieved maximum precision. This is defined to be a normalized floating-point number – the standard method in use. Consequently the mantissa values always lie in the range:

$0.1 \le$ mantissa < 1.0 decimal, that is

$0.5 \le$ mantissa < 1.0 binary

13.4 **Application software aspects**

13.4.1 Basic design and programming issues (or doing it right in the first place)

The advice given here is mainly intended to stop you getting into trouble in the first place, i.e. fault prevention. Almost all of the material has been covered already in the text, so this is somewhat like an *aide-memoire*.

- Use rigorous design techniques.
- Use well-ordered program structures.
- Develop and use good programming standards.
- Produce *readable* code.
- Where possible use programming languages designed for critical applications. For safety-critical work first consider Spark Ada.
- If this isn't possible use languages or language subsets which provide high levels of integrity (e.g. Ada 95, Modula-2, MISRA C).
- If even this isn't possible use appropriate development tools (e.g. Lint for C) to check for code quality (but if this is your chosen route for safety-critical projects, great care is needed).
- Do not, in normal code, use unconditional transfers of program control (these may be implemented explicitly as jumps and GOTOs or, in disguise, by raising exceptions).
- Do not use recursion.
- Avoid using pointers (*'the GOTO of the 1980s'* – *Tony Hoare*).
- Limit the use of inheritance.
- Limit the use of polymorphism (*'the GOTO of the 1990s'* – *from Les Hatton*).
- Don't use dynamic memory allocation in highly critical systems. For less critical applications use fixed memory allocation strategies controlled by a memory manager.
- Use static and dynamic code analysis techniques (strictly speaking these are *fault-removal* processes).

13.4.2 Dealing with run-time problems

There are three basic approaches to dealing with run-time problems:

- Exception handling (shorthand for detecting, handling and raising exceptions).
- Backward error recovery.
- *N*-version programming

Detecting and handling errors – exception handling

With the best will in the world, we cannot guarantee to stop errors getting into the software. In such cases we have to call fault-tolerance methods into action to contain the problem. Exception handling is, at the program level, one of the most effective methods for dealing with run-time problems. Regrettably, many languages do not include the exception construct. In such cases a work-around is needed, as shown in the following problem. Suppose we have designed a function to calculate the roots of a quadratic equation, but for real roots only. Could the algorithm produce imaginary roots? The answer is yes, even with legitimate input data values. This, of course, will produce a run-time error. To handle this specific problem, the following check can be used:

```
assert (((b*b) - (4*a*c)) >= 0)
```

In C, for example, this will call an abort function if the result isn't positive.

It makes good sense to always define pre- and post-conditions for encapsulated operations. The pre-condition may be translated into code to act as acceptance tests. If there is a test failure an exception may be raised. Alternatively, it may be sufficient to return an error indication to the calling unit.

Post-conditions can be used to specify expected results when carrying out unit testing.

Now this leads into an interesting topic – just what do we do when errors *are* detected? As a generalization:

- Normal operation ceases – control transfers to the exception handler. There may be levels of such handlers in slower systems. For fast systems (which, by definition, require fast responses) a single-level transfer of control should be used.

- Subsequent events are almost always application-specific. These are determined by functional needs, response times and system criticality.

In some situations it may be possible to set the system into a pre-determined acceptable state and then continue processing. For example, in a control system, the previous computed output could be used for just one iteration. This is a simple form of *forward error recovery*.

Maintaining continuous operation – backward error recovery

A technique called backward error recovery (*roll-back*) may also be used to maintain continuous operation when failures occur. One such method is that of recovery blocks, Figure 13.27. Here a section of program code consists of:

- A checkpoint (also called a recovery point).
- The main or primary algorithm.

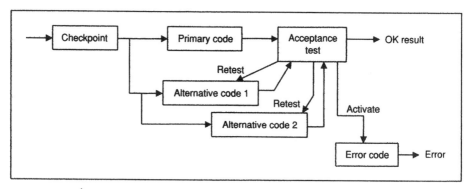

Figure 13.27 | Basic recovery block structure.

- Alternative algorithms.
- An acceptance tester.

System state (including data) is held at a checkpoint whilst the primary algorithm is executed. On completion an acceptance test is applied to the algorithm output. If it passes, processing continues using the current output. If not, the system first 'rolls-back' the program to the checkpoint. Using the stored state information it now executes the alternative code 1 and repeats the acceptance test. This it repeats until a good result is produced or else all alternatives fail. In the event of failure, a case error code is executed. Where the same acceptance test is applied to each computation, a typical recovery block error scheme is:

```
ENSURE    <AcceptanceTest>
BY        <PrimaryCode>
ELSEBY    <AlternativeCode1>
ELSEBY    <AlternativeCode2>
⋮
ELSEBY    <AlternativeCodeN>
ELSE      <ErrorCode>
```

In general roll-back techniques are more suited to mission-critical systems because:

- Program failures may cause operation to stop completely until some form of external recovery is put into action and
- Actual execution times may well vary from run to run, which can lead to performance problems. The processing time is indeterminate (within a defined worst-case upper-bound, of course).

However, given sufficient processing power, roll-back methods (Figure 13.28) can be used in fast systems. Tyrrell and Sillitoe [TYR91] applied them to a transputer-based robotic control system which had a 4 ms cycle time.

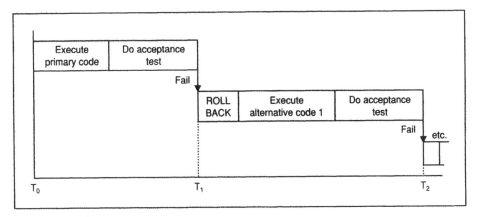

Figure 13.28 Timing aspects of backward recovery blocks.

One of the most difficult (and critical) aspects of backward error recovery is the design of the acceptance tester. Three different methods may be used:

- Test results against *pre-defined* values (e.g. checking that values lie within valid ranges).

- Test results against *predicted* values. In dynamical systems, for example, the maximum rates of change of parameters can be used for this purpose. Using this we can predict the maximum possible change of parameter values in any time interval. The actual value produced by the algorithm should not exceed the predicted amount.

- Using the output value, compute the input values which should have produced this output. Compare these with the checkpoint values to see if they agree. This technique (an inverse or 'reverse' algorithm check) can be applied in general to control and signal processing algorithms where time isn't a problem.

Note that we must have knowledge of system and/or software attributes in order to form acceptance tests.

Maintaining continuous operation – N-version programming

The fundamentals of *N*-version programming are shown in Figure 13.29. Here the input data to a section of code is processed by *N* versions of an algorithm. All *N* results are sent to an output checker which:

- Compares all results and votes on the comparison, then
  - If all agree, outputs the result, otherwise
  - Selects the result agreed by the majority and outputs this value (normally there are $N - 1$ agreements at any one time).

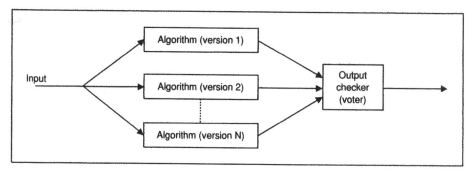

Figure 13.29 *N*-version programming.

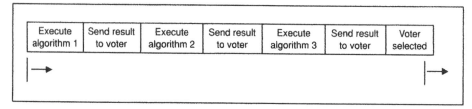

Figure 13.30 Timing aspects of sequential *N*-version programming.

Although this approach has its roots in electronic analogue control systems (especially flight control), it can be used effectively in single-processor applications. Its advantage is that we don't have to devise acceptance tests, the Achilles heel of roll-back techniques. Actual results don't matter as long as we have majority agreement. The down side for single-processor systems, however, is the time overhead, Figure 13.30. The *N*-version method fails when common-mode errors occur (i.e. all algorithms produce the same *wrong* result). To minimize such problems use as much diversity as possible between the *N* algorithms. For example, have each algorithm developed by a different designer.

A word of caution concerning diverse (dissimilar) methods and highly critical systems: don't be too trustworthy. Work by Susan Brilliant [BRI90] and Nancy Leveson [LEV90] showed flaws in the technique; even with diverse programming, significant common-mode errors can still occur.

13.5 Real-world interfacing

13.5.1 Background

Many design processes pay scant attention to handling of real-world interactions. Frequently OO techniques treat interfacing rather dismissively, using 'interface' or 'boundary' classes which are peripheral to the design (no pun intended). In some ways this view is understandable in desktop-type IT systems. But to take the same approach for real-time embedded systems is, at the best, risky; at worse it can be extremely dangerous. Lutz [LUT93] for example describes experiences gained in integration and system testing of the Voyager and Galileo spacecraft. He found that the misunderstanding of interface requirements and lack of detailed requirements for robustness were the primary causes of safety-related software errors. These accounted for 44% of all logged safety-related errors, as a result of:

- Out-of-range input values.

- Non-arrival of expected inputs.

- Unexpected arrival of inputs.

- Inconsistent code behaviour in response to input signals.

- Invalid input data time-frames.

- Out-of-range arrival rates.

- Lost events.

- Excessive output signal rates.

- Not all output data used.

- Effect of input signal arrival during non-operational modes (start-up/off-line/ shut-down).

The consequences of input signal errors are many and varied, ranging from irritating to catastrophic:

- Armstrong [ARM98] describes how electrical interference produced a false input signal to a radio-controlled crane. The crane dropped its load, crushing the operator (who, unfortunately, was standing below it) to death.

- The first Apollo Moon landing almost came to grief owing to a faulty sensor on the Lunar landing craft. In the final seconds of touchdown it fired off a rapid volley of interrupts, effectively disabling the control computer. Fortunately the astronauts were able to land under manual control.

13.5.2 Fault types and identification – inputs

Let us first consider input signals. The emphasis here is on using software to *detect* signal faults and so ensure safe system operation.

Embedded systems have to deal with a tremendous variety of devices, often needing specialized interfaces. Even so, device signals fall broadly into three categories: analogue, discrete (switch) and digital. When such inputs go faulty, the problem can originate in a number of places. These include external devices, connecting wiring or the interfacing and digitizing electronics. Well-known signal problems include:

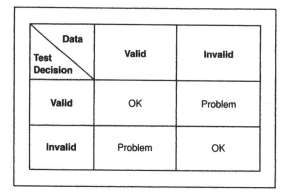

Figure 13.31 Fault detection logic.

- Switch inputs stuck in one state.
- Uncommanded change of switch state.
- Sensor signals going hard over to minimum or maximum positions.
- Analogue signals locking up (i.e. maintaining a constant digitized value).
- Invalid signals caused by noise.
- Bias on digitized signals owing to stuck bits.
- Sensor degradation (drift) with time.

What we have to do is to devise tests which *correctly* detect such problems, Figure 13.31. Provided the test decisions correspond to the data conditions then things are OK. There are two problem areas:

- Valid data being flagged as invalid and
- Invalid data considered to be valid.

The degree of severity depends on specific applications [LEV95], but in some situations may be catastrophic. (Personal experience: some years ago four military trainer aircraft were lost within the space of one week. The cause in each case was an invalid engine fire warning signal accepted as valid.)

13.5.3 Fault detection methods – inputs

Trying to describe in detail all possible detection methods is a challenging task; many are application specific. As a result, experienced designers usually build up a 'cook book' of fault detection methods. We, however, will only define a general set of tests which can be used to identify input errors. Broadly speaking, we can look for errors by checking against:

- Limit values – amplitude and time.
- Rate values.
- Predicted values.
- Redundant values.
- Time-related values.
- Inferred values.
- Estimated values.

Limit testing is the simplest, estimation the most complex. Some of these concepts have already been described, though not in the context of signal handling.

Limit testing

In limit testing the idea here is to compare actual values with known, practical limits of these values. For example, a conveyor belt might have a maximum speed of 4 miles per hour. Values outside the range 0 to 4 would clearly be invalid. Another example: key presses made by humans last for a minimum time, typically in the order of 50 milliseconds. Signals having a duration shorter than this are likely to be false, usually being noise-induced.

Limit testing is somewhat crude in that it tends to detect mainly the 'hard-over' type of fault. However, many faults actually fall into this category. Moreover, limit tests are both easy to implement and fast in operation.

Rate testing

Rate testing is based on the fact that things take time to happen. For example, the maximum turn rate of a ship might be 3 degrees per second: the time between key presses in the order of 250 milliseconds. By comparing actual rates of change with predetermined maxima, error conditions can be flagged up. The actual comparison testing is simple, but extracting rate information takes time and may be subject to error, as happened in the following case (personal experience). One of the main points of this story is to highlight the relationship between false alarms and error thresholds.

Rate testing was used on an airliner to detect faults in the flap selector system. In the event of a failure the system was designed to freeze the position of all relevant flight surfaces. However, when the aircraft first came into service many false freeze conditions (false alarms) were reported. Eventually it was established that the problem lay with how the flap selector switch was operated by the aircrew. Normally the switch toggle lay in a protected slot ('gate') at each selection. To set it to a new selection, it has to be moved out of the gate, pushed to the new position and then dropped into the new gate. All timings were based on this mode of operation. Unfortunately, human beings can be very creative at times, doing the most unexpected things. It turned out that what the co-pilots did was to extract the toggle out of the gate, slide it *almost* to the new gate, and then, on the command 'flaps down', flicked it with their fingers. This produced very fast toggling of the switch contact mechanism, which, of course, was judged to be a selection fault.

There may also be a further problem when using rate testing. When rate information is deduced from amplitude values, we actually perform differentiation. This has the unfortunate effect of magnifying the effects of noise; as a result calculated values may well be in error. Thus for noisy systems some extra digital filtering is needed, and this takes time.

Predicted values

The basic concepts involved in using predicted values have already been described in the section on acceptance testers. But be careful when dealing with real-world signals. Once again, if rates of change are used to predict future values, noise may be a problem.

In some control applications, techniques based on system modelling can be used. Here a mathematical model of the real system is built in software. For testing, the controller output signal is used to stimulate the model, which then produces a set of output signals. These output values are, of course, the predicted counterparts of the real input signals. By comparing the two sets of signals, errors can be identified.

Tests such as these do, however, start to blur the boundary between prediction and estimation.

Redundant inputs

Redundant systems use multiple versions of input signals, cross-checking these to identify faults. The technique is normally used with sensor signals and data from serial communications lines. For critical systems dual redundancy is commonplace, triple and quad redundancy being reserved for highly safety-critical applications.

Where it is important to detect that a system has developed a fault – but continued automatic operation isn't required – then dual redundancy is sufficient. Testing is done merely by comparing the two inputs. A disagreement indicates that we have a problem but doesn't, of course, identify the faulty signal. This approach has often been used where systems can revert to manual mode, for example.

Where continued operation is required, then triple or quad redundancy coupled with majority voting techniques is used.

Time-related values

The concept here is one of checking signals only at specific times, ignoring them otherwise. Thus signal errors which occur outside of the check time-frames have no effect on system behaviour.

- Dynamical systems have many states or modes of operation. Frequently only a subset of input signals are used in the individual modes. When a particular mode is active then, by looking only at relevant signals, many problems can be avoided. Take, for example, the start–stop control of a microwave oven. When the oven is stopped, the stop signal can be ignored. Likewise, once started, the start signal is irrelevant.

- Frequently signals are present continuously but are of interest only at specific times (e.g. passive sonar systems). By time-gating such signals, problems due to erroneous inputs and noise may be minimized.

- When synchronizing operations, especially of mechanical systems, it is important that valid state or status information is used. This is especially important in distributed systems which use LAN communication methods. Time stamping of such messages is critical.

Inferred values

In many real applications we can identify faulty signals using information provided by other input signals. For example, consider a room air conditioning unit that has temperature sensors in its inlet and outlet air ducts. The air conditioning controller is also wired to a room temperature sensor. Suppose that the sensors' signals indicate the following temperatures:

- Room temperature: 20 °C.
- Inlet temperature: 0 °C.
- Outlet temperature: 10 °C.

It doesn't take a genius to work out that there is something amiss here. Moreover, we can infer that the most likely culprit is the inlet temperature sensor.

Inferred techniques have been used in safety-critical applications (especially those using smart sensors) to minimize the number of sensors required. For instance, a classic quad-redundant system might have four temperature, four flow and four level sensors. By cross-correlating sensor information and using inference to detect faults, these numbers could be halved (leading to significant cost savings).

Estimated values

Estimation techniques are similar to model-based predictive methods. However, they are normally used in situations where the models cannot be predicted in advance. Instead they are built up 'on the fly', using advanced methods such as recursive least squares (RLS) and Kalman filters. An application example will best illustrate the use of these techniques. A submarine control system was optimized for normal (i.e. submerged) operation. However, when the vessel was on the surface, problems arose. Roll-motion caused by waves induced an excessive amount of control activity, significantly degrading system performance. In effect the wave noise swamped the true signal. Unfortunately the wave noise was well within the control bandwidth of the system. Even more unfortunately, wave frequency is highly variable (contrast the North Sea with the Atlantic Ocean). Thus traditional filtering methods were of limited use. However, advanced filtering was applied to estimate the true signal by digitally identifying, tracking and eliminating the noise content.

13.5.4 Fault handling – outputs

In critical systems, if we've done our job correctly, we shouldn't be issuing incorrect commands to the output world. Unfortunately, with the best will in the world . . . In reality, only a limited amount of protection can be provided by software. So for safety-critical systems extra (and perhaps external) hardware is likely to be used. But let us see what *can* be done.

(a) Don't use individual bits within a word to operate separate on–off type controls – *unless* you really do want to operate them simultaneously (yes, I know it's fast and simple; it's also dangerous). Instead use a specific, unique word for each control. Thus to operate a specific output, write the appropriate control word to a defined, unique memory-mapped (or I/O) location. Unfortunately this technique cannot be used unless the hardware supports such modes of operation.

(b) Where each bit of a single control word *does* operate an individual control, then use defensive measures:

- First, store the control word in memory. Then at least you can read it to see what state the outputs are supposed to be in.
- Second, when setting outputs, write to the stored control word; then output this to set the hardware state.
- Third, ensure that when setting a particular control you do not affect other controls; use AND and OR bit masking methods in the low-level software.

(c) Use state and sequence information where possible to limit the number of operations that may be invoked.

(d) Where operating a control incorrectly could produce dire effects, *never* use a single command. Multiple signalling is needed (this should really be tied in with proper hardware support so that true output status signals can be obtained).

(e) Apply rate-limiting to analogue output signals. While this won't stop wrong values being produced it will minimize their effects.

13.6 Operating systems aspects

13.6.1 General

The need to use robust, reliable operating systems in critical situations will be self-evident to users of desktop personal computers. Problems encountered in the PC world are many and varied. At the lower end of the frustration range is the shut-down of an application accompanied by the message 'This program has performed an illegal operation' (baffling when you haven't done anything). Applications may be launched automatically at the most unexpected times, causing havoc with existing work. And in extreme cases, machines completely lock up, needing to be switched off before operations can resume (a challenging task with a laptop). Well, enraging as this may be, the actual consequences are not especially harmful. However, it should be clear that such behaviour is quite unacceptable for mission-critical systems. (But not to everybody it seems; one well-known commercial OS was used within the machinery/propulsion systems of the US warship USS *Yorktown*. A failure on sea trials crippled the ship to such an extent that it had to be towed into port.)

What is needed then for all critical applications are operating systems that are robust, reliable and *predictable*. The key to success is to use, as before, a combination of fault prevention and fault tolerance. First, though, we need to understand how and why things go wrong. In very general terms, problems can be generated by:

- The OS software itself (including all pre-supplied software components such as device drivers, etc.).
- Application software (including library and middleware components).
- Malfunctioning hardware.

Practical experience has shown that the following items are the main causes of system malfunctions:

- Application software interfering with the OS.
- Tasks/applications interfering with other tasks/applications (in this context, an application may consist of one or more tasks).
- Unexpected functional behaviour of tasks or applications.
- Unexpected timing behaviour of tasks or applications.
- Design weaknesses or flaws in the OS software.

Interference aspects are best dealt with by using protection techniques. Behavioural problems can be minimized (in some cases eliminated) by applying appropriate tasking and/or scheduling principles. The final item is beyond your direct control; it depends entirely on the choice of operating system.

Certain fault modes are specific to distributed systems. They are discussed separately.

13.6.2 Protection techniques

Rogue applications or tasks can generate problems for others in a number of ways, including:

- Writing into the data area (e.g. RAM memory) of others.
- Writing into the code area (e.g. flash memory) of others.
- Sending messages to the wrong destinations.
- Reading/receiving messages from the wrong senders.
- Sending incorrect messages.
- Corrupting shared data items.
- Making invalid calls on OS functions.

Memory protection has been covered earlier in Chapter 6. Suffice it to say here that such techniques should always be used in safety-critical work.

As shown in Chapter 5, there are a number of ways to handle inter-task communication (also called inter-process communication, IPC). These, although they may vary in detail, have common features when used for critical work, Figure 13.32.

- Tasks should communicate using defined OS-supplied communication components. The use of shared (common) memory is to be avoided.
- All comms components must be shown on the tasking diagram (but see note below).
- Every component must be explicitly identified.
- Messaging should, wherever possible, be done on a one-to-one basis.
- Each component must, with one-to-to one signalling, have a designated sender and receiver. This provides us with secure 'circuits' for task-to-task communication.
- The OS must be able to check for invalid signalling.

Note: some OSs include comms components as integral parts of the tasks themselves. In such cases the tasking diagram will not, of course, contain comms items. Also, it is clear that there is no requirement to designate the receiver of a message; it is implicit in the tasking model.

Corruption of shared data (e.g. in data pools) can be prevented by using mutual exclusion techniques, as described in Chapter 5. It should be standard practice to apply such methods to *all* communication components (with the possible exception of flags).

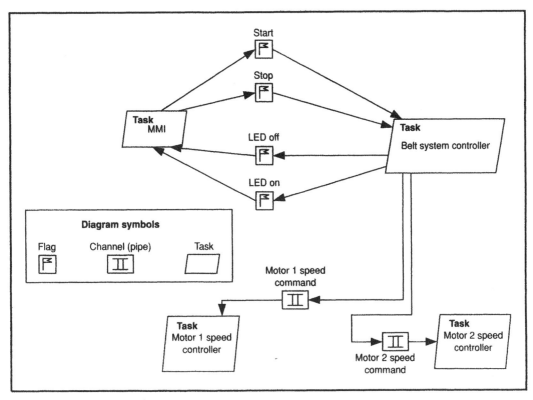

Figure 13.32 Secure inter-task communication features (example).

All calls by application software on OS services should be checked for correctness, e.g. caller validation, parameter checks, numerical range values, data length matching between senders and receivers, etc. It is highly desirable that all error handling is automatically invoked by the OS itself. This, by centralizing operations, guarantees that such problems *will* be attended to. It also means that cohesive, explicit and predefined exception-handling policies can be mandated. The alternative is to inform the application of the problem using some form of error message return. What happens in such cases depends entirely on the application software (at worst, nothing, say, due to ignoring the error message(s)).

There are other advantages in using OS features to provide exception handling. First, the OS can police itself. Second, it can check for problems with the use of run-time components (e.g. invalid use of library application programming interfaces, re-entrancy of subprograms, etc.). Third, it can handle problems originating in hardware, for example, an ADC refusing to perform a conversion (this implies that access to such devices is via a hardware abstraction layer integrated with the OS kernel, see Chapter 6).

13.6.3 Tasking models and scheduling

By using all the protection features listed above, applications will, *in general*, be sufficiently robust for mission-critical work. However, for safety-critical systems, the demands are much greater. Ideally we want systems which:

- Are functionally fully predictable.
- Are temporally (time) fully predictable.
- Guarantee to detect task failures.
- Guarantee to detect OS failures.
- Require a relatively small amount of memory (and use this in a deterministic manner).
- Can be formally certified if so required.

In reality we can only strive for this; practical techniques provide different levels of performance and safety. Tasking models suitable for the top two levels of criticality (see Figure 13.3) are covered here:

- Catastrophic severity level.
- Critical severity level.

Catastrophic severity level

We can attain this level of performance with systems which conform to the following rules:

- Task execution (task schedule) is a fully defined static one. There is no dynamic creation or deletion of tasks.
- All code can be fully statically analysed.
- Tasks execute in a run-to-completion mode, pre-emption is not allowed ('run to completion semantics').
- The code can be formally certified if so required.
- Watchdog techniques must be used to ensure that run-time bounds are not exceeded.

These requirements can be met by using cyclic scheduling based on rate-group techniques, see Chapter 5. This, in effect, transforms a design-level tasking model into a non-tasking implementation model (each task is run as an individual unit of sequential code, the sequence being controlled by the scheduler). With this design there are no calls by the application software to the OS. Moreover, the OS software, normally executed in response to a tick interrupt, can be fully statically analysed. Lastly, watchdog protection is straightforward as it only needs to be applied to each minor cycle of the schedule.

While cyclic scheduling is effective (used in practice, for example, by Rolls-Royce for electronic aero-engine control) it has a number of drawbacks:

- All tasks must be periodic.
- There is a limited choice of periodic (iteration) times.
- Proper allowance must be made for variations in actual run-times – overruns must not be allowed to happen.
- Schedules can become very rigid. In some cases it may be necessary to modify the original tasking design to fit the available resources (and so degrade the design).
- Through-life maintenance can be a very difficult and complicated job.

This last aspect is a major issue on long-life projects.

Critical severity level

The requirements at this level can be met by using a restricted subset of normal kernel functions, as for instance described in the Ravenscar profile [DOB99]. The salient features are:

- Both periodic and aperiodic tasks may be implemented.
- Fixed priority-based tasking is supported. Dynamically adjustable priorities are forbidden.
- Non-pre-emptive, co-operative and pre-emptive scheduling are allowed.
- All tasks are static – no dynamic creation or deletion is permitted.
- Periodic tasks are structured as infinite loops. Each task invocation runs the complete loop for that task.
- Worst-case execution times must be deterministic.
- Memory for all kernel components such as TCBs, stacks, etc. must be allocated statically.
- All code can be fully statically analysed.
- Priority inversion must be eliminated.
- Only scheduling algorithms which lend themselves to schedulability analysis (e.g. deadline monotonic scheduling) should be used.
- Watchdog techniques must be used to ensure that run-time bounds are not exceeded. These are more complex than those used with cyclic scheduling as every task needs to be checked.
- Code may be formally certified if so required.

The kernel itself must be supported by appropriate tools such as coverage and schedulability analysers and run-time scheduling tracers.

One safety-critical kernel designed to comply with these requirements is RAVEN, from Aonix Inc. [AON01].

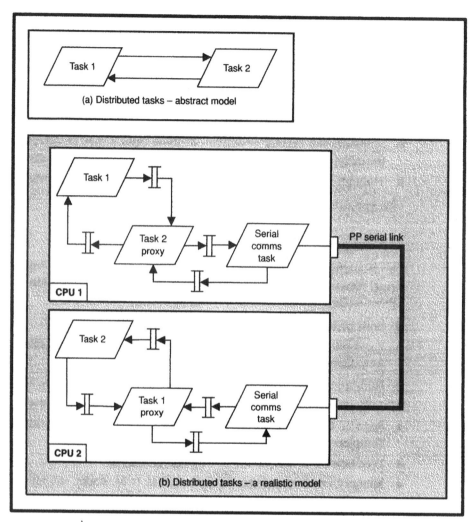

Figure 13.33 | Distributed tasks.

13.6.4   Operating systems and critical distributed applications

As pointed out in Chapter 5, operating system structures in most (if not all) practical distributed systems are similar. That is, each node of the system has its own RTOS kernel software, using message passing methods for communication. One of the cleanest ways of turning the abstract distributed tasking model of Figure 13.33a into a realistic one is shown in Figure 13.33b. Whether a 'home-grown' RTOS or a commercial one is used, we should provide service software to hide the details of:

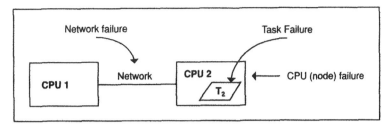

Figure 13.34 ┊ Potential failure points in distributed systems.

- Task location.
- CPU type and location.
- Network protocol aspects.
- Network physical interfacing and signal-handling features.

In effect these become 'transparent' to the applications programmer. Thus, at this level, the tasking model really does appear to be an abstract one.

Well, this is fine until problems arise. For example, our abstract model shows task 1 talking to task 2, as per Figure 13.33a. A message is sent from 1 to 2, one which requires a reply. But the reply never arrives. Clearly there has been some sort of failure in the system. But where? Figure 13.34 identifies the potential failure points in distributed systems:

- Network
- Node (or CPU)
- Task.

When task 1 sends out a message we can check that it actually gets launched onto the network using loopback techniques. However, if the network is faulty, the message may not get delivered.

Assuming a fault-free link, the message will arrive at the destination node. However, if the node has failed, no further progress will be made. Problems like these *can*, however, be identified by good system and protocol design.

All being well, the message will enter the node and be directed to the destination task 2. But just assume that because of sloppy programming task 2 has been halted. Once again a failure will ensue. And of course, even if the message does get to task 2, the answer still has to get back to task 1. Along with these potential failures we also have to consider:

- Synchronization of operation across the system.
- Addressing errors (wrong senders/receivers).
- Data errors (data corruption, wrong data, etc.).

- Message timing errors (e.g. messages arriving at unexpected times).
- Message sequence errors.
- Consistency of data (information) across the system.

For critical systems, methods *must* be implemented to handle such problems. It should also be clear that each node must be capable of looking after itself. Hence it makes sense to dedicate one task per node to look after such safety and security features. Features such as these are available in some RTOSs (such as OSE [ENE01]) devised for high-integrity applications.

 ## 13.7 Processor problems

13.7.1 Overview

This section is primarily concerned with processor-related run-time problems. It deals with issues resulting from either CPU register or memory malfunctions. Such malfunctions may be induced in a number of ways: electrical noise, aberrant program behaviour, excessive temperatures, hardware faults, etc. The techniques used seek to answer three questions:

(a) Is it OK to use the processor system in the first place?

(b) Is it safe to continue using the processor system in its normal running mode?

(c) If problems *are* detected, can we recover from the situation?

Questions (b) and (c) are closely interlinked and will be dealt with together as appropriate.

It is important to understand that these tests are not foolproof. Therefore they augment, not replace, hardware-based techniques (e.g. watchdogs and memory management units). Their advantages, when they work, are that they can:

- Warn us of processor and memory defects before we execute the application software.
- Warn us that things are going wrong before dangerous situations occur.
- Provide for more graceful and perhaps safer recovery from failures than watchdog-activated ones. Armstrong [ARM98] illustrates this point with the following story. The engine management system of a vehicle was reset while it was travelling at 70 mph on a multilane highway. It then executed the reset code, which was exactly the same as the power-on code. This assumed that the vehicle was stationary and parked. As a result of the power-on checks the management system decided that the wheel speed sensors had failed. It promptly shut down the engine. The driver's comments have not been recorded.

13.7.2 Power-on aspects

Two sets of tests are used to verify the goodness of the processor system:

● CPU tests (which may include various on-chip devices in the case of highly integrated microprocessors, complex microcontrollers, etc.).

● Permanent memory (e.g. ROM, EPROM, flash) tests.

In this section we'll restrict ourselves to the general principles of such tests. A fairly detailed description of these techniques is given by Brown [BRO99], applied to the Motorola 68332 microcontroller.

CPU tests

The basic purpose of these tests is to confirm that the CPU will (or should) function correctly. Checks carried out include:

● Verifying that the processor correctly executes its range of instructions.

● Ensuring that all condition flags can be operated and read correctly.

● Checking that all on-chip registers and devices can be written to and read from.

● Verifying, where applicable, the operation of maths co-processors.

In order to check the execution of individual instructions, tests must be written in assembler or machine code. While this may be feasible for RISC machines, the same may not be true of CISC devices. Brown recommends in this case that only those instructions used by the application need be tested. These may be obtained by parsing the output of the compiler to generate a list of related assembler instructions.

Testing procedures for on-chip devices such as timers, A/D converters, etc. tend to be specific to individual microcontroller structures.

Read-only memory tests

It is known that bit values in semiconductor memory may change state as a result of electromagnetic pulse effects and cosmic radiation. These, of course, occur only in quite specialized applications. For general applications there is a more pressing problem: to ensure that 'permanent' information in non-volatile read–write memory (e.g. flash) is valid. Devices like these can be programmed *in situ* and thus lend themselves to 'accidental' reprogramming (caused, for example, by poor electronic design, interference noise, etc.).

On power-up the information stored in these devices may be checked for validity. This includes both program code and data. Failure to pass such tests means that subsequent operations of the processor are unpredictable. In this situation the computer system should be put into a safe condition and – if possible – a warning generated. The technique used is to:

- Generate a check value based on the known, good contents of the memory devices.
- Store the check value in a defined location.
- On power-up, carry out a check of the current contents.
- Compare the resultant check value with the original one. If these don't agree take appropriate action (which may, for example, include shutting down the system).

Two techniques are in general use for calculating the check values: checksums and cyclic redundancy code (CRC) checks. Checksums are easy to implement and may be carried out very quickly. However, their error-detection properties are much less powerful than CRCs. To improve error-checking qualities, CRC techniques (also known as polynomial coding) should be used. These, though, are more complex and even the simplest ones take longer to perform than checksums. Fortunately, in most cases the time needed to carry out these tests during power-up isn't usually a problem.

13.7.3 Run-time issues

Three specific run-time issues are dealt with here:

- Stack overflow.
- Corruption of critical variables.
- Corruption of the processor instruction pointer register.

Stack overflow

Deciding how much RAM space to allocate to a stack is somewhat of a black art. There is an element of 'suck it and see'. Unfortunately, even extensive testing doesn't guarantee that, at some time, stack overflow won't occur. This is especially true for stacks used to hold processor context when interrupts occur. An unexpectedly high rate of interrupt arrivals can soon cause the stack to overflow, generally crashing the processor. Four possible ways of dealing with this are:

- Inhibit (disable) interrupts until the current one is serviced (not always feasible).
- Service the interrupt before the next one arrives (may not be possible).
- Use stack monitoring software.
- Use processor-based hardware stack monitoring and overflow detection (as, for example, provided on ARM processors).

Stack monitoring *may* be provided by languages and/or compilers. If so, use them. If not, develop your own. The concept is quite simple. On creating the stack, it is filled with a known pattern. As data is stored on the stack it overwrites the original pattern. By keeping track of this it is possible to calculate how much stack is in use (and thus how much is free). Hence impending overflow can be detected and corrective action applied.

Corruption of critical variables

It is always possible that data values can be corrupted as a result of electrical noise, power supply fluctuations, etc. This is especially true of dynamic, rather than static, memory. Because of this, critical variables should be treated with special care. Where it is important to detect but not correct errors then:

● Store the critical data items in a defined location and append a checksum or CRC value to the data set.

● Copy the critical data set, also using checksum or CRC methods (it is suggested that using a different data format for the copy makes the technique more reliable).

● Before using any of the variables, compare the two. If they don't agree, an error has occurred.

This scheme can be extended to include a third copy, incorporating majority voting. This enables the processor to both detect and correct errors.

Error correction techniques are rarely used in processor systems. However, they have been applied to long-life spacecraft missions, a process known as RAM scrubbing.

Corruption problems like this can also be caused by rampant pointers, another good reason for banning them.

Instruction pointer corruption

Electrical noise can cause corruption of binary information anywhere within the processor system. This includes values stored in the processor registers. Any such corruption is likely to lead to problems, but one register in particular is especially important: the instruction pointer, IP (also called the program counter). Two particular scenarios can be identified:

● The corrupted IP points to unprogrammed (unused) memory locations.

● The corrupted IP points to programmed code or data locations.

Vectoring to unprogrammed areas can be dealt with provided a no-operation (NOP) instruction can be input in one read cycle. Simply fill all unused locations up to the final one with NOPs. This last location should be programmed to make the processor jump to a defined error-recovery routine. Then, should the processor vector to an unused area, it just performs a series of NOPs. Finally it will end at the jump statement and thence to the recovery program.

However, should the processor vector to programmed code or data areas, behaviour is much less predictable (note that, to the CPU, code and data values are indistinguishable; they are merely bit patterns). There are three possible outcomes:

- Program control transfers to a valid instruction. In this case resulting operations depend on the code found at this point. Little can be done in software to protect against this problem.

- Program control transfers to a position *within* a multibyte instruction. In such situations processor behaviour is entirely unpredictable (for example, data values can be interpreted as op codes). Once again, software techniques offer little protection.

- Program control transfers to a valid instruction within a called software unit (e.g. task, function, routine).

In this last case a technique called 'token passing' [COU98] may give some protection. Its purpose is to ensure that such called units only execute if they have been invoked correctly (and not as a result of IP corruption, for example). One simple method is to use a flag as a token. The calling unit first sets this flag, then invokes the called unit. The called unit, during its execution, checks that the flag or token is correctly set. If so, it assumes that all is well and proceeds about its business. Otherwise recovery action is taken.

Token passing offers only a limited amount of protection. Moreover, the actual checking process itself adds to code size (estimated at between 10% and 20%) and execution times.

13.8 Hardware-based fault tolerance

13.8.1 General aspects

This section is concerned with the last line of defence in fault-tolerant systems: the use of hardware. Naturally enough, much of this hardware actually contains software. And it is at this level that hardware, software and system aspects become almost inseparable. The topic itself is a major one in its own right; all that can be done here is to give a very broad view of the subject. However, any software engineer involved in the development of real-time critical systems should understand these basics.

Three questions are central to the choice of fault-tolerant designs:

- What do we want to achieve?

- How can we achieve it?

- What are the pros and cons of the various solutions?

The first point is dealt with in this section whilst the others are discussed later.

There is a wide range of critical systems. Thus it is no surprise to find that their operational requirements – in terms of fault tolerance – vary considerably, Figure 13.35. The first point to consider is what is expected of a system when a fault occurs. Must

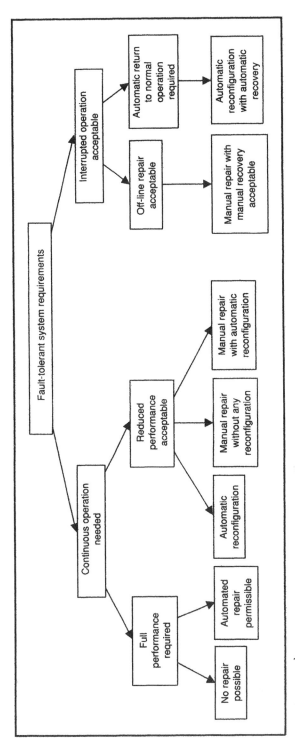

Figure 13.35 Operational requirements of hardware-based fault-tolerant systems.

it continue to carry on working without a break? In other words, must it operate continuously? Or is it acceptable for it to stop working correctly for a period of time but then resume operations?

Continuous operation

Where systems need to operate continuously, must they always deliver full performance (fail-operational – FO)? On the other hand, reduced performance may be acceptable (usually with some degree of graceful degradation), resulting in a fail-active (FA) system.

With most FO systems, it isn't possible to repair faulty units while the system is actually operational. Thus sufficient spare resources must be provided to keep the system working even if multiple failures occur. This approach has been used very successfully in, for example, flight control systems. However, even long-haul flights rarely exceed 24 hours. Thus the time at risk isn't excessively long. Contrast this with spacecraft systems, where the operational time runs into years. In such situations being able to repair faults automatically can be a major benefit.

Fail-active systems cannot afford to have (apparent) breaks in operation when faults occur. If it isn't possible to repair the system, then a degraded or 'limp-home' strategy must be invoked automatically. Generally, to the observer, the switch from normal to degraded mode should be instantaneous. In other applications, however (e.g. telecomms switches), it is essential to provide maintained operations even with faults present. This reduced level of service is maintained until such faults can be repaired. Normally repair is carried out by replacing the faulty board(s), a manual activity. Frequently (especially in the case of simple I/O boards), this is all that is required. In other cases, however, the system software must be updated (*reconfigured*) to take board changes into account. When systems are on-line, reconfiguration must be done automatically.

Interrupted operation

With interrupted operation, the computer system actually goes down and just stops working. Three important inter-linked questions are:

- What happens when the system goes down?
- How *does* the system get back to normal operation?
- How quickly must the failed system be brought back into service?

The first point is crucial in safety-critical systems. Here systems must generally go into a fail-safe mode; recovery is usually done manually. This is an off-line recovery method. In non-critical systems, failures (by definition) shouldn't create safety hazards. If time isn't pressing, then repair and return to normal operation is a manual process. However, the time taken to carry out manual repair may be too long for mission-critical systems. In many of these applications, acceptable down-times are measured in minutes or even seconds. To restore normal working that quickly, reconfiguration and recovery must be done automatically.

13.8.2 Fault-tolerant structures

A whole variety of fault-tolerant structures have been developed over the years, many predating the digital computer era. Broadly speaking, systems can be classed as one of the following:

- Passive redundant.
- Active redundant.
- Hybrid redundant.
- Very high availability.
- Hot-swap.

Passive redundant systems

Figure 13.36 shows one form of a passive redundant system where the redundancy is confined to the processors themselves (based on an actual feed-water control system for a nuclear reactor). In this case each processor carries out the same computation on the same set of input signals. The resulting outputs are sent to a majority voter, which selects one signal (the 'primary channel') to be output to the control actuator. The majority voter may be a simple logic device or, in more complex voting, a separate processor. Complex voters have the general structure shown in Figure 13.37. Its operation should be self-explanatory.

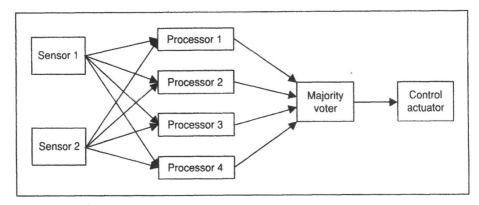

Figure 13.36 Four-channel passive redundant system.

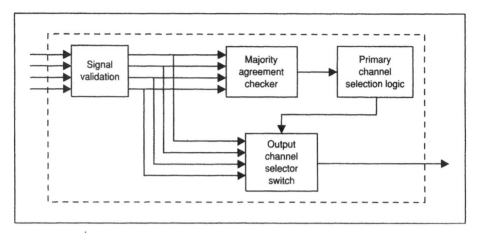

Figure 13.37 Software-based majority voter – logic diagram.

As described earlier, if channel disagreements are found, the primary channel is selected from the majority vote. Thus the design shown here can maintain full operation until three processors fail. System reconfiguration is essentially instantaneous, but the penalty to be paid for this performance is complexity (and cost). One version of this technique applied to telecomms systems is called 'lockstep processing' [MCK00].

Active redundant systems

The block diagram of an active redundant system (in this case a dual one) is given in Figure 13.38. Active redundancy typically involves the use of an operational (active) processor and a standby one. It also requires some form of fault detection, which may involve the use of a third processor. Should the active processor malfunction, the fault detection unit connects the output channel to the standby processor.

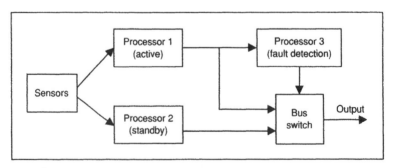

Figure 13.38 Dual-channel active redundant system.

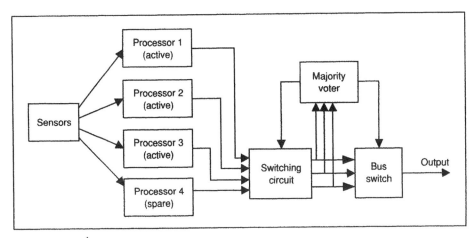

Figure 13.39 | Hybrid redundant system.

For 'seamless' transition of control, the standby processor not only needs to be running ('hot'); it also needs to be fully synchronized with the active processor. Where some down-time can be tolerated, a cold standby processor (i.e. unpowered) can be used. Active redundant systems strive to achieve a better balance of complexity, availability and cost than passive ones. They are frequently used in on-line transaction processing and have also been applied to aircraft and railway systems.

Hybrid redundant systems

A major purpose of a hybrid system is to improve the reliability of long-life missions. It does this by combining both active and spare processors as shown in Figure 13.39. Here processors 1–3 operate as a normal passive redundant system while processor 4 is the spare. However, the majority voter now has two basic functions to perform:

● To select one processor output as the primary channel.

● To disconnect a faulty processor and replace it with the spare one.

This is, of course, a simplified description of operation.

Very high availability (VHA) systems

As defined here, very high availability systems are designed (as the name implies) to provide extremely high levels of availability. Continuous, uninterrupted operation is not a basic design aim (though it's a bonus if this can be achieved). VHA systems are based on active redundant computer structures and come in different shapes and sizes. One form of active redundancy designed for database servers and similar applications is called 'clustered architectures' [MCK00]. These provide

- Very fast switch-over times ('failover times').
- Ready availability of disk data to standby systems.
- Simple fault management.

Another form is 'system-directed checkpointing' [MCK00]. This is aimed at applications where we can afford to lose current transaction information but restart rapidly (and in defined states, the checkpoints). For example, failover times in Motorola telecomm systems using checkpoint techniques are claimed to be less than 30 seconds (typically). However, failover times of under 1 second have been achieved with some designs.

Hot-swap systems

Hot-swap systems are those which rely on physical replacement of units to repair faults. With these designs boards can be removed, inserted or replaced while:

- The system is running (on-line) and
- Without disturbing on-going operations.

One particular hardware platform is used to illustrate the concepts, CompactPCI. The CompactPCI standard defines four levels of capability which systems may provide:

- Basic hot-swap.
- Full hot-swap.
- High-availability hot-swap (single-processor designs).
- High-availability hot-swap (multiprocessor designs).

For completeness, all levels will be described here.

Basic hot-swap systems

The structure of a basic hot-swap system is shown in Figure 13.40. Here it is safe to remove and insert boards without causing damage or affecting the running of

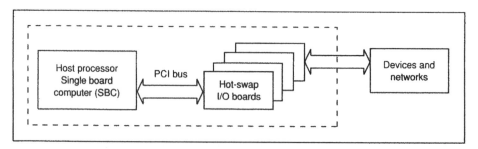

Figure 13.40 Basic hot-swap structure for CompactPCI systems.

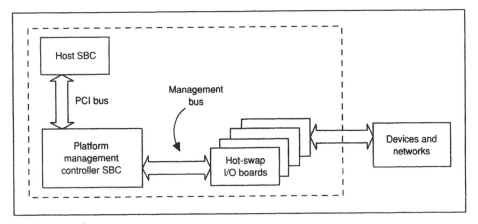

Figure 13.41 Structure of full and high-availability hot-swap CompactPCI systems (single-processor designs).

the system. However, no facilities are provided to allow the system to identify or configure newly inserted boards.

Full and high-availability hot-swap systems (single-processor designs)

Full and high-availability hot-swap facilities can be provided in single-processor systems using the structure of Figure 13.41. A full hot-swap implementation defines an interface to the system software which allows it to oversee the removal and insertion of boards. This includes board identification and configuration.

High-availability hot-swap extends this by allowing the system to monitor and control boards using platform management control software. This management software has the ability to reset or even power-down misbehaving boards. In more complex systems platform management may be carried out by a dedicated processor.

High-availability hot-swap systems (multiprocessor designs)

In multiprocessor systems, hot-swap facilities can be extended to the processors themselves, Figure 13.42. The multiprocessor structure is based on a primary (or host) processor to manage the system together with various other processors. These processors may perform a variety of tasks: distributed processing, I/O processing, dedicated control functions, etc. For distributed processing the structure has two potentially useful features. First, the processing load can be altered dynamically to achieve high performance ('load balancing'). Second, if a processor fails, its work can be allocated to another one. Fault diagnosis, repair and reconfiguration are, wherever possible, managed by the host computer.

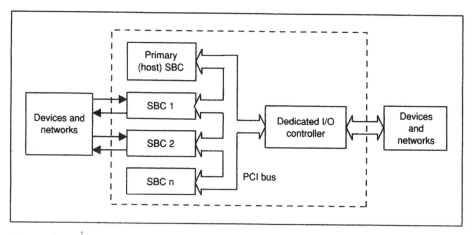

Figure 13.42   General structure – multiprocessor systems with hot-swap processor capability.

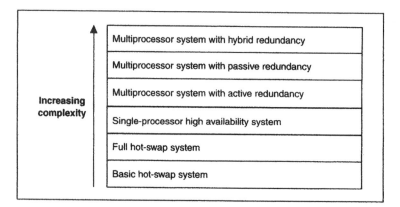

Figure 13.43   Relative complexity of fault-tolerant structures.

In summary, Figure 13.43 shows the fault-tolerant structure available to designers together with an indication of their relative complexities.

13.8.3   Matching structures to requirements

Figure 13.35 laid out the broad set of operational requirements of fault-tolerant systems. Figure 13.43 lists the range of fault-tolerant structures available to us. How can we go about matching structures to requirements? There isn't a unique answer, but a general guide is given in Figure 13.44. However, don't let this lull you into taking a cook-book approach to the subject. Many real practical systems are quite

System Requirements	Fault-Tolerant Structures	Hybrid redundancy	Passive redundancy	Active redundancy	High availability hot-swap	Full hot-swap	Basic hot-swap	Fail safe
Continuous operation needed	Full performance, no repair possible		X					
	Full performance, auto repair permissible	X						
	Reduced performance with automatic reconfiguration acceptable			X				
	Reduced performance, manual repair without reconfiguration						X	
	Reduced performance, manual repair with automatic reconfiguration				X	X		
Interrupted operation acceptable	Automatic reconfiguration with automatic recovery				X	X		
	Off-line repair with manual recovery acceptable							X

Figure 13.44 | Fault-tolerant systems – matching structures to requirements.

complex, often using variations on and combinations of these basic structures. To illustrate this point, see Figure 13.45, part of the Boeing 777 flight control system. Here the primary flight computer system uses a triple passive-redundant structure. Observe that all system interconnections are made using a triplex data bus (network). Closer examination of the primary flight computers shows that each one has a triple

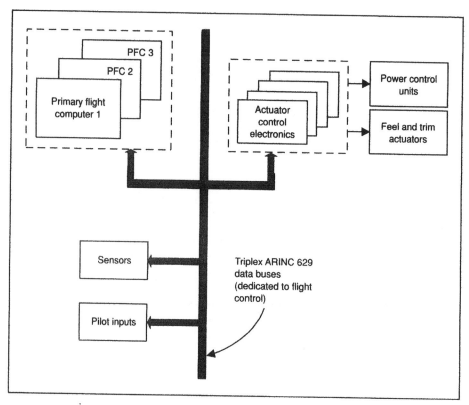

Figure 13.45 Example high-integrity system – Boeing 777 electronic flight control system (part).

'lane' structure, Figure 13.46. Every lane has its own processor, different compilers being used to generate run-time code, as follows:

PROCESSOR	COMPILER
AMD 29050	Verdix VADS
Intel 80486	DDC-I DACS 80X86
Motorola MC68040	Scicon XDAda

A final point: some authors have suggested using software patterns to develop critical software systems. This *may* be possible at the unit level (e.g. the majority voter of Figure 13.37), but even so one has to question the rationale for doing this. Exactly what will we gain? Applying the pattern concept to systems seems much less useful because of significant differences between designs. For example, the flight control system of the Airbus A320 differs considerably from that of the Boeing 777. Both perform pretty much the same function, yet they do it in quite different ways.

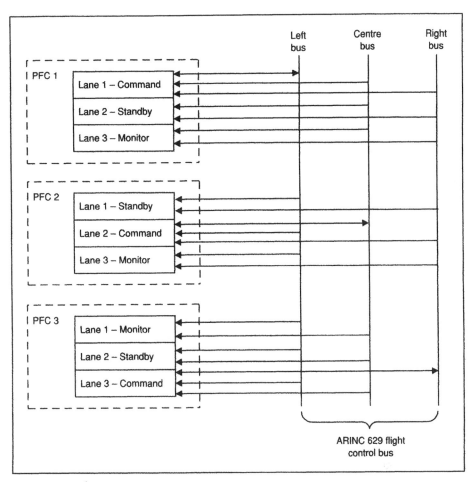

Figure 13.46 Primary flight computer lane structures.

Review

Having completed this chapter, you should now:

- Understand the key features and requirements of mission-critical and safety-critical systems.
- Be able to estimate appropriate severity levels, failure probabilities and failure rates for your own designs.
- Understand why and how formal methods are used in the specification of critical systems.
- Appreciate the many and varied errors that can arise when carrying out numerical (especially floating-point) computations.

- Be able to produce a set of basic guidelines for the production of high-quality application software.

- Appreciate why, in critical systems, special attention needs to be paid to the handling of real-world signals.

- Know how to apply fault detection and handling methods to such input–output signals.

- Realize that ordinary commercial RTOSs are unsuitable for use in safety-critical applications.

- Know what features are needed in RTOSs to provide secure operation.

- Understand how software techniques can alleviate problems caused by processor hardware malfunction.

- Recognize that the last line of defence against rogue software behaviour lies with hardware.

References and further reading

[AON01] *The Aonix real-time kernel, RAVEN*, Aonix, www.aonix.com, 2001.

[ARM98] *What EMC is, and some examples caused by software*, K. Armstrong, IEE Colloquium 1998/471 Electromagnetic compatibility of software, pp 1/1–1/10, Nov. 1998.

[BRI90] *Analysis of faults in an N-version software experiment*, S.S. Brilliant *et al.*, IEEE Transactions of Software Engineering, Vol. 16, No. 2, pp 238–247, 1990.

[BRO99] *Solving the software safety paradox*, D. Brown, Embedded Systems Programming Europe, pp 15–24, March 1999.

[COO94] *Formal specifications using animation prototyping*, J.E. Cooling and T.S. Hughes, Microprocessors and Microsystems, Vol. 18, No. 7, pp 385–391, 1994.

[COU98] *EMC techniques for microprocessor software*, D.R. Coulson, IEE Colloquium 1998/471 Electromagnetic compatibility of software, pp 2/1–2/5, Nov. 1998.

[DEN86] *Introduction to discrete mathematics for software engineers*, T. Denver, Macmillan Computer Science Series, ISBN 0-333-40737-7, 1986.

[DOB99] *The Ravenscar tasking profile for high integrity real-time programs*, B. Dobbing, Ada User Journal, Vol. 19, No. 4, pp 264–276, 1999.

[ENE01] *OSE – real-time operating system for embedded and fault tolerant applications*, ENEA OSE SYSTEMS AB, Sweden, www.enea.com, 2001.

[IEE85] *IEEE 754 standard for binary floating-point arithmetic (ANSI/IEEE Std 754-1985)* or IEC 559: *Binary floating-point arithmetic for microprocessor systems*.

[KEL91] *Implementing design diversity to achieve fault tolerance*, J.P. Kelly *et al.*, IEEE Software, Vol. 8, No. 4, pp 61–71, 1991.

[LEV90] *The use of self-checks and voting in software error detection: an empirical study*, N.G. Leveson, IEEE Transactions of Software Engineering, Vol. 16, No. 4, pp 432–443, 1990.

[LEV93] *An investigation of the Therac-25 accidents*, N.G. Leveson and C.S. Turner, IEEE Computer, Vol. 26, No. 7, pp 18–41, 1993.

[LEV95] *Safeware – system safety and computers*, N.G. Leveson, Addison-Wesley, ISBN 0-201-11972-2, 1995.

[LIG91] *Formal specification using Z*, D. Lightfoot, Macmillan Computer Science Series, ISBN 0-333-54408-0, 1991.

[LUT93] *Targeting safety-related errors during software requirements analysis*, R.R. Lutz, Sigsoft'93/12/93/CA, pp 99–106.

[MCK00] *Applying open systems to high-availability computing platforms*, D. McKinley, Embedded Systems Programming Europe, Vol. 3, No. 23, pp 14–21, 2000.

[NEL90] *Fault-tolerant computing: fundamental concepts*, V.P. Nelson, IEEE Computer, Vol. 23, No. 7, pp 19–25, 1990.

[ROL92] *Programming with VDM*, F.D. Rolland, Macmillan Computer Science Series, ISBN 0-333-56520-7, 1992.

[TYR91] Evaluation of fault tolerant structures for parallel systems in industrial control, A.M. Tyrrell and I.P.W. Sillitoe, IEE Conference Publication Control' 91, Vol. 1, No. 332, pp 393–398, Edinburgh, 1991.

Some important standards

- CENELEC EN 50128, European Committee for Electrotechnical Standardization Railway Applications: *Software for railway control and protection systems.*
- Defence Standard 00-55, UK MOD: *The procurement of safety critical software in defence equipment.*
- DOD-STD-2167A: *Military standard defense system software development.*
- IEC 61508, International Electrotechnical Commission: *Functional safety, safety related systems.*
- MIL-STD-498, *Military standard software development and documentation.*
- MISRA, UK Motor Industry Software Reliability Association: *Development guidelines for vehicle based software.*
- RTCA/DO-178B, EUROCAE/ED-12B: *Software considerations in airborne systems and equipment certification.*

Performance Engineering

Many projects have come to grief because the software couldn't cope with the demands of the real world. Problems have occurred in all sectors of industry, including aerospace, auto, medical, financial services and on-line booking systems. One point can be singled out as being dominant: the failure to deal with software performance requirements right from the start of projects.

The objectives of this chapter are to show:

- Why it is important to design for performance in real-time systems.
- Where performance requirements come from.
- How software performance relates to system performance.
- How performance targets get translated into performance achievables and deliverables.
- Why modelling and simulation are key techniques in performance analysis, prediction and evaluation.
- How doing 'top-down', 'bottom-up' and 'middle-out' performance analysis can reduce risk.

The core philosophy of this chapter is that software should be constructed to meet its performance objectives. This, in fact, is what people mean when they talk about software performance engineering [SMI90].

14.1 Why performance engineering is important

14.1.1 Time as a design driver

Many software developers – probably the majority, in fact – place great emphasis on producing designs that are functionally correct. This is especially true of OO-based projects, because OO techniques tend to concentrate on abstract logical features such as:

- Structure (class and class relationships).
- Encapsulation and information hiding.
- Object and class interfaces and dependencies.
- Object behaviour.

However, effective real-time embedded models concentrate on factors which are important in the real world itself. And unfortunately there is a significant mismatch between these two models. Real-world software designs are primarily shaped by:

- The natural simultaneous (concurrent) behaviour found in real systems.
- The need to co-ordinate and/or synchronize operations.
- The needs to respond to many and varied timing requirements (especially where potential solutions are heavily affected by project constraints).
- The real-world interaction and interfacing aspects of the software.

The essential difference is one of emphasis. Real-time software design is intrinsically driven by the need to meet *system* time requirements. These fall into five major categories, Figure 14.1:

- Control loop requirements:
  'The vehicle stabilizer control loops must be executed every 10 milliseconds.'

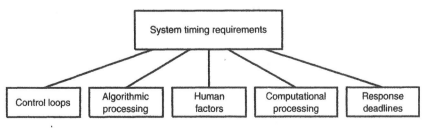

Figure 14.1 Major categories of system timing requirements.

- Algorithmic requirements:
  'Weapon delivery computation must be done X times per second in order to maintain numerical stability. This translates directly to the accuracy with which the target may be attacked.'

- Human factors requirements:
  'Active video displays must be updated at least 25 times per second to eliminate flicker effects.'
  'Keypad presses must be handled within 250 milliseconds to convince the operators that the system is responding correctly.'

- Computation requirements:
  'The throughput of the pipeline processor system is such that 50 aircraft can be handled simultaneously with a maximum display latency of 100 milliseconds.'

- Response requirements:
  'In auto mode a document must be extracted from the conveyor system within ±1 millisecond of the document arriving at the extraction datum point.'

14.1.2 Ignore performance at your peril – reactive vs. proactive techniques

How *important* is it to take system time performance factors into account? First, recognize that where performance needs aren't taken into account, they have little influence on design outcomes. The outcome is a classical example of a *reactive* solution to attaining performance (Figure 14.2), viz.:

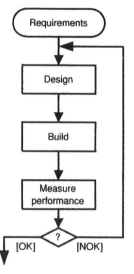

Figure 14.2 | A reactive design process.

- First design and build the system, then
- Measure the performance, and
- If unsatisfactory, modify the design, then repeat the process.

The fundamental weaknesses of reactive techniques are that:

- Performance is not addressed *prior* to system test and
- Systems are built on the premise that:
    - Tuning can be applied if necessary and/or
    - Faster hardware can be used if necessary and/or
    - A new version of software can be used if necessary.

Designers are (blindly) optimistic that performance problems – if they arise – can be easily overcome. Many reasons are given for not actively considering performance issues during design, including the following:

- It consumes valuable time and money that could be best spent elsewhere.
- The design/development phases will take longer to complete and the project can't afford the delay.
- Prediction results aren't of much value (we don't believe them).
- It's hard work.
- We don't have the necessary skills.
- In the end the work might not have been needed so it would have been a waste of money.

The problems with the reactive approach is that performance problems are not predicted, only *discovered*. If all goes well, fine. But if things do go wrong, however, the business consequences may be serious:

- Slipped release dates $\Rightarrow$ customer dissatisfaction.
- Roll-out with poor performance $\Rightarrow$ customer dissatisfaction.
- Greater cost of change $\Rightarrow$ dissatisfaction for whoever bears the costs.
- Project may be scrapped $\Rightarrow$ the worst scenario – dissatisfaction for all parties with probable long-term consequences for the software supplier.

It is also our experience that many performance problems have been quietly 'swept under the carpet', especially in the IT world.

In some cases problems can be remedied, but often at great expense. The phrase 'closing the stable door after the horse has bolted' springs to mind. The following examples [ROB01] show just how limiting this approach can be.

Example 1: A problem of hardware/software trade-offs – the professional recording console project

Background

Studio recording consoles have two key functions: to record

- Acoustic details of the performance session and
- The movements of all console faders and controls, i.e. how the real-time mix was done.

This makes it possible to play back not only the content of the recording (e.g. a piece of music) but also how the various sound channels were mixed dynamically during the recording process. It is then possible to listen to the recording and make fine adjustments to the overall sound picture.

In this case 'real time' means real time for a discerning recording engineer (or listener) to detect that the dynamics of the sound are wrong. What this translates to is the need for the recording timing to contain less than 1 ms of jitter (relative timing noise) in the mix data.

The problem

At a late stage in the project all the hardware had been designed, built and tested. Software had been developed to allow it to work with a single audio channel. Tests showed that with a single channel configuration, the mixer operations worked well. In fact the overall audio performance was wonderful. However, as channels were added, each channel's jitter performance degraded. The awful reality was that the console was unusable with more than one channel. And unfortunately it needed to support 32 channels in real time with no discernible timing distortion in the mix.

The diagnosis

On investigation, a number of problems were found:

- A full seven-layer ISO model had been implemented for communications between channel modules. Message formats had been designed purely on a logical but idealistic basis without concern for available bandwidth. The ISO model is designed for wide area communications over unreliable links, whereas in the console there is a very reliable local bus for communications (the protocol being SDLC, synchronous data link control).
- To save hardware cost the original designers decided to do without a hardware SDLC serial communications device. A hardware engineer programmed the SDLC controller functions on the main channel control processor. As a result its CPU utilization well exceeded 90% and its use became viciously constrained for application needs by the bit stuffing requirements, etc. of SDLC.

- No modelling was done of the shared bus bandwidth allocation and peak loading. There wasn't even a 'back of the envelope' communications model for the system (unbelievably, not even for a single channel).

The solution

At this stage it was too late to put the SDLC controller hardware chip into each channel. And all efforts by the original designers to solve the problem in software had come to nothing. It was now clear to the management that this project was on a 'death-march' to disaster; drastic steps were needed to stop the slide into oblivion. The project was saved only by calling in external experts who had extensive experience in handling performance-related problems. This they did by:

- Establishing clearly and fully the communications needs of the system.
- Allocating (prioritizing) the use of the total communication bandwidth across the various system transactions.
- Simplifying and tailoring the software structure to improve performance.

The rescue plan took approximately two months to complete. However, the net effect of the hardware 'cost saving' nearly killed the project and increased the time-to-market for the product by about one year. It also increased the development costs by about a factor of two. For the number of consoles sold, this was a ludicrous decision made at the wrong level by the wrong person.

Example 2: The non-expandable product – the document sorter

Background

This project involves a machine which:

- Pulls individual documents from a stack of documents, then
- Classifies them by pattern recognition, and finally
- Sorts and stacks them into separate silos.

The original design consisted of one physical 'control' module together with a set of stacker modules. The control module contained the input stack of documents, the classifier and the central processor. Stacker modules were responsible for the sorting and stacking functions. The overall system was designed so that small (four pocket) to large (16 pocket) machines could be configured and sold.

The problem

Unfortunately the interactions between the document handling, classifier and stacking mechanisms were not adequately defined before the machine was built.

Furthermore, management forced a short time scale on the project, leading to a 'do-before-think' approach to the work. The designers responded to management dictats by 'upgrading' an (existing) design of a smaller, slower machine. This, though, had been designed for a completely different set of cost and performance constraints.

After several *years* of struggle and 'fixes' the team realized that the machine had a basic flaw: it worked correctly only for a maximum of four output stacks of 'sorted' documents. Above that its behaviour became erratic. Every time a fix was made in one area other problems appeared (in one case most embarrassingly on the customer's site during crucial operational work). And fixes, by their nature, destroy design structures and build in further constraints so that future fixes are even harder to achieve.

The diagnosis

It was impossible to produce reliable operation for more than four stackers given the existing design. There was no alternative but to abandon the current project and start again.

The solution

The problem was completely solved by:

- Returning to the fundamental product requirements for the largest highest speed machine in the product family and then

- Designing the control system to handle *that* set of timing requirements and constraints.

- Specifically designing the architecture of the new system to be scalable, basing it on a distributed control system. The result was that as more physical stacking modules were added to the machine it acquired more processing power.

Designers of real-time (especially embedded) systems are normally conscious of the need to meet performance objectives. However, few actually integrate performance engineering into the development process. What is needed is the use of a proactive design technique which involves *building performance into the system*. It does this by developing and analysing models of systems throughout the project lifecycle, as follows (Figure 14.3):

- First, understand and quantify the system timing requirements. This will almost certainly involve modelling the real-world system behaviour.
- Design the system.
- Predict performance *during* system design.
- If unsatisfactory, modify the design and re-evaluate the predicted performance.
- Build the system.

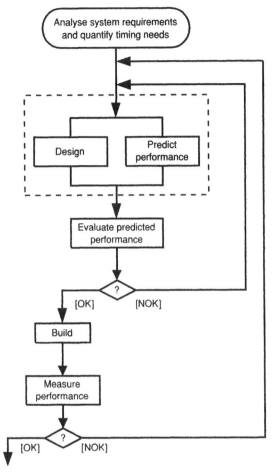

Figure 14.3 A proactive design process.

- Measure the performance.
- If unsatisfactory, modify the design and repeat the process.

The advantages of proactive techniques are that:

- They are fast and inexpensive ways to evaluate alternative designs and identify performance problems before they arise.
- They can provide performance estimates long before there is anything to measure.
- Useful testing can be carried out before the software is embedded into the real system.
- Experiments can be done that would be impractical in a real system.

14.2 Performance engineering – requirements, targets and achievables

Here performance requirements are taken to mean desired or specified perform-ance objectives, Figure 14.4. The highest level specifications, project performance requirements, are generated by the needs of the system itself. These, together with functional and other requirements, act as inputs to the system design activity. In developing system architectures to meet these needs, designers (even at this early stage) usually try to define *what actually can be achieved*. Take, for example, where the architectural model consists of two computers linked by a dedicated serial data link. Assume that the following items have been decided on:

> Link protocol: HDLC
> Transmission rate: 1 megabit/s
> Message length (minimum): 32 bytes
> Protocol overhead: 6 bytes.

Elementary calculations show that it will take at least 304 microseconds to trans-fer a message between the two computers. In other words, that is what can be achieved by the chosen system design. Such information is usually fed back to the opera-tional performance level to see how it impacts on performance requirements.

Software performance requirements are usually defined during system design, whilst program performance requirements are specified during software design. During each phase of work performance achievables can be established and fed up to higher levels. These may, of course, affect the performance requirements generated by these levels.

At the start of work, the requirements are aims or *targets*, Figure 14.5. Essentially targets are goals, things that we want to achieve but haven't actually done yet.

As work progresses, hard information is produced concerning the achievable per-formance. Thus the unknown quantity, the performance targets, reduces. Finally, when the project is finished, these initial aims will have been translated into achievables. And in an ideal world the final product would meet all its design requirements (reality may be somewhat different).

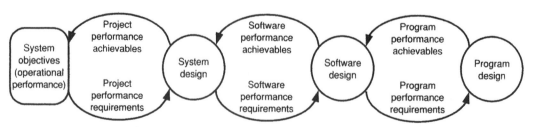

Figure 14.4 Performance requirements and achievables.

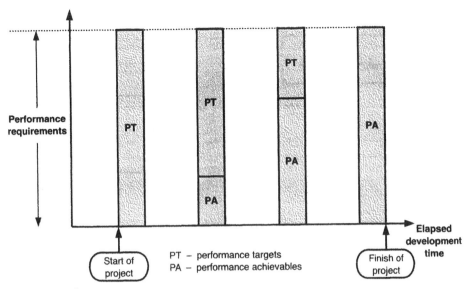

Figure 14.5 Performance targets and achievables -- a simplistic view.

Provided we continuously monitor and control these performance aspects, projects have a good chance of succeeding. It also helps identify projects that are going badly astray *early* in the development cycle. Using the information obtained we can set rescue plans into motion. In the worst case, however, performance evaluation may show that the project objectives just cannot be met. While this is a grim outcome, at least it is best to abandon a hopeless cause before too much money has been spent. (In 1987 the California Department of Motor Vehicles decided to computerize a merged driver and vehicle registration system. In December 1993 it abandoned the project, having spent $44.3 million.) So please, never forget that the reason for doing performance engineering is to minimize development risks.

Now, how does modelling and simulation fit into all of this? First, recognize that targets are essentially top-down requirements driven, whilst achievables are bottom-up results driven, Figure 14.6.

Three major questions need to be addressed here (there are, naturally, a host of minor ones). First, are the requirements realistic? Second, is the proposed design solution likely to meet these needs? Third, how accurate are the results taken from real testing? Modelling and simulation are techniques we can use to help answer these questions, specifically in terms of:

● Analysis of existing systems.

● Prediction of performance for new designs.

● Evaluation of performance using known data.

Note that a model is defined to be *an abstraction of an existing (or proposed) thing, process or structure.* This includes, for example:

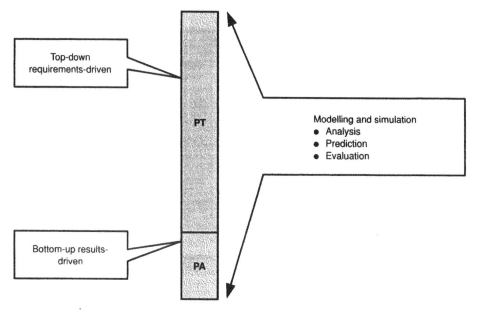

Figure 14.6 The role of modelling and simulation.

- Real physical scaled-down versions of aircraft, ships, buildings, etc.
- Mathematical descriptions of vehicle dynamics and control systems.
- Computer-based graphical descriptions of real-world devices (e.g. gearboxes, circuit boards, bridges, etc.).

Modelling (the process of producing a model of a system) is, however, merely a means to an end. What we really want to find out is how the system will perform. Thus there is a need to execute the model. This can be done in a number of ways (discussed later), but the most complex technique is that of simulation. For *our* purposes simulation is defined to be the execution of computer-based models.

14.3 Top-down (requirements-driven) performance modelling

14.3.1 Specifying targets – the project-management analogy

When taking a top-down modelling approach, the problem facing us can be stated quite simply, as follows:

Design input: Specifications (in particular, performance objectives).
Design output: Functional architecture.
Design performance: Who knows!

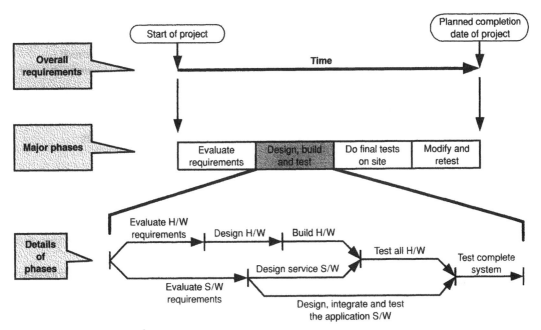

Figure 14.7 Defining targets – a project-management approach.

Now this is very similar to the issues faced when devising a project plan, Figure 14.7. The overall end-to-end project timescales are defined by the needs of the project itself. What must be done now is to produce a plan to ensure that the work gets finished on time. Such plans are developed first in their simplest form, concentrating on the major work phases. Each phase may then be further refined to show more detail. What we end up with is a model showing the work activities (and their relationships) of the project. Moreover, these activities have defined time allocations or targets. We can now *functionally* execute the model to see that it all hangs together, e.g. service software is produced in time to test the computer hardware, and all hardware is fully tested by the time the application software is finished. The model can then be 'walked-through' to validate overall timing *performance*. For example, a forward walk-through (start-to-finish) should produce the same result as a reverse one (finish-to-start). Further, all critical paths through the plan *must* be defined; these are the 'hot-spots' of the project.

In devising plans like this managers take into account many factors, including:

● History of previous projects.
● Available manpower and resources.
● Known capabilities.
● Risks and uncertainties.
● Spare time for handling unforeseen problems.
● Key deadlines.

But always remember that the timescales are *targets*; we don't actually know if the project will come in on time. Thus it is essential to regularly update the plan as work progresses. Only by doing this can we track and control the project.

We can apply these ideas directly to performance engineering in real-time software systems.

14.3.2 Performance targets and time budgeting in real-time systems

To show how the methods outlined above can be used in real-time applications, consider the system of Figure 14.8a. Here node 1 receives an input signal, event e_1, which provokes internal processing within the system. Some time later node 1 produces a response to the event, the upper-bound for this being specified as t_{req}, Figure 14.8b. What we have then is the highest level view of both system architecture and performance requirements.

During design a software model of the processing is produced, such processing being distributed across all nodes of the system (Figure 14.9). The sequence diagram shows the location, duration and intercommunication of the software processing functions. Each node now has specified processing and response requirements; for example, node 2 has a response requirement of t_{N2}.

Software allocation depends on many features, including:

● Arrival rates and response deadlines.

● Number of nodes.

● Processing capabilities of the individual nodes.

● Communication network details (e.g. data rates, access mechanisms, etc.).

● Internode message aspects (e.g. message size, blocking and non-blocking signalling).

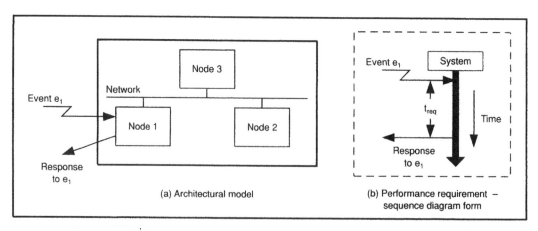

(a) Architectural model

(b) Performance requirement – sequence diagram form

Figure 14.8 System (network) level design – overall.

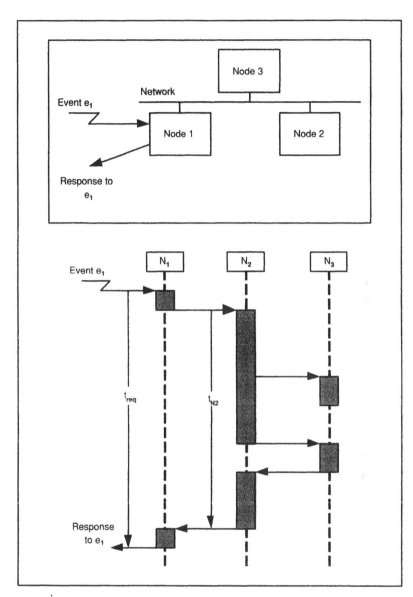

Figure 14.9 Time budgeting — system level design.

This allocation, an estimate of the time expenditure in each node, is in effect a time-budgeting model. The timing and dynamics of the model are defined in the sequence diagram, which can be 'executed' to check out performance. In this very simple example execution is not necessary; the pre-defined allocation is bounded by the t_{req} value. However, this wouldn't be the case where multiple, random events could occur – some form of modelling tool would be needed (see later).

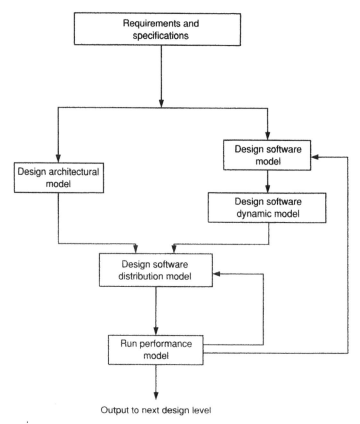

Figure 14.10 The generic design process.

Figure 14.10 describes the process outlined above, which can also be applied to node and processor design. If the system fails to meet its performance requirements then the software model design is revised, and the process repeated. At this stage we wouldn't normally modify the architectural model as the consequences may be serious (try telling your client 'sorry, we got our estimates wrong, the revised design needs six processors, not the four budgeted for' and see what happens). However, it *may* turn out that the requirements cannot be met given the defined architecture. Three options are open to us. One: redesign the architectural model and suffer the consequences. Two: negotiate a change in the specifications. Three: abandon the project.

Observe that we do not go down to more detailed levels until the performance requirements of the system *are* met.

The next level of refinement brings us to design of the nodes themselves, Figure 14.11. Here the software allocated to node 2 is now distributed across its individual processors P_1 and P_2. The original sequence diagram is extended to show details of processor-level processing, e.g. the response requirement t_{N2P2} of processor P_2.

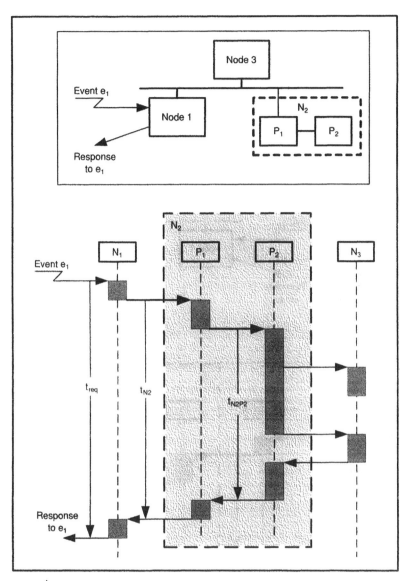

Figure 14.11 | Time budgeting – node level design.

Factors to be taken into account when distributing the software include:

- Arrival rates and response deadlines.
- Number of processors.
- Degree of parallelism required (e.g. array or pipeline processing).
- Processor organization (masters and slaves).

- Processing capabilities of the individual processors.
- Shared facilities (e.g. RAM boards, I/O devices, etc.).
- Communication network details.
- Inter-processor message aspects and synchronization requirements.

Having satisfied ourselves that the performance of the node is satisfactory, we can proceed to the processor-level design, Figure 14.12. Here the software is defined as

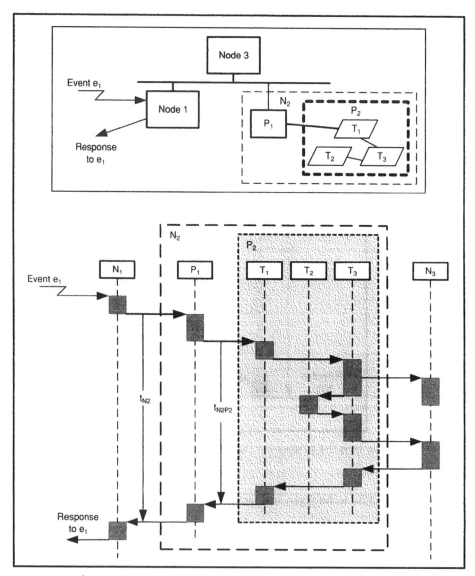

Figure 14.12 Time budgeting – processor-level design.

a set of tasks which usually communicate and co-operate with each other. Once again the sequence diagram can be elaborated to show the details of the revised software structure. The following items affect the way the software is partitioned across the tasks:

- Arrival rates and response deadlines.
- Number of tasks.
- Scheduling algorithms.
- Task synchronization requirements.
- Mutual exclusion and priority inheritance mechanisms.
- Inter-task communication aspects.
- Operating system overheads.

The processes described above are based on well-proven ideas expounded many times in this text: divide-and-conquer, top-down design, encapsulation and step-wise refinement.

14.4 Bottom-up (results-driven) performance modelling

Bottom-up modelling is based on using known data to predict system performance. To illustrate this approach, consider the small control system shown in Figure 14.13. Over time, performance data has been collected on the individual computing functions, such as the control algorithms. Using information like this it is possible to predict the total control program timing, as shown in Figure 14.14.

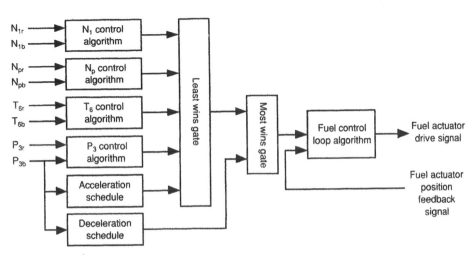

Figure 14.13 Example system I – marine gas turbine power loop controller.

Function	Execution time with 20 MHz clock
N_1 control algorithm	1 millisecond
N_p control algorithm	1 millisecond
T_6 control algorithm	1 millisecond
P_3 control algorithm	1 millisecond
Fuel control loop	1.5 milliseconds
Most wins gate	0.1 milliseconds
Least wins gate	0.1 milliseconds
TOTAL	5.7 milliseconds

Figure 14.14 Example system 1 – total control program execution times.

This technique can be used effectively in small systems or in subsystems of larger applications. However, the technique is not as foolproof as it may seem; the times *actually* produced in new designs depend on many factors, including:

- Processor type.
- Clock rate.
- Memory speeds and use of memory caches.
- Location of code in memory.
- Compiler efficiency.
- Compiler optimization techniques.

14.5 Middle-out (risk-driven) performance modelling

As pointed out earlier, performance modelling is all about risk reduction in general. Now, it isn't all that unusual during development to find certain areas which are critical to the design. They are ones which, should they fail, will bring the project crashing down. In areas like these we need great confidence (backed by evidence) that the design will (or should) meet its performance requirements. If our time-budgeting estimates can be supported with believable data (say information obtained from earlier projects), then we are on solid ground. If not, however, the project is exposed to tremendous risk of failure. So, in circumstances like this, what can be done to mitigate this risk? One solution is to take a 'middle-out' design approach (see Chapter 4), and apply it to the critical items. In such cases specific, localized modelling is done to provide confidence in the proposed design. Moreover, it must be done quite early in the design cycle. This technique is best illustrated by example, Figure 14.15, based on its use in a real project.

This shows the functional diagram for the control of power and pitch on a single propeller shaft of a ship. As such it forms only part of a complete propulsion control system. During initial design it was recognized that the power/pitch control was crucial to the design. From a performance perspective this was the most

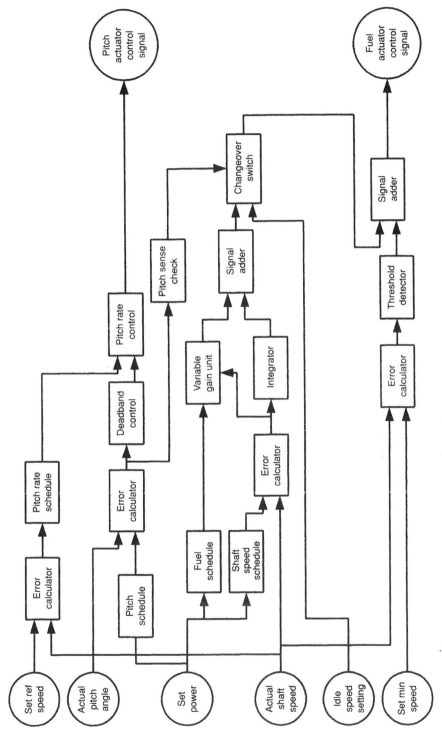

Figure 14.15 Example system 2 – single shaft power/pitch control system.

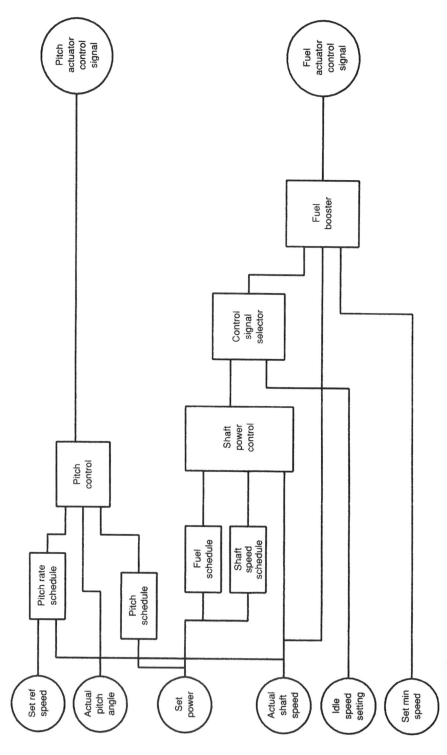

Figure 14.16 Example system 2 — software design.

Software machine	*Estimated* execution times, 8052 microcontroller with 20 MHz clock
Pitch rate schedule	2 milliseconds
Pitch schedule	2 milliseconds
Fuel schedule	2 milliseconds
Shaft speed schedule	2 milliseconds
Shaft power control	5 milliseconds
Pitch control	2 milliseconds
Control signal selector	0.2 milliseconds
Fuel booster	0.5 milliseconds
TOTAL	15.7 milliseconds

Figure 14.17 Example system 2 – estimated performance data.

demanding. Moreover, if this couldn't meet its performance objectives, the project would have to be scrapped. Thus a rapid development of 'first-cut' software design was put in motion, the objective of the work being to:

- Provide an *estimation* of the achievable processor performance and highlight time/complexity trade-offs.

- Provide a base reference for the software design effort of the total propulsion control system.

Note that the keyword here is *estimation*. We only do work sufficient to give a good confidence level in the design; it is not intended to be the final design itself.

In this case the software design implementing the functionality of Figure 14.15 is shown in Figure 14.16 (only outline details are given). Each software machine (or object) of Figure 14.17 is analysed and developed until useful, representative performance figures are obtained. For example, take the various schedules. The analysis of their computational requirements is as follows:

The five schedules are broadly similar, and can be implemented using one general-purpose schedule routine. Only the data which describes a specific schedule need be changed. If extremely fast execution is important, a look-up table technique should be used. In this case schedule execution times are trivial. However, it has an important bearing on store requirements. For 8 bit resolution each schedule will need 256 bytes of ROM; for 16 bit resolution 64 kBytes will be required per schedule. If this is beyond the capability of the proposed microcontrollers, then values must be calculated. These should be computed from a graph defined by a number of straight line segments, using interpolation within each segment. The most time-consuming part is the interpolation, involving the calculation:

$$Y = Y_{N-1} + [(X - X_{N-1})/(X_N - X_{N-1})][Y_N - Y_{N-1}]$$

This involves four additions/subtractions, one unsigned multiply (producing a double length product), and one unsigned divide (returning to normal length). Estimates of the worst-case total execution time are 2 milliseconds.

A similar process is applied to all software machines to generate the estimated performance data of Figure 14.17. Using this information we can estimate anticipated overall system performance with some degree of confidence.

14.6 Some practical issues in performance engineering

14.6.1 A general comment

Software performance engineering is a subject which can be handled at many levels. For in-depth work, a detailed knowledge of both tools and techniques is needed. Such topics are well beyond the scope of this book. Good material can be found in the texts by Connie Smith [SMI90], Raj Jain [JAI91] and Knepell and Arangno [KNE93]. Here, though, we'll limit ourselves to a brief outline of some important points.

The most important part of software performance engineering is *not* the modelling itself. It is to first establish:

- What you want to do.
- Why you want to do it.
- How the results will be used.
- Which modelling technique (or techniques) is best suited to the problem.
- How much it is going to cost in manpower, time and money (a sensible budget is 5% of the project costs).

Only when these points have been covered should a decision be made to develop performance models.

14.6.2 Modelling and simulation options

The methods used for performance engineering fall *roughly* into two camps: those used with deterministic data and those applied when data or operations are non-deterministic. Three techniques are in general use:

- Simple calculations (deterministic).
- Spreadsheet analysis (deterministic).
- Modelling tools (non-deterministic and deterministic).

Simple calculations

These can be applied to systems of the type shown in Figure 14.13, as demonstrated in Figure 14.14. The method is cheap and cheerful, doesn't take long to do, and can yield useful results. (One illustrative example: in a very 'political' project the software developer claimed that database information could be downloaded to local bureaux from a remote server in 7 seconds. A very brief calculation by the assessment consultant showed that it would be impossible do this in less than 30 seconds [FEA01].) Even if we can't produce precise values the method is often good enough to give us 'ball-park' figures.

Spreadsheet analysis

Suppose the system of Figure 14.13 is modified so that it can be operated in two modes, automatic and manual. How do we calculate its performance now? When using simple calculations it is necessary to identify (Figure 14.18):

- All modes of operation.
- The total set of functions performed by the software.
- The functions executed in each mode of operation.

In this case it is still relatively easy to get results by doing simple calculations. But take the case of a computer-based missile defence system on a naval vessel. Most of the time it will be in search mode, switching into tracking only if a potential threat is identified. Following this is the target acquisition and lock-on phase, leading into launch and then guidance modes. Thus the functions performed by the system are many and varied. However, those executed at any *particular* time depend on the mode of operation. Some will always be performed, some will apply to a number of modes, while others may be carried out only in specific modes. Clearly, a great amount of effort will be needed to produce performance figures for all possible scenarios. In cases like this spreadsheets can be very helpful, taking much of the drudgery out of the job.

Number-crunching techniques work well where data is deterministic. Unfortunately, as soon as things become indeterminate, we have a problem. The root of this is that data can, in many cases, be expressed only in statistical terms. Therefore in situations like this we need to resort to using appropriate modelling tools.

Modelling tools

There are many examples of indeterminate or aperiodic (loosely, 'random') operations in computer-based systems. Operator commands, alarms, mode changes, etc. are quite well-known examples. The basic problem here is that we cannot predict precisely when things have to be carried out. Wherever possible, to simplify things, we transform these aperiodic real-world operations into periodic computer-world operations. But if this can't be done then our modelling must be based on statistical techniques. The mathematical principles are well established, being extensively covered in numerous books [JAI91]. However, without computer-based tools it is virtually impossible to apply these ideas to real systems. Fortunately for the working engineer there are a number of software packages available for this, including:

Modes of operation
Automatic
Manual

(a) System modes of operation

Function	Execution time with 20 MHz clock
N_1 control algorithm	1 millisecond
N_p control algorithm	1 millisecond
T_6 control algorithm	1 millisecond
P_3 control algorithm	1 millisecond
Fuel control loop	1.5 milliseconds
Most wins gate	0.1 milliseconds
Least wins gate	0.1 milliseconds
Operator interface	10 milliseconds

(b) System software functions

Automatic mode functions	Execution time with 20 MHz clock
N_1 control algorithm	1 millisecond
N_p control algorithm	1 millisecond
T_6 control algorithm	1 millisecond
P_3 control algorithm	1 millisecond
Fuel control loop	1.5 milliseconds
Most wins gate	0.1 milliseconds
Least wins gate	0.1 milliseconds
TOTAL	5.7 milliseconds

(c) Functions performed in automatic mode

Manual mode functions	Execution time with 20 MHz clock
Fuel control loop	1.5 milliseconds
Operator interface	10 milliseconds
TOTAL	11.5 milliseconds

(d) Functions performed in manual mode

Figure 14.18   Program execution times – multimode operation.

- Graphical modelling tools (e.g. Simprocess [SIMP01]).
- Language-based tools (e.g. Simscript II.5 [SIMS01]).
- Mixed graphical and language-based tools [HYP00].

Note that many tools have animation features to show visually how the model behaves as it is executed.

A final point: if your system is a complex one, then think immediately of looking for tool support (even for deterministic operations).

Review

Having completed this chapter, you should now:

- Understand the various types of timing requirements of real-time (especially embedded) systems.
- Appreciate that neglecting to take performance into account during design can lead to disastrous results.
- Know the difference between reactive and proactive design processes.
- Understand what software performance engineering (SPE) is.
- Recognize its importance.
- Realize why and when you should use the techniques of SPE.
- Know what is meant by performance modelling and simulation.
- Know what is meant by performance requirements, performance targets and performance achievables.
- Understand the underlying concepts of top-down, bottom-up and middle-out performance modelling.
- See how these approaches can be used in isolation or in concert.
- Be able to do simple time budgeting for a software design.
- Be able to make a case for the use of performance modelling tools in the design of complex systems.

References and further reading

[FEA01] Personal correspondence with Niall Cooling, Feabhas Ltd, Real-time Training and Consultancy, Hungerford, Berks, UK, 2001.
[HYP00] SES/*workbench* simulation-modeling product, HyPerformix, Inc., www.hyperformix.com, 2000.
[JAI91] *The art of computer systems performance analysis*, R. Jain, John Wiley, ISBN 0-471-50336-3, 1991.
[KNE93] *Simulation validation – a confidence assessment methodology*, P. Knepell and D. Arangno, IEEE Computer Society Press, ISBN 0-8186-3512-6, 1993.
[ROB01] Personal correspondence with Brian Kirk, Robinson Associates, Painswick, Glos., UK, 2001.
[SIMP01] *SIMPROCESS – hierarchical process simulator*, CACI Inc., www.caciasl.com, 2001.
[SIMS01] *SIMSCRIPT II.5 simulation language product*, CACI Inc., www.caciasl.com, 2001.
[SMI90] *Performance engineering of software systems*, Connie Smith, Addison-Wesley, ISBN 0-201-53769-9, 1990.

chapter 15

Documentation

Documentation. Paperwork. Records. Words which induce instant apathy in any design team. Such things appeal to bureaucrats, not to creative designers. Maybe this is a slightly harsh judgement – apologies to dedicated bureaucrats – but it is true. Unfortunately, documentation is a key feature of all professional design and development activities. It can be regarded as the life-blood of the design body. Once it stops flowing properly, functions quickly deteriorate, eventually ending in rigor mortis. We just can't do without it. For some people, paperwork is an end in itself – but for the software engineer it is an essential component of the design process. The approach adopted here is essentially a pragmatic one. It explains:

- Why documentation is necessary.
- How documentation fits into, and supports, the various phases of the software life cycles.
- The content, structure and use of specific software documents.
- The concepts and use of configuration management and version control techniques.

Emphasized here are the underlying general aspects of system and software documentation, not specific techniques. There is, naturally enough, some overlap with material in earlier chapters.

15.1 Documentation – what and why?

15.1.1 The role of documentation

What precisely is the role of documentation in design engineering? Fundamentally it has three objectives: defining, communicating and recording information.

In the first instance a prospective customer must define what he wants, why he wants it, when it's needed, and, ultimately, how much he's prepared to pay. Likewise, the supplier needs to define what he intends to do, how he intends to do it, what the delivered product will do, and when it will be delivered. Later, many other points need elaborating and defining, ranging from performance aspects to maintenance features. These definition aspects basically determine the *contents* of engineering documents.

The second aspect, communication, is self-explanatory. But this has an impact on the *style* of presentation. To be really useful, documents need to communicate information effectively. Text is not an especially good medium, as engineers have long realized. What does work well is a combination of diagrams and text, organized to meet particular needs.

Recording, the third objective, is here regarded as a formal operation to capture specific aspects of the design process. The purpose is to rigorously document the following:

- What was wanted in the first place.
- What the supplier promised to do.
- What the supplier actually did.
- Design and performance features of the finished product.
- Installation, maintenance and test aspects.
- The modification history of the product when in service.

The amount of paperwork produced in any particular job depends on many factors. However, one general observation can be made. Where customers set up procurement organizations to handle the acquisition of products, paper mountains abound. And frequently these do little to improve the design of the final product. What they really do, to quote one anonymous quality control engineer, 'is show why we got a lousy job in the first place'. Documentation for its own sake is pointless. Therefore what is discussed here is useful documentation, applicable to professional design organizations.

15.1.2 Documentation – its structure

When devising documentation we should ask ourselves three basic questions: who, what and when, Figure 15.1. This shows that the documentation structure is

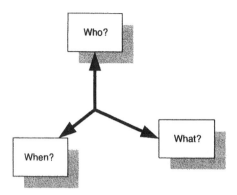

Figure 15.1 Documentation – the basic questions.

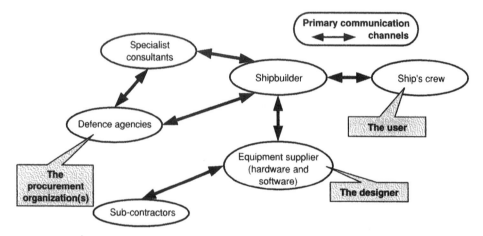

Figure 15.2 A complex project structure.

essentially a three-dimensional one. Unfortunately the axes are not independent ones.

Let's first consider who produces documents and who they're produced for. The answer to this is determined by two factors: the organizations involved, and the people concerned, with the project. Although the size of the project has some bearing on this, much more depends on the nature of the customer's organization. Consider defence projects. Here, whether we're dealing with large systems or small systems, the overall project structure is much the same. For instance, a typical naval project usually involves the bodies shown in Figure 15.2. All are concerned with system specification, design and development – but they usually have quite different requirements when it comes to documentation. The operator, for instance, couldn't care less about the supplier's design standards as long as the product works properly. What is vital to him is the paperwork needed for operation and mainten-ance of the installed equipment. On the other hand, procuring agencies have the

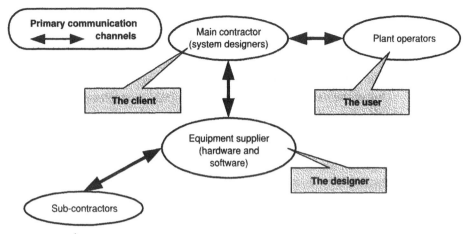

Figure 15.3 A simple project structure.

brief to ensure that proper design standards are maintained. Compliancy with such standards must be shown by proper recording of design techniques.

In such developments the paperwork becomes complex because the structure itself is complex. By contrast, where the customer's organization is simple (Figure 15.3), the documentation requirements are less formal. Here the people involved are usually technical rather than administrative. They have a very *direct* interest to see that the supplier delivers the final product on time, within budget, and working as promised. The lines of communication are short and clear, involving few people. This example (like the previous one) also highlights the fact that generally the body acquiring (procuring) the system is not necessarily the end-user.

Projects like these, which generate least paperwork, are frequently the most successful ones. At first this may seem paradoxical. If documentation is so important, why is this the case? The answer is that documentation is a hygiene factor. If standards are poor, projects limp along in a disorganized, uncontrolled fashion. Improving these standards produces instant benefits – but only up to a point. Beyond this little is gained. In fact there may well be a fall in productivity, with more time being spent on paperwork than on the job itself. Therefore it is essential to get the balance right and match documentation standards to project requirements. Regrettably, cook-book solutions to this problem aren't available; it takes experience to work these out.

15.1.3 A model for system documentation

In this chapter the reference model for system documentation is set at a fairly complex level, typified by those found in defence industries. Simpler models can be formed from this template by leaving out items which aren't needed in specific projects. Within this model three major bodies are concerned with documentation:

the customer, the supplier and the end-user. Figure 15.4 sets out *what* such documentation contains and *when* it is produced within the project programme.

Although this chapter is devoted mainly to software documentation, software is only one part of a real-time system. It is essential to see it in this light to appreciate how it fits into the overall project development, Figure 15.4.

One of the first documents to be generated is the preliminary statement of requirements. This, originated by the customer, basically defines the purpose and intended function of the proposed system. The supplier evaluates these requirements in terms of technical feasibility, cost and timescales. This may be a funded study. More often it is part of a contract bid reply. Using the results of this study/bid, the customer eventually awards a contract to a particular supplier. Details of the required work are defined in a contract specification. At this point the supplier begins serious work, usually involving a preliminary design study.

During this period several documents are produced by the supplier. These form part of a major proposal document, and include the following:

1. Extent of supply.

2. Commercial plan and costings.

3. Project plan and management structure.

4. Quality plan.

5. Overall technical description.

The first item, **extent of supply**, describes exactly what the supplier intends to provide to the customer. This includes:

- Hardware.
- Software.
- Documentation.
- Training.
- Post-design services.
- In-service support requirements.
- Environmental standards.
- Specialist ('type') testing of equipment.

The **commercial plan** defines:

- Overall costs.
- Estimated spend rates.
- Staging of payments.
- Contractual conditions.
- Arbitration procedures in the event of disputes.
- The company's commercial authority for the project.

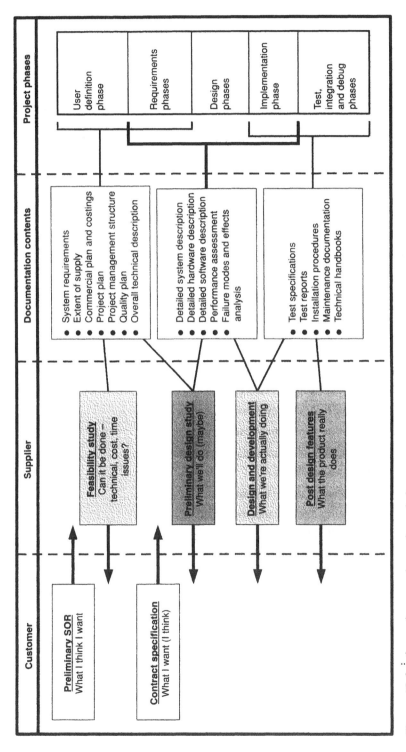

Figure 15.4 System documentation – what and when.

The **project plan** details how the design, development, manufacture, test and installation of the specified system is to be controlled. It defines the:

- Project administration management and structure – contractual.
- Project administration management and structure – technical.
- Lines for formal communication with the company.
- Division of responsibilities within the company.
- Project control techniques.
- Progress-reporting mechanisms and meeting arrangements.

The **quality plan** is designed to show that the company complies with accepted quality assurance (QA) techniques. It describes the:

- Supplier's QA organization.
- Standards with which the QA organization complies.
- Formal QA systems and procedures of the supplier.
- Design and manufacturing standards used by the supplier.
- Specific details of quality verification techniques.

Lastly, an **overall technical description** is produced. This is a wide-ranging and extensive document which includes:

- Overall system concepts.
- System design philosophy.
- System functional description.
- Equipment (hardware) description.
- Software structure.
- Software design techniques.
- System performance features.
- Testing and installation techniques.
- Man–machine interfacing.
- Maintenance and repair techniques.
- Reliability estimates.
- Failure mode behaviour.

This description represents what the supplier intends should happen (what happens in practice may be quite different). As design and development progress these items are translated from proposals to practicalities. The existing documentation is modified to reflect these developments; more detailed information is also produced. A substantial amount of design documentation is generated during this period, covering system, hardware and software aspects. Finally the post-design

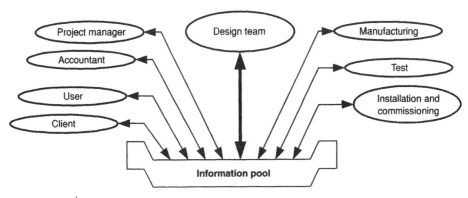

Figure 15.5 ⋮ The information pool.

documentation is produced, relating to test, installation and maintenance functions. The ultimate document is a set of technical handbooks which, for large systems, occupies many volumes.

A further consideration to be taken into account is how this information is used. We can visualize the situation as shown in Figure 15.5, where all information resides in a central 'pool' or store. Various bodies access this, providing inputs and obtaining outputs from the store. Note the following points:

- The major provider of information is the design team.
- All parties should have access to all information.
- Each party normally only uses specific sections of this information.
- Many parties use the same information, but need it presented in quite different forms.
- Consistency of the stored data is vital.
- Access to and use of the data store needs to be controlled to prevent unauthorized changes.

A centralized computer database is one of the most effective ways of implementing this information store.

15.2 Software life-cycle documentation – overview

In real-time systems there aren't always clear divisions between documents relating to system, hardware and software features. A better distinction is to group terms as they apply to specific aspects of the project development. In this chapter we're concerned mainly with the software life cycle and its associated documentation, Figure 15.6. As shown here each of the major phases has a set of associated documents which are generated as work proceeds on the project. This point needs to

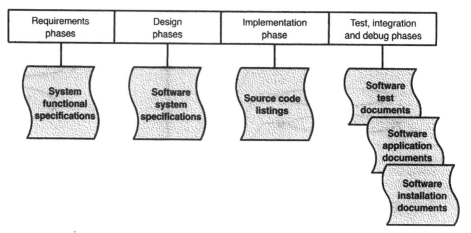

Figure 15.6 Software life-cycle documentation.

be stressed. The information is produced and recorded as a result of performing analysis, design and development. It should not be confused with that produced specifically to support '. . . in-service use, maintenance, and subsequent development of the software . . .' ([JSP88], 1980).

The system functional specification is created during the requirements phases. Essentially it is an extension of the earlier overall technical description, having two basic objectives. First, it defines the qualities of the proposed system from the customer's viewpoint: what it will do, how it will do it and how it is operated. Second, it acts as the design baseline for all subsequent work performed by the supplier.

During the design phases the software system specification documents are drafted. These describe the functions, structure and operation of the software system at an architectural level, being primarily a design working tool.

Program coding follows from this, using the structure definition documents as the design input guidelines. Source coding is documented in the usual form as a set of commented program listings.

The final phase of work is concerned with test, integration and debugging functions. These relate to two major activities. The first is the software/hardware test and integration actions performed by the supplier, prior to delivery. The other is the installation and commissioning of the delivered software at the customer's site. Appropriate documentation is needed to support this work. In a well-organized professional project, initial test documentation is produced right at the beginning of the project (very much driven by use case specifications to form the basis of acceptance testing). As development work progresses this documentation is extended, both in width of coverage and in depth of detail. Integration plans, likewise, should be developed in a staged manner. However, it isn't until we reach the end stages of the project that these are finalized. (Unfortunately, for many projects, this is the stage where such documents are produced in the first place. Human nature has much to answer for.)

Documentation required for in-service maintenance, etc. may readily be generated from the documents described here.

15.3 System functional specifications

15.3.1 Overview

System functions are described broadly in three ways: block diagrams, functional diagrams and requirements specifications, Figure 15.7.

15.3.2 Block diagram description

These are high-level documents, designed to give an overview of the total system. They consist of a series of block diagrams, augmented with text, their primary

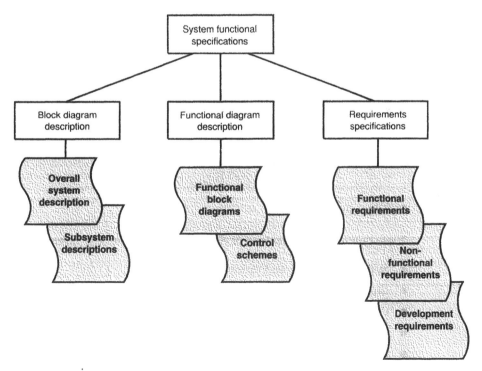

Figure 15.7 Documentation for the requirements phases.

purpose being to describe system operation. In large or complex systems these need to be expanded using a series of subsystem descriptions. Their purpose is to:

- Give a comprehensive description of the total system function and operation.
- Define the physical (hardware) composition of the total system.
- Identify the processor-based units within the total system.
- Define the operational features of all man–machine interfaces.
- Identify electronic communication methods used within the system.

15.3.3 Functional diagram description

This consists of block diagrams and flow diagrams – aided by text – describing precisely what the system is supposed to do. The block diagram depicts the overall system as a series of blocks, each one representing a particular function. Detailed operational aspects of each block (e.g. logic functions, sequencing, switching, closed-loop control, etc.) can be shown using control scheme diagrams. Specific details of all interfaces are given in text form. Individual blocks are connected to other blocks, hardware items or other systems.

In large systems a hierarchical diagram structure will have to be used. First, a single top-level diagram is produced. This is then decomposed by taking each block in turn and elaborating its functions on lower-level diagrams.

15.3.4 Requirements specification

These are described using three documents: functional, non-functional and development requirements specifications (see also Chapter 3). These are text descriptions, but may be amplified using diagrams.

Functional requirements

These describe the behaviour of the system, and cover the following topics:

- System processing and processes.
- Input signals.
- Output signals.
- Start-up and shut-down operations.
- Fault identification and recovery mechanisms.
- Communication aspects of networked systems.
- Communication aspects of multiprocessor systems.

Non-functional requirements

These are concerned with details of system performance and data, interfacing and system constraints. They include:

System performance and data

Processor cycle times and throughputs
Processor work load – periodic tasks
Response time – aperiodic events
Scheduling policy
Context switch times
Interrupt structures
Self-checking features and diagnostics
Fault detection and recovery techniques
Exception-handling policy

Storage capacity – non-volatile
Storage capacity – volatile
MTBF, MTTR, reliability, availability

Specific time-critical functions
System-operating profiles
System parameters – types and range limits

Control laws
Computation times
Computation accuracy
Resolution and accuracy of digitized signals
Signal filtering and linearization techniques

Alarm functions
Data logging and storage requirements.

Interfaces

MMI screen display contents and format
MMI panel displays (status, warnings, alarms)
Monitoring, trend and logging display presentations
Hard copy facilities
Operator facilities
Operator access security
System modification (e.g. control loop tuning)

Analogue sensors: Name, function, location, signal type,
signal range, electrical levels,
ADC resolution, accuracy and time,
signal bandwidth, noise bandwidth,
subsystem (control, monitoring, alarm).

Digital sensors: Name, function, location, signal type (serial, parallel), signal range, electrical levels, timing, frequency, subsystem type.

On–off switches: Name, function, location, electrical levels, response time to switch changes, subsystem type.

Processor output signals: Generally specified in the same way as the input signals.

Data communications networks:

Network structure (e.g. bus, star, ring), defining standard (Mil. Std.1553, IEEE 802.4, etc.), name of data link (control, surveillance, etc.), sources and sinks of data, specific data items, response times, network utilization, message structure, fault handling and recovery methods.

Software interfaces:

Real-time executives or operating systems, databases, screen formatters, input/output device drivers, communication packages.

System constraints

Programming languages
Operating systems
Specific software packages
Development techniques
Design tools
Processor type
Maximum memory capacity
Size, weight, environmental factors
Maintenance philosophy
Maintenance facilities and resources.

Development requirements

These apply to the methods and tools used in system design and development. As such there is some overlap with non-functional requirements; the boundary lines aren't always easy to specify. In essence they are a selective version of the original proposals, updated to reflect the current situation. They include:

- Deliverables: hardware, software, documentation.
- Test and installation procedures.
- Training, post-design services, in-service support requirements.
- Environmental standards, specialist ('type') testing of equipment.
- Cost monitoring, spend rates, staging of payments.
- Contractual conditions, arbitration procedures.
- Project administration structure – contractual and technical.
- Project control techniques (including configuration and version control, see later).
- Project milestones and progress-reporting mechanisms.
- Formal QA systems and procedures of the supplier.
- Design and manufacturing standards used by the supplier.
- Quality plan.

15.4   Software system specifications

As stated earlier, the software system specification is a full and complete description of the software architecture. It is a dynamic, technical document, produced by the design team for, and as a result of, software design. It starts life as the software section of the initial proposal document. In its final form it becomes a major document in its own right, describing precisely:

- What the design does.
- Why it does it.
- How it does it.

The contents of the structure specification documents are shown in Figure 15.8. Modern front-end integrated development environments and design tools play an important part here. Most of the required documentation can be produced automatically as part of the system design process. Chapter 10 ('Software analysis and design') emphasized the diagramming aspects of design methods, but now it can be seen that significant text input is also required. Such textual data is based mainly on the system non-functional requirements documents. Thus the total specification consists of text and diagrams describing the architectural and physical structures of the software.

Architectural structure

This is specified both at system and subsystem levels, as defined in Figure 15.8. The system level documents focus mainly on the interaction of the software and its

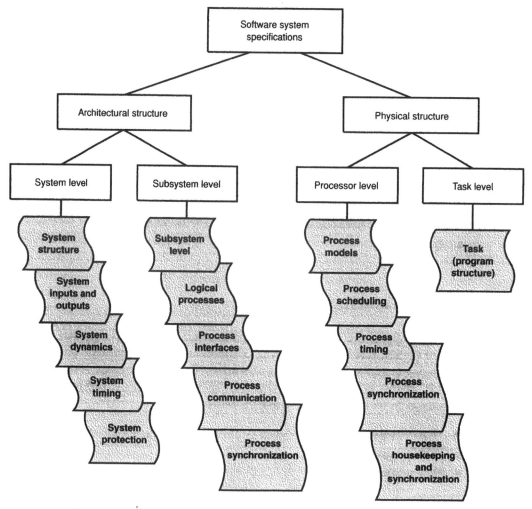

Figure 15.8 | Documentation for the design phases.

external environment. Subsystem design relates more to the internal structure of the software system itself. Descriptions are produced for the full set of logical processes, their interfaces and interprocess communication and synchronization.

Physical structure

Here the software structure devised in the architectural phase is mapped onto the hardware. In multiprocessor designs, functions are allocated to processors, every processor having its own description document. These processors each support one or more software processes. Thus a description of the individual process structures must be given, including:

- Process modelling technique.
- Scheduling, timing and synchronization of processes.
- Housekeeping and security aspects.

Finally, for each sequential task, a program structure document is generated.

How is information input to the design in the first place? How is it carried through the design from stage to stage? How is consistency maintained throughout the documentation? These depend almost entirely on the design methodology used – resulting in considerable variation at a detailed level. However, no matter which technique is used, the collective documentation should include the following:

General

- System and subsystem organization.
- Processing and processes.
- Input and output signals, system parameters – types and range limits.
- Start-up and shut-down operations.
- Fault identification and recovery mechanisms.
- Communication aspects (including networking).

Performance

- Scheduling policy and interrupt handling.
- Processor cycle times, throughputs, response times, context switch times, specific time-critical functions.
- Self-checking features and diagnostics.
- Specific fault detection and recovery techniques, exception-handling policies.
- Storage capacity.
- Performance profiles.
- Control laws.
- Computation times and accuracy.
- Resolution of digitized signals.
- Signal filtering and linearization techniques.

Detailed interface features

- Man–machine interfacing – content, format and facilities.
- Operator facilities and access security.

- System modification methods.

- Plant devices: name, function, location, signal type, signal range, electrical levels, ADC resolution, number representation, accuracy and timings, time response requirements.

- Data communication networks: network software model, name of data link, sources and sinks of data, specific data items, response times, message structure, fault handling and recovery methods.

- Software interfaces: hooks into, and use of, standard software packages such as real-time operating systems, databases, screen formatters, input/output device drivers and network managers.

It should be obvious that without automated design tools this task is an immense one.

15.5　Source code aspects

15.5.1　Source code documentation – a philosophy

Requirements. Design. Test. There are boundless numbers of small projects where no formal (sometimes just no) documentation exists for these items. However, *every* software project has source code. Thus it is worth looking at this topic in somewhat more detail (especially from the point of view of the individual programmer (you?)). The ideas expounded here are aimed at two groups in particular:

- Novice programmers and
- Experienced programmers who believe that documentation is for quiche-eaters and Pascal developers.

Both tend to have a very myopic, narrow view of program writing and development. Everything is done from *their* point of view, for *their* (often immediate) convenience, in the easiest, quickest fashion. In many cases the source code 'documentation' is the files submitted to the compiler. The content and format of such documentation depend on the whims of the programmer.

Well, this may be fine for companies where the cult of the 'hero-programmer' exists (though users of the software may have something else to say). However, this is totally unacceptable in professional companies where software quality, reliability and safety are concerned.

The key to excellent source code documentation is for it to be *reader*, not writer, oriented. Its quality can be assessed by asking just two (fundamental) questions:

- Is it easy to *use* the document?
- Is it easy to *understand* its contents?

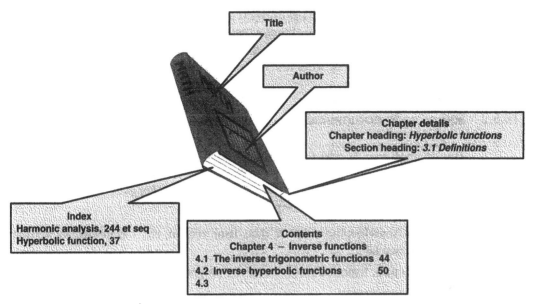

Figure 15.9 : Structure – an essential ingredient.

The first is concerned with structure, the second with readability and comprehension.

Let's look at a book example to see why structuring is so important. Now, the objective of any book is to communicate information. It doesn't matter whether the subject is 'Gardening for Beginners', a James Bond novel, or 'Electromagnetic Compatibility'; it's pointless printing it unless the reader can understand and use it. So, what structuring and organization features do we find in a book (Figure 15.9)?

First, when the individual pages have been printed we bind the book and put covers on it. On the cover we include the most important items of information: title, author name, publisher name and ISBN. Now it is easy to catalogue, store and reference the book. On opening the covers we find that the contents are arranged into chapters. For non-fiction work, logically related items are normally collected together in specific chapters. It then becomes a simple job to use the book as a reference source. But we still need to find our way around the book; that's where the contents list comes in. A quick glance at this will tell us immediately where the relevant information is held. It's also useful when we first come to decide whether or not to buy a book. When we get down to detailed referencing and cross-checking, the index comes into its own. Try using a technical working text which hasn't got an index; painful is the best description that can be applied to such a case. Finally, the text itself has to obey the rules of grammar and layout, that is, the syntax of the language.

We end up with an item that has a clearly understood function. If we go to the library we know how to track it down. Once in our hands we can quickly decide whether it's of interest to us from the contents list. Assuming that it is what we want, using it should be a straightforward task. Finally, we hope that it is written in a good, clear and correct style. If it does all these then it will truly convey information. To help you produce code that meets these criteria, I recommend you read a delightful paper 'How to write unmaintainable code', by Roedy Green [GRE00].

15.5.2 Source code documentation – practice

The simplest way to achieve consistency with source code documentation is to use pre-defined layout templates. These need to be tailored to specific types of program units (e.g. tasks, modules, classes, functions, etc.). For each program unit the following information should be produced:

- General housekeeping – author, date, issue version, etc. – as needed for version control (see later).
- The function, logic and structure of the program unit.
- Performance aspects.
- Detailed description of program functions (normally included as program comments).
- Inputs to, and exports from, the unit.
- Exception-handling procedures.
- Priority level (scheduled or interrupt-driven items).
- Initialization procedures.

Even where automated code generation is used, such information *must* be provided somewhere; without it, it is impossible to gain a true understanding of the software. Clearly, the specific format of the templates will depend on:

- The nature of the program unit.
- Language features.
- Tool support.
- Automatic code generation facilities.

In languages such as Ada most of this information is included in the interface (package) specification. With C or C++ it is likely to be housed in specific files.

Figure 15.10 is an example of a C program module-level layout template, while Figure 15.11 is a function-level one (courtesy of Hitex UK Ltd). Observe that the module template contains a summary of the templates for each function used in the module. This allows the reader to quickly identify all relevant functions together with their more significant properties. The function level template contains detailed information on the function's history, etc. together with activation details, memory resources used, run-times and test information.

```
/***************************************/
/* MODULE NAME:                      */
/* Project:                          */
/* Name:                             */
/* Filename                          */
/* Language:                         */
/* System:                           */
/* Rights:                           */
/*                                   */
/* Compiler:                         */
/* Assembler:                        */
/*                                   */
/***************************************/
/* Mo dfic ion histo ry:             */
/*                                   */
/***************************************/
/* Date:                             */
/* Name:                             */
/* Function:                         */
/* Test harness:                     */
/*                                   */
/* Modification details:             */
/*                                   */
/*                                   */
/* Date test performed:              */
/* Engineer:                         */
/*                                   */
/* Signed off by: _____     */
/*                                   */
/***************************************/
/***************************************/
/* Date:                             */
/* Name:                             */
/* Function:                         */
/* Test harness:                     */
/*                                   */
/* Modification details:             */
/*                                   */
/*                                   */
/* Date test performed:              */
/* Engineer:                         */
/*                                   */
/* Signed off by: _____     */
/*                                   */
/***************************************/
/***************************************/
```

Figure 15.10 Template for a software module.

```
/**********************/
/* FUNCTION No.      */
/*                   */
/* Function details: */
/******************** */
/* Function name:    */
/**********************/
/********************************************/
/*Pu pose:                                 */
/*                                         */
/*                                         */
/********************************************/
/********************************************/
/* Task o rinterrupt so ucre               */
/********************************************/
/* Reso ucre aage:                         */
/*                                         */
/* CODE CONST DATA STACK USER-STACK        */
/*                                         */
/*                                         */
/********************************************/
/* Performanc e analysis                   */
/* Max. run time:                          */
/* Min. run time:                          */
/* Av. run time:                           */
/*                                         */
/* Called from:                            */
/* Calls:                                  */
/*                                         */
/* Date test performed:                    */
/* Engineer:                               */
/*                                         */
/* Signed off by: _____           */
/*                                         */
/********************************************/
/********************************************/
/* Test harness details:                   */
/*                                         */
/* Purpose:                                */
/* Test harness:                           */
/*                                         */
/* % coverage obtained:                    */
/*                                         */
/* Date test performed:                    */
/* Engineer:                               */
/*                                         */
/* Signed off by: _____           */
/*                                         */
/********************************************/
/********************************************/
```

Figure 15.11 Layout template for a software function.

15.5.3 Source code review documentation

Of course, just because we provide programmers with templates doesn't mean that they're going to use them. A minimum of project policing will, of course, take care of that problem. Much more difficult to control is the *correct* use of the templates. What is needed here is a code review document, one example being that of Figure 15.12, courtesy of Robinson Associates.

CODE REVIEW CHECKLIST

Project:
Module:
Revision:
Module requirements:

Please tick each topic when it has been checked

General layout – is the module easy to read and understand

❑ Will the module print onto A4 paper without losing characters from the right hand side
❑ Are blank lines used to break up sections of code in a helpful way
❑ Is code indented in a helpful way
❑ Is the code commented in appropriate places and do the comments give a clear explanation

General structure and declarations

❑ Is the partitioning of the module sensible and is the purpose of each procedure clear
❑ Have meaningful names been used for all declarations, including functions, procedures and the module itself
❑ Have appropriate data types been used
❑ If global variables and/or included files are used is it clearly shown and can their use be justified

Module level

❑ Has this revision been booked into PVCS
❑ Does the module header include with correct details:
  • A copyright notice
  • A brief description of the module's purpose
  • The file name and path
  • The author, current revision number and date of last change
  • A list of all previous revisions and a useful description of the changes made

❑ Are the module requirements clear
❑ Does the code satisfy all of the requirements for the module
❑ Does the module adhere to the coding standard and guidelines and, if relevant, to the PDL standard
❑ Have any additional code requirements in the Project and Quality Plan been satisfied
❑ Does the module contain redundant or duplicated code other than for debugging purposes. In particular, are all procedures and declarations still used
❑ Is the module testable in a practical and cost-effective way
❑ If required, is there any provision for testing built into the module

Procedure level

❑ For each procedure, function, class or method:
  • Does it have a header
  • Is PDL provided if required
  • Is it clear which parameters are inputs, which are outputs and which are inouts
  • Are the purpose, pre and post conditions and actions defined
❑ Are all parameter types and ranges correct
❑ Do procedure and functions have a single exit point where possible
❑ For variables and parameters

Statement level

❑ Is the code well structured
❑ Do code constructs have a single entry and a single exit point where possible
❑ If not already covered by the compiler, is there reasonable provision for detecting run-time errors, e.g. range checks for variables, default actions for CASE statements, etc.

Reviewers comments

Figure 15.12 Code review checklist.

15.6 Configuration management and version control

15.6.1 General aspects

First, some definitions:

- Computer configuration is defined as 'the functional and/or physical characteristics of hardware/computer software as set forth in technical documentation and achieved in a product' [EIA82]. 'Version' refers to a specific variant of the software or hardware system.

- Configuration control may be defined as 'the discipline which ensures that any proposed change (modification or amendment) to a baseline definition (or build level) is prepared, accepted and controlled in accordance with set procedures'.

- Configuration management is 'a process for establishing and maintaining consistency of a product's performance, functional and physical attributes with its requirements, design and operational information throughout its life' [EIA98]. Simply stated, its purpose is to help managers deliver the right product, at the right time, in the right place. It is both a management discipline and a process.

- Version control is the activity of controlling the development and build of system components: hardware, software and documentation.

Configuration management and version control apply both to the product itself and to its documentation.

When configuration management is implemented properly it:

- Ensures that the current design and build state of the software and hardware is known and recorded.

- Provides an accurate historical record of system development (useful in debugging).

- Enables users to formally and safely record all change details including reasons for change, change requests and corresponding approvals or disapprovals, authorization for change, and dates.

- Ensures that documentation can be produced which truly describes the system as supplied to the customer.

- Enables the system to be rebuilt correctly in the event of catastrophes.

Documentation control is only one aspect of the complete subject. Yet the only way version control can be implemented is by using and controlling documentation. Thus it can be seen that version control is an essential ingredient of configuration management. The converse is not true; it can, and is, frequently used as a technique in its own right.

15.6.2   More on source code version control

The basic function of a version control system (VCS) is to keep a history of all changes made to a project. In terms of source code, it maintains a history of the changes made to the files within the project. Note this point well: changes made to the files. It doesn't have anything to do with code *per se*; in fact the files could contain whatever you like and the VCS wouldn't complain. Modern version control methods are based on the use of database-centred software packages. However, the principles are the same as manual systems, only the practices are different.

To be able to build up a view of the history of a file, certain core information is needed. Even the private work of an individual, at the very least, should include:

- Date of creation.
- Change date(s).
- Reason for change(s).
- Current status of the work.

When working within a team it is essential to know:

- Who did the original work and
- Who made the changes.

For the individual (lone) developer, a VCS tool would normally provide the following facilities:

- Add files (they will have been created as part of the code development work).
- Delete files.
- Read files.
- Modify (update) files.
- Set version numbers (label the files).
- Review the history of changes.
- Check the difference between versions.

When work is shared/exchanged within a team, it is essential to co-ordinate all changes. Thus when a user accesses a file, it is in a sense 'checked-out' of the database. The simplest, safest way of handling this is to lock all checked-out files. Thus only the current user can make changes; user accesses are mutually exclusive. However, this can lead to conflicts should other developers wish to work on the same file(s). One solution to this is to allow unrestricted access but rely on the VCS tool to automatically detect inconsistencies. This is one of the features in the open source tool 'Concurrent Versions Systems' [FOG99].

Review

At this stage you should:

- Understand that comprehensive, correct and usable documentation is an essential part of computer-based projects.

- Understand what documentation is produced, why it is needed, when it is generated and how it is used.

- Appreciate the roles, content and usage of system and software specification documents.

- Know how to produce a well-structured and readable source code document.

- Recognize that consistency, completeness and clarity of source code documents are much easier to achieve when document templates are used.

- Know what configuration management is and why it is needed, especially on larger projects.

- Understand what version control is, and appreciate that source code version control applies to projects of all sizes.

- See how version control relates to configuration management.

Applicable standards

This subject matter is essentially a practical one, being much less prescriptive than descriptive. The reason is simple. Test and documentation procedures are heavily influenced by many factors, including:

- The nature of the project (e.g. defence systems).
- The size of the project.
- Current practices.
- Current tool support.
- Company philosophy, structure and standards.
- Costs.

The following documents provide more than sufficient information for the implementation of effective test and documentation systems. The presentation of such information ranges from mildly exciting to rivetingly boring; but then, that's life.

[DEF83] UK Defence Standard 00-16/1 (1983), *Guide to the achievement of quality in software*, Procurement Executive, UK Ministry of Defence.
[DEF97] UK Defence Standard 00-55, *Requirements for safety related software in defence equipment*, Procurement Executive, UK Ministry of Defence.

[EIA82] *Configuration management definitions for digital computer programs*, Configuration Management Bulletin No. 4-1, Electronic Industries Association.

[EIA98] *National consensus standard for configuration management*, ANSI/EIA-649-1998, EIA.

[EIA01] EIA Bulletins on Configuration Management, EIA.

[IEEE98] IEEE Software Engineering Standards 730, 828, 829, 830, 1012, 1016, 1028, 1058, 1063. The Institute of Electrical and Electronic Engineers Inc.

[ISO97] ISO 9000-3 *Quality management and quality assurance standards. Guidelines for the application of ISO 9001 to the development, supply, and maintenance of software.*

[ISO98] ISO/IEC 12207: *Software life cycle processes.*

[JSP88] JSP188, Joint Services Publication 188 – *Requirements for the documentation of software in military operational real-time computer systems*, Procurement Executive, UK Ministry of Defence, 1980.

[RTC92] RTCA/DO-178B, *Software considerations in airborne systems and equipment certification.*

[STA87] *The STARTS guide – A guide to methods and software tools for the construction of large real-time systems*, NCC Publications, Manchester, ISBN 0-85012-619-3.

[STA88] *The STARTS purchasers' guide*, NCC Publications, Manchester, ISBN 0-85012-799-8.

References and further reading

[CVS01] Concurrent Versions System Web page, www.CVShome.org, 2001.

[FOG99] *Open source development with CVS*, K. Fogel, ISBN 1-576-104907, 1999.

[GRE00] *How to write unmaintainable code*, R. Green, Canadian Mind Products, www.mindprod.com, 2000.

[HIT93] *Coding, documenting and testing techniques for BS5750/Tickit-compliant software*, M. Beach, Hitex (UK) Ltd, 1993.

[ROB01] *Quality management system*, B. Kirk, Robinson Associates UK, 2001.

Glossary

....

ADC	Analogue to digital
ANSI	American National Standards Institute
ASIC	Application-Specific Integrated Circuit
BDM	Background Debug Mode
BSP	Board Support Package
CASE	Computer-Aided Software Engineering
CISC	Complex Instruction Set Computer
CORE	Controlled Requirements Expression
CPU	Central Processing Unit
CRC	Class-Responsibility-Collaboration
CT	Control Transformation
DAC	Digital to analogue
DDT	Dynamic Debugging Tool
DFD	Data Flow Diagram
DMA	Direct Memory Access
DOS	Disk Operating System
DP	Data Processing
DSD	Design Structure Diagram
DSP	Digital Signal Processor
DT	Data Transformation
EEPROM	Electrically Erasable Programmable Read Only Memory
EPROM	(UV) Erasable ROM
ERD	Entity Relationship Diagram
FIFO	First-In First-Out
FPGA	Field Programmable Gate Array
FRAM	Ferroelectric Random Access Memory
FSM	Finite State Machine
GDP	Graphics Display Processor
GUI	Graphical User Interface

HCI	Human-Computer Interface
HDLC	High-level Data Link Control
HLL	High-Level Language
HRRN	Highest Response Ratio Next
I/O	Input/Output
ICE	In-Circuit Emulator
IEEE	Institute of Electronic and Electrical Engineers
IP	Intellectual Property
ISO	International Standards Organisation
ISR	Interrupt Service Routing
JSP	Jackson Structured Programming
JTAG	Joint Test Action Group
LLC	Logical Link Control
LLF	Least Laxity First
LOC	Lines Of Code
MAC	Medium Access Control
MDS	Microprocessor Development System
Mflops	Mega floating point operations per second
MIPS	Millions of Instructions Per Second
MMI	Man-Machine Interface
MSC	Message Sequence Chart
MTBF	Mean Time Between Failures
MTTF	Mean Time To Fail
MTTR	Mean Time To Repair
NMI	Non-Maskable Interrupt
OCD	On-Chip Debug
OED	Oxford English Dictionary
OLTP	On-Line Transaction Processing
OOAD	Object-Oriented Analysis and Design
OOD	Object-Oriented design
OS	Operating System
OSI	Open Systems Interconnection
OTPROM	One Time PROM
PC	Personal Computer
PCI	Peripheral Component Interconnect
PD	Process Descriptor

PDF	Program Development Facility
PDU	Protocol Data Unit
POSIX	Portable Operating System Interface
PROM	Programmable Read Only Memory
PSD	Program Structure Diagram
QA	Quality Assurance
RAM	Random Access Memory
RISC	Reduced Instruction Set Computer
RMA	Rate Monotonic Analysis
RMS	Rate Monotonic Scheduling
ROM	Read Only Memory
RT-IDE	Real-Time Integrated Development Environment
RTOS	Real-Time Operating System
SAP	Service Access Point
SBC	Single-Board Computer
S-H	Sample-Hold
SC	Structure Chart
SDL	Specification and Description Language
SJF	Shortest Job First
SOC	System-On-Chip
SOR	Statement Of Requirements
SP	Structured Programming
SRT	Shortest Response Time
STD	State Transition Diagram
TCB	Task Control Block
TCP/IP	Transmission Control Protocol/Internet Protocol
TOD	Time Of Day
UML	Unified Modelling Language
VDM	Vienna Development Method
VDU	Visual Display Unit
VHDL	Very High Level Description Language
VME	Versa Module Europa
WAP	Wireless Application Protocol
WML	Wireless Markup Language (specification)
YSM	Yourdon Structured Methods

Index

....